Computational Mathematics

Computational Mathematics

Edited by **Lucas Lincoln**

Willford Press

New York

Published by Willford Press,
118-35 Queens Blvd., Suite 400,
Forest Hills, NY 11375, USA
www.willfordpress.com

Computational Mathematics
Edited by Lucas Lincoln

International Standard Book Number: 978-1-68285-155-5 (Hardback)

Printed in the United States of America.

Contents

Preface IX

Chapter 1 **Flow induced by non-coaxial rotations of porous disk and a fluid in a porous medium** 1
I. Ahmad

Chapter 2 **Results of symmetric groups S_n ($n \leq 7$) acting on unordered triples and ordered quadruples** 6
Stephen Kipkemoi Kibet, Kimutai Albert and Kandie Joseph

Chapter 3 **Improving the order selection of moving average time series model** 10
Ali Hussein Al-Marshadi

Chapter 4 **Einstein's equivalence principle has three further implications besides affecting time: T-L-M-Ch theorem ("Telemach")** 15
Otto E. Rossler

Chapter 5 **Temperature-dependent thermal stress determination of an isotropic circular annular fin** 19
Navneet Kumar Lamba, Warbhe M. S. and Khobragade N. W.

Chapter 6 **A sampling plan with producer's allowable risk (PAR) at maximum allowable proportion defective (MAPD)** 27
T. B. Ramkumar

Chapter 7 **Solving three-dimensional (3D) Laplace equations by successive over-relaxation method** 32
Mathias A. Onabid

Chapter 8 **Thermal deflection of a thin circular plate with radiation** 37
Hamna Parveen, N. K. Lamba and N. W. Khobragade

Chapter 9 **Utilization of mixture of $\bar{x}$, $\bar{x}_1$ and $\bar{x}_2$ in imputation for missing data in post-stratification** 42
D. Shukla, D. S. Thakur and N. S. Thakur

Chapter 10 **Mathematics as a sort of technology** 54
Xiong Zhang

Chapter 11 **Investigation on the effect of stent in unsteady blood flow** 58
Ibrahima Mbaye

Chapter 12 **Application of Bousinesq's and Westergaard's formulae in analysing foundation stress distribution for a failed telecommunication mast** 69
Ojedokun Olalekan Yinka and Olutoge Festus Adeyemi

Chapter 13 **Critical thinking: Essence for teaching mathematics and mathematics problem solving skills** 76
Ebiendele Ebosele Peter

Chapter 14 **Comparison of simulated annealing and hill climbing in the course timetabling problem** 81
Kenekayoro Patrick

Chapter 15 **Cross efficiency by using common weights for fuzzy data** 84
Sahand Daneshvar, Mojtaba Ramezani, Mozhgan Mansouri Kaleibar and Sharmin Rahmatfam

Chapter 16 **Statistical modeling of wastage using the beta distribution** 91
Ebuh G. U., Nwoke C. and Ebuh A. C.

Chapter 17 **A deterministic model for HIV infection incorporating identification rate in a heterosexual population: Mathematical analysis** 96
Abha Teguria, Manindra Kumar Srivastava and Anil Rajput

Chapter 18 **An inventory model for deteriorating items with different constant demand rates** 110
Trailokyanath Singh and Sudhir Kumar Sahu

Chapter 19 **Wu's algorithm and its possible application in cryptanalysis** 121
T. L. Grobler, A. J. van Zyl, J. C. Olivier, W. Kleynhans, B. P. Salmon and W. T. Penzhorn

Chapter 20 **Penalty function methods using matrix laboratory (MATLAB)** 129
Hailay Weldegiorgis Berhe

Chapter 21 **Scheme for solving ordinary differential equations with derivative discontinuities: A new class of semi- implicit rational, Runge-Kutta** 167
Bolarinwa Bolaji, Ademiluyi R. A., Oluwagunwa A. P. and Awomuse B. O.

Chapter 22 **Measuring strength of association in repeated samples** 174
Oyeka I. C. A. and Umeh E. U.

Chapter 23 **Logistic preference function for preference ranking organization method for enrichment evaluation (PROMETHEE) decision analysis** 178
S. K. Amponsah, K. F. Darkwah and A. Inusah

Chapter 24 **On three-dimensional generalized sasakian space - forms** 186
S. Yadav and D. L. Suthar

Chapter 25 **An overview of term rewriting systems** 192
Dasharath Singh, Ali Maianguwa Shuaibu and Adeku Musa Ibrahim

Chapter 26 **Egoists dilemma with fuzzy data** 197
Sahand Daneshvar, Mozhgan Mansouri Kaleibar and Mojtaba Ramezani

Chapter 27 **Two non-standard finite difference schemes for the Timoshenko beam** 205
Abdul Wasim Shaikh and Xiao-liang Cheng

Chapter 28 **Almost n-multiplicative maps** **210**
E. Ansari-Piri and N. Eghbali

Chapter 29 **A study on a novel method of mining fuzzy association using fuzzy correlation analysis** **214**
Karthikeyan T., Samuel Chellathurai A. and Praburaj B.

Permissions

List of Contributors

Preface

The world is advancing at a fast pace like never before. Therefore, the need is to keep up with the latest developments. This book was an idea that came to fruition when the specialists in the area realized the need to coordinate together and document essential themes in the subject. That's when I was requested to be the editor. Editing this book has been an honour as it brings together diverse authors researching on different streams of the field. The book collates essential materials contributed by veterans in the area which can be utilized by students and researchers alike.

Computational mathematics emerged as a distinct part of applied mathematics. This book provides a comprehensive study of computational mathematics, which forms an essential part of the modern numerical algorithms and scientific computing. It attempts to understand the multiple branches and research projects that fall under the field of computational mathematics. This book is an essential read for students, experts and mathematicians. It covers the significant aspects of this field ranging from fuzzy logic to non-linear differential equations.

Each chapter is a sole-standing publication that reflects each author´s interpretation. Thus, the book displays a multi-facetted picture of our current understanding of applications and diverse aspects of the field. I would like to thank the contributors of this book and my family for their endless support.

Editor

1

Flow induced by non-coaxial rotations of porous disk and a fluid in a porous medium

I. Ahmad

Department of Mathematics, Azad Kashmir University, Muzaffarabad 13100, Pakistan. E-mail: aaiftikhar@yahoo.com.

This paper deals with the flow of an incompressible, viscous and electrically conducting fluid in a porous medium when no slip condition is no longer valid. The fluid is bounded by a non-conducting porous disk. The flow is due to non-coaxial rotations of porous disk and a fluid at infinity. The fluid is electrically conducting in the presence of a constant applied magnetic field in the transverse direction. Analytic treatment for the arising problem is made for velocity components. An analytical solution of the problem is developed using Laplace transform method. A critical assessment is made for the case of partial slip and no-slip conditions and discussed these results in medium which is porous. Graphical results of velocity components are presented for various values of pertinent dimensionless parameters.

Key words: Viscous fluid, non-coaxial rotations, Laplace transform porous medium, partial slip condition.

INTRODUCTION

The equations which govern the flow of a Newtonian fluid are the Navier-Stokes equations. These equations are highly non-linear partial differential equations and known exact solutions are few in number. Exact solutions are very important not only because they are solutions of some fundamental flows but also because they serve as accuracy checks for experimental, numerical and asymptotic methods. Although computer techniques make the complete numerical integration of the Navier-Stokes equations feasible, the accuracy of the result can be established by a comparison with an exact solution. Exact solutions of the Navier-Stokes equations have been given by many authors, Berker (1963), Siddiquiet al. (2001), Erdogan (2000), Murthy and Ram (1978) and Rao and Kasiviswanathan (1987) in various situations. In continuation, Erdogan (2000) studied the flow due to non-coaxial rotations of a disk oscillating in its own plane and fluid at infinity. Hayat et al. (2001) discussed the magnetohydrodynamic (MHD) flow of a viscous fluid due to non-coaxial rotations of a porous disk and a fluid at infinity. Rajagopal (1992) presented a review for flows of Newtonian and non-Newtonian fluids between parallel disks rotating about a common axis.

However, no attempt has been made to discuss the MHD flow due to non-coaxial rotations of porous disk and a fluid through a porous medium when no slip condition is no longer valid. The aim of this paper is to present such attempt. Infect, the objective of the present work is to extend the analysis of reference, Hayatet al. (20017) in order to study the effects of partial slip on the flow in a porous medium. The disk and the fluid exhibit non-coaxial rotations. By using the Laplace transform method, the structures of the associated boundary layers are investigated in a porous medium when no-slip condition is no longer valid. The fluids exhibiting slip are very important from technological point of view. For example, the polishing of artificial heart valves and internal cavities in a variety of manufactured parts is achieved by imbedding such fluids with abrasives. The influence of various emerging parameters is discussed with the help of graphs.

Mathematical description of the problem

We consider an incompressible electrically conducting viscous fluid occupying the porous space $z > 0$. The fluid is in contact with a porous disk occupying the position $z = 0$. The disk and fluid are in a state of non-coaxial rotation with l being the distance between the axes of the rotations of the disk and fluid at infinity. A uniform magnetic field B_0 is applied in the transverse direction to flow. The magnetic Reynolds number is very small and thus the induced magnetic field is neglected. The electric field is taken zero. Initially the disk and fluid at infinity are rotating about z' -axis with constant angular velocity Ω. For $t = 0$, the disk starts to rotate impulsively about the z -axis and the fluid at infinity rotates about z' -axis with the same angular velocity Ω. For the flow under consideration, the boundary and initial considerations are;

$$u-\beta\frac{\partial u}{\partial z}=-\Omega y,\quad v-\beta\frac{\partial v}{\partial z}=\Omega x \quad \text{at} \quad z=0,\ t>0,$$

$$u=-\Omega(y-l),\quad v=\Omega x \quad \text{as} \quad z\to\infty \quad \text{for all} \quad t,$$

$$u=-\Omega(y-l),\quad v=\Omega x \quad \text{at} \quad t=0,\quad z>0, \tag{1}$$

Where β is slip coefficient and u and v are the x - and y -components of velocity defined by;

$$u=-\Omega y+f(z,t),\quad v=\Omega x+g(z,t). \tag{2}$$

Equation 2 together with continuity equation gives;

$$w=-W_0, \tag{3}$$

in which $W_0 > 0$ and $W_0 < 0$ respectively indicates the suction and blowing velocities.

After eliminating the pressure gradient, the momentum equation along with Equations (2) and (3) gives;

$$v\frac{\partial^3 w}{\partial z^3}+W_0\frac{\partial^2 w}{\partial z^2}-\frac{\partial^2 w}{\partial t\partial z}-(i\Omega+\frac{\sigma}{\rho}B_0{}^2+\frac{\phi}{k}\upsilon)\frac{\partial w}{\partial z}=0, \tag{4}$$

Where σ is the electrical conductivity of fluid, ρ is the density, υ is the kinematic viscosity, ϕ is the porosity, k is the permeability and;

$$W = f+ig. \tag{5}$$

The conditions in Equation (1) now become;

$$W(0,t)=\beta\frac{\partial w}{\partial z} \quad \text{at} \quad z=0,\quad t>0,$$

$$W(\infty,t)=\Omega l \quad \text{at} \quad z\to\infty \quad \text{for all} \quad t, \tag{6}$$

$$W(z,0)=\Omega l \quad \text{at} \quad t=0,\quad z>0.$$

Defining

$$G=\frac{w}{\Omega l},\quad \xi=\sqrt{\frac{\Omega}{2v}}z,\quad \tau=\Omega t, \tag{7}$$

In Equations (4) and (6) and then solving the resulting problem by Laplace transform procedure we obtain;

$$G(\xi,\tau)=1-e^{-\frac{s}{2}\xi}\left[\begin{matrix}\frac{1}{a^2-A}\left(\frac{1}{\sqrt{\pi\tau}}e^{-\frac{\xi^2}{4\tau}-A\tau}-ae^{\xi a+a^2\tau-A\tau}erfc\left(\frac{\xi}{2\sqrt{\tau}}+a\sqrt{\tau}\right)\right)\\+\frac{1}{2A-2a\sqrt{A}}\left(\frac{1}{\sqrt{\pi\tau}}e^{-\frac{\xi^2}{4\tau}-A\tau}-\sqrt{A}e^{\xi\sqrt{A}}erfc\left(\frac{\xi}{2\sqrt{\tau}}+\sqrt{A\tau}\right)\right)+\\\frac{1}{2A+2a\sqrt{A}}\left(\frac{1}{\sqrt{\pi\tau}}e^{-\frac{\xi^2}{4\tau}-A\tau}+\sqrt{A}e^{-\xi\sqrt{A}}erfc\left(\frac{\xi}{2\sqrt{\tau}}-\sqrt{A\tau}\right)\right)\end{matrix}\right], \tag{8}$$

Where;

$$A=\left(\frac{S}{2}\right)^2+N+i+\lambda,\quad a=1+\frac{\beta S}{2},\quad S=\frac{W_0}{\sqrt{2\Omega v}},$$
$$N=\frac{\sigma B_0{}^2}{\rho\Omega},\quad \lambda=\frac{\phi\upsilon}{k\Omega},\quad \beta=\beta\sqrt{\frac{\Omega}{2\upsilon}}, \tag{9}$$

and erfc (·) is the complementary error function. It should be noted that for $\lambda = \beta = 0$, we get the results of Hayat et al. (2001). Equation (8) for large time reduces.

$$G(\xi,\tau)=\left[\frac{1+\sqrt{A}e^{-\xi\sqrt{A}-\frac{s}{2}}}{a\sqrt{A}+A}\right]$$

$$-e^{-\frac{s}{2}\xi}\left[\begin{matrix}\frac{1}{a^2-A}\left(\frac{1}{\sqrt{\pi\tau}}e^{-\frac{\xi^2}{4\tau}-A\tau}-ae^{\xi a+a^2\tau-A\tau}erfc\left(\frac{\xi}{2\sqrt{\tau}}+a\sqrt{\tau}\right)\right)\\+\frac{1}{2A-2a\sqrt{A}}\left(\frac{1}{\sqrt{\pi\tau}}e^{-\frac{\xi^2}{4\tau}-A\tau}-\sqrt{A}e^{\xi\sqrt{A}}erfc\left(\frac{\xi}{2\sqrt{\tau}}+\sqrt{A\tau}\right)\right)+\\\frac{1}{2A+2a\sqrt{A}}\left(\frac{1}{\sqrt{\pi\tau}}e^{-\frac{\xi^2}{4\tau}-A\tau}+\sqrt{A}e^{-\xi\sqrt{A}}erfc\left(\frac{\xi}{2\sqrt{\tau}}-\sqrt{A\tau}\right)\right)\end{matrix}\right]. \tag{10}$$

The approximate forms of the real and imaginary parts of suction solution when $\xi << 2\sqrt{\tau}$ and $\tau >> 1$ are;

$$\frac{f}{\Omega 1}=1+\frac{e^{-\frac{S}{2}\xi+\xi\alpha_1}[(2\alpha_1+2+\beta S)\cos\xi\alpha_2-2\alpha_2 2\sin\xi\alpha_2]}{(2\alpha_1+2+\beta S)^2+(2\alpha_2)^2}$$

$$-\frac{e^{\left(\frac{S}{2}\xi+\alpha_2^2-\alpha_1^2\right)\tau}}{\sqrt{\pi\tau}}\frac{\left[\left(a^2+\alpha_2^2-\alpha_1^2\right)\{\cos 2\alpha_1 a_2\tau+2\alpha_1 a_2\sin 2\alpha_1 a_2\tau\}\left(1-e^{\xi a}\right)\right]}{\left(a^2+\alpha_2^2-\alpha_1^2\right)^2+\left(2\alpha_1 a_2\right)^2}$$

$$-\frac{e^{-\frac{S}{2}\xi+(a_2^2-\alpha_1^2)\tau}}{\sqrt{\pi\tau}}\frac{\left[\left(2\alpha_1^2-2\alpha_2^2-2a\alpha_1\right)\begin{Bmatrix}\left(1-e^{\xi\alpha_1}\cos\xi\alpha_2\right)\cos 2\alpha_1 a_2\tau\\ -e^{\xi\alpha_1}\sin\xi\alpha_2\sin 2\alpha_1 a_2\tau\end{Bmatrix}\right]}{\left(2\alpha_1^2-2\alpha_2^2-2a\alpha_1\right)^2+\left(2a\alpha_2+4\alpha_1 a_2\right)^2}$$

$$+\left(2a\alpha_2+4\alpha_1 a_2\right)\left[\left(1-e^{\xi\alpha_1}\cos\xi\alpha_2\right)\sin 2\alpha_1 a_2\tau+e^{\xi\alpha_1}\sin\xi\alpha_2\cos 2\alpha_1 a_2\tau\right]$$

$$-\frac{e^{\left(\frac{S}{2}\xi+a_2^2-\alpha_1^2\right)\tau}}{\sqrt{\pi\tau}}\left[\begin{matrix}\dfrac{\left(2\alpha_1^2-2\alpha_2^2-2a\alpha_1\right)\begin{Bmatrix}\left(1-e^{\xi\alpha_1}\cos\xi\alpha_2\right)\cos 2\alpha_1 a_2\tau\\ +e^{-\xi\alpha_1}\sin\xi\alpha_2\sin 2\alpha_1 a_2\tau\end{Bmatrix}}{\left(2\alpha_1^2-2\alpha_2^2-2a\alpha_1\right)^2+\left(2a\alpha_2+4\alpha_1 a_2\right)^2}+\\ \left(2a\alpha_2+4\alpha_1 a_2\right)\begin{pmatrix}\left(e^{-\xi\alpha_1}\sin\xi\alpha_2\right)\cos 2\alpha_1 a_2\tau-\\ (1-e^{-\xi\alpha_1}\cos\xi\alpha_2)\sin 2\alpha_1 a_2\tau\end{pmatrix}\end{matrix}\right], \quad (11)$$

$$\frac{g}{\Omega 1}=-\frac{e^{\frac{S}{2}\xi-\xi\alpha_1}}{\left(2\alpha_1+2+\beta S\right)^2+\left(2\alpha_2\right)^2}\left[2\alpha_2\cos\xi\alpha_2+\left(2\alpha_1+2+\beta S\right)\sin\xi\alpha_2\right]$$

$$-\frac{e^{\frac{S}{2}\xi+\left(\alpha_2^2-\alpha_1^2\right)\tau}}{\sqrt{\pi\tau}}\left[\frac{2\alpha_1\alpha_2\cos 2\alpha_1\alpha_2\tau-\left(a^2+\alpha_2^2-\alpha_1^2\right)\left(1-e^{\xi a}\right)\sin 2\alpha_1\alpha_2\tau}{\left(-a^2-\alpha_2^2+\alpha_1^2\right)^2+\left(2\alpha_1\alpha_2\right)^2}\right]$$

$$-\frac{e^{\frac{S}{2}\xi-\left(\alpha_2^2-\alpha_1^2\right)\tau}}{\sqrt{\pi\tau}}\left[\begin{matrix}\dfrac{\left(2a\alpha_2+4\alpha_1\alpha_2\right)\left\{1-e^{\xi\alpha_1}\cos\xi\alpha_2\right\}\cos 2\alpha_1\alpha_2\tau-e^{\xi\alpha_1}\sin\xi\alpha_2\sin 2\alpha_1\alpha_2\tau}{\left(2\alpha_1^2-2\alpha_2^2-2a\alpha_1\right)^2+\left(2a\alpha_2+4\alpha_1\alpha_2\right)^2}+\\ \left(2\alpha_1^2-2\alpha_2^2-2a\alpha_1\right)\left\{\left(1-e^{\xi\alpha_1}\cos\xi\alpha_2\right)\sin 2\alpha_1\alpha_2\tau+e^{\xi\alpha_1}\sin\xi\alpha_2\cos 2\alpha_1\alpha_2\tau\right\}\end{matrix}\right]$$

$$-\frac{e^{\frac{S}{2}\xi-\left(\alpha_2^2-\alpha_1^2\right)\tau}}{\sqrt{\pi\tau}}\left[\begin{matrix}\dfrac{\left(2a\alpha_2+4\alpha_1\alpha_2\right)\left\{e^{-\xi\alpha_1}\cos\xi\alpha_2-1\right\}\cos 2\alpha_1\alpha_2\tau-e^{-\xi\alpha_1}\sin\xi\alpha_2\sin 2\alpha_1\alpha_2\tau}{\left(2\alpha_1^2-2\alpha_2^2-2a\alpha_1\right)^2+\left(2a\alpha_2+4\alpha_1\alpha_2\right)^2}\\ +\left(2\alpha_1^2-2\alpha_2^2-2a\alpha_1\right)\left[e^{-\xi\alpha_1}\sin\xi\alpha_2\cos 2\alpha_1\alpha_2\tau-\left(1-e^{-\xi\alpha_1}\cos\xi\alpha_2\right)\sin 2\alpha_1\alpha_2\tau\right]\end{matrix}\right], \quad (12)$$

Where

$$\alpha_1=\left[\frac{1}{2}\sqrt{\left(\frac{S^2}{2}+N+\lambda\right)^2+1}+\left(\frac{S^2}{2}+N+\lambda\right)\right]^{\frac{1}{2}},$$

$$\alpha_2=\left[\frac{1}{2}\sqrt{\left(\frac{S^2}{2}+N+\lambda\right)^2+1}-\left(\frac{S^2}{2}+N+\lambda\right)\right]^{\frac{1}{2}}.$$

For blowing $S<0$, say $S=-\tilde{S}$, the solutions (11) and (12)

$$\frac{f}{\Omega 1}=1+\frac{e^{-\frac{\tilde{S}}{2}\xi+\xi\tilde{\alpha}_1}[2\tilde{\alpha}_1+2-\beta\tilde{S}]\cos\xi\tilde{\alpha}_2-2\tilde{\alpha}_2 2\sin\xi\tilde{\alpha}_2}{(2\tilde{\alpha}_1+2-\beta\tilde{S})^2+(2\tilde{\alpha}_2)^2}-$$

$$\frac{e^{\left(\frac{\tilde{S}}{2}\xi+\tilde{\alpha}_2^2-\tilde{\alpha}_1^2\right)\tau}}{\sqrt{\pi\tau}}\left\{\frac{\left(a^2+\tilde{\alpha}_2^2-\tilde{\alpha}_1^2\right)\left\{\cos 2\tilde{\alpha}_1\tilde{a}_2\tau+2\tilde{\alpha}_1\tilde{a}_2\sin 2\tilde{\alpha}_1\tilde{a}_2\tau\right\}\left(1-e^{\xi a}\right)}{\left(a^2+\tilde{\alpha}_2^2-\tilde{\alpha}_1^2\right)^2+\left(2\tilde{\alpha}_1\tilde{\alpha}_2\right)^2}\right\}$$

$$-\frac{e^{\left(-\frac{\tilde{S}}{2}\xi+\tilde{\alpha}_2^2-\tilde{\alpha}_1^2\right)\tau}}{\sqrt{\pi\tau}}\left\{\begin{matrix}\dfrac{\left(2\tilde{\alpha}_1^2-2\tilde{\alpha}_2^2-2a\tilde{\alpha}_1\right)\left\{\left(1-e^{\xi\tilde{\alpha}_1}\cos\xi\tilde{\alpha}_2\right)\cos 2\tilde{\alpha}_1\tilde{a}_2\tau-e^{\xi\tilde{\alpha}_1}\sin\xi\tilde{\alpha}_2\sin 2\tilde{\alpha}_1\tilde{a}_2\tau\right\}}{\left(2\tilde{\alpha}_1^2-2\tilde{\alpha}_2^2-2a\tilde{\alpha}_1\right)^2+\left(2a\tilde{\alpha}_2+4\tilde{\alpha}_1 a_2\right)^2}+\\ \left(2a\tilde{\alpha}_2+4\tilde{\alpha}_1\tilde{\alpha}_2\right)\left\{\left(1-e^{\xi\tilde{\alpha}_1}\cos\xi\tilde{\alpha}_2\right)\sin 2\tilde{\alpha}_1\tilde{a}_2\tau+e^{\xi\tilde{\alpha}_1}\sin\xi\tilde{\alpha}_2\cos 2\tilde{\alpha}_1\tilde{a}_2\tau\right\}\end{matrix}\right\}-$$

$$\frac{e^{\left(\frac{\tilde{S}}{2}\xi+\tilde{\alpha}_2^2-\tilde{\alpha}_1^2\right)\tau}}{\sqrt{\pi\tau}}\left\{\begin{matrix}\dfrac{\left(2\tilde{\alpha}_1^2-2\tilde{\alpha}_2^2-2a\tilde{\alpha}_1\right)\left(\left(1-e^{-\xi\tilde{\alpha}_1}\cos\xi\tilde{\alpha}_2\right)\cos 2\tilde{\alpha}_1\tilde{\alpha}_2\tau+e^{-\xi\tilde{\alpha}_1}\sin\xi\tilde{\alpha}_2\sin 2\tilde{\alpha}_1\tilde{a}_2\tau\right)}{\left(2\tilde{\alpha}_1^2-2\tilde{\alpha}_2^2-2a\tilde{\alpha}_1\right)^2+\left(2a\tilde{\alpha}_2+4\tilde{\alpha}_1\tilde{\alpha}_2\right)^2}+\\ \left(2a\tilde{\alpha}_2+4\tilde{\alpha}_1\tilde{\alpha}_2\right)\left(\left(e^{-\xi\tilde{\alpha}_1}\sin\xi\tilde{\alpha}_2\right)\cos 2\tilde{\alpha}_1\tilde{\alpha}_2\tau-(1-e^{-\xi\tilde{\alpha}_1}\cos\xi\tilde{\alpha}_2)\sin 2\tilde{\alpha}_1\tilde{a}_2\tau\right)\end{matrix}\right\}, \quad (13)$$

$$\frac{g}{\Omega 1}=-\frac{e^{\frac{\tilde{S}}{2}\xi-\xi\tilde{\alpha}_1}}{\left(2\tilde{\alpha}_1+2-\beta\tilde{S}\right)^2+\left(2\tilde{\alpha}_2\right)^2}\left[2\tilde{\alpha}_2\cos\xi\tilde{\alpha}_2+\left(2\tilde{\alpha}_1+2-\beta\tilde{S}\right)\sin\xi\tilde{\alpha}_2\right]$$

$$-\frac{e^{\frac{\tilde{S}}{2}\xi+\left(\tilde{\alpha}_2^2-\tilde{\alpha}_1^2\right)\tau}}{\sqrt{\pi\tau}}\left[\frac{2\tilde{\alpha}_1\tilde{\alpha}_2\cos 2\tilde{\alpha}_1\tilde{\alpha}_2\tau-\left(a^2+\tilde{\alpha}_2^2-\tilde{\alpha}_1^2\right)\left(1-e^{\xi a}\right)\sin 2\tilde{\alpha}_1\tilde{\alpha}_2\tau}{\left(-a^2-\tilde{\alpha}_2^2+\tilde{\alpha}_1^2\right)^2+\left(2\tilde{\alpha}_1\tilde{\alpha}_2\right)^2}\right]$$

$$-\frac{e^{\frac{\tilde{S}}{2}\xi-\left(\tilde{\alpha}_2^2-\tilde{\alpha}_1^2\right)\tau}}{\sqrt{\pi\tau}}\left[\begin{matrix}\dfrac{\left(2a\tilde{\alpha}_2+4\tilde{\alpha}_1\tilde{\alpha}_2\right)\left\{1-e^{\xi\tilde{\alpha}_1}\cos\xi\tilde{\alpha}_2\right\}\cos 2\tilde{\alpha}_1\tilde{\alpha}_2\tau-e^{\xi\tilde{\alpha}_1}\sin\xi\tilde{\alpha}_2\sin 2\tilde{\alpha}_1\tilde{\alpha}_2\tau}{\left(2\tilde{\alpha}_1^2-2\tilde{\alpha}_2^2-2a\tilde{\alpha}_1\right)^2+\left(2a\tilde{\alpha}_2+4\tilde{\alpha}_1\tilde{\alpha}_2\right)^2}+\\ \left(2\tilde{\alpha}_1^2-2\tilde{\alpha}_2^2-2a\tilde{\alpha}_1\right)\left\{\left(1-e^{\xi\tilde{\alpha}_1}\cos\xi\tilde{\alpha}_2\right)\sin 2\tilde{\alpha}_1\tilde{\alpha}_2\tau+e^{\xi\tilde{\alpha}_1}\sin\xi\tilde{\alpha}_2\cos 2\tilde{\alpha}_1\tilde{\alpha}_2\tau\right\}\end{matrix}\right]$$

$$-\frac{e^{\frac{\tilde{S}}{2}\xi-\left(\tilde{\alpha}_2^2-\tilde{\alpha}_1^2\right)\tau}}{\sqrt{\pi\tau}}\left[\begin{matrix}\dfrac{\left(2a\tilde{\alpha}_2+4\tilde{\alpha}_1\tilde{\alpha}_2\right)\left\{e^{-\xi\tilde{\alpha}_1}\cos\xi\tilde{\alpha}_2-1\right\}\cos 2\tilde{\alpha}_1\tilde{\alpha}_2\tau+e^{-\xi\tilde{\alpha}_1}\sin\xi\tilde{\alpha}_2\sin 2\tilde{\alpha}_1\tilde{\alpha}_2\tau}{\left(2\tilde{\alpha}_1^2-2\tilde{\alpha}_2^2-2a\tilde{\alpha}_1\right)^2+\left(2a\tilde{\alpha}_2+4\tilde{\alpha}_1\tilde{\alpha}_2\right)^2}\\ +\left(2\tilde{\alpha}_1^2-2\tilde{\alpha}_2^2-2a\tilde{\alpha}_1\right)\left[e^{-\xi\tilde{\alpha}_1}\sin\xi\tilde{\alpha}_2\cos 2\tilde{\alpha}_1\tilde{\alpha}_2\tau-\left(1-e^{-\xi\tilde{\alpha}_1}\cos\xi\tilde{\alpha}_2\right)\sin 2\tilde{\alpha}_1\tilde{\alpha}_2\tau\right]\end{matrix}\right] \quad (14)$$

With

$$\tilde{\alpha}_1=\left[\frac{1}{2}\sqrt{\left(\frac{\tilde{S}^2}{2}+N+\lambda\right)^2+1}+\left(\frac{\tilde{S}^2}{2}+N+\lambda\right)\right]^{\frac{1}{2}},$$

$$\tilde{\alpha}_2=\left[\frac{1}{2}\sqrt{\left(\frac{\tilde{S}^2}{2}+N+\lambda\right)^2+1}-\left(\frac{\tilde{S}^2}{2}+N+\lambda\right)\right]^{\frac{1}{2}}$$

RESULTS AND DISCUSSION

This area displays the graphical illustration of velocity profiles for the flow analyzed in this investigation .We interpret these results with respect to the variation of emerging parameters of interest and verify that they are consistent physically. Of particular interest here are the effects of the parameter λ, the slip parameter β and the suction/blowing parameter S.

In order to study the effects of various parameters of

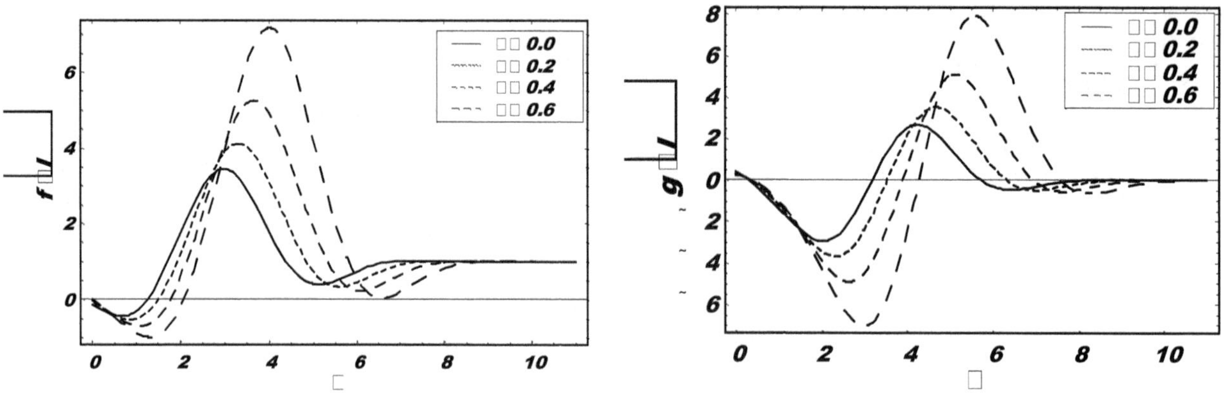

Figure 1. Variations of the velocity profiles for different values of λ when $S = 0.2, N = 0.1, \beta = 0.1 \, and \, \tau = 1.4$ are fixed.

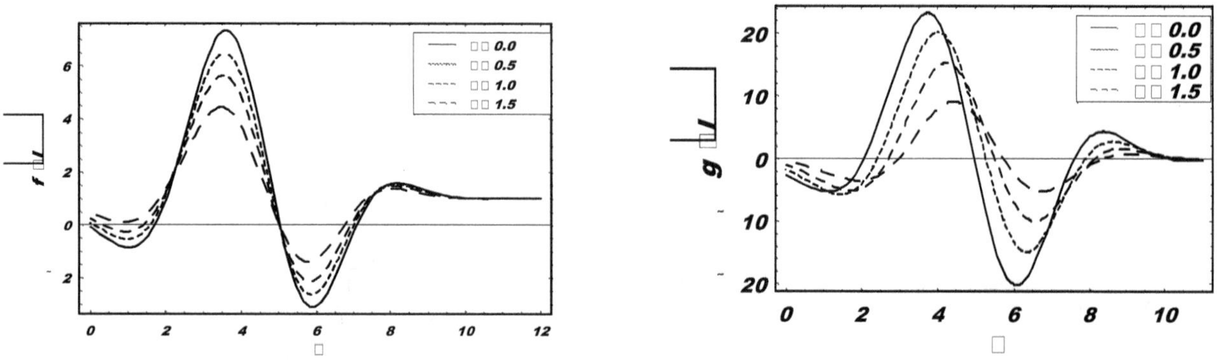

Figure 2. Variations of the velocity profiles for different values of β when $S = 0.2, N = 0.1, \beta = 0.1 \, and \, \tau = 1.4$ are fixed.

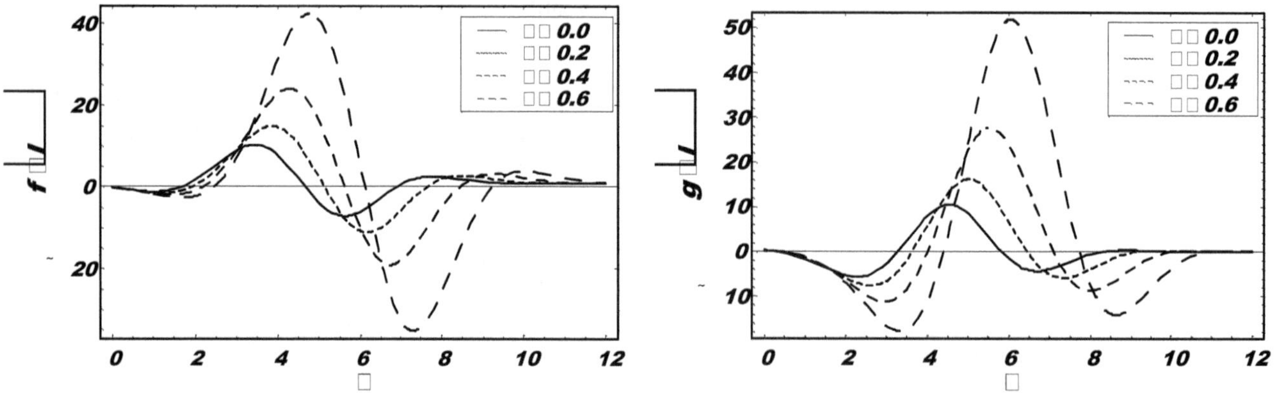

Figure 3. Variations of the velocity profiles for different values of λ when $S = -0.2, \; N = 0.1, \; \beta = 0.1 \; and \; \tau = 1.4$ are fixed.

interest on the velocity distributions we have plotted $\frac{f}{\Omega l}$ and $\frac{g}{\Omega l}$ against ξ in Figures 1 to 4. Figures 1 and 2 are for the suction case while Figures 3 and 4 are for blowing.

Figures 1 and 3 shows the effects of λ on the velocity profiles. It is noted that with the increase of λ the velocity profiles decreases near the disk in both cases (suction/blowing) by keeping other parameters fixed. This is in accordance with the fact that, the increase of the porosity of the porous medium increases the drag force

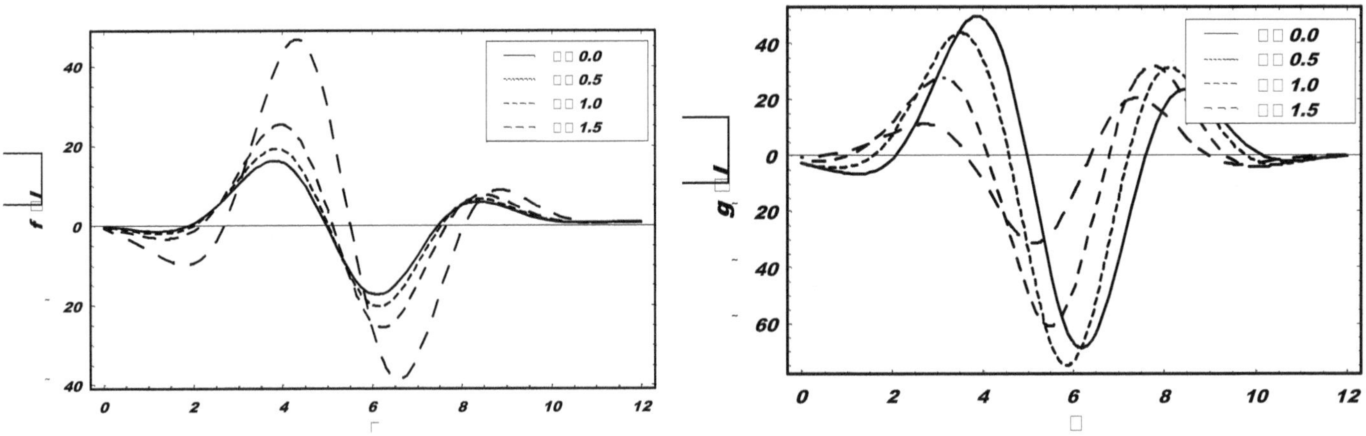

Figure 4. Variations of the velocity profiles for different values of β when $S=-0.2,\ N=0.1,\ \beta=0.1\ and\ \tau=1.4$ are fixed.

and hence causes the flow velocity to decrease. Thus, increasing the parameter λ yields an effect opposite to that of the permeability.

Figures 2 and 4 are prepared to elucidate the influence of the slip parameter β on the velocity profiles with fixed values of the other parameters. It is found that with the increase of slip parameter β, the velocity gradient decreases and hence the velocity profiles become flatter due to the decreasing shearing force from the slip boundary. It is also noted that the results of Hayat et al. (2001) can be recovered by taking $\beta=0=\lambda$.

CONCLUDING REMARKS

This article describes the unsteady flow of an incompressible electrically conducting fluid with partial slip characteristics in a porous medium. This is a theoretical study and may have applications in engineering. Mathematical analysis is performed in the presence of slip effects. The main points can be extracted from the present investigation.

1) It is found that with the increase of slip parameter β, the velocity gradient decreases.

2) The effects of λ yields effect opposite to that of the permeability k.

3) It is also noted that the results of Hayat et al. (2001) can be recovered by taking $\beta=0=\lambda$

REFERENCES

Berker R (1963). Integration des equation du mouvement d'u fluid visqueux incompressible, Hand Book of Fluid Dynamics, Vol. VIII/2, Springer, Berlin.

Siddiqui AM, Khan M, Asghar S, Hayat T (2001). Exact solutions in MHD rotating flow. Mech. Res. Comm., 28: 485-491.

Erdogan ME (2000). Unsteady flow between two eccentric rotating disks executing non-torsional oscillations, Int. J. Non-Linear Mech., 35: 691-699.

Murthy SN, Ram RKP (1978). Magnetohydrodynamic flows and heat transfer due to eccentric rotations of a porous disk and a fluid at infinity, Int. J. Eng. Sci., 16: 943-949.

Rao AR, Kasiviswanathan SR (1987). On exact solutions of unsteady Navier-Stokes equations. The vortex with instantaneous curvilinear axis, Int. J. Eng. Sci., 25: 337-349.

Erdogan ME (2000). Flow induced by non-coaxial rotation of a disk executing non-torsional oscillation and a fluid at infinity. Int. J. Eng. Sci., 38: 175-196.

Hayat T, Asghar S, Siddiqui AM, Haroon T (2001). Unsteady MHD flow due to non-coaxial rotations of a porous disk and a fluid at infinity. Acta Mech., 151: 127-134.

Rajagopal KR (1992). Flow of viscoelastic fluids between rotating disks, Theor. Comput. Fluid Dyn., 3: 185-206.

Results of symmetric groups S_n ($n \leq 7$) acting on unordered triples and ordered quadruples

Stephen Kipkemoi Kibet[1], Kimutai Albert[2*] and Kandie Joseph[3]

[1]Department of Mathematics, Kenyatta University, P. O. Box 43844-00100 Nairobi, Kenya.
[2]Kabianga University College, P. O. Box 2030-20200, Kericho, Kenya.
[3]Mathematics and Computer Science Department, Chepkoilel University College, P.O. Box 1125-30100, Eldoret.

In this paper, we examined the results of fixed point set of symmetric groups S_n ($n \leq 7$) acting on $X^{(3)}$ and $X^{[4]}$. In order to find the fixed point set| fix (g) | of these permutation groups, we used the method developed by Higman (1970) to compute the number of orbits, ranks and sub degrees of these actions. The results were used to find the number of orbits as proposed by Harary (1969) in Cauchy-Frobenius Lemma and hence deduce transitivity.

Key words: Cycles, | Fix (g) |, Lemma.

INTRODUCTION

In 1970, Higman calculated the rank and the sub-degrees of the symmetric group S_n acting on 2-elements subsets from the set X= {1, 2, 3... n.}. He showed that the rank is 3 and the sub-degrees are $1, 2\ n-2,\binom{n-2}{2}$. Faradžev and Ivanov (1990) calculated the subdegrees of primitive permutation representations of PSL (2, q). They showed that if G = PSL (2, q) acts on the cosets of its maximal sub-group H, then the rank is at least $\frac{|G|}{|H|^2}$ and if q>100, the rank is greater than 5.

In 1992, Kamuti devised a method for constructing some of the suborbital graphs of PSL (2,q) and PGL (2,q) acting on the cosets of their maximal dihedral subgroups of orders q-1 and 2(q-l) respectively. This method gave an alternative way of constructing the Coxeter graph which was first constructed by Coxeter (1986).

Neumann (1977) gave general properties of suborbital graphs. In this paper, he gave a construction of the famous Petersen graph which was first constructed by Petersen in 1898.

In 2001, Akbas investigated the suborbital graphs for the modular group. He proved the conjecture by Jones et al. (1991) that a suborbital graph for the modular group is a forest if and only if it contains no triangles. Kamuti (2006) calculated the sub degrees of primitive permutation representations of PGL (2,q). He showed that when PGL (2,q) acts on the cosets of its maximal dihedral subgroup of order 2 (q-1) then its rank is ½ (q+3) if q is odd, and ½ (q+2) if q is even.

This shows that finding the fixed point set | fix (g) |, for the action of S_n ($n \leq 7$) on $X^{(3)}$ and $X^{[4]}$ do not seem to have been published so far. Therefore, in this paper we find some formulas for fixed point set of these actions.

List of notations

S_n	- Symmetric group of degree n and order n!
| G |	- The order of a group G
{a, b, c}	- An unordered triple
[a, b, c, d]	-An ordered quadruple
$X^{(3)}$	- The set of all unordered triples from the set X = {1, 2... n}
$X^{[4]}$	- The set of all ordered quadruples from the set:

*Corresponding author. E-mail: kimutaialbert@yahoo.com.

$X = \{1, 2... n\}$

$\binom{r}{s}$ - r combinations

$|\text{Fix}(g)|$ - The number of elements in the fixed point set of g.

PRELIMINARY DEFINITIONS

In this area, we look briefly at some results and definitions on permutation groups which we are interested in.

Definition 1

Let X be a set; a group G acts on the left on X if for each $g \in G$ and each $x \in X$ there corresponds a unique element $gx \in X$ such that:

(i) $(g_1g_2) = g_1(g_2x)$, $\forall g_1, g_2 \in G$ and $x \in X$
(ii) For any $x \in X$, $1x=x$, where 1 is the identity in G.

Definition 2

Let G act on a set X. The set of elements of X fixed by $g \in G$ is called the fixed point set of g and is denoted by Fix (g). Thus Fix (g) = $\{x \in X \mid gx=x\}$.

Definition 3

If the action of a group G on a set X has only one orbit, then we say that G acts transitively on X. In other words, G acts transitively on X if for every pair of points $x, y \in X$, there exists $g \in G$ such that $gx = y$.

Theorem 1 (Harary, 1969:98)

Cauchy – Frobenius Lemma

Let G be a finite group acting on a set X. Then the number of orbits of G is:

$$\frac{1}{|G|}\sum_{g\in G}|Fix\ g|$$

Definition 4

If a finite group G acts on a set X with n elements, each $g \in G$ corresponds to a permutation б of X, which can be written uniquely as a product of disjoint cycles. If σ has α_1 cycles of length 1, α_2 cycles of length 2,... α_n cycles of length n, we say that σ and hence g has cycle type $\alpha_1, \alpha_2, \ldots, \alpha_n$.

Theorem 2 (Krishnamurthy, 1985:68)

Two permutations in S_n are conjugate if and only if they have the same cycle type; and if $g \in G$ has cycle type $\alpha_1, \alpha_2, \ldots, \alpha_n$, then the number of permutations in S_n conjugate to *g* is $\dfrac{n!}{\prod_{i=1}^{n}\alpha_i!\,i^{\alpha_i}}$.

RESULTS OF SYMMETRIC GROUPS S_n (n≤7) ACTING ON UNORDERED TRIPLES AND ORDERED QUADRUPLES

Lemma 1

Let the cycle type of $g \in S_n$ be $\alpha_1, \alpha_2, \ldots, \alpha_n$. Then | Fix (g) | in $X^{(3)}$ is given by the formula:

$$|\text{Fix}(g)| = \binom{\alpha_1}{3} + \alpha_2\ \alpha_1 + \alpha_3$$

Proof

Let $g \in S_n$ has cycle type $\alpha_1, \alpha_2, \ldots, \alpha_n$. $\{a, b, c\} \in X^{(3)}$ is fixed by g if each of a, b, and c come from a single cycle in g or one of a, b, or c come from single cycle in g and the other two come from a 2 – cycle in g or a, b, c come from a 3 – cycle in g. From the first case, the number of unordered triples fixed by g is $\binom{\alpha_1}{3}$; from the second case the number of unordered triples fixed by g is $\alpha_2\ \alpha_1$ and in the third case the number of unordered triples fixed by g is α_3. Therefore the number of unordered triples fixed by g is:

$$\binom{\alpha_1}{3} + \alpha_2\ \alpha_1 + \alpha_3$$

Lemma 2

Let $g \in S_n$ be a permutation with cycle type $\alpha_1, \alpha_2, \ldots, \alpha_n$ Then the number of permutations in S_n fixing $\{a, b, c\} \in X^{(3)}$ and having the same cycle type as g is given by:

$$\frac{n-3\,!}{\alpha_1-3\,!1^{\alpha_1-3}\prod_{i=2}^{n}\alpha_i!i^{\alpha_i}}+\frac{3\,n-3\,!}{\alpha_1-1\,!1^{\alpha_1-1}\,\alpha_2-1\,!2^{\alpha_2-1}\prod_{i=3}^{n}\alpha_i!i^{\alpha_i}}+\frac{2\,n-3\,!}{\alpha_1!1^{\alpha_1}\alpha_2!2^{\alpha_2}\,\alpha_3-1\,!3^{\alpha_3-1}\prod_{i=4}^{n}\alpha_i!i^{\alpha_i}}$$

Proof

A permutation $g\in S_n$ fixes an unordered triple say {a, b, c}$\in X^{(3)}$:

a) If g maps each element a, b and c onto itself, that is each of the elements a, b and c comes from a single cycle. To get the number of permutations in S_n that fix {a, b, c} and having the same cycle type as g, we apply Theorem 6 to a permutation of S_n-3 with cycle type $\alpha_1-3,\alpha_2,\alpha_3,\ldots,\alpha_n$ to get

$$\frac{n-3\,!}{\alpha_1-3\,!1^{\alpha_1-3}\prod_{i=2}^{n}\alpha_i!i^{\alpha_i}}$$ permutations.

b) If one of the elements a, b and c comes from a single cycle and other two comes from a 2 – cycle. In this case a, b and c may come from any of the following three permutations; (ab) (c)..., (ac) (b)...or (bc)(a)... Applying Theorem 6 to a permutation of S_n -3 with cycle type $\alpha_1-1,\alpha_2-1,\alpha_3,\alpha_4,\ldots,\alpha_n$

We get

$$\frac{n-3\,!}{\alpha_1-1\,!1^{\alpha_1-1}\,\alpha_2-1\,!2^{\alpha_2-1}\prod_{i=3}^{n}\alpha_i!i^{\alpha_i}}$$ permutations.

Considering the three cases pointed so far, we get

$$\frac{3\,n-3\,!}{\alpha_1-1\,!1^{\alpha_1-1}\,\alpha_2-1\,!2^{\alpha_2-1}\prod_{i=3}^{n}\alpha_i!i^{\alpha_i}}$$ permutations.

c) If the elements a, b and c come from a 3-cycle in g. In this case a, b and c may come from the permutation (abc),... or (acb)..... Applying Theorem 6 to a permutation of S_n -3 with cycle type $\alpha_1,\alpha_2,\alpha_3-1,\alpha_4,\ldots,\alpha_n$ we get

$$\frac{n-3\,!}{\alpha_1!1^{\alpha_1}\alpha_2!2^{\alpha_2}\,\alpha_3-1\,!3^{\alpha_3-1}\prod_{i=4}^{n}\alpha_i!i^{\alpha_i}}$$ permutations.

Considering the 2 cases pointed so far, we get

$$\frac{2\,n-3\,!}{\alpha_1!1^{\alpha_1}\alpha_2!2^{\alpha_2}\,\alpha_3-1\,!3^{\alpha_3-1}\prod_{i=4}^{n}\alpha_i!i^{\alpha_i}}$$

Combining cases (a), (b) and (c), we get the required result.

Lemma 3

Let g $\in$ S_n be a permutation with cycle type $\alpha_1,\alpha_2,\ldots,\alpha_n$. Then | Fix (g) | in X [4] is given by:

$$4!\binom{\alpha_1}{4}$$

Proof

Let [a, b, c, d] $\in X^{[4]}$ and $g\in S_n$. Then g fixes [a, b, c, d] if each of the elements a, b, c, d are mapped onto themselves, that is g [a, b, c, d] = [ga, gb, gc, gd] = [a, b, c, d] implying ga=a, gb=b, gc=c and gd=d. Each of a, b, c and d comes from single cycles. The number of unordered quadruples fixed by $g\in S_n$ is:

$$\binom{\alpha_1}{4}$$

But unordered quadruple, can be rearrange to give 24=4! distinct ordered quadruples. Thus the number of ordered quadruples fixed by $g\in S_n$ is'

$$4!\binom{\alpha_1}{4}$$

Lemma 4

Let g $\in$ S_n be a permutation with cycle type $\alpha_1,\alpha_2,\ldots,\alpha_n$ .Then the number of permutations in S_n fixing [a, b, c, d] $\in X^{[4]}$ and having the same cycle type as g is given by:

$$\frac{n-4\,!}{\alpha_1-4\,!1^{\alpha_1-4}\prod_{i=2}^{n}\alpha_i!i^{\alpha_i}}$$

Proof

Let $g\in S_n$ have cycle type $\alpha_1,\alpha_2,\ldots,\alpha_n$ and let g fix [a, b, c, d]. Then each of a, b, c and d must come from a single cycle in g. So to count the number of permutations in S_n having the same cycle type as g and fixing a, b, c and d, is the same as counting the number of permutations in S_n-4 having cycle type $\alpha_1 - 4, \alpha_2, \ldots, \alpha_n$.

By the Theorem 6, this number is:

$$\frac{(n-4)!}{(\alpha_1 - 4)!1^{\alpha_1 - 4}\prod_{i=2}^{n} \alpha_i ! i^{\alpha_i}}$$

REFERENCES

Akbas M (2001). Suborbital graphs for number group. Bull. London Math. Society 33:647-652.
Coxeter HSM (1986). My graph. Proc. London Math. Society 46:117-136.
Faradžev IA, Ivanov AA (1990). Distance-transitive representations of groups G with PSL (2,q)≤G≤PΓL(2,q). Eur. J. Combin. 11:347-356.
Harary F (1969). Graph Theory. Addison-Wesley. Publishing Company, New York.
Higman DG (1970). Characterization of families of rank 3 permutation groups by subdegrees I. Arch Math. 21:151-156.
Jones GA, Singerman D, Wicks K (1991). Generalized Farey graphs in groups, St. Andrews 1989, Eds. C. Campbell and E.F. Robertson, London mathematical society lecture notes series 160, Cambridge University Press, Cambridge pp. 316-338.
Kamuti IN (2006). Subdegrees of primitive permutation representation of $PGL(2,q)$, East Afr. J. Physic. Sci. 7(½): pp. 25-41.
Kamuti IN (1992). Combinatorial formulas, invariants and structures associated with primitive permutation representations of PSL (2,q) and PGL (2,q), Ph.D. Thesis, University of Southampton, U.K.
Krishnamurthy V (1985). Comb Theor Applic. Affiliatede East-West Press Private Limited, New Delhi.
Neumann PM (1977). Finite Permutation Groups, edge-coloured Graphs and. Matrices, in : M. P. J. Curran (Ed.), Topics in Group Theory and. Computation, Academic Press, London, New York, San Fransisco, 82-117.
Petersen J (1898). Sur le Theore' me de Tait Intermed. Math 5:225-227.

Improving the order selection of moving average time series model

Ali Hussein Al-Marshadi

Department of Statistics, Faculty of Science, King Abdulaziz University, Jeddah, Saudi Arabia.
E-mail: ALMarshadi-a@hotmail.com.

We propose an approach could be used to select the right order of moving average model. We used simulation study to compare four model selection criteria with and without the help of our approach. The comparison of the four model selection criteria was in terms of their percentage of number of times that they identify the right order of moving average model with and without the help of our approach. The simulation results indicate that overall, our approach showed improving in the performance of the four model selection criteria comparing to their performance without the help of our approach, where the Schwarz's Bayes information criteria (SBC) criterion provided the best performance for all the cases considered in the study. The main result of our article is that we recommend using our approach with SBC criterion as a standard procedure to identify the right order of moving average model.

Key words: Time series, moving average process, information criteria, MCB Procedure.

INTRODUCTION

An autoregressive moving average, {ARMA (p,q)}, model is a model for a time series that is originally stationary of order p,q with the form:

$$X_t = C + \sum_{k=1}^{p} \phi_k X_{t-k} + \sum_{m=1}^{q} \theta_m \varepsilon_{t-m} + \varepsilon_t , \qquad (1)$$

In this model the time series depends on p past values of itself and on q past random error terms ε that have $E(\varepsilon_t)=0,\ Var(\varepsilon_t)=\sigma^2$ and $Cov(\varepsilon_t,\varepsilon_{t-k})=0$, for all t, the parameters $\phi_1,\phi_2,...,\phi_p$ are the autoregressive parameters associated with the time series values, the parameters $\theta_1,\theta_2,...,\theta_q$ are moving average parameters associated with the error terms, p is the order of the autoregressive component of the time series process, and q is the order of the moving average component of the time series process (Box and Jenkins, 1976; Pankratz, 1983).

In this paper we are concerned with originally stationary moving average model {MA(q)} which is a special case of the autoregressive moving average {ARMA (p,q)} model. The selection of the suitable order of autoregressive moving average process is critical step in the analysis of time series since inappropriate order selection may result into inconsistent estimate of parameters and it increase the variance of the model when the order greater than the true value (Shibata, 1976). In practice statisticians recommend using information criterion to select the true model order among the class of candidate model orders (Hurvich and Tsai, 1991; Kadilar and Erdemir, 2002; Sen, and Shitan, 2002; Andr´es et al., 2004; Sak et al., 2005; Nakamura et al., 2006; Aladag et al., 2010). Statisticians often use information criteria such as Akaike's information criterion (AIC) by Akaike (1969), Schwarz's Bayes information criteria (SBC) by Schwarz (1978), Hannan's, and Quinn's information criterion (HQIC) by Hannan and Quinn (1979), and Bias-Corrected Akaike's information criterion (AICC) by Hurvich and Tsai (1989) to select the true model order. Lately, many studies have proposed and evaluated either new or modified criteria that are used to select the true model order (Padmanabhan and Rao, 1982; Wong and Li, 1998; Wu and Sepulveda, 1998; Jun-ichiro, 1999; Broersen and de Waele, 2002; Kadilar and Erdemir, 2002; Sen, and Shitan, 2002; Andr´es et al., 2004; Sak et al., 2005; Bengtsson and Cavanaugh, 2006; Nakamura et al., 2006;

Guoqi, and Xindong, 2007; Aladaget al., 2010; AL-Marshadi, 2011; Neelabh et al., 2011). Unfortunately, these criteria sometimes have low percentage of selecting the true model order.

Our research objective is to evaluate an approach which could be used to select the true moving average model order. Also, our research objective involves comparing four model selection criteria in terms of their ability to identify the right model order with and without the help of our approach.

METHODOLOGY

The ARMA procedure of the SAS system is a standard tool for fitting time series data. One of the main reasons that the ARMA procedure of the SAS system is very popular is the fact that it is a general-purpose procedure for time series data. In ARMA procedure, users find the following two model selection information criteria available, which can be used as tools to select the true model order. The two model selection information criteria are (SAS Institute Inc., 2008):

1) Akaike's Information Criterion (AIC) by Akaike (1969).
2) Schwarz's Bayes Information Criteria (SBC) by Schwarz (1978).

Two more model selection criteria will be considered in this study that are bias-corrected Akaike's information criterion (AICC) by Hurvich and Tsai (1989), and Hannan and Quinn Information Criterion (HQIC) by Hannan and Quinn (1979). Our study concerns with comparing the four information criteria in terms of their ability to identify the true moving average model order with and without the help of our approach.

Our approach involves using sequence sampling technique and the multiple comparisons with the best (MCB) procedure by Hsu (1984) as tools to help the four information criterion in identifying the right moving average model order (AL-Marshadi, 2011). The idea of our approach can be justified and applied in a very general context, one which includes the selection of the true moving average model order.

In the context of the moving average models, the algorithm for using the sequence sampling technique in our approach can be outlined as follows:

Let the observed order vector of data O_1 is defined as follows:

$$O_1 = \left[X_{(1)} \quad X_{(2)} \quad X_{(3)} \quad X_{(4)} \quad X_{(5)} \quad \ldots \quad X_{(n)}\right]',$$

1. Generate the new sequence samples $(O_1, O_2, \ldots., O_n)$ using the sequence sampling technique according to the order of the observed data (original sample) as follow:

$$O_1 = \left[X_{(1)} \quad X_{(2)} \quad X_{(3)} \quad X_{(4)} \quad X_{(5)} \quad \ldots \quad X_{(n)}\right]',$$

$$O_2 = \left[X_{(2)} \quad X_{(3)} \quad X_{(4)} \quad X_{(5)} \quad \ldots \quad X_{(n)} \quad X_{(1)}\right]',$$

$$O_3 = \left[X_{(3)} \quad X_{(4)} \quad X_{(5)} \quad \ldots \quad X_{(n)} \quad X_{(1)} \quad X_{(2)}\right]',$$

$$O_4 = \left[X_{(4)} \quad X_{(5)} \quad \ldots \quad X_{(n)} \quad X_{(1)} \quad X_{(2)} \quad X_{(3)}\right]',$$

$$O_n = \left[X_{(n)} \quad X_{(1)} \quad X_{(2)} \quad . \quad . \quad . \quad X_{(n-2)} \quad X_{(n-1)}\right]'$$

2. Fit all the class of candidate model orders of moving average model, which we would like to select the true model order among them, to the observed data, (O_1), thereby obtaining the AIC*, HQIC*, AICC*, and SBC* for each model order of the class of candidate model.

3. Repeat step (2) for each data sequence, $(O_2, \ldots., O_n)$.

4. Statisticians often use the previous collection of information criteria to select the right model order such as selecting the model with the smallest value of the information criteria (Pankratz, 1983). We will follow the same rule in our approach, but we have the advantage that each information criteria has (n) replication values result of fitting the different sequences of the observed data (from step 1, 2, and 3). To make use of this advantage, we propose using MCB procedure by Hsu (1984) to pick the winners (that is, selecting the best set of models or single model if possible), when we consider the replicates of the information criteria, that is produced by each of the candidate model, as group (AL-Marshadi, 2011).

THE SIMULATION STUDY

A simulation study of PROC ARMA's time series model analysis of data was conducted to compare the four model selection criteria with and without our approach in terms of their percentage of number of times that they identify the right model order.

Normal data were generated according to stationary moving average model with first and second orders. There were 24 scenarios to generate data involving four settings of the first order moving average, and four settings of the second order moving average, with three different sample sizes (n=25, 50, and 100 observations). The four settings of parameter values for first order moving average model and the four settings of parameter values for second order moving average model are given in Table 1. For those scenarios with sample size 25, we simulated 200 datasets, for those scenarios with sample size 50, we simulated 100 datasets, and for those scenarios with sample size 100, we simulated 50 datasets. SAS code was written to generate the datasets according to the described setup using the SAS®9.1.3 package (SAS Institute Inc., 2008). The algorithm of our approach was applied to each one of the generated data sets with each candidate model (MA(1), MA(2), MA(3), MA(4), MA(5), and MA(6), total of 6 models) for each one of the four information criteria in order to compare their performance with and without our approach. The objective of implanting MCB procedure by Hsu (1984) in our approach is to select models into a subset with a probability of correct selection $p(\text{correct selection})=(1\text{-}\alpha)$ that the "best" model is included in the subset where the subset could be single model if possible.

RESULTS AND DISCUSSION

The simulation results indicated that our procedure selects the right model order as member of the best subset hundred percent of the times from the class of candidate model orders for all the information criteria. Table 2 summarizes results of the percentage of number of times that the procedure selects the right model order alone from the class of candidate model orders (MA(1), MA(2), MA(3), MA(4), MA(5), and MA(6)) that is, out of 6 models for the four criteria with our approach and also, the percentage of number of times without our approach,

Table 1. The four settings of parameters for the two simulated moving average models used in the simulations.

Setting number	MA(1) model	MA(2) model	
	θ_1	θ_1	θ_2
1	0.8	0.5	0.4
2	-0.9	0.4	-0.5
3	0.5	0.4	-0.3
4	-0.6	0.7	0.28

Table 2. The Percentage of number of times that the procedure selects the right model order alone from the class of candidate model for the four criteria with the first parameters setting, and (nominal type I error=0.05).

Sample size	The right model	The four criteria							
		With the new approach				Without the new approach			
		AIC (%)	HQIC (%)	AICC (%)	SBC (%)	AIC (%)	HQIC (%)	AICC (%)	SBC (%)
25	MA(1)	79.00	84.00	92.00	95.00	51.50	56.00	72.00	80.50
	MA(2)	84.00	89.50	96.00	94.50	27.00	33.00	42.50	37.00
50	MA(1)	77.00	84.00	88.00	98.00	63.00	67.00	72.00	92.00
	MA(2)	72.00	81.00	88.00	91.00	45.00	47.00	51.00	68.00
100	MA(1)	50.00	60.00	60.00	98.00	64.00	66.00	66.00	88.00
	MA(2)	68.00	74.00	74.00	96.00	56.00	66.00	66.00	78.00

Table 3. The Percentage of number of times that the procedure selects the right model order alone from the class of candidate model for the four criteria with the second parameters setting, and (nominal type I error=0.05).

Sample size	The right model	The four criteria							
		With the new approach				Without the new approach			
		AIC (%)	HQIC (%)	AICC (%)	SBC (%)	AIC (%)	HQIC (%)	AICC (%)	SBC (%)
25	MA(1)	94.50	96.50	98.50	99.00	70.00	71.00	81.50	87.50
	MA(2)	96.50	97.00	99.00	99.50	52.00	56.00	63.00	59.50
50	MA(1)	96.00	97.00	99.00	100.0	68.00	71.00	75.00	92.00
	MA(2)	82.00	87.00	91.00	97.00	52.00	58.00	61.00	71.00
100	MA(1)	78.00	80.00	80.00	100.0	60.00	62.00	62.00	98.00
	MA(2)	70.00	76.00	76.00	98.00	62.00	68.00	66.00	90.00

using the first parameters setting when n=25, 50, and 100. Table 3 summarizes results of the percentage of number of times that the procedure selects the right model order alone from the class of candidate model orders (MA(1), MA(2), MA(3), MA(4), MA(5), and MA(6)) that is, out of 6 models for the four criteria with our approach and also, the percentage of number of times without our approach, using the second parameters setting when n=25, 50, and 100. Table 4 summarizes results of the percentage of number of times that the procedure selects the right model order alone from the class of candidate model orders (MA(1), MA(2), MA(3), MA(4), MA(5), and MA(6)) that is, out of 6 models for the four criteria with our approach and also, the percentage of number of times without our approach, using the third parameters setting when n=25, 50, and 100. Table 5 summarizes results of the percentage of number of times that the procedure selects the right model order alone from the class of candidate model orders (MA(1), MA(2), MA(3), MA(4), MA(5), and MA(6)) that is, out of 6 models for the four criteria with our approach and also, the percentage of number of times without our approach, using the fourth parameters setting when n=25, 50, and 100. Table 6 summarizes results of the average percentage of number of times that the procedure selects the right model order alone from the class of candidate model orders (MA(1), MA(2), MA(3), MA(4), MA(5), and MA(6)) that is, out of 6 models for the four criteria with our approach and also, the average percentage of number of times without our approach, averaging over

Table 4. The Percentage of number of times that the procedure selects the right model order alone from the class of candidate model for the four criteria with the third parameters setting, and (nominal type I error=0.05).

Sample size	The right model	The four criteria							
		With the new approach				Without the new approach			
		AIC (%)	HQIC (%)	AICC (%)	SBC (%)	AIC (%)	HQIC (%)	AICC (%)	SBC (%)
25	MA(1)	74.50	79.50	92.00	94.00	47.50	52.00	70.00	78.00
	MA(2)	93.00	97.00	98.50	96.00	33.50	35.50	40.50	35.00
50	MA(1)	67.00	73.00	86.00	98.00	58.00	62.00	67.00	92.00
	MA(2)	76.00	84.00	86.00	80.00	40.00	47.00	49.00	49.00
100	MA(1)	64.00	74.00	74.00	100.0	62.00	68.00	68.00	94.00
	MA(2)	70.00	74.00	74.00	92.00	66.00	68.00	68.00	74.00

Table 5. The Percentage of number of times that the procedure selects the right model order alone from the class of candidate model for the four criteria with the fourth parameters setting, and (nominal type I error=0.05).

Sample size	The right model	The four criteria							
		With the new approach				Without the new approach			
		AIC (%)	HQIC (%)	AICC (%)	SBC (%)	AIC (%)	HQIC (%)	AICC (%)	SBC (%)
25	MA(1)	89.00	92.50	97.50	98.00	64.00	67.00	76.00	84.00
	MA(2)	86.50	92.00	96.50	93.50	21.50	24.00	28.00	26.00
50	MA(1)	81.00	89.00	94.00	99.00	59.00	62.00	68.00	91.00
	MA(2)	71.00	81.00	90.00	87.00	32.00	39.00	42.00	35.00
100	MA(1)	70.00	76.00	76.00	100.0	62.00	66.00	66.00	96.00
	MA(2)	60.00	74.00	70.00	82.00	56.00	64.00	64.00	58.00

Table 6. The Average percentage of number of times that the procedure selects the right model order alone from the class of candidate model for the four criteria averaging over the four parameters settings, and (nominal type I error=0.05).

Sample size	The right model	The four criteria							
		With the new approach				Without the new approach			
		AIC(%)	HQIC (%)	AICC (%)	SBC (%)	AIC (%)	HQIC (%)	AICC (%)	SBC (%)
25	MA(1)	84.25	88.125	95.00	96.50	58.25	61.500	74.875	82.500
	MA(2)	90.00	93.875	97.50	95.87	33.50	37.125	43.500	39.375
50	MA(1)	80.25	85.750	91.75	98.75	62.00	65.500	70.500	91.750
	MA(2)	75.25	83.250	88.75	88.75	42.25	47.750	50.750	55.750
100	MA(1)	65.50	72.500	72.50	99.50	62.00	65.500	65.500	94.000
	MA(2)	67.00	74.500	73.50	92.00	60.00	66.500	66.000	75.000

the four parameters settings when n=25, 50, and 100.

Although our approach shows very good performance over all with all the criteria in all the cases, it was outstanding with SBC criterion.

Conclusion

In our simulation, we considered moving average process, looking at the performance of our approach for selecting the right moving average model order under different scenarios. Overall, our approach provided the best performance in selecting the right model order. Our approach showed outstanding performance with SBC criterion. Thus, our approach can be recommended to be used with the SBC criterion. Note for users of our approach: if the MCB procedure suggested the best subset of models contains more than one model, we recommend selecting the right model as the one with a smaller order since the examination of simulation results showed that in this case the other models are over fitted models, *i.e.* model that contains the right order of the true model and higher order terms. The main result of our article is that the SBC criterion is the best criteria in term of their ability to identifying the right model order with the help of our approach.

REFERENCES

Akaike H (1974). A new look at the statistical model identification. Trans. Autom. Control, 19: 716-723. DOI:10.1109/TAC.1974.1100705.

Aladag CH, Egrioglu E, Gunay S, Basaran MA (2010). Improving weighted information criterion by using optimization. J. Comput. Appl. Math., 233: 2683-2687. DOI:10.1016/j.cam.2009.11.016.

AL-Marshadi AH (2011). New Procedure to Improve the Order Selection of Autoregressive Time Series Model. J. Math. Stat., 7(4):270-274. http://thescipub.com /stat/10.3844 /jmssp.2011.270.274.

Andr´es MA, Daniel P, Juan R (2004). Introducing Model Uncertainty In Time Series Bootstrap. Statistica Sinica, 14: 155-174. http://www3.stat.sinica.edu.tw/statistica /oldpdf/A14n16.pdf.

Bengtsson T, Cavanaugh JE (2006). An Improved Akaike Information Criterion for State-Space Model Selection. Comput. Stat. Data Anal., 50(10): 2635-2654. DOI:10.1016/j.csda.2005.05.003.

Box GEP, Jenkins GM (1976). Time Series Analysis: Forecasting and Control. 1st Edn., Holden-Day, San Francisco, ISBN: 0816211043, p. 575. http://onlinelibrary.wiley.com/doi/10.1002/9780470316566.fmatter/pdf

Broersen PMT. de Waele S (2002). Costs of Order Selection in Time Series Analysis. IEEE Instrumentation and Measurement, Technology Conference, Anchorage, AK, USA, 21-23 May, 2002. DOI: 10.1109/IMTC.2002.1006858 http://ieeexplore.ieee.org/xpl /free abs_all.jsp?arnumber=1006858.

Guoqi Q, Xindong Z (2007). On time series model selection involving many candidate ARMA models. Comput. Stat. Data Anal., 51: 6180 – 6196. http://www.sdasinfo. org.cn/zjk/%E9%87%8D%E7%82%B9%E9%A2%86%E5%9F%9F%E6%95%B0%E6%8D%AE%E5%BA%93/wf3012.pdf.

Hannan EJ, Quinn BG (1979). The Determination of the order of an autoregression. J. Royal Stat. Soc., Ser. B., 41: 190–195. http://www.citeulike.org/user/fabiobayer/article/4647560.

Hsu JC (1984). Constrained simultaneous confidence intervals for multiple comparisons with the best. Ann. Stat., 12: 1136-1144. http://www.jstor.org/pss/2240990.

Hurvich CM, Tsai CL (1989). Regression and time series model selection in small samples. Biometrika, 76: 297-307. DOI: 10.1093/biomet/76.2.297.

Hurvich CM, Tsai CL (1991). Bias of the corrected AIC criterion for underfitted regression and time series models. Biometrika, 78(3): 499-509. DOI:10.1093/biomet/78.3.49.

Jun-ichiro F (1999). Subsampling and Model Selection in Time Series Analysis. Biometrika, 86(3): 591-604. http://www.jstor. org/pss/2673656.

Kadilar C, Erdemir C (2002). Comparison of performance among information criteria in var and seasonal var models. Hacettepe J. Math. Stat., 31: 127-137. http://www.mat.hacettepe.edu.tr/hjms/english/issues/vol31/full-text/127-137.pdf.

Nakamura T, Judd K, Mees AI, Small M (2006). A comparative study of information criteria for model selection. Int. J. Bifurcat. Chaos, 16(8): 2153-2175. http://www.eie.polyu.edu.hk/~ensmall/pdf/IJBC16-2.pdf.

Neelabh R, Ramanathan TV (2011). A study on the focused information criterion for order selection in ARMA models. Technical Report 1/2011, Department of Statistics and Centre for Advanced Studies University of Pune, 411 007, INDIA. http://stats.unipune.ernet.in /TVR-NR.pdf.

Padmanabhan G, Rao AR (1982). Order selection of AR models of Hydrologic Time Series. Nordic Hydrol., 13: 93-104. http://www.iwaponline.com/nh/013/0093/0130093.pdf.

Pankratz A (1983). Forcasting with Univariate Box-Jenkins Model: Concepts and Cases. 1st Edn., John Wiley & Sons, Inc., New York, ISBN 0-471-09023, p. 562. DOI: 10.1002/9780470316566.fmatter http://onlinelibrary.wiley.com/doi/10.1002/9780470316566.fmatter/pdf

Sak M, Dowe D, Ray S (2005). Minimum message length moving average time series data mining. Computational Intelligence Methods and Applications, 2005 ICSC Congress on, 6. DOI:10.1109/CIMA. 2005.1662352http://ieeexplore.ieee. org/Xplore/login.jsp?url=http%3A%2F%2Fieeexplore.ieee.org%2Fstamp%2Fstamp.jsp%3Ftp%3D%26arnumber%3D1662352&authDecision=-203.

SAS Institute Inc (2008). SAS OnlineDoc 9.1.3. SAS Institute Inc., Cary, NC. http://support.sas.com/onlinedoc/913/docMainpage.jsp.

Schwartz G (1978). Estimating the Dimension of a Model. Ann. Stat., 6: 461-464. http://projecteuclid.org/DPubS?service=UI&version=1.0&verb=Display&handle= euclid.aos/1176344136.

Sen LK, Shitan M (2002). The Performance of AICC as an Order Selection Criterion in ARMA Time Series Models. Pertanika J. Sci. Technol., 10(1): 25-33. http://psasir.upm.edu.my/3803/1/The_Performance_of_AICC_as_an_Order_Selection_Criterion_in.pdf.

Shibata R (1976). Selection of the order of an Autoregressive model by Akaike Information Criterion. Biometrika, 63: 117-126. DOI:10.1093/biomet/63.1.117.

Wong CS, Li WK (1998). A note on the corrected Akaike Information criterion for threshold Autoregressive models. J. Time Ser. Anal., 19(1): 113-124. DOI: 10.1111/1467-9892.00080.

Wu T-J, Sepulveda A (1998). The weighted average information criterion for order selection in time series and regression models. Stat. Prob. Lett., 39: 1-10. DOI:10.1016/S0167-7152(98)00003-0.

Einstein's equivalence principle has three further implications besides affecting time: T-L-M-Ch theorem ("Telemach")

Otto E. Rossler

Institute for Physical and Theoretical Chemistry, University of Tubingen, Auf der Morgenstelle18, 72076 Tubingen, F.R.G., Germany. E-mail: oeross00@yahoo.com.

General relativity is notoriously difficult to interpret. A "return to the mothers" is proposed to better understand the gothic-R theorem of the Schwarzschild metric of general relativity. It is shown that the new finding is already implicit in Einstein's equivalence principle of 1907 and hence in special relativity (with acceleration included). The TeLeMaCh theorem, named onomatopoetically after Telemachus, is bound to transform metrology if correct.

Key words: Equivalence principle, Telemach theorem, Schwarzschild metric, metrology, Large Hadron Collider (LHC).

INTRODUCTION

Recently it was shown that the Schwarzschild metric of general relativity admits at least one further canonical observable, the so-called gothic-R distance (Rossler, 2007). In terms of this distance, the speed of light c is globally constant. Is this result only a new mathematically allowed physical interpretation, or does it have deeper "ontological" significance?

A convenient way to find out is to pass over to an even more fundamental level of description. The "equivalence principle" between kinematic and gravitational acceleration, which still belongs to special relativity, is the oldest and in a sense most powerful element of general relativity since everything grew out of this "happiest thought of my life" as Einstein used to call it.

A famous "ontological" implication of the equivalence principle is the slower ticking rate of clocks at the rear end of a long constantly accelerating train or rocketship. It was deduced by Einstein in a chain of heuristic mental steps. The latter involved light-pulse emitting clocks and light-pulse detecting devices, in a mentally pictured scenario comprising long hollow cylinders releasable into free fall and sporting hooks and vertical slits in their sides to allow one to put in clocks and sensors at different height levels, before or after the release into free fall, cf. Pais (1982).

More than a half-century later, Rindler (1968) Succeeded in graphically retrieving all pertinent results described by Einstein in the famous Rindler metric. The latter describes a long collection of simultaneously ignited, infinitesimally short rocketships, or rather hollow rocket-rings that stay together spontaneously owing to a careful choice of their systematically varying constant accelerations. The most concise description of the resulting 2-D space-time diagram, with its "scrollable" simultaneity axes that all pass through a single point, can be found in Wald's (1984) famous, otherwise algebra-oriented book. For an independent re-discovery see Bell's (1976) intriguing paper.

THE SECRET POWER OF THE EQUIVALENCE PRINCIPLE

Clocks at the end of a long constantly accelerating rocket ship in outer space have elongated ticking intervals when their light pulses arrive at the rocket's tip because the latter has in the meantime acquired a well-defined positive velocity compared to the point of origin of the light pulses, as Einstein found out in 1907. The resulting special-relativistic redshift at first sight appears to be a mere observational effect: "in reality" the clocks in question ought to tick at their normal rate (but they do not).

We know how it is with Einstein's deceptively simple gedanken experiments: he has a knack for following them up to a breaking point where something "impossible" occurs. Remember his previous observation of an apparent clock slowdown of a constant-speed departing twin clock which, on returning with the same constant speed, possesses an equally accelerated pulse rate, considered in his seminal founding paper of special relativity of two years before: When the twin clock is back after this "symmetric" departure and return, everyone would have bet that the net effect must be zero when placing the two clocks side by side as physical twins. But to everyone's surprise, a net effect (a manifest lower age of the travelled clock) demonstrably remains: the famous "ontological mehrwert" of Einstein.

Here with the constantly accelerating rocketship, the same thing occurs once more: A clock that is carefully lowered from the tip to the slower-appearing rear-end of the accelerating long rocketship will, after having been hauled back up again,predictably fail to be as old as its stationary twin at the tip (Frolov and Novikov, 1998). This proves that the clocks "downstairs" indeed are ontologically slower-ticking there. Note that the philosophical term "ontological" is totally unfamiliar outside Einsteinian physics.

THREE ADDED IMPLICATIONS OF THE EQUIVALENCE PRINCIPLE

Everything that has been said so far is well known. If the clocks are genuinely slower-ticking downstairs, rather than just looking slower from above: how about the existence of further ontological implications valid at the rear end of the rocketship? This suspicion is justified it turns out. Einstein first found out – as described – that

T_tail = T_tip *(1+z), (1)

where T is the temporal wavelength of the light waves emitted by the equal clocks in question and (z+1) is the local gravitational redshift factor that applies in the Rindler metric; Einstein (1907) called this factor (1+Phi/c^2) with Phi being the gravitational potential.

With Einstein's result put into this simple form, one is immediately led to expect a spatial corollary: If all temporal unit wavelengths T are increased, the very same thing is bound to hold true for the spatial unit wavelengths L of the same light waves:

L_tail = L_tip *(1+z), (2)

And so by implication for all local lengths since everything appears normal locally as mentioned. Formally this conclusion follows from the constancy of the speed of light c (since L/T = c implies L = cT for light waves). If T is locally counterfactually increased by Equation (1) as we saw, L must be equally increased in Equation 2 if c is constant.

Although this is correct and we are here still in the realm of special relativity with its absolutely constant c despite the presence of acceleration, the conclusion just drawn is possibly premature since c is believed to be non-constant in general relativity (only "locally constant"). Therefore it is "safer" to first proceed to M and then from there back to L.

M, the mass of a particle that is locally at rest, is necessarily reduced by the very factor by which T is increased,

M_tail = M_tip /(1+z). (3)

This follows from the fact that all locally normal-appearing photons do by Equation 1 have a proportionally decreased frequency f, and hence have a proportionally reduced energy (by Planck's law E = h*f). They have so much less mass-energy by Einstein's E = mc^2. If all locally generated photons have so much less mass at the rocketship's tail in a locally counterfactual manner, it follows from quantum mechanics that all other masses – by virtue of their being locally inter-transformable into photons (like positronium) in principle – are reduced by the same factor. Hence Equation 3 is valid.

From the M of Equation 3, the L of Equation 2 can now be retrieved as announced - via the Bohr radius formula of quantum mechanics: a_0 = h/(m_e*c*2*pi*alpha), where m_e is the mass of the electron and alpha the dimensionless fine structure constant. But if the radius of the hydrogen atom is increased in proportion to 1/m_e, with m_e varying in accordance with Equation 3, then the size of all objects scales linearly with (1+z) and so does space itself. This was the content of Equation 2.

With Equations 1 to 3 we have arrived at the following abbreviated new law valid in the equivalence principle: "T-L-M." Einstein's old finding of T thus has acquired two corollaries of equal standing, L and M for short. What about the third candidate, Ch for charge?

If mass is counterfactually reduced locally and if charge stands in a fixed ratio to mass locally, then charge is bound to be counterfactually reduced in proportion for every class of charged particles. This follows – to give only one example – from the fact that locally, still two "511 keV" photons suffice to produce a positronium atom consisting of a locally normal-appearing electron and a locally normal-appearing positron. Since both these particles have a reduced mass content by Equation 3 as we saw, they must also have a proportionally reduced charge content, if all laws of nature are to remain intact locally. This latter condition is guaranteed by Einstein's principle of "general covariance" which states that the laws of nature are the same in every locally free-falling inertial system. Note that a freshly released free-falling particle (like our positronium atom) is still locally at rest. Therefore, charge is reduced in proportion to the stationary local mass:

Ch_tail = Ch_tip/(1+z). (4)

The herewith obtained "complete gravitational redshift law of Einstein" comprises 4 individual equations of equal importance. The new law can be condensed into four letters, T-L-M-Ch. Since the very same consonants pertain to a famous personality of mythological history, Ulysses's son Telemach (or Telemachus), the 4-letter result can be called the "Telemach theorem." To witness, the gravitational redshift (1+z) on the surface of a neutron star is of order of magnitude 2. And the gravitational redshift on the surface ("horizon" in Rindler's terminology) of a black hole is infinite. By virtue of Telemach, objects on the surface of a neutron star must be enlarged visibly in the vertical direction by a factor of about two which may be measurable (Kuypers, 2005). In the same vein the distance toward and from the horizon of a black hole has become infinite, as the corresponding light travel time is well-known to be (Frolov and Novikov, 1998: 20). Obviously, no known physical phenomenon contradicts the new result, which moreover retrieves angular momentum conservation (Kuypers, 2005).

DISCUSSION

Two points need to be discussed. First: Is the Telemach theorem derived from the equivalence principle robust enough to carry over to the Schwarzschild metric and from there on to all of general relativity? Second: Is the result acceptable in principle from the point of view of modern physics and specifically the science of metrology?

The first point is easy to answer. All arguments used above carry over to the Schwarzschild metric. The L of Equation 2 is nothing but a "poor man's version" of the gothic-R theorem of the Schwarzschild metric (Rossler, 2007). Conversely, the Schwarzschild metric would have a hard time if the "gothic-R" did not fit the "L" of the more basic theory of the equivalence principle.

Before we come to the testable second point announced, a brief digression into the literature is on line. As noted in Rossler (2007), similar propositions (sub-vectors of T-L-M-Ch as it were) are not unfamiliar. An analog of L was quite often conjectured to hold true in general relativity. For example, an engineer of the Global Positioning System who–in distrust of Einstein – had built-in a special switch in case Einstein's predictions were to prove true, later wrote a paper (Hatch, 2001) to come to grips with his own surprise; in one formula (his Equation 9 for the "local rest mass energy"), he is close to Equation 3. More recently, Cox (2009) in a preliminary paper independently arrived (in the present terminology) at T, L and M; he also was the first scientist to explicitly support Ch (personal communication 2010). Cook (2009) arrived independently at T-L-M (in these very symbols) in general relativity deriving in addition a variation in the gravitational constant G (by the factor (z+1)^2). He has since fully agreed to Ch (personal communication 2011). Ch proves to be the real crux in the present return to the roots of Einstein's theory. A discussion with members of the Albert-Einstein Institute in early 2009 highlighted the fact that validity of the Gauss-Stokes theorem of electrostatics (Wald, 1984: 432) is put at stake by any change in Ch. So is the Reissner-Nordström metric which combines the Schwarzschild metric with an added charge and which no general relativist would easily sacrifice. But this is not all. Even a change in L alone is bad enough already since it likely implies invalidity of the famous Kerr metric, as well as of certain cosmological solutions of the Einstein equation. Thus the aforementioned theory – while implicit in the equivalence principle and the Schwarzschild metric as the heart of general relativity – is by no means an easy-to absorb new implication of general relativity. This fact can explain some of the resistance the gothic-R theorem encountered when first proposed.

The announced second point in need of discussion is even more important because it makes the connection to measurement. Newton abandoned the "Ur-pound" as it were, but left the universal second ("Ur-second") unscathed. The latter was only toppled by Einstein's discovery of the gravity-dependent "local second" T of Equation 1. In the same vein, the universal meter ("Ur-meter") is toppled by the gravity-dependent "local meter" L of Equation 2. The same then holds true for the universal mass ("Ur-kilogram") which is toppled by the gravity-dependent "local mass" M of Equation 3, which now has become different on the moon, too. And finally the universal charge ("Ur-charge") of an electron is toppled by the gravity-dependent "local charge" Ch of Equation 4. The whole to be measured-out cosmos thereby acquires a new face – if Einstein's "happiest thought" (Equation 1) has been correctly elaborated with the newly implied Equations 2 to 4.

In return for this drawback (if it is one), four quantized physical variables must be distinguished, three of them new. Besides

(i) "Kilogram times second" (Leibniz's famous "action"), we now have:
(ii) "Kilogram times meter" ("cession"), Rossler and Giannetti (1997),
(iii) "Coulomb times second" ("el-action"),
and
(iv) "Coulomb times meter" ("el-cession"), Rossler and Fröhlich (2010).

The explanation for (ii) lies in the fact that time and space (Second and Meter) scale in strict parallelism by Equations 1 and 2. The explanation for (iii) and (iv) lies in the fact that rest mass and charge (Kilogram and Coulomb) scale in strict parallelism by Equations 3 and 4. The new quantized magnitudes (iii) and (iv) obey constants of nature and come in several force-specific varieties (Rossler and Fröhlich, 2010). Note that while both G and epsilon_o (and along with it mu_o) cease to be fundamental constants as a consequence of L-M-Ch, their ratio (more precisely the square root of the product of G and epsilon_o) becomes a new fundamental constant of nature which can be named "G_o":

(v) G_o = sqrt(G*epsilon_0) = 2.4308 *10^(-11) C/kg.

A particle-class-specific splitting of Equation (v) is predictable since there are more charges than the electrical one. Many experiments to test the newly derived results (ii-v) can be devised. Radically noveltechnological applications come in sight. Metrology predictably rises in the hierarchy of sciences.

CONCLUSION

In this study a minor revolution in physics was proposed. The skepticism shown by some members of the experimental profession towards the gothic-R theorem is hoped to be overcome with Equations 2 to 4 in view of their testable implications. A famous experiment is affected by the aforementioned results. Its detectors need replacement before continuation because the infinite distance of the horizon (Equation 2) makes black holes immune to Hawking evaporation, and the new unchargedness of black holes (Equation 4) makes them invisible at first. New dangers – even apocalyptic ones – have become recognizable by the Telemach theorem.

Electrons cannot be point masses any more by Equation 4 in empirical confirmation of string theory. This fact makes black hole production much more probable. And the new unchargedness of black holes renders artificial ones frictionless – until the first quark starts spiraling in at which point an exponentially growing "mini-quasar" is formed inside matter (earth). The super fluidity of neutron stars makes these densest objects immune to any natural fast mini black holes (so that all defenses of the LHC experiment collapse as if premeditated by Nature). However, Telemach's youthful and exotic character lets it still appear possible that he belongs more to Homer than to science. Einstein in the dusk of his life came to doubt everything he had done, the atomic bomb being the reason. Now his better understood "happiest thought" offers a rescuing effect.

ACKNOWLEDGEMENTS

Author thanks Eric Penrose, György Garvas and Kai-Long Hsiao for discussions and Peter Plath and Ese Origbo for stimulation. For J.O.R.

REFERENCES

Bell JS (1976). How to teach special relativity. Progress in Scientific Culture 1(2). Reprinted in: Bell.

Cook RJ (2009). Gravitational space dilation. http://arxiv.org/ PS_cache/arxiv/pdf/ 0902/0902.2811v1.pdf

Cox GW (2009).The complete theory of quantum gravity (draft). http://lhc-concern.info/wpcontent/uploads/2009/10/quantum fieldtheory31.pdf.

Einstein A (1907). On the relativity principle and the conclusions drawn from it (in German), in: The Collected Papers of Albert Einstein, Volume 2, The Swiss Years: Writings, 1900-1909, Princeton University Press, Princeton 1989, pp. 252-311, Eq.(30a):306.

Frolov VP, Novikov ID (1998). Black Hole Physics: Basic concepts and New Developments. Kluwer Academic Publishers, Dordrecht, p. 18.

Hatch RR (2001). Modified Lorentz ether theory, Infinite Energy, 39: 14-23.

Kuypers H (2005). Atoms in the Gravitational Field: Hints at a Change of Mass and Size (in German). PhD dissertation submitted to the University of Tubingen, Faculty of Natural Sciences.

Pais A (1982). Subtle is the Lord Oxford University Press, Oxford, pp. 180-181.

Rindler W (1968). Counterexample to the Lenz-Schiff argument. Am. J. Phys., 36: 540-544.

Rossler OE (2007). Abraham-like return to constant c in general relativity: gothic-R theorem demonstrated in Schwarzschild metric. Paper accepted for publication in Chaos, Solitons and Fractals. Revised 2009 version on: http://www.wissens navigator. com/documents/Chaos.pdf.
(Remark: Bernhard Umlauf kindly showed that Eq.9 contains a calculation error by stating correctly that "the numerator of the fraction under the natural logarithm must read r_0^(1/2)+(r_0-2m)^(1/2) and the denominator analogously must read r_i^(1/2)+(r_i-2m)^(1/2)"; this correction leaves the text unchanged.)

Rossler OE, Fröhlich D (2010).The weight of the Urkilogram.http://www.achtphasen.net/index.php/plasmaether/2010/12/11/p1890.

Rossler OE, Giannetti C (1997). Cession, twin of action (The assignment: action hermanagemela). Art in the electronic era (C Giannetti, ed.). Association of CulturaTemporániaL'Angelot and Goethe-Institute Barcelona, Barcelona, p. 124.

Wald RM (1984). General Relativity. University of Chicago Press, Chicago, p. 151.

Temperature-dependent thermal stress determination of an isotropic circular annular fin

Navneet Kumar Lamba*, Warbhe M. S. and Khobragade N. W.

Department of Mathematics P.G.T.D. RTM Nagpur University, Nagpur, India.

This paper is concerned with an inverse thermoelastic problem in which we need to determine the temperature distribution, unknown temperature gradient, displacement, stress functions and thermal stresses on the outer curved surface of a thin annular fin when the interior heat flux is known. Finite classical Marchi-Zgrablich transform and Laplace transform techniques have been utilized to obtain the solution for the problem. The results are obtained in the form of Marchi-Zgrablich series and depicted graphically.

Key words: Inverse transient problem, circular annular fin, Marchi-Zgrablich and Laplace transform.

INTRODUCTION

The typical problems of the transient thermal stresses in an annular fin have been investigated by Shang-Sheng (1997) and the solution has been obtained with the help of exponential-like solution. Deshmukh et al. (2003) analyzed the transient thermal stresses applying Hankel transform and Fourier transform techniques, where temperature transfer condition was prescribed on the surface of annular fin and the solution results at point interior to the body. The boundary value problem described by Wu et al. (1997) and then Deshmukh and Kedar (2011) occurs in design application, while interior value problem occurs in quenching studies and in the measurement of aerodynamic heating etc. Jaeger and Carslaw (1959) studied conduction of heat in solids. But for interior value problem, special methods are employed and it is necessary to provide invaluable check on the accuracy of numerical or approximate schemes and allow for widely applicable parametric studies. The temperature distribution for steady-state heat transfer and the thermal stresses induced by a temperature difference in a silicon carbide (SiC) ceramic tube with a circular fin are studied by Yasar (2004), and Lien-Tsai and Cha'o-Kuang (1998) presented the stresses distribution in a perfectly elastic isotropic annular fin. The Taylor transformation method is used to solve the nonlinear temperature field equation.

The stresses distribution are integrated obtain the results. Yu-Ching and Shao-Shu (2001) investigated the transient coupled thermoelasticity of an annular fin with its base suddenly subjected to a heat flux of a decayed exponential function of time. While neglecting the effect of the inertia term in the governing equation of motion, the thermo mechanical coupling effect is taken into account in the governing equation of heat conduction.

Correlation equations for optimum design of annular fins with temperature-dependent thermal conductivity are obtained by Cihat (2010). In this nonlinear fin equation which is associated with variable thermal conductivity condition is solved by Adomian decomposition method that provides an analytical solution in the form of an infinite power series. Mustafa et al. (2011) provided analytical solutions for temperature distribution and heat transfer rate for orthotropic two-dimensional, annular fins subject to convective-tip boundary condition and the contact resistance at the fin base. The generalized results are presented in terms of one geometric parameter (b/a) and three dimensionless fin parameters that relate the internal conductive resistance to three convective resistances discussed in terms of dimensionless variables such as contact, tip and axial Biot numbers (Bicr ; Bier ; Biz), in addition to the axial-to-radial conductivity ratio, K. Several special cases including the insulated tip boundary condition are presented. Chiu and Chen (2002) Investigated stress-field

*Corresponding author. E-mail: navneetkumarlamba@gmail.com.

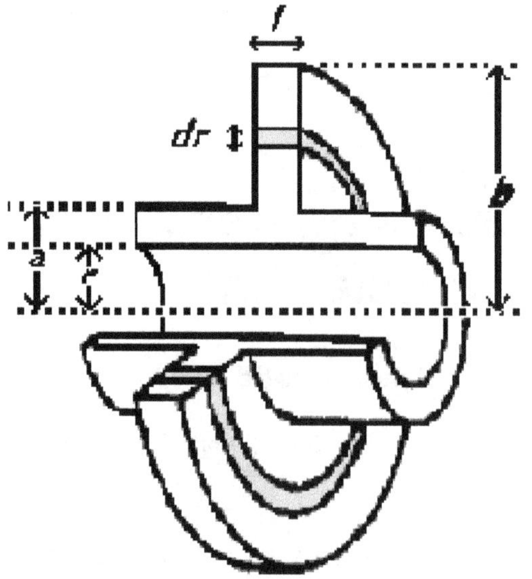

Figure 1. Cross-sectional view of an isotropic circular annular fin.

in an annular fin of temperature-dependent conductivity under a periodic heat transfer boundary condition is analyzed by the Adomian's decomposition method. The distribution of the transient thermal stress is obtained by direct integration of the temperature distribution.

The present paper attempts to generalize the problem considered by Shang-Sheng (1997) and obtain the exact solution of the inverse problem. This paper further investigates the transient thermal stresses by the use of finite Marchi- Zgrablich transform and Laplace transform techniques. The results are obtained in the form of Marchi-Zgrablich series.

Statement of the problem

Consider an isotropic annular fin occupying the space $D=\{(x, y, z)\in R^3: \quad a\le (x^2+y^2)^{1/2}\le b, \ \ 0\le z\le l\}$. The material of the fin is isotropic, homogenous and all properties are assumed to be constant. We assume that the fin is of a small thickness and its boundary surfaces remain traction free (Figure 1). The governing equations and boundary conditions for the stress field (Boley and Weiner, 1960) consist of: a non-zero stress strain-displacement equation:

$$\varepsilon_r = \frac{\partial u}{\partial r}, \ \ \varepsilon_\phi = \frac{u}{r} \tag{1}$$

A single equilibrium equation

$$\frac{d\sigma_r}{dr} + \frac{\sigma_r - \sigma_\phi}{r} = 0 \tag{2}$$

two equations of stress-strain-temperature relations:

$$\sigma_r = \frac{E}{1-\upsilon^2}\left[\varepsilon_r + \upsilon\varepsilon_\phi - (1+\upsilon)\alpha T\right] \tag{3}$$

$$\sigma_\phi = \frac{E}{1-\upsilon^2}\left[\varepsilon_\phi + \upsilon\varepsilon_r + (1+\upsilon)\alpha T\right] \tag{4}$$

and, two boundary conditions

$$\sigma_r = 0 \ \text{ at } \ r = a \tag{5}$$

$$\sigma_r = 0 \ \text{ at } \ r = b \tag{6}$$

Combining Equations 1 to 4, integrating twice with respect to r, and applying the boundary conditions (5, 6), one obtains the stress-displacement relations as;

$$\sigma_r = -\frac{\alpha E}{r^2}\int_a^r (T-T_\infty)\eta\, d\eta + \frac{\alpha E}{b^2-a^2}\left(1-\frac{a^2}{r^2}\right)\int_a^b (T-T_\infty)\eta\, d\eta \tag{7}$$

$$\sigma_\phi = -\alpha E(T-T_\infty) + \frac{\alpha E}{r^2}\int_a^r (T-T_\infty)\eta\, d\eta + \frac{\alpha E}{b^2-a^2}\left(1-\frac{a^2}{r^2}\right)\int_a^b (T-T_\infty)\eta\, d\eta \tag{8}$$

Substituting these expressions, for the radial and tangential stresses into the stress equilibrium Equation (2), leads to the following governing equation for the thermoelastic equilibrium of the circular annular fin in qualitative agreement with equations found earlier [3 and 6]:

$$k\left(\frac{\partial^2 T}{\partial r^2} + \frac{1}{r}\frac{\partial T}{\partial r} + \frac{\partial^2 T}{\partial z^2}\right) - \frac{2h}{l}\left(T - T_\infty\right) = \rho c\frac{\partial T}{\partial t}$$

$$a \le r \le b, \ 0\le z\le l \ \text{ and } \ t > 0 \tag{9}$$

Introducing the following dimensionless parameters as defined in the nomenclature (Appendix):

$$\theta = \frac{k(T-T_\infty)}{(q_b a)}, \ \ \xi = \frac{r}{a}, \ \ \zeta = \frac{z}{a}, \ \ L = \frac{l}{a}$$

$$\tau = \frac{(kt)}{\left(\rho c a^2\right)}, \ \ R = \frac{b}{a}, \ \ N^2 = \frac{2ha^2}{kl}$$

Equation 9 can be written in the dimensionless form as:

$$\frac{\partial^2\theta}{\partial\xi^2}+\frac{1}{\xi}\frac{\partial\theta}{\partial\xi}+\frac{\partial^2\theta}{\partial\zeta^2}-N^2\theta=\frac{\partial\theta}{\partial\tau}\quad 1\le\xi\le R,$$

$$0\le\zeta\le L,\ \tau>0 \tag{10}$$

The dimensionless radial and tangential stresses S_r and S_ϕ in terms of the dimensionless displacement function are,

$$S_r=-\frac{1}{\xi^2}\int_1^\xi \theta\xi\,d\xi+\frac{1}{\xi^2}\frac{\xi^2-1}{R^2-1}\int_1^R \theta\xi\,d\xi \tag{11}$$

$$S_\phi=-\theta+\frac{1}{\xi^2}\int_1^\xi \theta\xi\,d\xi+\frac{1}{\xi^2}\frac{\xi^2+1}{R^2-1}\int_1^R \theta\xi\,d\xi \tag{12}$$

The various dimensionless boundary conditions are defined to determine the influence of the thermal boundary conditions on the thermal stresses as:

The initial condition;

$\theta(\xi,\zeta,\tau)=0$, for all $1\le\xi\le R$, $0\le\zeta\le L$ and $\tau=0$ (13)

the boundary conditions;

$$\left[\theta(\xi,\zeta,\tau)+k_1\frac{\partial\theta(\xi,\zeta,\tau)}{\partial\xi}\right]_{\xi=1}=F_1(\zeta,\tau)$$

for all $0\le\zeta\le L$ and $\tau>0$ (14)

$$\left[\theta(\xi,\zeta,\tau)+k_2\frac{\partial\theta(\xi,\zeta,\tau)}{\partial\xi}\right]_{\xi=R}=F_R(\zeta,\tau)$$

for all $0\le\zeta\le L$ and $\tau>0$ (15)

where k_1 and k_2 are the radiation constants on the two annular fin surfaces;

$$\left[\theta(\xi,\zeta,\tau)+\frac{\partial\theta(\xi,\zeta,\tau)}{\partial\xi}\right]_{\xi=0}=0$$

for all $1\le\xi\le R$ and $\tau>0$ (16)

$[\theta(\xi,\zeta,\tau)]_{\zeta=L}=g(\xi,\tau)$ (unknown)

for all $1\le\xi\le R$ and $\tau>0$ (17)

The interior condition is;

$$\left[\frac{\partial\theta(\xi,\zeta,\tau)}{\partial\zeta}\right]_{\zeta=\frac{\eta}{a}}=f(\xi,\tau)$$

for all $1\le\xi\le R$ and $\tau>0$ (18)

where $F_1(\zeta,\tau)$ and $F_R(\zeta,\tau)$ are constants and here it is set to be zero, as this assumption, commonly made in the literatures [6] and [8], leads to considerable mathematical simplification and the function $f(\xi,\tau)$ is assumed to be known while the function $g(\xi,\tau)$ is not.

Equations 10 to 18 constitute the mathematical formulation of the problem under consideration.

SOLUTION OF THE PROBLEM

Applying finite Marchi-Zgrablich integral transform (Marchi and Zgrablich, 1964) to Equations 10 to 18, and then simultaneously utilizing Equations 14 and 15 in the operational property of finite Marchi-Zgrablich transform, one obtains;

$$-\mu_n^2\,\bar{\theta}(n,\zeta,\tau)+\frac{\partial^2\bar{\theta}(n,\zeta,\tau)}{\partial\zeta^2}-N^2\bar{\theta}(n,\zeta,\tau)=\frac{\partial\bar{\theta}(n,\zeta,\tau)}{\partial\tau} \tag{19}$$

Where μ_n are the positive roots of equation $J_p(k_1,\mu a).Y_p(k_2,\mu b)-J_p(k_2,\mu b).Y_p(k_1,\mu a)=0$.

Applying Laplace transform (Sneddon, 1972) to Equation 19 and boundary conditions 13, 16 to 18, one obtains

$$-\mu_n^2\,\bar{\theta}^*(n,\zeta,s)+\frac{\partial^2\bar{\theta}^*(n,\zeta,s)}{\partial\zeta^2}-N^2\bar{\theta}^*(n,\zeta,s)=s\bar{\theta}^*(n,\zeta,s) \tag{20}$$

Equation 20 is a second order differential equation whose solution is given by:

$$\bar{\theta}^*(n,\zeta,s)=Ae^{q\zeta}+Be^{-q\zeta} \tag{21}$$

Where $q=(\mu_n^2+N^2+s)^{1/2}$, s is the Laplace parameter, A and B are two arbitrary constants.

Using Equations 16 and 18 in 21, we obtain the values of A and B. Substituting these values in Equation 21one obtains;

$$\bar{\theta}^*(\xi,\zeta,s)=\frac{\bar{f}^*(n,s)}{q}\left(\frac{\sinh(q\zeta)-q\cosh(q\zeta)}{q\sinh q(\eta/a)\cosh q(\eta/a)}\right) \tag{22}$$

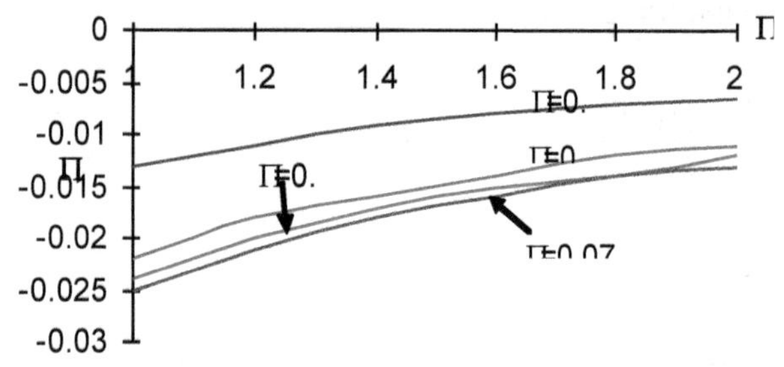

Figure 2. Distribution of the dimensionless temperature θ versus dimensionless radius ξ for different values of dimensionless time τ.

Applying inverse Laplace transform and finite Marchi-Zgrablich transform to the Equation (22) one obtains the expression of temperature distribution as;

$$\theta(\xi,\zeta,\tau)=\sum_{n=1}^{\infty}\frac{1}{C_n}\left[\sum_{m=0}^{\infty}(-1)^{m+1}m\left(\frac{2k\pi a^2}{\eta^2}\right)\left[\left(\frac{m\pi a}{\eta}\right)\cos\left(\frac{m\pi a\zeta}{\eta}\right)-\sin\left(\frac{m\pi a\zeta}{\eta}\right)\right]\right.$$

$$\times S_0(k_1,k_2,\mu_n,\xi)\times\int_0^{\tau}\bar{f}(n,t)e^{-\left[\left(\frac{m\pi a}{\eta}\right)^2+\mu_n^2+N^2\right](\tau-t)}dt$$

$$+\sum_{n=1}^{\infty}\frac{1}{C_n}\left[\sum_{m=0}^{\infty}(-1)^{m+(1/2)}(2m-1)\left(\frac{k\pi a^2}{\eta^2}\right)\left[\sin\left(\frac{(m-1/2)\pi a\zeta}{\eta}\right)-\left(\frac{(m-1/2)\pi a}{\eta}\right)\cos\left(\frac{(m-1/2)\pi a\zeta}{\eta}\right)\right]\right.$$

$$\times S_0(k_1,k_2,\mu_n,\xi)\times\int_0^{\tau}\bar{f}(n,t)e^{-\left[\left(\frac{(m-1/2)\pi a}{\eta}\right)^2+\mu_n^2+N^2\right](\tau-t)}dt \qquad (23)$$

Where

$$C_n=\frac{b^2}{2}\left\{S_p^2(k_1,k_2,\mu_n b)-J_{p-1}(k_1,k_2,\mu_n b).J_{p+1}(k_1,k_2,\mu_n b)\right\}$$

$$-\frac{a^2}{2}\left\{S_p^2(k_1,k_2,\mu_n a)-J_{p-1}(k_1,k_2,\mu_n a)J_{p+1}(k_1,k_2,\mu_n a)\right\}$$

And

$$S_p(k_1,k_2,\mu_n\xi)=J_p(\mu_n\xi)\left\{Y_p(k_1,\mu_n a)+Y_p(k_2,\mu_n b)\right\}$$

$$-Y_p(\mu_n\xi)\left\{Y_p(k_1,\mu_n a)+Y_p(k_2,\mu_n b)\right\}$$

(24)

Being

$$J_p(k_i,\mu\xi)=J_p(\mu\xi)+k_i\,\mu J'_p(\mu\xi)$$

and for $i=1,2$

$$Y_p(k_i,\mu\xi)=Y_p(\mu\xi)+k_i\,\mu Y'_p(\mu\xi)$$

Here $J_p(\mu x)$ and $Y_p(\mu x)$ $=\frac{1}{2}\pi\operatorname{cosec}(p\pi)[J_{-p}(\mu x)-e^{-ip\pi}J_p(\mu x)]$ are Bessel's functions of first and second kind respectively of order $p=0$.

The expression (23) is represented graphically, that is, Figure 2 to 5.

Substituting Equation 23 in 17, we obtain the expression for unknown temperature gradient as:

$$g(\xi,\tau)=\sum_{n=1}^{\infty}\frac{1}{c_n}\left\{\frac{2\pi ka^2}{\eta^2}\sum_{m=1}^{\infty}m(-1)^{m+1}\left[\left(\frac{m\pi a}{\eta}\right)\cos\left(\frac{m\pi al}{\eta}\right)-\sin\left(\frac{m\pi al}{\eta}\right)\right]\right.$$

$$\left.\times\int_0^{\tau}\bar{f}(n,t)\,e^{-\left[\left(\frac{m\pi a}{\eta}\right)^2+\mu_n^2+N^2\right](\tau-t)}dt\right\}S_0(k_1,k_2,\mu_n\xi)$$

$$+\frac{2\pi ka^2}{\eta^2}\sum_{m=1}^{\infty}(2m-1)(-1)^{m+1/2}\left[\sin\left(\frac{(m-1/2)\pi al}{\eta}\right)-\left(\frac{(m-1/2)\pi a}{\eta}\right)\cos\left(\frac{(m-1/2)\pi al}{\eta}\right)\right]$$

$$\left.\times\int_0^{\tau}\bar{f}(n,t)\,e^{-\left[\left(\frac{(m-1/2)\pi a}{\eta}\right)^2+\mu_n^2+N^2\right](\tau-t)}dt\right\}S_0(k_1,k_2,\mu_n,\xi)$$

(25)

Substituting the temperature distribution function in the given thermal stresses Equations 10 and 11, one obtains;

$$S_r=\frac{1}{\xi^2}\sum_{n=1}^{\infty}\frac{1}{c_n}\left\{\frac{2\pi ka^2}{\eta^2}\sum_{m=1}^{\infty}m(-1)^m\left[\left(\frac{m\pi a}{\eta}\right)\cos\left(\frac{m\pi a\zeta}{\eta}\right)-\sin\left(\frac{m\pi a\zeta}{\eta}\right)\right]\right.$$

$$\times\int_0^{\tau}\bar{f}(n,t)\,e^{-\left[\left(\frac{m\pi a}{\eta}\right)^2+\mu_n^2+N^2\right](\tau-t)}dt$$

$$-\frac{\pi ka^2}{\eta^2}\sum_{m=1}^{\infty}(2m-1)(-1)^{m+1/2}\left[\sin\left(\frac{(m-1/2)\pi a\zeta}{\eta}\right)-\left(\frac{(m-1/2)\pi a}{\eta}\right)\cos\left(\frac{(m-1/2)\pi a\zeta}{\eta}\right)\right]$$

$$\left.\times\int_0^{\tau}\bar{f}(n,t)\,e^{-\left[\left(\frac{(m-1/2)\pi a}{\eta}\right)^2+\mu_n^2+N^2\right](\tau-t)}dt\right\}\times\int_1^{R}\xi\,S_0(k_1,k_2,\mu_n\xi)\,d\xi$$

$$-\frac{1}{\xi^2}\left(\frac{\xi^2-1}{R^2-1}\right)\sum_{n=1}^{\infty}\frac{1}{c_n}\left\{\frac{2\pi ka^2}{\eta^2}\sum_{m=1}^{\infty}m(-1)^m\left[\left(\frac{m\pi a}{\eta}\right)\cos\left(\frac{m\pi a\zeta}{\eta}\right)-\sin\left(\frac{m\pi a\zeta}{\eta}\right)\right]\right.$$

$$\times\int_0^{\tau}\bar{f}(n,t)\,e^{-\left[\left(\frac{m\pi a}{\eta}\right)^2+\mu_n^2+N^2\right](\tau-t)}dt$$

$$+\frac{\pi ka^2}{\eta^2}\sum_{m=1}^{\infty}(2m-1)(-1)^{m+1/2}\left[\sin\left(\frac{(m-1/2)\pi a\zeta}{\eta}\right)-\left(\frac{(m-1/2)\pi a}{\eta}\right)\cos\left(\frac{(m-1/2)\pi a\zeta}{\eta}\right)\right]$$

$$\left.\times\int_0^{\tau}\bar{f}(n,t)\,e^{-k\left[\left(\frac{(m-1/2)\pi a}{\eta}\right)^2+\mu_n^2+N^2\right](\tau-t)}dt\right\}$$

$$\times\int_1^{R}\xi\,S_0(k_1,k_2,\mu_n\xi)\,d\xi \qquad (26)$$

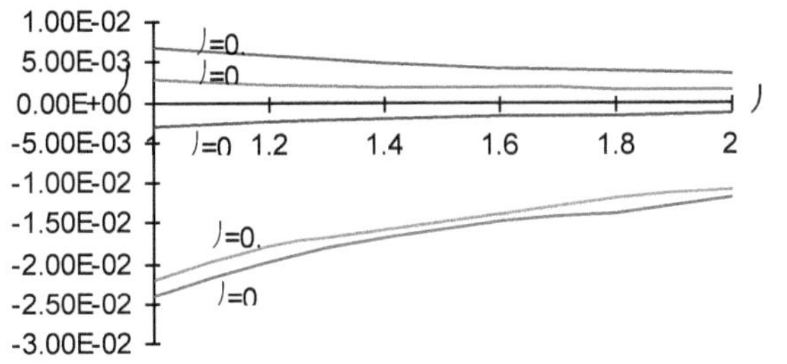

Figure 3. Distribution of the dimensionless temperature θ versus dimensionless radius ξ for different values of dimensionless thickness

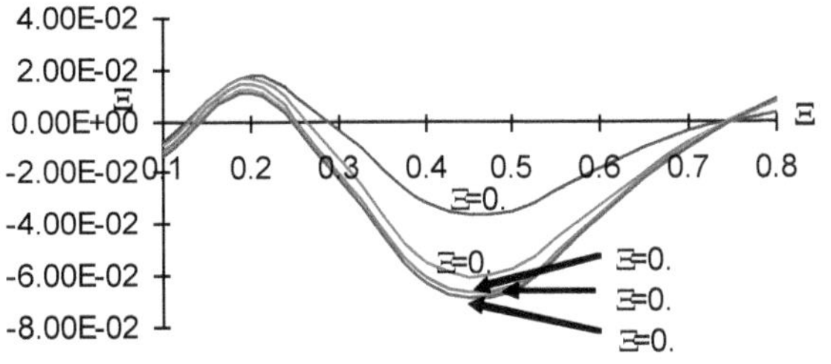

Figure 4. Distribution of the dimensionless temperature θ versus dimensionless thickness ζ for different values of dimensionless time τ.

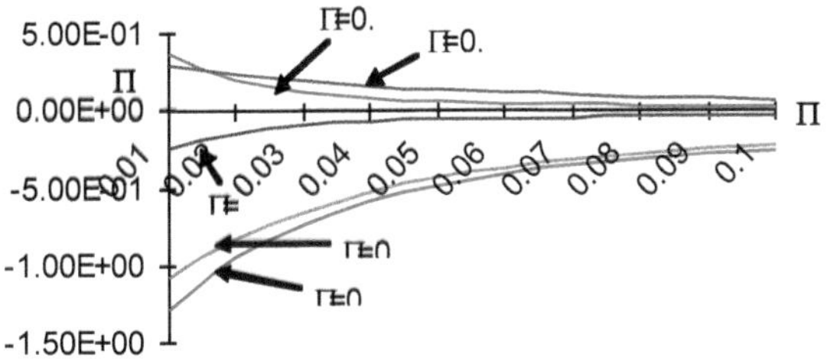

Figure 5. Distribution of the dimensionless temperature θ versus dimensionless time τ for different values of dimensionless thickness ζ.

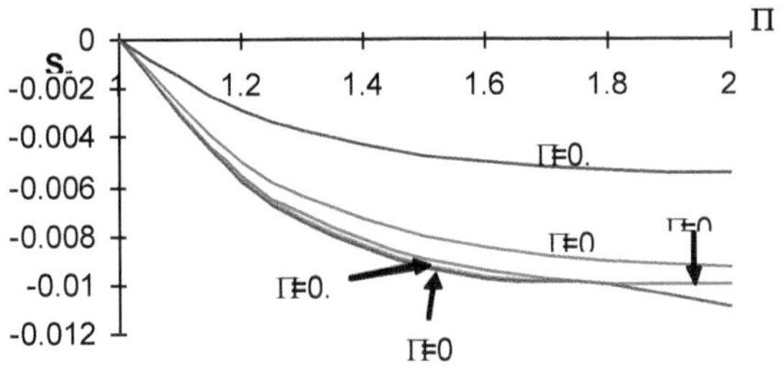

Figure 6. Distribution of the dimensionless radial stress S_r versus dimensionless radius ξ for different values of dimensionless time τ.

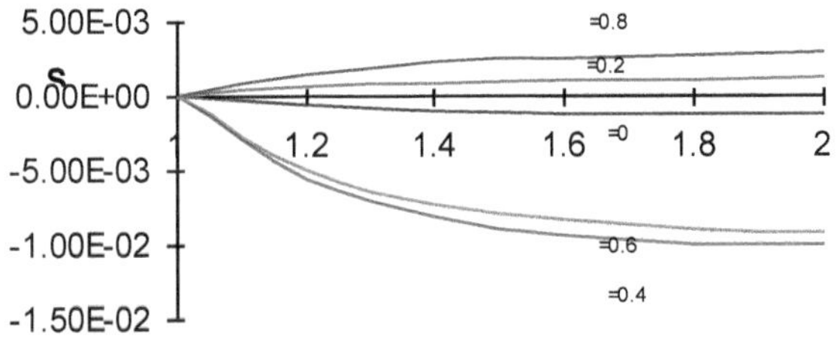

Figure 7. Distribution of the dimensionless radial stress S_r versus dimensionless radius ξ for different values of dimensionless thickness ζ.

The expression (26) is represented graphically, that is Figure 6 to 9.

$$
\begin{aligned}
S_\phi = \sum_{n=1}^{\infty}\frac{1}{c_n}\Bigg\{ & \frac{2\pi k a^2}{\eta^2}\sum_{m=1}^{\infty} m(-1)^m \left[\left(\frac{m\pi a}{\eta}\right)\cos\left(\frac{m\pi a\zeta}{\eta}\right) - \sin\left(\frac{m\pi a\zeta}{\eta}\right)\right] \\
& \times \int_0^{\tau}\bar{f}(n,t)\, e^{-\left[\left(\frac{m\pi a}{\eta}\right)^2+\mu_n^2+N^2\right](\tau-t)}\, dt \\
& -\frac{\pi k a^2}{\eta^2}\sum_{m=1}^{\infty}(2m-1)(-1)^{m+1/2}\left[\sin\left(\frac{(m-1/2)\pi a\zeta}{\eta}\right) - \left(\frac{(m-1/2)\pi a}{\eta}\right)\cos\left(\frac{(m-1/2)\pi a\zeta}{\eta}\right)\right] \\
& \times \int_0^{\tau}\bar{f}(n,t)\, e^{-\left[\left(\frac{(m-1/2)\pi a}{\eta}\right)^2+\mu_n^2+N^2\right](\tau-t)}\, dt\Bigg\} \times \int_1^R \xi\, S_0(k_1,k_2,\mu_n\xi)\, d\xi \\
-\frac{1}{\xi^2}\left(\frac{\xi^2+1}{R^2-1}\right)\sum_{n=1}^{\infty}\frac{1}{c_n}\Bigg\{ & \frac{2\pi k a^2}{\eta^2}\sum_{m=1}^{\infty} m(-1)^m \left[\left(\frac{m\pi a}{\eta}\right)\cos\left(\frac{m\pi a\zeta}{\eta}\right) - \sin\left(\frac{m\pi a\zeta}{\eta}\right)\right] \\
& \times \int_0^{\tau}\bar{f}(n,t)\, e^{-\left[\left(\frac{m\pi a}{\eta}\right)^2+\mu_n^2+N^2\right](\tau-t)}\, dt \\
& +\frac{\pi k a^2}{\eta^2}\sum_{m=1}^{\infty}(2m-1)(-1)^{m+1/2}\left[\sin\left(\frac{(m-1/2)\pi a\zeta}{\eta}\right) - \left(\frac{(m-1/2)\pi a}{\eta}\right)\cos\left(\frac{(m-1/2)\pi a\zeta}{\eta}\right)\right] \\
& \times \int_0^{\tau}\bar{f}(n,t)\, e^{-\left[\left(\frac{(m-1/2)\pi a}{\eta}\right)^2+\mu_n^2+N^2\right](\tau-t)}\, dt\Bigg\} \\
& \times \int_1^R \xi\, S_0(k_1,k_2,\mu_n\xi)\, d\xi \qquad (27)
\end{aligned}
$$

The expression (27) is represented graphically, that is Figures 10 to 13.

CONVERGENCE OF THE SERIES SOLUTION

In order for the solution to be meaningful, the series expressed in Equation 24 should be converge for all $D:\ 1 \le \xi \le R,\ 0 \le \zeta \le L$ and should further investigate

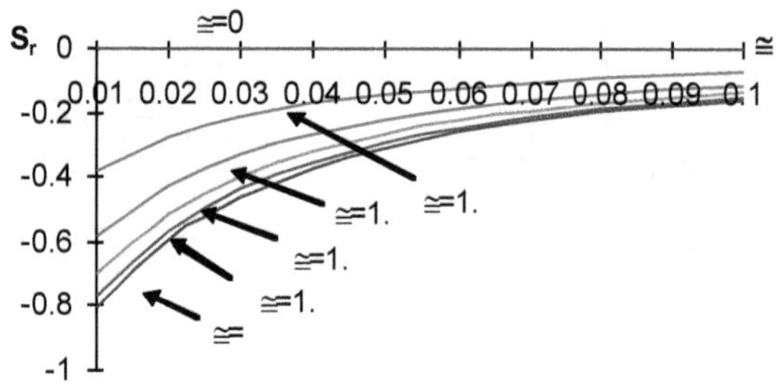

Figure 8. Distribution of the dimensionless radial stress S_r versus dimensionless time τ for different values of dimensionless radius ξ.

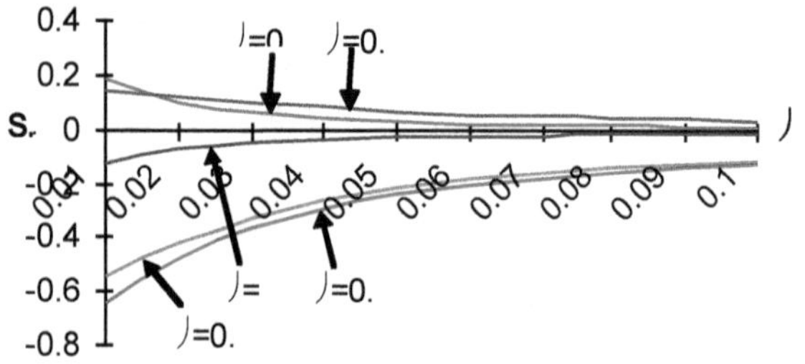

Figure 9. Distribution of the dimensionless radial stress S_r versus dimensionless time τ for different values of dimensionless thickness ζ.

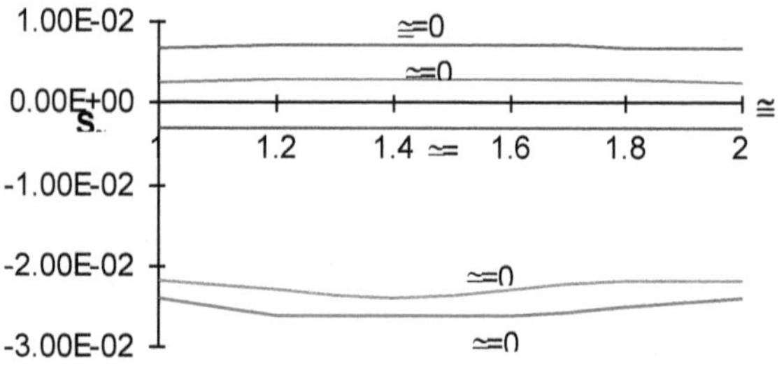

Figure 10. Distribution of the dimensionless axial stress S_θ versus dimensionless radius ξ for different values of dimensionless thickness ζ.

the conditions which has to be imposed on the functions $F_1(\zeta,\tau)$, $F_R(\zeta,\tau)$, $A(\xi,\tau)$, $B(\xi,\tau)$, and $f(\xi,\tau)$, so that the convergence of the series expansion for $\theta(\xi,\zeta,\tau)$ is valid. After taking into account the asymptotic behaviors of μ_n, $S_0(k_1,k_2,\mu_n,\xi)$, and C_n given in [8], it is observed that the series expansion (23) for $\theta(\xi,\zeta,\tau)$ will be convergent, if

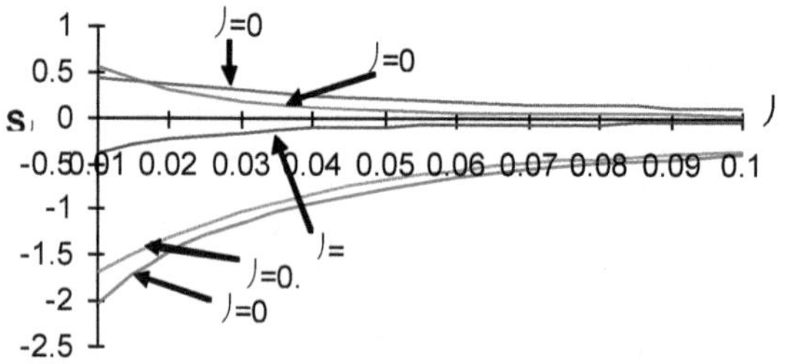

Figure 11. Distribution of the dimensionless axial stress S_θ versus dimensionless time τ for different values of dimensionless thickness ζ.

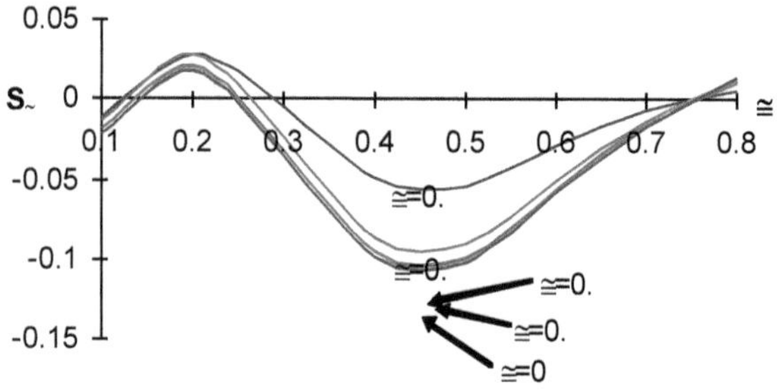

Figure 12. Distribution of the dimensionless axial stress S_θ versus dimensionless time ζ for different values of dimensionless time τ.

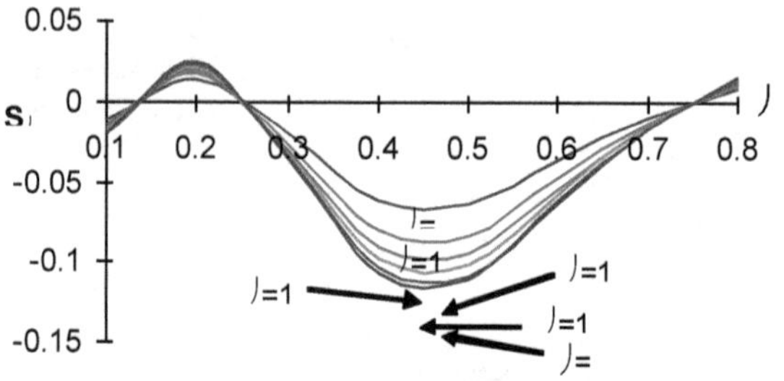

Figure 13. Distribution of the dimensionless axial stress S_θ versus dimensionless thickness ζ for different values of dimensionless radius ξ.

$$\int_0^{\tau} e^{-\left[(m\pi a/\eta)^2+\mu_n^2+N^2\right](\tau-x)}\bar{f}(n,t)\,dt = O\left(1/\mu_n^{\,k}\right), \quad k>0 \tag{28}$$

Here, $\bar{f}(n,t)$ in Equation 28 can be chosen as one of the following functions or the combinations thereof with addition or multiplication or both, as the laws of combination: *Constant, Sin(ωτ), Cos(ωτ),* e^{-kt} *or polynomials in* ξS_n, $J_0(\mu_n x)$, $Y_0(\mu_n x)$, Q_nC_{1n}, Q_nC_{2n} are convergent using Theorem 3.51 in the work of Warade and Deshmukh (2003) and thus, $\theta(\xi,\zeta,\tau)$ is convergent to a limit $\{\theta(\xi,\zeta,\tau)\}_{\xi=R,\zeta=L}$ using Theorem 3.28 in the work of Mustafa et al. (2011). Here, we consider that the convergence of a series for $\xi = R$ implies to the convergence for all $\xi \le R$, and $\zeta = L$ implies to the convergence for all $\zeta \le L$.

SPECIAL CASE AND NUMERICAL RESULTS

Set $f(r,t) = (1-e^{-t})(\xi - h)\,\delta(r - r_0)$, a = 0.5, b = 1, ξ = 0.75, r = 0.75, $k = 0.375$, $k_1 = 0.25$, $k_2 = 0.25$, t = 1 s and h = 1 in Equation 25 to obtain:

$$
\begin{aligned}
g(\xi,\tau) = \sum_{n=1}^{\infty} \frac{1}{c_n} \Bigg\{ & \frac{2\pi k a^2}{\eta^2} \sum_{m=1}^{\infty} m(-1)^{m+1} \left[\left(\frac{m\pi a}{\eta}\right) \cos\left(\frac{m\pi a l}{\eta}\right) - \sin\left(\frac{m\pi a l}{\eta}\right) \right] \\
& \times \int_0^{\tau} (1-e^{-t})(\xi - h)\, e^{-\left[\left(\frac{m\pi a}{\eta}\right)^2 + \mu_n^2 + N^2\right](\tau - t)}\, dt \Bigg\} \times S_0(k_1,k_2,\mu_n\xi) r_0 \; S_0(k_1,k_2,\mu_n r_0) \\
& + \frac{2\pi k a^2}{\eta^2} \sum_{m=1}^{\infty} (2m-1)(-1)^{m+1/2} \left[\sin\left(\frac{(m-1/2)\pi a l}{\eta}\right) - \left(\frac{(m-1/2)\pi a}{\eta}\right) \cos\left(\frac{(m-1/2)\pi a l}{\eta}\right) \right] \\
& \times \int_0^{\tau} (1-e^{-t})(\xi - h)\, e^{-\left[\left(\frac{(m-1/2)\pi a}{\eta}\right)^2 + \mu_n^2 + N^2\right](\tau - t)}\, dt \Bigg\} \times S_0(k_1,k_2,\mu_n,\xi) r_0 \; S_0(k_1,k_2,\mu_n r_0)
\end{aligned}
\tag{29}
$$

Conclusion

Thus, the temperature, displacements and thermal stresses on the outer curved surface of a thin annular fin have been obtained, when the interior heat flux and the other three boundary conditions are known with the aid of finite classical Marchi-Zgrablich transform and Laplace transform techniques. The results are obtained in terms of Bessel's function in the form of infinite Marchi-Zgrablich series.

The temperature distribution of the fin increases as the time increases; however, when the fin's temperature reaches the highest point, its temperature begins to decrease and finally reaches the steady state. This is because the heat source influenced by the decay exponential, results in the decrease of the fin's temperature. The temperature distribution of the fin decreases as the distance from the base of the fin increases. The temperature distribution on the base is higher than that of the fin.

The dimensionless radial and tangential stress distribution of the fin S_r and S_φ increases as the time increases; however, when the radial and tangential stress distribution of the fin reach the highest point, its stresses begin to decrease and finally reach the steady state.

The series of solutions converge provided takes sufficient number of terms in the series. Since the thickness of annular fin is very small, the series of solution given here will be definitely convergent. Assigning suitable values to the parameters and functions in the series of expressions, one can derive solutions in any particular case. The temperature, displacement and thermal stresses that are obtained can be applied to the design of useful structures or machines in engineering applications.

ACKNOWLEDGEMENTS

The authors express their sincere thanks to the reviewers for their expert comments. Also the authors are thankful to University Grant Commission, New Delhi for providing the partial financial assistance under major research project scheme.

REFERENCES

Boley BA, Weiner JH (1960). Theory of thermal stresses. Johan Wiley and Sons, New York.

Jaeger JC, Carslaw SH (1959). Conduction of heat in solids. 2nd ed. Oxford University Press, New York.

Chiu C-H, Chen C-K (2002). Thermal Stresses in Annular Fins with Temperature-Dependent conductivity Under Periodic Boundary Condition. J. Therm. Stress., 25(5): 475-492(18).

Cihat A (2010). Correlation equations for optimum design of annular fins with temperature dependent thermal conductivity. Heat Mass Transf., 45(4): 519-525, DOI: 10.1007/s00231-008-0446-9.

Deshmukh KC, Kedar GD (2011). Estimation of temperature distribution and thermal stresses in a thick circular plate. Afr. J. Math. Comp. Sci. Res., 4(13): 389-395.

Lien-Tsai Y, Cha'o-Kuang C (1998). Application of Taylor Transformation To The Thermal Stresses In Isotropic Annular Fins. J. Therm. Stress., 21(8): 781-809.

Marchi E, Zgrablich J (1964). Heat conduction in hollow cylinder with radiation. Proc. Edinburg Math. Soc., 14 (Series 11) Part 2: 159-164.

Mustafa MT, Syed MZ, Arif AFM (2011). Thermal analysis of orthotropic annular fins with contact resistance: A closed-form analytical solution. Appl. Therm. Eng., 31: 937e945.

Shang-Sheng W (1997). Analysis on transient thermal stresses in an annular fin. J. Therm. Stress.,, 20: 591-615.

Sneddon IN (1972). The use of integral transforms. Mc Graw Hill, New York.

Warade RW, Deshmukh KC (2003). Mathematical modeling on transient thermal stresses in an annular fin. Acta Ciencia Indica, XXIX M(3): 507-516.

Yasar I (2004). Numerical analysis of the influence of a circular fin with different profiles on the thermal characteristics in a ceramic tube of heat transfer equipment. Int. J. Press. Vessels Piping, 81(7): 583-587.

Yu-Ching Y, Shao-Shu C (2001). Transient coupled thermoelastic analysis of an annular fin. Int. Commun. Heat Mass Transf., 28(8): 1103-1114.

APPENDIX

Nomenclature

a, b: Inner and outer radii of the fin
c: Specific heat of material of the fin
C_1, C_2: Constants
E: Young's modulus of material of the fin
h: Heat transfer coefficient
k: Thermal conductivity of material of the fin
N: Dimensionless parameter
q_b: Heat flux from the base of the fin
R: Dimensionless outer radius,
S_r, S_ϕ: Dimensionless radial and tangential stresses
T: Temperature of the fin
T_∞: Ambient temperature
T: Time
U: Radial displacement
α: Linear thermal expansion coefficient of material of the fin
l: Thickness of the fin
ε_r -ε_ϕ: Radial and tangential strains
θ: Dimensionless temperature of the fin
ν: Poisson's ratio of material of the fin
σ_r, σ_ϕ: Radial and tangential stresses
τ: Dimensionless time
r, ϕ: Polar coordinates
ζ: Dimensionless thickness

6

A sampling plan with producer's allowable risk (PAR) at maximum allowable proportion defective (MAPD)

T. B. Ramkumar

Department of Statistics, St.Thomas' College, Thrissur, Kerala, India. 680001. E-mail: rktmidhuna@gmail.com.

This paper deals with sampling designs on incoming quality MAPD along with a specified probability of acceptance at this point called producer's allowable risk (PAR). It is defined as the minimum probability of acceptance of the lot with a maximum allowable proportion defective. Tables and graphs are presented, comparing the efficiency of new SSP as to protect AQL. An optimum criterion of sample size and acceptance number is suggested for a fixed ratio of PAR to MAPD within a plausible sample size region.

Key words: Single sampling plan (SSP), maximum allowable proportion defective (MAPD), operating characteristic curve, inflection point, producer's allowable risk (PAR), optimum sampling plan, decisive distance, steepness angle.

INTRODUCTION

Mayer (1956) and Mandelson (1962) suggested a consumer-producer-engineer friendly product quality – MAPD (p*) below which the proportion of acceptance of the lot was expected to decline stringently. Following poisson distribution by the number of defectives, the ratio c/n is efficient to divide the good and bad lots for the layman and industrialist. Norman (1953), Soundararajan (1975) Ramkumar and Suresh (1996) were derived some basic operating procedure to locate single sampling plan on MAPD and its properties. Ramkumar (2010) had formed a criterion for developing SSP on interval quality design in terms of MAPD in the p axis alike PAR in the Pa(p) axis. Also Ramkumar (2009) had suggested a sampling plan indexed through MAPD and discriminant distance, indicating the efficiency of OC curve on tangential distance and concept of optimum sampling plan under same operating ratio.

From Figure 1, PAR is the minimum probability of acceptance of a lot of quality having a maximum allowable proportion defective. In particular for a product with an incoming quality of MAPD <10%, more than 60% (PAR) lots were accepted saving the interest of producer. Inflection point is the turning point of OC curve with steepest declination tangent indicating the sharpness of OC curve ensuring protection to the consumers. The steepness angle θ is a sensitive measure to define the discrimination of the required OC curve. This angle will be wider for more stringent OC curve. Thus the parameters were capable of protecting both producer and consumer. So this plan is favorable in customer friendly, moderate costly, inspection oriented products like daily using items.

Selection of the plan

For a defined PAR the decisive distance d can be calculated (Equation 2). Inspect the range in which calculated d or PAR falls uniquely and locate c (greater than or equal to d) from Table 1. Hence for a prefixed MAPD, n=c/p*.The steepness angle θ subtended by d on the OC curve with the p axis at Pa(p*) and given MAPD can also provide d.(Equation 4).

Example 1

A toy quality is fixed at maximum allowable proportion defective 8% and PAR = 0.70. The decisive distance d = 1 - 0.70 = 0.30. From Table 1, 0.2642≤d<.0.3233 for c=2. Sampling plan (n, c) is (25. 2). And the steepness angle θ = 76.10.

Example 2

A textile company producing cotton and polyester yarn

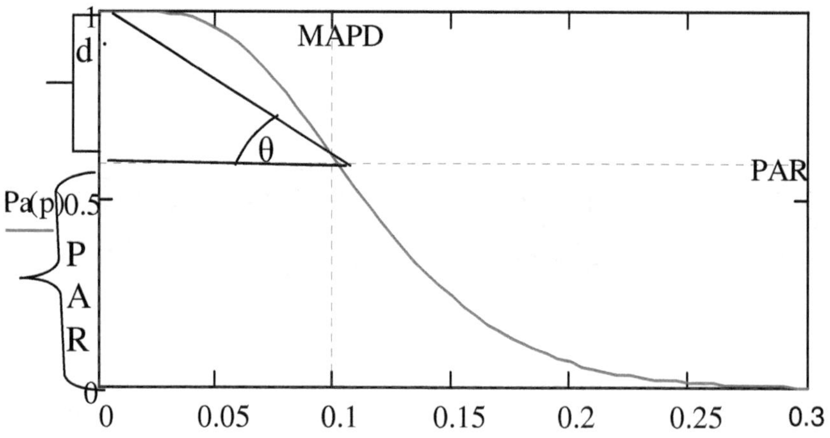

Figure 1. Optimum criterion (OC) curve showing maximum allowable proportion defective (MAPD) and producer's allowable risk (PAR).

Table 1. Values of PAR for c =1 to 20.

c	1	2	3	4	5	6	7	8	9	10
Pa(p^*)	0.7358	0.6767	0.6472	0.6289	0.6159	0.6063	0.5987	0.5926	0.5874	0.5830
d	0.2642	0.3233	0.3528	0.3711	0.3841	0.3937	0.4013	0.4074	0.4126	0.4170
c	11	12	13	14	15	16	17	18	19	20
Pa(p^*)	0.5793	0.5759	0.5731	0.5704	0.5681	0.5659	0.5640	0.5623	0.5606	0.5591
d	0.4207	0.4241	0.4269	0.4296	0.4319	0.4341	0.4360	0.4377	0.4394	0.4409

Table 2. Certain SSP for given PAR (or d) and MAPD.

c	Pa(p*)	d	p*									
			0.01	0.02	0.03	0.04	0.05	0.06	0.08	0.09	0.10	0.11
1	0.7358	0.2642	100	50	33	25	20	17	13	11	10	9
2	0.6767	0.3233	200	100	66	50	40	34	25	22	20	9
3	0.6472	0.3528	300	150	100	75	60	50	38	34	30	18
4	0.6289	0.3711	400	200	133	100	80	67	50	45	40	27
5	0.6159	0.3841	500	250	167	125	100	84	62	55	50	36
6	0.6063	0.3937	600	300	200	150	120	100	75	66	60	45
7	0.5987	0.4013	700	350	234	175	140	116	87	77	70	55
8	0.5926	0.4074	800	400	267	200	160	133	100	88	80	64
9	0.5874	0.4126	900	450	300	225	180	150	112	100	90	73
10	0.5830	0.4170	1000	500	333	250	200	166	125	111	100	82

fixes the MAPD =10% and steepness angle of OC curve as 74 and 68° respectively. Then decisive distances $d_1=p^*.\tan\theta_1$ = 0.1 × 3.487 =0.3487 and $d_2=p^*.\tan\theta_2$ =0.1x2.475 = 0.2475 on OC curve with sampling plans from Table 2 will be (30. 3) and (100.1)

Construction of the plan

Fix p* and Pa (p*) at suitable quality level in an OC curve.

Then

$$Pa\,(p^*) = \sum_{r=0}^{c} \frac{e^{-c} \cdot c^{r}}{r\,!} \qquad (1)$$

where the numbers of defectives follow Poisson

Table 3. Certain parametric combinations of PAR, MAPD and Angle θ.

c	d	PAR	p*									
			0.01	0.02	0.05	0.06	0.08	0.1	0.11	0.12	0.15	0.2
1	0.2642	0.7358	θ=87.8	85.67	79.2	77.20	73.15	69.26	67.3	65.57	60.4	52.87
2	0.3233	0.6767	88.22	86.69	81.20	79.48	76.10	72.8	71.2	69.6	65.1	58.25
3	0.3528	0.6472	88.37	86.75	81.93	80.34	77.22	74.1	72.6	71.2	66.96	60.45
4	0.3711	0.6289	88.45	86.55	82.32	80.8	77.8	74.9	73.4	72.08	67.99	61.67
5	0.3841	0.6159	88.50	87	82.58	81.12	78.2	75.4	74	72.6	68.6	62.49
6	0.3937	0.6063	88.52	87.09	82.76	81.3	78.5	75.7	74.3	73.04	69.1	63.06
7	0.4013	0.5987	88.57	87.14	82.89	81.49	78.7	76	74.6	73.35	69.5	63.5
8	0.4074	0.5926	88.59	87.18	83	81.62	78.8	76.2	74.8	73.58	69.78	63.8
9	0.4126	0.5874	88.61	87.2	83.09	81.72	79.02	76.3	75.07	73.78	70.02	64.13
10	0.4170	0.5830	88.62	87.25	83.16	81.8	79.1	76.5	75.22	73.9	70.2	64.23

distribution.

From Figure 1,

$$d = 1 - Pa;\ (p^*) = 1 - \sum_{r=0}^{c} \frac{e^{-c} \cdot c^r}{r!} \qquad (2)$$

which will be a function of c only, monotonically increasing, so that unique plan holds for each d. Find c matching with the given d (greater than or equal to the nearest d)

But $c=np^*$ .So that $n=c/p^*$. (3)

Also one can find d from the steepness angle θ opposite to distance d

$$\tan\theta = d/p^* \qquad (4)$$

Then $d= p^* \tan\theta$, can be found for given MAPD and θ.

$$d/np^*=d/c=\tan\theta /n \qquad (5)$$

From $Pa(p^*)$ or d and θ using (5) $\tan\theta/n$ is determined and substitute for $\tan\theta$,n can be found or equivalently

$$n= (c/d)^*\tan\theta \qquad (6)$$

Construction of table

Table 1 is constructed by substituting c=1,2,.., in(1) and (2). Table 2 represents SSPs for various combinations of p* and d. Find c for each d from Table 1 and then n is determined by (3). Table 3 is the declination angle for various values p* and PAR. Finding d from (2), c is fixed from Table 1 and tanθ is found. It is useful to identify (n,c) for given (p*,θ) Table 4 is the suitable sampling plans at various steepness angles and PA. For PAR and θ, n can be evaluated by the relation d/c=(tanθ)/n from Table 4.

Significance of the sampling plan

Acceptable quality level (AQL) is a quality measure fixing producers risk at 5, 10 and 1% in usual practice. But in an assemblage of components it is not good to prefix only one level of AQL at a fixed producer's risk. Also keeping at a level may exert pressure on the consumers as well as the producer because different items require different levels of acceptance. Thus fixed AQL sampling plans deteriorate the confidence of the vendor and the customer. This is the limitation of all probability based indices with fixed levels as they are inadequate to specify the quality aspiration of the customer. Fixing various level of probability of acceptance at MAPD on the OC curve is called the producers allowable risk (PAR). PAR is probability liberalization to 70, 85 and 93% etc. instead of 95 and 10%. MAPD is an engineer's quality level with steepest declination beyond p*, so that the utmost quality of acceptance is prefixed by MAPD. Thus MAPD and PAR gives a balanced design for both consumer and producer keeping information on steepness of OC. This is the only one point OC plan and may be flexible for various components. The steepness angle produced by d is a direct measure of efficiency of OC curve so the designs are possible in terms of required steepness. Also in the composite production units or in the components, different MAPD and PAR can be fixed. Thus MAPD-PAR sampling plan is a flexible strategy of inspection of different components in a composite product with one point OC curves. Also angleθ and PAR has a strong power of discrimination of lot as good and bad. Considering an example one can show the significance of this sampling plan. Fix the PAR=0.635, (d=0.365) and angle of steepness 80° (1). Then c = 4 and n = 62 with

Table 4. Finding n for given PAR/ (or d) and angle θ.

c	1	2	3	4	5	6	7
d	0.2642	0.3233	0.3528	0.3711	0.3841	0.3937	0.4013
Pa(p*)	0.7358	0.6767	0.6472	0.6289	0.6159	0.6063	0.5987
tanθ/n	0.2642	0.1616	0.1176	0.0927	0.0768	0.0656	0.0573
c/d	3.7850	6.1862	8.5034	10.7787	13.0174	15.2400	17.4433
c	8	9	10	11	12	13	14
d	0.4074	0.4126	0.417	0.4207	0.4241	0.4269	0.4296
Pa(p*)	0.5926	0.5874	0.583	0.5793	0.5759	0.5731	0.5704
tanθ/n	0.0509	0.0458	0.0417	0.0382	0.0353	0.0328	0.0306
c/d	19.6367	21.8128	23.9808	26.1468	28.2952	30.4520	32.5884
c	15	16	17	18	19	20	21
d	0.4319	0.4341	0.436	0.4377	0.4394	0.44	0.4419
Pa(p*)	0.5681	0.5659	0.564	0.5623	0.5606	0.56	0.5581
tanθ/n	0.0287	0.0271	0.0256	0.0243	0.0231	0.022	0.0210
c/d	34.7302	36.8578	38.9908	41.1240	43.2407	45.4545	47.5220

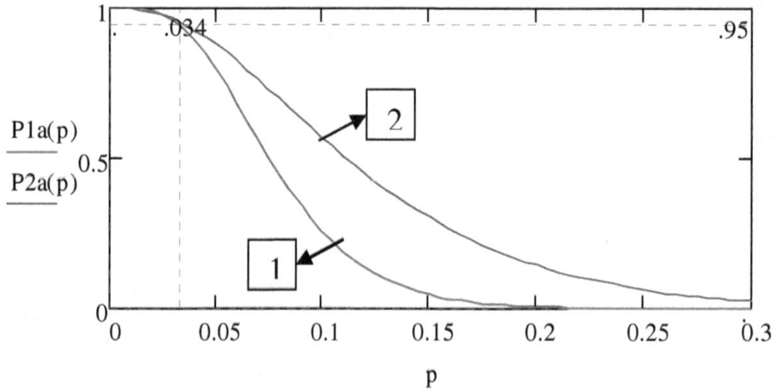

Figure 2. Optimum criterion (OC) curves for fixed acceptable quality level (AQL) defined on producer's allowable risk (PAR) and steepness angle.

MAPD=0.065 and AQL=0.032. For keeping the same AQL, with steepness angle 75°, PAR will be 0.6767, (d=0.3233) (2) and MAPD 0.083 satisfying a sampling plan (24.2) (Figure 2). Thus fixing AQL it is better to adjust PAR and the steepness angle so as to get required quality.

Comparison of OC curves

Figure 2 shows OC curves stringent or moderate at the same quality of AQL which can be finalized on PAR and steepness angle. When PAR is less and angle is more there exists a more discriminating OC curve than higher PAR and lower angle. Also for such parameters MAPD increases on PAR increase. Figure 3 is the feasible acceptance numbers within a sample size 50 to 100 keeping operating ratio d/p* a constant, from which maximum and minimum efficient OC curves can be derived. Figure 4 shows the OC curves satisfying the defined OR=8.0 so that switching rules could be implemented.

Optimum sampling plan

Practically this idea can be used when the producer had little information about the resultant quality, but he is ready to inspect a range of sample size for final decision. Pa(p*) or d is a good measure of efficiency of OC curve, and MAPD is a suitable quality measure so that a ratio of this is fixed as constant and sampling plans were developed on this criteria. There exists a set of plans within a range of sample size and one can start with

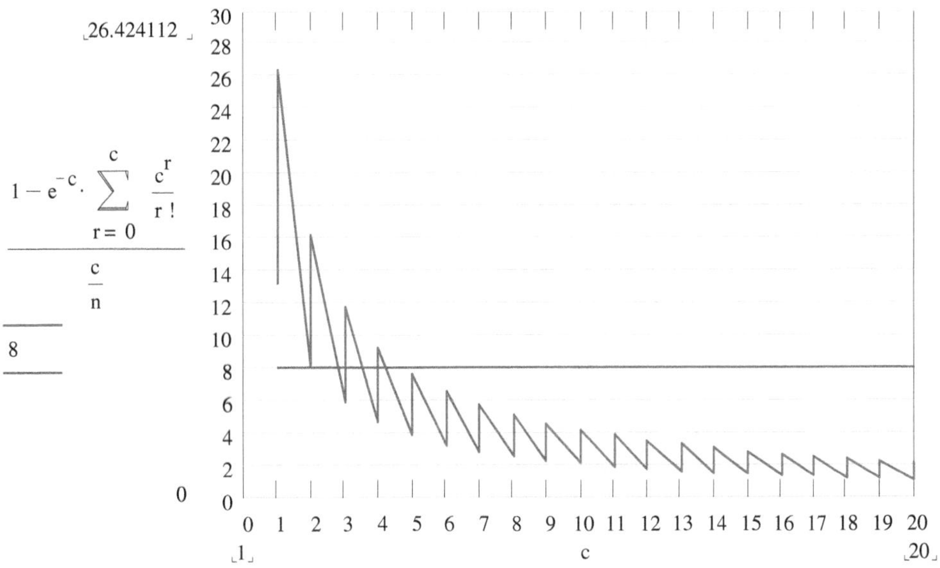

Figure 3. Feasible acceptance numbers for a fixed OR=8.

suitable sampling plan.

Example 3, a yarn industry fix a quality index OR = 8 based on MAPD and decisive distance, provided they are ready to bear an inspection cost of 50 to 100 units. Then what will be the optimum sampling plan?

Since the quality index is fixed at R=8, for a range of sample n = 50 to 100 and c = 1 to 20. Then the various sampling plans obtained were (50.2), (67.3) and (85.4), (Figure 4). Among these sampling plans, optimum is reached at (85.4), and they can start with (50.2) and switch over to (67.3) on successive completion of fixed number of lots. From the OC curves (85. 4), has a optimum probability of acceptance at maximum allowable proportion defective (Figure 4).

Conclusion

The suggestion of this plan is efficient to contain MAPD oriented AQL protection satisfactory for both consumer and producer. Decisive distance and declining angle is a concept to exhibit the quality of OC curve. Switching over of the sampling plans will not highly affect the OC curve even cost reduction is possible.

REFERENCES

Mayer PL (1956). Some Properties of inflection Point of an OC curve for Single Sampling Plan. Proceedings of 2nd Statistical Engineering Symposium, Published in Chemical Corps, Engineering Command.

Mandelson J (1962). The Statistician, Engineer and Sampling Plans. Ind. Qual. Control, 19: 12-15.

Norman B (1953) A method of discrimination for Single and Double sampling OC Curves utilizing of the point of inflection. ENASR Report No.P.R.7 Engineering Agency.

Ramkumar TB, Suresh KK 1996). Selection of sampling plan indexed with Maximum Allowable Average Outgoing Quality. J. Appl. Stat., 23(6): 645-654.

Ramkumar TB (2009). Design of Single Sampling Plan by discriminant at MAPD. Probstat Forum, 2: 104-114.

Ramkumar TB (2010). Designing a Quality Interval Single Sampling Plan. Int. J. Oper. Res. Optim., 1(1): 27-40.

Soundararajan V (1975). Maximum Allowable Percent Defective (MAPD) single sampling inspection by attributes plan. J. Qual. Technol., 7(4): 173-182.

7

Solving three-dimensional (3D) Laplace equations by successive over-relaxation method

Mathias A. ONABID

Department of Mathematics and Computer Sciences, Faculty of Sciences, P. O. Box 67 Dschang, University of Dschang, Cameroon. E-mail: mathakong@yahoo.fr.

Motivated by the assertion that all physical systems exist in three space dimensions, and that representation in one or two space dimensions entails a large degree of approximations. The main objective of this paper is to extend the successive over-relaxation (SOR) method which is one of the widely used numerical methods in solving the Laplace equation, the most often encountered of the Elliptic partial differential equations (PDEs) in two dimensions to solving it in three dimensions. This is done by providing an easier procedure to obtain proper estimates to the SOR parameter and the stability criterion which are the two determinant elements used in facilitating convergence to the solution when solving PDEs by the SOR method. The hope is that, with the emergence of this finding, the representation of physical and environmental science problem will be closer to reality by representing them in three dimensions.

Key words: Stability criterion, over relaxation parameter, Laplace equation, finite differencing, successive over-relaxation.

INTRODUCTION

To describe changes in a most physical system, there is a need to study partial differential equations (PDEs). The general linear equations governing physical fields take the form:

$$A\frac{\partial^2 U}{\partial x^2} + 2B\frac{\partial^2 U}{\partial x\,\partial y} + C\frac{\partial^2 U}{\partial y^2} = D\frac{\partial U}{\partial x} + E\frac{\partial U}{\partial y} + FU + G \qquad (1)$$

By letting the parameters A to G assume positive, negative or zero magnitude, the PDE could be classified as being hyperbolic, parabolic or elliptic. For instance, if $AC > B^2$, the equation is termed elliptic. The same situation will arise if B is 0, and A and C are positive. This classification of PDEs into these three categories is necessary because the basic analytical and numerical methods for treating field problems are different for the three types of equations (Vemuri and Karplus, 1981). It is also possible for an equation to be of more than one type, depending on the values of the coefficients. As an example, the equation $y\frac{\partial^2 U}{\partial x^2} + \frac{\partial^2 U}{\partial x\,\partial y} = 0$, is elliptic for $y > 0$, parabolic for $y = 0$, and hyperbolic for $y < 0$ (Kallin, 1971b).

In this research, interest is in the elliptic type of equation and specifically in the Poisson equation. The most often encountered of the elliptic PDE, and indeed of all PDEs in applied physical sciences and physics, is Laplace's equation as stated by Brandt and Diskin (1999). This is a special case of the Poisson equation and it arises when all the terms on the right hand side of the Poisson equation equal zero. The prototypical elliptic equation in three dimensions is the Poisson equation of the form:

$$\frac{\partial^2 U}{\partial x^2} + \frac{\partial^2 U}{\partial y^2} + \frac{\partial^2 U}{\partial z^2} = \rho(x, y, z), \qquad (2)$$

where the source term ρ is given. Thus, if this source term is equal to zero, the equations become Laplace's equation. The cross product term is not included because there is no theoretical foundation to expect convergence in such a case as seen in Kallin (1971a).

The advantage of the Poisson equation as stated by Reynolds (1988) lies in its mode of solution. That is, the

Poisson equation also has the important benefit of behaving well numerically. Thus, when the equations are expanded by finite differencing into a set of linear algebraic equations, they can be solved iteratively to obtain a unique solution. This behaviour is especially convenient since the set of equations varies as the boundary points respond to changes.

SOLVING THE THREE-DIMENSIONAL (3D) LAPLACE EQUATION

In order to solve the Laplace equation which is also an example of a boundary value problem, it is necessary to:

1) Specify boundary values along the perimeter of the region of interest,
2) Set the forcing term ρ to the Laplacian; otherwise ρ is set to zero.

One of the methods of solving this equation is the finite difference method as stated by Kallin (1971a). The resulting set of simultaneous equation can be solved either by elimination or by iterative methods as shown in Dorn and McCracken (1972). It is worth noting that solving simultaneous equations by elimination is not a simple task, especially with a large system of algebraic equations. In fact, even for computers, the solution of a large system of algebraic equations by elimination may not be practicable because of storage requirements and accumulation of round-off errors. McCracken (1974) and Edgar (1992) provided some guidelines on how to build computer codes to solve systems of algebraic equations. Therefore, the best approach is to use an iterative method. This has the advantage over elimination in that it is self-correcting in the sense that the arithmetic error at any stage is eventually suppressed as described by Kallin (1971b).

Since the resulting matrix arising from this finite-differencing is sparse, it can be solved easily using the relaxation method. A somewhat more physical way of looking at the relaxation method, which also enhances convergence, is by making use of the diffusion equation. Therefore writing Equation 2 as a diffusion equation, with t as the time-step, the following equation is obtained.

$$\frac{\partial U}{\partial t} = \frac{\partial^2 U}{\partial x^2} + \frac{\partial^2 U}{\partial y^2} + \frac{\partial^2 U}{\partial z^2} - \rho(x,y,z), \qquad (3)$$

As $t \rightarrow \infty$, the solution to this problem is a solution to the original elliptic Equation 2.
This can then be represented using finite differencing as:

$$U_{i,j,k}^{n+1} = U_{i,j,k}^{n} + \frac{\Delta t}{\Delta^2}(U_{i+1,j,k}^{n} + U_{i-1,j,k}^{n} + U_{i,j+1,k}^{n} + U_{i,j-1,k}^{n} + U_{i,j,k+1}^{n} + U_{i,j,k-1}^{n} - 6U_{i,j,k}^{n}) - \Delta t \rho_{i,j,k}$$

Where Δ represents the difference between two points in either the i, j or k directions and Δt represents the time-step from one iteration to another. The solution of the system of linear simultaneous equations, resulting from this expression when all the boundary conditions have been applied, can be obtained by the relaxation method.

The concern here shall be to establish the procedures for obtaining the stability criterion and the over-relaxation parameter which are the two determinant elements used in facilitating convergence to the solution when solving PDEs by the successive over-relaxation (SOR) method.

Obtaining the stability criterion for 3D finite differencing

The stability criterion for one-dimensional finite differencing of the diffusion equation is $\frac{\Delta t}{\Delta^2} \leq \frac{1}{2}$ and in the two-dimensional case, it is $\frac{\Delta t}{\Delta^2} \leq \frac{1}{4}$, where Δt represents the time-step from one iteration to another. Empirically, the criterion for higher-dimensions can be obtained as follows:

1) Let the number of dimensions (the number of spatial variables) be k and
2) Let y be the order of the partial derivative,
3) Then the stability criterion can be calculated as $\frac{\Delta t}{\Delta^2} \leq \frac{1}{ky}$.

Following this procedure, it is easy to see that the condition for stability for the 3D case when calculated will be $\frac{\Delta t}{\Delta^2} \leq \frac{1}{6}$. This matches with the suggestion of Roberts (2001) on the multi-grid solution of Poisson's equation using diagonally oriented grids.

Obtaining the over-relaxation parameter for 3D finite differencing

To the best of my knowledge, the only attempt to estimate the optimum SOR parameter for higher order Laplace's equation has been made by T.J. Randall, Department of Physics and Mathematics, John Dalton College of Technology, Manchester 1 Technical report, 400–401. This was for the case of 3D region with axial symmetry. The approach used here is from Frankel (1950) point of view. From his formula for obtaining the over-relaxation parameter in two dimensions, an

Table 1. The values obtained for the over-relaxation parameter in the 3D case, with varying dimensions.

m	n	l	α
10	10	10	1.528
15	20	10	1.621
40	35	20	1.796
200	100	50	1.920
230	65	46	1.907
1000	1000	1000	1.994
2000	2000	2000	1.997
10000	10000	10000	1.999

In all the cases, the value obtained lies between 1 and 2. This falls in line with the fact that the over-relaxation parameter should always lie between this ranges.

extension to obtain this parameter for the 3D case was approached intuitively as follows:

1) A close observation of the formula indicates that the calculation of the parameter does not depend on any other variable except the number of grid points and the number of spatial variables. This means that, if $k = 2$ is the number of spatial variables (that is, in the 2D case), and m and n are the number of grid points in the various directions (that is, the area is of dimension $m \times n$), then a general rule for obtaining the over-relaxation parameter could be given as: $\alpha = 2[1 + sincos^{-1}\frac{1}{k}\left(cos\frac{\pi}{m} + cos\frac{\pi}{n}\right)]^{-1}$.

To extend this to three dimensions, the following modifications can be made.

2) In the parentheses containing $\left(cos\frac{\pi}{m} + cos\frac{\pi}{n}\right)$, a third term was added containing the number of grid points in the third spatial variable, say l. This became $\left(cos\frac{\pi}{m} + cos\frac{\pi}{n} + cos\frac{\pi}{l}\right)$,

3) The multiplying factor of $\frac{1}{k}$, is $\frac{1}{2}$ when k = 2 in the 2D case, therefore, in three dimensions, k= 3 and thus the multiplier becomes $\frac{1}{3}$.

4) Thus, the formula for calculating the over-relaxation parameter in the 3D case can then be written as: $\alpha = 2[1 + sincos^{-1}\frac{1}{3}\left(cos\frac{\pi}{m} + cos\frac{\pi}{n} + cos\frac{\pi}{l}\right)]^{-1}$, or in the case where $m = n = l$, the shorter formula used was: $\alpha = \frac{2}{(1 + \sin\frac{\pi}{n})}$. This matches what is described in Thompson (1961).

NUMERICAL ILLUSTRATION

Table 1 shows the values of over-relaxation parameters obtained using the idea proposed in the work for solving 3D problems with some selected numbers of grid points. The numbers of grid points in each dimension are given as m, n and l and the relaxation parameter (α) is then calculated as previously described.

To test whether the over-relaxation parameters so obtained are optimum, the following example of 3D problem was solved using different numbers of equally sized grid points from 10 to 100. The convergence criterion was set to 1×10^{-6} and the maximum number of iterations allowed was 10000. The numbers of iterations at the point of convergence were recorded at different over-relaxation parameters and then compared to the numbers of iterations at convergence when the over-relaxation parameter calculated using the developed formula was used.

Example 1

Let $u = x^2z + 3z^3y^2 + y^3x^2z + 1$, found in Spiegel (1974), be considered in the interval [(0; 1); (0; 1); (0; 1)], with the x-axis divided into $i = 1,...,m$, the y-axis into $j= 1,...,n$ and the z-axis into $k=1,...,l$ grid points. The working surface is thus of dimension $m \times n \times l$. To solve this problem, it is necessary to start by looking for the derivatives with regards to all the spatial variables. That is,

$$\frac{\partial u}{\partial x} = 2xz + 2xy^3z\,; \qquad \frac{\partial^2 u}{\partial^2 x} = 2x(1 + y^3);$$

$$\frac{\partial u}{\partial y} = 6z^3y + 3x^2y^2z\,; \qquad \frac{\partial^2 u}{\partial^2 y} = 6z^3 + 6yx^2z);$$

$$\frac{\partial u}{\partial z} = x^2 + 9z^2y^2 + y^3x^2\,; \qquad \frac{\partial^2 u}{\partial^2 z} = 18z^2y^2;$$

The boundary conditions are:

$$f(x_0, y_0, z_0) = 1$$

$$f(x_1, y_1, z_1) = 6$$

Table 2. The comparison of the rate of convergence when using different fixed over-relaxation parameters and those calculated using the formula herein developed.

Relaxation coefficient	α							
	1.99	**1.9**	**1.8**	**1.7**	**1.6**	**1.5**	$2/\sin(\pi/n)$	
Grid points	**Iteration**	**Iteration**	**Iteration**	**Iteration**	**Iteration**	**Iteration**	α	**iteration**
10	1500	146	74	54	35	30	1.528	31
20	1504	172	79	70	110	148	1.728	65
30	1499	178	96	175	248	326	1.811	97
40	1534	162	192	309	430	561	1.854	129
50	1508	166	302	473	653	849	1.881	160
60	1494	192	431	666	916	1188	1.901	192
70	1519	261	577	886	1215	1575	1.914	223
80	1520	350	741	1132	1551	2007	1.924	254
90	1607	446	922	1404	1920	2483	1.932	285
100	1538	550	1119	1701	2323	3001	1.939	316

$$f(x_0, y_j, z_k) = 3z_k^3 y_j^2 + 1$$

$j = 2,...,n-1;\ k = 2,..., l-1$

$$f(x_1, y_j, z_k) = z_k + 3z_k^3 y_j^2 + y_j^3 z_k + 1$$

$j = 2,...,n-1;\ k = 2,..., l-1$

$$f(x_i, y_0, z_k) = x_i^2 z_k + 1;$$

$i = 2,...,m-1;\ k = 2,..., l-1$

$$f(x_i, y_1, z_k) = 2x_i^2 z_k + 3z_k^3 + 1;$$

$i = 2,...,m-1;\ k = 2,..., l-1$

$$f(x_i, y_j, z_0) = 1$$

$i = 2,...,m-1;\ j = 2,..., n-1$

$$f(x_i, y_j, z_1) = x_i^2 + 3y_j^2 + y_j^3 x_i^2 + 1$$

$l=2,...,m-1; j=2,...,n-1$

$$f(x_i, y_j, z_k) = 2z_k + 2y_j^3 z_k + 6z_k^3 + 6y_j x_i^2 z_k + 18y_j^2 z_k;$$

$i = 2,...,m-1;\ j = 2,\ ...,n$

$-1; k = 2,\ ...,l-1$

The calculated over-relaxation parameter was the same irrespective of whether the long form or the short form of the formula was used. The number of grid points was assumed equal in all the axes.

Table 2 shows the results obtained. From Table 2, it is clear that when using the over-relaxation parameter computed from the formula given, convergence is attained faster than when fixed values are used. Note the closeness in iteration numbers between relaxation parameters very close to those obtained using the formula. Thus, this formula gives an effective choice of the parameter and shall be used throughout the rest of this research when necessary. After having obtained the stability criterion and the over-relaxation parameter for the 3D case, the Gauss-Seidel scheme for solving the system of simultaneous equations resulting from this can be written in its extrapolated Liebmann form as follows:

$$U_{i,j,k}^{n+1} = U_{i,j,k}^{n} + \alpha(\frac{1}{6}(U_{i+1,j,k}^{n} + U_{i-1,j,k}^{n+1} + U_{i,j+1,k}^{n} + U_{i,j-1,k}^{n+1} + U_{i,j,k+1}^{n} + U_{i,j,k-1}^{n+1} - 6U_{i,j,k}^{n}) - \frac{\Delta^2}{6}\rho_{i,j,k}).$$

This can be written in short form as:

$$U_{i,j,k}^{n+1} = U_{i,j,k}^{n} + \alpha R_{i,j,k}^{n},$$

This matches with what is shown in Oort (1983) and Southwell (1946), where:

(1) $R_{i,j,k} = \nabla^2 U_{i,j,k} - \rho_{i,j,k}$ is the residual which must be less than a stated tolerance limit ε for convergence to be attained, and $\nabla^2 U_{i,j,k}$ is calculated from the recently obtained U as: $\nabla^2 U_{i,j,k} = (U_{i+1,j,k}^{n} + U_{i-1,j,k}^{n+1} + U_{i,j+1,k}^{n} + U_{i,j-1,k}^{n+1} + U_{i,j,k+1}^{n} + U_{i,j,k-1}^{n+1}$

2) The superscript *n* is the iteration number, while

3) α is the over-relaxation parameter.

The choice of the over-relaxation parameter determines the rapidity of convergence. If the parameter is equal to 1, the method reduces to the Gauss-Seidel scheme as described by Ames (1972). If the parameter is less than 1, then there is under-correction as seen in Press et al. (1992). This scheme is then iterated until convergence is attained. The convergence set thus obtained is the solution field of the process.

Conclusion

We have been able to provide intuitively a procedure for obtaining the stability criterion and the over-relaxation parameter which are the two determinant elements used in facilitating convergence to the solution when solving PDEs by the SOR. These parameters were obtained for the 3D case by a natural extension of the one and 2D formulae developed by Frankel (1950).

Since the approach is intuitive, the main focus was to match this with reality. Thus, the detail derivation by Frankel (1950) has not been included. Instead, comparisons to the conditions of optimality posed by Frankel (1950) were tested on the obtained values. The performances of the parameters obtained from the procedure herein developed can be seen clearly in Table 2. The belief is that, with this development, many physical problems which were hitherto approximated by the use of 1D or 2D PDEs shall be explicitly expressed in three dimensions and be solved easily.

REFERENCES

Ames WF (1972). Numerical methods for partial differential equation, 2nd edn. Thomas and Sons Limited. pp. 206-213.

Brandt A, Diskin B (1999). Multigrid solvers for nonaligned sonic flows. SIAM J. Sci. Comput. 21(2):473-501.

Dorn SW, McCracken DD (1972). Numerical methods with Fortran IV Case Studies. John Wiley and Sons, Inc. pp. 305-331.

Edgar SL (1992). FORTRAN for the '90s problem solving for Scientists and Engineers. Computer Science press USA.

Frankel SP (1950). Convergence rates of iterative treatments of partial differential equations. Math. Tables Aids Computation 4:65-75.

Kallin S (1971a). An Introduction to FORTRAN, AUERBACH publisher Inc.

Kallin S (1971b). Numerical methods and FORTRAN programming. AUERBACH publisher Inc. pp. 365-391.

McCracken DD (1974). A simplified guide to FORTRAN programming. John Wiley & Sons Inc. pp. 163-187.

Oort AH (1983). Global atmospheric circulation statistics. *NOAA prof paper 14 180pp* Nat. Oceanic and Atmospheric Administration, (Silver spring. Md.). p. 180.

Press WH, Tenkolsky SA, Vetterling WT, Flanney BP (1992). Numerical recipes in C programming Language. C. U. P. pp. 827-888.

Reynolds RW (1988). A real-time global sea surface temperature analysis. J. Clim. 1(2):75-86.

Roberts AJ (2001). 'Simple and fast multigrid solution of poissons equation using diagonally oriented grids'. ANZIAM J. 43(E):E1-E36.

Southwell R (1946). Relaxation methods in theoretical Physics. Clarendon Press, Oxford. P. 248.

Spiegel MR (1974). Advanced calculus. McGraw Hill Book Co.

Thompson P (1961). Numerical Weather Analysis and Prediction. The Macmillan Company, New York. pp. 89-98.

Vemuri V, Karplus W (1981). Digital Computer Treatment of PDE, Prentice Hall Inc. pp. 17-35.

8

Thermal deflection of a thin circular plate with radiation

Hamna Parveen, N. K. Lamba* and N. W. Khobragade

Department of Mathematics P.G.T.D. RTM Nagpur University, Nagpur, India.

This paper deals with the determination of thermal deflection of a thin circular plate defined as $0 \le r < a; -h \le z \le h$. A circular plate is considered having arbitrary initial temperature and subjected to radiation type boundary condition which is fixed at $(r = a)$. The non homogeneous type boundary conditions are maintained at plane surfaces of the plate. The governing heat conduction equation has been solved by using integral transform technique. The results are obtained in series form in terms of Bessel's functions. As a special case, aluminum metallic plate has been considered and the results for temperature distribution and thermal deflection have been computed numerically and are illustrated graphically.

Key words: Heat generation, non homogeneous heat conduction equation, thermal deflection, thermoelastic problem.

INTRODUCTION

Nowacki (1957) has determined steady-state thermal stresses in a circular plate subjected to an axisymmetric temperature distribution on the upper face with zero temperature on the lower face and the circular edge respectively. Roy (1973) discussed the normal deflection of a thin clamped circular plate due to ramp type heating of a concentric circular region of the upper face. This satisfies the time – dependent heat conduction equation. Recently Kedar and Deshmukh (2005) have determined the thermal deflection of a thin circular plate.

In this paper, the work of Deshmukh et al. (2005) has been extended for two-dimensional non-homogeneous boundary value problem of heat conduction and studied the thermal deflection of the plate defined as $0 \le r \le a; -h \le z \le h$. This inverse problem deals with the determination of temperature distribution, unknown temperature gradient and thermal deflection.

The plate is considered having arbitrary initial temperature and subjected to radiation type boundary conditions which are fixed at $(r = 0)$ and $(r = a)$. The non homogeneous type boundary conditions are maintained on plane surfaces of the disc. The governing heat conduction equation has been solved by using integral transform technique. The results are obtained in series form in terms of Bessel's functions. The results for thermal deflection have been computed numerically and are illustrated graphically. It is believed that this particular problem has not been considered by any one. This is new and novel contribution to the field. According to Lamba and Khobragade (2011), analytical approach is establish to construct solution in terms of stresses in a thin circular plate subjected to steady and unsteady state thermoelasticity due to diametrical compression. In this approach stress distribution are expressed by means of theoretical technique. The result is obtained as series of Bessel functions.

The results presented here will be useful in engineering problems particularly in aerospace engineering for stations of a missile body not influenced by nose tapering. The missile skill material is assumed to have physical properties independent of temperature, so the temperature $T(r, z, t)$ is a function of radius, thickness and time only.

STATEMENT OF PROBLEM

Consider a circular plate of thickness $2h$ occupying space

*Corresponding author. E-mail: kimutaialbert@yahoo.com.

D defined by $0 \le r \le a$;$-h \le z \le h$. The plate is considered having arbitrary initial temperature and subjected to radiation type boundary condition which is fixed at $(r = a)$. The non homogeneous type boundary conditions are maintained at plane surfaces of the plate.

The differential equation satisfying the deflection function $w(r,t)$ is given by:

$$\nabla^4 \omega = \frac{\nabla^2 M_T}{D(1-v)} \quad (1)$$

where M_T is the thermal moment of the plate which is defined as;

$$M_T = a_t E \int_{-h}^{h} T(r,z,t) z \quad dz \quad (2)$$

D is the flexural rigidity of the disc denoted as;

$$D = \frac{Eh^3}{12(1-v^2)} \quad (3)$$

$a_{t,}$ $_E$ and v are the coefficients of the linear thermal expansion, Young's modules and Poisson's ratio of the disc material respectively and

$$\nabla^2 = \frac{\partial^2}{\partial r^2} + \frac{1}{r}\frac{\partial}{\partial r} \quad (4)$$

Since the edge of an annular disc is fixed and clamped,

$$\omega = \frac{\partial \omega}{\partial r} = 0 \text{, at } r = a \quad (5)$$

Initially $T = \omega = F(r,z)$, at $t = 0$

The temperature $T(r,z,t)$ of the plate at time t satisfies the differential equation,

$$\frac{\partial^2 T}{\partial r^2} + \frac{1}{r}\frac{\partial T}{\partial r} + \frac{\partial^2 T}{\partial z^2} = \frac{1}{\alpha}\frac{\partial T}{\partial t} \quad (6)$$

with the boundary conditions,

$$[T(r,z,t)]_{r=0} = g_1(z,t) \text{, } t > 0 \quad (7)$$

$$[T(r,z,t)]_{r=a} = g_2(z,t) \text{, } -h \le z \le h \quad (8)$$

$$\left[T + k_1 \frac{\partial T}{\partial z}\right]_{z=-h} = f_1(r,t) \text{, } t > 0 \quad (9)$$

$$\left[T + k_2 \frac{\partial T}{\partial z}\right]_{z=h} = f_2(r,t) \text{, } t > 0 \quad (10)$$

and initial condition is;

$$T(r,z,t) = F(r,z) \text{, } 0 \le r \le a, \ -h \le z \le h \text{, } t = 0 \quad (11)$$

where k_1 and k_2 are radiation constants on the plane surfaces of the plate respectively and α is thermal diffusivity of the material of the plate. Equations 1 to 11 constitute the mathematical formulation of the problem under consideration.

SOLUTION OF THE PROBLEM

Applying Marchi-Fasulo transform (Marchi and Fasulo, 1964] (Appendix) to Equation 6, one obtains;

$$\frac{d^2\overline{T}}{dr^2} + \frac{1}{r}\frac{d\overline{T}}{dr} - a_n^2\overline{T} = \frac{1}{k}\frac{d\overline{T}}{dt} + \Psi \quad (12)$$

Further applying finite Hankel transform to Equation 12, we get:

$$\frac{d\overline{T}^*}{dt} + kp^2\overline{T}^* = \Psi_1{}^* \quad (13)$$

where $a_n^2 + \mu_m{}^2 = p^2$, $-k\Psi^* = \Psi_1{}^*$

Equation 13 is a first order differential equation, whose solution is given by:

$$\overline{T}^*(m,n,t) = e^{-kp^2t}\left[\int_0^t \psi_1{}^* e^{kp^2t^1}\, dt^1 + \overline{f}^*(m,n)\right] \quad (14)$$

Applying inversion of Hankel transform and Marchi-Fasulo transform to Equation 14, one obtains;

$$T(r,z,t) = \frac{2}{a^2}\sum_{m=1}^{\infty}\frac{J_0(\mu_m r)}{[J_1(\mu_m a)]^2}$$

$$\sum_{n=1}^{\infty}\frac{P_n(z)}{\lambda_n} e^{-kp^2t}\left[\int_0^t \psi_1{}^* e^{kp^2t^1}\, dt^1 + \overline{f}^*(m,n)\right] \quad (15)$$

Equation 15 is the desired solution of the given problem.

DETERMINATION OF THERMAL DEFLECTION

Using the value of temperature distribution from Equation 15 into Equation 2, one obtains;

$$M_T(r,t) = \frac{2a_t E}{a^2} \sum_{m=1}^{\infty} \frac{J_0(\mu_m r)}{[J_1(\mu_m a)]^2} \sum_{n=1}^{\infty} e^{-kp^2 t} \left[\int_0^t \psi_1{}^* e^{kp^2 t^1} dt^1 + \bar{f}^*(m,n) \right] \int_{-h}^{h} \frac{z P_n(z)}{\lambda_n} dz \quad (16)$$

We assume the solution of Equation 1, satisfying condition 5 as;

$$\omega(r,t) = \sum_{m=1}^{\infty} C_n(t)\, Sin\left(\frac{m\pi r}{a}\right) r(r-a) \quad (17)$$

where μ_m are the positive roots of the transcendental equation,

$$J_1(\mu_m a) = 0 \quad (18)$$

It can be easily seen that

$$\omega = \frac{\partial \omega}{\partial r} = 0 \text{ at } r = a$$

Hence solution 17 satisfies condition 5.

Now

$$\nabla^4 \omega = \left(\frac{\partial^2}{\partial r^2} + \frac{1}{r}\frac{\partial}{\partial r} \right)^2 \sum_{m=1}^{\infty} c_m [J_0(\mu_m r)] \quad (19)$$

We use the well known result,

$$\left(\frac{\partial^2}{\partial r^2} + \frac{1}{r}\frac{\partial}{\partial r} \right) J_0(\mu_m r) = -\mu_m^2 J_0(\mu_m r) \quad (20)$$

In Equation 19, we get;

$$\nabla^4 \omega = \sum_{m=1}^{\infty} c_m \mu_m^4 J_0(\mu_m r) \quad (21)$$

Also

$$\nabla^2 M_T = -a_t E \sum_{m=1}^{\infty}\sum_{n=1}^{\infty} [J_0(\mu_m r) \frac{1}{\lambda_n^2} (\bar{F}^* + \int_0^t e^{\alpha p^2 t^1} \bar{\Psi}^* dt^1)(z-1) \int_{-h}^{h} P_n(z)\, dz] \quad (22)$$

Using Equations 21 and 22 in Equation 1, one obtains;

$$\sum_{m=1}^{\infty} c_m \mu_m^4 J_0(\mu_m r) = -\frac{a_t E}{D(1-v)} \times \sum_{m=1}^{\infty}\sum_{n=1}^{\infty} [J_0(\mu_m r) \frac{1}{\lambda^2} (\bar{F}^* + \int_0^t \bar{\Psi}^* e^{\alpha p^2 t^1} dt^1)(z-1) \int_{-h}^{h} P_n(z)\, dz] \quad (23)$$

On solving Equation 23 we get;

$$c_m(t) = -\frac{a_t E}{D(1-v)} \sum_{n=1}^{\infty} \left[\frac{1}{\lambda_n^2 \mu_m^4} (\bar{F}^* + \int_0^t \bar{\Psi}^* e^{\alpha p^2 t^1} dt^1)(z-1) \int_{-h}^{h} P_n(z)\, dz \right] \quad (24)$$

Substituting Equation 24 into Equation 17, we get

$$\omega(r,t) = -\frac{a_t E}{D(1-v)} \sum_{m=1}^{\infty}\sum_{n=1}^{\infty} \left[\frac{1}{\lambda_n^2 \mu_m^4} (\bar{F}^* + \int_0^t \bar{\Psi}^* e^{\alpha p^2 t^1} dt^1)(z-1) \int_{-h}^{h} P_n(z)\, dz \right] \times [J_0(\mu_m r)] \quad (25)$$

The expression (25) is represented graphically, that is Figures 1 and 2.

SPECIAL CASE AND NUMERICAL RESULTS

Setting

$$F(r,z) = \delta(r - r_0) \times (z-h)^2 \times (z+h)^2 \quad (26)$$

where r is the radius of the disc and δ is the Dirac – delta function.

$$\Rightarrow \bar{F}^* = 3(k_3 + k_4) J_0(\mu_m r_0) \left[\frac{a_n h \cos^2(a_n h) - \cos(a_n h)\sin(a_n h)}{a_n{}^2} \right] \quad (27)$$

Using Equation 27 in Equation 16, one obtains;

$$T = \sum_{m=1}^{\infty} \frac{1}{\mu_m} J_0(\mu_m r) \left[\sum_{n=1}^{\infty} \frac{1}{\lambda_n} P_n(z) \left(\bar{F}^* + \int_0^t \bar{\Psi}^* e^{\alpha p^2 t^1} dt^1 \right) \right] \quad (28)$$

The expression (28) is represented graphically, that is Figures 3 and 4.

CONCLUSION

In this paper, the temperature distribution and thermal

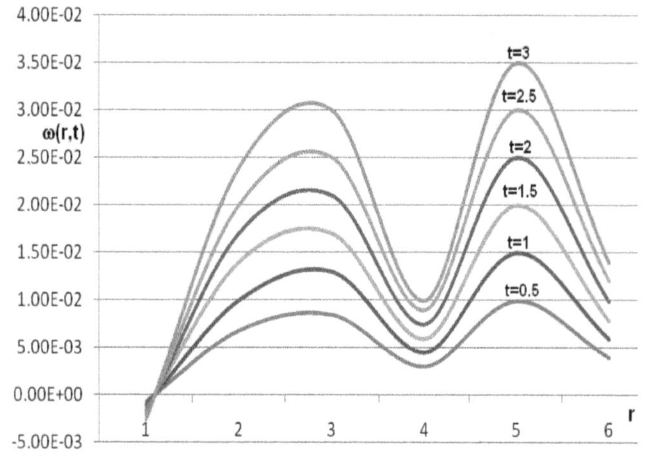

Figure 1. Thermal deflection ω(r,t) versus r for different values of t.

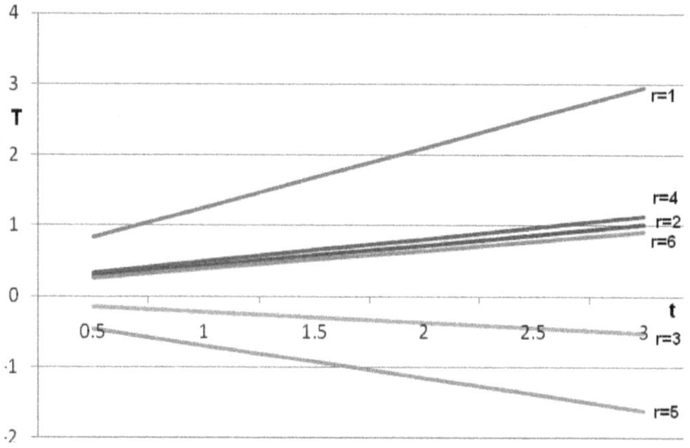

Figure 2. Thermal deflection ω(r,t) versus t for different values of r.

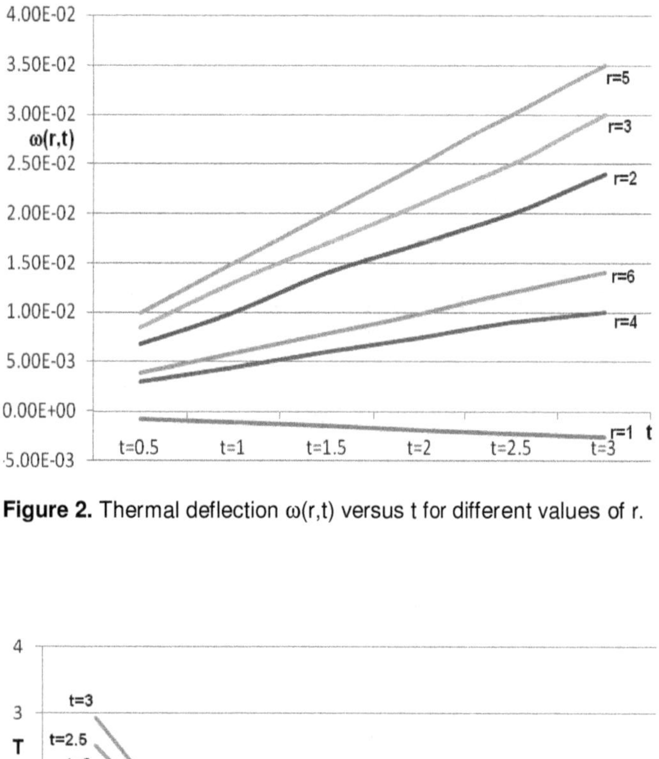

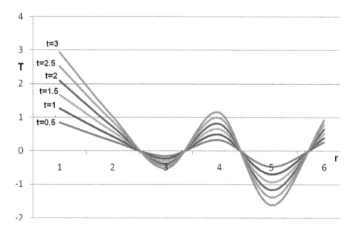

Figure 3. Temperature distribution T versus r for different values of t.

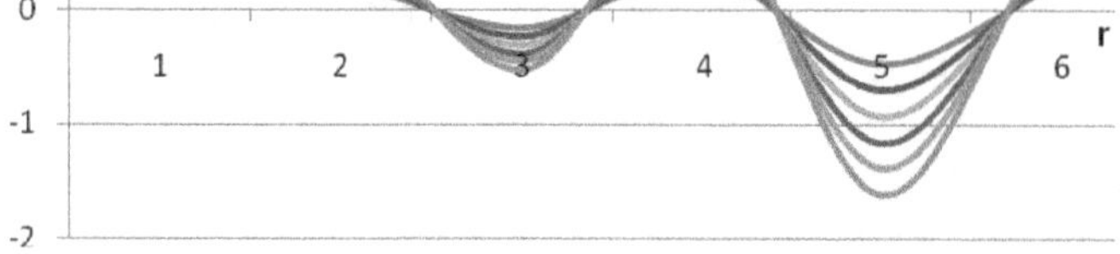

Figure 4. Temperature distribution T versus t for different values of r.

deflection have been investigated and the results are depicted graphically. Mathematical calculations have been made in MathCAD, and graphs have been plotted for temperature distribution and thermal deflection versus r, t and z for different values of time and radius.

The temperature distribution and thermal deflection of a thin circular plate made of aluminium have been determined by using the conditions given in the problem and applying integral transform techniques.

ACKNOWLEDGEMENTS

Authors express their sincere thanks to the reviewers for their expert comments. Also the authors are thankful to University Grant Commission, New Delhi for providing the partial financial assistance under major research project scheme.

REFERENCES

Deshmukh KC, Khobragade NL (2005). An inverse quasi-static thermal deflection problem for a thin clamped circular plate. J. Therm.Stress., 28: 353-361.

Kedar GD, Deshmukh KC (2011). Estimation of temperature distribution and thermal stresses in a thick circular plate. Afr. J. Math. Comp. Sci. Res., 4(13): 389-395, Dec.

Marchi E, Fasulo A (1967). Heat conduction in sector of hollow cylinder with radiation. Atti, della Acc. Sci. di. Torino, 1: 373-382.

Lamba N, Khobragade NW (2011). Analytical Thermal Stress Analysis in a Thin Circular Plate Due to Diametrical Compression. Int. J. Latest Trend Math., 1(1): 12-17.

Nowacki W (1957). The state of stress in thick circular plate due to temperature field. Ball. Sci. Acad. Polon Sci. Tech., 5: 227.

Roy CSK (1973). A note on quasi-static thermal deflection of a thin clamped circular plate due to ramp-type heating on a Concentric circular region of the upper face. J. Franklin. Inst., 206: 213-219.

APPENDIX

The finite Marchi-Fasulo integral transform of f (z), -h < z < h is defined to be

$$\overline{F}(n) = \int_{-h}^{h} f(z) P_n(z)\, dz \qquad (29)$$

then at each point of (-h, h) at which f(z) is continuous,

$$f(z) = \sum_{n=1}^{\infty} \frac{\overline{F}(n)}{\lambda_n} P_n(z) \qquad (30)$$

where

$$P_n(z) = Q_n \cos(a_n z) - W_n \sin(a_n z)$$
$$Q_n = a_n(\alpha_1 + \alpha_2)\cos(a_n h) + (\beta_1 - \beta_2)\sin(a_n h)$$
$$W_n = (\beta_1 + \beta_2)\cos(a_n h) + (\alpha_2 - \alpha_1) a_n \sin(a_n h)$$
$$\lambda_n = \int_{-h}^{h} P_n^2(z)\, dz = h\left[Q_n^2 + W_n^2\right] + \frac{\sin(2a_n h)}{2a_n}\left[Q_n^2 - W_n^2\right]$$

The Eigen values a_n are the solutions of the equation

$$\left[\alpha_1 a \cos(ah) + \beta_1 \sin(ah)\right] \times \left[\beta_2 \cos(ah) + \alpha_2 a \sin(ah)\right] = \left[\alpha_2 a \cos(ah) - \beta_2 \sin(ah)\right] \times \left[\beta_1 \cos(ah) - \alpha_1 a \sin(ah)\right]$$

α_1, α_2, β_1 and β_2 are constants.

Moreover the integral transform has the following property:

$$\int_{-h}^{h} \frac{\partial^2 f(z)}{\partial z^2} P_n(z)\, dz = \frac{P_n(h)}{\alpha_1}\left[\beta_1 f(z) + \alpha_1 \frac{\partial f(z)}{\partial z}\right]_{z=h} - \frac{P_n(-h)}{\alpha_2}\left[\beta_2 f(z) + \alpha_2 \frac{\partial f(z)}{\partial z}\right]_{z=-h} - a_n^2 \overline{F}(n).$$

Utilization of mixture of $\bar{x}$, $\bar{x}_1$ and $\bar{x}_2$ in imputation for missing data in post-stratification

D. Shukla[1], D. S. Thakur[2] and N. S. Thakur[3]

[1]Department of Mathematics and Statistics, Dr. H. S. Gour Central University, Sagar, (M.P.), India.
[2]School of Excellence, Sagar (M.P.), India.
[3]Centre for Mathematical Sciences (CMS), Banasthali University, Rajasthan, India.

To estimate the population mean using auxiliary variable there are many estimators available in literature like-ratio, product, regression, dual-to-ratio estimator and so on. Suppose that all the information of the main variable is present in the sample but only a part of data of the auxiliary variable is available. Then, in this case none of the aforementioned estimators could be used. This paper presents an imputation based factor-type class of estimation strategy for population mean in presence of missing values of auxiliary variables. The non-sampled part of the population is used as an imputation technique in the proposed class. Some properties of estimators are discussed and numerical study is performed with efficiency comparison to the non-imputed estimator. An optimum sub-class is recommended.

Key words: Imputation, non-response, post-stratification, simple random sampling without replacement (SRSWOR), respondents (R).

INTRODUCTION

In sampling theory, the problem of mean estimation of a population is considered by many authors like Srivastava and Jhajj (1980, 1981), Sahoo (1984, 1986), Singh (1986), Singh et al. (1987), Singh and Singh (1991), Singh et al. (1994), Sahoo et al. (1995), Sahoo and Sahoo (2001), and Singh and Singh (2001). Sometimes in survey situations, a small part of sample remains non-responded (or incomplete) due to many practical reasons. Techniques and estimation procedures are needed to develop for this purpose. The imputation is a well defined methodology by virtue of which this kind of problem could be partially solved. Ahmed et al. (2006), Rao and Sitter (1995), Rubin (1976) and Singh and Horn (2000) have given applications of various imputation procedures. Hinde and Chambers (1990) studied the non-response imputation with multiple source of non-response. The problem of non-response in sample surveys immensely looked into by Hansen and Hurwitz (1946), Grover and Couper (1998), Jackway and Boyce (1987), Khare (1987), Khot (1994), Lessler and Kalsbeek (1992).

When the "response" and "non-response" part of the sample is assumed into two groups, it is closed to call upon as post-stratification. Estimation problem in sample survey, in the setup of post-stratification, under non-response situation is studied due to Shukla and Dubey (2001, 2004, and 2006). Some other useful contributions to this area are by Holt and Smith (1979), Jagers et al. (1985), Jagers (1986), Smith (1991), Agrawal and Panda (1993), Shukla and Trivedi (1999, 2001, 2006), Wywial (2001), Shukla et al. (2002, 2006). When a sample is full of response over main variable but some of auxiliary values are missing, it is hard to utilize the usual estimators. Traditionally, it is essential to estimate those missing observations first by some specific estimation techniques. One can think of utilizing the non-sampled part of the population in order to get estimates of missing observations in the sample. These estimates could be imputed into actual estimation procedures used for the population mean. The content of this research work takes into account the similar aspect for non-responding values of the sample assuming post-stratified setup and utilizing

*Corresponding author. E-mail: nst_stats@yahoo.co.in.

the auxiliary source of data.

Symbols and setup

Let $U = (U_1, U_2, \ldots\ldots\ldots, U_N)$ be a finite population of N units with Y as a main variable and X the auxiliary variable. The population has two types of individuals like N_1 as number of "respondents (R)" and N_2 "non-respondents (NR)", ($N = N_1+N_2$). Their population proportions are expressed like $W_1 = N_1/N$ and $W_2 = N_2/N$. Quantities W_1 and W_2 could be guessed by past data or by experience of the investigator. Further, let $\overline{Y}$ and $\overline{X}$ be the population means of Y and X respectively. Some symbols are as follows:

R-group, Respondents group or group of those who responses in survey;
NR-group, Non-respondents group or group of those who denied to response during survey;
$\overline{Y}_1$, Population mean of R-group of Y;
$\overline{Y}_2$, Population mean of NR-group of Y;
$\overline{X}_1$, Population mean of R-group of X;
$\overline{X}_2$, Population mean of NR-group of X;
S_{1Y}^2, Population mean square of R-group of Y;
S_{2Y}^2, Population mean square of NR-group of Y;
S_{1X}^2, Population mean square of R-group of X;
S_{2X}^2, Population mean square of NR-group of X;
C_{1Y}, Coefficient of variation of Y in R-group;
C_{2Y}, Coefficient of variation of Y in NR-group;
C_{1X}, Coefficient of variation of X in R-group;
C_{2X}, Coefficient of variation of X in NR-group;
ρ, Correlation coefficient in population between X and Y;
N, Sample size from population of size N by SRSWOR;
n_1, Post-stratified sample size coming from R-group;
n_2, Post-stratified sample size from NR-group;
$\bar{y}_1$, Sample mean of Y based on n_1 observations of R-group;
$\bar{y}_2$, Sample mean of Y based on n_2 observations of NR-group;
$\bar{x}_1$, Sample mean of X based on n_1 observations of R-group;
$\bar{x}_2$, Sample mean of X based on n_2 observations of NR-group;
ρ_1. Correlation Coefficient of population of R-group;
ρ_2, Correlation Coefficient of population of NR-group

Further, consider few more symbolic representations:

$$D_1 = E\left(\frac{1}{n_1}\right) = \left[\frac{1}{nW_1} + \frac{(N-n)(1-W_1)}{(N-1)n^2W_1^2}\right]; \qquad D_2 = E\left(\frac{1}{n_2}\right) = \left[\frac{1}{nW_2} + \frac{(N-n)(1-W_2)}{(N-1)n^2W_2^2}\right]$$

$$\overline{Y} = \frac{N_1\overline{Y}_1 + N_2\overline{Y}_2}{N}; \quad \overline{X} = \frac{N_1\overline{X}_1 + N_2\overline{X}_2}{N}$$

ASSUMPTIONS

Consider following in light of Figure 1 before formulating an imputation based estimation procedure:

1) The sample of size n is drawn by SRSWOR and post-stratified into two groups of size n_1 and n_2 ($n_1 + n_2 = n$) according to R and NR group respectively
2) The information about Y variable in sample is completely available.
3) The sample means of both groups $\bar{y}_1$ and $\bar{y}_2$ are known such that

$$\bar{y} = \frac{n_1\bar{y}_1 + n_2\bar{y}_2}{n}$$ which is sample mean on n units.

4) The population means $\overline{X_1}$ and $\overline{X}$ are known.
5) The population size N and sample size n are known. Also, N_1 and N_2 are known by past data, past experience or by guess of the investigator ($N_1 + N_2 = N$).
6) The sample mean of auxiliary information $\bar{x}_1$ is only known for R-Group, but information about $\bar{x}_2$ of NR-group is missing. Therefore

$$\bar{x} = \frac{n_1\bar{x}_1 + n_2\bar{x}_2}{n}$$ could not be obtained due to absence of $\bar{x}_2$.

7) Other population parameters are assumed known, in either exact or in ratio from except the $\overline{Y}$, $\overline{Y}_1$ and $\overline{Y}_2$.

PROPOSED CLASS OF ESTIMATION STRATEGY

To estimate population mean $\overline{Y}$, in setup of Figure 1, a problem to face is of missing observations related to $\bar{x}_2$, therefore, usual ratio, product and regression estimators are not applicable. Singh and Shukla (1987) have proposed a factor type estimator for estimating population mean $\overline{Y}$. Shukla et al. (1991), Singh and Shukla (1993) and Shukla (2002) have also discussed properties of factor-type estimators applicable for estimating population mean. But all these cannot be useful due to unknown information $\bar{x}_2$. In order to solve this, an imputation $(\bar{x}_2^*)_4$ is adopted as:

$$(\bar{x}_2^*)_4 = \left[\frac{N\overline{X} - n\{f\overline{X}_1 + (1-f)\overline{X}_2\}}{N-n}\right] \qquad (1)$$

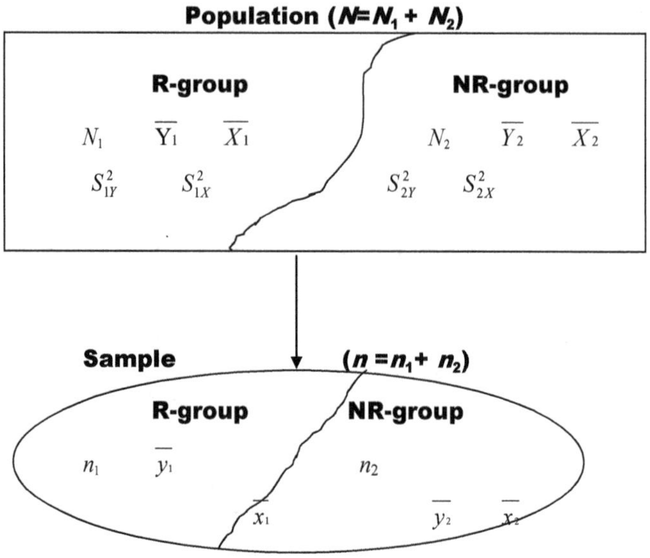

Figure 1. Setup to estimate population mean $\overline{Y}$.

The logic for this imputation is to utilize the non-sampled part of the population of X for obtaining an estimate of missing $\bar{x}_2$ and generate $\bar{x}^{(2)}$ for $\bar{x}$ as describe as follows:

And

$$\bar{x}^{(4)} = \left[\frac{N_1\bar{x}_1 + N_2\left(\bar{x}_2^{*}\right)_4}{N_1 + N_2}\right] \tag{2}$$

The proposed class of imputed factor-type estimator is:

$$[(\bar{y}_{FT})_D]_k = \left(\frac{N_1\bar{y}_1 + N_2\bar{y}_2}{N}\right)\left[\frac{(A+C)\bar{X} + fB\bar{x}^{(4)}}{(A+fB)\bar{X} + C\bar{x}^{(4)}}\right] \tag{3}$$

Where $0 < k < \infty$ and k is a constant and

$A = (k-1)(k-2);\ B = (k-1)(k-4);\ C = (k-2)(k-3)(k-4);\ f = n/N.$

LARGE SAMPLE APPROXIMATION

Consider the following for large n:

$$\left.\begin{aligned} \bar{y}_1 &= \bar{Y}_1(1+e_1) \\ \bar{y}_2 &= \bar{Y}_2(1+e_2) \\ \bar{x}_1 &= \bar{X}_1(1+e_3) \\ \bar{x}_2 &= \bar{X}_2(1+e_4) \end{aligned}\right\} \tag{4}$$

where, e_1, e_2, e_3 and e_4 are very small numbers $e_i > 0$ (i = 1,2,3,4).

Using the basic concept of SRSWOR and the concept of post-stratification of the sample n into n_1 and n_2 (Cochran, 2005; Hansen et al., 1993; Sukhatme et al., 1984; Singh and Choudhary, 1986; Murthy, 1976), we get

$$\left.\begin{aligned} E(e_1) &= E\left[E(e_1)\ |n_1\right] = 0 \\ E(e_2) &= E\left[E(e_2)\ |n_2\right] = 0 \\ E(e_3) &= E\left[E(e_3)\ |n_1\right] = 0 \\ E(e_4) &= E\left[E(e_4)\ |n_2\right] = 0 \end{aligned}\right\} \tag{5}$$

Assume the independence of R-group and NR-group representation in the sample, the following expression could be obtained:

$$E\left[e_1^2\right] = E\left[E\left(e_1^2\right)\ |n_1\right]$$

$$= E\left[\left\{\left(\frac{1}{n_1} - \frac{1}{N}\right)C_{1Y}^2\right\}\middle| n_1\right]$$

$$= \left[\left\{E\left(\frac{1}{n_1}\right) - \frac{1}{N}\right\}C_{1Y}^2\right]$$

$$= \left[\left(D_1 - \frac{1}{N}\right)C_{1Y}^2\right] \tag{6}$$

$$E\left[e_2^2\right] = E\left[E\left(e_2^2\right) \mid n_2\right]$$

$$= E\left[\left\{\left(\frac{1}{n_2} - \frac{1}{N}\right) C_{2Y}^2\right\} \middle| n_2\right]$$

$$= \left[\left(D_2 - \frac{1}{N}\right) C_{2Y}^2\right] \tag{7}$$

$$E\left[e_3^2\right] = E\left[E\left(e_3^2\right) \mid n_1\right]$$

$$= \left[\left(D_1 - \frac{1}{N}\right) C_{1X}^2\right] \tag{8}$$

and

$$E\left[e_4^2\right] = \left[\left(D_2 - \frac{1}{N}\right) C_{2X}^2\right] \tag{9}$$

$$E\left[e_1 e_3\right] = E\left[E\left(e_1 e_3\right) \mid n_1\right]$$

$$= E\left[\left\{\left(\frac{1}{n_1} - \frac{1}{N}\right) \rho_1 C_{1Y} C_{1X}\right\} \middle| n_1\right]$$

$$= \left[\left(D_1 - \frac{1}{N}\right) \rho_1 C_{1Y} C_{1X}\right] \tag{10}$$

$$E\left[e_1 e_2\right] = E\left[E\left(e_1 e_2\right) \mid n_1, n_2\right] = 0 \tag{11}$$

$$E\left[e_1 e_4\right] = 0 \tag{12}$$

$$E\left[e_2 e_3\right] = E\left[E\left(e_2 e_3\right) \mid n_1, n_2\right] = 0 \tag{13}$$

$$E\left[e_2 e_4\right] = \left(D_2 - \frac{1}{N}\right) \rho_2 C_{2Y} C_{2X} \tag{14}$$

$$E\left[e_3 e_4\right] = 0 \tag{15}$$

The expressions (11), (12), (13) and (15) are true under the assumption of independent representation of R-group and NR-group units in the sample. This is introduced to simplify mathematical expressions.

Theorem 1

The estimator $[(\bar{y}_{FT})_D]_k$ could be expressed under large sample approximation in the form:

$$[(\bar{y}_{FT})_D]_k = \delta_3 \bar{Y}[1 + s_1 W_1 e_1 + s_2 W_2 e_2][1 + (\alpha_3 - \beta_3)e_3 - (\alpha_3 - \beta_3)\beta_3 e_3^2 + (\alpha_3 - \beta_3)\beta_3^2 e_3^3 \ldots$$

Proof

Rewrite $\bar{x}^{(4)}$ as in Equation 2:

$$\bar{x}^{(4)} = \left[\frac{N_1 \bar{x}_1 + N_2 \left(\bar{x}_2^*\right)_4}{N_1 + N_2}\right]$$

Where,

$$\left(\bar{x}_2^*\right)_4 = \left[\frac{N\bar{X} - n\left\{f\bar{X}_1 + (1-f)\bar{X}_2\right\}}{N-n}\right]$$

$$\Rightarrow \quad \bar{x}^{(4)} = \frac{1}{N}\left[N_1 \bar{X}_1 (1+e_3) + N_2 \left\{\frac{N\bar{X} - n\left\{f\bar{X}_1 + (1-f)\bar{X}_2\right\}}{N-n}\right\}\right]$$

$$= \frac{N_1 \bar{X}_1 (1+e_3) + p\left[N\bar{X} - n\left(f\bar{X}_1 + (1-f)\bar{X}_2\right)\right]}{N}$$

$$= \left[\frac{N_1 \bar{X}_1 + pN\bar{X} - pnf\bar{X}_1 - pn(1-f)\bar{X}_2 + N_1 \bar{X}_1 e_3}{N}\right]$$

$$= \left[\frac{pN\bar{X} + (N_1 - pnf)\bar{X}_1 - pn(1-f)\bar{X}_2 + N_1 \bar{X}_1 e_3}{N}\right]$$

$$= \bar{X}\left[p + \left(W_1 - pf^2\right)r_1 - pf(1-f)r_2 + W_1 r_1 e_3\right]$$

$$= \bar{X}\left[\mu + W_1 r_1 e_3\right] \tag{16}$$

Where,

$p = \dfrac{N_2}{N-n}$; $\mu = p + (W_1 - pf^2)r_1 - pf(1-f)r_2$.

Now, the estimator $[(\bar{y}_{FT})_D]_k$ under approximation and using (16) is

$$[(\bar{y}_{FT})_D]_k = \left(\frac{N_1 \bar{y}_1 + N_2 \bar{y}_2}{N}\right)\left[\frac{(A+C)\bar{X} + fB\bar{x}^{(4)}}{(A+fB)\bar{X} + C\bar{x}^{(4)}}\right]$$

$$= \left[\frac{N_1 \bar{Y}_1 (1+e_1) + N_2 \bar{Y}_2 (1+e_2)}{N}\right]\left[\frac{(A+C)\bar{X} + fB(\mu + W_1 r_1 e_3)\bar{X}}{(A+fB)\bar{X} + C(\mu + W_1 r_1 e_3)\bar{X}}\right]$$

$$= \bar{Y}[1 + s_1 W_1 e_1 + s_2 W_2 e_2]\left[\frac{(A + fB\mu + C) + fBW_1 r_1 e_3}{(A + fB + C\mu) + CW_1 r_1 e_3}\right]$$

$$= \bar{Y}[1 + s_1 W_1 e_1 + s_2 W_2 e_2]\left[\frac{\xi_1 + \xi_2 e_3}{\xi_3 + \xi_4 e_3}\right]$$

$$= \delta_3 \bar{Y}[1 + s_1 W_1 e_1 + s_2 W_2 e_2](1 + \alpha_3 e_3)(1 + \beta_3 e_3)^{-1}$$

Where,

$\xi_1 = A + fB\mu + C$; $\xi_2 = fBW_1r_1$; $\xi_3 = A + fB + C\mu$; $\xi_4 = CW_1r_1$;

$r_1 = \dfrac{\overline{X}_1}{\overline{\overline{X}}}$; $r_2 = \dfrac{\overline{X}_2}{\overline{\overline{X}}}$; $s_1 = \dfrac{\overline{Y}_1}{\overline{\overline{Y}}}$; $s_2 = \dfrac{\overline{Y}_2}{\overline{\overline{Y}}}$; $\alpha_3 = \dfrac{\xi_2}{\xi_1}$; $\beta_3 = \dfrac{\xi_4}{\xi_3}$; $\delta_3 = \dfrac{\xi_1}{\xi_3}$.

We can further express the above into following:

$= \delta_3 \overline{Y} [1 + s_1W_1e_1 + s_2W_2e_2] (1 + \alpha_3 e_3) (1 - \beta_3 e_3 + \beta_3^2 e_3^2 - \beta_3^3 e_3^3 \ldots\ldots)$

$= \delta_3 \overline{Y} [1+s_1W_1e_1+s_2W_2e_2][1+(\alpha_3-\beta_3)e_3-(\alpha_3-\beta_3)\beta_3 e_3^2 +(\alpha_3 - \beta_3) \beta_3^2 e_3^3 \ldots.]$

BIAS AND MEAN SQUARED ERROR

Define E(.) for expectation, B(.) for bias and M(.) for mean squared error, then the first order of approximations could be established for *i*, *j* = 1, 2, 3, ... as

$$\left.\begin{array}{lll} \mathrm{E}\left[e_1^i e_2^j\right] = 0 & \text{when} & i+j > 2 \\ \mathrm{E}\left[e_1^i e_3^j\right] = 0 & \text{when} & i+j > 2 \\ \mathrm{E}\left[e_2^i e_3^j\right] = 0 & \text{when} & i+j > 2 \end{array}\right\} \quad (17)$$

Theorem 2

The $[(\overline{y}_{FT})_D]_k$ is a biased estimator of $\overline{Y}$ with the amount of bias to the first order of approximation:

$$\mathrm{B}[(\overline{y}_{FT})_D]_k = \overline{Y}\left[(\delta_3 - 1) - \delta_3 C_{1X}(\alpha_3 - \beta_3)\left(D_1 - \frac{1}{N}\right)\{\beta_3\, C_{1X} - s_1W_1\, \rho_1 C_{1Y}\}\right]$$

Proof

$$\mathrm{B}[(\overline{y}_{FT})_D]_k = \mathrm{E}[\{(\overline{y}_{FT})_D\}_k - \overline{Y}]$$

Using theorem 1 and taking expectations

$\mathrm{E}[(\overline{y}_{FT})_D]_k = \delta_3 \overline{Y}\, \mathrm{E}[1 + (\alpha_3 - \beta_3)e_3 - (\alpha_3 - \beta_3)\beta_3 e_3^2 + s_1W_1e_1\{1 + (\alpha_3 - \beta_3)e_3 - (\alpha_3 - \beta_3)\beta_3 e_3^2\}$

$+ s_2W_2e_2\{1 + (\alpha_3 - \beta_3)e_3 - (\alpha_3 - \beta_3)\beta_3 e_3^2\}]$

$= \delta_3 \overline{Y}[1 - (\alpha_3 - \beta_3)\beta_3 \mathrm{E}(e_3^2) + s_1W_1(\alpha_3 - \beta_3)\mathrm{E}(e_1e_3) + s_2W_2(\alpha_3 - \beta_3)\mathrm{E}(e_2e_3)]$

$$= \delta_3 \overline{Y}\left[1 - (\alpha_3 - \beta_3)\beta_3\left(D_1 - \frac{1}{N}\right)C_{1X}^2 + (\alpha_3 - \beta_3)s_1W_1\left(D_1 - \frac{1}{N}\right)\rho_1 C_{1Y}C_{1X}\right]$$

$$= \delta_3 \overline{Y}\left[1 - (\alpha_3 - \beta_3)\left(D_1 - \frac{1}{N}\right)C_{1X}\{\beta_3 C_{1X} - s_1W_1\rho_1 C_{1Y}\}\right]$$

Therefore,

$$\mathrm{B}[(\overline{y}_{FT})_D]_k = \mathrm{E}[\{(\overline{y}_{FT})_D\}_k - \overline{Y}]$$

$$= \overline{Y}\left[(\delta_3 - 1) - \delta_3 C_{1X}(\alpha_3 - \beta_3)\left(D_1 - \frac{1}{N}\right)\{\beta_3 C_{1X} - s_1W_1\rho_1 C_{1Y}\}\right]$$

Theorem 3

The mean squared error of $[(\overline{y}_{FT})_D]_k$ is

$\mathrm{M}\,[(\overline{y}_{FT})_D]_l$

$$= \overline{Y}^2\left[(\delta_3 - 1)^2 + \left(D_1 - \frac{1}{N}\right)\{J_1 s_1^2 C_{1Y}^2 + J_2 C_{1X}^2 + 2J_3 s_1 \rho_1 C_{1Y} C_{1X}\} + \left(D_2 - \frac{1}{N}\right)\delta_3^2 s_2^2 W_2^2 C_{2Y}^2\right]$$

Where

$$J_1 = \delta_3^2 W_1^2,\ J_2 = \delta_3(\alpha_3 - \beta_3)\{\delta_3(\alpha_3 - \beta_3) - 2(\delta_3 - 1)\beta_3\};\ J_3 = W_1\delta_3(2\delta_3 - 1)(\alpha_3 - \beta_3$$

Proof

$$\mathrm{M}\,[(\overline{y}_{FT})_D]_k = \mathrm{E}[\{(\overline{y}_{FT})_D\}_k - \overline{Y}]^2$$

Using Theorem 1, we can express

$\mathrm{M}[(\overline{y}_{FT})_D]_k = \mathrm{E}[\delta_3 \overline{Y}\{1 + s_1W_1e_1 + s_2W_2e_2\}\{1 + (\alpha_3 - \beta_3)e_3 - (\alpha_3 - \beta_3)\beta_3 e_3^2 + (\alpha_3 - \beta_3)\beta_3^2 e_3^3$

$\ldots\} - \overline{Y}]^2$

Using large sample approximations of (17) we could express

$= \overline{Y}^2 \mathrm{E}\,[(\delta_3 - 1) + \delta_3\{(\alpha_3 - \beta_3)e_3 - (\alpha_3 - \beta_3)\beta_3 e_3^2 + (s_1W_1e_1 + s_2W_2e_2) + (\alpha_3 - \beta_3)(s_1W_1e_1 + s_2W_2e_2)$

$e_3\}]^2$

$= \overline{Y}^2 \mathrm{E}\,[(\delta_3 - 1)^2 + \delta_3^2\{(\alpha_3 - \beta_3)^2 e_3^2 + s_1^2 W_1^2 e_1^2 + s_2^2 W_2^2 e_2^2 + 2s_1s_2W_1W_2e_1e_2$

$+ 2(\alpha_3 - \beta_3)(s_1W_1e_1 e_3 + s_2W_2e_2e_3)\} + 2\delta_3(\delta_3 - 1)\{(\alpha_3 - \beta_3)e_3 - (\alpha_3 - \beta_3)\beta_3 e_3^2$

$+ (s_1W_1e_1 + s_2W_2e_2) + (\alpha_3 - \beta_3)(s_1W_1e_1e_3 + s_2W_2e_2e_3)\}]$

Using (5), (11) and (12) we rewrite,

$= \overline{Y}^2[(\delta_3 - 1)^2 + \delta_3^2\{(\alpha_3 - \beta_3)^2 \mathrm{E}(e_3^2) + s_1^2 W_1^2 \mathrm{E}(e_1^2) + s_2^2 W_2^2 \mathrm{E}(e_2^2) + 2(\alpha_3 - \beta_3) s_1W_1 \mathrm{E}(e_1 e_3)\}$

$+ 2\delta_3(\delta_3 - 1)\{-(\alpha_3 - \beta_3)\beta_3 \mathrm{E}(e_3^2) + (\alpha_3 - \beta_3)s_1W_1 \mathrm{E}(e_1e_3)\}]$

$$= \overline{Y}^2\left[(\delta_3 - 1)^2 + \delta_3^2\left\{(\alpha_3 - \beta_3)^2\left(D_1 - \frac{1}{N}\right)C_{1X}^2 + s_1^2W_1^2\left(D_1 - \frac{1}{N}\right)C_{1Y}^2\right.\right.$$

$$\left. + s_2^2W_2^2\left(D_2 - \frac{1}{N}\right)C_{2Y}^2 + 2(\alpha_3 - \beta_3)s_1W_1\left(D_1 - \frac{1}{N}\right)\rho_1 C_{1Y}C_{1X}\right\}$$

$$\left. + 2\delta_3(\delta_3 - 1)\left\{-(\alpha_3 - \beta_3)\beta_3\left(D_1 - \frac{1}{N}\right)C_{1X}^2\right\} + (\alpha_3 - \beta_3)s_1W_1\left(D_1 - \frac{1}{N}\right)\rho_1 C_{1Y}C_{1X}\right]$$

$$= \overline{Y}^2\left[(\delta_3 - 1)^2 + \left(D_1 - \frac{1}{N}\right)\{\delta_3^2 s_1^2W_1^2C_{1Y}^2 + \delta_3(\alpha_3 - \beta_3)\{\delta_3(\alpha_3 - \beta_3) - 2(\delta_3 - 1)\beta_3\}C_{1X}^2\right.$$

$$\left. + 2\delta_3(\delta_3 - 1)(\alpha_3 - \beta_3)s_1W_1\rho_1 C_{1Y}C_{1X}\} + \left(D_2 - \frac{1}{N}\right)\delta_3^2 s_2^2W_2^2C_{2Y}^2\right]$$

$$= \overline{Y}^2\left[(\delta_3 - 1)^2 + \left(D_1 - \frac{1}{N}\right)\{J_1 s_1^2 C_{1Y}^2 + J_2 C_{1X}^2 + 2J_3 s_1 \rho_1 C_{1Y}C_{1X}\} + \left(D_2 - \frac{1}{N}\right)\delta_3^2 s_2^2 W_2^2 C_{2Y}^2\right]$$

SOME SPECIAL CASES

The term A, B and C are functions of k. In particular, there are some special cases:

Case 1

When $k = 1$

$A = 0$; $B = 0$; $C = -6$; $\xi_1 = -6$; $\xi_2 = 0$; $\xi_3 = -6\mu$; $\xi_4 = -6r_1w_1$; $\alpha_3 = 0$; $\beta_3 = \frac{r_1W_1}{\mu}$; $\delta_3 = \mu^{-1}$;

$J_1 = \frac{W_1^2}{\mu^2}$; $J_2 = \frac{r_1^2W_1^2(3-2\mu)}{\mu^4}$; $J_3 = \frac{r_1W_1^2(\mu-2)}{\mu^3}$;

The estimator $[(\bar{y}_{FT})_D]_k$ along with bias and m.s.e. under case i is:

$$[(\bar{y}_{FT})_D]_{k=1} = \left[\frac{N_1\bar{y}_1 + N_2\bar{y}_2}{N}\right]\left[\frac{\bar{X}}{\bar{x}^{(4)}}\right] \tag{18}$$

$$B[(\bar{y}_{FT})_D]_{k=1} = \bar{Y}\mu^{-3}[(1-\mu)\mu^2 + \left(D_1 - \frac{1}{N}\right) r_1W_1^2 C_{1X}\{r_1C_{1X} - \mu s_1\rho_1C_{1Y}\}] \tag{19}$$

$$M[(\bar{y}_{FT})_D]_{k=1} = \bar{Y}^2\mu^{-4}[(1-\mu)^2\mu^2 + W_1^2\left(D_1 - \frac{1}{N}\right)\{\mu^2 s_1^2 C_{1Y}^2 + (3-2\mu) r_1^2 C_{1X}^2$$
$$+ 2(\mu-2)\mu r_1s_1\rho_1C_{1Y}C_{1X}\} + \left(D_2 - \frac{1}{N}\right)\mu^2W_2^2 s_2^2 C_{2Y}^2] \tag{20}$$

Case 2

When $k = 2$

$A = 0$; $B = -2$; $C = 0$; $\xi_1 = -2f\mu$; $\xi_2 = -2fW_1r_1$; $\xi_3 = -2f$, $\xi_4 = 0$;

$\alpha_3 = r_1W_1\mu^{-1}$; $\beta_3 = 0$; $\delta_3 = \mu$; $J_1 = W_1^2\mu^2$; $J_2 = r_1^2W_1^2$; $J_3 = r_1W_1^2(2\mu-1)$;

$$[(\bar{y}_{FT})_D]_{k=2} = \left[\frac{N_1\bar{y}_1 + N_2\bar{y}_2}{N}\right]\left[\frac{\bar{x}^{(4)}}{\bar{X}}\right] \tag{21}$$

$$B[(\bar{y}_{FT})_D]_{k=2} = \bar{Y}\left[(\mu-1) + \left(D_1 - \frac{1}{N}\right)W_1^2r_1s_1\rho_1C_{1Y}C_{1X}\right] \tag{22}$$

$$M[(\bar{y}_{FT})_D]_{k=2} = \bar{Y}^2[(\mu-1)^2 + W_1^2\left(D_1 - \frac{1}{N}\right)\{\mu^2 s_1^2 C_{1Y}^2 + r_1^2C_{1X}^2 + 2(2\mu-1)s_1r_1\rho_1C_{1Y}C_{1X}\}$$
$$+ \left(D_2 - \frac{1}{N}\right)\mu^2W_2^2 s_2^2 C_{2Y}^2] \tag{23}$$

Case 3

When $k = 3$

$A = 2$; $B = -2$; $C = 0$; $\xi_1 = 2(1-f\mu)$; $\xi_2 = -2fW_1r_1$; $\xi_3 = 2(1-f)$; $\xi_4 = 0$; $\alpha_3 = \frac{-fW_1r_1}{1-f\mu}$

$\beta_3 = 0$; $\delta_3 = \frac{1-f\mu}{1-f}$; $J_1 = \frac{(1-f\mu)^2W_1^2}{(1-f)^2}$; $J_2 = \frac{f^2W_1^2r_1^2}{(1-f)^2}$; $J_3 = \frac{fW_1^2r_1\{2f\mu - f - 1\}}{(1-f)^2}$;

$$[(\bar{y}_{FT})_D]_{k=3} = \left(\frac{N_1\bar{y}_1 + N_2\bar{y}_2}{N}\right)\left[\frac{\bar{X} + f\bar{x}^{(4)}}{(1-f)\bar{X}}\right] \tag{24}$$

$$B[(\bar{y}_{FT})_D]_{k=3} = \bar{Y}f(1-f)^{-1}\left[(1-\mu) - \left(D_1 - \frac{1}{N}\right)W_1^2r_1s_1\rho_1C_{1Y}C_{1X}\right] \tag{25}$$

$$M[(\bar{y}_{FT})_D]_{k=3} = \bar{Y}^2(1-f)^{-2}[f^2(1-\mu)^2 + \left(D_1 - \frac{1}{N}\right)W_1^2\{(1-f\mu)^2 s_1^2 C_{1Y}^2 + f^2r_1^2 C_{1X}^2$$
$$+ 2(2f\mu - f - 1)fr_1s_1\rho_1C_{1Y}C_{1X}\} + \left(D_2 - \frac{1}{N}\right)(1-f\mu)^2W_2^2 s_2^2 C_{2Y}^2] \tag{26}$$

Case 4

When $k = 4$;

$A = 6$; $B = 0$; $C = 0$; $\xi_1 = 6$; $\xi_2 = 0$; $\xi_3 = 6$; $\xi_4 = 0$; $\alpha_3 = 0$; $\beta_3 = 0$; $\delta_3 = 1$; $J_1 = W_1^2$; $J_2 = 0$; $J_3 = 0$;

$$[(\bar{y}_{FT})_D]_{k=4} = \left[\frac{N_1\bar{y}_1 + N_2\bar{y}_2}{N}\right] \tag{27}$$

$$B[(\bar{y}_{FT})_D]_{k=4} = 0 \tag{28}$$

$$V[(\bar{y}_{FT})_D]_{k=4} = \left(D_1 - \frac{1}{N}\right)W_1^2\bar{Y}_1^2C_{1Y}^2 + \left(D_2 - \frac{1}{N}\right)W_2^2\bar{Y}_2^2C_{2Y}^2 \tag{29}$$

ESTIMATOR WITHOUT IMPUTATION

Throughout the discussion, the assumption is unknown value of $\bar{x}_2$. This is imputed by the term $\left(\bar{x}_2^*\right)_4$, to provide the generation of $\bar{x}^{(4)}$ [Equations (1) and (2)]. Suppose the $\bar{x}_2$ is known, then there is no need of imputation and the proposed (2) and (3) reduces into:

$$\bar{x}^{(*)} = \left(\frac{N_1\bar{x}_1 + N_2\bar{x}_2}{N}\right) \tag{30}$$

$$[(\bar{y}_{FT})_w]_k = \left(\frac{N_1\bar{y}_1 + N_2\bar{y}_2}{N}\right)\left(\frac{(A+C)\bar{X} + fB\bar{x}^{(*)}}{(A+fB)\bar{X} + C\bar{x}^{(*)}}\right) \quad (31)$$

Where, k is a constant , $0 < k < \infty$ and

$A = (k-1)(k-2)$; $B = (k-1)(k-4)$; $C = (k-2)(k-3)(k-4)$; $f = n/N$.

Theorem 4

The estimator $[(\bar{y}_{FT})_w]_k$ is biased for $\bar{Y}$ with the amount of bias

$$B[(\bar{y}_{FT})_w]_k = (\xi_1' - \xi_2')\Big[\left(D_1 - \frac{1}{N}\right)W_1^2 r_1 C_{1X}\{s_1\rho_1 C_{1Y} - \xi_2' r_1 C_{1X}\}$$

$$+\left(D_2 - \frac{1}{N}\right)W_2^2 r_2 C_{2X}\{s_2\rho_2 C_{2Y} - \xi_2' r_2 C_{2X}\}\Big]$$

Where,

$$\xi_1' = fB/(A + fB + C); \qquad \xi_2' = C/(A + fB + C).$$

Proof

The estimator $[(\bar{y}_{FT})_w]_k$ could be approximate like:

$$[(\bar{y}_{FT})_w]_k = \left(\frac{N_1\bar{y}_1 + N_2\bar{y}_2}{N}\right)\left(\frac{(A+C)\bar{X} + fB\bar{x}^{(*)}}{(A+fB)\bar{X} + C\bar{x}^{(*)}}\right)$$

$$= \left[\frac{N_1\bar{Y}_1(1+e_1) + N_2\bar{Y}_2(1+e_2)}{N}\right]\left[\frac{N(A+C)\bar{X} + fB\{N_1\bar{X}_1(1+e_3) + N_2\bar{X}_2(1+e_4)\}}{N(A+fB)\bar{X} + C\{N_1\bar{X}_1(1+e_3) + N_2\bar{X}_2(1+e_4)\}}\right]$$

$$= [\bar{Y} + W_1\bar{Y}_1 e_1 + W_2\bar{Y}_2 e_2]\left[\frac{(A+fB+C) + fB(W_1 r_1 e_3 + W_2 r_2 e_4)}{(A+fB+C) + C(W_1 r_1 e_3 + W_2 r_2 e_4)}\right]$$

$$= [\bar{Y} + W_1\bar{Y}_1 e_1 + W_2\bar{Y}_2 e_2][1 + \xi_1'(W_1 r_1 e_3 + W_2 r_2 e_4)]\,[1 + \xi_2'(W_1 r_1 e_3 + W_2 r_2 e_4)]^{-1}$$

Expanding above using binominal expansion, and ignoring $(e_i^k e_j^l)$ terms for $(k + l) > 2$, $(k, l = 0, 1, 2 \ldots\ldots)$, $(i, j = 1, 2, 3, 4)$; the estimator result into

$$[(\bar{y}_{FT})_w]_k = \bar{Y} + \bar{Y}(\Delta_1 - \Delta_2) + W_1\bar{Y}_1 e_1(1 + \Delta_1 - \Delta_2) + W_2\bar{Y}_2 e_2(1 + \Delta_1 - \Delta_2) \quad (32)$$

Where,

$\Delta_1 = (\xi_1' - \xi_2')(W_1 r_1 e_3 + W_2 r_2 e_4)$; $\Delta_2 = \xi_2'(\xi_1' - \xi_2')(W_1 r_1 e_3 + W_2 r_2 e_4)^2$

And

$W_1 r_1 + W_2 r_2 = 1$ holds.

Further, one can derive up to first order of approximation according to the following;

(i) $E[\Delta_1] = 0$

(ii) $E[\Delta_1^2] = (\xi_1' - \xi_2')^2\left[W_1^2 r_1^2\left(D_1 - \frac{1}{N}\right)C_{1X}^2 + W_2^2 r_2^2\left(D_2 - \frac{1}{N}\right)C_{2X}^2\right]$

(iii) $E[\Delta_2] = \xi_2'(\xi_1' - \xi_2')\left[W_1^2 r_1^2\left(D_1 - \frac{1}{N}\right)C_{1X}^2 + W_2^2 r_2^2\left(D_2 - \frac{1}{N}\right)C_{2X}^2\right]$

(iv) $E[e_1\Delta_1] = (\xi_1' - \xi_2')\, W_1 r_1\left(D_1 - \frac{1}{N}\right)\rho_1 C_{1X} C_{1Y}$

(v) $E[e_2\Delta_1] = (\xi_1' - \xi_2')\, W_2 r_2\left(D_2 - \frac{1}{N}\right)\rho_2 C_{2X} C_{2Y}$

(vi) $E[e_1\Delta_2] = 0$ [under $0(n^{-1})$]

(vii) $E[e_2\Delta_2] = 0$ [under $0(n^{-1})$]

The bias of estimator without imputation is

$$B[(\bar{y}_{FT})_w]_k = E[\{(\bar{y}_{FT})_w\}_k - \bar{Y}]$$

$$= E[\bar{Y}(\Delta_1 - \Delta_2) + W_1\bar{Y}_1 e_1(1 + \Delta_1 - \Delta_2) + W_2\bar{Y}_2 e_2(1 + \Delta_1 - \Delta_2)]$$

$$= [W_1\bar{Y}_1 E(e_1\Delta_1) + W_2\bar{Y}_2 E(e_2\Delta_1) - \bar{Y}E(\Delta_2)]$$

$$= (\xi_1' - \xi_2')\Big[\left(D_1 - \frac{1}{N}\right)W_1^2 r_1 C_{1X}\{\bar{Y}_1\rho_1 C_{1Y} - \bar{Y}\xi_1' r_1 C_{1X}\}$$

$$+\left(D_2 - \frac{1}{N}\right)W_2^2 r_2 C_{2X}\{\bar{Y}_2\rho_2 C_{2Y} - \bar{Y}\xi_1' r_2 C_{2X}\}\Big]$$

$$= \bar{Y}(\xi_1' - \xi_2')\Big[\left(D_1 - \frac{1}{N}\right)W_1^2 r_1 C_{1X}\{s_1\rho_1 C_{1Y} - \xi_2' r_1 C_{2X}\}$$

$$+\left(D_2 - \frac{1}{N}\right)W_2^2 r_2 C_{2X}\{s_2\rho_2 C_{2Y} - \xi_2' r_2 C_{2X}\}\Big]$$

Theorem 5

The mean squared error of the estimator $[(\bar{y}_{FT})_w]_k$ is

$$M[(\bar{y}_{FT})_w]_k = \bar{Y}^2\Big[\left(D_1 - \frac{1}{N}\right)W_1^2\{T_1^2 C_{1Y}^2 + T_2^2 C_{1X}^2 + 2T_1 T_2\,\rho_1 C_{1Y} C_{1X}\}$$

$$+\left(D_2 - \frac{1}{N}\right)W_2^2\{S_1^2 C_{2Y}^2 + S_2^2 C_{2X}^2 + 2S_1 S_2\rho_2 C_{2Y} C_{2X}\}\Big]$$

Where,

$T_1 = s_1$; $T_2 = (\xi_1' - \xi_2')r_1$; $S_1 = s_2$; $S_2 = (\xi_1' - \xi_2')r_2$;

Proof

$$\mathrm{M}\left[\left(\bar{y}_{FT}\right)_w\right]_k = \mathrm{E}\left[\left\{\left(y_{FT}\right)_w\right\}_k - \bar{Y}\right]^2$$

$$[(\bar{y}_{FT})_w]_k = \mathrm{E}\left[\bar{Y}(\Delta_1 - \Delta_2) + W_1\bar{Y}_1 e_1(1+\Delta_1-\Delta_2) + W_2\bar{Y}_2 e_2(1+\Delta_1-\Delta_2)\right]^2$$

$$= \bar{Y}^2\mathrm{E}\left(\Delta_1^2\right) + W_1^2\bar{Y}_1^2\mathrm{E}\left(e_1^2\right) + W_2^2\bar{Y}_2^2\mathrm{E}\left(e_2^2\right) + 2W_1\,\bar{Y}\bar{Y}_1\mathrm{E}\left(e_1\Delta_1\right)$$

$$+ 2W_2\,\bar{Y}\bar{Y}_2\mathrm{E}\left(e_2\Delta_1\right) + 2W_1\,W_2\bar{Y}_1\bar{Y}_2\mathrm{E}\left(e_1e_2\right)$$

$$= \bar{Y}^2\left[\left(\xi_1' - \xi_2'\right)^2\left\{W_1^2r_1^2\left(D_1 - \frac{1}{N}\right)C_{1X}^2 + W_2^2r_2^2\left(D_2 - \frac{1}{N}\right)C_{2X}^2\right\}\right.$$

$$+ \left\{W_1^2s_1^2\left(D_1 - \frac{1}{N}\right)C_{1Y}^2 + W_2^2s_2^2\left(D_2 - \frac{1}{N}\right)C_{2Y}^2\right\}$$

$$+ 2W_1s_1\left(\xi_1' - \xi_2'\right)\left\{W_1r_1\left(D_1 - \frac{1}{N}\right)\rho_1C_{1Y}C_{1X}\right\}$$

$$\left. + 2W_2s_2\left(\xi_1' - \xi_2'\right)\left\{W_2r_2\left(D_2 - \frac{1}{N}\right)\rho_2C_{2Y}C_{2X}\right\}\right]$$

$$= \bar{Y}^2\left[\left(D_1 - \frac{1}{N}\right)W_1^2\left\{T_1^2C_{1Y}^2 + T_2^2C_{1X}^2 + 2T_1T_2\,\rho_1C_{1Y}C_{1X}\right\}\right.$$

$$\left. + \left(D_2 - \frac{1}{N}\right)W_2^2\left\{S_1^2C_{2Y}^2 + S_2^2C_{2X}^2 + 2S_1S_2\rho_2C_{2Y}C_{2X}\right\}\right]$$

Remark 1

At $k = 1$, $k = 2$, $k = 3$ and $k = 4$, there are some special cases of non-imputed estimators with the respective bias and mean squared error as laid down with the following

Case 5

When $k = 1$

$A = 0$; $B = 0$; $C = -6$; $\xi_1' = 0$; $\xi_2' = 1$; $T_1 = s_1$;

$T_2 = -r_1$; $S_1 = s_1$; $S_2 = -r_2$;

$$[(\bar{y}_{FT})_w]_{k=1} = \left(\frac{N_1\bar{y}_1 + N_2\bar{y}_2}{N}\right)\left(\frac{\bar{X}}{\bar{x}^{(*)}}\right)$$

$$\mathrm{B}[(\bar{y}_{FT})_w]_{k=1} = -\bar{Y}\left[\left(D_1 - \frac{1}{N}\right)W_1^2r_1C_{1X}\left\{s_1\rho_1C_{1Y} - r_1C_{1X}\right\} + \left(D_2 - \frac{1}{N}\right)W_2^2r_2C_{2X}\left\{s_2\rho_2C_{2Y} - r_2C_{2X}\right\}\right]$$

$$\mathrm{M}[(\bar{y}_{FT})_w]_{k=1} = -\bar{Y}^2\left[\left(D_1 - \frac{1}{N}\right)W_1^2\left\{s_1^2C_{1Y}^2 + r_1^2C_{1X}^2 - 2s_1r_1\,\rho_1C_{1Y}C_{1X}\right\}\right.$$

$$\left. + \left(D_2 - \frac{1}{N}\right)W_2^2\left\{s_2^2C_{2Y}^2 + r_2^2C_{2X}^2 - 2s_2r_2\,\rho_2C_{2Y}C_{2X}\right\}\right]$$

Case 6

When $k = 2$

$A = 0$; $B = -2$; $C = 0$; $\xi_1' = 1$; $\xi_2' = 0$; $T_1 = s_1$; $T_2 = r_1$; $S_1 = s_2$; $S_2 = r_2$.

$$[(\bar{y}_{FT})_w]_{k=2} = \left(\frac{N_1\bar{y}_2 + N_2y_2}{N}\right)\left(\frac{\bar{x}^{(*)}}{\bar{X}}\right)$$

$$\mathrm{B}[(\bar{y}_{FT})_w]_{k=2} = \bar{Y}\left[\left(D_1 - \frac{1}{N}\right)W_1^2s_1r_1\rho_1C_{1X}C_{1Y} + \left(D_2 - \frac{1}{N}\right)W_2^2s_2r_2\rho_2C_{2X}C_{2Y}\right]$$

$$\mathrm{M}[(\bar{y}_{FT})_w]_{k=2} = \bar{Y}^2\left[\left(D_1 - \frac{1}{N}\right)W_1^2\left\{s_1^2C_{1Y}^2 + r_1^2C_{1X}^2 + 2s_1r_1\,\rho_1C_{1Y}C_{1X}\right\}\right.$$

$$\left. + \left(D_2 - \frac{1}{N}\right)W_2^2\left\{s_2^2C_{2Y}^2 + r_2^2C_{2X}^2 + 2s_2r_2\,\rho_2C_{2Y}C_{2X}\right\}\right]$$

Case 7

When $k = 3$

$A = 2$; $B = -2$; $C = 0$; $\xi_1' = -f/(1-f)^{-1}$; $\xi_2' = 0$; $T_1 = s_1$; $T_2 = r_1 f(1-f)^{-1}$;

$S_1 = s_2$; $S_2 = r_2 f(1-f)^{-1}$;

$$[(\bar{y}_{FT})_w]_{k=3} = \left(\frac{N_1\bar{y}_1 + N_2\bar{y}_2}{N}\right)\left(\frac{\bar{X} - \bar{x}^{(*)}}{(1-f)\bar{X}}\right)$$

$$\mathrm{B}[(\bar{y}_{FT})_w]_{k=3} = -\bar{Y}f(1-f)^{-1}\left[\left(D_1 - \frac{1}{N}\right)W_1^2r_1s_1\rho_1C_{1Y}C_{1X} + \left(D_2 - \frac{1}{N}\right)W_2^2r_2s_2\rho_2C_{2Y}C_{2X}\right]$$

$$\mathrm{M}[(\bar{y}_{FT})_w]_{k=3} = \bar{Y}^2\left[\left(D_1 - \frac{1}{N}\right)W_1^2\left\{s_1^2C_{1Y}^2 + (1-f)^{-2}f^2r_1^2C_{1X}^2 - 2(1-f)^{-1}fs_1\rho_1C_{1Y}C_{1X}\right\}\right.$$

$$\left. + \left(D_2 - \frac{1}{N}\right)W_2^2\left\{s_2^2C_{2Y}^2 + (1-f)^{-2}f^2r_2^2C_{2X}^2 - 2(1-f)^{-1}fs_2r_2\rho_2C_{2Y}C_{2X}\right\}\right]$$

Case 8

When $k = 4$, then

$A = 6$; $B = 0$; $C = 0$; $\xi_1' = 0$; $\xi_2' = 0$; $T_1 = s_1$; $T_2 = 0$; $S_1 = s_2$; $S_2 = 0$;

$$[(\bar{y}_{FT})_w]_{k=4} = \left(\frac{N_1\bar{y}_1 + N_2\bar{y}_2}{N}\right)$$

$$\mathrm{B}[(\bar{y}_{FT})_w]_{k=4} = 0$$

$$\mathrm{V}[(\bar{y}_{FT})_w]_{k=4} = \bar{Y}^2\left[\left(D_1 - \frac{1}{N}\right)W_1^2s_1^2C_{1Y}^2 + \left(D_2 - \frac{1}{N}\right)W_2^2s_2^2C_{2Y}^2\right]$$

NUMERICAL ILLUSTRATION

Consider two populations I and II given in Appendix A and B. Both populations are divided into two parts as R-group and NR-group having size N_1 and N_2 respectively ($N = N_1 + N_2$). The population parameters are displayed in Tables 1 to 6.

DISCUSSION

Using the imputation for $\bar{x}_2$ by the mixture of three

Table 1. Parameters of population - I (from Appendix A).

Parameter	Entire population	For R-group	For NR-group
Size	$N = 180$	$N_1 = 100$	$N_2 = 80$
Mean *Y*	$\bar{Y} = 159.03$	$\bar{Y}_1 = 173.60$	$\bar{Y}_2 = 140.81$
Mean *X*	$\bar{X} = 113.22$	$\bar{X}_1 = 128.45$	$\bar{X}_2 = 94.19$
Mean square *Y*	$S_Y^2 = 2205.18$	$S_{1Y}^2 = 2532.36$	$S_{2Y}^2 = 1219.90$
Mean square *X*	$S_X^2 = 1972.61$	$S_{1X}^2 = 2300.86$	$S_{2X}^2 = 924.17$
Coefficient of variation of *Y*	$C_Y = 0.295$	$C_{1Y} = 0.2899$	$C_{2Y} = 0.248$
Coefficient of variation of *X*	$C_X = 0.392$	$C_{1X} = 0.373$	$C_{2X} = 0.323$
Correlation coefficient	$\rho_{XY} = 0.897$	$\rho_{1XY} = 0.857$	$\rho_{2XY} = 0.956$

Table 2. Parameters of population - ii (from Appendix B).

Parameter	Entire population	For R-group	For NR-group
Size	$N = 150$	$N_1 = 90$	$N_2 = 60$
Mean *Y*	$\bar{Y} = 63.77$	$\bar{Y}_1 = 66.33$	$\bar{Y}_2 = 59.92$
Mean *X*	$\bar{X} = 29.2$	$\bar{X}_1 = 30.72$	$\bar{X}_2 = 26.92$
Mean Square *Y*	$S_Y^2 = 299.87$	$S_{1Y}^2 = 349.33$	$S_{2Y}^2 = 206.35$
Mean Square *X*	$S_X^2 = 110.43$	$S_{1X}^2 = 112.67$	$S_{2X}^2 = 100.08$
Coefficient of Variation of *Y*	$C_Y = 0.272$	$C_{1Y} = 0.282$	$C_{2Y} = 0.2397$
Coefficient of Variation of *X*	$C_X = 0.3599$	$C_{1X} = 0.345$	$C_{2X} = 0.3716$
Correlation coefficient	$\rho_{XY} = 0.8093$	$\rho_{1XY} = 0.8051$	$\rho_{2XY} = 0.8084$

Let samples of size n = 40 and n = 30 are drawn from population I and II respectively by SRSWOR and post-stratified into R and NR-groups. The sample values are in Tables 3 and 4.

Table 3. Sample values for population – i.

Parameter	Entire sample	R-group	NR-group
Size	$n = 40$	$n_1 = 28$	$n_2 = 12$
Fraction	$f = 0.22$	-	-

Table 4. Sample values for population – ii

Parameter	Entire sample	R-group	NR-group
Size	$n = 30$	$n_1 = 20$	$n_2 = 10$
Fraction	$f = 0.2$	-	-

population means is performed. The proposed class is in Equation (3) with bias in theorem 2 and mean squared error in theorem 3. The class contains some special imputed estimators for value $k = 1$, $k = 2$, $k = 3$ and $k = 4$. A non-imputed class of estimator is also developed which has bias and mean squared error derived in theorem 4 and 5. This class also has some special cases. The computation over two population is made whose description is given in appendix. The two random sample of size n = 40 and n = 30 are drawn from populations I and II respectively and post-stratified into two groups. The Tables 5 and 6 are presenting a numerical comparison between imputation and non-imputation class over the two populations in terms of their bias and m. s. e. The imputation technique (1) is effective because there is not much increase in the mean squared error due to

Table 5. Bias and M.S.E. comparisons of $[(\bar{y}_{FT})_D]_k$.

Estimator	Population I		Population II	
	Bias	M.S.E.	Bias	M.S.E.
$[(\bar{y}_{FT})_D]_{k=1}$	-2.8775	18.6000	-1.1874	9.8618
$[(\bar{y}_{FT})_D]_{k=2}$	3.3127	232.4162	3.4360	41.4794
$[(\bar{y}_{FT})_D]_{k=3}$	-4.0370	8.4710	-0.6377	6.3540
$[(\bar{y}_{FT})_D]_{k=4}$	0	43.6500	0	9.2675

Table 6. Bias and MSE comparison of $[(\bar{y}_{FT})_w]_k$.

Estimator	Population I		Population II	
	Bias	M.S.E.	Bias	M.S.E.
$[(\bar{y}_{FT})_w]_{k=1}$	0.1433	12.9589	0.1095	6.0552
$[(\bar{y}_{FT})_w]_{k=2}$	0.3141	216.3024	0.1599	46.838
$[(\bar{y}_{FT})_w]_{k=3}$	−0.096	4.327	−0.031	5.2423
$[(\bar{y}_{FT})_w]_{k=4}$	0	43.65	0	9.2662

imputation. The k = 3 seems to be a good choice. The k = 2 performs worst for both sots of data.

CONCLUSIONS

The technique of mixture of $\bar{X}$, $\bar{X}_1$, $\bar{X}_2$ performs well and the imputed factor-type estimator is very close to non-imputed in terms of mean squared error when k = 1, 2, and 3 holds. The choice k = 3 is better over the other two. Performance over population II is superior than I. it seems that factor type lass is able to replace the non-responded observation in a nice manner.

ACKNOWLEDGEMENT

Authors are thankful to the referee for his valuable suggestions.

REFERENCES

Agrawal MC, Panda KB (1993). An efficient estimator in post-stratification. Metron, 51(3-4): 179-187.
Ahmed MS, Al-titi O, Al-Rawi Z, Abu-dayyeh W (2006). Estimation of a population mean using different imputation method. Stat. Transit., 7(6): 1247-1264.
Cochran WG (2005). Sampling Techniques. Third Edition, John Willey & Sons, New Delhi.
Grover RM, Couper MP (1998). Non-response in household surveys. John Wiley and Sons, New York.
Hansen MH, Hurwitz WN (1946). The problem of non-response in sample surveys. J. Am. Stat. Assoc., 41: 517-529.
Hansen MH, Hurwitz WN, Madow WG (1993). Sample Survey Methods and Theory. John Wiley and Sons, New York.
Hinde RL, Chambers RL (1990). Non-response imputation with multiple source of non-response. J. Off. Stat., 7: 169-179.
Holt D, Smith TMF (1979). Post-stratification. J. R. Stat. Soc., Ser. A., 143: 33-46.
Jackway PT, Boyce RA (1987). Response including techniques of mail surveys. Aus. J. Stat., 29: 255-263.
Jagers P (1986). Post-stratification against bias in sampling. Int. Stat. Rev., 54: 159-167.
Jagers P, Oden A, Trulsoon L (1985). Post-stratification and ratio estimation. Int. Stat. Rev., 53: 221-238.
Khare BB (1987). Allocation in stratified sampling in presence of non-response. Metron, 45(I/II): 213-221.
Khot PS (1994). A note on handling non-response in sample surveys. J. Am. Stat. Assoc., 89: 693-696.
Lessler JT, Kalsbeek WD (1992). Non-response error in surveys. John Wiley and Sons, New York.
Murthy MN (1976). Sampling Theory and Methods. Statistical Publishing Society, Calcutta.
Rao JNK, Sitter RR (1995). Variance estimation under two phase sampling with application to imputation for missing data. Biometrika, 82: 453-460.
Rubin DB (1976). Inference and missing data. Biometrika, 63: 581-593.
Sahoo LN (1984). A note on estimation of the population mean using two auxiliary variables. Ali. J. Stat., pp. 3-4, 63-66.
Sahoo LN (1986). On a class of unbiased estimators using multi auxiliary information. J. Ind. Soc. Ag. Stat, 38(3): 379-382.
Sahoo LN, Sahoo RK (2001). Predictive estimation of finite population mean in two-phase sampling using two auxiliary variables. Ind. Soc. Ag. Stat., 54(4): 258-264.

Sahoo LN, Sahoo J, Mohanty S (1995). New predictive ratio estimator. J. Ind. Soc. Ag. Stat., 47(3): 240-242.
Shrivastava SK, Jhajj HS (1980). A class of estimators using auxiliary information for estimation finite population variance. Sankhya C, 42: 87-96.
Shrivastava SK, Jhajj HS (1981). A class of the population mean in a survey sampling using auxiliary information. Biometrika, 68: 341-343.
Shukla D (2002). F-T estimator under two phase sampling. Metron, 59(1-2): 253-263.
Shukla D, Dubey J (2001). Estimation in mail surveys under PSNR sampling scheme. Ind. Soc. Ag. Stat., 54(3): 288-302.
Shukla D, Dubey J (2004). On estimation under post-stratified two phase non-response sampling scheme in mail surveys. Int. J. Manage. Syst., 20(3): 269-278.
Shukla D, Dubey J (2006). On earmarked strata in post-stratification. Stat. Transit., 7(5): 1067-1085.
Shukla D, Trivedi M (1999). A new estimator for post-stratified sampling scheme. Proceedings of NSBA-TA (Bayesian Analysis), Eds. Rajesh Singh, pp. 206-218.
Shukla D, Trivedi M (2001). Mean estimation in deeply stratified population under post-stratification. Ind. Soc. Ag. Stat., 54(2): 221-235.
Shukla D, Trivedi M (2006). Examining stability of variability ratio with application in post-stratification. Int. J. Manage. Syst., 22(1): 59-70.
Shukla D, Bankey A, Trivedi M (2002). Estimation in post-stratification using prior information and grouping strategy. Ind. Soc. Ag. Stat., 55(2): 158-173.
Shukla D, Singh VK, Singh GN (1991). On the use of transformation in factor type estimator. Metron, 49(1-4): 359-361.
Shukla D, Trivedi M, Singh GN (2006). Post-stratification two-way deeply stratified population. Stat. Transit., 7(6): 1295-1310.
Singh GN, Singh VK (2001). On the use of auxiliary information in successive sampling. J. Ind. Soc. Ag. Stat., 54(1): 1-12.
Singh D, Choudhary FS (1986). Theory and Analysis of Sample Survey Design. Wiley Eastern Limited, New Delhi.
Singh HP (1986). A generalized class of estimators of ratio product and mean using supplementary information on an auxiliary character in PPSWR scheme. Guj. Stat. Rev., 13(2): 1-30.
Singh HP, Upadhyaya LN, Lachan R (1987). Unbiased product estimators. Guj. Stat. Rev., 14(2): 41-50.
Singh S, Horn S (2000). Compromised imputation in survey sampling. Metrika, 51: 266-276.
Singh VK, Shukla D (1987). One parameter family of factor type ratio estimator. Metron, 45(1-2): 273-283.
Singh VK, Shukla D (1993). An efficient one-parameter family of factor type estimator in sample survey. Metron, 51(1-2): 139-159.
Singh VK, Singh GN (1991). Chain type estimator with two auxiliary variables under double sampling scheme. Metron, 49: 279-289.
Singh VK, Singh GN, Shukla D (1994). A class of chain ratio estimator with two auxiliary variables under double sampling scheme. Sankhya, Ser. B., 46(2): 209-221.
Smith TMF (1991). Post-stratification. Statisticians, 40: 323-330.
Sukhatme PV, Sukhatme BV, Sukhatme S, Ashok C (1984). Sampling Theory of Surveys with Applications. Iowa State University Press, I.S.A.S. Publication, New Delhi.
Wywial J (2001). Stratification of population after sample selection. Stat. Transit., 5(2): 327-348.

Appendix A. Population I (N= 180); R-group: (N_1=100).

Y:	110	75	85	165	125	110	85	80	150	165	135	120	140	135	145
X:	80	40	55	130	85	50	35	40	110	115	95	60	70	85	115
Y:	200	135	120	165	150	160	165	145	215	150	145	150	150	195	190
X:	150	85	80	100	25	130	135	105	185	110	95	75	70	165	160
Y:	175	160	165	175	185	205	140	105	125	230	230	255	275	145	125
X:	145	110	135	145	155	175	80	75	65	170	170	190	205	105	85
Y:	110	110	120	230	220	280	275	220	145	155	170	195	170	185	195
X:	75	80	90	165	160	205	215	190	105	115	135	145	135	110	145
Y:	180	150	185	165	285	150	235	125	165	135	130	245	255	280	150
X:	135	110	135	115	125	205	100	195	85	115	75	190	205	210	105
Y:	205	180	150	205	220	240	260	185	150	155	115	115	220	215	230
X:	110	105	110	175	180	215	225	110	90	95	85	75	175	185	190
Y:	210	145	135	250	265	275	205	195	180	115					
X:	170	85	95	190	215	200	165	155	150	175					

NR-group: (N_2=80)

Y:	85	75	115	165	140	110	115	13.5	120	125	120	150	145	90	105
X:	55	40	65	115	90	55	60	65	70	75	80	120	105	45	65
Y:	110	90	155	130	120	95	100	125	140	155	160	145	90	90	95
X:	70	60	85	95	80	55	60	75	90	105	125	95	45	55	65
Y:	115	140	180	170	175	190	160	155	175	195	90	90	80	90	80
X:	75	105	120	115	125	135	110	115	135	145	45	55	50	60	50
Y:	105	125	110	120	130	145	160	170	180	`145	130	195	200	160	110
X:	65	75	70	80	85	105	110	115	130	95	65	135	130	115	55
Y:	155	190	150	180	200	160	155	170	195	200	150	165	155	180	200
X:	115	130	110	120	125	145	120	105	100	95	90	105	125	130	145
Y:	160	155	170	195	200										
X:	120	115	120	135	150										

Appendix B. Population II (N=150); R-group (N_1=90).

Y:	90	75	70	85	95	55	65	80	65	50	45	55	60	60	95
X:	30	35	30	40	45	25	40	50	35	30	15	20	25	30	40
Y:	100	40	45	55	35	45	35	55	85	95	65	75	70	80	65
X:	50	10	25	25	10	15	10	25	35	55	35	40	30	45	40
Y:	90	95	80	85	55	60	75	85	80	65	35	40	95	100	55
X:	40	50	35	45	35	25	30	40	25	35	10	15	45	45	25
Y:	45	40	40	35	55	75	80	80	85	55	45	70	80	90	55
X:	15	15	20	10	30	25	30	40	35	20	25	30	40	45	30
Y:	65	60	75	75	85	95	90	90	45	40	45	55	60	65	60
X:	25	40	35	30	40	35	40	35	15	25	15	30	30	25	20
Y:	75	70	40	55	75	45	55	60	85	55	60	70	75	65	80
X:	25	20	35	30	45	10	30	25	40	15	25	30	35	30	45

NR-group (N_2=60)

Y:	40	90	95	70	60	65	85	55	45	60	65	60	55	55	45
X:	10	30	30	30	25	30	40	25	15	20	30	30	35	25	20
Y:	65	80	55	65	75	55	50	55	60	45	40	75	75	45	70
X:	35	45	30	30	40	15	15	20	30	15	10	40	45	10	30
Y:	65	70	55	35	35	50	55	35	55	60	30	35	45	55	65
X:	30	40	30	10	15	25	30	15	20	30	10	20	15	30	30
Y:	75	65	70	65	70	45	55	60	85	55	60	70	75	65	80
X:	30	35	40	25	45	10	30	25	40	15	25	30	35	30	45

Mathematics as a sort of technology

Xiong Zhang

Department of Mathematics, Shaanxi Institute of Education, Xi'an 710061, China.
E-mail: zhangxiong799@yahoo.com.cn.

Mathematics has double characters including science and technology. The direct research object of mathematics is mode which is the carrier of information, and the evolvement of mode is the process of information processing and information conversion. This paper has described the three characters of mathematic: operation, instrument and invention, which shows mathematic is a sort of technology. In addition to some expels have been put forwarded. Therefore, mathematics is the technology of information processing and information conversion.

Key words: Mathematical mode, information carrier, mathematical activities, information processing, information conversion, mathematical technology.

INTRODUCTION

Mathematics has been regarded as pure and rational science for a long time, but comparing with other natural sciences, the mathematics science has its unique characters. Many subjects such as physics, chemistry, and life science generally are theories or laws of theoretical generalization about certain natural law based on experiments, but mathematics is the mode coming from abstract thinking which can be evolved. With the development of mathematics and the change of social mathematical demands, the characters of mathematics are also changing. In the day of informationization and high technology, people have more realized that mathematics is not only the science, but also the technology. Academician of American Academy of Sciences, J. C. Glimm said that "mathematics is very important for the economic competition, and it is a sort of pivotal and universal technology which can offer ability for people".

Mathematics is regarded as a sort of technology, but what sort of technology it is?

HIGH AND NEW TECHNOLOGY AS A SORT OF MATHEMATICAL TECHNOLOGY IN NATURE

In 1981, American Council of State called experts in mathematics science and relative subjects together and founded a special committee, and though three years' observation and analysis, this committee put forward the report of "further flourishing the mathematics of US". The report pointed out that "the appearance of high technology has pushed our society into the new time of mathematical engineering technology". The president of the special committee, the applied mathematician, E. David said that "only few people can realize that the high technology is a sort of mathematics technology in nature".

Since the second half of the 20th century, the technology character of mathematics is more and more dominant, and the new and high technology more and more depends on the mathematics technology. There are three causes. Firstly, the new and high technology generally has high science and technology content, and generally speaking, the high science and technology degree has high abstraction degree, and the possibility to apply mathematics to solve problems is higher. Secondly, with the development of modern applied mathematics, mathematics fully presents powerful function and technology power when solving human and nature problems. Thirdly, because of the appearance of computer, the fourth peak of mathematics occurs, that is, the information-based mathematics. In the time of information, mathematics could be everywhere, and it becomes into the universally applied technology.

For example, the Nobel Prize in medicine of 1979 was

awarded to American Cormack and British Hounsfield, and praised that they designed the computed tomography (CT) by the mathematical Radon Transform principle. The basic process of preventing CT can be descried as follows: it can not directly confirm the absorption quantity of x-rays on each point in the 3D space (such as brain scanning), but Cormack regarded this problems as the solution of the tri-function defined on D, $F(x, y, z)$, and the instrument can measure the average absorption quantity of x-ray on any line segment *l* on D, $\hat{F}$ (it can be denoted by definite integral), and the problem is that when many different values of $\hat{F}$ are measured, whether F can be confirmed completely. According to the theory of Radon Transform in mathematics, F can be confirmed completely, so CT is invented in principle. The CT which can benefit human beings can be regarded as an implementation of mathematical technology.

For another example, before 1990s, Japan is the big country of TV. To develop the TV mode with high definition, Japan and Western European countries invested billions dollars in the simulated mode. However, in 1993, after the digitalized TV plan of US was pushed, the simulated mode plan immediately became into a piece of waster paper. The mathematical technology supporting TV digitalization is the wavelet technology, and it can compress enormous data to the minimum, and realize the digital transfer of images. In this way, the leading right of world TV industry in the 21st century is grasped in US. The positioning of plane needs the Kalman filtering technology when the plane takes off and touches down, the auto design needs the computer simulation, the enterprise management needs the mathematical model, the drug effect depends on the statistics analysis, the fluctuation of stock needs mathematical estimation, the software design depends on the disperse mathematics, the base of AI is the mathematical method, the computer simulation technology makes the plane design need not all be implemented in the wind tunnel, the big gun performance test needs not adopt ball firing, and underground nuclear test such as A-bomb can be simulated in computer, and the war game even can be implemented in computer.

Incalculable facts have proved scientists' judgments, "the base of high and new technology is the applied science, and the base of applied science is the mathematics", "high technology is a sort of mathematical technology in nature", "in a sense, the modernization is the mathematization".

CHARACTERS OF OPERATION, INSTRUMENT, AND INVENTION OF MATHEMATICS

By analyzing the dynamic process of mathematics converting from theory and method to technology, it is obvious that the formation between mathematics and technology is not "either-or", but "both-and" (Zhang, 1995). Technology is a human rational activity taking efficiency as target, and its target is to design and invent the process, program, instrument and products which do not exist in the nature but are required by people. Science is the knowledge about the object is "what" and "why it is", and technology is the method and measure about "what to do" and "how to do", both are rational activities, but the sense in technology "emphasizes the logic, practical and disciplined method which can solve problems to deal with subjective matters, and it depends on computation, exactness, measurement and system concepts" (Rapp, 1986).

Mathematics is generally thought as the abstract quantitative mode of the nature, and it is not only the explanation of the nature, but the method and measure to engage in other technical activities, which can mainly confirm the rationality of the technology. The confirmation of mathematics in the efficiency and rationality of technology indicates an important advancement of human sense. Just as Weber said, except that the computation could grasp all powers, there was not any one misery power to function. For example, Urbain Le Verrier found the Neptune by computation in 1946. In addition, Newton's law of gravity and Einstein theory were established all depending on mathematics. The utilization of mathematical methods such as computation and modeling could solve kinds of practical problems and technical problems, which fully proves that mathematics is a kind of universal technology of information processing and conversion. Mathematics is science, but science knowledge will not be pure and absolute for ever, and it contains practical histories and practices, and the technology needs to play the media between the fact and science.

Mathematics is an instrumental subject, and it can not only be understood, but also has certain character of operation, especially, it comes down to the establishment skill and operation law of mathematical mode, and the mathematical contents full of inventions such as positive and negative numbers, decimal system, Gauss-Legendre's least square method, Riemann surface of multi-valued complex function uniformization, calculus invented by Newton and Leibniz, and computer, and these contents all have obvious technology component.

The appearance of computer rapidly spreads the modern mathematics to various domains in modern society by the mode of technology, and many people think that the appearance of high technology has pushed our society into the new time of mathematical technology. In modern physics, a series of new phenomena did not occur in the lab or high-energy accelerator, but were found by the computer. For example, in 1963, the strange attractor was discovered, and the chaos phenomenon of the conservative system was discovered in 1964, and the solution was discovered in 1965, and the bifurcation and the universality of the over all model were discovered in 1978, which all owned to the scientific computation of computer.

Technology includes the technology with knowledge form and the technology with materialized form, and mathematics is a sort of technology with knowledge form (Zhang, 2001). Without mathematics, high and new technology can not be composed and accumulated, and without high and new technology, mathematics will lose the dwelling place, and can not be developed. For example, without the mathematical theory of time sequence, there is not the oil geography exploitation industry with large scale nowadays. Any one plane or space ship needs to install the automatic navigation equipment designed according to the Kalman Filtering Theory in mathematics. The wing form of Boeing-767 was obtained according to the new approximate solution and computation geometric method of the nonlinear PDE. The main theoretical base of the x-ray technology which pushed the revolution in medicines and medical diagnosis technology is the Radon transform in mathematics. The extension and application of the optimized method and the orthogonal experiment designing method have promoted the enterprise management rule and the technology reform in China.

In addition, the character of technology of mathematics is also represented that it was invented by human being. Mathematics is the abstract description of the nature, and though it accords with the objective rules, but the mathematical contents are not objective and real things in the nature, and they are the abstract mode of the objects invented by mathematicians under the law of scientific thinking.

In a word, these three characters of mathematics all accord with the meaning of technology, so when affirming the character of science of mathematics, the character of technology of mathematics can not be denied.

MATHEMATICS IS THE TECHNOLOGY OF INFORMATION PROCESSING AND INFORMATION CONVERSION

Mathematics is the abstract description of objective practice, and its result certainly is the abstract mode. The main characters of mode include "formalization" and "generalization". The formalization means that the research object of mathematics is divorced from the actual background to certain meaning, and it is not the concrete review of natural things and it needs not to compare with physical experiences, but it only studies the structure form of a sort of things relationship on general meaning. The generalization indicates the universality and catholicity of the thing reflected by the mode. Both the formalization and the generalization reflect that the mode is the carrier of information. The large numerous of concrete and practical contents in mathematical mode, or certain concrete things are the information contained in the mode. In reverse, the formalized mode is just the carrier of large numerous of information which are processed collectively (Zhang, 2000).

Information is contained in the mode carrier, and any mathematical mode is the carrier of information. If it is not that, mathematics will lose its all complete meanings, but only dead symbols, and in the interior of mathematics, there is not any axiom, and before mathematical mode, there is not any idea.

A series of mathematical activities including the establishment, composing and conversion of mathematical mode are the process of mode deduction. Though mathematical mode is the carrier of information, so the deduction of mode is the process of information processing and information conversion. Therefore, mathematics is the technology of information processing and information conversion.

In this way, whether the mathematical model used by engineers even the mathematical method in science technology, or the deduction adopted by mathematicians to solve mathematical problems even any one small transformation in the mathematical deduction process, all can be summarized as the mathematical technology in nature.

For example, Belgium physicist J. Plateau put forward a problem in 1847, that is, in a spatial closed curve C, whether the curve face with minimum area and in C can be found? This problem has been defined as the Plateau Problem. In 1873, in the book of "Experiment and Theory of Hydrostatics in the Single-molecule Model", Plateau pointed out that if people emerged the wire with the closed curve form into the glycerite or suds, and then took the wire out, and there would surely be the membrane with minimum curve face on the wire. In this way, Plateau utilized the principle of liquid surface tension to solve this problem, but it was not satisfactory for mathematicians. In the 19th century, many mathematicians including Riemann and Karl Weierstrass tried to use mathematical method to solve this problem, but none of them succeed. About 60 years later, US mathematician J. Douglas accidentally published the thesis of "the solution of Plateau problem" in January 1931, and he regarded the Plateau problem as the first boundary value problem of a nonlinear ellipse PDE, and solved this problem in the range of generalized solution. Because of this thesis, Douglas obtained the first Fields Medal in 1936. So the key of Douglas' success is an important reduction that is, the technology of information conversion.

Each step of the reduction process is to implement the mathematical reduction formally, and its essential is to

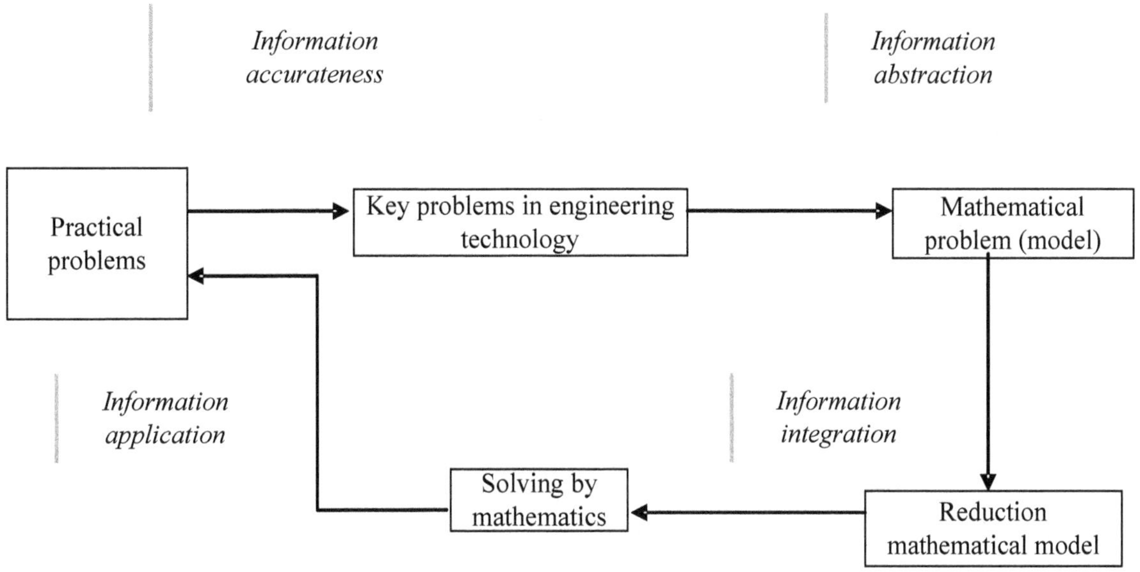

Figure 1. Five Stages of the Implementation Process of Mathematics Technology.

continually implement information processing or information conversion.

In a word, the research object of mathematics is abstract mode, and the mode is the carrier of information, and the mathematical activity is the reduction of mode, and the mode reduction is the process of information processing and information conversion. Therefore, mathematics is the technology of information processing and information conversion. Generally speaking, the science technology or the mathematical method universally utilized in other domains is a sort of mathematics technology in fact. The implementation process of mathematics technology mainly includes five main stages (Figure 1).

REFERENCES

Rapp F (1986). Technical Introduction to Philosophy. Liu Wu- translation, Shenyang: Liaoning Science and Technology Publishing House.

Zhang X (1995). On technology, culture, personality triple purpose of mathematics education. J. Math. Educ., 3(4): 21-25.

Zhang X (2000). Mathematics: The Technology of Information Processing and Information Transforming. J. Stud. Dialect. Nat., 16(8): 27-29.

Zhang X (2001). Introduction to Mathematics Education. Science and Technology Press of China Shaanxi. ISBN 7-5369-3385-1. http: //www.snstp.com.

Investigation on the effect of stent in unsteady blood flow

Ibrahima Mbaye

Department of Mathematics, University of Thies, Thies, Senegal. E-mail: ibambaye2000@yahoo.fr.

In this work, we tried to determine the fact that an interest in optimal stents shapes helps to minimize fluid swirl and to maximize shear stress on the wall artery in order to reduce the risk of the restenosis in stented segments. Our study deals with three geometric parameters of the stent, namely the strut spacing l, the strut height h and the strut width w. These parameters have direct effect on blood flow. A multi-objective optimization based on genetic algorithm is used to determine an optimal stent.

Key words: Multiobjective optimization, stent, Navier-Stokes, genetic algorithm.

INTRODUCTION

Stent placement in stenosis artery perturbs is more often in blood flow. Stent shape in artery can provoke the presence of recirculation zones, blood stagnation zones, thrombosis and embolism. The aim of this work is to find optimal stents shapes in order to reduce blood stagnation and recirculation zones. As it has already been observed Berry et al. (2000), Moore et al. (2002), a stent associated with a higher value of shear stress is preferred because it lowers the risk of the late restenosis by reducing the presence of blood stagnation. A former paper Quarteroni et al. (2003), Blouza et al. (2008) had shown that a stent associated with a lower value of vorticity is preferred. Qualitative study Blouza et al. (2008) shows that the variation of vorticity and shear stress depend entirely on the variation of three parameters l, h and w. Using multiobjective optimization approach we minimize the vorticity and maximize the shear stress on the wall artery simultaneous. Indeed, we propose the multiobjective optimization approach because our two criteria compete.

A former paper Blouza et al. (2008), we had supposed that the fluid is modeled by the stoke equation for steady flow. In the work, the fluid is modeled by two dimensional Navier-Stoks equations for unsteady flow and we also suppose that the wall artery is rigid.

MATHEMATICAL FRAMEWORK

Let Ω_F the domain occupied by the fluid (Figure 1). The boundary of Ω_F is decomposed by:

$$\partial\Omega_F = \Sigma_{in} \cup \Sigma_{out} \cup \Sigma_{stent}$$

The fluid which is viscous, incompressible and Newtonian is modeled by two dimensional Navier Stokes equations.

Let $v:[0,T]\times\Omega_F \rightarrow R^2$

The fluid velocity vector and

$p:[0,T]\times\Omega_F \rightarrow R$

The fluid pressure.

We will find the couple (v,p) such as:

$$\begin{cases} \rho^F(\frac{\partial v}{\partial t} + (v.\nabla)v) - \mu\Delta v + \nabla p = f \text{ in } [0,\mathrm{T}]\times\Omega_F \ (1) \\ \nabla.v = 0 \text{ in } [0,T]\times\Omega_F \ (2) \\ v(t=0) = v_0 \text{ in } \Omega_F \ (3) \\ -pIn + \mu\nabla v.n = p_{in}In \text{ on } [0,T]\times\Sigma_{in} \ (4) \\ -pIn + \mu\nabla v.n = 0 \text{ on } [0,T]\times\Sigma_{out} \ (5) \\ v = 0 \text{ on } [0,T]\times\Sigma_{stent} \ (6) \end{cases}$$

Where

1) I is the identity matrix,

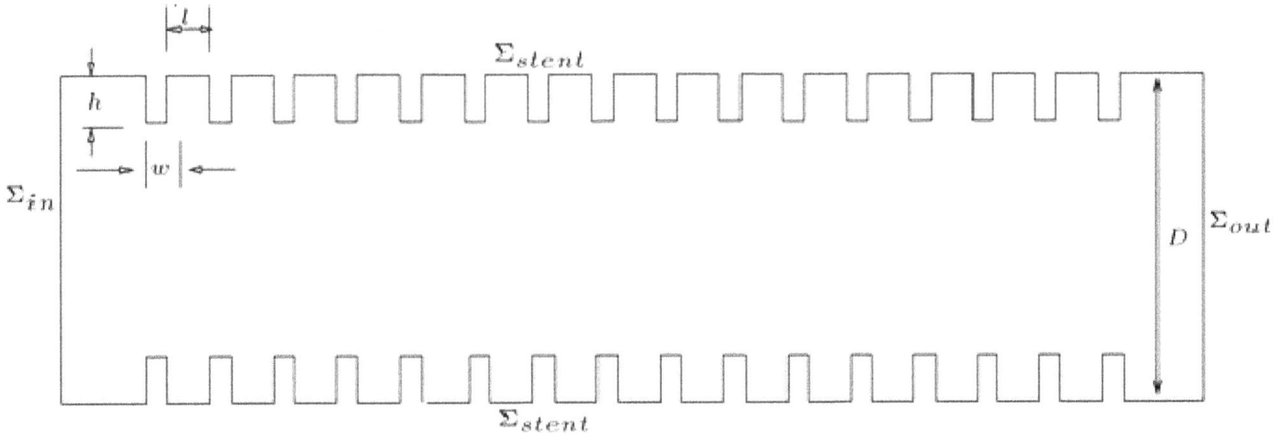

Figure 1. Simplified 2d-geometry of a stent and associated fluid domain Ω_F .

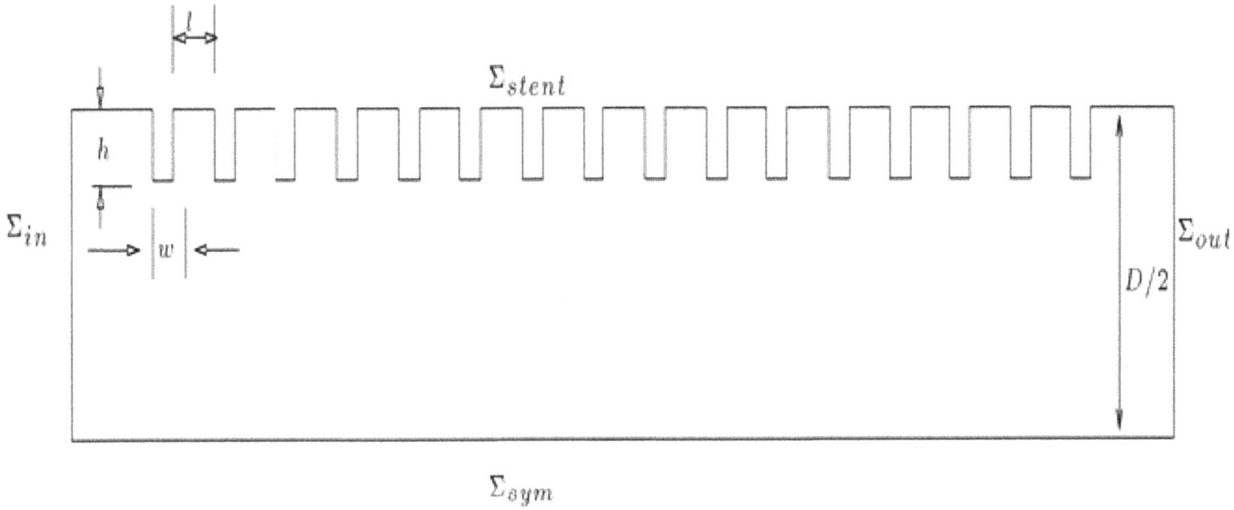

Figure 2. Half fluid domain Ω .

2) n is the unit outward vector normal to $\partial\Omega_F$
3) v_0 is the initial condition of the fluid
4) μ is the viscosity of the fluid,
5) ρ^F the density of the fluid,
6) f is the volume force of the fluid,
7) p_{in} is the boundary conditions imposed of the pressure,
8) Concerning the outflow Σ_{out} , we impose free boundary condition of the pressure.

The symmetric properties of the problem imply us to take in the following work the half fluid domain Ω (Figure 2) to solve the Navier-Stokes equations.
Let the Navier-Stokes equations in Ω:

$$\begin{cases} \rho^F(\frac{\partial v}{\partial t}+(v.\nabla)v)-\mu\Delta v+\nabla p=f \text{ in } [0,T]\times\Omega \ (1) \\ \nabla.v=0 \text{ in } [0,T]\times\Omega \ (2) \\ v(t=0)=v_0 \text{ in } \Omega \ (3) \\ -pIn+\mu\nabla v.n=p_{in}In \text{ on } [0,T]\times\Sigma_{in} \ (4) \\ -pIn+\mu\nabla v.n=0 \text{ on } [0,T]\times\Sigma_{out} \ (5) \\ v=0 \text{ on } [0,T]\times\Sigma_{stent} \ (6) \\ v_2=0 \text{ on } [0,T]\times\Sigma_{sym} \ (7) \\ \frac{\partial v_1}{\partial x_2}=0 \text{ on } [0,T]\times\Sigma_{sym} \ (8) \end{cases}$$

Where

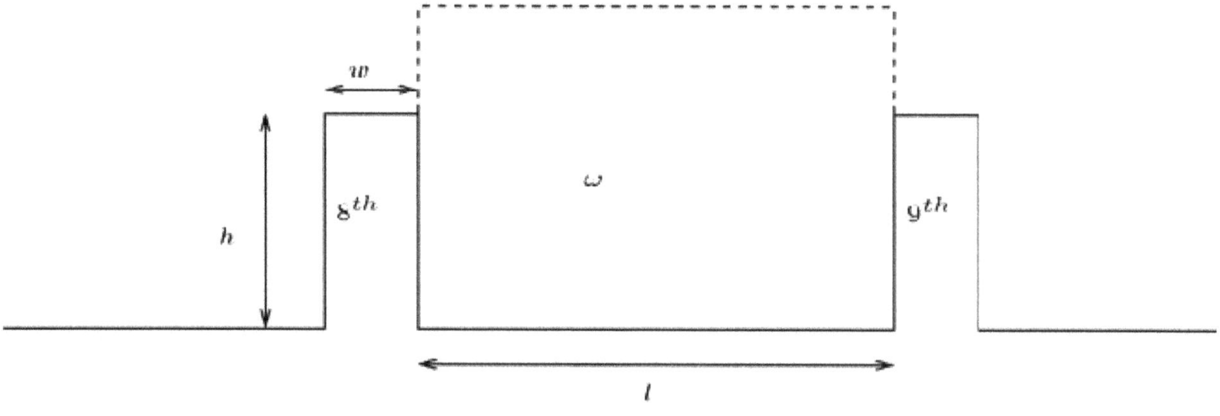

Figure 3. Definition of the integration domains ω and Γ_ω.

1) v_1 is the first component of vector *v*,
2) v_2 is the second component of vector *v*,
3) Σ_{sym} is the symmetric axis,
4) on Σ_{sym} the no penetration condition $v.n = v_2 = 0$ and the continuity stress tensor

$$\sigma.n = \frac{\partial v_1}{\partial x_2} = 0$$ are imposed.

Variational formulation for the fluid equations

Let W and Q the variational spaces:

$$W = \{w \in (H^2(\Omega))^2 : w = 0 \text{ on } \Sigma_{stent}, w_2 = 0 \text{ on } \Sigma_{sym}\}$$

$$Q = L^2(\Omega).$$

Where

1) w_2 is the second component of w.

Now, we can introduce the variational formulation for the fluid equations for all $t \in [0,T]$, we find the velocity $v \in W$ and the pressure $p \in Q$ such that:

$$\int_\Omega \rho^F v.wdt + c(v,v,w) + a(v,w) + b(w,p) = F(w),\ w \in W$$

$$b(v,q) = 0, \forall q \in Q.$$

Where

$$c(v,v,w) = \int_\Omega \rho^F (v.\nabla v)v.wdx$$

$$a(v,w) = \int_\Omega \mu \nabla v.\nabla w dx$$

$$b(w,p) = -\int \nabla.w\, p\, dx$$

$$F(w) = \int_\Omega f.w\, dx + \int_{\Sigma_{in}} p_{in} w.n\, d\sigma.$$

Position of the problem

The vorticity is given by:

$$\nabla \times v = \frac{\partial v_2}{\partial x_1} - \frac{\partial v_1}{\partial x_2},$$

and the shear stress by:

$$\tau_\omega = \mu\left(\frac{\partial v_2}{\partial x_1} + \frac{\partial v_1}{\partial x_2}\right)$$

Let J_1 the first cost functional which measures the mean square wall shear stress between two struts, that is:

$$J_1(l,h,w) = \frac{1}{length(\Gamma_w)} \sqrt{\int_0^T \int_{\Gamma_\omega} \tau_w^2 d\Gamma_\omega dt}$$

and let J_2 the second cost functional which measures the mean swirl value near the struts, that is:

$$J_2(l,h,w) = \frac{1}{area(w)} \sqrt{\int_0^T \int_\omega |\nabla \times v|^2 d\Omega dt}$$

Where ω is the integration domain, Figure 3.

We use the multiobjective optimization approach based

on genetic algorithm Deb et al. (2003) so as to minimize J_1 and maximize J_2 simultaneously. This method is chosen here because it has already obtained, in many applicative fields, robust and global optimal solutions (Dumas and Alaoui, 2007; Dumas et al., 2005). Moreover, it is well adapted to determine a set of optimal solution located on the Pareto front. More precisely, the Є-multiobjective evolutionary algorithm developed by Deb et al. (2003) and freely available at the site http://www.iitk.ac.in/kangal/soft.htm, is used for all the computations done here. It is based on the ε dominance principle that relaxes the classic dominance principle with a factor ε and also on the use of two co-evolving populations (an EA population and archive population). A good diversity is ensured by allowing on the Pareto front only one solution in each hyper box.

NUMERICAL RESULTS

Spatial discretisation

Let W_h be the finite element approximation spaces for the fluid velocity obtained from W by using the mixed finite element $P^1 + bubble / P^1$, and let Q_h be also the finite element approximation spaces for the fluid pressure obtained from Q by using the finite element P^1 :

$$W_h = \left\{ \begin{matrix} w_h \in (C^0(\Omega))^2 : \forall K \in \tau_h, w_h \in P^1 + bubble, \\ (w_2)_h = 0 \text{ on } \Sigma_{sym}, w_h = 0 \text{ on } \Sigma_{stent} \end{matrix} \right\}$$

and

$$Q_h = \{ q_h \in C^0(\Omega) : \forall K \in \tau_h, q_h \in P^1 \}$$

Time discretisation

The time integration scheme is based on the implicit Euler approximation.

Knowing $v_h^n \in W_h$, we find $v_h^{n+1} \in W_h$ and $p_h^{n+1} \in Q_h$ such as:

$$\begin{cases} \frac{\rho^F}{\Delta t} \int_\Omega (v^{n+1} - v^n \circ \chi^n).w dx + a(v^{n+1}, w) + \\ b(w, p^{n+1}) = F^{n+1}(w), \forall w \in W \\ b(v^{n+1}, q) = 0, \quad \forall q \in Q \end{cases}$$

Where

$$F^{n+1}(w) = \int_\Omega f^{n+1}.w dx + \int_{\Sigma_{in}} p_{in}^{n+1} w.n d\sigma$$

1) Δt is the time step,

2) The term $v^n \circ \chi^n \approx v^n(x - v^n(x)\Delta t)$ will be computed by the operator "convect" Hecht et al. (2005).

Boundary conditions

Boundary conditions imposed to the pressure

$$p_{in}(x_1, x_2, t) = 10^4(1 - \cos(pi \times t / 0.005)), t \in [0, 0.005] \quad p_{in}(x_1, x_2, t) = 0, t \in [0.005, T]$$

(Mbaye and Murea, 2008).

Parameters values related to fluid

The fluid viscosity is $\mu = 0.035 g / cm.s$, the density of the fluid is $\rho^F = 1 g / cm^3$, the volume forces $f = (0,0)$ and the width of artery is $D = 0.4 cm$ and the length of the artery is between $[0.492, 3.944]$. Time step is $\Delta t = 0.1 ms$ and $v_0 = 0$ (Mbaye and Murea, 2008).

Parameters values related to stent

The three stent design parameters l, h, w lie in a rather large domain $(l, h, w) = [0.02, 0.2] \times [0.01, 0.04] \times [0.007, 0.009]$ Andreas et al. (2002).

Parameter values related to genetic algorithm

We use the following parameters for the genetic algorithm: a population of 120 individuals, number of generations 100, the probability of mutation $p_m = 0.33$, the probability of crossover $p_c = 0.9$ and the seed $p_s = 0.123$.

NUMERICAL SIMULATIONS

Figure 4 displays the initial population and the Pareto front after 100 generations and 50 iterations in time (5 ms).

Figure 5 displays Pareto front after 100 generations and 50 iterations in time (5 ms). Figure 6 displays the initial population and the Pareto front after 100 generations and 100 iterations in time (10 ms). Figure 7 displays Pareto front after 100 generations and 100 iterations in time (10 ms). Figure 8 displays the initial population and the Pareto front after 100 generations and 150 iterations in time (15 ms). Figure 9 displays Pareto front after 100 generations and 150 iterations in time (15 ms). Figure 10 represents Pareto front at t = 5, 10 and 15 ms, respectively after 100

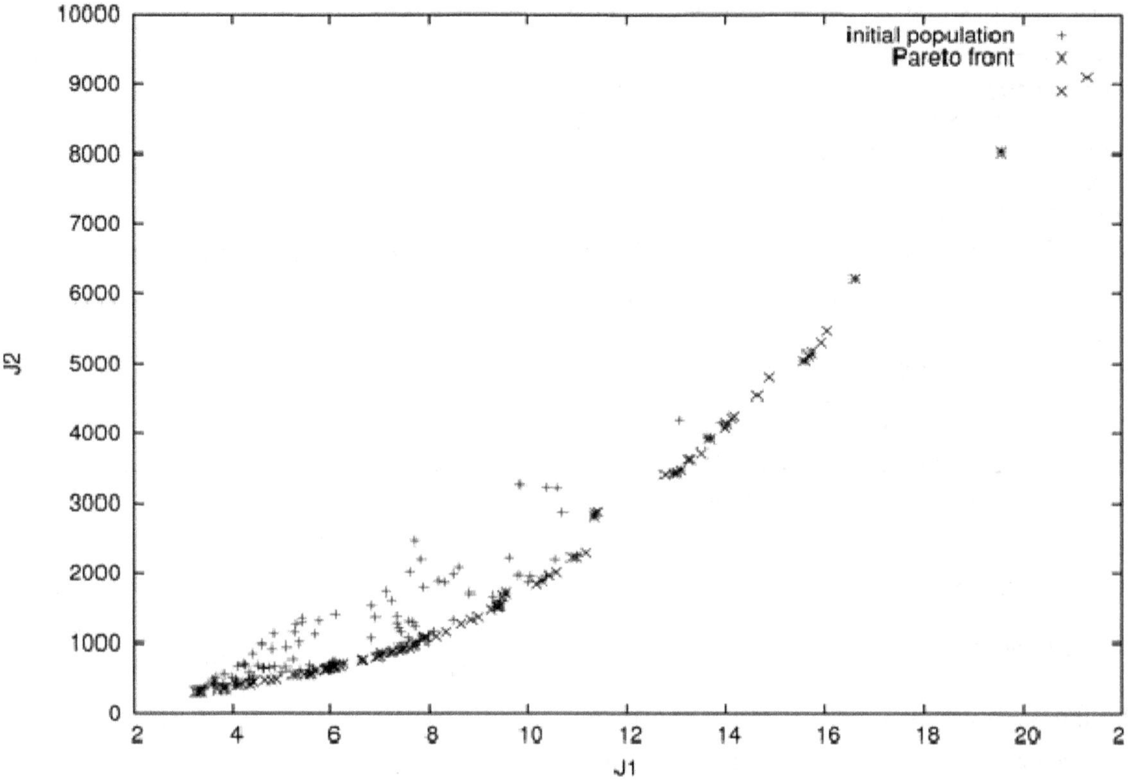

Figure 4. Initial population and pareto front after 100 generations.

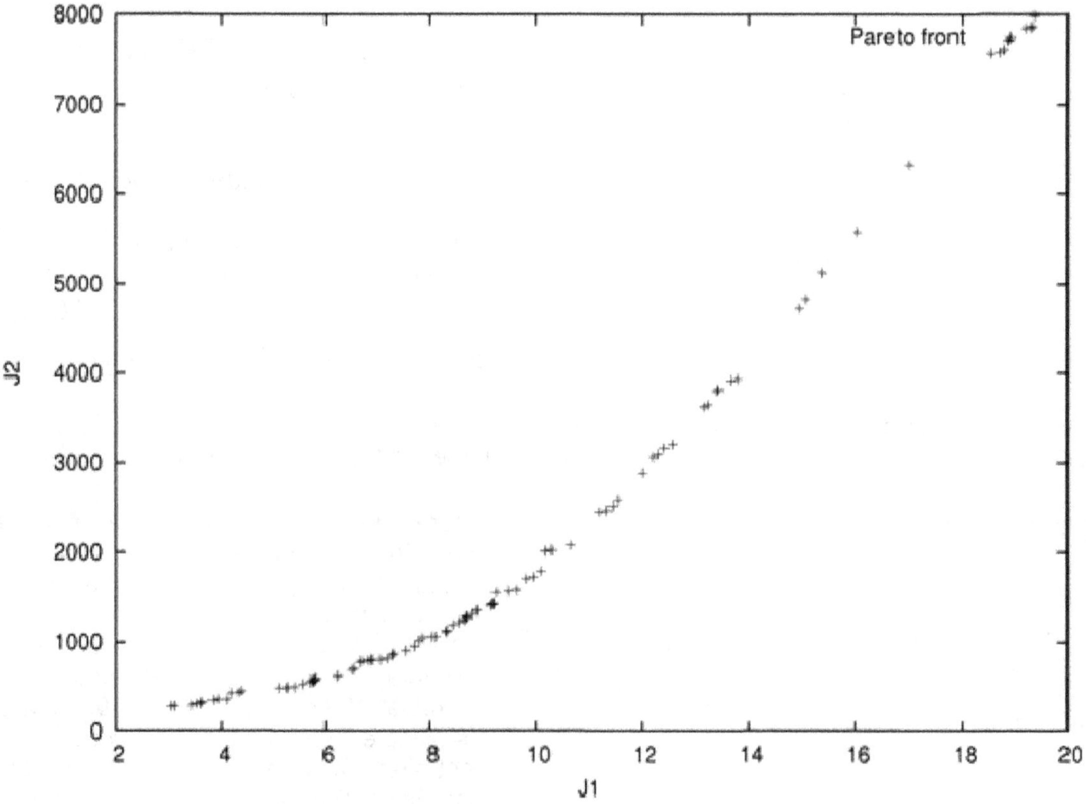

Figure 5. Pareto front after 100 generations.

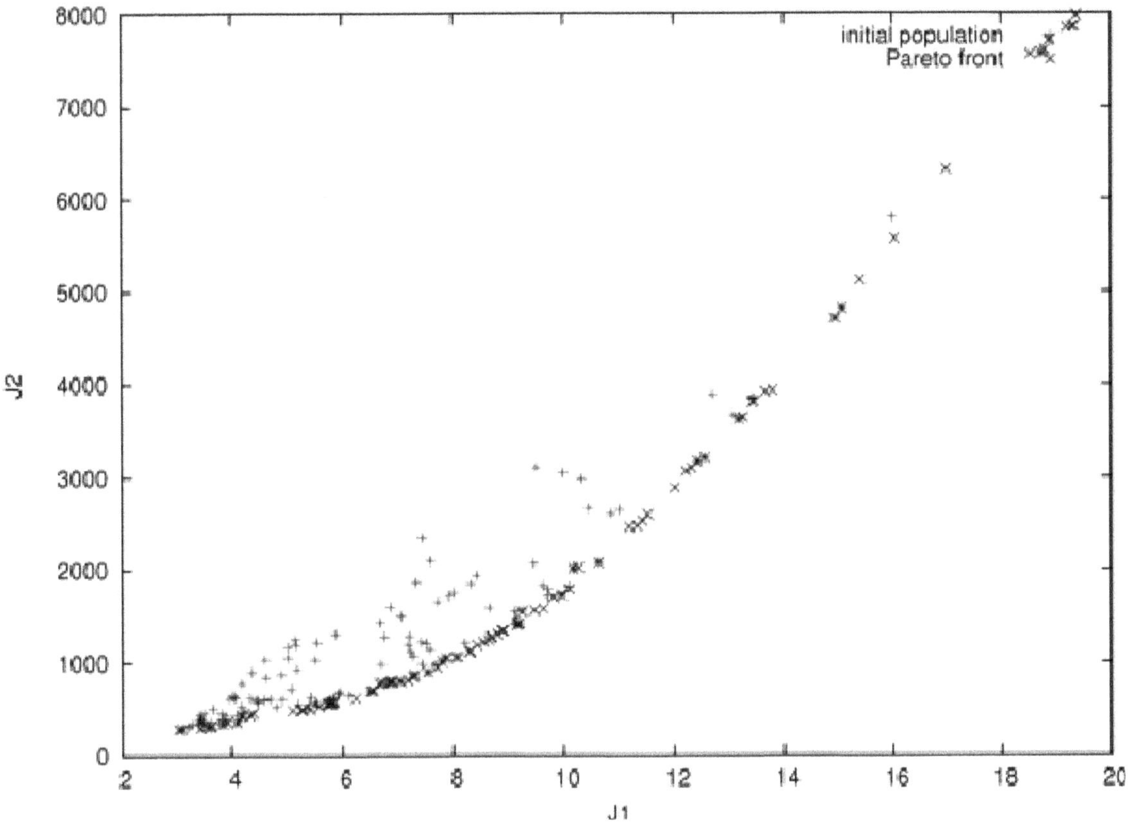

Figure 6. Initial population and Pareto front after 100 generations

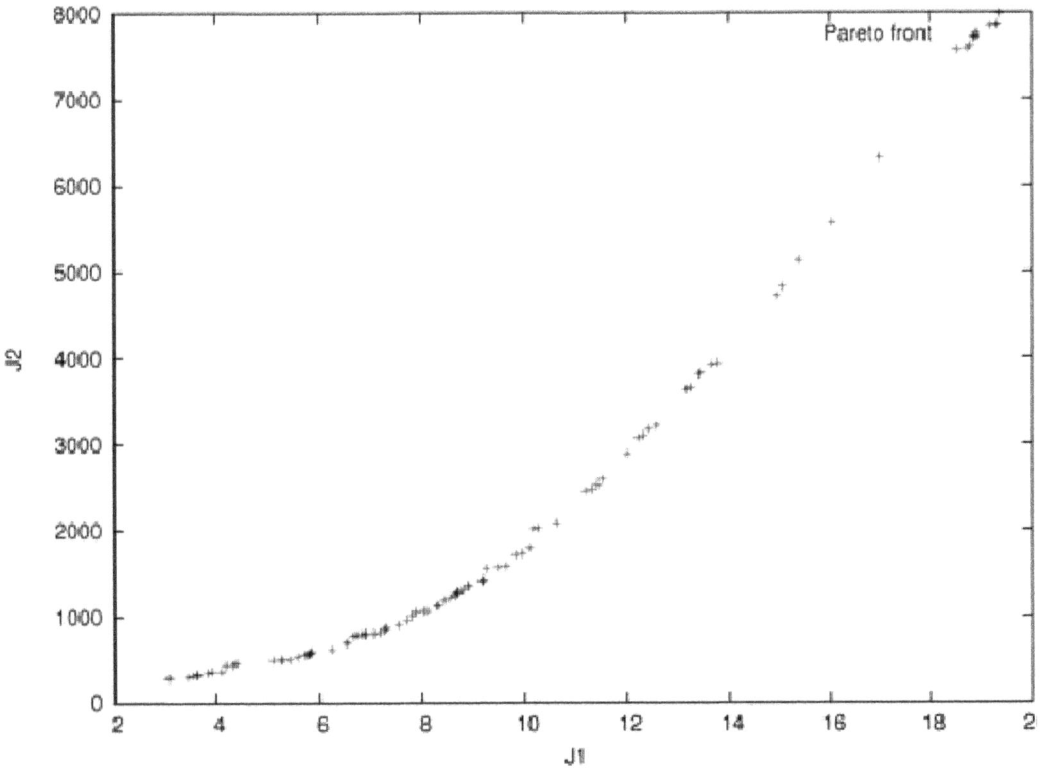

Figure 7. Pareto front after 100 generations.

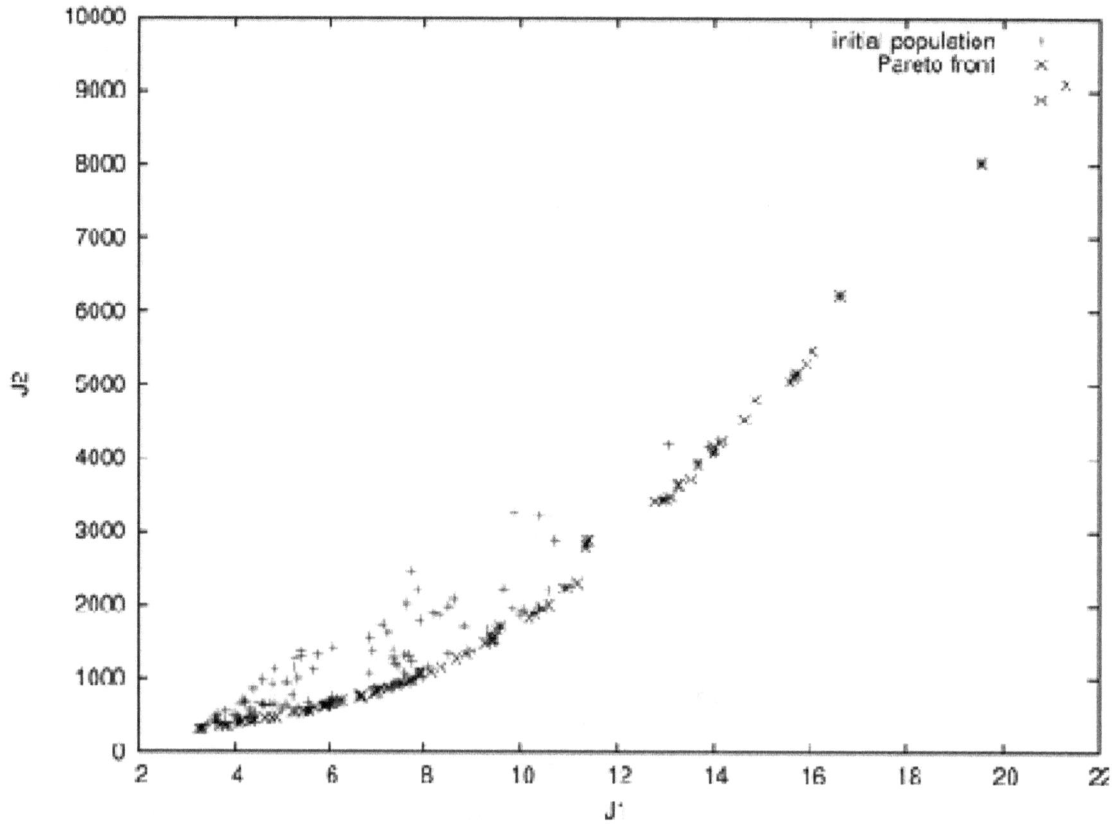

Figure 8. Initial population and Pareto front after 100 generations.

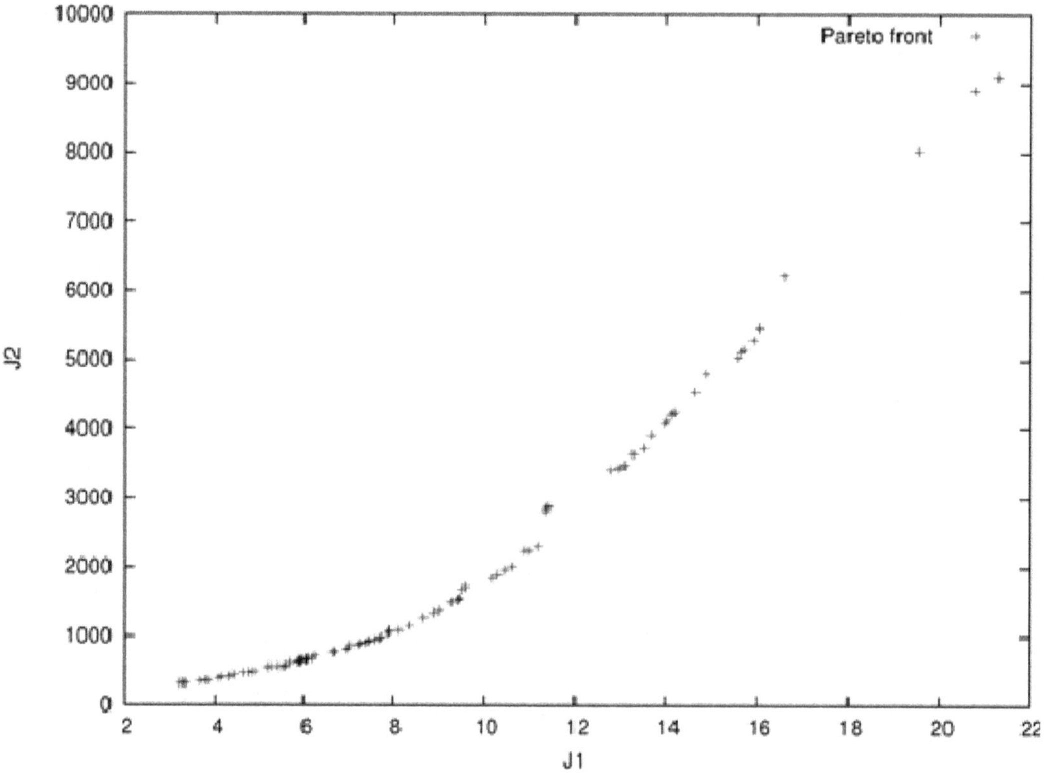

Figure 9. Pareto front after 100 generations.

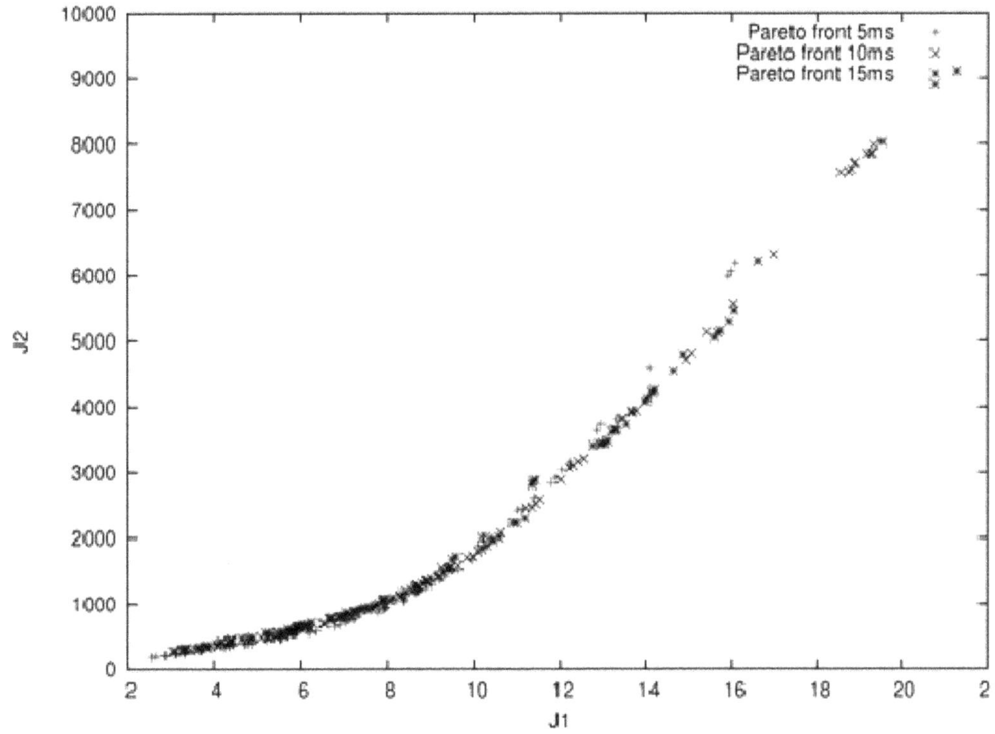

Figure 10. Pareto front at t=5, 10 and 15 ms.

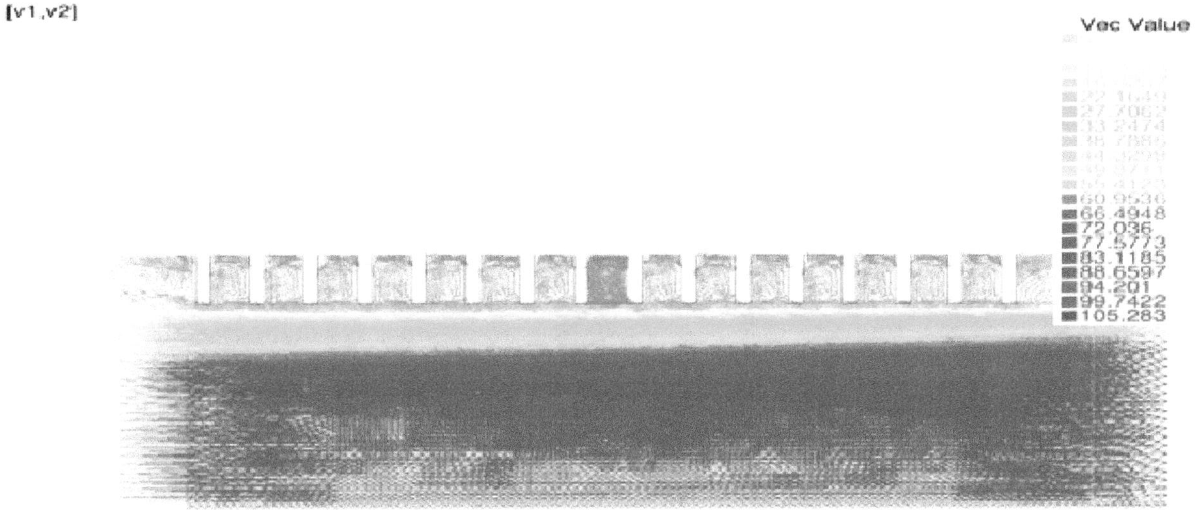

Figure 11. Velocity streamlines.

generations.

Some optimal stent shapes at t = 5 ms after 100 generations

According to optimal parameters l, h and w, we represent in Figures 11 to 18 after 100 generations some optimal stents.

1) For $l = 0.021360, w = 0.008317, \quad h = 0.038598.$

2) For $l = 0.187011, w = 0.007466, \quad h = 0.039841.$

3) For $l = 0.020842, w = 0.008683, \quad h = 0.012138.$

Figure 12. Velocity streamlines between two struts.

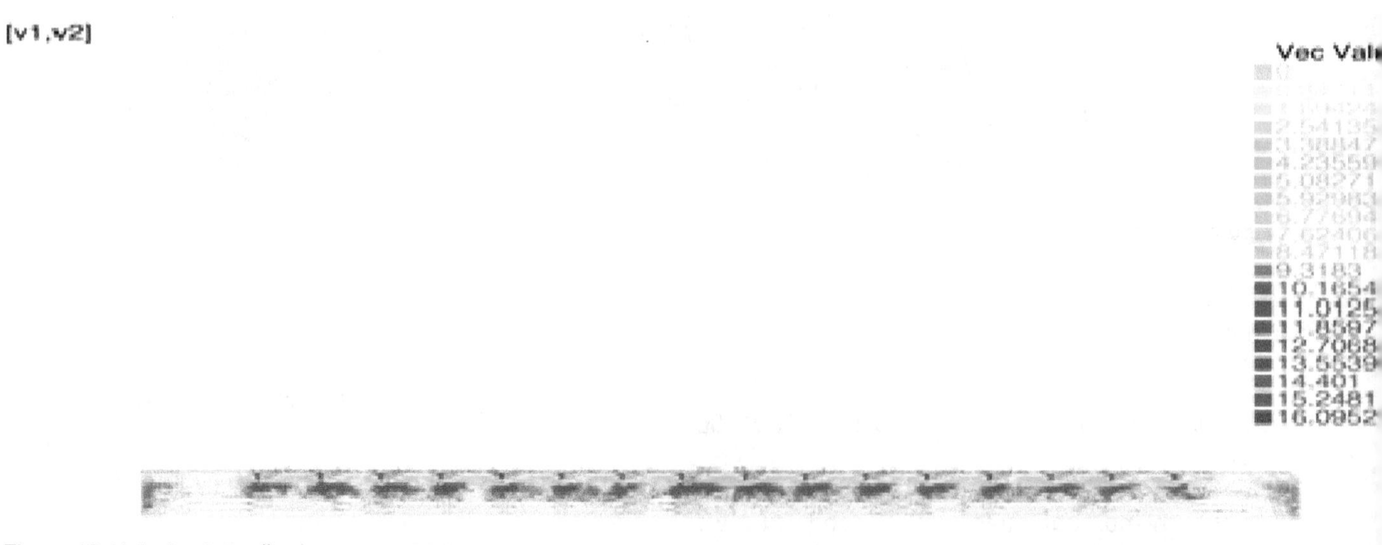

Figure 13. Velocity streamlines.

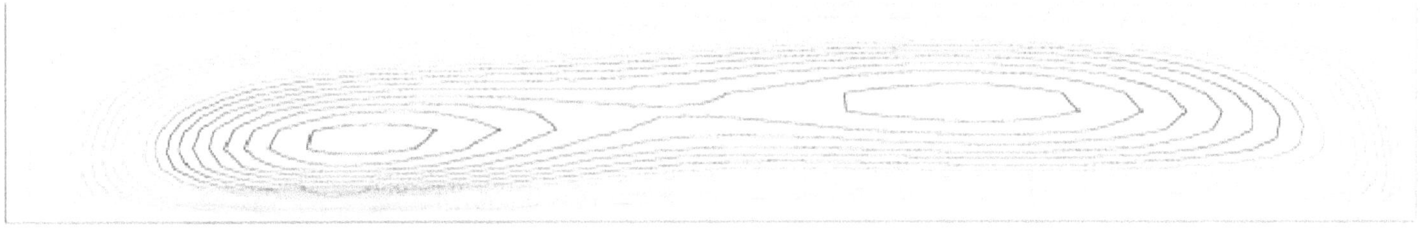

Figure 14. Velocity streamlines between two struts.

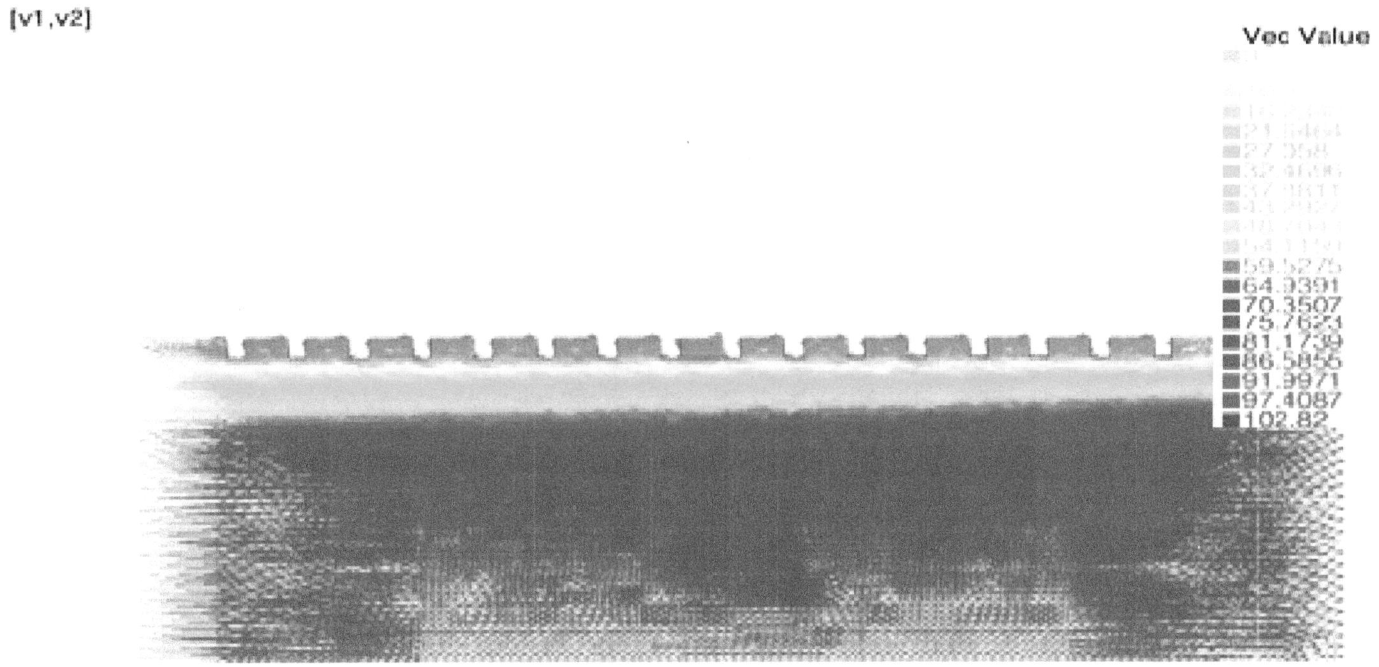

Figure 15. Velocity streamlines.

Figure 16. Velocity streamlines between two struts.

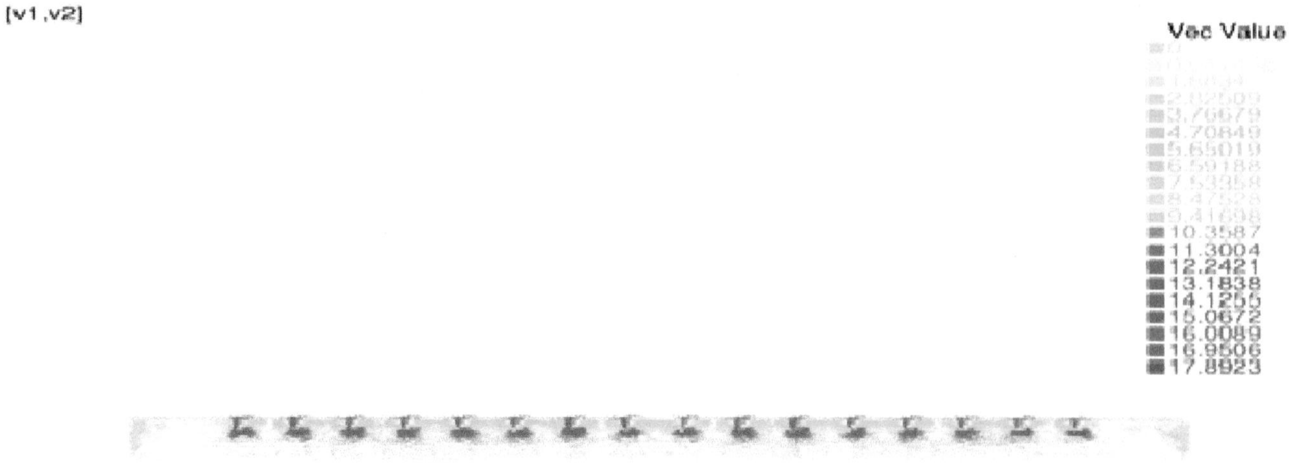

Figure 17. Velocity streamlines.

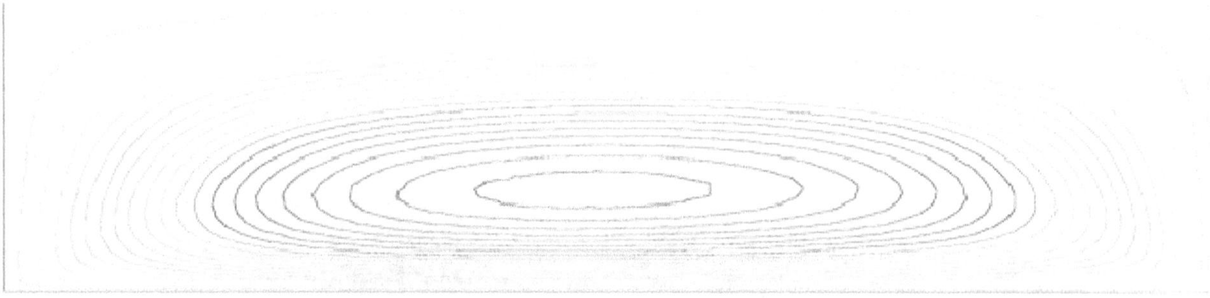

Figure 18. Velocity streamlines between two struts.

4) For $l = 0.049559, w = 0.007901, \ h = 0.018499$.

Conclusion

A multiobjective optimization based on genetic algorithm is used to find optimal stent. A curve of exchange named Pareto front is given. The latter gives a large inquiry during the phase of design when the designer submits several criteria for arbitration. The current results using a 2d computational fluid modeling and multiobjective optimization loop indicate that there exists some important rules to fulfill in order to design appropriate stents which may avoid or at least reduce restenosis. In this paper, we suppose that the wall artery is rigid. That hypothesis simplifies the problem. In a future work, the wall artery will be modeled by an elastic structure.

ACKNOWLEDGEMENT

Author wish to thank Professor Djaraf Seck for fruitful discussion on this subject.

REFERENCES

Andreas OF, Peter WW, Moore Jr JE (2002). Computational fluid dynamics and stent design. Artificial Organs, 26(7): 614-621.

Berry JL, Santamarina A, Moore Jr JE, Roychowdhury S, Routh WD (2000). Experimental and computational flow evaluation of coronary stents. Ann. Biomed. Eng., 28: 386-398.

Blouza A, Dumas L, Mbaye I (2008). Multiobjective optimization of a stent in fluid structure context. Proc. GECCO, 11: 2056-2060.

Deb K, Tuveri M, Veneziani A (2003). A fast multiobjective evolutionary algorithm for finding well-spread Pareto optimal solutions. KanGAL Report 002.

Dumas L, Herbert V, Muyl F (2005). Comparaison of global optimization methods for dragreduction in the automotive industry. Lect. Note Comput Sci., 3483: 948-954.

Dumas L, Alaoui El (2007). How genetic algorithms can improve a pa cemaker efficiency. Proceedings of GECCO, pp. 2681-2686.

Hecht F, Pironneau O (2005). A finite element software for PDE: FreeFem++. www.rocq-inria.fr/Frederic.Heccht.

Mbaye I, Murea C (2008). Numerical procedure with analytic derivative in unsteady fluid-structure interaction. Commun. Meth. Eng., 11: 1257-1275.

Moore Jr JE, Berry JL (2002). Fluid and solid mechanical implications of vascular stenting. Ann. Biomed.Eng., 30: 498-508.

Quarteroni A, Rozza G (2003). Optimal control and shape optimization in aorto-coronaric baypass anastomoses. Math. Models Meth. Appl. Sci., p. 13.

12

Application of Bousinesq's and Westergaard's formulae in analysing foundation stress distribution for a failed telecommunication mast

OJEDOKUN Olalekan Yinka[1]* and OLUTOGE Festus Adeyemi[2]

[1]Department of Civil Engineering, Faculty of Engineering, the Polytechnic, Ibadan, Oyo State, Nigeria.
[2]Department of Civil Engineering, Faculty of Engineering, University of Ibadan, Oyo State, Nigeria.

The concurrent foundation failure of telecommunication masts in Nigeria and all over the world which endanger the lives and properties of residents situated within the fall distance of the telecommunication mast is a thing of great concern. In this study, a GSM mast that underwent foundation failure at Ibadan, Oyo State, Nigeria was critically examined with a view to providing engineering solution. The soil investigation at the global system for mobile communications (GSM) telecommunication tower comprised of laboratory tests: sieve analysis, Atterberg limits and moisture content tests were carried out on the soil samples obtained while Dutch cone penetrometer test was performed on the site to a depth of refusal to determine the allowable bearing pressure at various depths of the soil. The application of Boussineq's and Westergard's formulae for point loads using Java programme to simulate and compute the stress distribution at various predetermined depths showed the stress distribution pattern beneath the failed foundation of the structure. The stress distribution pattern revealed that the soil strength was lower than the imposed loadings from the structure thereby resulting in differential settlements and cracks at the foundation. A variety of engineering solutions were recommended to improve the soil strength and thus prevent such occurrences in future.

Key words: Telecommunication mast, Bousinesq's and Westergraard's formula, stress distribution.

INTRODUCTION

A telecommunication mast installation comprises of a mast supporting telecommunications antenna and a foundation structure supporting the mast, the foundation structure being in the form of an enclosed chamber situated at least partially underground and defining an internal space which is accessible to personnel and which accommodates electronic equipment associated with operation of the antenna. The telecommunication mast has a foot at its lower end which is supported on a base of the chamber, the base acting as a structural foundation for the mast. The foot of the mast is seated on the base, the seat restraining lateral movements of the foot of the mast at the base without transfer of bending moments between the mast and the foundation structure (Creighton, 2002).

Numerous investigations have been carried out on the design and erection techniques of telecommunication towers. Comparatively little attention has been directed toward the behaviour and deterioration of tower foundations. It should be pointed out that the design of tower foundations is more involved than that of other steel structures. In the latter case, the foundations are usually subjected to static compressive force with uniform stress distribution on soil (Abdalla, 2002).

Communication masts are used for all types of wireless communication and come in many different shapes and sizes. From a structural point of view, a lattice construction has been shown to provide a strong durable structure upon which to locate antennae of different types and size. However, many people consider lattice

*Corresponding author. E-mail: daniely2kus@yahoo.com.

constructions to be unattractive and in the recent past this has resulted in slim tubular constructions being utilized in order to reduce the visual impact of the mast (Heslop, 2002).

In an engineering sense, failure may occur long before the ultimate load or the load at which the bearing resistance of the soil is fully mobilized since the settlement will have exceeded tolerable limits. Terzaghi (1967) suggested that, for practical purposes, the ultimate load can be defined as that which causes a settlement of one-tenth of the pile diameter or width which is widely accepted by engineers. In most cases where the piles are acting as structural foundations, the allowable load is governed solely from considerations of tolerable settlement at the working load. An ideal method of calculating allowable loads on piles would be one which would enable the engineer to predict the load-settlement relationship up to the point of failure, for any given type and size of pile in any soil or rock conditions (Tomlinson, 1994).

Estimation of vertical stresses at any point in a soil-mass due to external vertical loadings is of great significance in the prediction of settlements of buildings, bridges, embankments and many other structures. Equations have been developed to compute stresses at any point in a soil mass on the basis of the theory of elasticity. According to elastic theory, constant ratios exist between stresses and strains. For the theory to be applicable, the real requirement is not that the material necessarily be elastic, but there must be constant ratios between stresses and the corresponding strains. Therefore, in non-elastic soil masses, the elastic theory may be assumed to hold so long as the stresses induced in the soil mass are relatively small. Since the stresses in the subsoil of a structure having adequate factor of safety against shear failure are relatively small in comparison with the ultimate strength of the material, the soil may be assumed to behave elastically under such stresses. When a load is applied to the soil surface, it increases the vertical stresses within the soil mass. The increased stresses are greatly directly under the loaded area, but extend indefinitely in all directions. Many formulae based on the theory of elasticity have been used to compute stresses in soils. They are all similar and differ only in the assumptions made to represent the elastic conditions of the soil mass. The formulae that are most widely used are the Boussinesq and Westergaard formulas (Murthy, 1992).

METHODOLOGY

Collection of samples

The soil investigation at the GSM telecommunication tower at Ibadan, Oyo State, Nigeria comprised of and was carried out in three parts; field work: (tests two boreholes), laboratory analysis of borehole samples obtained and analysis of the test results. The scope of work executed involved the performance of two boreholes to depth of refusal. The samples obtained from the borehole test were also subjected to laboratory analysis. The laboratory tests carried out on the samples are: grain size analysis, moisture content, atterberg limits, dutch cone penetrometer tests.

Pile details

Mass of tower ad ladder, W	= 12796 Kg
Height of tower, Ht	= 55 m
Maximum force/leg, Rv	= 524.43 kN
Maximum uplift/leg, Wv	= -461.67 kN
Leg spacing heal-heal	= 6502 mm
R.C. Stud section	= 700 × 700 mm
Load factor	= 1.3

Safe working loads

Pile depth, Lp = -6.00 m

Pile requirement

Piles required/leg = Max forces per leg/(Qs + Qb)

300 mm	= 524.43/108 = 4.8558333 ~ 5No
400 mm	= 524.43/182 = 2.8814835 ~ 3No

Provision per leg
400 mm = 3No

Load per pile

Wp = 174.81 kN
Wp (factored) = 174.81 x 1.3 = 227.253 KN

Pile design

Designed as a short braced column min. steel required = 0.4%ACol

Acol = $(3.142 \times 400^2) / 4 = 125680 \text{ mm}^2$

Ast = $(0.4 \times 125680) / 100 = 502.72 \text{ mm}^2$

Provide = 6 No. 16 mm diameter bar

Asc(pro) = 1206 mm^2

Load capacity N = 0.35 Fcu x Acol + 0.67Ast x Fy
N = 0.35 x 25 x 125680 + 0.67 x 1206 x 380
N = 1406.70kN

RESULTS AND DISCUSSION

Physical properties of soil samples

The analysis of total load to be carried by the piles is presented in Table 1. The results of the tests carried out on the soil specimens are given in Table 2. Sample 4 had the highest value of plastic and liquid limits while samples 1, 3, 5, 7 and 8 had no plastic and liquid limits. Generally, liquid limits vary widely, but values of 40 to 60% and above are typical of clay soils and values of 25 to 50% can be expected for silty soil so clays soils with liquid limits between 30 and 50% exhibit medium plasticity while liquid limits less than 30% infer low plasticity and liquid limits greater than 50% indicate high plasticity. High liquid limit is an indication of soils with high clay content and low bearing capacity.

Sample 8 had the highest moisture content which indicated poor drainage property while sample 1 had the lowest moisture content indicating that the drainage property is good at that depth.

Allowable bearing pressure at predetermined depths

The allowable bearing capacity at predetermined depths were determined for borehole 1 and tabulated in Table 3.

The highest bearing capacity of the soil which was at 7.50 m depth was 220 kN/m^2. The derived allowable bearing capacity of the soil in relationship to the actual load of the telecommunication mast would be used in the simulation using Java programme to determine the cause of failure.

Application of Bousinesq's formula for stress distribution

$$\sigma_B = \frac{3N}{2\Pi Z^2}\,\frac{1}{[1+(r/Z)^2]^{5/2}} = \frac{N\,I_B}{Z^2}$$

$$I_B = \frac{3}{2\Pi}\,\frac{1}{[1+(r/Z)^2]^{5/2}}$$

Where σ_B = Bousinesq stress coefficient
I_B = Bousinesq vertical stress
N = Point load from the end bearing pile
Z = Vertical distance from the end point of pile
r = The radial distance from Z (Murthy, 1992).

Application of Westergaard's formula for stress distribution

$$\sigma_W = \frac{N}{\Pi Z^2}\,\frac{1}{[1+2(r/Z)^2]^{3/2}} = \frac{N\,I_W}{Z^2}$$

$$I_W = \frac{(1/\Pi)}{[1+2(r/Z)^2]^{3/2}}$$

Where σ_W = Westergaard stress coefficient
I_W = Westergaard vertical stress
N = Point load from the end bearing pile
Z = Vertical distance from the end point of pile
r = Radial distance from Z (Murthy, 1992).

Stress distribution at predetermined depths

Based on the Bousinesq's and Westergaard's formulae stated, the Java coding for determining the various stresses at predetermined depths was used to analyse the experimental data. The result of the analysis is shown in Table 4.

Figure 1: Graph of values of I_B and I_W showed the values obtained from the Table 4: Stress distribution at predetermined depths when I_B and I_W were plotted against r/z. The graph (Figure 1) showed that both Bousinesq vertical stress and Westergaard vertical stress decreased as the depths moves further away from the point load. In other words, as the values of radial and vertical distances increased, both values of Bousinesq vertical stress and Westergaard vertical stress decreased.

Figure 2: Graph of values of σ_B and σ_W showed the values obtained from the Table 3: Stress distribution at predetermined depths when σ_B and σ_W were plotted against r/z. The graph (Figure 2) showed that both Bousinesq vertical stress coefficient and Westergaard vertical stress coefficient decreased as the depths moved further away from the point load. In other words, as the values of radial and vertical distances increased, both values of Bousinesq Vertical Stress and Westergaard Vertical Stress decreased.

Figure 3: Graph of values of σ_B/σ_W showed the values obtained from the Table 4: Stress distribution at predetermined depths when σ_B/σ_W is plotted against r/z. The graph (Figure 3) showed that σ_B/σ_W decreased as the depths moved further away from the point load. In other words, as the values of radial and vertical distances increased, σ_B/σ_W decreased.

Conclusion

From the analysis of the results obtained from *in-situ* and laboratory tests carried out on the soil samples at the telecommunication mast site, the following conclusions can be drawn.

(1) The telecommunication mast was erected at a distance of two metres to the nearby building thereby violating the Nigerian Communication Commission guidelines of observing a clear fall distance to any nearby building.

The stress distribution at predetermined depths revealed:

Table 1. Load classification on piles.

Pile diameter (mm)	End bearing, Qb (kN)	Skin friction, Qs (kN)	Total load {Qb (kN) +Qs(kN)}
300	84	24	108
400	150	32	182

Table 2. Physical properties of soil samples.

BH number	Sample number	Depth (m)	Soil type	Natural moisture content (%)	Atterberg limits (%)			Grading analysis percentage passing										
					LL	PL	PI	9.5	6.3	4.75	2.36	1.18	600	425	300	212	150	75
1	1	0.15	SM	13							100	98	89	80	75	61	48	34
	2	2.25	SC	17	44	18	26				100	97	88	80	71	65	55	48
	3	3.75	SC	16							100	97	88	80	71	61	54	47
	4	5.25	SC	19	46	19	27				100	98	92	85	77	67	58	49
	5	7.50	GP/SM	20				85	81	80	72	67	56	48	41	34	29	23
2	6	0.75	SM/SC	18	31	13	18		100	99	96	90	77	68	59	48	41	34
	7	3.00	SM/SC	18						100	98	94	81	69	58	47	39	32
	8	6.00	SC	23					100	99	98	94	83	74	66	57	50	45
	9	8.25	SC	16	45	17	28			100	99	93	81	73	66	58	53	48

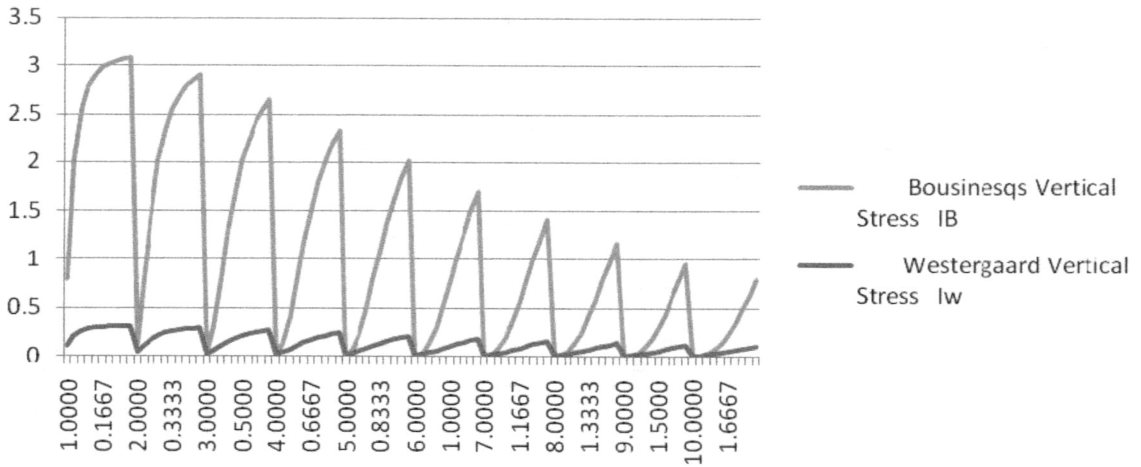

Figure 1. Graph of I_B and I_W.

Table 3. Allowable bearing pressure at predetermined depths.

Depth (m)	Allowable bearing pressure (kN/m^2)
0.00 - 0.15	50
0.15 - 2.25	108
2.25 - 3.75	140
3.75 - 5.25	190
5.25 - 7.50	220

Table 4. Stress distribution at predetermined depths based on Java coding.

Radial distance, r(m)	Vertical distance z (m)	r/z	Bousinesq's vertical stress (I_B)	Bousnesq's stress coefficient, σ_B(N/m^2)	Westergaard vertical stress (I_w)	Westergaard stress coefficient, σ_w (N/m^2)	σ_B/σ_w
1	1	1.0000	0.7854	1104745.006	0.1061	149245.4289	7.4022
1	2	0.5000	2.0106	2828147.216	0.2122	298490.8577	9.4748
1	3	0.3333	2.5447	3579373.82	0.2604	366329.689	9.7709
1	4	0.2500	2.7829	3914390.61	0.2829	397987.8103	9.8355
1	5	0.2000	2.9046	4085595.437	0.2947	414570.6357	9.855
1	6	0.1667	2.9741	4183344.129	0.3016	424171.2189	9.8624
1	7	0.1429	3.0172	4243988.416	0.3058	430178.0009	9.8657
1	8	0.1250	3.0457	4284057.321	0.3087	434168.5203	9.8673
1	9	0.1111	3.0654	4311857.219	0.3106	436947.4604	9.8681
1	10	0.1000	3.0797	4331908.661	0.3121	438957.1437	9.8686
2	1	2.0000	0.1257	176759.201	0.0354	49748.4763	3.5531
2	2	1.0000	0.7854	1104745.006	0.1061	149245.4289	7.4022
2	3	0.6667	1.5057	2117972.675	0.1685	237036.8576	8.9352
2	4	0.5000	2.0106	2828147.216	0.2122	298490.8577	9.4748
2	5	0.4000	2.3347	3284022.016	0.2411	339194.1565	9.6818
2	6	0.3333	2.5447	3579373.82	0.2604	366329.689	9.7709
2	7	0.2857	2.6853	3777134.582	0.2736	384896.106	9.8134
2	8	0.2500	2.7829	3914390.61	0.2829	397987.8103	9.8355
2	9	0.2222	2.8529	4012861.999	0.2897	407490.3283	9.8477
2	10	0.2000	2.9046	4085595.437	0.2947	414570.6357	9.855
3	1	3.0000	0.0314	44189.8002	0.0168	23565.0677	1.8752
3	2	1.5000	0.2974	418364.9728	0.0579	81406.5976	5.1392
3	3	1.0000	0.7854	1104745.006	0.1061	149245.4289	7.4022
3	4	0.7500	1.2868	1810014.218	0.1498	210699.429	8.5905

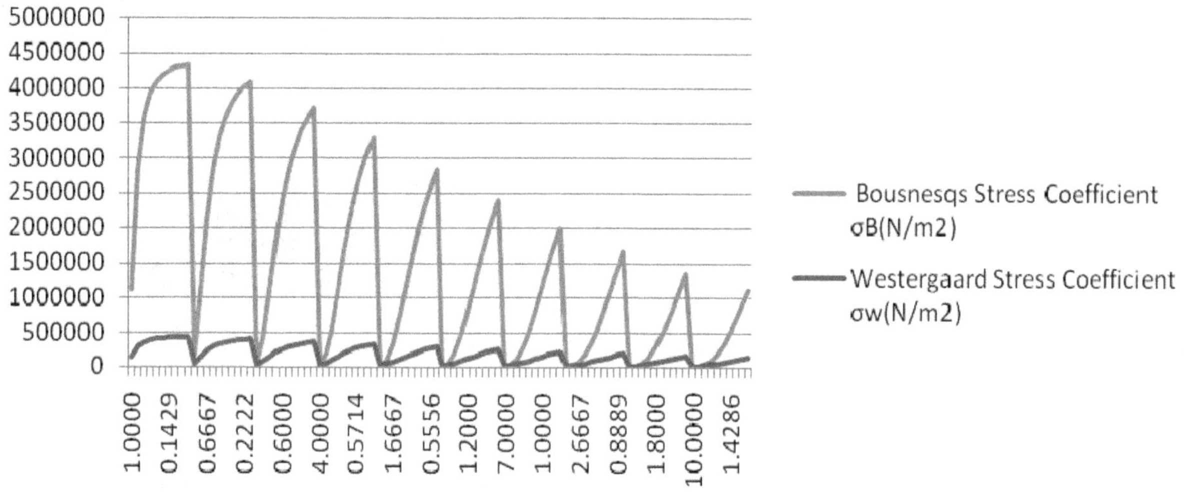

Figure 2. Graph of σ_B and σ_W.

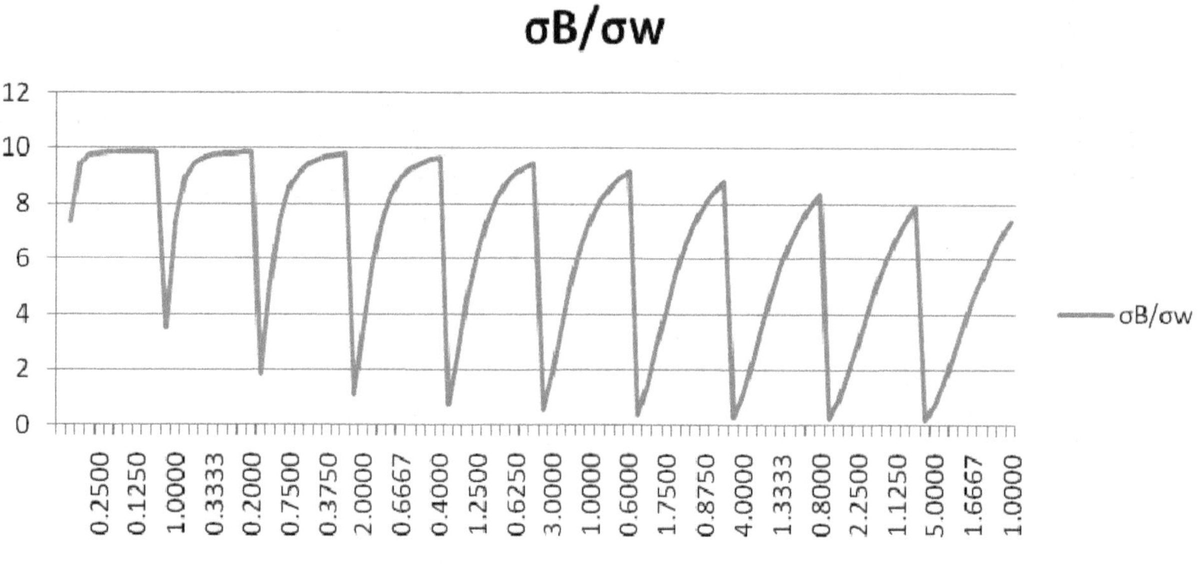

Figure 3. Graph of $\sigma_{B/}\sigma_W$.

1) Bousinesq vertical stress, Westergaard vertical stress, Bousinesq vertical stress coefficient and Westergaard vertical stress coefficient decreased as the depths moved further away from the point load. In other words, as the values of radial and vertical distances increased, the values of Bousinesq vertical stress, Westergaard vertical stress, Bousinesq vertical stress coefficient and Westergaard vertical stress coefficient decreased.

2) The total weight of the structure transmitted by the end bearing of the pile foundation unto the soil which is 389.47 kN/m^2 in relationship to the soil bearing capacity at the depth of the pile foundation which is 220 kN/m^2 has caused a differential settlement to occur at the foundation. This differential settlement has resulted to cracks occurring at the pile caps and also a clearance at the base plate which would eventually result to a total collapse if not attended to.

Based on the conclusions arrived at, the following recommendations could be adopted;

1) The telecommunication mast should be dismantled because it violated the Nigeria Communication Commission guidelines for safe erection of telecommunication mast of observing a clear fall distance.

2) The soil bearing pressure could be improved by adopting any of the following soil improvement methods: Application of vertical or wick drains, vacuum consolidation, cement deep mixing, vibroflotation techniques, application of geotextiles.

REFERENCES

Abdalla HA (2002). Repair of Cracked Concrete Foundations of Telecommunication Structures. 4th Structural Specialty Conference of the Canadian Society for Civil Engineering, June 5-8.

Creighton BR (2002). Telecommunications mast installation. Free Patents Online, pp. 1-2.

Heslop P (2002). Communications mast. Free Patents Online, Great Britain, pp. 1-2.

Murthy VNS (1992). Principles and Practices of Soil Mechanics and Foundation Engineering, Marcel Dekker Inc., New York, pp. 173-175.

Terzaghi K, Peck RB (1967). Soil Mechanics in Engineering. 2nd Edition, John Wiley, New York.

Tomlinson MJ (1994). Foundation Design and Construction. Singapore, Longman, pp. 267-268.

13

Critical thinking: Essence for teaching mathematics and mathematics problem solving skills

Ebiendele Ebosele Peter

Department of Mathematics and Computer Science, Lagos State University, Isolo Campus, Lagos, Nigeria.
E-mail: peter.ebiendele@yahoo.com.

Critical thinking is a learned skill that requires instruction and practice. Mathematics education instructors at both the secondary and post-secondary levels can enhance students' critical thinking skills by (i) using instructional strategies that actively engage students in the learning process rather than relying on lecture and note memorization, (ii) focusing instruction on the process of learning rather than solely on the content, and (iii) using assessment techniques that provide students with an intellectual challenge rather than memory recall. Several barriers can impede critical thinking instruction. Lack of training, limited resources, biased preconceptions and time constraints conspire to negate learning environments that promote critical thinking. However, actively engaging students in project-based or collaborative activities can encourage students' critical thinking development if instructors model the thinking process, use effective questioning techniques and guide students' critical thinking processes. The examples provided challenge instructors to think of students as users of information rather than receivers of information. 'It is possible to store the mind with a million facts and still be entirely uneducated."

Key words: Mathematics, problem solving skills, instructional strategies, critical thinking.

INTRODUCTION

What is critical thinking and why is it so important? The critical thinking community defined critical thinking as "the intellectually disciplined process of actively and skillfully conceptualizing, applying, analyzing, synthesizing, and/or evaluating information gathered from, or generated by observation, experience, reflection, reasoning, or communication as a guide to belief and action" (Scriven and Paul, 2007). Critical thinking has also been referred to as met cognition (Tempelaar, 2006) or the process of "thinking about thinking" as defined and originally purposed by Flavell (1979). Critical thinking skills are important because they enable students "to deal effectively with social, scientific, and practical problems" (Shakirova, 2007). Simply put, students who are able to think critically are able to solve problems effectively. Merely having knowledge or information is not enough. To be effective in the workplace (and in their personal lives), students must be able to solve problems to make effective decisions, they must be able to think critically.

Yet many teachers continually struggle to engage students in critical thinking activities (Templeaar, 2006), and students seldom use critical thinking skills to solve complex, real-world problems (Bartlett, 2002; Rippin et al., 2002). Why?

The answer may be in our instructional methods. Two quotes that are often cited together reflect this supposition (Schafersman, 1991). First, Clement (1979) stated that "we should be teaching students how to think. Instead, we are teaching them what to think". Secondly, Norman (1981) noted that "it is strange that we expect students to learn, yet seldom teach them anything about learning." Although content is important, the process of how students learn the material is equally important.

Objective

The main objective of this article is to analyze and synthesize secondary research to provide best practices for incorporating critical thinking instructional methods into mathematics education classrooms at both the secondary and post-secondary levels. The underlisted areas will be discussed in this article:

1) Relation of critical thinking to Bloom et al.'s taxonomy of the cognitive domain;
2) Relation of critical thinking to instructional design;
3) Modeling critical thinking skill;
4) Questioning techniques;
5) Guiding student critical thinking
6) Barriers to critical thinking.

RELATION OF CRITICAL THINKING TO BLOOM ET AL.'S TAXONOMY OF THE COGNITIVE DOMAIN

Bloom and his colleagues in 1956 produced one of the most often cited documents in establishing educational outcomes - The taxonomy of the cognitive domain. They proposed that knowing is actually composed of six successive levels arranged in a hierarchy: knowledge, comprehension, application, analysis, synthesis and evaluation. Research over the past 40 years has generally confirmed that the first four levels are indeed a true hierarchy. That is, knowing at the knowledge level is easier than and subsumed number, the level of comprehension and so forth up to the level of analysis. However, research is mixed on the relationship of synthesis and evaluation. It is possible that these two are reversal or they could be two separate, though equally difficult activities. Synthesis and evaluation are two types of thinking that have much in common (the first four levels of Bloom's taxonomy, but are quite different in thinking) requires an individual to look at parts and well purpose. Evaluation, which might be considered equivalent to critical thinking as used in this paper focuses on making an assessment or judgment based on an analysis of a statement or proposition. Synthesis, which might be considered more equivalent to creative thinking requires an individual to look at parts and relationships (analysis) and then to put these together in a new and original way.

There is some evidence to suggest that this equivalent but different relationship between critical/ evaluative and creative synthesis thinking is appropriate. Huitt (1992) classified techniques used in problem solving and decision making into two groups roughly corresponding to the critical/creative dichotomy. One set of techniques tended to be more linear and serial, more structured, more rational and analytical and more goal-oriented, these techniques are often taught as part of critical thinking exercises. The second set of techniques tended to be more holistic and parallel, more emotional and intuitive, more creative, more visual and more tactual/ kinesthetic, these techniques are more often taught as part of creative thinking exercises. This distinction also corresponds to what is sometimes referred to as left brain thinking analytic, serial, logical, objective as compared to right brain thinking global, parallel, emotional and subjective.

RELATION OF CRITICAL THINKING TO INSTRUCTIONAL DESIGN

Those who have the ability to hear, do not always actively listen. Similarly, those who have the ability to know, do not always critically think. The premise that critical thinking is to knowing as listening is to hearing implies that critical thinking is a learned skill that must be developed, practiced, and continually integrated into the curriculum to engage students in active learning. To support this premise, focused attention needs to be placed on the application of content, the process of learning, and methods of assessment.

In terms of the application of content, teaching techniques that promote memorization offer temporary knowledge do not support critical thinking. Although some content, such as vocabulary definitions, do require memory, it is the application of the content that stimulates thinking. Instruction that supports critical thinking uses questioning techniques that require students to analyze, synthesize, and evaluate information to solve problems and make decisions (think) rather than merely to repeat information (memorize). Because critical thinking is a mental habit that requires students to think about their thinking and about improving the process, it requires students to use higher-order thinking skills, not memorize data or accept what they read or are told without critically thinking about it (Scriven and Paul, 2007; Schafersman, 1991; Templeaar, 2006). Therefore, critical thinking is a product of education, training, and practice.

To link critical thinking skills to content, the instructional focus should be on the process of learning. How will the students get the information? Research supports the premise that lecture and memorization do not lead to long term knowledge or the ability to apply that knowledge to new situations (Celuch and Slama, 1999; Daz-Lefebvre, 2004; Kang and Howren, 2004). Traditional instructional methods use too many facts and not enough conceptualization; too much memorizing and not enough thinking. Therefore, lecture and note memorization do not promote critical thinking. Instructional strategies that employ students' higher order thinking skills lead to improved critical thinking skills (Duplass and Ziedler, 2002; Hemming, 2000; Wong, 2007).

Additionally, assessments should emphasize thinking rather than facts (Ennis, 1993). Graded assignments, quizzes, or tests should become intellectual challenges rather than memory recall (Schafersman, 1991). Subjective tools such as essay questions and case studies require students to apply their knowledge to new situations and are better indicators of understanding than objective true/false or standardized multiple choice assessments. However, instructors can create multiple choice questions that require critical thinking. For example, a question that asks students to identify the example that best applies a specific concept requires more critical thinking and analysis than a question that asks students to identify the correct term for a given definition. Ennis (1993) stated that although they are more labour intensive to create than equally effective open ended critical thinking assessments, multiple choice tests are easier to grade. To enhance students' processing skills, it is important to review test questions and explain correct answers by modeling the critical thinking process (Brown and Kelly, 1986; Duplass and Ziedler, 2002; Schafersman,1991).

MODELING CRITICAL THINKING SKILLS

Although mathematics education students perceive critical thinking as an important skill (Davis et al., 2003), they typically do not know how to think critically. Students are not born with the ability to think critically, and their prior learning experiences often do not require them to think critically. Therefore, instructors who wish to integrate this skill in their classroom experiences must first model the behavior (Hemming, 2000). Students must learn how to think critically before they can apply the skill to content scenarios. Modeling can be demonstrated in a discussion setting by asking a question and "walking students through" the process of critically thinking.

Further, critical thinking activities should be based on a structure that includes four elements; "ill-structured problems, criteria for assessing thinking, student assessment of thinking and improvement of thinking" (Broadbear, 2003). Ill-structured problems are questions, case studies, or scenarios that do not have a definite right or wrong answer, they include debatable issues that require reflective judgment. For example, asking students to evaluate comparable websites, such as Wal-Mart and Target, requires them to think about the content of the websites, their format and their usability. Right and wrong answers do not exist as long as the student's choice is supported by logical reasoning. The second element, criteria for assessing thinking, provides students with a framework for thinking about their thinking. Why do you think Target's navigational menus are easier to use than Wal-Mart's? Why do you like one's colour scheme over the other? What is your perspective based upon? Providing students with individualized feedback based on their responses allows them to address specific criteria upon which they can assess their thinking, which is the third element. If instructors model the criteria for assessing thinking and provide a framework, students will eventually apply these techniques on their own (Lundquist, 1999).

Finally, the process concludes with improvement of thinking. By creating a culture of inquiry where students can think about their thinking processes and practice logical constructs, students will become more willing to reconsider and revise their thinking (Duplass and Ziedler, 2002).

QUESTIONING TECHNIQUES

In their research, Haynes and Bailey (2003) emphasized the importance of asking the right questions to stimulate students' critical thinking skills. Other researchers (Brown and Kelley, 1996; Hemming, 2000) also focused on integrating questioning techniques into class discussions to support an educational environment where students can demonstrate and practice critical thinking skills. Brown and Kelley's book, Asking the Right Questions: A guide to critical thinking, documented the premise that students' critical thinking is best supported when instructors use critical questioning techniques to engage students actively in the learning process. Sample questions from all these studies include the following:

1) What do you think about this?
2) Why do you think that?
3) What is your knowledge based upon?
4) What does it imply and presuppose?
5) How are you viewing it?
6) Should it be viewed differently?

These questions require students to evaluate the clarity and accuracy of their thinking as well as the depth and breadth of their thinking. Have they considered all the alternatives? Do they know why they think the way they do? Students need to determine whether the content they are using is relevant and if their thinking process is logical. By questioning their thought process, students can begin thinking about their thinking. Research on questioning methodology also suggests that instructors should wait for student responses (Brown and Kelley, 1986; Hemming, 2000). Too often, the students' silence is filled by the instructor rewording the question or asking a different student for a response. However, most students need at least 8 to 12 s to process and formulate their response, especially in critical thinking situations (Schafersman, 1991). If a question is based on note memory recall, speed may be relevant. However, thinking requires time and patience. Give students the time they need to think critically.

Research also provides strategies for using questioning methods in online learning environments (Astleitner, 2002; MacKnight 2000). Discussion boards, virtual chat rooms and instant messages provide forums for questioning and critical thinking. In synchronous environments, instructors can question students as they construct their responses. Although this is not possible with asynchronous communication, instructors can model the critical thinking process and assign activities that utilize questioning techniques and critical thinking responses. In all learning environments, it is important to guide students through the critical thinking process.

GUIDING STUDENTS' CRITICAL THINKING

When students are accustomed to being passive learners by merely memorizing and recalling information, it may be difficult at first to engage them in active learning situations that require critical thinking skills (Brown and Kelley, 1986). Instructors should be aware of students' initial resistance and guide them through the process to create a learning environment where students feel comfortable thinking through an answer rather than simply having an answer. For example, peer coaching techniques can engage students in active learning and critical thinking opportunities (Ladyshewsky, 2006). Assign students to two-person teams; one student is the problem solver, and the other is the peer coach. Using the six steps to effective thinking and problem solving, or "IDEALS" (Facione, 2007), the problem solver works through a case study or activity by responding to questions from the peer coach. The IDEALS are to identify, define, enumerate, analyze, list and self correct:

I – Identify the problem: What is the real question we are facing?
D – Define the context: What are the facts that frame this problem?
E – Enumerate the choices: What are plausible options?
A – Analyze options: What is the best course of action?
L – List reasons explicitly: Why is this the best course of action?
S – Self correct: look at it again, what did we miss?

This problem solving technique guides students through the critical thinking process and utilizes learner collaboration. Similar strategies include integrating project based learning activities that require students to apply their knowledge by constructing a real world product. As a final guide to students' practice, use peer assessments to facilitate students' critical thinking and meta cognitive skills (Hou et al., 2007).

BARRIERS TO CRITICAL THINKING

Several researchers (Landsman and Gorski, 2007; Sandholtz et al., 2004; Sheldon and Biddle, 1998; Wong, 2007) suggest that the current educational trend to standardize curricula and focus on test scores undermines instructors' ability to address critical thinking in the classroom. The emphasis on "teaching to the test" distracts the learning process from student centered instruction and places the emphasis on the content. If the focus is on learning, students should be given the freedom (and responsibility) to explore content, analyze resources, and apply information.

Unfortunately, students are not typically taught to think or learn independently, and they rarely pick up these skills on their own (Ladsman and Gorski, 2007; Lundquist, 1999; Rippen et al., 2002). Critical thinking is not an innate ability. Although some students may be naturally inquisitive, they require training to become systematically analytical, fair and open-minded in their pursuit of knowledge. With these skills, students can become confident in their reasoning and apply their critical thinking ability to any content area or discipline (Lundquist, 1999). Critical thinking is often compared to the scientific method, it is a systematic and procedural approach to the process of thinking (Scriven and Paul, 2007). Just as students learn the process of the scientific method, they must also learn the process of critical thinking.

Four barriers often impede the integration of critical thinking in education: (i) lack of training, (ii) lack of information, (iii) preconceptions and (iv) time constraints. First, teachers often are not trained in critical thinking methodology (Broadbear, 2003). Elementary and secondary teachers know their content and receive training in the methods of instruction, but little if any of their training is devoted specifically on how to teach critical thinking skills. Post secondary instructors pursue additional content based instruction during graduate school, but often have no formal methodological training, much less skill based instructions. Secondly, few instructional materials provide critical thinking resources (Scriven and Paul, 2007). Some textbooks provide chapter based critical thinking discussion questions, but instructional materials often lack additional critical thinking resources. Thirdly, both teachers and students have preconceptions about the content that blocks their ability to think critically about the material. Preconceptions such as personal bias partiality prohibit critical thinking because they obviate analytical skills such as being fair, open minded and inquisitive about a topic (Kang and Howren, 2004). For example, many mathematics educators still continue using two spaces after ending punctuation even though typeface experts have documented that today's proportional fonts are designed for one space (American Psychological Association, 2001: Chicago Manual of Style Online, 2007). A critical analysis of the information provided on this typesetting topic would support the use of a single space. However, strong biases for two spaces preclude many mathematics teachers predominantly typing teachers from changing their opinion and adopting the acceptable procedure.

Finally, time constraints are barriers to integrating critical thinking skills in the classroom. Instructors often have a great deal of content to cover within a short time period. When the focus is on content rather than student learning, shortcuts such as lectures and objective tests become the norm. Lecturing is faster and easier than integrating project based learning opportunities. Objective tests are faster to take and grade than subjective assessments. However, research indicates that lecturing is not the best method of instruction and objective tests are not the best method of assessment (Broadbear, 2003; Brodie and Irving, 2007).

CONCLUSION

The goal for mathematics educators who want to instill critical thinking skills in their classrooms is to think of their students not as receivers of information, but as users of information. Learning environments that actively engage students in the investigation of information and the application of knowledge will promote students' critical thinking skills. However, as with any skill, critical thinking requires training, practice, and patience. Students may initially resist instructional questioning techniques if they previously have been required only to remember information and not think about what they know. They may struggle with assessment questions that are not taken verbatim from the book. However, by encouraging students throughout the process and modeling thinking behaviors, students' critical thinking skills can improve. The effort is worth the reward; students who can critically think for themselves and solve real world problems.

REFERENCES

American Psychological Association (2001). Publication manual of the American Psychological Association, 5th eds. Washington, DC: Am. Psychol. Assoc., pp. 290-291.

Astleitner H (2002). Teaching critical thinking online. J. Instr. Psychol., 29(2): 53-77.

Bartlett JE (2002). Analysis of motivational orientation and learning strategies of high school business students. Bus. Educ. Forum, 56(4): 18-23.

Broadbear JT (2003). Essential elements of lessons designed to promote critical thinking. J. Scholarsh. Teach. Learn., 3(3): 1-8.

Brodie P, Irving K (2007). Assessment in work based learning: Investigating a pedagogical approach to enhance student learning. Assess. Eval. High. Educ., 32(1): 11-19.

Brown MN, Kelley SM (1986). Asking the right questions: A guide to critical thinking, 7th ed. Englewood Cliffs, NJ: Prentice Hall.

Celuch K, Slama M (1999). Teaching critical thinking skills for the 21st century: An advertising principles case study. J. Educ. Bus., 74(3): 134.

Chicago Manual of Style Online (2007). Retrieved January 2, 2008, from http:// www.chicagomanualofstyle.org/home.html.

Clement J (1979). Introduction to research in cognitive process instruction. In Lochhead, J. and Clement, J. (Eds.), Cognitive process instruction. Hillsdale, NJ: Lawrence Erlbaum Associates.

Davis L, Riley M, Fisher DJ (2003). Business students' perceptions of necessary skills. Bus. Educ. Forum, 57(4): 18-21.

Daz-Lefebvre R (2004). Multiple intelligences, learning for understanding, and creative assessment: Some pieces to the puzzle of learning. Teachers Coll. Record, 106(l): 49-57.

Duplass JA, Ziedler DL (2002). Critical thinking and logical argument. Social Educ., 66(5): 10-14.

Ennis RH (1993). Critical thinking assessment. Theory Pract., 32(3): 179-186.

Facione PA (2007). Critical thinking: What it is and why it counts. Retrieved January 2, 2008, from http://www.telacommunications.com/nutshell/ cthinking7.htm.

Flavell JH (1979). Metacoguition and cognitive monitoring: A new area of cognitive-development inquiry. Am. Psychol., 34: 906-911.

Haynes T, Bailey G (2003). Are you and your basic business students asking the right questions? Bus. Educ. Forum, 57(3): 33-37.

Hemming HE (2000). Encouraging critical thinking: "But..what does that mean?" J. Educ., 35(2): 173.

Hou H, Chang K, Sung Y (2007). An analysis of peer assessment online discussions within a course that uses project based learning. Interact. Learn. Environ., 15(3): 237-251.

Kang N, Howren C (2004). Teaching for conceptual understanding. Sci. Child., 42(1): 28-32.

Ladyshewsky RK (2006). Peer coaching: A constructivist methodology for enhancing critical thinking in postgraduate business education. High. Educ. Res. Dev., 25(1): 67-84.

Landsman J, Gorski P (2007). Countering standardization. Educ. Leadersh., 64(8): 40-41.

Lundquist R (1999). Critical thinking and the art of making good mistakes. Teach. High. Educ., 4(4): 523-530.

MacKnight CB (2000). Teaching critical thinking through online discussions. Educause Quart., 23(4): 38-41.

Norman DA (Ed.) (1981). Perspectives on cognitive science. Hillsdale, NJ: Erlbaum.

Rippen A, Booth C, Bowie S, Jordan J (2002). A complex case: Using the case study method to explore uncertainty and ambiguity in undergraduate business education. Teach. High. Educ., 7(4): 429.

Sandholtz J, Ogawa RT, Scribner SP (2004). Standards gaps: Unintended consequences of local standards-based reform. Teachers Coll. Record, 106(6): 1177-1202.

Schafersman SD (1991). An introduction to critical thinking. Retrieved January 2, 2008, from http://www.freeinquiryconVcritical-thinking.html.

Scriven M, Paul R (2007). Defining critical thinking. The Critical Thinking Community: Foundation for Critical Thinking. Retrieved January 2, 2008, from http://www.criticalddnking.org/aboutCT/define_criticat_thinking.cfm.

Shakirova DM (2007). Technology for the shaping of college students' and upper-grade students' critical thinking. Russ. Educ. Soc., 49(9): 42-52.

Sheldon KM, Biddle BJ (1998). Standards, accountability, and school reform: Perils and pitfalls. Teachers Coll. Record, 100(1): 164-180.

Tempelaar DT (2006). The role of metacognition in business education. Ind. High. Educ., 20(5): 291-297.

Wong D (2007). Beyond control and rationality: Dewey, aesthetics, motivation, and educative experiences. Teachers Coll. Record, 109(1): 192-220.

14

Comparison of simulated annealing and hill climbing in the course timetabling problem

Kenekayoro Patrick

Department of Mathematics and Computer Science, Niger Delta University, Wilberforce Island, P. M. B. 071, Amassoma, Bayelsa State, Nigeria. E-mail: patrick.kenekayoro@outlook.com.

Course timetabling is a task that must be performed by all higher institutions. It is very difficult doing this manually and even classified as nondeterministic polynomial (NP) complete in five independent ways. Several methods (heuristics) are used to solve this problem including local search optimization methods like simulated annealing and hill climbing. This paper compares these methods used to solve the university course timetabling problem.

Key words: Hill climbing, simulated annealing, course timetabling, local search optimization.

INTRODUCTION

Designing any type of schedule manually is an arduous task, an example is the university course timetables among others like duty rosters, job shops etcetera. Doing this automatically has proven to be difficult as well. It is classified as a nondeterministic polynomial (NP) hard problem (Even et al., 1976), and proven to be NP complete in five independent ways (Cooper and Kingston, 1995). In NP complete problems, as the size of input increases linearly, the time it takes to find a solution increases exponentially. It is difficult to find a solution to these types of problems in worst case, and a popular way to solve these problems is with heuristics. Course timetabling falls within this group of problems. Course timetabling involves assigning events to time slots and venues while meeting several constraints; constraints could either be hard or soft. A feasible timetable is reached when all hard constraints are met, while a good timetable meets all the hard constraints as well as most of the soft constraints.

Several ways to solve this timetabling problem have been published; some of these methods involve the use of local search optimization techniques like the simulated annealing and hill climbing. Hill climbing and annealing have different variants, depending on the way successive nodes are chosen. This paper compares these methods when used to solve a university course timetabling problem. Subsequent sections describe the course timetabling problem, current techniques used to solve it, with emphasis on simulated annealing and hill climbing, and then results gotten when compared are shown.

COURSE TIMETABLING PROBLEM (CTP)

"Timetabling is the allocation, subject to constraints, of given resources to objects being placed in space time, in such a way as to satisfy as nearly as possible a set of desirable objectives" (Wren, 1996). A university course timetable is a function of students, rooms, lecturers, events and time slots. The constraints used to compare results are same as published by Dawood et al. (2011) that a student cannot attend more than one event simultaneously.

The room size must be able to contain all students. At any given time slot, only one event can take place in a room. The timetable to be generated is similar to the ones used in Nigerian universities. It has 5 events a day, hence 25 time slots. The problem instance is similar to the problem in the School of Mathematics and Computer Science, Niger Delta University with 10 groups of students taking 70 courses in 6 available rooms.

CTP SOLVING TECHNIQUES

One of the earliest methods to solve timetabling problems was with graph coloring. A graph consists of a set of vertices and edges. Two vertices are said to be adjacent if they are connected by an edge. Solving the CTP with graph coloring involves assigning colors to vertices where all adjacent vertices are assigned different colors. Each vertices is a course and all vertices adjacent to it are courses that should not be placed in the same time slot. The CTP problem has been solved by Burke et al. (1995) and Kenekayoro (2011). Although they solved the examination timetabling problem (ETP), which is similar to the CTP, in the ETP, students may be in different rooms but in CTP all students must be in the same room. Other methods are local search optimization methods like hill climbing; where an initial solution is chosen randomly and then gradually improved. Hill climbing has a tendency to get stuck in a local maxima but with exception of known methods like stochastic hill climbing, a variation of hill climbing as well as simulated annealing improving result significantly (Bertsimas and Tsitsiklis, 1993), Tabu Search (Alvarez-Valdes et al., 2002). Other methods are ants colony optimization (Mayer et al., 2007) and others based on the theory of natural selection; genetic algorithms (Yu and Sung, 2002), evolutionary approach (Dawood et al., 2011) and (Datta et al., 2007), fuzzy genetic heuristics (Chaudhuri and De, 2010).

In genetic algorithms, a group initial solutions are generated randomly or using a local search method. The group is called a population and each solution in the population is a chromosome. New chromosomes (offspring) are generated by mutation (modifying a chromosome in a generation) or crossover (merging chromosomes in a generation). A fitness function evaluates each chromosome, and a new generation is formed by some of the parents and offspring based on the fitness functions. A relative new approach is hyper heuristics. Meta heuristic approaches like the ones mentioned earlier are problem specific too, a slight change in the problem domain causes massive change in the results. The aim of hyper heuristic is to be able to get a solution that may not be as good as the best meta heuristic approach but it is good enough and also generic. Hyper heuristic in a broad sense is using a meta-heuristic technique to select other lower level heuristics to solve a problem. Hyper heuristic could have top level meta-heuristic as simulated annealing (Bai et al., 2006), Tabu Search (Burke et al., 2003), case based reasoning (Burke et al., 2006). These techniques do not perform as good as the best heuristic approach in a specific problem domain but across several domains they outperform meta-heuristic approaches.

HILL CLIMBING AND SIMULATED ANNEALING

Hill climbing gradually improves a solution recursively by selecting the best neighbor based on an evaluation function recursively, until there is not a neighbor better than the current. If there is more than one best successor, a random from the set of best successors is selected.

Popular variants of hill climbing are: (i) First choice: the first successor better than the current is selected and (ii) Stochastic: any random uphill move is selected. The successor is not necessarily the best neighbor. Hill climbing is incomplete because it usually gets stuck in a *local maxima*; a state that is not the optimal but no neighbor is better than the current, *ridges*; a state where neighbors are series of local maxima, *plateau or flat top*; a state where all successors are equal. To escape from a local maxima random restart hill climbing is a good choice. In this case, the hill climbing algorithm is run several times with a randomly selected initial state. The random restart hill climbing algorithm is proven to be quite efficient, it solves the N queen problem almost instantly even for very large number of queens.

Hill climbing always gets stuck in a local maxima because downward moves are not allowed. Simulated annealing is technique that allows downward steps in order to escape from a local maxima. Annealing emulates the concept in metallurgy; where metals are heated to very high temperature and then gradually cooled so its structure is frozen at a minimum energy configuration. Applying this to the hill climbing optimization method, the probability of allowing a downward move is high (at very high temperatures) and this probability is gradually reduced with time (as it cools). The idea behind annealing is that, at high temperatures the algorithm should jump out of a local maxima.

CTP SOLUTION

For the CTP problem as earlier specified, a penalty of 1 (one) was given for a violation of each of the constraints in the final schedule. For each iteration, 25 neighbors were generated by moving a course in time_slot[i] to time_slot[i+1]. In the last time slot, 25; the neighbor is time slot 1. In the initial state, a random time slot and room that can contain students is assigned to a course.

Simulated annealing (random) where the successor is a randomly selected neighbor of the current as suggested by Russel and Norvig (2003) performed poorly in this case. It rarely outperformed the initial state. On the other hand, simulated annealing (best) where the successor is the best neighbor produced good results. At over 50 iterations, simulated annealing (best) performs better than hill climbing, although there were a few instances when hill climbing performed better (Figure 1).

Random restart hill climbing always performs better than the regular hill climbing, which is no surprise as random restart is the best out of successive regular hill climbing's. Random restart also outperforms simulated annealing because with random restart, a larger space is searched. It is worth noting that the best result was achieved with simulated annealing.

Although, no solution with penalty = 0 was reached, simulated annealing (best) got a penalty of less than 6 in 5 instances and a penalty = 1 (one) in an instance. Random restart always had a penalty less than 10. The best solution from random restart and regular hill climbing

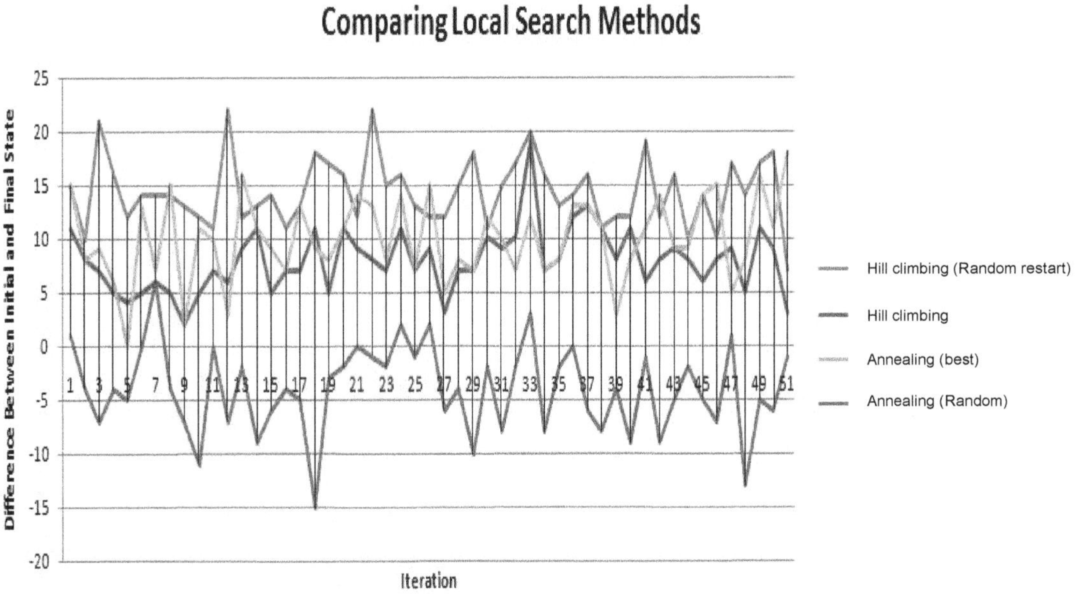

Figure 1. A comparison of hill climbing and simulated annealing for 50 iterations.

was penalty = 4.

When a solution with such low penalty is reached, a simple repair method that removes a course in a time slot that causes a collision and places it in a new time slot that does not increase the penalty produces a feasible solution. The solutions were reached almost instantly for regular hill climbing and simulated annealing with random restart hill climbing taking longer time to run.

CONCLUSION

Using simulated annealing or hill climbing is a good choice because of its ease of implementation. A solution was reached by generating only 25 neighbors. Alternative methods should be used only when simulated annealing or hill climbing is not good enough. Other methods like the genetic algorithm and hyper heuristics techniques still use these method at some point in their algorithm; either to generate the initial population or as a higher level heuristic.

The poor performance of simulated annealing (random) shows how problem specific meta-heuristic techniques are. It highlights importance of the new direction in operational research; hyper heuristics – *one size fits all* as opposed to meta-heuristics – *tailor made*. Tests were run on Windows Vista 32 Bit Operating system, MinGW c++ compiler.

REFERENCES

Alvarez-Valdes R, Crespo E, Tamarit J (2002). Design And Implementation of A Course Scheduling System Using Tabu Search. Eur. J. Oper. Res. 137:512-523.

Bai R, Burke E, Kendall G, McCollum G (2006). A Simulated Annealing Hyper-heuristic for Univ. Course Timetabling Problem. Nottingham Pract. Theory Autom. Timetabling pp. 345-350.

Bertsimas D, Tsitsiklis J (1993). Simulated Annealing. J. Stat. Sci. 8(1):10-15.

Burke EK, Petrovic S, Qu R (2006). Case-Based Heuristic Selection for Timetabling Problems. J. Scheduling 9(2):115-132.

Burke E, Elliman DG, Weare RF (1995). The Automation of the Timetabling Process in Higher Education. J. Educ. Technol. Syst. 23(4):257-266.

Burke E, Kendall G, Soubiega E (2003). A Tabu-Search Hyperheuristic for Timetabling and Rostering. J. Heuristics pp. 451-470.

Chaudhuri A, De K (2010). Fuzzy Genetic Heuristic for University Course Timetable Problem. Int. J. Adv. Soft Comput. Appl. 2(1):100-123.

Cooper TB, Kingston JH (1995). The complexity of timetable construction problems. Proceedings of PATAT. Springer-Verlag. pp. 283-295.

Datta D, Deb K, Fonseca CM (2007). Multi-objective evolutionary algorithm for Univ. Class Timetabling Problem. In Dahal, K. P., Tan, K. C., and Cowling, P. I. (eds.), Evolutionary Scheduling, Springer. pp. 197-236.

Dawood A, Awad Y, Badr A (2011). An Evolutionary Immune Approach for University Course Timetabling. Int. J. Comput. Sci. Netw. Secur. 11(2):127-136.

Even S, Itai A, Shamir A (1976). Complexity of Timetable and Multicommodity Flow Problems. SIAM J. Comput. 5(4):691-703.

Kenekayoro PT (2011). Automation of Examination Timetabling using Graph Coloring. West Afr. J. Sci. Technol. Soc. Sci. 1(1):53-56.

Mayer A, Nothegger C, Chwatal A, Raidl GR (2007). Solving the Post Enrolment Course Timetabling Problem by Ant Colony Optimization. Austria.

Russel SJ, Norvig P (2003). Local Search Algorithms and Optimization Methods. In Artificial Intelligence, A Modern Approach (2nd Edition) Prentice Hall, pp. 110-119.

Wren A (1996). Scheduling, timetabling and rostering - a special relationship? (E. Burke, and P. Ross, Eds.) Practice and Theory of Automated Timetabling, volume LNCS 1153 of Lecture Notes in Comput. Sci. pp. 46-75.

Yu E, Sung KS (2002). A genetic algorithm for a university's weekly courses timetabling problem. Int. Trans. Oper. Res. pp. 703-717.

Cross efficiency by using common weights for fuzzy data

Sahand Daneshvar[1], Mojtaba Ramezani[2]*, Mozhgan Mansouri Kaleibar[1] and Sharmin Rahmatfam[3]

[1]Islamic Azad University, Tabriz Branch, Tabriz, Iran.
[2]Islamic Azad University, Bonab Branch, Bonab, Iran.
[3]Islamic Azad University, Tehran Central Branch, Tehran, Iran.

This paper firstly revists the cross efficiency evaluation method which is an extention tool of data envelopment analysis (DEA), then analyzes the potential flawes which happens when the ultimate average cross efficiency scores are used. In this paper, we consider the decision making units (DMUs) as the players in a cooperative fuzzy game, where the characteristic function values of coalitions are defined to compute the Shapley value of each DMU with fuzzy data, and the common weights associate with the imputation of the Shapley values are used to determine the ultimate cross efficiency scores. In this paper cross efficiency defined with fuzzy data for solving fuzzy parameters problems.

Key words: Cross efficiency, cooperative game, common weights, data envelopment analysis (DEA), fuzzy game, fuzzy linear programming, Shapley value.

INTRODUCTION

As a non-parametric programming efficiency-rating technique for a set of decision making units (DMUs) with multiple inputs and multiple outputs, data envelopment analysis (DEA) (Cooper et al., 2000) is receiving more and more importance for evaluating and improving the performance of manufacturing and service operations. It has been extensively applied in performance evaluation and benchmarking of schools, hospitals, bank branches, production plants, etc (Charnes et al., 1994). However, traditional DEA models are not very appropriate for ranking DMUs since they simply classify the units into two groups: efficient and inefficient (Charnes et al., 1978). Moreover, it is often possible in DEA that some inefficient DMUs are in fact better overall performers than some efficient ones. This is because of the unrestricted weight flexibility problem in DEA by being involved in an unreasonable self-rated scheme (Dyson and Thannassoulis, 1988). The DMU under evaluation heavily weighs few favorable measures and completely ignores other inputs and outputs in order to maximize its own DEA efficiency. In the fuzzy game, each DMU will be a player, the characteristic function value of each coalition is defined, and the solution of Shapley value is computed to determine the ultimate cross efficiency of each DMU by Despotis (2002). However, there are still several limitations for utilizing the average cross efficiency measure to evaluation, like the losing association with the weights by averaging among the cross efficiencies. In most real-world situations, the possible values of parameters of mathematical models are often only imprecisely or ambiguously known to the experts. It would be certainly more appropriate to interpret the experts understanding of the parameters as fuzzy numerical data which can be represented by means of fuzzy sets of the real line known as fuzzy numbers. In this study, we deal with problems with fuzzy parameters from the viewpoint of experts imprecise of the nature of

*Corresponding author. E-mail: Mojtaba.Ramezani.53@gmail.com.

parameters in a problem- formulation process. The fuzzy parameters issue can thus be solved in this paper.

CROSS EFFICIENCY EVALUATION

Adopting the conventional nomenclature of DEA, assume that there are n DMUs that are to be evaluated in terms of m inputs and s outputs of triangular fuzzy number. We denote the ith input and rth output for $DMU_j (j = 1,2,...,n)$ as $\tilde{x}_{ij} (i = 1,2,...,m)$ and $\tilde{y}_{rd} (r = 1,2,...,s)$, respectively. The efficiency rating for any given DMU_d, can be computed using the following CCR model in the form of fuzzy linear programming:

$$Max \sum_{r=1}^{s} \mu_r \tilde{y}_{rd} = \theta_d$$
$$\text{s.t.} \sum_{i=1}^{m} w_i \tilde{x}_{ij} - \sum_{r=1}^{s} \mu_r \tilde{y}_{rj} \geq 0, j = 1,2,...,n, \sum_{i=1}^{m} w_i \tilde{x}_{id} = 1$$
$$w_i \geq 0, i = 1,2,...,m, \mu_r \geq 0, r = 1,2,...,s \quad (1)$$

Where $\tilde{x}_{ij}, \tilde{y}_{rd}$ are triangular fuzzy numbers, in this paper, we employ a parametric approach to solving the linear programming problem with fuzzy parameters in order to construct the values of coalitions Sakawa (1993). First we introduce the α-level of the fuzzy numbers $\tilde{x}_{ij}, \tilde{y}_{rd}$ defined as the set $(\tilde{x}_{ij})_\alpha, (\tilde{y}_{rd})_\alpha$ in which the degree of their membership functions exceeds the level α:

$$(\tilde{x}_{ij})_\alpha = \{(x_{ij})\ \mu_{\tilde{x}_{ij}}(x_{ij}) \geq \alpha,\ k = 1,...,n\ ,i = 1,...,m\}$$
$$(\tilde{y}_{rd})_\alpha = \{(y_{rd})\ \mu_{\tilde{y}_{rd}}(y_{rd}) \geq \alpha,\ k = 1,...,n\ ,i = 1,...,m\} \quad (2)$$

Now suppose that all players consider that the degree of all the membership functions of the fuzzy number involved in the linear programming problem should be greater than or equal to a certain degree α. Then, for such a degree α, the problem can be interpreted as the following non fuzzy linear programming problem which depends on a coefficient vector $(x_{ij}) \in (\tilde{x}_{ij})_\alpha, (y_{rd}) \in (\tilde{y}_{rd})_\alpha$ Sakawa (1993).

$$Max \sum_{r=1}^{s} \mu_r y_{rd} = \theta_d$$
$$\text{s.t.} \sum_{i=1}^{m} w_i x_{ij} - \sum_{r=1}^{s} \mu_r y_{rj} \geq 0, j = 1,2,...,n, \sum_{i=1}^{m} w_i x_{id} = 1$$
$$w_i \geq 0, i = 1,2,...,m, \mu_r \geq 0, r = 1,2,...,s \quad (3)$$

Observe that there exists an infinite number of such a problem (3) depending on the coefficient vector $(x_{ij}) \in (\tilde{x}_{ij})_\alpha, (y_{rd}) \in (\tilde{y}_{rd})_\alpha$ and the values of $(x_{ij}), (y_{rd})$ are arbitrary for any $(x_{ij}) \in (\tilde{x}_{ij})_\alpha, (y_{rd}) \in (\tilde{y}_{rd})_\alpha$ in the sense that the degree of all the membership functions for the fuzzy number in the problem (3) exceeds the level α. However, if the players think that the problem should be solved by taking an optimistic view, the coefficient vector $(x_{ij}) \in (\tilde{x}_{ij})_\alpha, (y_{rd}) \in (\tilde{y}_{rd})_\alpha$ in the problem (4) would be chosen so as to maximize the objective functions under the constraints. From such a point of view, for a certain degree α, it seems to be quite natural to have understood the linear programming problem with fuzzy parameters as the following non fuzzy α-linear programming problem:

$$Max \sum_{r=1}^{s} \mu_r y_{rd} = \theta_d$$
$$\text{s.t.} \sum_{i=1}^{m} w_i x_{ij} - \sum_{r=1}^{s} \mu_r y_{rj} \geq 0, j = 1,2,...,n, \sum_{i=1}^{m} w_i x_{id} = 1$$
$$w_i \geq 0, i = 1,2,...,m, \mu_r \geq 0, r = 1,2,...,s$$
$$(x_{ij}) \in (\tilde{x}_{ij})_\alpha, (y_{rd}) \in (\tilde{y}_{rd})_\alpha \quad (4)$$

It should be noted that the coefficient vectors $(x_{ij}), (y_{rd})$ are treated as decision variables rather than constants. Therefore, the problem (4) is not a linear programming problem. However, from the properties of the α-level set for the vectors of fuzzy number $\tilde{x}$ and $\tilde{y}$ it follows that the feasible regions for $\tilde{x}$ and $\tilde{y}$ can be denoted respectively by the closed intervals $[x^L, x^R], [y^L, y^R]$. Thus, we can obtain an optimal solution to the problem (4) by solving the following linear programming problem by Sakawa (1993).

$$Max \sum_{r=1}^{s} \mu_r y_{rd}^R = \theta_d$$
$$\text{s.t.} \sum_{i=1}^{m} w_i x_{ij}^R - \sum_{r=1}^{s} \mu_r y_{rj}^R \geq 0, j = 1,2,...,n, \sum_{i=1}^{m} w_i x_{id}^R = 1$$
$$w_i \geq 0, i = 1,2,...,m, \mu_r \geq 0, r = 1,2,...,s \quad (5)$$

Conversely the players may think that the problem should be solved by taking a pessimistic view. Then taking opposite extreme points of the closed intervals $[x^L, x^R], [y^L, y^R]$, we can formulate the following problem which yields a value of the objective function smaller than that the problem (5):

$$Max \sum_{r=1}^{s} \mu_r y_{rd}^L = \theta_d$$
$$\text{s.t.} \sum_{i=1}^{m} w_i x_{ij}^L - \sum_{r=1}^{s} \mu_r y_{rj}^L \geq 0, j = 1,2,...,n, \sum_{i=1}^{m} w_i x_{id}^L = 1$$
$$w_i \geq 0, i = 1,2,...,m, \mu_r \geq 0, r = 1,2,...,s \quad (6)$$

We obtain a set of optimal weights $w_{1d}^*, ..., w_{md}^*, \mu_{1d}^*, ..., \mu_{sd}^*$. Then the cross efficiency of any DMU_j $(j = 1,2,...,n)$ for fuzzy data, using the weights that DMU_d has chosen in

Table 1. A generalized cross efficiency matrix (CEM) for first and end of interval.

Rating DMU	Rated DMU			
	1	2	...	n
1	$E_{11}^L\ E_{11}^R$	$E_{12}^L\ E_{12}^R$	...	$E_{1n}^L\ E_{1n}^R$
2	$E_{21}^L\ E_{21}^R$	$E_{22}^L\ E_{22}^R$	...	$E_{2n}^L\ E_{2n}^R$
3	$E_{31}^L\ E_{31}^R$	$E_{32}^L\ E_{32}^R$	...	$E_{3n}^L\ E_{3n}^R$
...	... ...	... ...	...	...
n	$E_{n1}^L\ E_{n1}^R$	$E_{n2}^L\ E_{n2}^R$	...	$E_{nn}^L\ E_{nn}^R$
Mean	$\bar{E}_1^L\ \bar{E}_1^R$	$\bar{E}_2^L\ \bar{E}_2^R$	...	$\bar{E}_n^L\ \bar{E}_n^R$

models (5) and (6) can be calculated as:

$$E_{dj}^L = \sum_{r=1}^{s} \mu_{rd}^* y_{rj}^L / \sum_{i=1}^{m} w_{id}^* x_{ij}^L, \; j = 1, 2, \ldots, n$$

$$E_{dj}^R = \sum_{r=1}^{s} \mu_{rd}^* y_{rj}^R / \sum_{i=1}^{m} w_{id}^* x_{ij}^R, \; j = 1, 2, \ldots, n \tag{7}$$

For DMU the average of all $E_{dj}^L, E_{dj}^R \ (d = 1, \ldots, n)$, namely $\bar{E}_j = 1/n \sum_{d=1}^{n} E_{dj}$ with same weights can be used as a new efficiency measure for DMU_j and will be referred to as the cross efficiency score for DMU_j.

As seen in Table 1, when we move along the *d*th row of the matrix E of cross efficiencies, each element E_{dj} is the efficiency that DMU_d accords to DMU_j, given the computed weighting scheme described above. The leading diagonal is the special case where DMU_d rates itself. Each of the columns of the cross efficiency matrix (CEM) in Table 1 is then averaged to get a mean cross efficiency measure for each DMU. In fuzzy environment for $DMU_j \ (j = 1, 2, \ldots, n)$, the average of all $E_{dj} (d = 1, \ldots, n)$, namely $\overline{E_j^L} = \frac{1}{n} \sum_{d=1}^{n} E_{dj}^L$ and $\overline{E_j^R} = \frac{1}{n} \sum_{d=1}^{n} E_{dj}^R$ can be used as a new efficiency measure for DMU_j, and will be referred to as the cross efficiency score for DMU_j (Table 1).

DETERMINATION OF ULTIMATE CROSS EFFICIENCY USING FUZZY DEA GAME MODEL

Here, we will use the fuzzy DEA game model and Shapley value in, for determine the ultimate cross efficiency of each DMU.

Definition of DEA game

As defined in Table 1, matrix $E^L = (E_{dj}^L) \in R_+^{n \times n}$ and $E^R = (E_{dj}^R) \in R_+^{n \times n}$ are the cross efficiency matrix (CEM), and the elements of E_{dj}^L, E_{dj}^R represents the efficiency that DMU_d accords to DMU_j. Analogously to the models in, we normalize the data set E^L, so that it is row-wise normalized,that is $\sum_{p=1}^{n} E_{dp}^L = 1, \ \sum_{p=1}^{n} E_{dp}^R = 1$. For this purpose, we divide the row $(E_{d1}^L, \ldots E_{dn}^L)$ by the row-sum $\sum_{p=1}^{n} E_{dp}^L$ for $d = 1, \ldots, n$, and denote the *d*th row after row-wise normalizing as $(E'^L_{d1}, \ldots E'^L_{dn})$. Similarly we can normalize data set E^R. After using Charnes-Cooper transformation scheme, the linear program to select the most preferable weights for each DMU can be expressed as follows:

$$c^L(j) = \operatorname{Max} \sum_{d=1}^{n} w_d^j E'^L_{dj}$$
$$s.t. \ \sum_{d=1}^{n} w_d^j = 1$$
$$w_d^j \geq 0 (\forall d) \tag{8}$$

$$c^{L}(j)=Max\sum_{d=1}^{n}w_{d}^{j}E'^{R}_{dj}$$
$$st.\ \sum_{d=1}^{n}w_{d}^{j}=1$$
$$w_{d}^{j}\geq 0(\forall d) \qquad (9)$$

Let the coalition S be a subset of player set N=(1,…,n). The record of the coalition S is defined by

$$E'^{L}_{d}(S)=\sum_{j\in s}E'^{L}_{dj},\quad d=1,...,n.$$
$$E'^{R}_{d}(S)=\sum_{j\in s}E'^{R}_{dj},\quad d=1,...,n. \qquad (10)$$

This coalition aims at obtaining the maximal outcome $c(S)$:

$$c^{L}(S)=Max\sum_{d=1}^{n}w_{d}E'^{L}_{d}(S)$$
$$st.\ \sum_{d=1}^{n}w_{d}=1$$
$$w_{d}\geq 0(\forall d) \qquad (11)$$

$$c^{R}(S)=Max\sum_{d=1}^{n}w_{d}E'^{R}_{d}(S)$$
$$st.\ \sum_{d=1}^{n}w_{d}=1$$
$$w_{d}\geq 0(\forall d) \qquad (12)$$

The $c(S)$, with $c(\varphi)=0$ defines a characteristic function of the coalition S. thus, we have a game in coalition form with transferable utility, as represented by (N,c). We can easily find that the characteristic function c is a sub-additive, so we consider the opposite side of the game (N,c), which is defined by replacing *max* in (11) and (12) by *min* as follows:

$$d^{L}(j)=Min\sum_{d=1}^{n}w_{d}^{j}E'^{L}_{dj}$$
$$st.\ \sum_{d=1}^{n}w_{d}^{j}=1,$$
$$w_{d}^{j}\geq 0(\forall d) \qquad (13)$$

$$d^{R}(j)=Min\sum_{d=1}^{n}w_{d}^{j}E'^{R}_{dj}$$
$$st.\ \sum_{d=1}^{n}w_{d}^{j}=1,$$
$$w_{d}^{j}\geq 0(\forall d) \qquad (14)$$

The optimal value $d(j)$ assures the minimum division that player j can expect from the game. Analogously to the game (N,c), for the coalition $S\subset N$ we define

$$d^{L}(S)=Min\sum_{d=1}^{n}w_{d}E'^{L}_{d}(S)$$
$$st.\ \sum_{d=1}^{n}w_{d}=1,$$
$$w_{d}\geq 0(\forall d) \qquad (15)$$

$$d^{R}(S)=Min\sum_{d=1}^{n}w_{d}E'^{R}_{d}(S)$$
$$st.\ \sum_{d=1}^{n}w_{d}=1,$$
$$w_{d}\geq 0(\forall d) \qquad (16)$$

Game (N,d) is super-additivethat is we have $d(S\cup T)\geq d(S)+d(T)$ for any $S\subset N$ and $T\subset N$ with $S\cap T=\phi$.

From the description in 'Nakabayashi and Tone (2006)' we have the following proposition between the games (N,c) and (N,d): $d(S)+c(N\setminus S)=1,\ \forall S\subsetneqq N$, so ($N$,$c$) and ($N$,$d$) are dual games.

Shapley value of the DEA game

For DEA game (N,d) above, its imputation is a vector $z=(z_{1},...,z_{n})$ that satisfies the following individuals and grand coalition rationalities:

Individuals rationality: $z_{j}\geq d(j), j=1,...,n$

Grand coalition rationality: $\sum_{j=1}^{n}z_{j}=d(N)=1$

In this paper, we consider the Shapley value as the representative imputations of the cooperative game above. The Shapley value $\phi_{i}(d)$ of player I for the game (N,d) is defined by (Liang and Ynag 2009):

$$\phi_{i}(d)=\sum_{S\setminus i\in S\subset N}\frac{(s-1)!(n-s)!}{n!}\{d(S)-d(S\setminus\{i\})\}, \qquad (17)$$

Where s is the number of members of coalition S. From the introduction above, we can get the conclusion that the games (N,c) and (N,d) are dual games, so they have the same Shapley value.

Table 2. Five DMUs, with two inputs x_1,x_2 and one output y_1 in fuzzy environment.

Variable	X_1	X_2	Y_1
DMU1	(5,7,9)	(4.7,5,5.1)	(5.2,5.4,5.7)
DMU2	(2,5,7)	(6.9,7.2,7.3)	(6.3,6.5,6.8)
DMU3	(2,3,6)	(7.8,8,8.4)	(7.5,7.9,8)
DMU4	(3,5,6)	(10.8,11,11.3)	(4.7,5,5.2)
DMU5	(4,6,7)	(8.7,8.8,9)	(9.9,10,10.2)

Table 3. Values of first input.

Variable	$\alpha=1$	$\alpha=0.5$	$\alpha=0$
DMU1	[7,7]	[6,8.5]	[5,10]
DMU2	[5,5]	[3.5,6]	[2,7]
DMU3	[3,3]	[2.5,4.5]	[2,6]
DMU4	[3,3]	[4,4.5]	[3,6]
DMU5	[5,5]	[4.5,6]	[4,7]

Determination of common weights

Now we return to the subject incorporating our knowledge of imputation $z=(z_1,...,z_n)$ induced by coalitions and allocations of the Shapley value in fuzzy environment. The weight $w=(w_1,...,w_n)\in R^n$ associates with the imputation $z=(z_1,...,z_n)\in R^n$ through $wE'\in R^n$. In an effort to determine w in away that wE'^L, wE'^R approximates z as close as possible, we formulate the following LP with variables

$w\in R^n,\ s^+\in R^n,\ s^-\in R^n,\ p\in R$

$$\begin{aligned}
&\text{Min}\, p\\
&\text{s.t. } wE_j'^L+s_j^+-s_j^-=z_j, j=1,2,...,n\\
&\quad w_1+w_2+w_3+..w_m=1,\\
&\quad 0\le s_j^+\le p,\ 0\le s_j^-\le p, j=1,2,...,n,\\
&\quad w_i\ge 0, i=1,2,...,m
\end{aligned} \tag{18}$$

$$\begin{aligned}
&\text{Min}\, p\\
&\text{s.t. } wE_j'^R+s_j^+-s_j^-=z_j, j=1,2,...,n\\
&\quad w_1+w_2+w_3+..w_m=1,\\
&\quad 0\le s_j^+\le p,\ 0\le s_j^-\le p, j=1,2,...,n,\\
&\quad w_i\ge 0, i=1,2,...,m
\end{aligned} \tag{19}$$

Where $E_j'^L$, $E_j'^R$ denotes the *j*th column vector of E'^L and E'^R respectively. Let an optimal solution of this program be (p^*,w^*,s^{+*},s^{-*}). Then we have two cases:

Case 1: $p^*=0$. In this case, it holds that $z=w^*E'^L$, $z=w^*E'^R$, and so the imputation z is explained by the common weight w^*.

All players will accept the solution since it represents the common value judgment corresponding to the cooperative game solution.

Case 2: $p^*>0$. In this case, we have no common weight w^* which can express z as $z=w^*E'^L$, $z=w^*E'^R$ perfectly, while the optimal weight vector w^* can approximate the solution of the game within the tolerance p^*.

The common weights, that is the optimal value of *w* in model (18) and (19), can be used to determine the ultimate cross efficiency of each DMU is expressed as follows:

$$\begin{aligned}
E_j^{(L)cross}&=\sum_{d=1}^{n} w_d^* E_{dj}^L, j=1,...n\\
E_j^{(R)cross}&=\sum_{d=1}^{n} w_d^* E_{dj}^R, j=1,...n
\end{aligned} \tag{20}$$

NUMERICAL EXAMPLE

To illustrate the proposed approach above, we consider a simple numerical example given in Table 2 involving five DMUs, with two inputs x_1,x_2 and one output y_1 in fuzzy environment. Suppose that the parameters are characterized by triangular fuzzy numbers as shown in Table 2. By varying parameter α from 0.0 to 1.0 at intervals of 0.5, we construct the fuzzy values of row normalizing and cross efficiency for first and end of intervals (Tables 4 and 5). Cross efficiency values calculated in Tables 6, 7 and 8 for three different parameter by using the introduced model. Comparing the cross efficiency values in three interval shows DMU5 with $\alpha=0.5$ having better efficient value.

Table 4. Values of second input.

Variable	$\alpha=1$	$\alpha=0.5$	$\alpha=0$
DMU1	[5,5]	[4.85,5.05]	[4.7,5.1]
DMU2	[7.2,7.2]	[7.05,7.25]	[2,7]
DMU3	[8,8]	[7.9,8.2]	[7.8,8.4]
DMU4	[11,11]	[10.9,11.15]	[10.8,11.3]
DMU5	[8.8,8.8]	[8.75,8.9]	[8.7,9]

Table 5. Values of output.

Variable	$\alpha=1$	$\alpha=0.5$	$\alpha=0$
DMU1	[5.4,5.4]	[5.3,5.55]	[5.2,5.7]
DMU2	[6.5,6.5]	[6.4,6.665]	[6.3,6.8]
DMU3	[7.9,7.9]	[7.7,7.95]	[7.5,8]
DMU4	[5,5]	[4.85,5.1]	[4.7,5.2]
DMU5	[10,10]	[9.95,10.1]	[9.9,10.2]

Table 6. Cross efficiency in parameter $\alpha=1$.

E	DMU1	DMU2	DMU3	DMU4	DMU5
DMU1	0.9504, 0.9504	0.7916, 0.7916	0.869, 0.869	0.4, 0.4	1, 1
DMU2	0.0703, 0.0703	0.7943, 0.7943	0.8688, 0.8688	0.3999, 0.3999	1, 1
DMU3	0.6079, 0.6070	0.7322, 0.7322	1, 1	0.5004, 0.5004	1, 1
DMU4	0.3300, 0.3300	0.4938, 0.4938	0.5000, 0.5000	0.3165, 0.3165	0.7597, 0.7597
DMU5	0.9474, 0.9474	0.7948, 0.7948	0.8693, 0.8693	0.4001, 0.4001	1, 1

Table 7. Cross efficiency in parameter $\alpha=0.5$.

E	DMU1	DMU2	DMU3	DMU4	DMU5
DMU1	0.9605, 0.7965	0.7982,0.1000	0.8681,0.7026	0.3912,0.3315	1, 0.8225
DMU2	0.6038,0.4193	0.8076,0.7644	1,1	0.4337,0.7280	1,1
DMU3	0.6037,0.4193	0.8076,0.7644	1,1	0.4337,0.7279	1,1
DMU4	0.6044,0.4193	0.7959,0.7644	0.9676,1	0.4203,0.7279	1,1
DMU5	0.9610,0.4191	0.7982,0.7640	0.8681,1	0.3912,0.7274	1,1

Table 8. Cross efficiency in parameter $\alpha=0.5$.

E	DMU1	DMU2	DMU3	DMU4	DMU5
DMU1	0.3509,0.8099	0.9992,0.7039	0.3050,0.5003	0.1381, 0.3334	0.3609, 0.9356
DMU2	0.3314,0.8095	1, 0.7036	1, 0.5001	0.4284, 0.3333	0.5284, 0.9352
DMU3	0.3314,0.3659	1, 0.6232	0.9334,0.6205	0.4275, 0.2954	0.7324, 0.6119
DMU4	0.3315,0.3659	1, 0.6232	1, 0.6205	0.4249, 0.2954	0.7296, 0.6119
DMU5	0.3317,0.9703	1, 0.6002	1, 0.4484	0.4253, 0.6538	0.7300, 0.5226

CONCLUSIONS

In this paper, we have studied the ultimate average cross efficiency scores in fuzzy environment. We eliminate the assumption of average and consider the DMUs as the players in a cooperative game, the characteristic function value of coalitions are defined to compute the Shapley value of each DMU, and the common weights associate with the imputation of the Shapley values are used to determine the ultimate cross efficiency scores. Regarding this subject, we have proposed a method for compute cross efficiency for fuzzy data, and transform fuzzy programs to non fuzzy for solving fuzzy numbers problem by α -level set of the fuzzy numbers.

REFERENCES

Charnes A, Cooper WW, Levin AY, Seaford LM (1994). "Data envelopment analysis: Theory, methodology and applications," Boston: Kluwer.

Charnes A, Cooper WW, Rhodes E (1978). "Measuring the efficiency of decision Making units." Eur. J. Oper. Res., 2: 429-444.

Cooper WW, Seiford LM, Tone K (2000). "Data Envelopment Analysis." Boston: Klawer Academic publishers.

Despotis DK (2002). "Improving the discriminating power of DEA: Focus on globally efficient units." J. Oper. Res. Soc., 53: 314-323.

Dyson RG, Thannassoulis E (1988). "Reducing weight flexibility in data envelopment analysis." J. Oper. Res. Soc., 39: 563-576.

Liang Liang JW, Ynag F (2009). "Determination of the weights for the ultimate cross efficiency using Shapley value in cooperative game." Expert Syst. Appl., 36: 872-876.

Nakabayashi K, Tone K (2006). "Egoist's dilemma: A DEA game." Int. Manage. Sci., 36: 135-148.

Sakawa M (1993). Fuzzy sets and Interactive Multiobjective Optimization, Plenum Press, New York.

Statistical modeling of wastage using the beta distribution

Ebuh G. U.[1]*, Nwoke C.[1] and Ebuh A. C.[2]

[1]Department of Statistics, Faculty of Physical Sciences, Nnamdi Azikiwe University, Awka, Anambra State, Nigeria.
[2]Department of Computer Science, Faculty of Physical Sciences, Nnamdi Azikiwe University, Awka, Anambra State, Nigeria.

This work attempts to fit a set of observed industrial wastage to the beta distribution using the Chi-square goodness of fit test and it was found to fit the beta distribution at 1% significance level. The mean and the variance of the wastage proportion were found to be 0.429 and 0.0395, respectively. The parameters of the beta distribution were α = 2.25 and β = 2.97. The skewness of the beta distribution is 0.286 confirming the claim that the distribution is skewed to the right whenever β > α and the distribution is a unimodal distribution since α and β is greater than 1.

Key words: Parameter, goodness of fit, chi-square, probability, random variable, distribution.

INTRODUCTION

It is believed that in management of a firm, there must be proportionate wastage out of the general output or yield. These wastages can be seen as loss of money, time and manpower. The beta distribution has two positive parameters denoted as α and β. It is a continuous distribution defined on the interval (0, 1). In Bayesian statistics, It can be seen as the posterior distribution of the parameter P of the binomial distribution after observing α-1 independent events with probability P and β-1 with probability 1-P, if the prior distribution of P was uniform (Oyeka, 2009). The beta distribution can be of two kinds, the beta distribution of the first kind and the second kind. According to Feller (1968), a random variable X is said to have a beta distribution of the first kind if and only if its probability density is

$$F(x)=\frac{1}{\beta(\alpha,\beta)} X^{\alpha-1} 1-X^{\beta-1}, 0 elsewhere 0 < X < 1 \alpha,\beta > 0 \quad (1)$$

The mean of the distribution is $\frac{\alpha}{\alpha+\beta}$ (2)

Its variance is $\frac{\alpha\beta}{(\alpha+\beta+1)(\alpha+\beta)}$ (3)

The beta distribution can take on different shapes depending on the values of the two parameters of α and β. When α = 1 and β = 1, the distribution is uniform over (0, 1) when α>1 and β>1, the distribution is unimodal when α = β, the beta distribution is symmetric about ½ whenever β > α, the distribution is skewed to the right while if α > β, the distribution is skewed to the left.

METHOD OF ANALYSIS

The major statistical tool that was used for this paper is the Chi-square goodness of fit test.

Hypothesis

H_0: The data fits the Beta distribution
H_1: The data does not fit the Beta distribution

The test statistics is given by

$$\chi^2_{cal} = \sum_{i=1}^{k}\left[\frac{(O_i - e_i)^2}{e_i}\right] \quad (4)$$

*Corresponding author. E-mail: ablegod007@yahoo.com.

where o_i is the observed frequency, e_i is the expected frequency and $e_i = nP_x$ where P_x is the expected relative frequency.

Decision rule

From the test statistics, if the calculated χ^2 is greater than the tabulated χ^2, the null hypothesis is rejected, that is rejected H_o if $\chi^2_{cal} > \chi^2_{1-\alpha,\ k-m-1}$ at significance level of α, otherwise the null hypothesis is rejected when k-m-1 is the degree of freedom.

K is the number of categories or class interval for which the observed and the expected frequency is available and m is the number of parameters estimated for the hypothesized distribution.

Relationship between the beta and other distribution using cumulating moment generating function (CMGF)

According to Oyeka et al. (2008), the CMGF is the weighted sum or cumulating of a set of its constituent moments of the distribution of the random variable of interest about zero. It is denoted by $g_n(c)$. The CMGF of the beta distribution is

$$g_n(c) = \sum_{t=0}^{n} \binom{n}{t} \frac{\lambda^{n-t}\Gamma(\alpha+\beta)\Gamma(ct+\alpha)}{\Gamma(\alpha)\Gamma(ct+\alpha)} \tag{5}$$

where c is the power of the distribution, α and β are the parameters of the distribution, n and t are the moments of the distribution. To get the CMGF of the gamma distribution (Equation 7) from the CMGF of the beta distribution, we put Equation (6) into (5)

$$\frac{\Gamma(\alpha+\beta)}{\Gamma(ct+\alpha)} = \beta^{ct} \tag{6}$$

$$g_n(c) = \sum_{t=0}^{n} \binom{n}{t} \frac{\lambda^{n-t}\Gamma(\alpha+\beta)\Gamma(ct+\alpha)}{\Gamma(\alpha)\Gamma(ct+\alpha)} \tag{7}$$

Similarly to get the CMGF of an exponential distribution (Equation 8) from the CMGF of a beta distribution, we put α = 1 and $\frac{\Gamma(\alpha+\beta)}{\Gamma(ct+\alpha)} = \beta^{ct}$ into Equation (7) to obtain:

$$g_n(c) = \sum_{t=0}^{n} \binom{n}{t} \lambda^{n-t} \beta^{ct} \Gamma(ct+1) \tag{8}$$

To also get a chi-square distribution from the beta

$$g_n(c) = \sum_{t=0}^{n} \binom{n}{t} \frac{\lambda^{n-t} 2^{ct} \Gamma\left(ct+\frac{k}{2}\right)}{\Gamma\left(\frac{k}{2}\right)} \tag{9}$$

ANALYSIS

Data presentation on the total number of items produced and the number of defective products for thirty-one randomly selected days is shown in Table 1. Table 2 shows the group frequency table for Table 1.

Parameter estimation

Mean, $\bar{x} = \frac{\sum fx}{\sum f} = \frac{13.295}{31} = 0.429$

Variance, $s^2 = \frac{\sum f(x-\bar{x})^2}{N-1} = \frac{1.186352}{31-1} = \frac{1.186352}{30}$

$= 0.0395$

Where the relationship among the mean, alpha and beta distributions is given by the

$$\bar{x} = \frac{\alpha}{\alpha+\beta},$$

and the relationship among the variance, alpha and beta distributions is given by the

$$s^2 = \frac{\alpha\beta}{(\alpha+\beta)^2(\alpha+\beta+1)}$$

Thus

$$\bar{x} = \frac{\alpha}{\alpha+\beta} = 0.429 \tag{10}$$

$$s^2 = \frac{\alpha\beta}{(\alpha+\beta)^2(\alpha+\beta+1)} = 0.0395 \tag{11}$$

From Equation 10, α = 0.429(α+β)

$$\therefore\ \alpha = 0.751\beta \tag{12}$$

Substituting Equation 12 into (11) gives

Table 1. Data presentation on the total number of items produced and the number of defective products for thirty-one randomly selected days.

S/N	Total number produced (X)	Total number of defective products	Proportion of defective products
1	5900	2320	0.393
2	5628	1830	0.325
3	5954	1480	0.249
4	6000	2400	0.400
5	5488	2090	0.381
6	4800	900	0.188
7	5004	1760	0.352
8	4570	2080	0.455
9	6400	3200	0.500
10	4870	2980	0.612
11	6030	1680	0.279
12	6200	1920	0.310
13	6077	2420	0.398
14	5320	1978	0.372
15	5328	2368	0.444
16	4600	2840	0.609
17	5368	3404	0.634
18	5523	1800	0.326
19	4830	2000	0.414
20	6380	3276	0.513
21	5418	2800	0.517
22	5540	1540	0.298
23	4836	2380	0.492
24	5930	2168	0.366
25	4634	1480	0.319
26	4800	1200	0.250
27	5892	2000	0.475
28	5085	4082	0.803
29	5251	1238	0.236
30	5450	3418	0.627
31	5974	3348	0.560
	163240	71060	

$$s^2 = \frac{0.751\beta^2}{(0.751\beta+\beta)^2(0..751\beta+\beta+1)} = 0.0395$$

$\beta = 2.97$

From Equation 12, $\alpha = 0.751 \times 3 = 2.25$. Therefore, $\alpha = 2.25$, $\beta = 2.97$.

COMPUTATION OF THE OBSERVED VALUES OF WASTAGE PROPORTION INTO THE BETA DISTRIBUTION

From Equation 1

$$f(x) = \begin{cases} \dfrac{\Gamma(\alpha+\beta)}{\Gamma(\alpha)\Gamma(\beta)} x^{\alpha-1}(1-x)^{\beta-1} & \text{for } 0<x<1 \ \alpha,\beta>0 \\ 0 & \text{elsewhere} \end{cases}$$

Substitute the values of $\alpha = 2$ and $\beta = 3$ in the above equation

$$= \frac{\Gamma 5}{\Gamma 2 \Gamma 3} = \frac{4!}{1!2!} = 12$$

$$\therefore f(x) = \begin{cases} 12\,x\,(1-x)^2 & 0<x<1 \ \alpha,\beta>0 \\ 0 & \text{Elsewhere} \end{cases} \qquad (13)$$

Calculation of the expected frequencies

We first calculate the probability corresponding to the

Table 2. A group frequency table for Table 1.

Class interval	Tally	Frequency (f)	Class mark (x)	Fx	x-$\bar{x}$	(x-$\bar{x}$)^2	f(x-$\bar{x}$)^2	Class boundaries
0.10 – 0.19	I	1	0.145	0.145	-0.284	0.080655	0.080655	0.095 – 0.195
0.20 – 0.29	IIII	4	0.245	0.980	-0.184	0.033856	0.135424	0.195 – 0.295
0.30 – 0.39	~~IIII~~ ~~IIII~~	10	0.345	3.450	-0.084	0.007056	0.07056	0.295 – 0.395
0.40 – 0.49	~~IIII~~ II	7	0.445	3.115	0.016	0.000256	.001792	0.395 – 0.495
0.50 – 0.59	IIII	4	0.545	2.180	0.116	0.013456	0.53824	0.495 – 0.595
0.60 – 0.69	IIII	4	0.645	2.580	0.216	0.046656	0.186624	0.595 – 0.695
0.70 – 0.79		0	0.745	0	0.316	0.099856	0	0.695 – 0.795
0.80 – 0.89	1	1	0.845	0.845	0.416	0.173056	0.173056	0.795 – 0.895
		31		13.295			1.186352	

Table 3. Calculation of expected frequencies and $\frac{(O_i - e_i)^2}{e_i}$.

Class interval	Class boundaries	Observed frequency (O$_i$)	Expected relative frequency P(x)	Expected frequency e_i = nPx	$(O_i - e_i)^2$	$\frac{(O_i - e_i)^2}{e_i}$
0.10 – 0.29	0.095 – 0.195	5	0.291955688	9.050626328	16.40757365	1.8128661
0.30 – 0.39	0.295 – 0.395	10	0.17665135	5.47619185	20.46484018	3.737056834
0.40 – 0.49	0.395 – 0.495	7	0.163820369	5.078431129	3.6924269	0.72708024
0.50 – 0.59	0.495 – 0.595	4	0.135029352	4.185909912	0.034562495	0.008256866
0.60 – 0.89	0.595 – 0.895	5	0.180742044	5.603003364	0.363613057	0.064896098
						6.350156

lower upper class boundaries of each interval, and then calculate their expected frequency for each interval.

The expected frequency for the first class interval 0.10 to 0.29 is

$$P(0.095<x<0.295) = 12\int_{0.095}^{0.295} x - 2x^2 + x^3 \partial x =$$

$$12\left[\frac{x^2}{2} - \frac{2x^3}{3} + \frac{x^4}{4}\right]_{0.095}^{0.295}$$

= 12(0.02829092 – 0.0039612793) = 0.291955688.

The expected frequency for this class interval is calculated as

np(x) = 31(0.291955688) = 9.050626328

The expected frequencies for the other class interval are computed as shown in Table 3.

CHI-SQUARE (χ^2) GOODNESS OF FIT TEST AND HYPOTHESIS

Chi-Square would be used to see if this data fits the beta distribution at 1% level of significance. H_o: the data fits the beta distribution, H_1: the data does not fit the beta distribution

$$\chi^2 = \sum\left(\frac{(O_i - e_i)^2}{e_i}\right) = 6.350156$$

Chi-square tabulated = $\chi^2_{\alpha,k-m-1}$ where $X^2_{0.01,\,5-2-1}$ = 9.210

Decision and conclusion

Since 6.350156 <9.210, we accept that the null hypothesis, hence implying that the data fits the Beta distribution with its parameter α = 2.25 and β = 2.97 at 1% level of significance.

Calculation of skewness

The skewness of the Beta distribution is given as

$$\frac{2(\beta-\alpha)\sqrt{(\alpha+\beta+1)}}{(\alpha+\beta+2)\sqrt{\alpha\beta}} = \frac{2(3-2)\sqrt{(2+3+1)}}{(2+3+2)\sqrt{(2)(3)}} = \frac{2\sqrt{6}}{7\sqrt{6}} = 0.286$$

Conclusion

From the results obtained, the mean and variance of the wastage proportion are 0.429 and 0.0395, respectively, the parameters of the distribution are α = 2.25 and β = 2.97, the skewness of the distribution is 0.286, the observed proportion of wastage (defective) fits the Beta distribution with a chi-square calculated value of 6.350156 which is less than the tabulated chi-square value of 9.210 at 1% significance level.

It also shows that the values of the wastage proportion fit the beta distribution at 1% significance level and that the density of the distribution is skewed to the right with α = 2.25 and β = 2.97. The mean and the wastage proportion are 0.429 and 0.0395, respectively, which is high and therefore need to be minimized.

REFERENCES

Feller W (1968). An Introduction to Probability Theory and its Applications. Wiley, New York. pp. 123-124.

Oyeka ICA (2009). An Introduction to Applied Statistics Methods, (Eight Edition) Nobern Avocation Publishing Company, Enugu. pp. 56-141.

Oyeka ICA, Ebuh GU, Nwosu CR, Utazi EC, Ikpebu PA, Obiora-Ilouno HO (2008). "The nth moment of x^c " ISSN 0331-9504. J. Niger. Stat. Assoc., 20: 24-33.

17

A deterministic model for HIV infection incorporating identification rate in a heterosexual population: Mathematical analysis

Abha Teguria[1], Manindra Kumar Srivastava[2]* and Anil Rajput[3]

[1]Department of Mathematics, Government M.L.B. PG girl Autonomous College, Bhopal, India.
[2]Department of Mathematics, School of Management Sciences, Technical Campus, Lucknow, India.
[3]Department of Mathematics, Sadhu Basbani PG College, Bhopal, India.

In this research, we developed a model for investigating the spread of HIV infection, which can result in acquired immunodeficiency syndrome (AIDS), through vertical and horizontal transmissions and introduced the concept of identification program by considering identification rate in heterosexual population which was qualitatively and numerically analyzed. We obtained equilibrium points of the model at two states (infection-free and Endemic). Thereafter, we investigated the criteria for existence of the endemic equilibrium point of the model. We determined local and global dynamics of the steady states of the system using stability theory and computer simulation before concluding.

Key words: Vertical and horizontal transmissions, heterosexual community, asymptotic stability, epidemiological parameters.

INTRODUCTION

Today, acquired immunodeficiency syndrome (AIDS), which is caused by human immunodeficiency virus (HIV) has shown a very high degree of prevalence in populations all over the world. The nature of human interactions, the uncertainties in the current estimates of epidemiological parameters and the lack of enough and reliable data makes it extremely difficult to understand the dynamics of the virus transmission without the frame works provided by mathematical modeling. The study of mathematical modeling is also helpful in determining the demographic and economic impact of the epidemic which in turn helps us to develop reasonable scientific and socially sound investigation plans in order to reduce the spread of the infection (NACO, 2004).

In recent decades, several mathematical modeling studies have been conducted to describe the transmission dynamics of HIV infection for homogeneous and heterogeneous populations (Anderson et al., 1986, 1988; Bailey, 1986; Knox, 1986; Pickering et al., 1986; May and Anderson, 1987, 1989; Grant et al., 1987; Hethcote, 1987; Anderson, 1988; May, 1988; Castillo-Chavez et al., 1989a, b, c; Sun, 1995; Hethcote and Yorke, 1984; Rapatski et al., 2006).

In particular, Anderson et al. (1986) described some preliminary attempts to use mathematical models for transmission of HIV in a homosexual community. May and Anderson (1987) presented simple HIV transmission models to help clarify the effects of various factors on the overall pattern of AIDS epidemic. Blythe and Anderson (1988) considered HIV transmission models with four forms for the distribution of incubation period by assuming that the infectious period is equal to the incubation period. Castillo-Chavez et al. (1989) analyzed a model where the mean rate of acquisition of new partners depends on the size of the sexually active population. Most of the above mentioned models consider only one population but HIV transmission takes place in the population that are heterogeneous in a

*Corresponding author. E-mail: mohitmanindra83@yahoo.co.in.

variety of ways and this aspect should be taken in modeling HIV (Knox, 1986; Colgete et al., 1989; Jacquez et al., 1989; Koopman et al., 1989; Srinivasa Rao, 2003; Abbas et al., 2007; Korobeinikov et al., 2001; Kribs-Zaleta et al., 2005; Arazoza et al., 2002; Smith et al., 2001).

MODEL FORMULATION

Let us consider a heterosexual community of size *P* with uniform promiscuous behavior and taking only heterosexual encounters and assume that the birth and death rates are same, making community size to be a constant. We have assumed that infection is transmitted in the studied population, through the member of one male or female class to the other female or male class respectively. The infection can also be transmitted vertically to the offspring of an infected mother.

Let any instant of time *t* for the illustrated community be subdivided into five classes of $S_1(t)$ male susceptibles, $I_1(t)$ male infectives having HIV infection, $S_2(t)$ female susceptibles, $I_2(t)$ female infectives having HIV infection, $R(t)$ removed infected hosts after identification. The susceptibles become infected with transmission efficiency *k* and the rate at which the HIV infected individuals are removed from the population after being identified is *c*. This leads to the following system of ordinary differential equations

$$\frac{dS_1}{dt} = -kS_1I_2 + b\alpha(S+R) + pb'\beta I - bS_1$$
$$\frac{dS_2}{dt} = -kS_2I_1 + b(1-\alpha)(S+R) + pb'(1-\beta)I - bS_2$$
$$\frac{dI_1}{dt} = kS_1I_2 + qb'lI - (b'+c)I_1$$
$$\frac{dI_2}{dt} = kS_2I_1 + qb'(1-l)I - (b'+c)I_2 \qquad (1)$$
$$\frac{dR}{dt} = cI - bR$$

with initial data

$$S_1(0)=S_{10}>0;\; S_2(0)=S_{20}>0;$$
$$I_1(0)=I_{10}>0;\; I_2(0)=I_{20}>0;$$
$$R(0)=R_0\geq 0,\; P=S+I+R;\; S=S_1+S_2;\; I=I_1+I_2;$$
$$1=p+q;\; 0<\alpha,\beta,l<1. \qquad (2)$$

where

$\left[\begin{matrix}(1-\alpha),(1-\beta)\\ \text{and}\,(1-l)\end{matrix}\right] = \alpha, \beta$ and l = The fraction of male hosts in population under consideration.

b and b' = Birth rates of susceptibles and infectives respectively.

p = The fraction of newborn offsprings of infective parents, who are susceptible at birth.

q = The fraction of newborn offsprings of infective parents, who are infective at birth.

b and b' = Death rate of susceptibles and infectives respectively.

The mathematical modeling as seen in 2 can be understood by following Figure 1.

EQUILIBRIUM POINTS OF MODEL

The equilibrium points of the model can be derived from the following set of equations

$$-kS_1^*I_2^* + b\alpha(S_1^*+S_2^*+R^*) + pb'\beta(I_1^*+I_2^*) - bS_1^* = 0$$
$$-kS_2^*I_1^* + b(1-\alpha)(S_1^*+S_2^*+R^*) + pb'(1-\beta)(I_1^*+I_2^*) - bS_2^* = 0$$
$$kS_1^*I_2^* + qb'l(I_1^*+I_2^*) - (b'+c)I_1^* = 0 \qquad (3)$$
$$kS_2^*I_1^* + qb'(1-l)(I_1^*+I_2^*) - (b'+c)I_2^* = 0$$
$$c(I_1^*+I_2^*) - bR^* = 0$$
$$S_1^*+S_2^*+I_1^*+I_2^*+R^* = P$$

Infection free equilibrium point

$$E_0(S_1^*,I_1^*,S_2^*,I_2^*,R^*):$$
$$I_1^* = I_2^* = R^* = 0;$$
$$S_1^* = \alpha P;\; S_2^* = (1-\alpha)P$$

Endemic equilibrium point

$$E_1(S_1^*,I_1^*,S_2^*,I_2^*,R^*):$$
$$S_1^* = \frac{b\alpha P - a_1(I_1^*+I_2^*)}{kI_2^*+b};$$

$S_1^*>0$, if $b\alpha P + pb'\beta(I_1^*+I_2^*) > b\alpha(I_1^*+I_2^*)$

$$S_2^* = \frac{b(1-\alpha)P - a_2(I_1^*+I_2^*)}{kI_1^*+b};$$

$S_2^*>0$, if $b(1-\alpha)P + pb'(1-\beta)(I_1^*+I_2^*) > b(1-\alpha)(I_1^*+I_2^*)$

$$R^* = \frac{c}{b}(I_1^*+I_2^*)$$

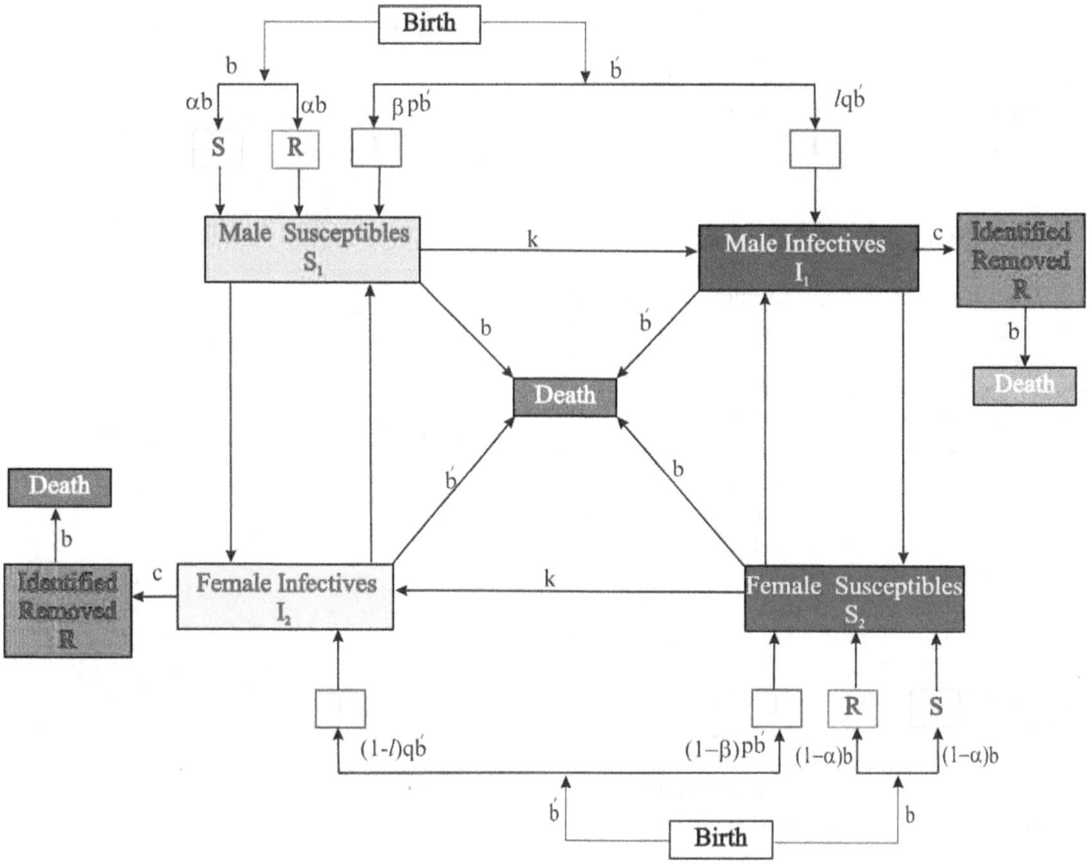

Figure 1. Five classes of S1(t) male susceptibles, I1(t) male infectives having HIV infection, S2(t) female susceptibles, I2(t) female infectives having HIV infection, and R(t) removed infected hosts.

$\boldsymbol{R^* > 0}$, if $\boldsymbol{I_1^* > 0, I_2^* > 0}$

Now, we investigate criteria for endemic steady state E_1 to exist. We require the system of equations (3) has a positive solution.

From the set of equations (3) we get:

$$(a_3 I_2^* + a_4) I_1^{*2} + (a_5 I_1^* + a_6) I_2^{*2} + a_7 I_1^* I_2^* - a_8 (I_1^* + I_2^*) + a_9 = 0 \quad (4)$$

which implies

$$I_1^* = \frac{a_8 + \sqrt{a_8^2 - 4a_4 a_9}}{2a_4}; \text{ when } I_2^* = 0$$

$\boldsymbol{I_1^* > 0}$, if $\boldsymbol{a_8^2 > 4a_4 a_9}$, $\boldsymbol{a_8 > 0}$, $\boldsymbol{a_4 > 0}$ and $\boldsymbol{a_9 > 0}$

Thus $I_1^* \to z_1(let)$ when $I_2^* \to 0$

and

$$I_2^* = \frac{a_8 + \sqrt{a_8^2 - 4a_6 a_9}}{2a_6}; \text{ when } I_1^* = 0$$

$\boldsymbol{I_2^* > 0}$, if $\boldsymbol{a_8^2 > 4a_6 a_9}$, $\boldsymbol{a_8 > 0}$, $\boldsymbol{a_6 > 0}$ and $\boldsymbol{a_9 > 0}$

Thus $I_2^* \to z_2(let)$ when $I_1^* \to 0$

We can also obtain

$$\frac{dI_2^*}{dI_1^*} = -\frac{2a_3 I_1^* I_2^* + 2a_3 I_1^* + a_5 I_2^{*2} + a_7 I_2^* - a_8}{a_3 I_1^{*2} + 2a_5 I_1^* I_2^* + 2a_6 I_2^* + a_7 I_1^* - a_8};$$

$\boldsymbol{\frac{dI_2^*}{dI_1^*} < 0}$, if $\boldsymbol{2a_3 (I_1^* I_2^* + I_1^*) + a_5 I_2^{*2} + a_7 I_2^* > a_8}$ and $\boldsymbol{a_3 I_1^{*2} + 2a_5 I_1^* I_2^* + 2a_6 I_2^* + a_7 I_1^* > a_8}$

Hence, we find that I_2^* is decreasing function of I_1^*.

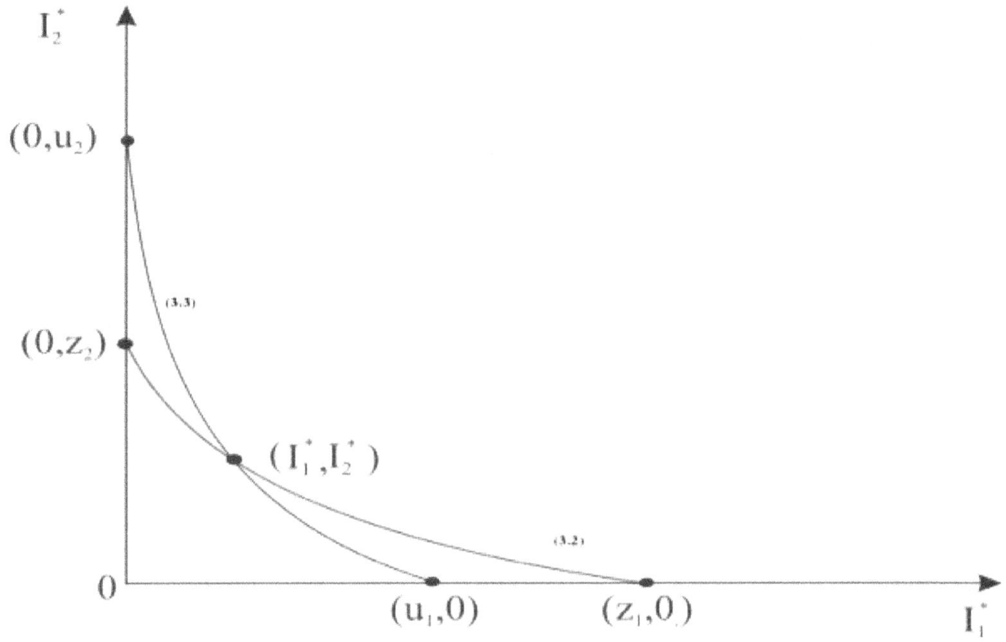

Figure 2. Intersection graph of the two isoclines.

Also, from the set of equations (3) we get:

$$a_{10}I_1^{*2} + a_{11}I_2^{*2} + a_{12}\left(I_1^{*2}I_2^* + I_1^*I_2^{*2}\right) + a_{13}I_1^*I_2^* - a_{14}I_1^* - a_{15}I_2^* = 0 \qquad (5)$$

which implies

$I_1^* = \dfrac{a_{14}}{a_{10}}$; when $I_2^* = 0$ $\boldsymbol{I_1^* > 0}$, if $\boldsymbol{a_{14} > 0}$ and $\boldsymbol{a_{10} > 0}$

Thus $I_1^* \to u_1(let)$ when $I_2^* \to 0$

and

$I_2^* = \dfrac{a_{15}}{a_{11}}$; when $I_1^* = 0$ $\boldsymbol{I_2^* > 0}$, **if** $\boldsymbol{a_{15} > 0}$ **and** $\boldsymbol{a_{11} > 0}$

Thus $I_2^* \to u_2(let)$ when $I_1^* \to 0$

We can also obtain

$$\frac{dI_2^*}{dI_1^*} = -\frac{2a_{10}I_1^* + a_{13}I_2^* + 2a_{12}I_1^*I_2^* + a_{12}I_2^{*2} - a_{14}}{a_{13}I_1^* + 2a_{11}I_2^* + 2a_{12}I_1^*I_2^* + a_{12}I_1^{*2} - a_{15}};$$

$\dfrac{dI_2^*}{dI_1^*} < 0$,if $\left\{2a_{10}I_1^* + a_{13}I_2^* + a_{12}\left(2I_1^*I_2^* + I_2^{*2}\right)\right\} > a_{14}$ and

$$\left\{a_{13}I_1^* + 2a_{11}I_2^* + 2a_{12}I_1^*I_2^* + a_{12}I_1^{*2}\right\} > a_{15}$$

Hence, we find that I_2^* is decreasing function of I_1^*. From the foregoing equation, we see that the two isoclines given by (4) and (5) will intersect provided that $z_1 > u_1$ and $u_2 > z_2$. Hence, with this consideration, isocline (4) represents I_2^* as decreasing from z_2 and isocline (5) represents I_2^* as decreasing from u_2.

Therefore, two isoclines must intersect provided intersection values $0 < I_1^* \le z_1$ and $0 < I_2^* \le u_2$, then endemic equilibrium point E_1 exists in the positive $I_1^* - I_2^*$ plane, shown in Figure 2.

Note: The values of constants a_i (i = 1, 2, ..., 15) are given in appendix.

QUALITATIVE ANALYSIS

Now to determine local and global dynamics of steady states E_0 and E_1 of system (1) we used Lyapunov's second method. First we analyzed local dynamic of above steady states (E_0 and E_1). So that we can find sufficient conditions under which E_0 and E_1 are locally asymptotically stable in the form of the following theorems (6) and (7) respectively.

Theorem 6

Let the following inequalities hold:

$$(b+b\alpha A_1) > \frac{1}{2}\left[kS_1^* + 2pb'\beta + 4b\alpha + bA_1\right] \quad (6a)$$

$$(4b\alpha + pb'\beta)A_1 > \left[b\alpha + kS_2^* + 2b + 2pb'\right]A_1 \quad (6b)$$

$$(b'+c) > \frac{1}{2}(kS_1^* + 3qb'l) \quad (6c)$$

$$(b'+c) > \frac{1}{2}\left[kS_2^* + 3qb'(1-l)\right] \quad (6d)$$

$$b > c \quad (6e)$$

Then E_0 is locally and asymptotically stable. Here A_1 is arbitrary positive constant.

Proof

Let us take the following positive definite function of system (1) is:

$$V_1 = \frac{1}{2}\left[n_1^2 + A_1 n_2^2 + A_2 n_3^2 + A_3 n_4^2 + A_4 n_5^2\right] \quad (7)$$

Here, A_i is arbitrary positive constants (i = 1,2,….,5).

Using linearized form of system (1) in time derivative of V_1 and applying the inequality $\pm(a+b) \le \frac{1}{2}(a^2+b^2)$ and after some manipulations, we get:

$$\frac{dV_1}{dt} \le -\left[A_{11}n_1^2 + A_{12}n_2^2 + A_{13}n_3^2 + A_{14}n_4^2 + A_{15}n_5^2\right] \quad (8)$$

Where

$$A_{11} = (b + b\alpha A_1) - \frac{1}{2}\left[kS_1^* + 2pb'\beta + 4b\alpha + bA_1\right];$$

$$A_{12} = \frac{1}{2}(4b\alpha + pb'\beta)A_1 - \frac{1}{2}\left[b\alpha + kS_2^* + 2b + 2pb'\right]A_1;$$

$$A_{13} = (b'+c)A_2 - \frac{1}{2}\left[pb'\beta + \left(pb'(1-\beta) + kS_2^*\right)A_1 + (kS_1^* + 3qb'l)A_2 + \left(qb'(1-l) + kS_2^*\right)A_3 + cA_4\right];$$

$$A_{14} = (b'+c)A_3 - \frac{1}{2}\left[pb'\beta + kS_1^* + pb'(1-\beta)A_1 + \left(kS_1^* + qb'l\right)A_2 + \left(kS_2^* + 3qb'(1-l)\right)A_3 + cA_4\right];$$

$$A_{15} = bA_4 - \frac{1}{2}\left[b\alpha + (1-\alpha)bA_1 + 2cA_4\right];$$

Here $A_{11}>0, A_{12}>0, A_{13}>0, A_{14}>0, A_{15}>0,$ are holding under the conditions (6[a-e]). Thus the time derivative of V_1 is negative definite under the conditions (6). Hence from theory of stability E_0 is locally asymptotically stable.

Theorem (7)

Steady state E_1 of the system (1) is locally asymptotically stable if

$$(kI_2^* + b + b\alpha B_1) > \frac{1}{2}\left[kS_1^* + 2pb'\beta + 4b\alpha + bB_1 + kI_2^*B_2\right] \quad (8a)$$

$$(kI_1^* + 4b\alpha + pb'\beta)B_1 > b\alpha + (kS_2^* + 2pb' + 2b)B_1 + kI_1^*B_3 \quad (8b)$$

$$(b'+c) > \frac{1}{2}(kS_1^* + kI_2^* + 3qb'l) \quad (8c)$$

$$(b'+c) > \frac{1}{2}\left[kS_2^* + kI_1^* + 3qb'(1-l)\right] \quad (8d)$$

$$b > c \quad (8e)$$

uniformed. Where B_1, B_2, B_3 are arbitrary positive constants.

Proof of the theorem (7) is similar to the above theorem (6).

Now to show that steady states E_0 and E_1 of system (1) are globally asymptotically stable, we consider a region of attraction for the system (1) in the form of the following lemma,

Lemma (1)

The set

$$R_1 = \left\{ \begin{array}{lll} (S_1, S_2, I_1, I_2, R): & 0 < S_{1m} \le S_1 \le P; & 0 < S_{2m} \le S_2 \le P; \\ & 0 < I_{1m} \le I_1 \le P; & 0 < I_{2m} \le I_2 \le P; \\ & 0 \le R; & \end{array} \right\}$$

Here, $S_{1m} = S_{2m} = I_{1m} = I_{2m}$ are positive constants. This is a region of attraction for all solutions initially in the positive orthant.

Now we obtain here the conditions for asymptotic stability of positive steady states E_0 and E_1 of system (1) in non-linear (global) case in form of the following theorem (8).

Theorem (8)

The steady state E_0 of system (1) is non-linearly (globally) asymptotically stable in a region R_1 given by lemma (1) where the following conditions are satisfied:

$$(b+b\alpha K_1) > \frac{1}{2}(kS_{1m}+2pb'\beta+4b\alpha+bK_1) \tag{9a}$$

$$(4b\alpha+pb'\beta)K_1 > [b\alpha+(kS_{2m}+2b+2pb')K_1] \tag{9b}$$

$$(b'+c) > \frac{1}{2}(kP+3qb'l) \tag{9c}$$

$$(b'+c) > \frac{1}{2}[kP+3qb'(1-l)] \tag{9d}$$

$$b > c \tag{9e}$$

where K_1 is arbitrary positive constant.

Proof

Again consider the following positive definite function about E_0 of system (1)

$$V_2 = \frac{1}{2}[v_1^2+K_1v_2^2+K_2v_3^2+K_3v_4^2+K_4v_5^2] \tag{10}$$

Here, K_i are arbitrary positive constants $(i=1,2,.....5)$. Take small perturbations in $E_0(S_1^*,S_2^*,I_1^*,I_2^*,R^*)$ as $v_1(t), v_2(t), v_3(t), v_4(t)$ and $v_5(t)$ respectively on putting $S_1=S_1^*+v_1(t)$, $S_2=S_2^*+v_2(t)$, $I_1=I_1^*+v_3(t)$, $I_2=I_2^*+v_4(t)$, $R=R^*+v_5(t)$ in the set of equations (1).

We get following equivalent nonlinear system of model (1):

$$\frac{dv_1}{dt} = -(1-\alpha)bv_1+b\alpha v_2+pb'\beta v_3-k(S_1^*+v_1)v_4+pb'\beta v_4+b\alpha v_5 \tag{11a}$$

$$\frac{dv_2}{dt} = (1-\alpha)bv_1-b\alpha v_2-k(S_2^*+v_2)v_3+pb'(1-\beta)v_3+pb'(1-\beta)v_4 \\ +(1-\alpha)bv_5 \tag{11b}$$

$$\frac{dv_3}{dt} = [qb'l-(b'+c)]v_3+k(S_1^*+v_1)v_4+qb'lv_4 \tag{11c}$$

$$\frac{dv_4}{dt} = k(S_2^*+v_2)v_3+qb'(1-l)v_3+[qb'(1-l)-(b'+c)]v_4 \tag{11d}$$

$$\frac{du_5}{dt} = bu_1+pb'u_2+bu_3+pb'u_4-mu_5 \tag{11e}$$

Differentiating V_2 with respect to t along the solution of (1) and using lemma (1), we get:

$$\begin{aligned}\frac{dV_2}{dt} = & -(1-\alpha)bv_1^2-\alpha bK_1v_2^2-[(b'+c)-qb'l]K_2v_3^2-[(b'+c)-qb'(1-l)]K_3v_4^2 \\ & -bK_4v_5^2+[b\alpha+K_1b(1-\alpha)]v_1v_2-kS_{1m}v_1v_4+pb'\beta v_1v_3+pb'\beta v_1v_4 \\ & +b\alpha v_1v_5-kS_{2m}K_1v_2v_3+pb'(1-\beta)K_1v_2v_3+pb'(1-\beta)K_1v_2v_4 \\ & +(1-\alpha)bK_1v_2v_5+[(kP+qb'l)K_2+(kP+qb'(1-l))K_3]v_3v_4 \\ & +cK_4v_3v_5+cK_4v_4v_5\end{aligned} \tag{12}$$

Applying inequality $\pm ab \le \frac{1}{2}(a^2+b^2)$ and a lengthy algebraic manipulation yields:

$$\frac{dV_2}{dt} \le -[K_{11}v_1^2+K_{12}v_2^2+K_{13}v_3^2+K_{14}v_4^2+K_{15}v_5^2] \tag{13}$$

Where

$$K_{11} = (b+b\alpha K_1)-\frac{1}{2}(kS_{1m}+2pb'\beta+4b\alpha+bK_1)$$

$$K_{12} = \frac{1}{2}(4b\alpha+pb'\beta)K_1-\frac{1}{2}[b\alpha+(kS_{2m}+2b+2pb')K_1]$$

$$\begin{aligned}K_{13} = (b'+c)K_2-\frac{1}{2}[& pb'\beta+(kS_{2m}+pb'(1-\beta))K_1+(kP+3qb'l)K_2 \\ & +(qb'(1-l)+kP)K_3+cK_4]\end{aligned}$$

$$\begin{aligned}K_{14} = (b'+c)K_3-\frac{1}{2}[& kS_{1m}+pb'\beta+pb'(1-\beta)K_1+(kP+qb'l)K_2 \\ & +(kP+3qb'(1-l))K_3+cK_4]\end{aligned}$$

$$K_{15} = bK_4-\frac{1}{2}[b\alpha+(1-\alpha)bK_1+2cK_4];$$

Here $K_{11}>0, K_{12}>0, K_{13}>0, K_{14}>0, K_{15}>0$, are existing under the conditions (9[a-e]). From (13), it can be shown that, $\frac{dV_2}{dt}$ is negative definite under the following conditions (9[a-e]). Hence, disease free steady state E_0 of system (1) is non-linearly (globally) asymptotically stable in the region R_1 under the conditions given by (9[a-e]), proving theorem (8).

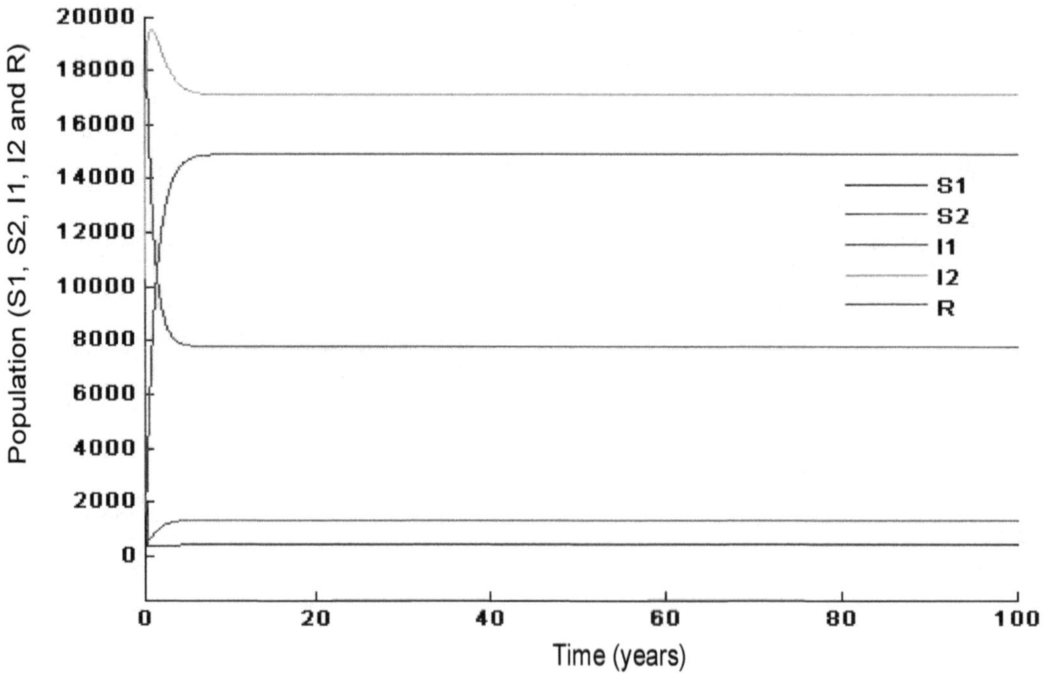

Figure 3. Variation of population at large time scale.

Similarly we also determined that endemic steady state E_1 of system (1) is also globally asymptotically stable in a region R_1 given by lemma (1) under the conditions as follows:

$$(kI_{2m}+b+b\alpha T_1) > \frac{1}{2}\{kS_1^* + 2pb'\beta + 4b\alpha + bT_1 + kPT_2 \tag{14a}$$

$$(kI_{1m}+4b\alpha+pb'\beta)T_1 > b\{\alpha + k\{S_2^* + 2b + 2pb'\}T_4 + kPT_3 \tag{14b}$$

$$(b'+c) > \frac{1}{2}(kS_1^* + kP + 3qb'l) \tag{14c}$$

$$(b'+c) > \frac{1}{2}\{kS_2^* + kP + 3qb'(1-l) \tag{14d}$$

$$b > c \tag{14e}$$

Where T_1, T_2, T_3 are arbitrary positive constants.

NUMERICAL ANALYSIS

To study the dynamical behavior of the model system (1), numerical simulation of the model is done by MATLAB 7.0 using the parameter values $k=0.01, \alpha=0.4, \beta=0.4, b=0.5, b'=1, p=0.4, q=0.6, l=0.2, c=0.3$ with initial values:

$$S_1(0)=500, S_2(0)=500, I_1(0)=100, I_2(0)=100, R(0)=100$$

The endemic equilibrium values of different variables are computed as follows:

$$S_1^* = 43.7300579, S^*_2 = 125.6327342, I_1^* = 226.6570323, I^*_2 = 479.9861267, R^* = 423.989101$$

The results of numerical simulation are displayed graphically in Figures 3 to 12. In Figures 3 to 6 the distribution of population with time at large and small scales respectively, are shown in different classes. It is seen that the susceptible male and female populations decreases continuously as the population is closed which results in an increase in infective male and female populations and then it decreases as all infective males and females will be identified as AIDS (HIV Positive) individuals and some of them may die by disease-induced deaths which results as the variation in all subpopulations are being stopped due to the endemicness of HIV virus.

The variation of infective male population is shown in

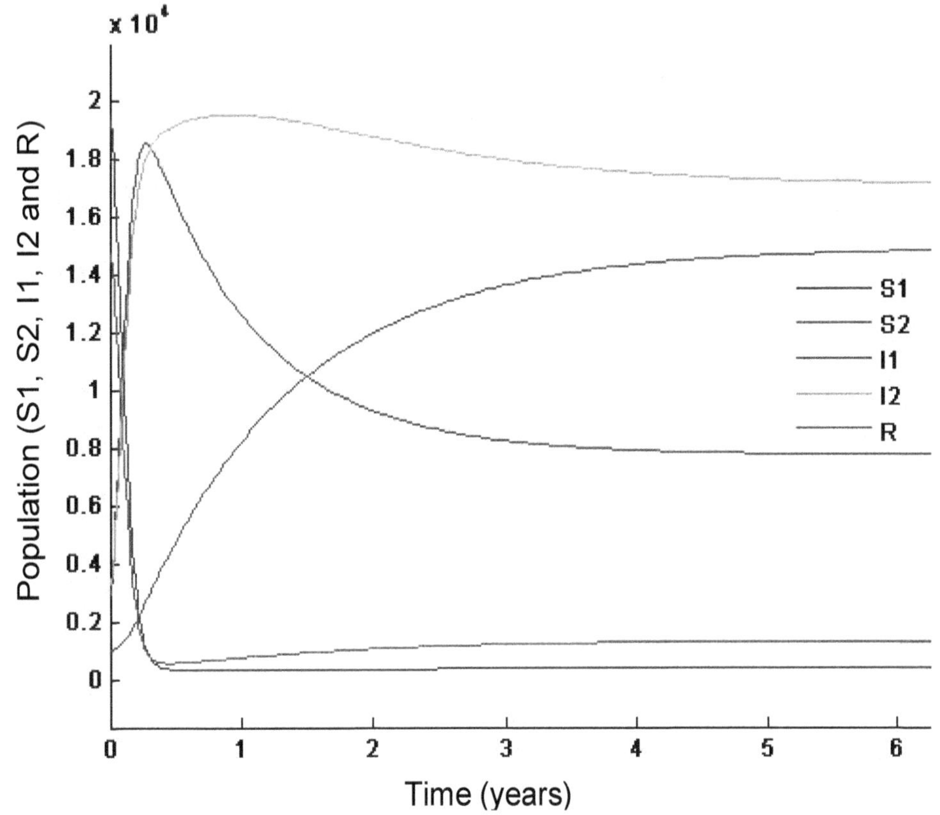

Figure 4. Variation of population at small time scale.

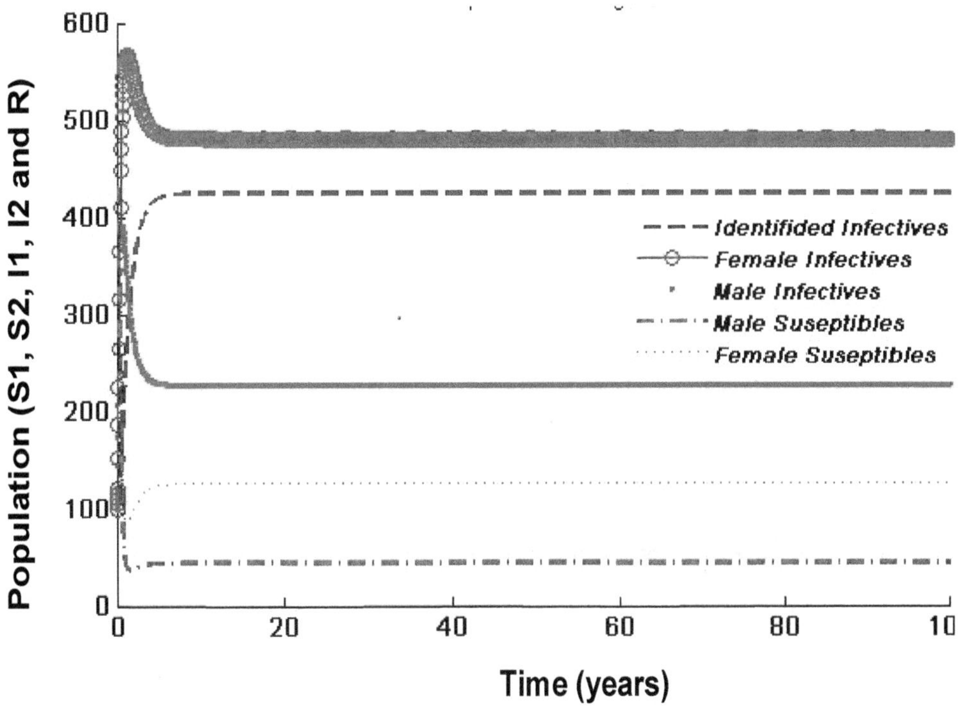

Figure 5. Variation of infective and susceptibles population at large time scale.

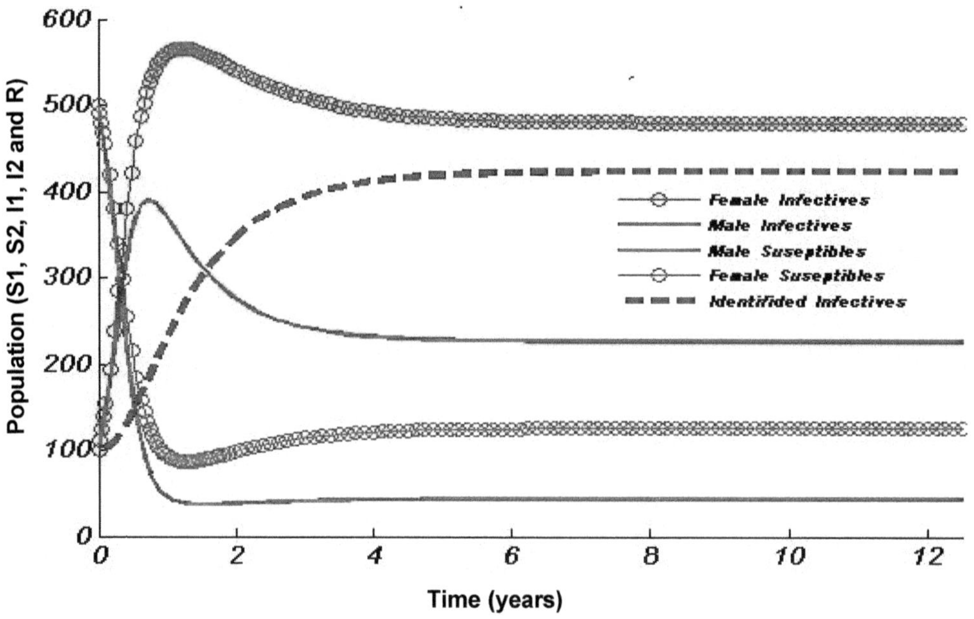

Figure 6. Variation of population at small time scale.

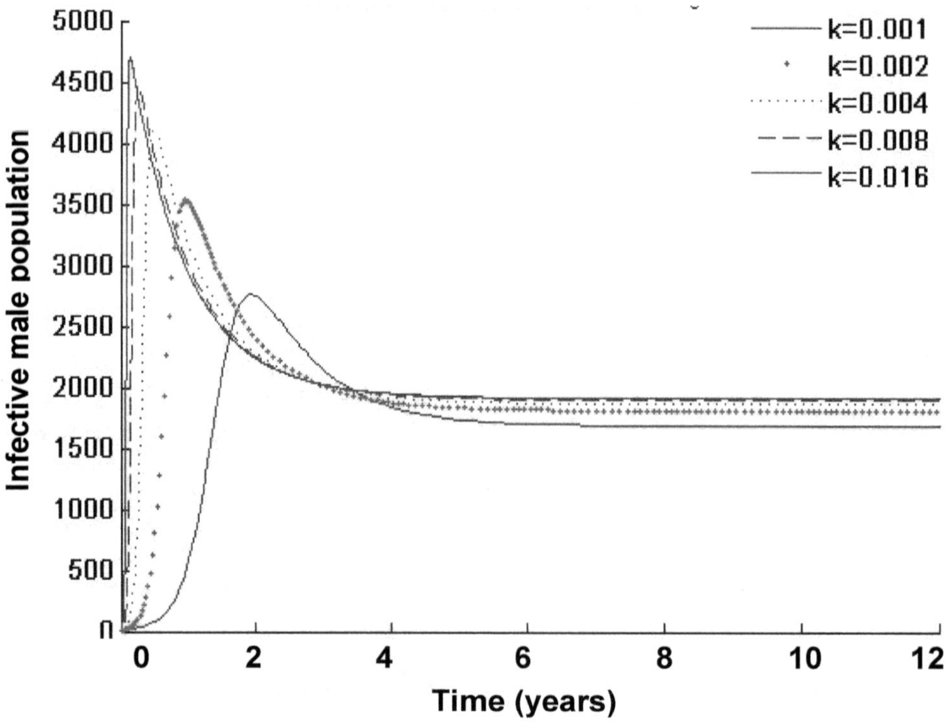

Figure 7. Variation of infectives male due to change in k.

Figures 7 to 9, infective female population and identified infective population respectively at different level of horizontal transmission rates as $k = 0.001$to 0.016. It is found that all infective subpopulations including identified sub-population, first increased with time and then reached on its equilibrium position.

The variation of identified infective population at various increasing level of identification strategy of infective

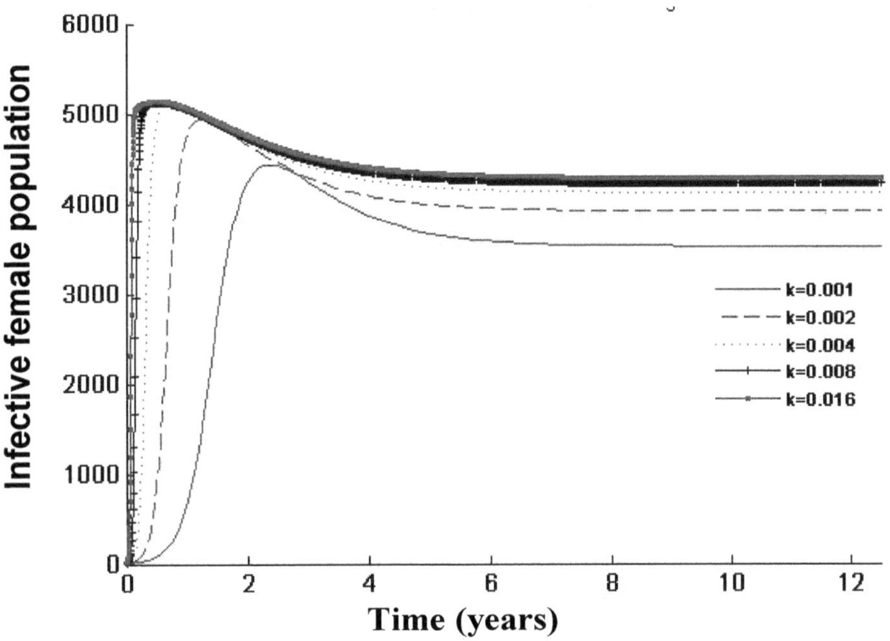

Figure 8. Variation of infectives female due to change in k.

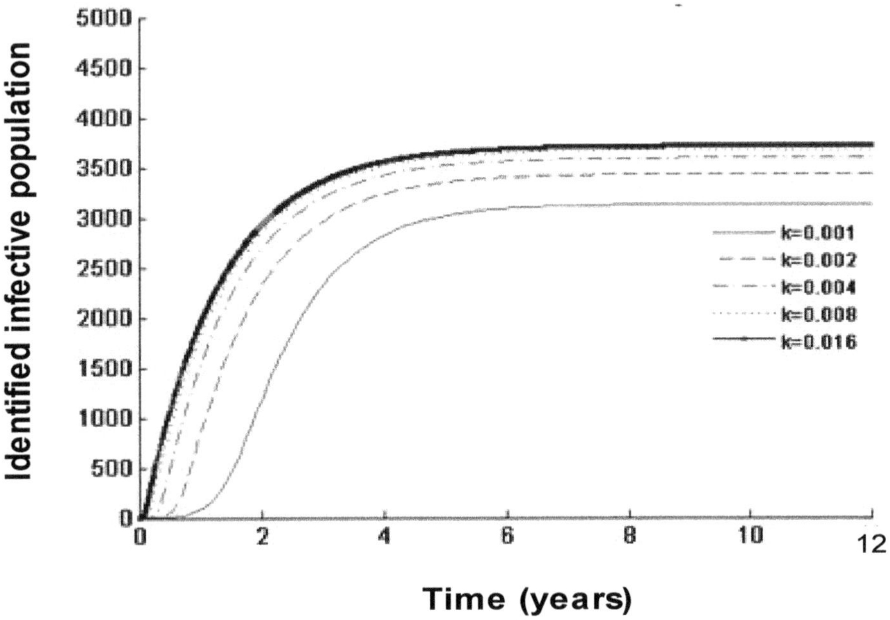

Figure 9. Variation of identified infectives due to change in k.

individuals (males and females) as $c = 0.01$ to 0.48 is reflected in Figure 10. It is observed that identification program runs successfully at first then increases with time and then arrives at its equilibrium position. For the most part, when the level of identification rate c is increased more than 0.6 the identified population increased slowly at first having low peak and decreases rapidly with time and then achieves an equilibrium position. However, this happens due to the complexity of identification strategy which should be appropriate and properly correlate with distribution and transmission related aspects of infection.

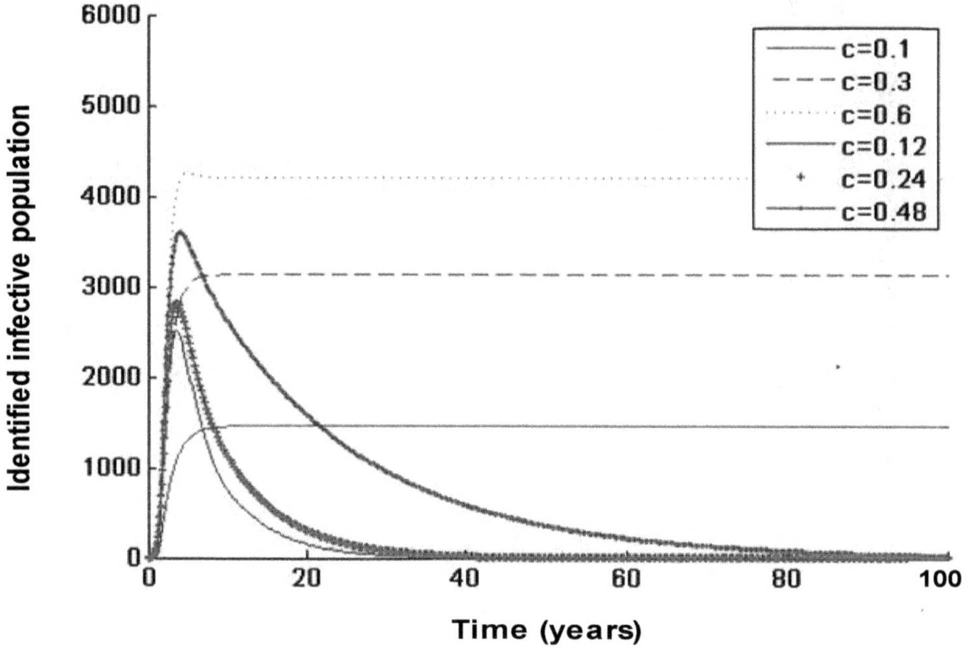

Figure 10. Variation of identified infectives due to change in c.

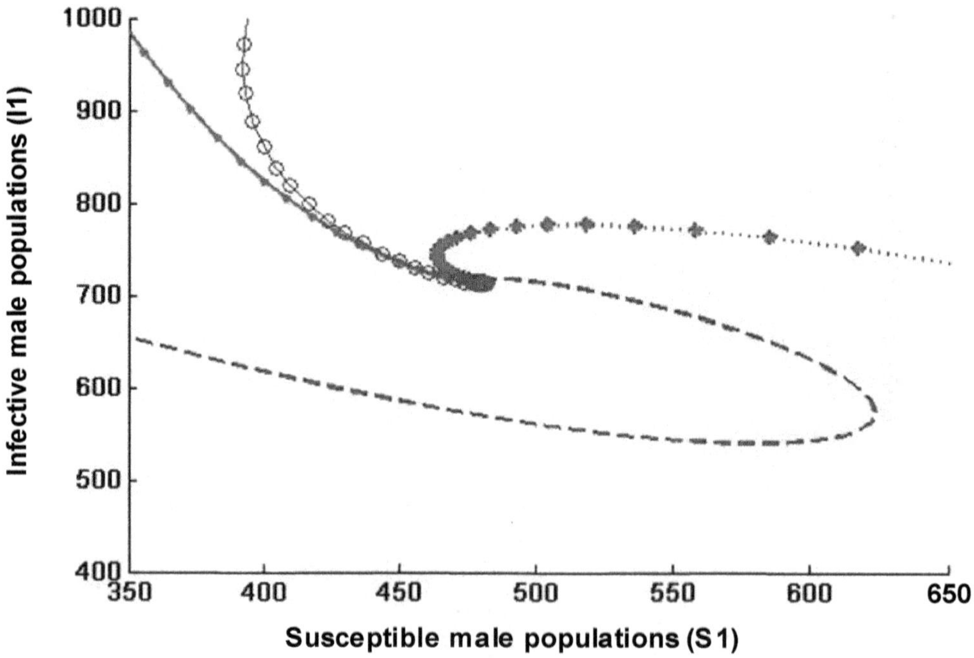

Figure 11. Male population plane.

In Figures 11 to 12, the infective male and female populations are plotted against the susceptible male and female populations respectively. We see from these figures that for any initial start, the solution curves tend to endemic equilibrium point. Hence, we infer that the system (1) may be globally asymptotically stable about this endemic equilibrium point for the above set of parameter values.

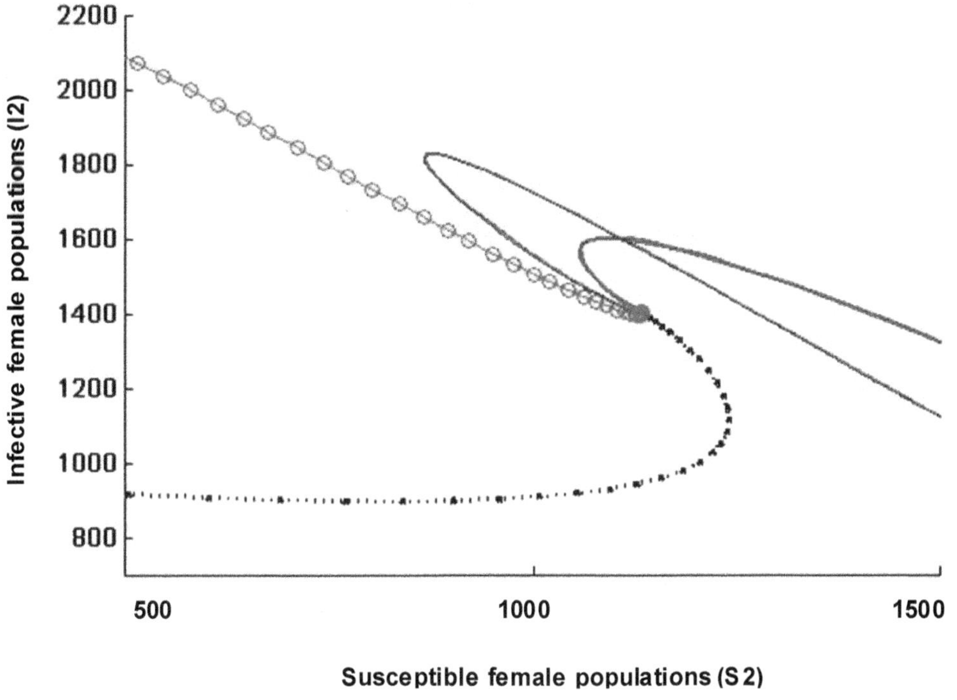

Figure 12. Female population plane.

Conclusions

In this paper, a deterministic mathematical model is formulated and analyzed qualitatively and numerically, to study the transmission dynamics of HIV/AIDS in a heterosexual population, which is of constant size, by assuming constant births and deaths of males and females. Since, the vertical transmission of infection, due to sexual interaction of susceptible (male/female) with infective (female/male), there is also increase in the population level of susceptible (male/female) and infective (male/female) subpopulations by recruiting their offspring's according to their susceptibility or infectiousness at the time of birth. To analyze the effect of identification program of seropositves on the dynamics of infection, the model incorporated an identification rate.

The model has two non-negative equilibriums namely the infection-free equilibrium and the endemic equilibrium. It is found that the infection-free equilibrium point and the endemic equilibrium point are locally and globally asymptotically stable under the conditions involving infection related parameters respectively. From stability analysis of infection-free equilibrium point, it may be concluded that the infection would eventually die-out in the population. From the analysis of endemic equilibrium point, it may be concluded that the infection will remain always in the population provided

(i) $bcP > (b^2 - pb')R^*$

(ii) $(p\beta + ql)b' > [b' + (1-\alpha)c + 2\alpha bP]$

(iii) $[\alpha(1-\alpha)P + pb'] > b$

(iv) $(p\beta + ql)b' + \alpha\{(1-\alpha)b + c\} \alpha\beta pb'$

(v) $(p\beta + ql)b' + (1-\alpha)b\alpha > b' + (1-\alpha)(pb'\beta + c)$

(vi) $b >$ is being satisfied.

The study of the model (1) suggested that the vertical spread of the infection should be controlled by rigid use of condom or other effective treatment to keep the overall infective population under control. It may also be speculated that if the HIV infection is suppressed at an early stage by effectively treating the infectives; this can become more effective if we identify infectives by choosing the right identification strategy, which may help not only in initial treatment of infective but also helpful in controlling vertical spread of infection.

The progression to the AIDS disease can be slowed down and the life span of HIV infectives can be increased.

ACKNOWLEDGEMENT

Authors are grateful to Prof. O. P. Misra, School of Mathematics and Allied Sciences, Jiwaji University Gwalior (M.P.), India for his constructive comments and valuable suggestions during the preparation of this paper.

REFERENCES

Abbas UL, Anderson RM, Mellors JW (2007). Potential Impact of Antiretroviral Chemoprophylaxis on HIV-1 Transmission in Resource-Limited Settings. PLOS ONE 2; E875 Doi: 10.1371 (1-11).

Anderson RM, Medley GF, May RM, Johnson AM (1986). IMA Jl. Math. Appl. Med. Biol. 3:229-263.

Anderson RM, May RM, McLean AR (1988). Natures, 332(6161):228-234.

Arazoza HD, Lounes R (2002). A nonlinear model for sexually transmitted disease with contact tracing, IMA J. Math. Appl. Med. Biol. pp. 19221-19234.

Bailey NTJ (1986). Use of simulation models to help control AIDS In: Blum, B., Jorgansen, M. eds. Medinfo. Elsevier 86:741-744.

Castillo-Chavez CK, Cooke W, Huang W, Levin SA (1989a). On the Role of Long Periods of Infectiousness in the Dynamics of Acquired Immunodeficiency Syndrome (AIDS), Mathematical Approaches to Problems in Resource Management and Epidemiology (eds. C. Castillo-Chavez, S. A. Levin and Shoemaker), Lecture Notes in Biomathematics, Springer Verlag, New York, 81:177-189.

Castillo-Chavez C, Cooke K, Huang W, Levin SA (1989c). On the Role of Long Incubation Periods in the Dynamics of Acquired Immunodeficiency Syndrome (AIDS), Part 1, Single Population Models, J. Math. Biol. 27:373-398.

Castillo-Chavez C, Cooke K, Huang W, Levin SA (1989b). On the Role of Long Incubation Periods in the Dynamics of Acquired Immunodeficiency Syndrome (AIDS), Part 2, Multiple Group Models, Mathematical and Statistical Approaches of ADIS Epidemiology (eds. C. Castillo-Chavez,), Lecture Notes in Biomathematics, No. 83, Springer Verlag, New York. pp. 200-217.

Grant R, Willey J, Winklestein W (1987). Infectivity of the human immunodeficiency virus:estimates from a prospective study of homosexual men. J. Inf. Dis. 156:189-193.

Hethcote HW (1987). AIDS modeling work in the United States. In: Future Trends in AIDS, Her Majesty's Stationery Office, London. pp. 35-40.

Jacquez JA, Simon CP, Koopmam J (1989). Mathematical and Statistical Approaches to AIDS Epidemiology. C. Castillo-Chavez (ed) Lecture Notes in Biomathematics, 83, Springer-Verlag. pp. 301-315.

Korobeinikov A, Wake GC (2002). Lyapunov functions and global stability for SIR, SIRS and SIS epidemiological models. Appl. Math. Lett.15:955-960.

Kribs-Zaleta CM, Lee M, Roman C, Wiley S, Hernandez-Suarez CM (2005). The effect of the HIV/AIDS epidemic on Africa's truck drivers. Math. Bios. Eng. 2(4):771-788.

Knox EG (1986). A transmission model for AIDS. Eur. J. Epidemiol. 2:165-177.

May RM, Anderson RM (1987). Transmission dynamics of HIV infection. Nature 326:137-142.

May RM (1988). HIV infection in heterosexuals. Nature 331:665-666.

May RM, Anderson RM (1989). Biomathematics, Simon, A. Levin, Thomas, G. Hallam and Louis, J. Gross (eds.). Appl. Math. Ecol. p.18, Springer-Verlag.

National AIDS Control Organization (2004). Country Scenario AIDS, Published by NACO, Ministry of Health, Government of India, New Delhi,

Pickering J. Wiley JA, Padian NS, Lieb L, Ekenberg D, Walker J (1986). Modeling the incidence of A .I .D.S. in San Francisco, Los Angeles, and New York . Math Modeling 7, 661-688 .

Rapatski B, Klepac P, Dueck S, Liu M, Weiss LI (2006). Mathematical epidemiology of HIV/AIDS in Cuba during the period 1986-2000. Math. Bios. Eng. 3(3):545-556.

Smith MY, Li HL, Wang L (2001). Global dynamics of an SEIR epidemic with vertical transmission. SIAM J. Appl. Math. 62(1):58-69.

Srinivasa Rao ASR (2003). Mathematical Modeling of AIDS Epidemic in India. Curr. Sci. 84:1192-1197.

Sun J (1995). Empirical Estimation of a Distribution Function with Truncated and Doubly Interval-Censored Data and Its Application to AIDS Studies. Biometrics 51(3):1096-1104.

APPENDIX.

$$a_1 = \alpha - pb'\beta ;\; a_2 = (1-\alpha) - pb'(1-\beta) ;\; a_3 = {}^2 \; P\beta + ql \; b' - b + (-\alpha \; c$$

$$a_4 = b \; p\beta + ql \; b' + (-\alpha \; \alpha - pb'\beta - b + c(-\alpha \;\; a_5 = {}^2 \; p\beta + ql \; b' + \alpha c$$

$$a_6 = b \; p\beta + ql \; b' + \alpha c + \alpha \; b(1-\alpha) - pb'(-\beta$$

$$a_7 = b \; 2 \; p\beta + ql \; b' + (-\alpha \; \alpha - pb'\beta + \alpha \; b(1-\alpha) + c \; b + (-\alpha \; c + pb'\alpha(-\beta$$

$$a_8 = b\alpha(-\alpha \; P - b(- pb' ;\; a_9 = {}^2 \; p\beta + ql \; b' - b + (-\alpha \; c + 2\alpha(-\alpha \; bP ;$$

$$a_{10} = k \; (+ c \; + pb'\beta \; kb^2\alpha ;\; a_{11} = k \; (+ c \; + pb'(1-\beta) \; kb^2 (-\alpha ;\; a_{12} = {}^2 \; (+ c ;$$

$$a_{13} = k \; (+ c \; + pb' - (+ kP ;\; a_{14} = {}^2 \; 2b + c \; + kP \; pb' + k^2\alpha P ;$$

$$a_{15} = {}^2 \; (-\alpha \; P + pb' \; 2b + c \; + kP$$

18

An inventory model for deteriorating items with different constant demand rates

Trailokyanath Singh[1]* and Sudhir Kumar Sahu[2]

[1]Department of Mathematics, Sir Chandrasekhara Venkata Raman College of Engineering, Bhubaneswar, India.
[2]Department of Statistics, Sambalpur University, Sambalpur, India.

In this paper, we study the inventory model for deteriorating items with different constant demand rates, that is, the demand rate is piecewise linear function. The deterioration rate is assumed as constant. We have proposed an inventory replenishment policy for this type of inventory model. The numerical solution of the model is also obtained and examined.

Key words: Inventory, deteriorating items, constant demand rate.

INTRODUCTION

In real life deterioration of goods is a common process. Food items, vegetables, fruits, medicines, drugs are a few examples of such items. Physical goods, fashions goods, pharmaceuticals, electronics components etc., undergo deterioration overtime. Therefore, the loss due to damage, decay, spoilage or deterioration can not be neglected. As inventory is defined as decay change, damage or spoilage of these items can not be used for its original purposes. The important problem for any modern organization is the control and maintenance of inventories of deteriorating items. In the classical EOQ (Economic Order Quantity) model developed in 1915, the demand of an item was assumed as constant, therefore, many researchers, considered the demand of these items as constant. Two earliest researchers, Ghare and Schrader (1963) considered the continuously decaying inventory for a constant demand. However, in real situation, the demand rate of items should vary with time. Silver and Meal (1969) suggest a simple modification of the EOQ model with varying demand. Researchers like Ritchie (1984), considered the inventory models about constant, linear and time-dependent demand. Bahari-Kashani (1989) and Goswami and Chaudhuri (1991), developed the EOQ models for deteriorating items with trended demand. The inventory model with ramp ty rate was first proposed by Hill (1995). The ramp type demand is commonly seen when some fresh fruits are brought to the market. In the case of ramp type demand rate, the demand increases linearly at the beginning and then the market grows into a stable stage such that the demand becomes a constant until the end of the inventory cycle. Hill (1995) first considered the inventory models for increasing demand followed by a constant demand. Mandal and Pal (1998) extended the inventory model with ramp type demand for deterioration items and allowing shortage. Wu and Ouyang (2000) extended the inventory model to include two different replenishment policies: (a) models starting with no shortage and (b) models starting with shortage. Deng et al. (2007) point out some questionable results of Mandal and Pal (1998) and Wu and Ouyang (2000), and then resolved the similar problem by offering a rigorous and efficient method to derive the optimal solution. Wu (2001) further investigated the inventory model with ramp type demand rate such that the deterioration followed the Weibull distribution. Giri et al. (2003) and Cheng and Wang (2009) extended the ramp type demand inventory model with a more generalized Weibull deterioration

*Corresponding author. E-mail: trailokyanaths108@gmail.com.

distribution.Various types of order-level inventory model for deteriorating items at a constant rate with a time-dependent were discussed recently.

In the following, we have worked on constant-constant-constant demand rates where the value differs with different time intervals. We assumed that the inventory system considered here has several replenishments and all the ordering cycles are of fixed length. Such type of demand pattern is generally seen in case of seasonal goods like vegetables, fruits and electronics components coming to market. We think that such types of demand are quite realistic and a useful inventory replenishment policy for such type of inventory model is also proposed.

The rest of the paper is organized as follows. Subsequently, this study describes the assumptions and notations used throughout this paper, after which it establishes the mathematical model with shortage in inventory and the necessary conditions to find an optimal solution. This is followed by the use of some numerical examples to illustrate the solution procedure. Finally, the study is summarized and some suggestions are provided for further research.

NOTATION AND ASSUMPTION

In this paper, we extend trapezoidal type demand rate type to different demand rate. The fundamental assumption and notation used in this paper are given as:

1. The replenishment rate is infinite, thus, replenishment is instantaneous.
2. The demand rate, $\mathbf{D(t)}$, which is positive and consecutive, is assumed to be a constant-constant-constant type function of time, that is:

$$\mathbf{D(t)} = \begin{cases} A_1, & t \le \mu_1, \\ D_0, & \mu_1 \le t \le \mu_2, \\ A_2, & \mu_2 \le t \le T. \end{cases}$$

where A_1 is the constant distribution, $A_1 > 0$; $-A_2$ is the negative constant distribution, $A_2 > 0$; μ_1 is the time point changing from the increasing linearly demand to the constant demand and μ_2 is the time point changing from the constant demand to the decreasing linearly demand.

3. $I(t)$ is the level of inventory at time t , $0 \le t \le T$.
4. T is the fixed length of each ordering cycle.
5. θ is the constant deteriorating rate, $0 < \theta < 1$.
6. t_1 is the time when the inventory level reaches zero.
7. t_1^* is the optimal point.
8. A_0 is the fixed ordering cost per order.
9. c_1 is the cost of each deteriorated items.
10. c_2 is the inventory holding cost per unit per unit of time.
11. c_3 is the shortage cost per unit per unit of time.
12. S is the maximum inventory level for the ordering cycle, such that $S = I(0)$.
13. Q is the ordering quantity per cycle.
14. $C_1(t_1)$ is the average total cost per unit time under the condition $t_1 \le \mu_1$.
15. $C_2(t_1)$ is the average total cost per unit time under the condition $\mu_1 \le t_1 \le \mu_2$.
16. $C_1(t_1)$ is the average total cost per unit time under the condition $\mu_2 \le t_1 < T$.

MATHEMATICAL FORMULATION

We consider the deteriorating inventory model with trapezoidal type demand rate. Replenishment occurs at time $t = 0$ when the inventory level attains its maximum. From $t = 0$ to t_1, the inventory level reduces due to demand and deterioration. At t_1, the inventory level achieves zero, then the shortage is allowed to occur during the time interval (t_1, T), and all of the demand during the shortage period (t_1, T) is completely backlogged. The total number of backlogged items is replaced by the next replenishment. According to the notations and assumptions mentioned above, the behavior of inventory system at any time can be described by the following differential equations:

$$\frac{dI(t)}{dt} = -\theta I(t) - D(t), \quad 0 < t < t_1 \tag{1}$$

and

$$\frac{dI(t)}{dt} = -D(t), \quad t_1 < t < T \tag{2}$$

with the boundary condition $I(t_1) = 0$.

In follows, we consider three possible cases based on values of t_1, μ_1 and μ_2. These three cases are shown as follows:

Case 1. $0 < t_1 \le \mu_1$.

Due to reasons of deteriorating items and trapezoidal type market demand, the inventory gradually diminishes during the period [0, t_1] and ultimately falls to zero at time t_1 Figure 1. Then from equation (1), we have

$$\frac{dI(t)}{dt} = -\theta I(t) - A_1 \quad 0 < t < t_1 \tag{3}$$

$$\frac{dI(t)}{dt} = -A_1 \quad , t_1 < t < \mu_1 , \tag{4}$$

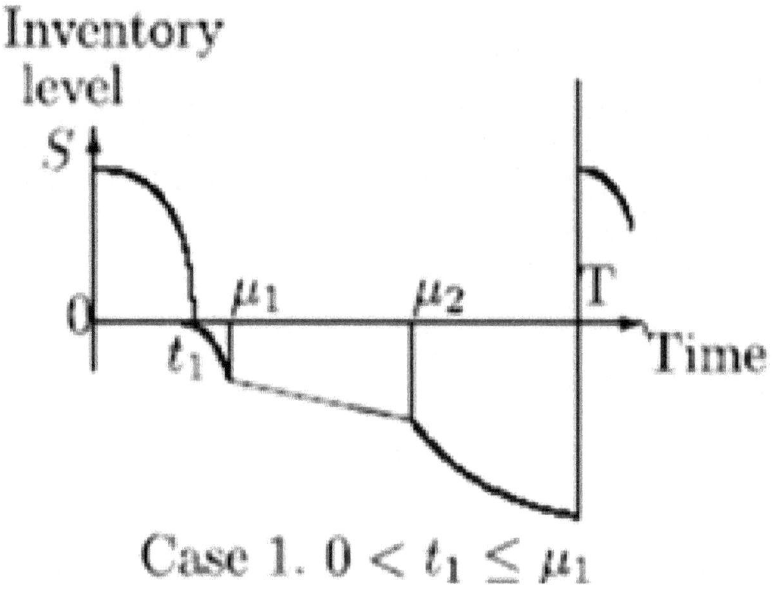

Figure 1. Graphical representation of inventory level over the cycle for case 1.

$$\frac{dI(t)}{dt} = -D_0 \quad , \mu_1 < t < \mu_2 \ , \tag{5}$$

and

$$\frac{dI(t)}{dt} = -A_2 \quad , \ \mu_2 < t < T \ . \tag{6}$$

Solving the differential equations from (3) to (6) with $I(t_1) = 0$, we have:

$$I(t) = \frac{A_1}{\theta}(e^{\theta(t_1-t)} - 1) , 0 \le t \le t_1 \tag{7}$$

$$I(t) = A_1(t_1 - t), t_1 \le t \le \mu_1 , \tag{8}$$

$$I(t) = D_0(\mu_1 - t) + A_1(t_1 - \mu_1), \mu_1 \le t \le \mu_2 \tag{9}$$

$$I(t) = A_2(\mu_2 - t) - D_0(\mu_2 - \mu_1), + A_1(t_1 - \mu_1) \quad \mu_2 \le t \le T \ . \tag{10}$$

The beginning inventory level can be computed as:

$$S = I(0) = \frac{A_1}{\theta}(e^{\theta t_1} - 1) \ . \tag{11}$$

The total number of items which perish in the interval [0, t_1], say D_T , is:

$$\begin{aligned} D_T &= S - \int_0^{t_1} D(t)dt \\ &= S - \int_0^{t_1} A_1 dt \\ &= \frac{A_1}{\theta}(e^{\theta t_1} - 1) - A_1 t_1 \ . \end{aligned} \tag{12}$$

The total number of inventory carried during the interval [0, t_1], say H_T , is:

$$\begin{aligned} H_T &= \int_0^{t_1} I(t)dt \\ &= \int_0^{t_1} \left[\frac{A_1}{\theta}(e^{\theta(t_1-t)} - 1)\right] dt \\ &= \frac{A_1}{\theta^2}(e^{\theta t_1} - \theta t_1 - 1) \end{aligned} \tag{13}$$

The total shortage quantity during the interval [0, t_1], say B_T , is:

$$\begin{aligned} B_T &= -\int_{t_1}^{T} I(t)dt \\ &= -\int_{t_1}^{\mu_1} [A_1(t_1 - t)]dt - \int_{\mu_1}^{\mu_2} [D_0(\mu_1 - t) + A_1(t_1 - \mu_1)]dt \\ &\quad - \int_{\mu_2}^{T} [A_2(\mu_2 - t) - D_0(\mu_2 - \mu_1) + A_1(t_1 - \mu_1)]dt \\ &= \frac{A_1}{2}(t_1 - \mu_1)(t_1 + \mu_1 - 2T) + \frac{A_2}{2}(\mu_2 - T)^2 \\ &\quad + \frac{D_0}{2}(\mu_1 - \mu_2)(\mu_1 + \mu_2 - 2T) \ . \end{aligned} \tag{14}$$

Then, the average total cost per unit time under the condition $t_1 \le \mu_1$ can be given by

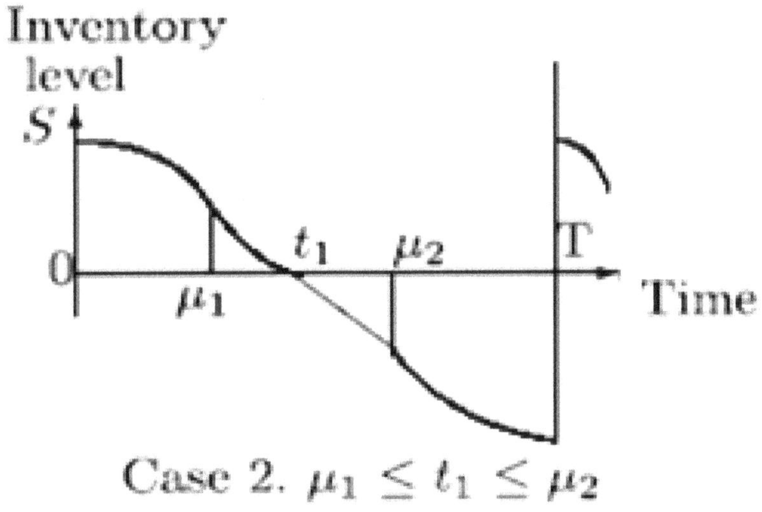

Figure 2. Graphical representation of inventry level over the cycle for case 2.

$$C_1(t_1) = \frac{1}{T}[A_0 + c_1 D_T + c_2 H_T + c_3 B_T] \tag{15}$$

The first order differential of $C_1(t_1)$ with respect to t_1 is as follows:

$$\frac{dC_1(t_1)}{dt_1} = \frac{1}{T}\left[\left(c_1 + \frac{c_2}{\theta}\right)(e^{\theta t_1} - 1) + c_3(t_1 - T)\right]A_1 \tag{16}$$

The necessary condition for $C_1(t_1)$ in (15) to be minimized is $\frac{dC_1(t_1)}{dt_1} = 0$, that is:

$$\left[\left(c_1 + \frac{c_2}{\theta}\right)(e^{\theta t_1} - 1) + c_3(t_1 - T)\right]A_1 = 0 \tag{17}$$

Let $f(t_1) = \left(c_1 + \frac{c_2}{\theta}\right)(e^{\theta t_1} - 1) + c_3(t_1 - T)$, Since $f(0) = -c_3 T < 0$, $f(T) = \left(c_1 + \frac{c_2}{\theta}\right)(e^{\theta T} - 1) > 0$ and $f'(t_1) = (\theta c_1 + c_2)e^{\theta t_1} + c_3 > 0$, it implies that $f(t_1)$ is a strictly monotone increasing function and equation (17) has a unique solution as t_1^*, for $t_1^* \epsilon (0, T)$. Therefore, we have:

Property 1

The deteriorating inventory model under the condition $0 < t_1 \leq \mu_1$, $C_1(t_1)$ obtains its minimum at $t_1 = t_1^*$, where $f(t_1^*) = 0$ if $t_1^* < \mu_1$. On the other hand, $C_1(t_1)$ obtains its minimum at $t_1^* = \mu_1$ if $t_1^* \geq \mu_1$.

From property 1, we know that the total back-order amount at the end of the cycle is $\Delta_1 = A_1(\mu_1 - t_1^*) + D_0(\mu_2 - \mu_1) + A_2(T - \mu_2)$.

Therefore, the optimal order quantity, denoted by Q^*, is $Q^* = S^* + \Delta_1$, where S^* denotes the optimal value of S.

Case 2. $\mu_1 \leq t_1 \leq \mu_2$.

If the time $t_1 \epsilon (\mu_1, \mu_2)$, then, the differential equations governing the inventory model can be expressed as follows Figure 2:

$$\frac{dI(t)}{dt} = -\theta I(t) - A_1, 0 < t < \mu_1 \tag{18}$$

$$\frac{dI(t)}{dt} = -\theta I(t) - D_0, \mu_1 < t < t_1 \tag{19}$$

$$\frac{dI(t)}{dt} = -D_0, t_1 < t < \mu_2, \tag{20}$$

and

$$\frac{dI(t)}{dt} = -A_2, \mu_2 < t < T. \tag{21}$$

Solving the differential equations from (18) to (21) with $I(t_1) = 0$, we have

$$I(t) = \frac{D_0}{\theta}(e^{\theta t_1} - e^{\theta \mu_1})e^{-\theta t} + \frac{A_1}{\theta}(e^{\theta(\mu_1 - t)} - 1), 0 \leq t \leq \mu_1 \tag{22}$$

$$I(t) = \frac{D_0}{\theta}(e^{\theta(t_1 - t)} - 1), \mu_1 \leq t \leq t_1 \tag{23}$$

$$I(t)=D_0(t_1-t),t_1\le t\le\mu_2, \tag{24}$$

$$I(t)=A_2(\mu_2-t)+D_0(t_1-\mu_2),\mu_2\le t\le T \tag{25}$$

The beginning inventory level can be computed as:

$$S=I(0)=\frac{D_0}{\theta}(e^{\theta t_1}-e^{\theta\mu_1})+\frac{A_1}{\theta}(e^{\theta\mu_1}-1). \tag{26}$$

The total number of items which perish in the interval [0, t_1] is:

$$\begin{aligned}D_T&=S-\int_0^{t_1}D(t)dt\\&=S-\left[\int_0^{\mu_1}A_1dt+\int_{\mu_1}^{t_1}D_0dt\right]\\&=\frac{D_0}{\theta}(e^{\theta t_1}-e^{\theta\mu_1})+\frac{A_1}{\theta}(e^{\theta\mu_1}-1)-D_0t_1.\end{aligned} \tag{27}$$

The total number of inventory carried during the interval [0, t_1] is:

$$\begin{aligned}H_T&=\int_0^{t_1}I(t)dt\\&=\int_0^{\mu_1}\left[\frac{D_0}{\theta}(e^{\theta t_1}-e^{\theta\mu_1})e^{-\theta t}+\frac{A_1}{\theta}(e^{\theta(\mu_1-t)}-1)\right]dt\\&\quad+\int_{\mu_1}^{\mu_2}\left[\frac{D_0}{\theta}(e^{\theta(t_1-t)}-1)\right]dt\\&=\frac{D_0}{\theta^2}(e^{\theta t_1}-e^{\theta\mu_1})+\frac{A_1}{\theta^2}(e^{\theta\mu_1}-1)-\frac{D_0}{\theta}t_1.\end{aligned} \tag{28}$$

The total shortage quantity during the interval $[t_1,T]$ is:

$$\begin{aligned}B_T&=-\int_{t_1}^{T}I(t)dt\\&=-\int_{t_1}^{\mu_2}[D_0(t_1-t)]dt-\int_{\mu_2}^{T}[A_2(\mu_2-t)+D_0(t_1-\mu_2)]dt\\&=\frac{D_0}{2}(t_1-\mu_2)(t_1+\mu_2-2T)+\frac{A_2}{2}(\mu_2-T)^2.\end{aligned} \tag{29}$$

Then, the average total cost per unit under the condition

$\mu_1\le t_1\le\mu_2$, can be given by:

$$C_2(t_1)=\frac{1}{T}[A_0+c_1D_T+c_2H_T+c_3B_T]. \tag{30}$$

The first order differential of $C_2(t_1)$ with respect to t_1 is as follows:

$$\frac{dC_2(t_1)}{dt_1}=\frac{D_0}{T}\left[\left(c_1+\frac{c_2}{\theta}\right)(e^{\theta t_1}-1)+c_3(t_1-T)\right]. \tag{31}$$

The necessary condition for $C_2(t_1)$ in (30) to be minimized is $\frac{dC_2(t_1)}{dt_1}=0$, that is:

$$\left[\left(c_1+\frac{c_2}{\theta}\right)(e^{\theta t_1}-1)+c_3(t_1-T)\right]=0. \tag{32}$$

Similar to the first case, we have:

Property 2

The inventory model under the condition $\mu_1<t_1\le\mu_2$, $C_2(t_1)$ obtains its minimum at $t_1=t_1^*$, where $f(t_1^*)=0$ if $\mu_1<t_1^*<\mu_2$; $C_2(t_1)$ obtains its minimum at $t_1^*=\mu_1$ if $t_1^*<\mu_1$; and $C_2(t_1)$ obtains its minimum at $t_1^*=\mu_2$ if $\mu_2<t_1^*$.

From property 2, we know that the total back-order amount at the end of the cycle is $\Delta_2=D_0(\mu_2-t_1^*)+A_2(T-\mu_2)$. Therefore, the optimal order quantity, denoted by Q^*, is $Q^*=S^*+\Delta_2$, where S^* denotes the optimal value of S.

Case 3. $\mu_2\le t_1\le T$

If the time $t_1\in[\mu_2,T)$, then, the differential equations governing the inventory model can be expressed as follows Figure 3:

$$\frac{dI(t)}{dt}=-\theta I(t)-A_1,\quad 0<t<\mu_1, \tag{33}$$

$$\frac{dI(t)}{dt}=-\theta I(t)-D_0,\quad \mu_1<t<\mu_2 \tag{34}$$

$$\frac{dI(t)}{dt}=-\theta I(t)-A_2,\quad \mu_2<t<t_1, \tag{35}$$

and

$$\frac{dI(t)}{dt}=-A_2,\quad t_1<t<T \tag{36}$$

Solving the differential equations from (33) to (36) with $I(t_1)=0$, we have

$$I(t)=\frac{A_1}{\theta}(e^{\theta(\mu_1-t)}-1)+\left[\frac{D_0}{\theta}(e^{\theta\mu_2}-e^{\theta\mu_1})+\frac{A_2}{\theta}(e^{\theta t_1}-e^{\theta\mu_2})\right]e^{-\theta t},$$

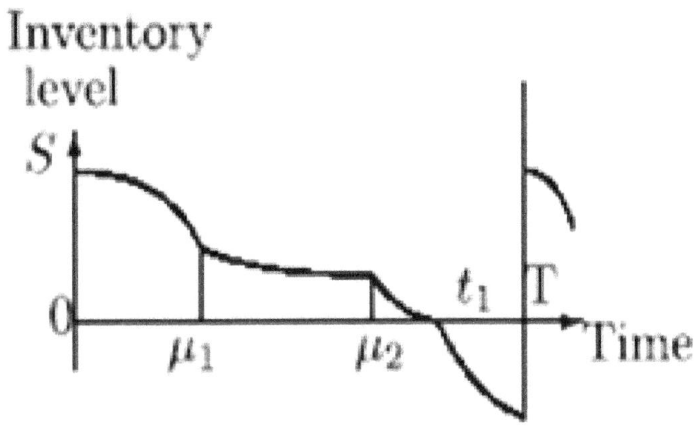

Case 3. $\mu_2 \le t_1 < T$

Figure 3. Graphical representation of inventry level over the cycle for case 3.

$0 \le t \le \mu_1$ (37)

$$I(t) = \frac{D_0}{\theta}\left(e^{\theta(\mu_2 - t)} - 1\right) + \left[\frac{A_2}{\theta}\left(e^{\theta t_1} - e^{\theta \mu_2}\right)\right] e^{-\theta t},$$

$\mu_1 \le t \le \mu_2$, (38)

$$I(t) = \frac{A_2}{\theta}\left(e^{\theta(t_1 - t)} - 1\right), \mu_2 \le t \le t_1 \quad (39)$$

$$I(t) = A_2(t_1 - t), t_1 \le t \le T \quad (40)$$

The beginning inventory level can be computed as

$$S = I(0) = \frac{A_1}{\theta}\left(e^{\theta\mu_1} - 1\right) + \frac{D_0}{\theta}\left(e^{\theta\mu_2} - e^{\theta\mu_1}\right) + \frac{A_2}{\theta}\left(e^{\theta t_1} - e^{\theta\mu_2}\right) \quad (41)$$

The total number of items which perish in the interval [0, t_1], say D_T, is:

$$D_T = S - \int_0^{t_1} D(t)dt = S - \left[\int_0^{\mu_1} A_1 dt + \int_{\mu_1}^{\mu_2} D_0 dt + \int_{\mu_2}^{t_1} A_2 dt\right] = \frac{D_0}{\theta}\left(e^{\theta\mu_2} - e^{\theta\mu_1}\right) + \frac{A_1}{\theta}\left(e^{\theta\mu_1} - 1\right) + \frac{A_2}{\theta}\left(e^{\theta t_1} - e^{\theta\mu_2}\right) - A_2 t_1 \quad (42)$$

The total number of inventory carried during the interval [0, t_1], say H_T, is:

$$H_T = \int_0^{t_1} I(t)dt = \int_0^{\mu_1}\left[\frac{A_1}{\theta}\left(e^{\theta(\mu_1 - t)} - 1\right) + \left[\frac{D_0}{\theta}\left(e^{\theta\mu_2} - e^{\theta\mu_1}\right) + \frac{A_2}{\theta}\left(e^{\theta t_1} - e^{\theta\mu_2}\right)\right] e^{-\theta t}\right] dt + \int_{\mu_1}^{\mu_2}\left[\frac{D_0}{\theta}\left(e^{\theta(\mu_2 - t)} - 1\right) + \left[\frac{A_2}{\theta}\left(e^{\theta t_1} - e^{\theta\mu_2}\right)\right] e^{-\theta t}\right] dt + \int_{\mu_2}^{t_1}\left[\frac{A_2}{\theta}\left(e^{\theta(t_1 - t)} - 1\right)\right] dt = \frac{D_0}{\theta^2}\left(e^{\theta\mu_2} - e^{\theta\mu_1}\right) + \frac{A_1}{\theta^2}\left(e^{\theta\mu_1} - 1\right) + \frac{A_2}{\theta}\left(e^{\theta t_1} - e^{\theta\mu_2}\right) - \frac{A_2}{\theta} t_1 \quad (43)$$

The total shortage quantity during the interval [0, t_1], say B_T, is:

$$B_T = -\int_{t_1}^{T} I(t)dt = -\int_{t_1}^{T}\left[A_2(t_1 - t)\right]dt = \frac{A_2}{2}(t_1 - T)^2 \quad (44)$$

Then, the average total cost per unit time under the condition $\mu_2 \le t_1 \le T$, can be given by:

$$C_3(t_1) = \frac{1}{T}\left[A_0 + c_1 D_T + c_2 H_T + c_3 B_T\right] \quad (45)$$

The first order differential of $C_1(t_1)$ with respect to t_1 is as follows:

$$\frac{dC_3(t_1)}{dt_1} = \frac{A_2}{T}\left[\left(c_1 + \frac{c_2}{\theta}\right)(e^{\theta t_1} - 1) + c_3(t_1 - T)\right] \quad (46)$$

The necessary condition for $C_1(t_1)$ in (45) to be minimized is $\frac{dC_3(t_1)}{dt_1} = 0$, that is:

$$A_2\left[\left(c_1 + \frac{c_2}{\theta}\right)(e^{\theta t_1} - 1) + c_3(t_1 - T)\right] = 0 \quad (47)$$

Similar to the first case, we have:

Property 3

The inventory model under the condition $\mu_2 \le t_1 < T$, $C_3(t_1)$ obtains its minimum at $t_1 = t_1^*$,
where $f(t_1^*) = 0$ if $\mu_2 < t_1^*$. On the other hand, $C_3(t_1)$ obtains its minimum at $t_1^* = \mu_2$ if $t_1^* < \mu_2$.

From Property 3, we know that the total back-order amount at the end of the cycle is $\Delta_3 = A_2(T - t_1^*)$. Therefore, the optimal order quantity, denoted by Q^*, is $Q^* = S^* + \Delta_3$, where S^* denotes the optimal value of S.

Remark 1: The previous analysis shows that Equations (16), (31) and (46) can be expressed as $\frac{dC_j(t)}{dt_1} = \frac{D_{j[(t]_1)}}{T} f(t_1), j = 1,2,3.$ which denotes the total marginal cost function under different demand rate conditions, respectively.

Combining the above properties, we know that $C_1(\mu_1) = C_2(\mu_1)$, and $C_2(\mu_2) = C_3(\mu_2)$. Therefore, we can derive the following result.

Theorem 1: For the deteriorating inventory model with trapezoidal type demand rate, the optimal replenishment time is t_1^* and $C_1(t_1)$ obtains its minimum at $t_1 = t_1^*$, if and only If $t_1^* < \mu_1$. On the other hand, $C_2(t_1)$ obtains its minimum at t_1^* if and only if $\mu_1 < t_1^* < \mu_2$ and $C_13\ (t_11$) obtains its minimum at t_1^* if and only if $\mu_2 < t_1^*$, where t_1^* is the unique solution of the equation $f(t_1) = 0$.

NUMERICAL EXAMPLES

In this section, we provide several numerical examples to illustrate the above theory.

Example 1

The parameter values are given as follows: $T = 15$ weeks, $\mu_1 = 5$ weeks, $\mu_2 = 10$ weeks, $A_1 = 150$ units, $A_2 = 210$ units, $\theta = 0.2$, $A_0 = \$200$, $c_1 = \$2$ per unit, $c_2 = \$4$ per unit, $c_3 = \$3$ per unit, $D_0 = \$360$. Based on the solution procedure as aforementioned, we have $f(\mu_1) = 7.8022 > 0$, then it yields that the optimal replenishment time $t_1^* = 4.4556227$ weeks, the optimal order quantity, Q^*, is 4010.06 unit and the minimum cost $C_1(t_1^*) = 4007.51$

Example 2

The parameter values are given as follows: $T = 15$ weeks, $\mu_1 = 2$ weeks, $\mu_2 = 10$ weeks, $A_1 = 150$ units, $A_2 = 210$ units, $\theta = 0.2$, $A_0 = \$200$, $c_1 = \$2$ per unit, $c_2 = \$4$ per unit, $c_3 = \$3$ per unit, $D_0 = \$360$. Based on the solution procedure as aforementioned, we have $f(\mu_1) = -28.1799 < 0$ and $f(\mu_2) = 125.559 > 0$, then it yields that the optimal replenishment time $t_1^* = 4.4556227$ weeks, the optimal order quantity, Q^*, is 5117.73 unit and the minimum cost $C_2(t_1^*) = 4326.95$.

Example 3

The parameter values are given as follows:

$T = 15$ weeks, $\mu_1 = 2$ weeks, $\mu_2 = 4$ weeks, $A_1 = 150$ units, $A_2 = 210$ units, $\theta = 0.2$, $A_0 = \$200$, $c_1 = \$3$ per unit, $c_2 = \$2$ per unit, $c_3 = \$5$ per unit, $D_0 = \$360$. Based on the solution procedure as above, we have $f(\mu_2) = -30.4892 < 0$, then it yields that the optimal replenishment time $t_1^* = 5.922857$ weeks, the optimal order quantity, Q^*, is 4691.69 unit and the minimum cost $C_3(t_1^*) = 4952.73$

SENSITIVITY ANALYSIS

We study the effects of changes in the system parameter T, μ_1, μ_2, A_1, A_2, θ, A_0, c_1, c_2, c_3, and D_0 on the optimal values of t_1, the optimal order quantity Q^* and the minimal optimal costs $C_1(t_1^*)$, $C_2(t_1^*)$ and $C_3(t_1^*)$ on the three tables. The sensitivity analysis is performed by changing each of the parameters by +25, +10, -10 and -25% on taking one parameter at a time and keeping the remaining parameters unchanged. The results are shown in Tables 1, 2 and 3.

On the basis of the results in Table 1, the following observations are taken into account:

Table 1. Based on Example 1.

Parameter changing	Change (%)	t_1^*	Q^*	$C_1(t_1^*)$	Percentage change in $C_1(t_1^*)$
T	+25	-	-	-	-
	+10	4.775294	4397.83	4479.1	+11.7677
	-10	4.11914	3626.538	3519.72	-12.1719
	-25	3.579408	3060.082	2741.2	-31.5984
μ_1	+25	4.4556227	3747.56	3515.33	-12.2814
	+10	4.4556227	3905.06	3802.75	-5.10941
	-10	4.4556227	4115.06	4222.75	+5.37092
	-25	4.4556227	4272.56	4565.33	+13.9194
μ_2	+25	4.4556227	4385.06	4288.75	+7.01782
	+10	4.4556227	4160.06	4142.51	+3.36868
	-10	4.4556227	3860.06	3842.51	-4.11727
	-25	4.4556227	3635.06	3538.75	-11.697
A_1	+25	4.4556227	4300.07	4199.81	+4.79849
	+10	4.4556227	4126.06	4084.43	+1.9194
	-10	4.4556227	3894.052	3930.59	-1.9194
	-25	4.4556227	3720.042	3815.22	-4.79824
A_2	+25	4.4556227	4272.56	4138.75	+3.27485
	+10	4.4556227	4115.06	4060.01	+1.31004
	-10	4.4556227	3905.06	3955.01	-1.31004
	-25	4.4556227	3747.56	3876.25	-3.27535
θ	+25	4.13413	4066.47	4069.09	+1.53662
	+10	4.321147	4034.15	4033.01	+0.636305
	-10	4.598762	3983.71	3980.73	-0.668245
	-25	4.831456	3939.43	3938.01	-1.73424
A_0	+25	4.4556227	4010.06	4010.85	+0.0833435
	+10	4.4556227	4010.06	4008.85	+0.0334372
	-10	4.4556227	4010.06	4006.18	-0.0331877
	-25	4.4556227	4010.06	4004.18	-0.083094
c_1	+25	4.403952	3999.01	4020.99	+0.336368
	+10	4.434786	4005.58	4012.95	+0.135745
	-10	4.476688	4014.62	4002.01	-0.137242
	-25	4.5087249	4021.53	3993.65	-0.345851
c_2	+25	3.9940306	3918.064	4127.82	+3.00211
	+10	4.256916	3968.62	4059.34	+1.29332
	-10	4.677329	4059.70	3949.63	-1.44429
	-25	-	-	-	-
c_3	+25	4.9807361	4133.76	4834.66	+20.64
	+10	4.677329	4059.70	4343.26	+8.37802
	-10	4.2154887	3960.345	3664.46	-8.56018
	-25	3.8135331	3886.023	3134.38	-21.7873
D_0	+25	4.4556227	4460.06	4692.51	+17.0929
	+10	4.4556227	4055.06	4277.51	+6.73735
	-10	4.4556227	3830.06	3737.51	-6.73735
	-25	4.4556227	3560.06	3332.51	-16.8434

Table 2. Based on Example 2.

Parameter changing	Change (%)	t_1^*	Q^*	$C_2(t_1^*)$	Percentage change in $C_2(t_1^*)$
T	25	5.2263	6359.1	5461.8	26.228
	10	4.7753	5607.4	4791.4	10.735
	-10	4.1191	4638.3	3824.9	-11.6
	-25	3.5794	3940.3	2962.8	-31.53
μ1	25	4.4556	4953	4085.3	-5.584
	10	4.4556	5053.8	4233.2	-2.167
	-10	4.4556	5179.2	4417	2.0818
	-25	4.4556	5266.8	4533.6	4.7754
μ2	25	4.4556	5492.7	4608.2	6.5002
	10	4.4556	5267.7	4462	3.12
	-10	4.4556	4967.7	4162	-3.813
	-25	4.4556	4742.7	3858.2	-10.83
A1	25	4.4556	5210	4467.5	3.2489
	10	4.4556	5154.6	4381.1	1.2503
	-10	4.4556	5080.8	4272.9	-1.25
	-25	4.4556	5025.5	4191.7	-3.126
A2	25	4.4556	5380.2	4458.2	3.0336
	10	4.4556	5222.7	4379.5	1.2133
	-10	4.4556	5012.7	4274.5	-1.213
	-25	4.4556	4855.2	4195.7	-3.033
θ	25	4.1341	5224.6	4578.3	5.8083
	10	4.3211	5164.4	4435.7	2.5142
	-10	4.5988	5065.4	4203.7	-2.848
	-25	4.8315	4974.8	3981.5	-7.984
A0	25	4.4556	5117.7	4330.3	0.077
	10	4.4556	5117.7	4328.3	0.0307
	-10	4.4556	5117.7	4325.6	-0.031
	-25	4.4556	5117.7	4323.6	-0.077
C_1	25	4.404	5091.2	4342.1	0.3499
	10	4.4348	5107	4333.1	0.1426
	-10	4.4767	5128.7	4320.6	-0.146
	-25	4.5087	5145.5	4310.9	-0.371
C_2	25	3.994	4896.9	4443.5	2.6941
	10	4.2569	5018.3	4382.5	1.2836
	-10	4.6773	5236.9	4284.3	-0.986
	-25	5.0642	5466.6	4117.8	-4.835
C_3	25	4.9807	5414.6	5183.4	19.793
	10	4.6773	5236.9	4681.3	8.1885
	-10	4.2155	4998.4	3955.1	-8.593
	-25	3.8135	4820	3360.2	-22.34
D_0	25	4.4556	6042.4	5138.9	18.764
	10	4.4556	5487.6	4651.7	7.5055
	-10	4.4556	4747.8	4002.2	-7.506
	-25	4.4556	4193	3515	-18.76

Table 3. Based on Example 3.

Parameter changing	Change (%)	t_1^*	Q^*	$C_3(t_1^*)$	Percentage Change in $C_3(t_1^*)$
T	+25	6.888121	6007.47	6158.35	+24.3425
	+10	6.3256856	5210.11	5421.12	+9.45721
	-10	5.4951019	4185.06	4506.83	-9.00312
	-25	4.80104	3449.87	3891.70	-21.4229
μ_1	+25	5.922857	4526.95	4733.08	-4.43493
	+10	5.922857	4627.76	4867.49	-1.72107
	-10	5.922857	4753.11	5034.62	+1.65343
	-25	5.922857	4840.75	5151.48	+4.01294
μ_2	+25	5.922857	5061.25	5445.47	+9.94886
	+10	5.922857	4830.71	5138.09	+3.74258
	-10	5.922857	4563.36	4781.62	-3.45486
	-25	5.922857	4389.12	4549.3	-8.14561
A_1	+25	5.922857	4783.91	5075.69	+2.48267
	+10	5.922857	4728.58	5001.91	+0.992988
	-10	5.922857	4654.80	4903.54	-.99319
	-25	5.922857	4599.47	4829.77	-2.48267
A_2	+25	5.922857	5442.22	5624.39	+13.5614
	+10	5.922857	4991.90	5221.39	+5.42448
	-10	5.922857	4391.48	4684.06	-5.42468
	-25	5.922857	3941.16	4281.07	-13.5614
θ	+25	5.244098	4811.16	5337.94	+7.77773
	+10	5.6332	4743.12	5111.73	+3.21035
	-10	6.240075	4633.23	4786.61	-3.35411
	-25	6.774499	4527.33	4523.89	-8.65866
A_0	+25	5.922857	4691.69	4956.06	+0.0672356
	+10	5.922857	4691.69	4954.06	+0.0268539
	-10	5.922857	4691.69	4951.4	-0.0268539
	-25	5.922857	4691.69	4949.4	-0.0672356
c_1	+25	5.6287167	4557.34	5198.08	+4.95383
	+10	5.8006196	4634.45	5053.57	+2.03605
	-10	6.051904	4754.34	4847.89	-2.11681
	-25	6.259809	4860.24	4682.29	-5.46042
c_2	+25	5.6287167	4557.34	5198.08	+4.95383
	+10	5.8006196	4634.45	5053.57	+2.03605
	-10	6.051904	4754.34	4847.89	-2.11681
	-25	6.259809	4860.24	4682.29	-5.46042
c_3	+25	6.48752	4983.52	5628.25	+13.6393
	+10	6.16304	4810.17	5233.43	+5.66758
	-10	5.659581	4570.9	4656.04	-5.99043
	-25	5.2109858	4385.64	4176.26	-15.6776
D_0	+25	5.922857	5021.86	5392.96	+8.88863
	+10	5.922857	4823.76	5128.82	+3.55541
	-10	5.922857	4559.62	4776.64	-3.55541
	-25	5.922857	4361.52	4512.5	-8.88863

--- indicates the solutions are infeasible.

1) With increase in the value of parameter T and $c_3 : t_1$, the optimal values of Q^* and $C_1(t_1^*)$ increase.
2) With increase in the value of parameter c_1 and c_2 : t_1 and the optimal values of Q^* decrease and $C_1(t_1^*)$ increase.
3) With increase in the value of parameter: t_1 decreases and the optimal values of Q^* and $C_1(t_1^*)$ increase.
4) With increase in the value of parameter μ_2, A_1, A_2 and $D_0 : t_1$ remains constant and the optimal values of Q^* and $C_1(t_1^*)$ increase.
5) With increase in the value of parameter $\mu_1 : t_1$ remains constant and the optimal values of Q^* and $C_1(t_1^*)$ decrease.
6) With increase in the value of parameter $A_0 : t_1$ and the optimal values of Q^* remains constant and $C_1(t_1^*)$ increase.

Similar results are obtained from Tables 2 and 3:

1) The changes in values of t_1^* , Q^* and $C_i(t_1^*)$ where i = 1, 2 and 3 more seen when we increase the percentage of μ_1. So μ_1 is more sensitive.
2) With increase in the value of parameter μ_2, A_1, A_2, θ , A_0 , c_1, c_2, and D_0 ,the optimal values of t_1^* , Q^* and $C_i(t_1^*)$ where $i = 1$, 2 and 3 are moderately sensitive.
3) With increase in the value of parameter T and c_3 , the optimal values of t_1^*, Q^* and $C_i(t_1^*)$ where i = 1, 2 and 3 are less sensitive.

CONCLUDING REMARKS

In this paper, we study the inventory model for deteriorating items with constant-constant-constant type demand rate, that is, the demand rate is a piecewise constant function. We proposed an inventory replenishment policy for this type of inventory model. Such type of demand pattern is generally seen in case of seasonal goods like vegetables, fruits and electronics components coming to market. We think that such types of demand are quite realistic and a useful inventory replenishment policy for such type of inventory model is also proposed. From the market information, we can find that this type of demand rate model is some applicable than trapezoidal type demand rate model in the stage of product life cycle. This paper provides an interesting topic for the future study of such kind of important inventory models and we extend to quadratic demand, stock-dependent demand and time-dependent demand. We also extend constant deterioration rate to variable deterioration rates, Weibull two parameter deterioration rates, Weibull three parameters deterioration rate and also Gamma deterioration rate.

REFERENCES

Bahari-Kashani H (1989). Replenishment schedule for deteriorating items with time-proportional demand. J. Oper. Res. Soc. 40:75-81.
Cheng M, Wang G (2009). A note on the inventory model for deteriorating items with trapezoidal type demand rate. Comput. Ind. Eng. 56:1296-1300.
Deng P, Shaohua L, Robert HJ, Chu P (2007). A note on the inventory model with deteriorating items with ramp type demand rate. Eur. J. Oper. Res. 178:112-120.
Ghare PM, Schrader SF (1963). Model for Exponentially decaying inventory. J. Ind. Eng. 14(5):238.
Giri BC, Jalan AK, Chaudhuri KS (2003). Economic order quantity model with Weibull deterioration distribution, shortage and ramp-type demand. Int. J. Syst. Sci. 34:237-243.
Goswami A, Chaudhuri KS (1991). An EOQ model for deteriorating items with shortages and a linear trend in demand. J. the Operational Res. Soc. 42:1105-1110
Hill RM (1995). Inventory model for increasing demand followed by level demand. J. Operational Res. Soc. 46:1250-1269.
Mandal B, Pal AK (1998). Order level inventory system with ramp-type demand rate for deteriorating items. J. Interdiscip. Math. 1:49-66.
Ritchie E (1984). The EOQ for linear increasing demand: a simple optimal solution, J. Oper. Res. Soc. 35:949-952.
Silver EA, Meal HC (1969). A simple modification of the EOQ for the case of a varying demand rate. Prod. Inventory Manag. 10(4):52-65.
Wu KS (2001). An EOQ inventory model for items with Weibull distribution deterioration, ramp-type demand rate and partial backlogging. Prod. Plann. Control 12:787-793.
Wu KS, Ouyang Ly (2000). A replenishment policy for deteriorating items with ramp-type demand rate. Proceedings of National Sci. Council ROC (A), 24: 279-286[Short Communication].

Wu's algorithm and its possible application in cryptanalysis

T. L. Grobler[1,2]*, A. J. van Zyl[3], J. C. Olivier[4], W. Kleynhans[1,5], B. P. Salmon[1,5] and W. T. Penzhorn[1]

[1]Department of Electrical, Electronic and Computer Engineering, University of Pretoria, South-Africa.
[2]Defence, Peace, Safety and Security, Council for Scientific and Industrial Research, South-Africa.
[3]Department of Mathematics and Applied Mathematics, University of Pretoria, South-Africa.
[4]School of Engineering, University of Tasmania, Hobart, Australia.
[5]Meraka Institute, Council for Scientific and Industrial Research, South-Africa.

In this paper we reviewed Wu's algorithm and introduced it as a cryptanalysis technique. This study reveals that when Wu's algorithm is used for cryptanalysis it simplifies. This is true because Wu's algorithm has to be applied to binary polynomials only, when used for cryptanalysis. To summarize, we gave a full description of Wu's algorithm in the binary case and also a basic example of using binary Wu to break an s-box.

Key words: Wu-Ritt decomposition algorithm, s-box, binary polynomials, cryptanalysis.

INTRODUCTION

Cryptographic algorithms use s-boxes to introduce non-linearity into a method. Such an s-box can be represented by a set of non-linear binary polynomials. A non-linear s-box is difficult to reverse. If the output is known it is difficult to derive the input. This is true due to the fact that reversing an s-box is the same as solving a set of non-linear polynomials (finding the roots of such a set). Wu's algorithm is a mechanical method to solve non-linear polynomial sets and can thus be used as a cryptanalysis technique.

The algorithm was originally developed by J. F. Ritt in the late forties (See his now classic book Differential Algebra: Ritt (1950). Later it was independently rediscovered and improved by the Chinese mathematician Wu Wen-Tsün in the late seventies (Wen-Tsün, 1978, 1984, 1986). Other resources describing Wu's algorithm include, Bayram and Celik, (2002), and Kapur and Mundy (1988). The cornerstone of this algorithm is the generation of a Ritt-Wu characteristic set, which is a triangular set that is constructed from a polynomial set so that the characteristic set shares some of the properties of the original set (Gallo and Mishra, 1990b; Ritt, 1950). The algorithm has found wide usage in mechanical theorem proving (Wen-Tsün, 1986; Kapur and Mundy, 1988) and solving polynomial sets (Bayram, 2002) to name a few applications. Improved variations on the original algorithm can be found in Gallo and Mishra (1990b), and Chou and Gao, (2008). The computational complexity of the algorithm is thoroughly analyzed in Gallo and Mishra (1990a, b).

It has been speculated that the reason Wu has failed to make a large impact is that it has been overshadowed by the Gröbner base algorithm (Buchberger, 1985). A debate regarding the respective power of these two algorithms has sprung up. Experimental data is available for both algorithms in Buchberger (1985), Chou (1985), and Kapur (1986). The complexity of the Gröbner base algorithm is analyzed in Möller and Mora (1984). This paper however does not investigate which of these two algorithms would

*Corresponding author. E-mail: trienkog@gmail.com.

make a better cryptanalysis method. It only introduces Wu's original algorithm (Wen-Tsün, 1986) as a cryptanalysis technique without the improvements of Gallo and Mishra (1990b), and Chou and Gao, (2008).

Wu's algorithm is used to solve polynomial sets in the decimal number system. This paper will investigate Wu's algorithm in the binary case with the hope that the algorithm will simplify greatly so that it can be used as an effective non-linear attack on s-boxes.

The paper begins by introducing multivariate polynomials. This is followed by a discussion of polynomial sets. These are then used to introduce Wu's algorithm. Once Wu's algorithm is introduced it is modified for the binary case. The paper ends with an example of how Wu can be used as a non-linear attack and a final conclusion discussing the future research required for possible successful implementation of this approach.

MULTIVARIATE POLYNOMIALS

Basic definitions

Multivariate polynomials are polynomials consisting of more than one variable, $x_1, x_2, \cdots, x_r$. Without loss of generality one may assume that the ordering of the above mentioned variables are $x_1 < x_2 < \cdots < x_r$. A multivariate polynomial *f* is denoted by (1) if x_m is selected as *master variable*

$$f = I_n x_m^n + I_{n-1} x_m^{n-1} + \cdots + I_0 \qquad (1)$$

where $I_k \in \{x_1, x_2, \cdots, x_{m-1}, x_{m+1}, \cdots, x_r\}$, $0 \le k \le n$. I_k is a multivariate polynomial itself and may contain a number in its coefficient.

The *class* of a multivariate polynomial is defined as the greatest subscript *c* of any x contained in *f* and is denoted by $c = class(f)$. The class of a constant is defined to be naught.

When the master variable is equal to x_c (1) becomes

$$f = I_n x_c^n + I_{n-1} x_c^{n-1} + \cdots + I_0 \qquad (2)$$

The variable x_c is the *leading variable* and I_n is the *leading or initial coefficient* of *f*. The leading variable is denoted by $x_c = lv(f)$, while the initial is denoted by $I_n = lc(f)$.

The *degree* of a polynomial is the highest degree of the leading variable. The degree of *f* is denoted by *n* = *deg*(*f*). One can also determine the degree of any variable; this is denoted by *deg*(*f*, x_i).

These definitions are described in greater detail in Bayram et al. (2002), Wen-Tsün (1986), and Kapur and Mundy (1986).

Reduction

A polynomial *g* is said to be *reduced* with respect to *f* if the highest degree of x_c $[lv(f)]$ in *g* (if any) is less than the *deg*(*f*). The above does not imply that *g* is of a lesser class than *f*, x_c is only the master variable of *g* and not necessarily its leading variable. If *g* is reduced with respect to *f* we denote it as *g red f*. If *g* is not reduced with respect to *f* we denote it as *g* ~~*red*~~ *f*. The action of reducing *g* with respect to *f* is known as *reduction*.

Reduction is provided by the *pseudo division algorithm*. In normal polynomial mathematics any polynomial $g(x)$ can be written as $g(x) = f(x) \cdot q(x) + r(x)$. When working with multivariate polynomials the above equation becomes

$$I_n^s g = q \cdot f + r \qquad (3)$$

where $f = I_n x_c^n + I_{n-1} x_c^{n-1} + \cdots + I_0$ with $I_k \in \{x_1, x_2, \cdots, x_{c-1}\}$ and $g = L_j x_c^j + L_{j-1} x_c^{j-1} + \cdots + L_0$ with $L_k \in \{x_1, x_2, \cdots, x_{c-1}, x_{c+1}, \cdots x_r\}$. Note that $j \ge n$. The polynomial I_n is thus the leading coefficient of *f* and must be non-zero. Also *q* and *r* are multivariate polynomials and *s* is an integer with the following added condition $s \le n - j + 1$. If the integer *s* is the smallest possible power that satisfies (3) and *q* as well as *r* was uniquely determined by some means then *r* is known as the *pseudo remainder* of *g* with respect to *f*. The pseudo remainder has one additional property reduced with respect to *f*, meaning *deg*(*f*, x_c) > *deg*(*r*, x_c). If $n > j$ then *g* is already reduced with respect to *f* and $s = 0, q = 0$ are chosen so that $r = g$ and the above equation still holds.

Pseudo division algorithm

Input to the algorithm is the polynomials *g* and *f* in x_c, thus one can write *g* and *f* as $g = L_j x_c^j + \cdots + L_0$, $f = I_n x_c^n + \cdots + I_0$. Output of the algorithm is the pseudo remainder of *g* with respect to *f* and is denoted by $prem(g, f) = r$.

Set $r = g$.

While *k* = *deg*(r, x_c) $\ge n$

$r = I_n r - C_k x_c^{k-n} f$, where C_k is the leading coefficient of r in x_c .
Return *r*.

This algorithm is discussed in greater detail in Chou and Gao, (2008).

Partial order on polynomials

One can define a *partial order on polynomials*. The polynomial *g* has a higher rank than *f* if one of the following two cases holds:

1) $class(f) < class(g)$;
2) $class(f) = class(g)$ and the *deg*(*f*) < *deg*(*g*).

It is denoted as $g > f$ (*g* has a higher rank than *f*). The expression $g > f$ can also be interpreted as *f* has a lower rank than *g*. When neither of the above conditions is met one says that *f* and *g* are of the same rank. This is donated as $f \sim g$. This happens when $class(f) = class(g)$ and the *deg*(*f*) = *deg*(*g*) or when both polynomials are constants.

One has to note here that reduction is not parallel to the partial order. If $g > f$ it does not mean that *g* is not reduced with respect to *f*. Reduction concentrates on a single variable, while the partial order concentrates on the entire polynomial.

POLYNOMIAL SETS

A *polynomial set* is defined as a collection of polynomials and is denoted by $F = \{f_1, f_2, \cdots, f_p\}$.

Polynomial ideal

Let *F* be a set of polynomials in variables $x_1, x_2 \cdots, x_r$. Let P_i be the totality of linear combinations of polynomials in *F* with polynomials in *K* as coefficients, where *K* consist of all possible polynomials in variables $x_1, x_2 \cdots, x_r$. Then P_i is a *polynomial ideal* generated by *F*.

Let P_i be a prime ideal in variables $x_1, x_2 \cdots, x_r$. Then there may be some x_i such that no non-zero polynomial in P_i involves only x_i , that is every polynomial in which x_i appears effectively also involves some x_j with $i \neq j$. If there exist such a x_i , let us pick one of them and call it u_1 . There may be another x_k distinct from u_1 such that no non-zero polynomial in P_i involves only u_1 and the new x_k . If there exist such a x_k , pick one of them and call it u_2 . Continuing, one finds a set $u_1, \cdots, u_w (w < r)$. This set is known as *the parametric set of indeterminates* for P_i . The value *w* is known as the *dimension* of P_i and is denoted as *dim* P_i . More information on polynomial ideals can be found in Ritt (1950).

Ascending set

A polynomial set $F = \{f_1, f_2, \cdots, f_p\}$ is said to be an *ascending set* if either of the following two conditions hold:

1) *p* = 1, and $f_1 \neq 0$.
2) *p* > 1, $0 < class(f_1) < class(f_2) < \cdots < class(f_p)$, and f_j is reduced with respect to f_i for each pair $j > i$.

An ascending set is said to be *contradictory* if *p* = 1, $f_1 \neq 0$ with $class(f_1) = 0$. It is clear from the above that *p* ≤ *r*.

Reducing a polynomial with respect to an ascending set

Let $F = \{f_1, f_2, \ldots, f_r\}$ be an ascending set with $class(f_1) > 0$ and *g* a polynomial. We define $prem(g; F)$ inductively to be $prem(prem(g, f_r); f_1, f_2, \ldots, f_{r-1})$. Let the answer be *R*. Note that $prem(g; F)$ means we reduce *g* with respect to *F*. In other words *g* is reduced with respect to all polynomials in *F*. This definition leads to the *remainder equation.*

$$\prod_{i=1}^{r} I_i^{s_i} g = \sum_{i=1}^{r} Q_i f_i + R \qquad (4)$$

which is derived in Wen-Tsün (1986).

Partial order for ascending sets

One can extend the partial order on polynomials to provide a *partial order for ascending sets*. Let $F = (f_1, f_2, \ldots, f_p)$ and $G = (g_1, g_2, \ldots g_s)$ be ascending sets. We define $F < G$ whenever there is either a $j \leq \min\{p, s\}$ such that $f_i \sim g_i$ for all *i* < *j*, but $f_j < g_j$, or *p* > *s* and $f_i \sim g_i$ for all $i \leq s$. This means that $F < G$ if either of two cases holds:

1) When f_i and g_i are incomparable up to a point *j*

($j \leq \min\{p, s\}$), but $f_j < g_j$.

2) When F is longer than G, and each g_i is incomparable to the corresponding f_i.

For incomparable ascending sets we write $F \sim G$. When $F < G$ we say that G has a higher rank than F or that F has a lower rank than G. When $F \sim G$ we say F and G are of the same rank. The ascending sets will be of the same rank when $p = s$, $f_1 \sim g_1, \cdots, f_p \sim g_p$. Note from above that the larger ascending set may have the lower rank.

Minimal ascending set

A *minimal ascending set* is defined as any set from a collection of ascending sets that has the lowest rank of all the sets in the collection. What is meant by the lowest rank is that no other set in the collection may be of a lower rank than a minimal ascending set. There may however be some sets that have the same rank than a minimal ascending set. These sets are minimal ascending sets of the collection as well. Thus one can say a set F_i is a minimal ascending set of the collection of ascending sets $F_1, \cdots, F_v$ if $F_i < F_j$ or $F_i \sim F_j$ for all $1 \leq j \leq v, i \neq j$.

The formal definition of a minimal ascending set is given by the following lemma (Wen-Tsün, 1986).

Lemma 1

Let $F_1, F_{2,} \cdots, F_q, \cdots$ be a sequence of ascending sets F_q for which the rank never increases, or for any q we have either $F_{q+1} < F_q$ or $F_{q+1} \sim F_q$. Then there is an index q' such that for any $q > q'$ we have $F_q \sim F_{q'}$. In other words, there is some q' such that any F_q for which $q \geq q'$ is a minimal ascending set of the above sequence.

Because any ascending collection can be written as the sequence described in the above lemma (due to the partial order for ascending sets) one can deduce that every ascending collection has at least one minimal ascending set.

Basic set

The *basic set* of a non-empty polynomial set F is any ascending subset from F that is a minimal ascending set of all the possible ascending subsets that can be constructed of F. In other words there will be no other ascending subset from F with a lower rank than the basic set of F. Any ascending subset of F that has the same rank as a basic set of F is a basic set of F as well. Please note that a basic set is an ascending set by construction. So let $\Omega = \{F_1, F_2, \cdots, F_v\}$ be a set consisting of all possible ascending subsets of F, so that $F_j \subset F$ for all $(1 \leq j \leq v)$. Then any F_i such that $F_i < F_j$ or $F_i \sim F_j$ for all $(1 \leq j \leq v)$ is a basic set of F. The main difference between a basic set and a minimal ascending set is the fact that a basic set is an ascending set one constructs from a single polynomial set, while a minimal ascending set is a set belonging to an existing collection of ascending sets.

Constructing a basic set of a polynomial set

The input to the algorithm is a polynomial set F. The output of the algorithm is B a basic set of F. This is denoted as B = *basic_set*(F).

Set $F_1 = F$, B is equal to an empty set.
k = 1
While (B not the basic set of F)
Find the first polynomial f from F_k of lowest rank and add it to B.
F_{k+1} is equal to an empty set.
If (*class*(f) = 0 and k = 1) then B is a basic set of F,
Else
For (i = 1, $i \leq size(F_k)$, i++)
If ((f_i *red* f) and ($f_i \neq f$)) add f_i to F_{k+1}
end{for}
If (F_{k+1} is empty) B is a basic set of F.
k++
end {else}
end {while}
Return B.

In simpler terms what this algorithm does is it constructs the longest possible ascending set of lowest rank. Remember there is more than one basic set, this algorithm uses the first polynomial of lowest rank; if you use the second you would get a completely different basic set.

Characteristic set

The *characteristic set* of a polynomial set F is a set that is constructed in a special manner so that this new set contains all the zeros (solutions) of F and is triangular in form. What is meant by the solutions of F is all those numbers that would make F = 0 true. A triangular form (ascending set) is an easy form to solve for instance $\{y^3 - y^2, xy + x + y\}$ is easier to solve than $\{xy + x + y, xy^2 + x + y\}$, because it is triangular in form, in other words direct back substitution is possible. A more formal definition of a characteristic set is as follow. Let P_i be the prime ideal generated by *F*. Then the characteristic set of *F* is the basic set of P_i.

Constructing a characteristic set from a polynomial set

The input to the algorithm is a polynomial set *F*. The output of the algorithm is *C* a characteristic set of *F*. This is denoted as *C* = *char_set*(*F*).

C is an empty set, *T* is an empty set.
While (*C* not the characteristic set of *F*)
B = *basic_set*(*F*).
If (*class*(*B*) = 0) then *C* = {1} and is the characteristic set of *F*,
Else
T = *F* - *B*, *T* is thus the difference between the sets *F* and *B*. Those polynomials that are in *F* but not in *B*.
T_2 is an empty set, and *R* is a polynomial.
For (*i* = 1, $i \leq size(T)$, *i*++), {Forms the set of remainders of polynomials in *T* with respect to *B*}
$R = prem(t_i; B)$, where t_i is the ith polynomial in *T*.
If ($R \neq 0$) then add *R* to T_2.
end{for}
If (T_2 is empty) then *C* = *B* and is the characteristic set of *F*.
Else add T_2 to *F*.
end{else1}
end{while}
Return *C*.

The following theorem from Wen-Tsün (1986) is thus briefly summarized.

Ritt's theorem also known as the Well-Ordering theorem

There is an algorithm which permits us to get, after a mechanically finite number of steps, either a polynomial set C = {1}, or a non-contradictory ascending set $C = \{c_1, \cdots, c_v\}$ with initials $I_1, \cdots, I_v$ such that any zero of F is also a zero of C, and any zero of C which is not a zero of any of the initials I_i, will also be a zero of F. The set C obtained in this manner is known as the characteristic set of F.

The size of a characteristic set *C* can be calculated using Equation 5 as stated by Gallo and Mishra (1990b)

$$n \geq |C| \geq n - \dim P_i \quad (5)$$

where *C* is the characteristic set of *F*, *n* is the size of *F*, and P_i is the polynomial ideal generated by *F*.

WU'S ALGORITHM

So far, we know that the roots of *F* are pretty much the roots of *C* if $I \neq 0$. But how do we find those zeros of *F* for the case when *I* = 0? This is quite easy when one calculates the characteristic set of $F \cup \{I\}$. We recursively call the characteristic set algorithm to investigate this case. It may produce more roots, or it may proclaim that the set $F \cup \{I\}$ has no roots. Hence

$$Zeros(F) = [Zeros(C) - Zeros(I)] \cup \bigcup Zeros(F \cup \{I_i\}) \quad (6)$$

where I_i is an initial of $c_i \in C$ and $I = \prod I_i$. One does not know how deep this recursion goes but that it must terminate is for certain due to the fact that the basic sets decrease in rank. We write $[Zeros(C) - Zeros(I)]$ for the set of zeros of *C* subject to the condition that $I \neq 0$. So the zeros of *F* are those zeros of *C* which are not zeros of *I*, together with the zeros of $F \cup \{I_i\}$. The last term captures those zeros that are simultaneous solutions of *F* and *I*. We stop pursuing a branch whenever we get that the *Zeros*($F \cup \{I_i\}$) is an empty set. Wu's complete algorithm is described below. Given a set of polynomials *F*, return a set of ascending sets of solutions *Z*.

Z is an empty set, *G* = *F*.
While (*G* is non-empty)
Pick a set of polynomials F' from *G*.
G = *G* - F', Let *G* be the polynomials that are in *G* but not in F'.
$C = Char\_set(F')$.
If ($C \neq \{1\}$) $Z = Z \cup C$.
T is an empty set.
For (All initials I_i of *C*)
If (I_i are non-constant) Add I_i to *T*.
end{for}
If (*T* is not empty) $G = G \cup F' \cup T$.
end{while}
Return *Z*.

A complete theoretical analysis of Wu's method can be found in Gallo and Mishra (1990a, b).

WU'S ALGORITHM IN THE BINARY CASE

There are quite a few simplifications that occur when Wu's algorithm is applied to binary multivariate polynomials.

Binary multivariate polynomials

A *binary multivariate polynomial* consists of binary variables $x_1, x_2 \cdots, x_r$. These variables can assume only one of two values a '0' or a '1'. Equation (2) transforms to (10) when the variables $x_1, x_2 \cdots, x_r$ are binary.

$$f = I_1 x_c \oplus I_0 \qquad (10)$$

Note that plus becomes XOR and multiplication becomes AND. The value of *f* can thus either be a '1' or a '0'. Also the degree of *f* is always one. All the definitions stay exactly the same in the binary case except for a few which will be highlighted below.

The definition of reduction does simplify. A binary polynomial *g* is said to be *reduced* with respect to a binary polynomial *f* if x_c $[lv(f)]$ is not present in *g*. The above facts simplify the pseudo division algorithm to one single equation

$$bprem(g, f) = r = I_1 g \oplus L_1 f \qquad (7)$$

Where *g* and *f* are binary polynomials in x_c $[lv(f)]$, I_1 is the initial of *f* and L_1 is the initial of *g*. Also the variable *r* denotes the binary pseudo remainder. The notation $bprem(g, f)$ is used to show that the binary pseudo remainder is being calculated. Also remember if *g* is already reduced with respect to *f* then *g* is the pseudo remainder and not (7). The partial order for polynomials is also affected by the binary condition; and is redefined as follow. The binary polynomial *g* has a higher rank than a binary polynomial *f* if the $class(f) < class(g)$ and is denoted by *f* < *g*. When the $class(f) = class(g)$ we say *g* and *f* are of the same rank, and denote it by $f \sim g$.

All other algorithms and definitions stay exactly the same except when it uses the original definitions of the above. Then the algorithm or definition must use the above instead. For instance when an algorithm or definition uses *prem* one should use *bprem*. Also for linear combinations one should use XOR and not standard addition and AND instead of multiplication.

Influence on WU's algorithm

Wu's algorithm itself simplifies as well, hence Wu's complete algorithm is not needed. One only needs one iteration of the characteristic set algorithm to obtain the roots of a binary polynomial set that has a unique solution. The reason for this is explained below.

When the characteristic set algorithm is applied to a binary polynomial set one gets either one of three possible outcomes.

1) A characteristic set of {1} is returned, showing that the system has no solution.
2) A characteristic set of the following form is returned

$$\begin{Bmatrix} x_1 \oplus a_1, \\ x_2 \oplus a_2, \\ \vdots \\ x_n \oplus a_n \end{Bmatrix} \qquad (8)$$

showing that the system has a unique solution. Equation (8) has a size that equals the size of the original set. Remember a_i can be either a '1' or a '0'.

3) A characteristic set that has a smaller size than (8) is returned, showing that the system has more than one solution.

From Ritt's theorem it is clear that when a system has no solutions it will generate a characteristic set of {1}.

The reason for (8) is as follows, if a binary polynomial set has only one unique solution then the polynomial ideal that is generated by such a set will be a zero dimensional ideal. This is so, because there is no interdependence between the variables in such a system. The linear combinations that form the polynomial ideal can eliminate all variables except one, without changing the roots of the original system when the system has a unique solution. As stated before, the size of a characteristic set can be calculated using (5). Thus because the set generates a zero dimensional ideal, (5) becomes $|C| = n$.

Now because, the characteristic set is also a binary ascending set and must have a size that is equal to the original set it will be of the form stated in (8). In the case of (8) the unique solution can be determined directly and is equal to $\{a_1, a_2, \cdots, a_n\}$. In this case one characteristic set iteration is required to compute the unique solution.

When a system has more than one unique solution it does not generate a zero dimensional ideal, and therefore generates a characteristic set that is smaller than the original set. It does not do this because the linear combinations that form the polynomial ideal can not eliminate all the variables except one without changing the roots of the original system. This is impossible due to the way a polynomial ideal is constructed; it preserves the original roots (linear combinations). Thus Ritt's theorem can be restated for the binary case as follow.

Ritt's theorem in the binary case

There is an algorithm which permits us to get, after a mechanically finite number of steps, either a binary polynomial set C = {1}, or a non-contradictory binary ascending set $C=\{c_1,\cdots,c_v\}$ with initials that are all equal to 1 such that any zero of F is also a zero of C, and any zero of C is also a zero of F, or a non-contradictory ascending set $C=\{c_1,\cdots,c_v\}$ with initials $I_1,\cdots,I_v$ such that any zero of F is also a zero of C, and any zero of C which is not a zero of any of the initials I_i, will also be a zero of F. The set C obtained in this manner is known as the binary characteristic set of F.

In the remainder of the paper we will concentrate on the case when *F* has a unique solution, because this has direct applicability to cryptography.

Example

It is time to illustrate the use of Wu as an attack. Let us investigate the following set.

$$F=\begin{Bmatrix} x_3\oplus x_1\oplus x_1x_3\oplus x_2x_3\oplus x_2x_1=y_1, \\ x_3\oplus x_1x_2=y_2, \\ x_3\oplus x_2\oplus x_2x_3\oplus x_1=y_3 \end{Bmatrix} \tag{9}$$

Assuming that the output vector (y_1,y_2,y_3) and the input vector (x_1,x_2,x_3) of an s-box is related by (9). The concept is thus represented graphically as in Figure 1.

In Figure 1 the variables y_1,y_2,y_3,x_1,x_2,x_3 represent the bits of a binary number where the lowest subscript is the LSB, while the highest subscript represents the MSB.

Assuming the output vector (y_1,y_2,y_3) is known as well as the transformation function *F*. The following procedure can be used to calculate the input vector. If it is known that the output vector is equal to $(1,0,0)$ then (9) transforms to

$$\begin{aligned} R_{1_1} &= (x_2\oplus x_1\oplus 1)\cdot(x_3\oplus x_1x_2)\oplus(1)\cdot f_1 \\ &= x_1\oplus 1 \end{aligned} \tag{10}$$

where each polynomial is equal to naught. Set (10) was constructed by substituting the output vector into (9) and equating each polynomial to naught. Now the input vector is actually the root of (10). We know from "Wu's algorithm in the binary case" that we only require one iteration of the characteristic set algorithm to calculate the root of (10), because (10) has a unique solution. The first thing one needs to calculate is the basic set of F_1. The basic set is calculated as follow. First retrieve the first polynomial of lowest rank from F_1. In this case it will be

$$f_{1_1}=x_3\oplus x_1\oplus x_1x_3\oplus x_2x_3\oplus x_2x_1\oplus 1.$$

Now make a separate polynomial set containing all the polynomials in F_1 that are already reduced with respect to f_{1_1}. Because in this case this new set is empty; f_{1_1} is the basic set of F_1. Thus

$$B_1=\{x_3\oplus x_1\oplus x_1x_3\oplus x_2x_3\oplus x_2x_1\oplus 1\} \tag{11}$$

Now remove the basic set from F_1 to form T_{1_1}.

$$T_{1_1}=\begin{Bmatrix} x_3\oplus x_1x_2, \\ x_3\oplus x_2\oplus x_2x_3\oplus x_1 \end{Bmatrix} \tag{12}$$

Now calculate $R_{1_{11}}=bprem(t_{1_1};B_1)$ using (7) and the section "Reducing a polynomial with respect to an ascending set" under "Polynomial sets".

$$\begin{aligned} R_{1_{11}} &= (x_2\oplus x_1\oplus 1)\cdot(x_3\oplus x_1x_2)\oplus(1)\cdot f_{1_1} \\ &= x_1\oplus 1 \end{aligned} \tag{13}$$

Because B_1 consists of only one polynomial there is no recursion. Now because $R_{1_{11}}$ is not equal to naught it gets added to T_{1_2}. Now we need to calculate

$$R_{1_{21}}=bprem(t_{1_2};B_1)=x_1x_2\oplus x_2\oplus x_1\oplus 1 \tag{14}$$

which is also not equal to naught and is thus added to T_{1_2}. Now T_{1_2} is equal to

$$T_{1_2}=\begin{Bmatrix} x_1\oplus 1, \\ x_1x_2\oplus x_2\oplus x_1\oplus 1 \end{Bmatrix} \tag{15}$$

Because T_{1_2} is not empty it gets added to F_1 to form F_2 which is now equal to

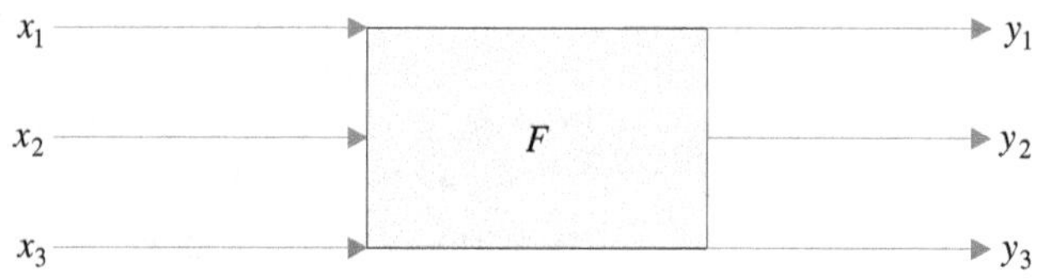

Figure 1. Graphical representation of (9).

$$F_2 = \begin{Bmatrix} x_1 \oplus 1, \\ x_1x_2 \oplus x_2 \oplus x_1 \oplus 1, \\ x_3 \oplus x_1 \oplus x_1x_3 \oplus x_2x_3 \oplus x_2x_1 \oplus 1, \\ x_3 \oplus x_1x_2, \\ x_3 \oplus x_2 \oplus x_2x_3 \oplus x_1 \end{Bmatrix} \qquad (16)$$

Next we need to recalculate the basic set of F_2. In this case it is equal to $B_2 = \{x_1 \oplus 1\}$. Also T_{2_1} is recalculated by removing B_2 from F_2. Applying the same procedure as above one can calculate T_{2_2}. For convenience sake let's define a new syntax.

$$bprem\{T_{n_1}; B_n\} = \begin{Bmatrix} bprem(t_{n_1}; B_n), \\ bprem(t_{n_2}; B_n), \\ \vdots \\ bprem(t_{n_r}; B_n) \end{Bmatrix} \qquad (17)$$

Please note that if $bprem(t_{n_i}; B_n)$ is equal to naught it does not get added to T_{n_2}.

Using (17) we can calculate T_{2_2}

$$T_{2_2} = non\_zero(bprem(T_{2_1}; B_2)) = \begin{Bmatrix} x_2x_3 \oplus x_2, \\ x_3 \oplus x_2, \\ x_2x_3 \oplus x_3 \oplus x_2 \oplus 1 \end{Bmatrix} \qquad (18)$$

Now F_3 is equal to $F_3 = F_2 \bigcup T_{2_2}$.

Continuing as before one calculates T_{3_2}. Now $F_4 = F_3 \bigcup T_{3_2}$. $B_5 = \begin{Bmatrix} x_1 \oplus 1 \\ x_2 \oplus 1 \\ x_3 \oplus 1 \end{Bmatrix}$. We calculate T_{5_1} with $T_{5_1} = F_5 - B_5$ and then we calculate the set T_{5_2} wit $T_{5_2} = non\_zero(bprem(T_{5_1}; B_5))$. This leads to $T_{5_2} = \{\}$. Now because T_{5_2} is an empty set we know B_5 is the characteristic set *F*. The input vector can now be determined directly and is equal to (1,1,1).

CONCLUSION

What is clear from this article is the fact that Wu's original algorithm does work and can be used as a cryptanalysis method.

REFERENCES

Bayram M, Çelik E (2002). Simultaneous solutions of polynomial equations. Appl. Math. Comput., 113: 533-538.

Buchberger B (1985). Gröbner basis: An Algorithmic method in Polynomial Ideal Theory. Recent Trends in Multidimensional System Theory. Reidel.

Chou SC (1985). Proving and Discovering Theorems in Elementary Geometries Using Wu's Method. Phd dissertation, Department of Mathematics , University of Texas at Austin.

Chou SC, Gao X (2008). Ritt-Wu's Decomposition Algorithm, Department of Computer Sciences. The University of Texas at Austin, Texas 78712 USA, pp. 1-15.

Gallo G, Mishra B (1990a). Efficient Algorithms and Bounds for Wu-Ritt Characteristic Sets. In Proceedings of MEGA 90: Meeting on Effective Methods in Algebraic Geometry, Castiglioncello, Livorno, Italy.

Gallo G, Mishra B (1990b). Wu-Ritt characteristic sets and their complexity, Courant Institute, New York University, pp. 1-25.

Kapur D (1986). Geometry Theorem Proving for Gröbner Bases. J. Symb. Comput., 2: 399-412.

Kapur D, Mundy JL (1988). Wu's method and it's application to perspective viewing. Artif. Intell., 37: 15-36.

Möller HM, Mora F (1984). Upper and Lower Bounds for the Degree of Gröbner basis. Lecture Notes in Computer Sciences. Springer Verlag, pp. 172-183.

Ritt JF (1950). Differential Algebra, American Mathematical society, New York.

Wen-Tsün W (1978). On the decision problem and the mechanization of theorem proving in elementary geometry. Sci. Sinica, 21: 157-179.

Wen-Tsün W (1986). Basic principles of mechanical theorem proving in geometries. J. Autom. Reasoning, *2:* 221-252.

Wen-Tsün W (1984). Some Recent Advances in Mechanical Theorem-Proving of Geometries, of Automated Theorem Proving: After 25 Years. Contemp. Math. Am. Math. Soc., 29: 235-242.

Penalty function methods using matrix laboratory (MATLAB)

Hailay Weldegiorgis Berhe

Department of Mathematics, Haramaya University, Ethiopia. E-mail: hailaywg@yahoo.com.

The purpose of the study was to investigate how effectively the penalty function methods are able to solve constrained optimization problems. The approach in these methods is to transform the constrained optimization problem into an equivalent unconstrained problem and solved using one of the algorithms for unconstrained optimization problems. Algorithms and matrix laboratory (MATLAB) codes are developed using Powell's method for unconstrained optimization problems and then problems that have appeared frequently in the optimization literature, which have been solved using different techniques compared with other algorithms. It is found out in the research that the sequential transformation methods converge to at least to a local minimum in most cases without the need for the convexity assumptions and with no requirement for differentiability of the objective and constraint functions. For problems of non-convex functions it is recommended to solve the problem with different starting points, penalty parameters and penalty multipliers and take the best solution. But on the other hand for the exact penalty methods convexity assumptions and second-order sufficiency conditions for a local minimum is needed for the solution of unconstrained optimization problem to converge to the solution of the original problem with a finite penalty parameter. In these methods a single application of an unconstrained minimization technique as against the sequential methods is used to solve the constrained optimization problem.

Key words: Penalty function, penalty parameter, augmented lagrangian penalty function, exact penalty function, unconstrained representation of the primal problem.

INTRODUCTION

Optimization is the act of obtaining the best result under given circumstances. In design, construction and maintenance of any engineering system, engineers have to take many technological and managerial decisions at several stages. The ultimate goal of all such decisions is either to minimize the effort required or to maximize the desired benefit. Since the effort required or the benefit desired in any practical situation can be expressed as a function of certain decision variables, optimization can be defined as the process of finding the conditions that give the maximum or minimum value of a function. It can be taken to mean minimization since the maximum of a function can be found by seeking the minimum of the negative of the same function.

Optimization can be of constrained or unconstrained problems. The presence of constraints in a nonlinear programming creates more problems while finding the minimum as compared to unconstrained ones. Several situations can be identified depending on the effect of constraints on the objective function. The simplest situation is when the constraints do not have any influence on the minimum point. Here the constrained minimum of the problem is the same as the unconstrained minimum, that is, the constraints do not have any influence on the objective function. For simple optimization problems it may be possible to determine before hand, whether or not the constraints have any influence on the minimum point. However, in most of the practical problems, it will be extremely difficult to identify it. Thus, one has to proceed with general assumption that the constraints will have some influence on the optimum point. The minimum of a nonlinear programming problem will not be, in general, an extreme point of the feasible region and may not even be on the boundary. Also, the problem may have local minima even if the corresponding unconstrained problem is not having local minima. Furthermore, none of the local minima may correspond to the global minimum of the unconstrained problem. All these characteristics are direct consequences of the introduction of constraints and hence, we should have general algorithms to overcome these kinds of minimization problems.

The algorithms for minimization are iterative procedures that require starting values of the design variable x. If the objective function has several local minima, the initial choice of x determines which of these will be computed. There is no guaranteed way of finding the global optimal point. One suggested procedure is to make several computers run using different starting points and pick the best. Majority of available methods are designed for unconstrained optimization where no restrictions are placed on the design variables. In these problems, the minima exist if they are stationary points (points where gradient vector of the objective function vanishes). There are also special algorithms for constrained optimization problems, but they are not easily accessible due to their complexity and specialization.

All of the many methods available for the solution of a constrained nonlinear programming problem can be classified into two broad categories, namely, the direct methods and the indirect methods approach. In the direct methods the constraints are handled in an explicit manner whereas in the most of the indirect methods, the constrained problem is solved as a sequence of unconstrained minimization problems or as a single unconstrained minimization problem. Here we are concerned on the indirect methods of solving constrained optimization problems. A large number of methods and their variations are available in the literature for solving constrained optimization problems using indirect methods. As is frequently the case with nonlinear problems, there is no single method that is clearly better than the others. Each method has its own strengths and weaknesses. The quest for a general method that works effectively for all types of problems continues. The main purpose of this research is to present the development of two methods that are generally considered for solving constrained optimization problems, the sequential transformation methods and the exact transformation methods.

Sequential transformation methods are the oldest methods also known as sequential unconstrained minimization techniques (SUMT) based upon the work of Fiacco and McCormick (1968). They are still among the most popular ones for some cases of problems, although there are some modifications that are more often used.

These methods help us to remove a set of complicating constraints of an optimization problem and give us a frame work to exploit any available methods for unconstrained optimization problems to be solved, perhaps, approximately. However, this is not without a cost. In fact, this transforms the problem into a problem of non smooth (in most cases) optimization, which has to be solved iteratively. The sequential transformation method is also called the classical approach and is perhaps the simplest to implement. Basically, there are two alternative approaches. The first is called the exterior penalty function method (commonly called penalty function method), in which a penalty term is added to the objective function for any violation of constraints. This method generates a sequence of infeasible points, hence its name, whose limit is an optimal solution to the original problem. The second method is called interior penalty function method (commonly called barrier function method), in which a barrier term that prevents the points generated from leaving the feasible region is added to the objective function. The method generates a sequence of feasible points whose limit is an optimal solution to the original problem.

Penalty function methods are procedures for approximating constrained optimization problems by unconstrained problems. The approximation is accomplished by adding to the objective function a term that prescribes a high cost for the violation of the constraints. Associated with this method is a parameter μ that determines the severity of the penalty and consequently the degree to which the unconstrained problem approximates the original problem. As $\mu \to \infty$ the approximation becomes increasingly accurate.

Thus, there are two fundamental issues associated with this method. The first has to do how well the unconstrained problem approximates the constrained one. This is essential in examining whether, as the parameter μ is increased towards infinity, the solution of the unconstrained problem converges to a solution of the constrained problem. The other issue, most important from a practical view point, is the question of how to solve a given unconstrained problem when its objective function contains a penalty term. It turns out that as μ is increased yields a good approximating problem; the corresponding structure of the resulting unconstrained problem becomes increasingly unfavorable thereby slowing the convergence rate of many algorithms that may be applied. Therefore it is necessary to device acceleration procedures that circumvent this slow convergence phenomenon. To motivate the idea of penalty function methods consider the following nonlinear programming problem with only inequality constraints:

Minimize f(x), subject to $g(x) \leq 0$ (P) $x \in X$;

Whose feasible region we denote by $S = \{x \in X \mid g(x) \leq 0\}$. Functions $f: R^n \to R$ and $g: R^n \to R^m$ are assumed to be continuously differentiable and X is a nonempty set in R^n. Let the set of minimum points of problem (P) be denoted by M (f, S), where M (f, S) $\neq \emptyset$. And we consider a real sequence $\{\mu_k\}$ such that $\mu_k \geq 0$. The number μ_k is called penalty parameter, which controls the degree of penalty for violating the constraints. Now we consider functions $\theta: X \times (R_+ \cup \{0\}) \to R$, as defined by

$$\theta(x, \mu) := f(x) + \mu p(x),\ (x, \mu) \in \{(X)\times(R_{+}\cup\{0\})\}, \quad (1.1)$$

where $X \subseteq R^n$ and p(x) is called penalty function, to be used throughout this paper, and μp(x) is called penalty term. μ is a strictly increasing function. Throughout this paper we use penalty function methods for exterior penalty function methods

Another apparently attractive idea is to define an exact penalty function in which the minimizer of the penalty function and the solution of the constrained primal problem coincide. The idea in these methods is to choose a penalty function and a constant penalty parameter so that the optimal solution of the unconstrained problem is also a solution of the original problem. This avoids the inefficiency inherent in sequential techniques. The two popular exact penalty functions are l_1 exact penalty function and augmented Lagrangian penalty function.

More emphasis is given here for sequential transformation methods and practical examples, which appeared frequently in the optimization literature (which have been solved using different methods.) and facility locations are solved using the MATLAB code given in the appendix with special emphasis given to facility location problems.

Some important techniques in the approach of the primal problem and the corresponding unconstrained penalty problems will be discussed later. We also discuss properties of the penalty problem, convergence conditions and the structure of the Hessian objective function of the penalty problem and the methods for solving unconstrained problems; the general description of the algorithm for the penalty function problems in addition to the considerations for the implementation of the method. A major challenge in the penalty function methods is the ill-conditioning of the Hessian matrix of objective function as the penalty parameter approaches to infinity, the choice of the initial starting points, penalty parameters and subsequent values of the penalty parameters.

In the later part of this study, the exact penalty methods, the exact l_1 penalty function and the augmented Lagrangian penalty function methods will be discussed in detail. The sequential methods suffer from numerical difficulties in solving the unconstrained problem. Furthermore, the solution of the unconstrained problem approaches the solution of the original problem in the limit, but is never actually equal to the exact solution. To overcome these shortcomings, the so-called exact penalty functions have been developed.

Statement of the problem

The focus of this research paper is on investigating constraint handling to solve constrained optimization problems using penalty function methods and thereby indicating ways of revitalizing them by bringing to attention.

Objectives of the research

General objective

The purpose of the research is generally to see how the penalty methods are successful to solve constrained optimization problems.

Specific objectives

The specific objectives of the research are to:

i. Describe the essence of penalty function methods,
ii. Clearly identify the procedures in solving constrained optimization problems using penalty function methods,
iii. Develop an algorithm and MATLAB code for penalty function methods,
iv. Solve real life application problems which frequently appeared in the optimization literature and facility location problems using the investigated code and compare with other methods,
v. Compare the effectiveness of the penalty methods.

Significance of the research

i. All algorithms for constrained optimization are unreliable to a degree. Any one of them works well on one problem and fails to another. Thus, this work will be having its own contribution in bridging the gap,
ii. It will also pave way and serves as an eye opener to other researchers to carry out an extensive and/or detail study along the same or other related issue.

PENALTY FUNCTION METHODS

In this section, we are concerned with exploring the computational properties of penalty function methods. We present and prove an important result that justifies using penalty function methods as a means for solving constrained optimization problems. We also discuss some computational difficulties associated with these methods and present some techniques that should be used to overcome such difficulties. Using the special structure of the penalty function, a special purpose one-dimensional search procedure algorithm is developed. The procedure is based on Powell's method for unconstrained minimization technique together with bracketing and golden section for one dimensional search.

When solving a general nonlinear programming problem in which the constraints cannot easily be eliminated, it is necessary to balance the aims of reducing the objective function and staying inside or close to the feasible region, in order to induce global convergence (that is convergence to a local solution from any initial approximation). This inevitably leads to the idea of a penalty function, which is a combination of the some constraints that enables the objective function to be minimized whilst controlling constraint violations (or near constraint violations) by penalizing them. The philosophy of penalty methods is simple; you give a "fine" for violating the constraints and obtain approximate solutions to your original problem by balancing the objective function and a penalty term involving the constraints. By increasing the penalty, the approximate solution is forced to approach the feasible domain and hopefully, the solution of the original constrained problem. Early penalty functions were smooth so as to enable efficient techniques for smooth unconstrained optimization to be used.

The use of penalty functions to solve constrained optimization problems is generally attributed to Courant. He introduced the earliest penalty function with equality constraint in 1943. Subsequently, Pietrgykowski (1969) discussed this approach to solve nonlinear problems. However, significant progress in solving practical problems by use of penalty function methods follows the classic work of Fiacco and McCormick under the title sequential unconstrained minimization technique (SUMT). The numerical problem of how to change the parameters of the penalty functions have been investigated by several authors.

Fiacco and McCormick (1968) and Himmelblau (1972) discussed effective unconstrained optimization algorithms for solving penalty function methods. According to Fletcher, several extensions to the concepts of penalty functions have been made; first, in order to avoid the difficulties associated with the ill-conditioning as the penalty parameter approaches to infinity, several parameter-free methods have been proposed. We will discuss some of the effective techniques in reducing these difficulties in the following sections.

The concept of penalty functions

Consider the following problem with single constraint $h(\mathbf{x}) = 0$:

Minimize $f(x)$,
subject to $h(x) = 0$.

Suppose this problem is replaced by the following unconstrained problem, where $\mu > 0$ is a large number:

Minimize $f(x) + \mu h^2(x)$,
subject to $x \in \mathbb{R}^n$

we can intuitively see that an optimal solution to the above problem must have $h^2(x)$ close to zero, otherwise a large penalty term $\mu h^2(x)$ will be incurred and hence $f(x) + \mu h^2(x)$ approaches to infinity which makes it difficult to minimize the unconstrained problem (Bazaraa et al. (2006).

Now consider the following problem with single inequality constraint $g(x) \leq 0$:

Minimize $f(x)$,
subject to $g(x) \leq 0$.

It is clear that the form $f(x) + \mu g^2(x)$ is not appropriate, since a penalty will be incurred where $g(x) < 0$ or $g(x) > 0$; that is a penalty is added to the objective function whether x is inside or outside the feasible region. Needless to say, a penalty is desired only if the point is not feasible, that is, if $g(x) > 0$. A suitable unconstrained problem is therefore given by:

Minimize $f(x) + \mu\text{maximum}\{0, g(x)\}$,
subject to $x \in R^n$.

Note that if $g(x) \leq 0$, then maximum $\{0, g(x)\} = 0$, and no penalty is incurred on the other hand, if $g(x) > 0$, then maximum $\{0, g(x)\} > 0$, and the penalty term $\mu g(x)$ is realized. However, it is observe that at points x where $g(x) = 0$, the forgoing objective function might not be differentiable, even though g is differentiable.

Example 1

Minimize x,
subject to $-x + 2 \leq 0$,

the constraint, $g(x) = -x + 2 \leq 0$ is active at $x = 2$ and the corresponding forgoing objective function is:

$$f(x) + \mu\text{maximum}\{0, g(x)\} = \begin{cases} x + \mu(-x+2), \text{if } x < 2 \\ x, \text{if } x \geq 2. \end{cases}$$

Clearly this is not differentiable at $x = 2$. If differentiability is desirable in such cases, then one could, for example, consider instead a penalty function term of the type $\mu(\text{maximum}\{0, g(x)\})^2$.

In general, a suitable penalty function must incur a positive penalty for infeasible points and no penalty for feasible points. If the constraints are of the form $g_i(x) \leq 0$ for $i = 1. . . m$, then a suitable penalty function p is defined by

$$p(x) = \sum_{i=1}^{m} \Phi(g_i(\mathbf{x})), \quad (2.1a)$$

where:

Φ is a continuous function satisfying the following properties:

$$\Phi(y) = 0 \text{ if } y \leq 0 \text{ and } \Phi(y) > 0 \text{ if } y > 0. \quad (2.1b)$$

Typically Φ is of the form

$\Phi(y) = (\text{maximum}\{0, y\})^q$,

where q is a nonnegative real number. Thus, the penalty function p is usually of the form $p(\mathbf{x}) = \sum_{i=1}^{m}(\text{maximum}\{0, g_i(\mathbf{x})\})^q$.

Definition 1. A function $p : R^n \rightarrow R$ is called a penalty function if p satisfies

i. p(x) is continuous on R^n
ii. p(x) = 0 if $g(x) \leq 0$ and
iii. p(x) > 0 if $g(x) > 0$.

An often-used class of penalty functions for optimization problems with only inequality constraints is:

$p(\mathbf{x}) = \sum_{i=1}^{m}(\text{maximum}\{0, g_i(\mathbf{x})\})^q$, where $q \geq 1$

We refer to the function f(x) + μp(x) as the auxiliary function. Denoting $\theta(x, \mu): = f(x) + \mu\sum_{i=1}^{m}(\text{maximum}\{0, g_i(\mathbf{x})\})^q$, for the auxiliary function. The effect of the second term on the right side is to increase θ(x, μ) in proportion to the qth power of the amount by which the constraints are violated. Thus there will be a penalty for violating the constraints and the amount of penalty will increase at a faster rate compared to the amount of violation of a constraint (for $q > 1$) Rao (2009). Let us see the behavior of θ(x, μ) for various values of q.

i. q = 0,

$$\theta(x, \mu) = f(x) + \mu\sum_{i=1}^{m}(\text{maximum}\{0, g_i(\mathbf{x})\})^0$$

$$= \begin{cases} f(\mathbf{x}) + m\mu, \text{if all } g_i(\mathbf{x}) > 0 \\ f(\mathbf{x}), \text{if all } g_i(\mathbf{x}) \leq 0. \end{cases}$$

This function is discontinuous on the boundary of the acceptable region and hence it will be very difficult to minimize this function.

ii. $0 < q < 1$

Here the θ-function will be continuous, but the penalty for violating a constraint may be too small. Also the derivatives of the function are discontinuous along the boundary. Thus, it will be difficult to minimize the θ-function.

iii. q = 1

In this case, under certain restrictions, it has been shown that there exists a μ_o large enough that the minimum of θ is exactly the constrained minimum of the original problem for all $\mu_k > \mu_o$; however, the contours of the θ-function posses discontinuous first derivatives along the boundary.

Hence, in spite of the convenience of choosing a single μ_k that yields the constrained minimum in one unconstrained minimization, the method is not very attractive from computational point of view.

iv. $q > 1$

The θ-function will have continuous first derivatives. These derivatives are given by

$$\frac{d\theta}{dx_i} = \frac{df}{dx_i} + \mu\sum_{i=1}^{m} q(\text{maximum}\{0, g_i(\mathbf{x})\})^{q-1}\frac{dg_i(\mathbf{x})}{dx_i}.$$

Generally, the value of q is chosen as 2 in practical computations and hence, will be used as q = 2 in the subsequent discussion of the penalty method with

$$p(x) = \sum_{i=1}^{m}(\text{maximum}\{0, g_i(\mathbf{x})\})^2.$$

Example 2

Consider the optimization problem in example1,
Let $p(x) = (\text{maximum}\{0, g_i(\mathbf{x})\})^2$, then,

$$p(x) = \begin{cases} 0, \text{if } x \geq 0 \\ (-x+2)^2, \text{if } x < 2. \end{cases}$$

Note that the minimum of f + μp occurs at the point $2 - (\frac{1}{2\mu})$ and approaches the minimum point x = 2 of the original problem as $\mu \rightarrow \infty$. The penalty and auxiliary functions are as shown in Figure 1.

If the constraints are of the form $g_i(\mathbf{x}) \leq 0$ for I = 1, . . . , m and $h_i(\mathbf{x}) = 0$ for I = 1, . . . , l, then a suitable penalty function p is defined by

$$p(\mathbf{x}) = \sum_{i=1}^{m}\Phi(g_i(\mathbf{x})) + \sum_{i=1}^{l}\psi(h_i(\mathbf{x})), \quad (2.2a)$$

where Φ and ψ are continuous functions satisfying the following properties:

$$\Phi(y) = 0 \text{ if } y \leq 0 \text{ and } \Phi(y) > 0 \text{ if } y > 0. \quad (2.2b)$$
$$\psi(y) = 0 \text{ if } y = 0 \text{ and } \psi(y) > 0 \text{ if } y \neq 0.$$

Typically, Φ and ψ are of the forms

$\Phi(y) = (\text{maximum}\{0, y\})^q$
$\psi(y) = |y|^q$

where q is a nonnegative real number. Thus, the penalty function p is usually of the form

$$p(\mathbf{x}) = \sum_{i=1}^{m}(\text{maximum}\{0, g_i(\mathbf{x})\})^q + \sum_{i=1}^{l}|h_i(\mathbf{x})|^q.$$

Definition 2

A function $p : R^n \rightarrow R$ is called a penalty function if p satisfies

i. p(x) is a continuous function on R^n
ii. p(x) = 0 if $g(x) \leq 0$ and h(x) = 0 and
iii. p(x) > 0 if $g(x) > 0$ and $h(x) \neq 0$.

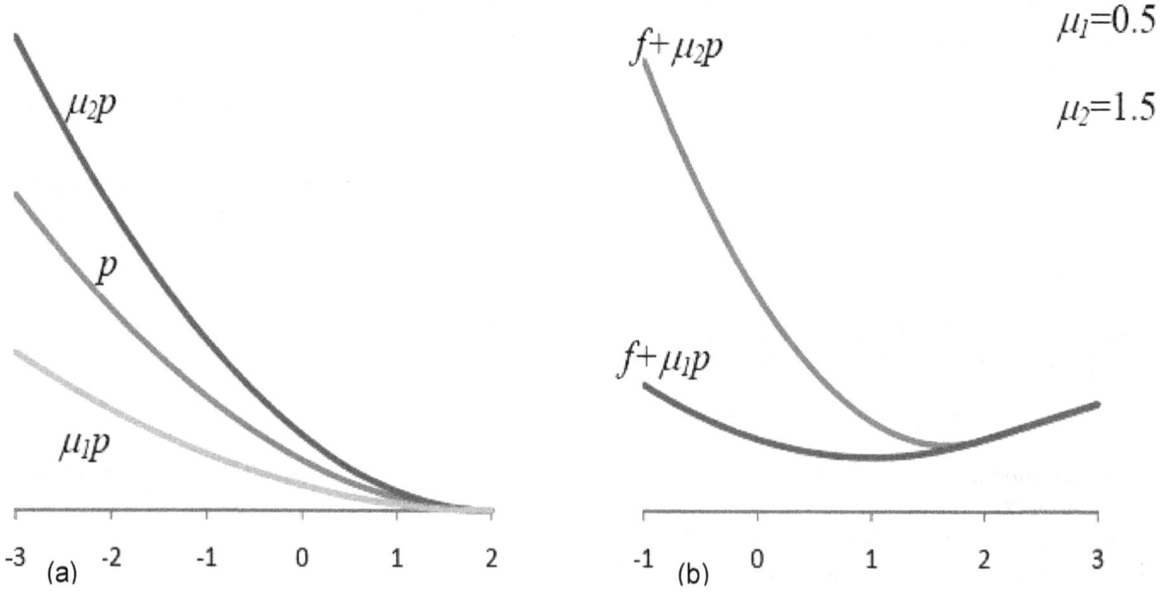

Figure 1. Penalty and auxiliary functions.

An often used class of penalty functions for this is:

$p(x) = \sum_{i=1}^{m} (\text{maximum}\{0, g_i(\mathbf{x})\})^q + \sum_{i=1}^{l} |h_i(\mathbf{x})|^q$, where $q \geq 1$.

We note the following:

If q = 1, p(x) is called "linear penalty function." This function may not be differentiable at points where $g_i(x) = 0$ or $h_i(x) = 0$ for some i.

Setting q = 2 is the most common form that is used in practice and is called the "quadratic penalty function".

We focus here mainly on the quadratic penalty function and investigate how penalty function methods are useful to solve constrained optimization problems by changing into the corresponding unconstrained optimization problems.

Penalty function methods for mixed constraints

Consider the following constrained optimization problem:

Minimize f(x) (P)
subject to $g_i(\mathbf{x}) \leq 0$, I = 1, . . . , m
$h_i(\mathbf{x}) = 0$, I = 1, . . . , l,

where functions f, $h_i(x)$, I = 1, . . . , l and g_i, I = 1, . . . , m are continuous and usually assumed to posses continuous partial derivatives on R^n. For notational simplicity, we introduce the vector-valued functions $h = (h_1, h_2, \ldots, h_l)^T \in R^l$ and $g = (g_1, g_2, \ldots, g_m)^T \in R^m$ and rewrite (P) as:

Minimize f(x)
subject to $g(x) \leq 0$
h(x) = 0 (P)
$x \in X$,

whose feasible region we denote by S: $= \{\mathbf{x} \in \mathbf{X}, g(\mathbf{x}) \leq \mathbf{0}, h(\mathbf{x}) = \mathbf{0}\}$. The constraints h(x) = 0 and $g(x) \leq 0$ are referred to as functional constraints, while the constraint $x \in X$ is a set constraint. The set X is a nonempty set in R^n and might typically represent simple constraints that could be easily handled explicitly, such as lower and upper bounds on the variables. We emphasize the set constraint, assuming in most cases that either X is in the whole R^n or that the solution to (P) is in the interior of X.

By converting the constraints "$h_i(x) = 0$" to "$h_i(x) \leq 0, -h_i(\mathbf{x}) \leq 0$" or considering only problems with inequality constraints we can assume that (P) is of the form:

Minimize f(x) (P)
subject to $g(x) \leq 0$
$x \in X$,

whose feasible region we denote by S: $= \{\mathbf{x} \in \mathbf{X} \mid g(\mathbf{x}) \leq 0\}$. We then consider solving the following penalty problem,

$\theta(\mu)$: Minimize $f(x) + \mu p(x)$
subject to $x \in X$,

and investigate the connection between a sequence $\{\mathbf{x}_\mu\}, \mathbf{x}_\mu \in M(f, X)$, a minimum point of θ and a solution of the original problem (P), where the set of minimum points of θ is denoted by M(f, X) and the set of all minimum points of (P) is denoted by M(f, S).

The representation of penalty methods above has assumed either that the problem (P) has no equality constraints, or that the equality constraints have been converted into inequality constraints. For the latter, the conversion is easy to do, but the conversion usually violates good judgments in that it unnecessarily complicates the problem. Furthermore, it can cause the linear independence condition to be automatically violated for every feasible solution. Therefore, instead let us consider the constrained optimization problem (P) with both inequality and equality constraints since the above can be easily verified from this. To describe penalty methods for problems with mixed constraints, we denote the penalty parameter by $l(\mu) = \mu \geq 0$, which is a monotonically increasing function and the penalty function $P(\mathbf{x}) = \sum_{i=1}^{m} \Phi(g_i(\mathbf{x})) + \sum_{i=1}^{l} \psi(h_i(\mathbf{x}))$, satisfying the properties given in (2.2b) and then consider the following Primal and Penalty problems:

Primal problem

Minimize f(x)
subject to g(x)
≤ 0 h(x) = 0 (P) $x \in X$.

Penalty problem

The basic penalty function approach attempts to solve the following problem:

Maximize θ(μ)
subject to $\mu \geq 0$,

where $\theta(\mu) = \inf\{f(x) + \mu p(x) : x \in X\}$. The penalty problem consists of maximizing the infimum (greatest lower bound) of the function $\{f(x) + \mu p(x) : x \in X\}$; therefore, it is a max-min problem. Therefore the penalty problem can be formulated as:

Find $\sup_{\mu \geq 0} \inf_{\mathbf{x} \in X}\{f(\mathbf{x}) + \mu p(\mathbf{x})\}$ which is equivalent to the form;

Find $\inf_{\mathbf{x} \in X} \sup_{\mu \geq 0}\{f(\mathbf{x}) + \mu p(\mathbf{x})\}$. We remark here that, strictly speaking, we should write the penalty problem as $\sup\{\theta(\mu), \mu \geq 0\}$, rather than $\text{maximum}\{\theta(\mu), \mu \geq 0\}$, since the maximum may not exist. The main theorem of this section states that:

$\inf\{f(x) : x \in S\} = \sup_{\mu \geq 0} \theta(\mu) = \lim_{\mu \to \infty} \theta(\mu)$.

From this result, it is clear that we can get arbitrarily close to the optimal objective value of the original problem by computing θ(μ) for a sufficiently large μ.This result is established in Theorem 2. First, the lemma theorem is needed.

Lemma 1 (Penalty Lemma)

Suppose that f, $g_1, \ldots, g_m, h_1, \ldots, h_l$ are continuous functions on R^n, and let X be a nonempty set in R^n. Let p be a continuous function on R^n as given by definition 1, and suppose that for each μ, there exists an $x_\mu \in X$, which is a solution of θ(μ), where $\theta(\mu) := f(x_\mu) + \mu p(x_\mu)$.
Then, the following statements hold:

1. $p(x_\mu)$ is a non-increasing function of μ.
2. $f(x_\mu)$ is a non-decreasing function of μ.
3. θ(μ) is a non-decreasing function of μ.
4. $\text{nf}\{f(x) : x \in S\} \geq \sup_{\mu \geq 0} \theta(\mu)$, where $\theta(\mu) = \inf\{f(x) + \mu p(x) : x \in X\}$, and g, h are vector valued functions whose components are $g_1, g_2, \ldots, g_m$ and $h_1, h_2, \ldots, h_l$ respectively.

Proof: Assume that μ and λ are penalty parameters such that $\lambda < \mu$.

1. By the definition of θ(λ), x_λ is a solution of θ(λ) such that,

$\theta(\lambda) = f(x_\lambda) + \lambda p(x_\lambda) \leq \inf\{f(x) + \lambda p(x), \text{ for all } x \in X\}$, which follows

$$f(x_\lambda) + \lambda p(x_\lambda) \leq f(x_\mu) + \lambda p(x_\mu), \text{ since } x_\mu \in X. \quad (2.3a)$$

Again by the definition of θ(μ)

$\theta(\mu) = f(x_\mu) + \mu\, p(x_\mu) \leq \inf\{f(x) + \mu\, p(x), \text{ for all } x \in X\}$ which follows that

$$f(x_\mu) + \mu p(x_\mu) \leq f(x_\lambda) + \mu p(x_\lambda), \text{ since } \mathbf{x}_\lambda \in X. \quad (2.3b)$$

Adding equation (2.3a) and (2.3b) holds:

$$f(x_\lambda) + \lambda p(x_\lambda) + f(x_\mu) + \mu p(x_\mu) \leq f(x_\mu) + \lambda p(x_\mu) + f(x_\lambda) + \mu p(x_\lambda)$$

and simplifying like term, we get

$$\lambda p(x_\lambda) + \mu\, p(x_\mu) \leq \lambda p(x_\mu) + \mu p(x_\lambda),$$

which implies by rearranging that

$$(\lambda - \mu)[p(x_\lambda) - p(x_\mu)] \leq 0.$$

Since $\lambda - \mu \leq 0$ by assumption, $p(x_\lambda) - p(x_\mu) \geq 0$. Then, $p(x_\lambda) \geq p(x_\mu)$.

Therefore, $p(x_\mu)$ is a non increasing function of μ.

2. By (2.3a) above

$f(x_\lambda) + \lambda p(x_\lambda) \le f(x_\mu) + \lambda p(x_\mu)$.

Since $p(x_\lambda) \ge p(x_\mu)$ by part 1, we concluded that

$f(x_\lambda) \le f(x_\mu)$.

3. $\theta(\lambda) = f(x_\lambda) + \lambda p(x_\lambda) \le f(x_\mu) + \lambda p(x_\mu)$
$\le f(x_\mu) + \mu p(x_\mu) = \theta(\mu)$.

4. Suppose x^* be any feasible solution to problem (P) with

$g(x^*) \le 0$, $h(x^*) = 0$ and $p(x^*) = 0$, where $x^* \in X$. Then,
$f(x^*) + \mu p(x^*) = \inf\{f(x), x \in S\}$ which implies that
$f(x^*) = \inf\{f(x), x \in S\}$. (2.3c)

By the definition of $\theta(\mu)$

$\theta(\mu) = f(x_\mu) + \mu p(x_\mu) \le f(x^*) + \mu p(x^*) = \inf\{f(x), x \in S\}$, for all $\mu \ge 0$.

Therefore, $\sup_{\mu \ge 0} \theta(\mu) \le \{\inf\{f(x), x \in S\}\}$.

The next result concerns convergence of the penalty method. It is assumed that f(x) is bounded below on the (nonempty) feasible region so that the minimum exists.

Theorem 2 (Penalty convergence theorem)

Consider the following Primal problem:

Minimize f(x)
subject to $g(x) \le 0$
$h(x) = 0$ (P)
$x \in X$,

where f, g, h are continuous functions on R^n and X is a nonempty set in R^n. Suppose that the problem has a feasible solution denoted by x^*, and p is a continuous function of the form (2.2). Furthermore, suppose that for each μ, there exists a solution $x_\mu \in X$ to the problem to minimize $\{f(x) + \mu p(x)$ subject to $x \in X\}$, and $\{x_\mu\}$ is contained in a compact subset X then,

$\inf\{f(x) : x \in S\} = \sup_{\mu \ge 0} \theta(\mu) = \lim_{\mu \to \infty} \theta(\mu)$,

where $\theta(\mu) = \inf\{f(x) + \mu p(x) : x \in X\} = f(x_\mu) + \mu p(x_\mu)$. Furthermore, the limit $\bar{x}$ of any convergent subsequence of $\{x_\mu\}$ is an optimal solution to the original problem, and $\mu p(x_\mu) \to 0$ as $\mu \to \infty$.

Proof

We first show that $p(x_\mu) \to 0$ as $\mu \to \infty$. Let y be any feasible point and $\varepsilon > 0$.

Let x_1 be an optimal solution to the problem minimize $\{f(x) + \mu p(x), x \in X\}$, for $\mu = 1$.
If we choose $\mu \ge \frac{1}{\varepsilon}|f(y) - f(x_1)| + 2$, then by part 2 of Lemma 1 we have $f(x_\mu) \ge f(x_1)$.
We now show that $p(x_\mu) \le \varepsilon$. By contradiction, suppose $p(x_\mu) > \varepsilon$. Noting part 4 of lemma 1, we get

$\inf\{f(x), x \in S\} \ge \theta(\mu) = f(x_\mu) + \mu p(x_\mu) \ge f(x_1) + \mu p(x_\mu)$
$> f(x_1) + (\frac{1}{\varepsilon}|f(y) - f(x_1)| + 2)\varepsilon$
$= f(x_1) + |f(y) - f(x_1)| + 2\varepsilon > f(y)$

it follows that $\inf\{f(x), x \in S\} > f(y)$. This is not possible in the view of feasibility of y.

Thus, $p(x_\mu) \le \varepsilon$ for all $\mu \ge \dfrac{1}{\varepsilon}|f(y) - f(x_1)| + 2$. Rearranging the above we get $\varepsilon \ge \frac{1}{\mu}|f(y) - f(x_1))| + \frac{2\varepsilon}{\mu}$, since $\varepsilon > 0$ is arbitrary, $p(x_\mu) \to 0$ as $\mu \to \infty$.
To show $\inf\{f(x) : x \in S\} = \sup_{\mu \ge 0} \theta(\mu) = \lim_{\mu \to \infty} \theta(\mu)$.
Let $\{x_{\mu_k}\}$ be any arbitrary convergent sequence of $\{x_\mu\}$, and let $\bar{x}$ be its limit. Then,

$\sup_{\mu \ge 0} \theta(\mu) \ge \theta(\mu_k) = f(x_{\mu_k}) + \mu_k p(x_{\mu_k}) \ge f(x_{\mu_k})$.

Since $x_{\mu_k} \to \bar{x}$ and f is continuous function with $\lim_{\mu_k \to \infty} f(x_{\mu_k}) = f(\bar{x})$, then the above inequality implies that

$\sup_{\mu \ge 0} \theta(\mu) \ge f(\bar{x})$. (2.4)

Since $p(x_\mu) \to 0$ as $\mu \to \infty$, then $p(\bar{x}) = 0$, that is, $\bar{x}$ is a feasible solution to the original problem (P) which follows that $\inf\{f(x) : x \in S\} = f(\bar{x})$.

By part 3 of Lemma 1 $\theta(\mu)$ is a nondecreasing function of μ, then

$\sup_{\mu \ge 0} \theta(\mu) = \lim_{\mu \to \infty} \theta(\mu)$. (2.5a)

x^* is an optimal solution to (P) by assumption implies that

$\inf\{f(x) : x \in S\} = f(x^*)$ (2.5b)

and by part 4 of the Lemma 1 above

$\sup_{\mu \ge 0} \theta(\mu) \le \inf\{f(x) : x \in S\}$. (2.5c)

Equating (2.4), (2.5a), (2.5b) and (2.5c), we get
$\inf\{f(x) : x \in S\} = \sup_{\mu \ge 0} \theta(\mu) = \lim_{\mu \to \infty} \theta(\mu)$

To show $\mu p(x_\mu) \to 0$ as $\mu \to \infty$.
$\theta(\mu) = f(x_\mu) + \mu p(x_\mu)$
$\mu p(x_\mu) = \theta(\mu) - f(x_\mu)$.

Taking the limit as $\mu \to \infty$ to both sides

$\lim_{\mu\to\infty} \mu p(x_\mu) = \lim_{\mu\to\infty} \theta(\mu) - \lim_{\mu\to\infty} f(x_\mu)$
$= \sup_{\mu\geq 0} \theta(\mu) - f(\bar{x})$
$= f(\bar{x}) - f(\bar{x})$
$= 0$.

So that $\mu p(x_\mu) \to 0$ as $\mu \to \infty$.

Note: It is interesting to observe that this result is obtained in the absence of differentiability or Karush Kuhn-Tucker regularity assumptions.

Corollary 3

If $p(x_\mu) = 0$ for some μ, then x_μ is an optimal solution to the original problem (P)

Proof

If $p(x_\mu) = 0$,then x_μ is a feasible solution to the problem (P). Furthermore, since
$\inf\{f(x), x \in S\} \geq \theta(\mu) = f(x_\mu) + \mu p(x_\mu) = f(x_\mu)$ it follows that
$\inf\{f(x), x \in S\} \geq f(x_\mu)$

it immediately follows that x_μ is an optimal solution to (P). Note the significance of the assumption that $\{x_\mu\}$ is contained in a compact subset X. obviously, this assumption holds if X is compact. Without this assumption, it is possible that the optimal objective values of the primal problem and the penalty problems are not equal. This assumption is not restricted in most practical cases, since the variables usually lie between finite lower and upper bounds.

From the above theorem, it follows that the optimal solution x_μ to the problem to minimize $f(x) + \mu p(x)$ subject to $x \in X$ can be made arbitrarily close to the feasible region by choosing μ large enough. Furthermore, by choosing μ large enough, $f(x_\mu) + \mu p(x_\mu)$ can be made arbitrarily close to the optimal objective value of the original problem. One popular scheme for solving the penalty problem is to solve a sequence of problems of the form:

Minimize $f(x) + \mu p(x)$
subject to $x \in X$,

for an increasing sequence of penalty parameters. The optimal points $\{x_\mu\}$ are generally infeasible as seen in proof of the Theorem 2, as the penalty parameter μ is made large, the points generated approach an optimal solution from outside the feasible region.

Hence, as mentioned earlier, this technique is also referred to as an exterior penalty function method.

Karush Kuhn Tucker multipliers at optimality

Under certain conditions, we can use the solutions to the sequence of penalty problems to recover the KKT Lagrange multipliers associated with the constraints at optimality. Suppose $X = R^n$ for simplicity and consider the primal problem (P) and the penalty function given in (2.2). In the penalty methods we solved, for various values of μ, the unconstrained problem is

Minimize $f(x) + \mu p(x)$ (2.6)
subject to $x \in X$.

Most algorithms require that the objective function has continuous first partial derivatives. Hence we shall assume that $f, g, h \in C^1$. It is natural to require, that the penalty function $p \in C^1$. As we explained earlier, the derivative of maximum $\{0, g_i(x)\}$ is usually discontinuous at points where $g_i(x) = 0$ and thus, some restrictions must be placed on ϕ in order to guarantee $p \in C^1$. We assume that the functions ϕ and ψ are continuously differentiable and satisfy:

$\phi'(y) = 0$ if $y \leq 0$ and $\phi'(y) \geq 0$ for all y. (2.7)

In view of this assumption p is differentiable whenever f, g, h are differentiable, that is, $f, g, h \in C^1$ implies $p \in C^1$ and we can write

$\nabla p(x) = \sum_{i=1}^{m} \phi'(g_i(x_\mu)) + \sum_{i=1}^{l} \psi'(h_i(x_\mu))$.

Assuming that the conditions of Theorem 2 hold true, since x_μ solves the problem to minimize $\{f(x) + \mu p(x), x \in X\}$, the gradient of the objective function of this penalty problem must vanish at x_μ. This gives

$\nabla f(x_\mu) + \nabla p(x_\mu) = 0$ for all μ,

that is,

$\nabla f(x_\mu) + \mu \sum_{i=1}^{m} \phi'(g_i(x_\mu)) \nabla g_i(x_\mu) + \sum_{i=1}^{l} \psi'(h_i(x_\mu)) \nabla h_i(x_\mu)$
$= 0$.

Now let $\bar{x}$ be an accumulation point of the generated sequence $\{x_\mu\}$. Without loss of generality, assume that $\{x_\mu\}$ itself converges to $\bar{x}$ and so $\bar{x}$ is an optimal solution

to (P).

Denoted by:

$I = \{I : g_i(\bar{x}) = 0\}$ to be the set of inequality constraints that are binding at $\bar{x}$ and
$N = \{I : g_i(\bar{x}) < 0\}$ for all constraints not binding at $\bar{x}$.

Since $g_i(\bar{x}) < 0$ for all elements of N then by Theorem 2.2, We have $g_i(x_\mu) < 0$ for sufficiently large μ which results $\phi'(g_i(x_\mu)) = 0$ (by assumption). Hence, we can write the foregoing identity as

$$\nabla f(x_\mu) + \mu \sum_{i \in I}^{m} (u_\mu)_i \nabla g_i(x_\mu) + \sum_{i=1}^{m} (v_\mu)_i \nabla h_i(x_\mu) = 0, \quad (2.8a)$$

for all μ large enough, where u_μ and v_μ are vectors having components

$(u_\mu)_i = \mu\phi'(g_i(x_\mu)) \geq 0$ for all I ∈ I and $(v_\mu)_i = \mu\psi'(h_i(x_\mu))$ for all I = 1, . . . , l. (2.8b)

Let us now assume that $\bar{x}$ is a regular solution such that $\nabla g_i(x_\mu)$ and $\nabla h_i(x_\mu)$ are linearly independent then, we know that there exist unique scalars $\bar{u}_i \geq 0$, I ∈ I and $\bar{v}_i$, I = l, . . . , l such that

$$\nabla f(x_\mu) + \sum_{i \in I}^{m} \bar{u}_i \nabla g_i(x_\mu) + \sum_{i=1}^{m} \bar{v}_i \nabla h_i(x_\mu) = 0.$$

Since g, h, ϕ, ψ are all continuously differentiable and since $\{x_\mu\} \rightarrow \bar{x}$, which is a regular point, we must then have in (2.8) that

$(u_\mu)_i \rightarrow \bar{u}_i$, for all I ∈ I and $(v_\mu)_i \rightarrow \bar{v}_i$, for all I = 1, . . . , l.

For sufficiently large values of μ, the multipliers given in (2.8) can be used to estimate KKT Lagrange multipliers at optimality and so we can interpret u_μ and v_μ as a sort of vector of Karush-Kuhn-Tucker multipliers. The result stated in next lemma insures that $u_\mu \rightarrow \bar{u}$ and $v_\mu \rightarrow \bar{v}$.

Lemma 4

Suppose $\phi(y)$ and $\psi(y)$ are continuously differentiable and satisfy (2.7), and that f, g, h are differentiable. Let (u_μ, v_μ) be defined by (2.8). Then, if $x_\mu \rightarrow \bar{x}$, and $\bar{x}$ satisfies the linear independence condition for gradient vectors of active constraints ($\bar{x}$ is a regular solution), then $(u_\mu, v_\mu) \rightarrow (\bar{u}, \bar{v})$, where $(\bar{u}, \bar{v})$ are vectors of KKT multipliers for the optimal solution $\bar{x}$ of (P).

Proof: From the Penalty Convergence Theorem, $\bar{x}$ is an optimal solution of (P).

Let

I = {I | $g_i(\bar{x}) = 0$} and

N = {I | $g_i(\bar{x}) < 0$}.

For I ∈ N, $g_i(x_\mu) < 0$ for all μ sufficiently large, so $(u_\mu)_i = 0$ for all μ sufficiently large, whereby $\bar{u}_i = 0$ for I ∈ N.

From (2.8b) and the definition of a penalty function, it follows that $(u_\mu)_i \geq 0$ for I ∈ I, for all μ sufficiently large.

Suppose $(u_\mu, v_\mu) \rightarrow (\bar{u}, \bar{v})$ as $\mu \rightarrow \infty$. Then $\bar{u}_i = 0$ for I ∈ N. From the continuity of all functions involved,

$\nabla f(x_\mu) + \mu \sum_{i \in I}^{m} (u_\mu)_i \nabla g_i(x_\mu) + \sum_{i=1}^{l} (v_\mu)_i \nabla h_i(x_\mu) = 0$, implies $\nabla f(\bar{x}) + \sum_{i \in I}^{m} \bar{u}_i \nabla g_i(\bar{x}) + \sum_{i=1}^{m} \bar{v}_i \nabla h_i(\bar{x}) = 0$.

From the above remarks, we also have $\bar{u} \geq 0$ and $\bar{u}_i = 0$ for all I ∈ N. Thus $(\bar{u}, \bar{v})$ are vectors of Karush-Kuhn-Tucker multipliers. It therefore remains to show $(u_\mu, v_\mu) \rightarrow (\bar{u}, \bar{v})$ as $\mu \rightarrow \infty$ for some unique $(\bar{u}, \bar{v})$.

Suppose $\{(u_\mu, v_\mu)\}_{\mu=0}^{\infty}$ has no accumulation point, then $\|(u_\mu, v_\mu)\| \rightarrow \infty$. But then define $(W_\mu, \lambda_\mu) = (\frac{(u_\mu, v_\mu)}{\|(u_\mu, v_\mu)\|})$, and then $\|(W_\mu, \lambda_\mu)\| = 1$ for all μ, and so the sequence $\{(u_\mu, v_\mu)\}_{\mu=0}^{\infty}$ has some accumulation point $(\bar{w}, \bar{\lambda})$ point. For all I ∈ N, $(w_\mu)_i = 0$ for all μ large, where by $\bar{w}_i = 0$ for all I ∈ N, and

$$\sum_{i \in I}^{m} (w_\mu)_i \nabla g_i(x_\mu) + \sum_{i=1}^{l} (\lambda_\mu)_i \nabla h_i(x_\mu) = \sum_{i=1}^{m} (w_\mu)_i \nabla g_i(x_\mu) + \sum_{i=1}^{l} (\lambda_\mu)_i \nabla h_i(x_\mu)$$

$$= \sum_{i=1}^{m} \frac{(u_\mu)_i}{\|(u_\mu, v_\mu)\|} \nabla g_i(x_\mu) + \sum_{i=1}^{l} \frac{(v_\mu)_i}{\|(u_\mu, v_\mu)\|} \nabla h_i(x_\mu)$$

$$= -\frac{\nabla f(x_\mu)}{\|(u_\mu, v_\mu)\|}$$

for μ large. As $\mu \rightarrow \infty$, we have $x_\mu \rightarrow \bar{x}$, $(W_\mu, \lambda_\mu) \rightarrow (\bar{w}, \bar{\lambda})$, and $\|(u_\mu, v_\mu)\| \rightarrow \infty$ by assumption, and so the above equation becomes;

$\sum_{i \in I}^{m} (w_\mu)_i \nabla g_i(x_\mu) + \sum_{i=1}^{l} (\lambda_\mu)_i \nabla h_i(x_\mu) = 0$, and $\|(W_\mu, \lambda_\mu)\| = 1$, which violates the linear independence condition. Therefore $\{(u_\mu, v_\mu)\}$ is bounded sequence, and so has at least one accumulation point.

Now suppose that $\{(u_\mu, v_\mu)\}$ has two accumulation points, $(\bar{u}, \bar{v})$ and $(\hat{u}, \hat{v})$. Note $\bar{u}_i = 0$ and $\hat{u}_i = 0$ for I ∈ N, and so

$$\sum_{i \in I} \bar{u}_i \nabla g_i(\bar{x}) + \sum_{i=1}^{l} \bar{v}_i \nabla h(\bar{x}) = -\nabla f(\bar{x}) = \sum_{i \in I} \hat{u}_i \nabla g_i(\bar{x}) + \sum_{i=1}^{l} \hat{v}_i \nabla h(\bar{x}),$$

so that

$$\sum_{i \in I} (\bar{u}_i - \hat{u}_i) \nabla g_i(\bar{x}) + \sum_{i=1}^{l} (\bar{v}_i - \hat{v}_i) \nabla h(\bar{x}) = 0.$$

But by the linear independence condition, $\bar{u}_i - \hat{u}_i = 0$ for all I ∈ I, and $\bar{v}_i - \hat{v}_i$. This implies that $(\bar{u}, \bar{v}) = (\hat{u}, \hat{v})$.

Remark: The quadratic penalty function satisfies the condition (2.7), but the linear penalty function does not satisfy.

As a final observation we note that in general if $x_\mu \rightarrow \bar{x}$, then since $(u_\mu)_i = \mu\phi'(g_i(x_\mu)) \rightarrow \bar{u}_i$ and $(v_\mu)_i = \mu\psi'(h_i(x_\mu)) \rightarrow \bar{v}_i$, the sequence x_μ approaches $\bar{x}$ from outside the constraint region. Indeed as $x_\mu \rightarrow \bar{x}$ all constraints that are active at $\bar{x}$ and have positive Lagrange multipliers will be violated at x_μ because the corresponding $\Phi'(g_i(x_\mu))$ are positive. Thus, if we assume that the active constraints are non degenerate (all Lagrange multipliers are strictly positive), every active constraint will be approached from outside of the feasible region.

Consider the special case if p is the quadratic penalty function given by:

$p(x) = \sum_{i=1}^{m}(\text{maximum}\{0, g_i(x)\})^2 + \sum_{i=1}^{m}(h_i(x))^2$, then $p(y) = \sum_{i=1}^{m}(\text{maximum}\{0, y_i\})^2 + \sum_{i=1}^{m} y_i^2$, $\Phi'(y) = 2\text{maximum}\{0, y\}$ and $\psi'(y) = 2y$. Hence, from (2.8), we obtain

$(u_\mu)_i = 2\mu(\text{maximum}\ \{0, g_i(x_\mu)\})$, for all I ∈ I, and
$(v_\mu)_i = 2\mu h_i(x_\mu)$ for all I = 1, . . . , l. (2.9)

In particular, observe that if $\bar{u}_i > 0$ for some I ∈ I, then $(u_\mu)_i > 0$ for μ large enough and then $g_i(x_\mu) > 0$ and by our assumption $\Phi'(g_i(x_\mu)) > 0$ for $g_i(x_\mu) > 0$. This means that $g_i(x) \le 0$ is violated all along the trajectory leading to $\bar{x}$, and in the limit $g_i(\bar{x}) = 0$. Hence, if $\bar{u}_i > 0$ for some I ∈ I, $\bar{v}_i \ne 0$ for all I, then all the constraints binding at $\bar{x}$ are violated along the trajectory $\{x_\mu\}$ leading to $\bar{x}$.

Example 3

Consider the following optimization problem:

Minimize $x_1^2 + x_2^2$
subject to $x_1 + x_2 = 1$

and the corresponding penalty problem:

Minimize $x_1^2 + x_2^2 + \mu(x_1 + x_2 - 1)^2$
subject to $(x_1, x_2) \in R^2$,

where μ is a large number.

$\mathbf{X}_\mu = [\frac{\mu}{2\mu+1}, \frac{\mu}{2\mu+1}]$ is the solution for the penalty problem.
And
$h(\mathbf{x}_\mu) = \frac{\mu}{2\mu+1} + \frac{\mu}{2\mu+1} - 1 = \frac{-1}{2\mu+1}$; and so,

$(v_\mu)_i = (v_\mu) = 2\mu h(\mathbf{x}_\mu) = 2\mu(\frac{-1}{2\mu+1})$

Implies

$v_\mu = \frac{-2\mu}{2\mu+1}$ from (2.8)

As $\mu \to \infty$, $v_\mu \to -1$, which is the optimal value of the Lagrange multiplier for this example.

Example 4

Minimize x
subject to $-x + 2 \le 0$.

The corresponding penalty problem is:

Minimize $x + \mu(-x + 2)^2$
subject to x ∈ R,
$\nabla_x \theta(x_\mu) = 1 + 2\mu[\text{maximum}\{0, -x_\mu + 2\}](-1) = 0$, for x < 2
which implies that $1 + 2\mu x_\mu - 4\mu = 0$.
Therefore, $x_\mu = 2 - \frac{1}{2\mu}$, and
$(u_\mu)_i = 2\mu(g_i(x_\mu))$, for I ∈ I
$= 2\mu(-(\frac{4\mu+1}{2\mu}) + 2)$
$= 1$
It follows that $U_\mu = 1$.

Note that, as $\mu \to \infty$, $u_\mu = 1$, the optimal value of the Lagrange multiplier for the primal problem.

Example 5

Minimize $x_1^2 + 2x_2^2$
subject to $-x_1 - x_2 + 1 \le 0$, $x \in R^2$.

For this problem the Lagrangian is given by $L(x, u) = x_1^2 + 2x_2^2 + u(-x_1 - x_2 + 1)$. The KKT conditions yield:

$\frac{\partial L(x,u)}{\partial x_1} = 2x_1 - u = 0$ and $\frac{\partial L(x,u)}{\partial x_2} = 4x_2 - u = 0$; $u(-x_1 - x_2 + 1) = 0$.

Solving these results in $x_1^* = 2/3$; $x_2^* = 2/3$; $\bar{u} = 4/3$; (u = 0 yields an infeasible solution).
To consider this example using penalty method, define the penalty function

$$p(x) = \begin{cases} (-x_1 - x_2 + 1)^2, \text{if } g_i(x) > 0 \\ 0, \text{if } g_i(x) \le 0. \end{cases}$$

The unconstrained problem is then,

minimize $x_1^2 + 2x_2^2 + \mu p(x)$.
If p(x) = 0, then the optimal solution is x* = (0, 0) which is infeasible.

Therefore, $p(x) = (-x_1 - x_2 + 1)^2$, $\theta(x, \mu) = x_1^2 + 2x_2^2 + \mu(-x_1 - x_2 + 1)^2$, and the necessary conditions for the optimal solution yield the following:

$\frac{\partial \theta(x,\mu)}{\partial x_1} = 2x_1 + 2\mu((-x_1 - x_2 + 1)(-1)$, and
$\frac{\partial \theta(x,\mu)}{\partial x_2} = 2x_1 + 2\mu(-x_1 - x_2 + 1)(-1) = 0$.

Thus, $x_{\mu_1} = \frac{2\mu}{(1+3\mu)}$ and $x_{\mu_2} = \frac{\mu}{(2+3\mu)}$ for any fixed μ.
When $\mu \to \infty$, this converges to the optimum solution of $x^* = (\frac{2}{3}, \frac{1}{3})$.
Now suppose we use (2.8) to define

$(u_\mu)_i = 2\mu(\text{maximum } \{0, g_i(x_\mu)\})$, then

$u_\mu = 2\mu(1 - \{2\mu/(2+3\mu)\} - \{\mu/(2+3\mu)\})$
$= 2\mu(1 - \{3\mu/(2+3\mu)\})$
$= (4\mu/(2+3\mu))$.

Then it is readily seen that $\lim_{\mu\to\infty}(4\mu/(2+3\mu)) = 4/3 = \bar{u}$ (the optimal Lagrangian multiplier for this example). Therefore the above Lemma 4 is true under some regularity conditions.

III-Conditioning of the Hessian matrix

Since the penalty function method must, for various (large) values of μ, solve the unconstrained problem:

Minimize f(**x**) + μp(**x**)
subject to x ∈ **X**,

It is important, in order to evaluate the difficulty of such a problem, to determine the eigenvalue structure of the Hessian of this modified objective function. The motivation for this is that the eigenvalue structure of the Hessian of the objective function determines the natural rates of convergence for algorithms designed for unconstrained optimization problems. We show here that the structure of the eigenvalue of the corresponding unconstrained problem becomes increasingly unfavorable as μ increases. Although, one usually insists for computational as well as theoretical purposes that the function $p \in c^1$, one usually does not insist that $p \in c^2$. In particular, the most popular penalty function $p(x) = (\text{maximum } \{0, y\})^2$, has discontinuity in its second derivative at any point where the component of g is zero, that is, $\phi'(y) = 2(\text{maximum}\{0, y\})$, but $\phi''(y)$ would have been undefined at y = 0 (as shown below). Hence, the Hessian of the unconstrained problem would be undefined at points having binding inequality constraints. At first this might appear to be a serious drawback, since it means the Hessian is discontinuous at the boundary of the constraint region-right where, in general, the solution is expected to lie.

However, as pointed out above, the penalty method generates points that approach a boundary solution from the outside the constraint region. Thus, except for some possible chance occurrences, the sequence will, as $x_\mu \to \bar{x}$, be at points where the Hessian is well-defined. Furthermore, in iteratively solving the above unconstrained problem with a fixed μ, a sequence will be generated that converges to x_μ which is (for most value of μ) a point where the Hessian is well-defined, and the standard type of analysis will be applicable to the tail of such a sequence (Luenberger, 1974).

Consider the constrained optimization problem:

Minimize {f(x), x ∈ S}

whose feasible region we denote by S: = {x ∈ X | g(x) ≤ 0, h(x)} and the corresponding unconstrained problem:

$\theta(\mathbf{x}, \mu) = f(x) + \mu p(x)$, $p(x) = \sum_{i=1}^{m} \phi(g_i(\mathbf{x})) + \sum_{i=1}^{l} \psi(h_i(\mathbf{x}))$,

where f, g, h, φ, ψ are assumed to be twice continuously differentiable at $\mathbf{x}_\mu$. Then denoting by ∇ and ∇^2 the gradient and the Hessian operators for the functions Q, f, g, h, respectively, and denoting the first and second derivatives of φ and ψ as ϕ', ψ' and ϕ'',ψ'' (all with respect to x) we have,

$\nabla_x \theta(\mathbf{x}_\mu, \mu) = \nabla f(\mathbf{x}_\mu) + \mu \sum_{i=1}^{m} \phi'(g_i(\mathbf{x}_\mu)) \nabla g_i(\mathbf{x}_\mu) + \mu \sum_{i=1}^{l} \psi'(h_i(\mathbf{x}_\mu)) \nabla h_i(\mathbf{x}_\mu)$
And

$$Q(x, \mu) = \nabla_x^2 \theta(x_\mu) = [\nabla^2 f(x_\mu) + \mu \sum_{i=1}^{m} \phi'(g_i(x_\mu)) \nabla^2 g_i(x_\mu) + \sum_{i=1}^{l} \psi'(h_i(x_\mu)) \nabla^2 h_i(x_\mu)] + \mu \sum_{i=1}^{m} \phi''(g_i(x_\mu)) \nabla g_i(x_\mu) \nabla (g_i(x_\mu))^t + \mu \sum_{i=1}^{l} \psi''(h_i(x_\mu)) \nabla h_i(x_\mu) \nabla h_i(x_\mu)^t. \quad (2.10)$$

To estimate the convergence rate of algorithms designed to solve the modified objective function let us examine the eigenvalue structure of (2.10) as $\mu \to \infty$, and under the conditions of Theorem 2.2, as $x \equiv x_\mu \to \bar{x}$, an optimum solution to the given problem. Assuming that $\{x_\mu\} \to \bar{x}$ and $\bar{x}$ is a regular solution, we have from (2.8) that,

$\mu\phi'(g_i(\mathbf{x}_\mu)) \to \bar{u}_i \geq 0$ for $i \in I$ and $\mu\psi'(h_i(\mathbf{x}_\mu)) \to \bar{v}_i$, i = 1, . . . , l,

where the optimal Lagrange multipliers associated with the ith constraint. Hence, the term in [.] approaches the Hessian of the Lagrangian function of the original problem as $x_\mu \to \bar{x}$, which is

$\nabla^2 L(\bar{x}) = \nabla^2 f(\bar{x}) + \sum_{i=1}^{m} \bar{u}_i \nabla^2 h_i(\bar{x}) + \sum_{i=1}^{m} \bar{v}_i \nabla^2 h_i(\bar{x})$,

and has a limit that is independent of μ. The other term in (2.10), however, is strongly tied in with μ, and is potentially explosive.

For example, if $\phi(y) = (\text{maximum}\{0, y\})^2$ and $\psi(y) = y^2$, as the popular quadratic penalty functions for the inequality and equality constraints and considering a primal problem with equality or inequality constraints separately we have two matrices.

$$\Phi''(g_i(\mathbf{x}_\mu)) = 2\begin{bmatrix} e_1 & 0 & . & . & . & 0 \\ 0 & e_2 & . & . & . & 0 \\ \vdots & \vdots & & & & \vdots \\ 0 & 0 & . & . & . & e_m \end{bmatrix}$$

where

$$e_i = \begin{cases} 1 \text{ if } g_i(\mathbf{x}_\mu) > 0 \\ 0 \text{ if } g_i(\mathbf{x}_\mu) < 0 \\ \text{undefined if } g_i(\mathbf{x}_\mu) = 0. \end{cases}$$

Thus,

$$\mu\sum_{i=1}^{m}\Phi''(g_i(\mathbf{x}_\mu))\,\nabla g_i(\mathbf{x}_\mu)\nabla g_i(\mathbf{x}_\mu)^t = 2\mu\sum_{i=1}^{m}\nabla g_i(\mathbf{x}_\mu)\nabla g_i(\mathbf{x}_\mu)^t,$$

which is 2μ times a matrix that approaches $\sum_{i=1}^{m}\nabla g_i(\bar{\mathbf{x}})\nabla g_i(\bar{\mathbf{x}})^t$. This matrix has rank equal to the rank of the active constraints at $\bar{\mathbf{x}}$ (Luenberger, 1974).

Assuming that there are r_1 active constraints at the solution $\bar{\mathbf{x}}$, then for well behaved Φ the matrix Q(x, μ) with only inequality constraints has r_1 eigenvalues that tend to ∞ as $\mu \to \infty$, but the $n - r_1$ eigenvalues, though varying with μ, tend to finite limits. These limits turnout to be the eigenvalues of $L(\bar{\mathbf{x}})$ restricted to the tangent subspace M of the active constraints. The other matrix $2\mu\sum_{i=1}^{l}\nabla h_i(\mathbf{x}_\mu)\nabla h_i(\mathbf{x}_\mu)^t$ with l equality constraints has rank l. As $\mu \to \infty$, $\mathbf{x}_\mu \to \bar{\mathbf{x}}$, the matrix Q(x, μ) with only equality constraints has l eigenvalues that approach infinity while the n - l eigenvalues approach some finite limits. Consequently, we can expect a severely ill-conditioned Hessian matrix for large values of μ.

Considering equation (2.10) with both equality and inequality constraints we have as $\mathbf{x}_\mu \to \bar{\mathbf{x}}$, is a local solution to the constrained minimization problem (P) and that it satisfies

$$\mathbf{h}(\bar{\mathbf{x}}) = 0 \text{ and } \mathbf{g}_A(\bar{\mathbf{x}}) = 0 \text{ and } \mathbf{g}_I(\bar{\mathbf{x}}) < 0,$$

where g_A and g_I, is the induced partitioning of g into r_1 active and r_2 inactive constraints, respectively. Assuming that the l gradients of h and the r_1 gradients of g_A evaluated at $\bar{\mathbf{x}}$ together are linearly independent, then $\bar{\mathbf{x}}$ is said to be regular. It follows from this expression that, for large μ and for $\mathbf{x}_\mu$ close to the solution of (P) the matrix Q has $l + r_1$, eigenvalues of the order of μ. Consequently, we can expect a severely ill-conditioned Hessian matrix for large values of μ. Since the rate of convergence of the method of steepest descent applied to a functional is determined by the ratio of the smallest to the largest eigenvalues of the Hessian of that functional, it follows in particular that the steepest descent method applied to θ converges slowly for large μ.

In examining the structure of Q is therefore; first, as μ is increased, the solution of the penalty problem approaches the solution of the original problem, and, hence, the neighborhood in which attention is focused for convergence analysis is close to the true solution. This means that the structure of the Lagrangian in the neighborhood of interest is close to that of Lagrangian at the true solution. Secondly, we conclude that, for large μ, the matrix Q is positive definite. For any μ, Q must be at least positive semi definite at the solution to the penalty problem: it is indicated that a stronger condition holds for large μ.

Example 6

Consider the auxiliary function, $\theta(x, \mu) = x_1^2 + 2x_2^2 + \mu(-x_1^2 - x_2^2 + 1)^2$, of example 2.5. The Hessian is:

$$H = \begin{bmatrix} 2+2\mu & 2\mu \\ 2 & 4+2\mu \end{bmatrix}.$$

Suppose we want to find its eigenvalues by solving det $|H - \lambda I| = 0$,

$$|H - \lambda I| = (2 + 2\mu - \lambda)(4 + 2\mu - \lambda) - 4\mu^2$$
$$= \lambda^2 - (6 + 4\mu)\lambda + 8 + 12\mu.$$

This quadratic equation yields

$$\lambda = (3 + 2\mu) \pm \sqrt{4\mu^2 + 1},$$
$$\lambda_1 = (3 + 2\mu) - \sqrt{4\mu^2 + 1} \text{ and } \lambda_2 = (3 + 2\mu) + \sqrt{4\mu^2 + 1}.$$

Note that $\lambda_2 \to \infty$ as $\mu \to \infty$, while λ_1 is finite; and, hence, the condition number of H approaches ∞ as $\mu \to \infty$. Taking the ratio of the largest and the smallest eigenvalue yields

It should be clear that as $\mu \to \infty$, the limit of the preceding ratio also goes to ∞. This indicates that as the iterations proceed and we start to increase the value of μ, the Hessian of the unconstrained function that we are minimizing becomes increasingly ill-conditioned. This is a common situation and is especially problematic if we are using a method for the unconstrained optimization that requires the use of the Hessian.

Unconstrained minimization techniques and penalty function methods

In this we mainly concentrate on the problems of efficiently solving the unconstrained problems with a penalty method. The main difficulty as explained above is the extremely unfavorable eigenvalue structure. Certainly straight forward application of the method of steepest descent is out of the question.

Newton's method and penalty function methods

One method for avoiding slow convergence for the problems is to apply Newton's method (or one of its variations), since the order two convergence of Newton's method is unaffected by the poor eigenvalue structure.

In applying the method, however, special care must be devoted to the manner by which the Hessian is inverted, since it is ill-conditioned. Nevertheless, if second order information is easily available, Newton's method offers an extremely attractive and effective method for solving modest size penalty and barrier optimization problems.

When such information is not readily available, or if data handling and storage requirements of Newton's method are excessive, attention naturally focuses on zero order or first order methods.

Conjugate gradients and penalty function methods

According to Luenberger (1984) the partial conjugate gradient method for solving unconstrained problems is ideally suited to penalty and barrier problems having only a few active constraints. If there are l active constraints, then taking cycles of 1+1 conjugate gradient steps will yield a rate of convergence that is independent of μ. For example, consider the problem having only equality constraints:

Minimize f(x) (P)
subject to h(x) = 0,

where $x \in R^n$, $h(x) \in R^l$, $l < n$. Applying the standard quadratic penalty method, we solve instead the unconstrained problem:

minimize $f(x) + \mu|h(\mathbf{x})|^2$,

for large μ. The objective function of this problem has a Hessian matrix that has l eigenvalues that are of order μ in magnitude, while the remaining n – l eigenvalues are close to the eigenvalues of the matrix L_M, corresponding to the primal problem (P). Thus, letting $x_{\mu+1}$ be determined from x_μ by making l + 1 steps of a (nonquadratic) conjugate gradient method, and assuming $x_\mu \rightarrow \bar{\mathbf{x}}$, a solution to $\theta(\mu)$, the sequence $\{f(x_\mu)\}$ converges linearly to $f(\bar{\mathbf{x}})$ with a convergence ratio equal to approximately

$$\left(\frac{\beta - \alpha}{\beta + \alpha}\right)^2$$

where α and β are, respectively, the smallest and largest eigenvalues of $L_M(\bar{\mathbf{x}})$. This is an extremely effective technique when l is relatively small. The method can be used for problems having inequality constraints as well but it is advisable to change the cycle length, depending on the number of constraints active at the end of the previous cycle.

Here we will use Powell's method which is the zero order method. Powell's method is an extension of the basic pattern search methods. It is the most widely used direct search method and can be proved to be a method of conjugate directions. This is as effective as the first order methods like the gradient method for solving unconstrained optimization problems. The reason why we use it here is:

a. First, it is assumed that the objective and constraint functions be continuous and smooth (continuously differentiable). Experience has shown this to be a more theoretical than practical requirement and this restriction is routinely violated in engineering design and in some facility location problems. Therefore it is better to develop a general code that solves both differentiable and non-differentiable problems.
b. The input of the derivative if it exists is tiresome for problems with large number of variables. In spite of its advantages, Newton's method for example is not generally used in practice due to the following features of the method:

i. It requires the storing of the $n \times n$ Hessian matrix of the objective function,
ii. It becomes very difficult and sometimes, impossible to compute the elements of the Hessian matrix of the objective function,
iii. It requires the inversion of the Hessian matrix of the objective function at each step,
iv. It requires the evaluation of the product of inverse of the Hessian matrix of the objective function and the negative of the gradient of the objective function at each step.

Because of the above reasons I do not prefer first and second order methods and I did not give more emphasis on these methods and their algorithms.

Finally, we should not use second-order gradient methods (e.g., pure Newton's method) with the quadratic loss penalty function for inequality constraints, since the Hessian is discontinuous (Belegundu and, Chandrupatla, 1999). To see this clearly, consider:

Minimize f(x) = 100/x
subject to $g = x - 5 \leq 0$,

with f(x) being a monotonically decreasing function of x. At the optimum $\bar{x} = 5$, the gradient of p(x) is $2\mu\max(0, x - 5)$. Regardless of whether we approach $\bar{x}$ from the left or right, the value of $\frac{dp}{dx}$ at $\bar{x}$ is zero. So, p(x) is first-order differentiable. However, $\frac{\partial p^2}{\partial x^2} = 0$ when approaching $\bar{x}$ from the left while $\frac{\partial p^2}{\partial x^2} = 2\mu$ when approaching from the right. Thus, the penalty function is not second-order differentiable at the optimum.

Powell's method and penalty function methods

Powell's method is a zero-order method, requiring the evaluation of f(x) only. If the problem involves n design variables, the basic algorithm is (Kiusalaas, 2005):

Choose a point x_0 in the design space.

Choose the starting vectors v_i , i = 1, 2, . . . , n(the usual choice is $v_i = e_i$, where e_i is the unit vector in the x_i-coordinate direction).
Cycle
do with i = 1, 2, . . . , n
Minimize f(x) along the line through x_{i-1} in the direction of v_i. Let the minimum point be x_i.

end
do $v_{n+1} \leftarrow x_n - x_0$ (this vector is conjugate to v_{n+1} produced in the previous loop).
Minimize f(x) along the line through x_0 in the direction of v_{n+1}. Let the minimum point be x_{n+1}.
if $|x_{n+1} - x_0| < \varepsilon$ exit loop
do with i = 1, 2, . . . , n
$v_i \leftarrow v_{i+1}$ (v_1 is discarded, the other vectors are reused)
end do end cycle.

Powell (1997) demonstrated that the vectors $\mathbf{v}_{n+1}$ produced in successive cycles are mutually conjugate, so that the minimum point of a quadratic surface is reached in precisely n cycles. In practice, the merit function is seldom quadratic, but as long as any function can be approximated locally by quadratic function, Powell's method will work. Of course, it usually takes more than n cycles to arrive at the minimum of a non quadratic function. Note that it takes n line minimizations to construct each conjugate direction.

Powell's method does have a major flaw that has to be remedied; if f(x) is not a quadratic, the algorithm tends to produce search directions that gradually become linearly dependent, thereby ruining the progress towards the minimum. The source of the problem is the automatic discarding of v_1 at the end of each cycle. It has been suggested that it is better to throw out the direction that resulted in the largest decrease of f(x), a policy that we adopt. It seems counter intuitive to discard the best direction, but it is likely to be close to the direction added in the next cycle, thereby contributing to linear dependence. As a result of the change, the search directions cease to be mutually conjugate, so that a quadratic form is not minimized in n cycles any more. This is not a significant loss since in practice f(x) is seldom a quadratic anyway. Powell suggested a few other refinements to speed up convergence. Since they complicate the bookkeeping considerably, we did not implement them.

General description of the penalty function method algorithm

The detail of this and a MATLAB computer program for implementing the penalty method using Powell's method of unconstrained minimization is given in the appendix.

Algorithm 1 (Algorithm for the penalty function method)

To solve the sequence of unconstrained problems with monotonically increasing values of μ_k, let $\{\mu_k\}$, k = 1, . . . be a sequence tending to infinity such that $\mu_k \geq 0$ and $\mu_{k+1} > \mu_k$. Now for each k we solve the problem

Minimize $\{\theta(x, \mu_k), x \in X\}$. (2.11)

To obtain x_k, the optimum it is assumed that problem (2.11) has a solution for all positive values of μ_k. A simple implementation known as the sequential unconstrained minimization technique (SUMT) is given below.

Step 0: (Initialization) Select a growth parameter $\beta > 1$ and a stopping parameter $\varepsilon > 0$ and an initial value of the penalty parameter μ_0. Choose a starting point $\mathbf{x}_0$ that violates at least one constraint and formulate the augmented objective function $\theta(x, \mu_k)$. Let k = 1.

Step 1: Iterative - Starting from x_{k-1}, use an unconstrained search technique to find the point that minimizes $\theta(x, \mu_{k-1})$ and call it x_k.

Step 2: Stopping Rule - If the distance between x_{k-1} and x_k is smaller than ε, that is, $\| x_{k-1} - x_k \| < \varepsilon$ or the difference between two successive objective function values is smaller than ε, that is, $|f(x_{k-1}) - f(x_k)| < \varepsilon$, stop with x_k an estimate of the optimal solution otherwise, put $\mu_k = \beta\mu_{k-1}$, and formulate the new $\theta(x, \mu_k)$ and put k = k+1 and return to the iterative step.

Considerations for implementation of the penalty function method

Starting point x_1

First in the solution step is to select a starting point. A good rule of thumb is to start at an infeasible point. By design then, we will see that every trial point, except the last one, will be infeasible (exterior to the feasible region). A reasonable place to start is at the unconstrained minimum. Always we should ensure that the penalty does not dominate the objective function during initial iterations of penalty function method.

Selecting the initial penalty parameter (μ_0)

The initial penalty parameter μ_0 should be fixed so that the magnitude of the penalty term is not much smaller than the magnitude of objective function. If an imbalance exists, the influence of the objective function could direct the algorithm to head towards an unbounded minimum even in the presence of unsatisfied constraints. Because the exterior penalty method approach seems to work so well, it is natural to conjecture that all we have to do is set μ to a very large number and then optimize the resulting augmented objective function $\theta(\mathbf{x}, \mu_k)$ to obtain the solution to the original problem. Unfortunately, this conjecture is not correct. First, "large" depends on the particular model. It is almost always impossible to tell how large μ must be to provide a solution to the problem without creating numerical difficulties in the computations. Second, in a very real sense, the problem is dynamically changing with the relative position of the current value of **x** and the subset of the constraints that are violated. The third reason why the conjecture is not correct is associated with the fact that large values of μ create enormously steep valleys at the constraint boundaries. Steep valleys will often present formidable if not insurmountable convergence difficulties for all preferred search methods unless the algorithm starts at a point extremely close to the minimum being sought. Fortunately, there is a direct and sound strategy that will overcome each of the difficulties mentioned above. All that needs to be done is to start with a relatively small value of μ. The most frequently used initial penalty parameters in the literature are 0.01, 0.1, 2, 5, and 10. This will assure that no steep valleys are present in the initial optimization of $\theta(\mathbf{x}, \mu_k)$. Subsequently, we will solve a sequence of unconstrained problems with monotonically increasing values of μ chosen so that the solution to each new problem is "close" to the previous one. This will preclude any major difficulties in finding the minimum of $\theta(x, \mu_k)$ from one iteration to the next.

Subsequent values of the penalty parameter

Once the initial value of the μ_k is chosen, the subsequent values of μ_k have to be chosen such that $\mu_{k+1} > \mu_k$.

For convenience, the value of μ_k is chosen according to the relation:

$\mu_{k+1} = \beta\mu_k$.
where $\beta > 1$. The value of β can be taken as in most literatures 2, 5, 10,100 etc.

Various approaches to selecting the penalty parameter sequence exist in the literature. The simplest is to keep it constant during all iterations and we consider here the penalty parameter as same for all constraints.

Normalization of the constraints

An optimization may also become ill-conditioned when the constraints have widely different magnitudes and thus badly affect the convergence rate during the minimization of θ-function. Much of the success of SUMT depends on the approach used to solve the intermediate problems, which in turn depends on their complexity. One thing that should be done prior to attempting to solve a nonlinear programming using a penalty function method is, to scale the constraints so that the penalty generated by each is about the same magnitude. This scaling operation is intended to ensure that no subset of the constraints has an undue influence on the search process. If some constraints are dominant, the algorithm will steer towards a solution that satisfies those constraints at the expense of searching for the minimum. In either case, convergence may be exceedingly slow. Discussion on how to normalize constraints is given on barrier function methods.

Test problems (Testing practical examples)

As discussed in previous sections, a number of algorithms are available for solving constrained nonlinear programming problems. In recent years, a variety of computer programs have been developed to solve engineering optimization problems. Many of these are complex and versatile and the user needs a good understanding of the algorithms/computer programs to be able to use them effectively. Before solving a new engineering design optimization problem, we usually test the behavior and convergence of the algorithm/computer program on simple test problems. Eight test problems are given in this section. All these problems have appeared in the optimization and on facility location literature and most of them have been solved using different techniques.

Example 1

Consider the optimization problem:

Minimize $f(x) = (x_1 - 5)^2 + (x_2 - 6)^2$
subject to $x_1^2 - 4 \le 0$
$e^{-x_1} - x_2 \le 0$
$x_1 + 2x_2 - 4 \le 0$
$x_1 \ge 0$
$x_2 \ge 0$

We consider the sequence of problems:

$\theta(\mathbf{x}, \mu) = f(x) + \mu[(\text{maximum}\{0, x_1^2 - 4\})^2 + (\text{maximum}\{0, e^{-x_1} - x_2\})^2 + (\text{maximum}\{0, -x_1\})^2\ ] + (\text{maximum}\{0, -x_2\})^2 + (\text{maximum}\{0, x_1 + 2x_2 - 4\})^2]$

Optimum solution point using Mathematica is x = (1.67244, 1.21942) and Optimum solution is at $f^* = 34.1797$
Optimum solution point using MATLAB is x = (2.000000003129, 1.000000123435) and
Optimum solution is at $f^* = 34.0000050125$

The graph of the feasible region and steps of a computer program (Deumlich, 1996) with the contours of the objective function are shown in Figure 2.

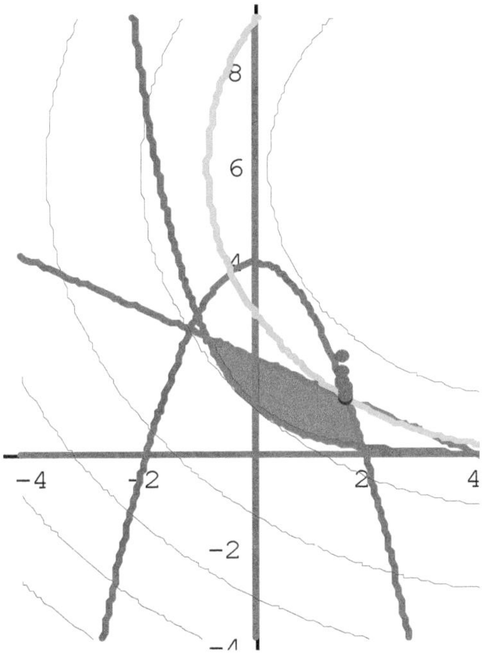

Figure 2. The sequence of unfeasible results from outside the feasible region. And the iteration step using MATLAB for penalty and the necessary data are given.

Table 1. The iteration step using MATLAB.

μ	x_{min}	f_{min}	aug_{min}
1.00	(-10.000000000000,-10.000000000000)	481.00	485615721.72568649
10.00	(2.055936255098, 1.977625505064)	24.847007912	65.8104676667
100.00	(2.003470085541, 1.120258484331)	32.791068788	38.7633368822
1000.00	(2.000316074133, 1.012311179827)	33.875143422	34.4986676000
10000.00	(2.000031285652, 1.001234049950)	33.987473310	34.0500992010
100000.00	(2.000003125478, 1.000123433923)	33.998746923	34.0050122192
1000000.00	(2.000000312552, 1.000012343760)	33.999874687	34.0005012538
10000000.00	(2.000000031250, 1.000001234352)	33.999987469	34.0000501229
100000000.00	(2.000000003129, 1.000000123435)	33.999998747	34.0000050125

And the iteration step using MATLAB for penalty method and the necessary data are given as follows:

Initial:

x_1 = [2; 5];
μ = 1; beta = 10;
tol = 1.0e-4; tol1 = 1.0e-6; h = 0.1;N = 10 (Table 1).

Example 2

Consider the optimization problem:

Minimize f(x) = $(x_1 - 3)^2 + (x_2 - 4)^2$

subject to $x_1^2 - x_2 \leq 0$

$e^{-x_1} - x_2 \leq 0$
$-x_1 + 2x_2 - 2 \leq 0$

We consider the sequence of problems:
$\theta(x, \mu)$ = f(x) + μ[$(\text{maximum}\{0, x_1^2 - x_2\})^2 + (\text{maximum}\{0, e^{-x_1} - x_2\})^2 + (\text{maximum}\{0, -x_1 + 2x_2 - 2\})^2$]
Optimum solution point using Mathematica is x = (1.33271, 1.7112) and Optimum solution is at f^* = 8.26363
Optimum solution point using MATLAB is x = (1.280776520285, 1.640388354297) and Optimum solution is at f^* = 8.5235020151.

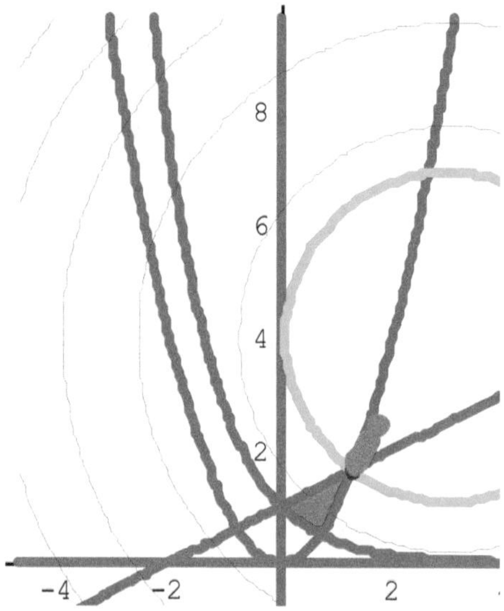

Figure 3. The sequence of unfeasible results.

Table 2. The iteration step using MATLAB.

μ	x_{min}	f_{min}	aug_{min}
1.00	(10.00000000000, 10.00000000000)	85.000000000	8249.000000000
10.00	(1.762313021963, 2.438395531128)	3.9704775728	20.8446729268
100.00	(1.376888913083, 1.774431551334)	7.5876445202	12.0187470067
1000.00	(1.291940370698, 1.655287557366)	8.4151441359	8.9534555697
10000.00	(1.281912903137, 1.641896920522)	8.5124734059	8.5675584019
100000.00	(1.280890263154, 1.640539267595)	8.5223932351	8.5279146690
1000000.00	(1.280787794313, 1.640403311676)	8.5233871397	8.5239394231
10000000.00	(1.280777545189, 1.64038971403)	8.5234865508	8.5235417778
100000000.00	(1.280776520285, 1.64038835429)	8234964917	8.5235020150

The graph of the feasible region and steps of a computer program (based on Mathematica) with the contours of the objective function are shown in Figure 3.

And the iteration step using MATLAB for penalty method and the necessary data are given as follows:

Initial:

x = [10; 10];
μ = 1; beta = 10;
tol = 1.0e-3; tol1 = 1.0e-5; h = 0.1; N = 10 (Table 2).

Example 3

Consider the optimization problem:

Minimize $f(x) = -\ln(\sqrt{x_1} + \sqrt{x_2})$
subject to $x_1 \geq 0$
$x_2 \geq 0$
$2x_1 + 3x_2 \leq 6$

Solution

The θ-function of the corresponding unconstrained problem is:

$$\theta(\mathbf{x}, \mu) = f(x) + \mu[(\text{maximum}\{0, -x_1\})^2 + (\text{maximum}\{0, -x_2\})^2 + (\text{maximum}\{0, 2x_1 + 3x_2 - 6\})^2]$$

The Exterior penalty function method, coupled with the Powell method of unconstrained minimization and golden

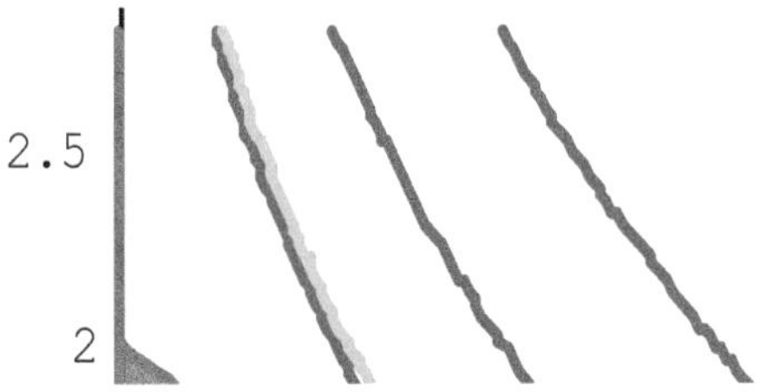

Figure 4. The sequence of unfeasible results from outside the feasible region.

Table 3. The iteration step using MATLAB.

μ	x_{min}	f_{min}	aug_{min}
1.00000	(100.0000000000, 100.0000000000)	-2.9957322736	244033.0042677264
1.50000	(1.812414390011, 0.805517491028)	-0.8081555566	-0.805586944500
2.25000	(1.812414390377, 0.805517490784)	-0.8081555566	-0.804302638400
3.37500	(1.812414395786, 0.805517487178)	-0.8081555566	-0.802376179003
5.06250	(1.803696121437, 0.801642712659)	-0.8057446020	-0.804976156000

bracket and golden search method of one-dimensional search, is used to solve this problem.
Optimum solution point using Mathematica is **x** = (1.80125, 0.800555) and
Optimum solution is at f^* = -0.804892

Optimum solution point using MATLAB is **x** = (1.803696121437, 0.801642712659) and
Optimum solution is at f^* = -0.8057446020
The graph of the feasible region and steps of a computer program (Deumlich, 1996) with the contours of the objective function are shown in Figure 4. And the iteration step using MATLAB for penalty method and the necessary data are given as follows:

Initial:

x_1 = [100; 100];
μ = 1; beta = 1.5;
tol = 1.0e-9; tol1 = 1.0e-3; h = 0.1;N = 10; Table 3

Example 4

Consider the optimization problem:

Minimize f(**x**) = $(x_1 - 2)^2 - 5\ln((x_2 - 2)^2 + 1)$
subject to $x_1^2 + x_2 - 4 \leq 0$
$e^{-x_1} - x_2 \leq 0$.

We consider the sequence of problems:

$$\theta(\mathbf{x}, \mu) = (x_1 - 2)^2 - 5\ln((x_1 - 2)^2 + 1) + \mu[(\text{maximum}\{0, x_1^2 + x_2 - 4\})^2 + (\text{maximum}\{0, e^{-x_1} - x_2\})^2].$$

We can solve this problem numerically. Since the function f is not convex we can expect local minimum points depending on the choice of the initial point.

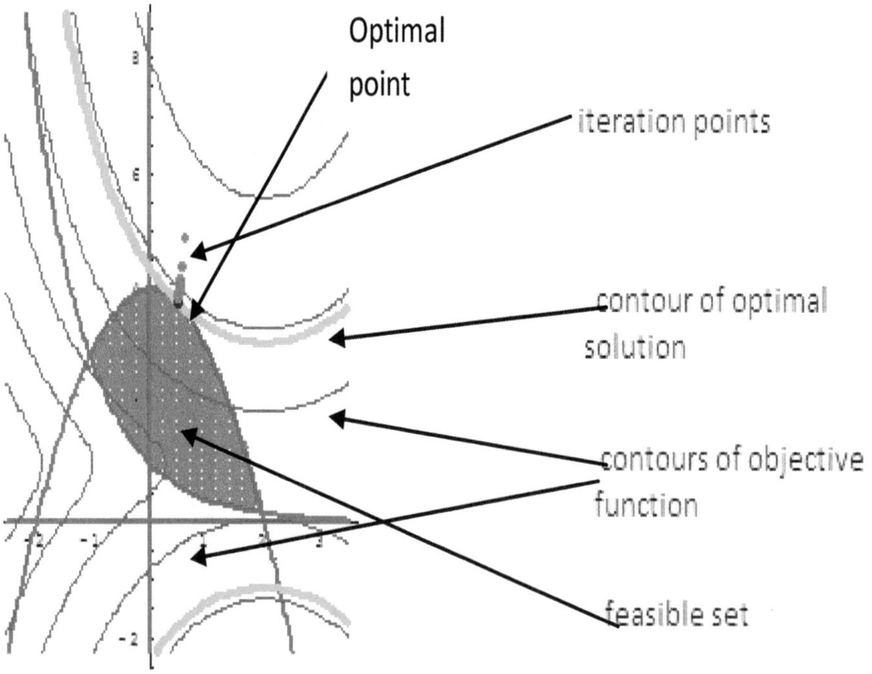

Figure 5. The sequence of unfeasible results from outside the feasible region.

Table 4. The iteration step using MATLAB.

μ	x_{min}	f_{min}	aug_{min}
1.0	(2 .000000000000, 3.000000000000)	-8.0471895622	0.9528104378
10.0	(0.584383413070, 4.869701406514)	-11.851026032	2.8191586927
100.0	(0.491210873054, 3.912290440909)	-8.9702340739	-6.6115965813
1000.0	(0.478587312848, 3.786849015552)	-8.5400072779	-8.2873616072
10000.0	(0.477272005299, 3.773806675110)	-8.4944671131	-8.4690191379
100000.0	(0.477139883021, 3.772497114149)	-8.4898858321	-8.4873391868
1000000.0	(0.477126692178, 3.772366078499)	-8.4894274297	-8.4891727436
10000000.0	(0.477125354746, 3.772352991728)	-8.4893815863	-8.4893561184

Optimum solution point using Mathematica is x = (0.472776, 3.80538) and
Optimum solution is at f^* = -8.52761
Optimum solution point using MATLAB is x = (0.477125354746, 3.772352991728) and
Optimum solution is at f^* = -8.4893815863

The graph of the feasible region and steps of a computer program (Deumlich 1996) with the contours of the objective function are shown in Figure 5. And the iteration step using MATLAB for penalty method and the necessary data are given as follows:

Initial:
$\mathbf{x}_1$ = [2; 3];
μ = 1; beta = 10;
tol = 1.0e-4; tol1 = 1.0e-6; h = 0.1;N = 10 (Table 4).

Example 5

A new facility is to be located such that the sum of its distance from the four existing facilities is minimized. The four facilities are located at the points (1, 2), (-2, 4), (2, 6), and (-6,-3). If the coordinates of the new facility are x_1 and x_2, suppose that x_1 and x_2 must satisfy the restrictions $x_1 + x_2 = 2$, $x_1 \geq 0$, and $x_2 \geq 0$.

Formulate the problem
Solve the problem by a penalty function method using a suitable unconstrained optimization technique.

Minimize f(x) = $\sqrt{(x_1-1)^2+(x_2-2)^2} + \sqrt{(x_1-2)^2+(x_2-6)^2} + \sqrt{(x_1+2)^2+(x_2-4)^2} + \sqrt{(x_1+6)^2+(x_2+3)^2}$

subject to $x_1 + x_2 = 2$

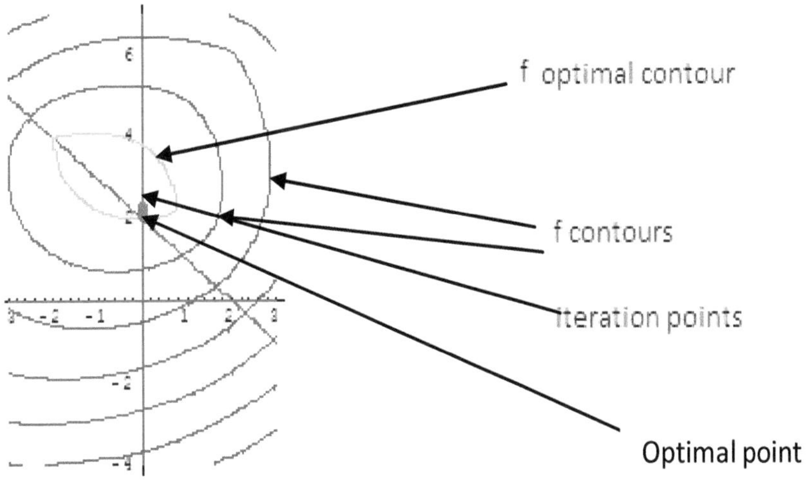

Figure 6. The sequence of unfeasible results from outside the feasible region.

Table 5. The iteration step using MATLAB.

μ	x_{min}	f_{min}	aug_{min}
0.1	(-100000.0000000,-100000.0000000)	565688.2534900	6000645688.6535
1.0	(-0.504816443491, 2.941129889320)	5.6534514664	16.0986605310
10.0	(-0.235317980540, 2.465609185550)	15.7843894418	16.8684753525
100.0	(-0.043496067432, 2.086197027712)	16.0316892765	16.4032172656
1000.0	(-0.004877163871, 2.009622311363)	16.1014887806	16.1477919328
10000.0	(0.000981076620, 2.000347630256)	16.1105064270	16.1281610467
100000.0	(0.003030519805, 1.997102981748)	16.1136901197	16.1154723862
1000000.0	(0.003236508228, 1.996776847061)	16.1140109620	16.1141893257

$x_1 \geq 0$
$x_2 \geq 0$

The corresponding unconstrained optimization problem

is:

$\theta(\mathbf{x}, \mu) = f(x) + \mu[(\text{maximum}\{0, x_1 + x_2 - 2\})^2 + (\text{maximum}\{0, -x_1\})^2 + (\text{maximum}\{0, -x_2\})^2]$.

Optimum solution point using Mathematica is x $=\{3.087 \text{x} 10^{-32}, 2.02328\}$

Optimum solution is at $f^* = 16.0996$.

Optimum solution point using MATLAB is x = (0.003236508228, 1.996776847061) and

Optimum solution is at $f^* = 16.1140109620$.

The graph of the feasible region and steps of a computer program (Deumlich 1996) with the contours of the objective function are shown in Figure 6.

And the iteration step using MATLAB for penalty method and the necessary data are given as follows:

Initial:
x = [-100000; -100000]; μ = 0.1; beta = 10;
tol = 1.0e-6; tol1 = 1.0e-3; h = 0.1;N = 10 (Table 5).

Example 6

A new facility is to be located such that the sum of its distance from the four existing facilities is minimized. The four facilities are located at the points (1, 2), (-2, 4), (2, 6), and (-6,-3). If the coordinates of the new facility are x_1 and x_2, suppose that x_1 and x_2 must satisfy the restrictions $x_1 + x_2 = 2$, $x_1^2 + x_2^2 \leq 2$, $-x_1^2 - 2x_2^2 \leq -3$, $x_1 \geq 0$, and $x_2 \geq 0$.

Formulate the problem
Solve the problem by a penalty function method using a suitable unconstrained optimization technique.

Minimize $f(\mathbf{x}) = \sqrt{(x_1-1)^2+(x_2-2)^2} + \sqrt{(x_1-2)^2+(x_2-6)^2} + \sqrt{(x_1+2)^2+(x_2-4)^2} + \sqrt{(x_1+6)^2+(x_2+3)^2}$

subject to $x_1 + x_2 = 2$
$x_1^2 + x_2^2 \leq 2$
$-x_1^2 - 2x_2^2 \leq -3$
$-x_1 \leq 0$
$-x_2 \leq 0$

The corresponding unconstrained optimization

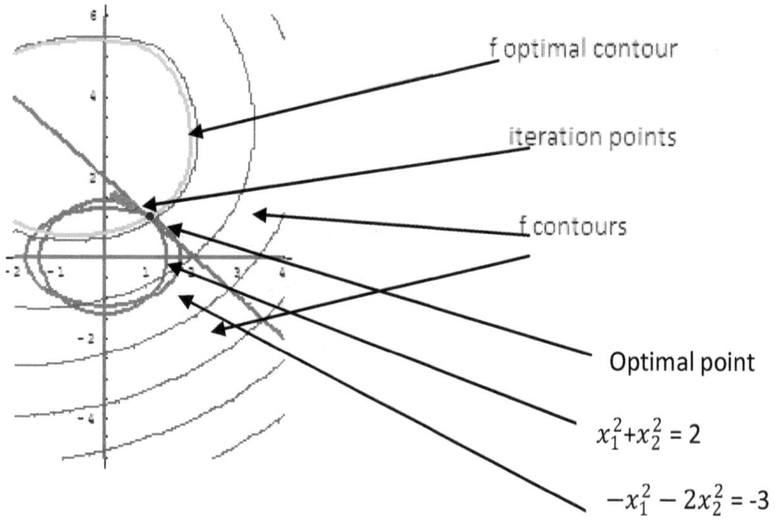

Figure 7. The sequence of unfeasible results from outside the feasible region.

Table 6. The iteration step using MMATLAB.

μ	x_{min}	f_{min}	aug_{min}
0.01	(-100.00000000000,-100.0000000000)	568.62244178640	4000376.7024418
0.10	(-0.204074540511, 2.488615905901)	15.7748455724	17.5805067419
1.00	(-0.005676255570, 1.87710924673)	16.2384983466	18.5763296826
10.0	(0.208853398412, 1.519794991416)	16.7514115057	18.7366197410
100.0	(0.541258580758, 1.337453329403)	17.2205864696	19.3598462433
1000.0	(0.774045018932, 1.191529581681)	17.7152204663	19.2571015793
10000.0	(0.894859224075, 1.097008320463)	18.0550540479	18.8928463977
100000.0	(0.951465363246, 1.046723818830)	18.2363926667	18.6484042954
1000000.0	(0.977561265017, 1.022043406130)	18.3250429734	18.5208297859
10000000.0	(0.989607061234, 1.01030727942)	18.3670763153	18.4588852580

problem is:

$$\theta(\mathbf{x},\mu) = f(\mathbf{x}) + [(x_1 + x_2 - 2)^2 + (\text{maximum}\{0,-x_1\})^2 + (\text{max imum}\{0,-x_2\})^2 +$$
$$+ (\text{maximum}\{0, x_1^2 + x_2^2 - 2\})^2 + (\text{max imum}\{0, -x_1^2 - 2x_2^2 + 3\})^2]$$

Optimum solution point using Mathematica is **x** = {0.624988, 1.28927} and
Optimum solution is at $f^* = 17.579$.
Optimum solution point using MATLAB is **x** = (0.989607061234, 1.010307279416) and
Optimum solution is at $f^* = 18.3670763153$.
The graph of the feasible region and steps of a computer program (Deumlich 1996) with the contours of the objective function are shown in Figure 7.

And the iteration step using MATLAB for penalty method and the necessary data are given as follows:

Initial:

$\mathbf{x}_1$ = [-100; -100];

μ = 0.01; beta = 10;
tol = 1.0e-6; tol1 = 1.0e-3; h = 0.1; N = 10; Table 6

Example 7

The detail of this location problem is given in example 1 of the barrier method.

Minimize

$$3600\sqrt{(x_1)^2 + (x_2 - 2)^2} + 2500\sqrt{(x_1 - 2)^2 + (x_2 - 4)^2} + 1800\sqrt{(x_1 - 5)^2 + (x_2 - 6)^2}$$
$$+ \quad 2200\sqrt{(x_1 - 5)^2 + (x_2 - 10)^2} \quad + \quad 1000\sqrt{(x_1 - 7)^2 + (x_2 - 15)^2}$$
$$+$$
$$4500\sqrt{(x_1 - 10)^2 + (x_2 - 15)^2} + 5600\sqrt{(x_1 - 12)^2 + (x_2 - 10)^2} + 1400\sqrt{(x_1 - 12)^2 + (x_2 - 6)^2}$$
$$+ 1800\sqrt{(x_1 - 15)^2 + (x_2 - 4)^2} + 3000\sqrt{(x_1 - 20)^2 + (x_2 - 2)^2}$$

subject to $x_1^2 + x_2^2 \le 25$

Table 7. The iteration step using MMATLAB.

μ	x_{min}	fmin	aug_{min}
10.0	(-100.000000,-100.0000000)	4201299.48370	3994823869.4837
100.0	(5.18664531200, 5.613234562710)	217725.1471	335935.8823
1000.0	(3.874734526, 3.94912345612000)	243622.3686	306218.6111
10000.0	(4.28341223, 2.646232345145123)	256672.3825	399517.2275
100000.0	(4.175642351, 0.46232345145100)	293524.5216	342434.4427
1000000.0	(4.01825125, 0.047812341001001)	302445.1718	307672.3810
10000000.0	(4.001831234, 0.00479123410010)	303387.2635	303913.3990
100000000.0	(4.000181234, 0.00047912341001)	303481.9797	303534.6277
1000000000.0	(4.000018123, 0.00004791234100)	303491.4564	303496.7216
10000000000.0	(4.0000018123, 0.0000047912340)	303492.4042	303492.9307
100000000000.0	(4.0000001812, 0.0000004790123)	303492.4989	303492.5516
100000000000.0	(4.000000018, 0.00000004812331)	303492.5084	303492.5137
10000000000000.0	(4.0000000018, 0.000000048123)	303492.5100	303492.5099
100000000000000.0	(4.000000000185, 0.00000000048)	303492.5095	303492.5095
1000000000000000.0	(4.00000000002, 0.00000000005)	303492.5095	303492.5095

$x_1 + x_2 = 4$
$x_1 - x_2 = 4$
$-x_1 \leq 0$
$-x_2 \leq 0$

The corresponding unconstrained optimization problem is:

$\theta(\mathbf{x}, \mu) = f(x) + \mu[(\text{maximum}\{0, -x_1\})^2 + (\text{maximum}\{0, -x_2\})^2 + (\text{maximum}\{0, x_1^2 + x_2^2 - 25\})^2 + (x_1 + x_2 - 4)^2 + (x_1 - x_2 - 4)^2]$.

Optimum solution point using Mathematica is x = (4, $1\text{x}10^{-12}$)

Optimum solution is at f^* = 303493.0.

Optimum solution point using MATLAB is x = (4.000000000018, 0.000000000048) and

Optimum solution is at f^* = 303492.50947.

And the iteration step using MATLAB for penalty method and the necessary data are given as follows:

Initial:

x = [-100; -100];
μ = 10; beta = 10;
tol = 1.0e-6; tol1 = 1.0e-6; h = 0.1; N = 20 (Table 7).

Example 8

Here, we test the well studied welded beam design problem, which has been solved by using a number of classical optimization methods and by using Genetic Algorithms [Deb, 128 to 129]. The welded beam is designed for minimum cost subject to constraints on shear stress in weld (τ), bending stress in the beam (σ), buckling load on the bar (Pc), end deflection of the beam (δ), and side constraints. It has four design variables $\mathbf{x} = (h, l, t, b)$.

Design vector: $\begin{pmatrix} h \\ l \\ t \\ b \end{pmatrix} = \begin{pmatrix} x_1 \\ x_2 \\ x_3 \\ x_4 \end{pmatrix}$

Objective function: $f(x) = 1.10471x_1x_2 + 0.04811x_3x_4(14.0 + x_2)$

Constraints:
$g_1(x) = \tau(x) - \tau_{max} \leq 0$
$g_2(x) = \sigma(x) - \sigma_{max} \leq 0$
$g_3(x) = x_1 - x_4 \leq 0$
$g_4(x) = 0.10471x_1 + 0.04811x_3x_4 (14.0 + x_2) - 5.0 \leq 0$
$g_5(x) = 0.125 - x_1 \leq 0$
$g_6(x) = \delta(x) - \delta_{max} \leq 0$
$g_7(x) = P - Pc(x) \leq 0$
$g_8(x)$ to $g_{11}(x)$: $0.1 \leq x_i \leq 2.0$, i = 1, 4
$g_{12}(x)$ to $g_{15}(x)$: $0.1 \leq x_i \leq 10.0$, i = 2, 3
where

$$\tau(\mathbf{x}) = \sqrt{(\tau'(x))^2 + (\tau''(x))^2 + l\tau'(x)\tau''(x)/\sqrt{0.25[l^2 + (h+t)^2]}}$$

$$\sigma(x) = \frac{504000}{t^2b},$$

$$p_c(\mathbf{x}) = 64746.022(1 - 0.0282346t)tb^3,$$

$$\delta(\mathbf{x}) = \frac{2.1952}{t^3b},$$

$$\tau'(\mathbf{x}) = \frac{6000}{\sqrt{2}hl},$$

$$\tau''(\mathbf{x}) = \frac{6000(14 + 0.5l)\sqrt{0.25[l^2 + (h+t)^2]}}{2\left\{0.707hl[\frac{l^2}{12} + 0.25(h+t)^2]\right\}}$$

Table 8. The iteration step using MMATLAB.

μ	x_{min}	f_{min}	aug_{min}
0.01	(2.00000, 3.00000, 0.100000, 0.050000)	13.2606093500	10160035228635306
0.02	(0.3634872, 2.7826082, 10.558957, 0.232105300)	2.3849380	2.39159576770
0.04	(0.3634872, 2.7826082, 10.55895716, 0.2321053)	2.3849380	2.39825371460
0.08	(0.3738517, 2.8145296, 10.10980684, 0.2340900)	2.3490380	2.35157651770
0.16	(0.375852754, 2.8212375, 10.0249324, 0.234488)	2.3426482	2.34679527470

P = 6000 lb, τ_{max} =13,600 psi, σ_{max} = 30,000 psi, and δ_{max} = 0.25 in.

Starting and optimum solutions:

$x_{start} = \begin{pmatrix} h \\ l \\ t \\ b \end{pmatrix} = \begin{pmatrix} 10 \\ 10 \\ 10 \\ 10 \end{pmatrix}$, f_{start} = 5.398 and $\mathbf{X}^* = \begin{pmatrix} 0.2415 \\ 6.3568, \\ 8.25539 \\ 0.24651 \end{pmatrix}$ and

fsolution^* = $2.3810

Optimum solution point given by Rao (2009) is x = (0.2444, 6.2177, 8.2915, 0.2444) and Optimum solution is at f^* = 2.3810. Optimum solution point using MATLAB is x = (0.375852754, 2.8212375, 10.0249324, 0.234488) and Optimum solution is at f^* = 2.3467952747.

And the iteration step using MATLAB for penalty method and the necessary data are given as follows:

Initial:

x_1 = [2; 3; 0.1; 0.05];
μ = 0.01; beta = 2;
tol = 1.0e-2; tol1 = 1.0e-6; h = 0.1; N = 5 (Table 8).

Using other starting point we have different solution but the difference is not significant as given below.

Initial:

$\mathbf{x}_1$ = [0.4; 6; 0 .01; 0.05];
μ = 0.1; beta = 2;
tol = 1.0e-2; tol1 = 1.0e-6; h = 0.1;N = 30 (Table 9).

EXACT PENALTY FUNCTION METHODS

In this chapter, we analyze two important extensions of the transformation methods, which are called exact penalty functions and have been most frequently used. In these methods a single unconstrained minimization problem, with a reasonable sized penalty parameter can yield an optimum solution to the original problem. This suggests an algorithm which attempts to locate the optimum value of θ whilst keeping μ finite and so avoids the ill-conditioning in the limit μ goes to infinity that we face in penalty function methods.

For the types of penalty functions considered thus far, we have seen that we need to make the penalty parameter infinitely large in a limiting sense to recover an optimal solution. This can cause numerical difficulties and ill-conditioning effects. To alleviate the computational difficulties associated with having to take the penalty parameter to infinity in order to recover an optimal solution to the original problem, we present below two penalty functions that possess this property and are known as exact penalty functions. These are exact absolute value (l_1 penalty function) and augmented Lagrangian penalty function method.

The exact absolute value or l_1 penalty function

An attractive approach to nonlinear programming is to attempt to determine an exact penalty function θ by which is meant a function defined in terms of the objective function and constraints. This holds out the possibility that the solution can be found by a single application of an unconstrained minimization technique to θ, as against the sequential processes described above cannot be used. Consider problem (P) to minimize f(x) subject to $g_i(\mathbf{x}) \leq 0$, i = 1, . . . , m, and $h_i(\mathbf{x}) = 0$, i = 1, . . . , l, and a penalty parameter μ > 0.

Roughly speaking, an exact penalty function for problem (P) is a function $\theta_E(\mathbf{x}, \mu)$, where μ > 0 is the penalty parameter, with the property that there exists a lower bound $\bar{\mu} > 0$ such that for $\mu \geq \bar{\mu}$ any local minimizer of (P) is also a local minimizer of the penalty problem. Exact penalty functions can be divided into two classes: continuously differentiable and non-differentiable exact penalty functions. Continuously differentiable exact penalty functions were introduced by Fletcher (1987) for equality constrained problems and by Gland and Polak (1979) for problems with inequality constraints; further contributions have been assumed in Di Pillo. Non-differentiable exact penalty functions were introduced by Zangwill (1967); Pietrgykowski (1969). The most frequently used type of exact penalty function is the l_1 exact penalty function. This function has been researched widely, for example by Pietrgykowski (1969); Coleman and Conn (1982); in nonlinear programming applications amongst others. Unfortunately the many effective techniques for smooth minimization cannot adequately be used because of its non-differentiability and the best way of using this penalty function is currently being researched. A more realistic approach is to use this function as a criterion function to be used in conjunction with other iterative methods for nonlinear programming. The most satisfactory approach of all is to apply methods of non-smooth optimization.

A class of non-differentiable exact penalty functions associated to (P) for $X = R^n$ was analyzed by Charalambous in 1978. It is assumed by

$$\theta_q(x, \alpha, \beta) = f(x) + q\left(\sum_{i=1}^{m}[\beta_i g_i^+(x)]^q + \sum_{i=1}^{l}[\alpha_i |h_i(x)|]^q\right)^{\frac{1}{q}},$$

where $q \geq 1$, $\beta_i, \alpha_i > 0$, $i = 1, \ldots, m$ and $i = 1, \ldots, l$. For $q = 1$ and considering all the penalty parameters equal to μ; we have the l_1 penalty function, introduced by Pietrgykowski (1969),

$$\theta_E(x, \mu) = f(x) + \mu\sum_{i=1}^{m}[\max\{0, g_i(x)\}] + \sum_{i=1}^{l}|h_i(x)|, \quad (4.1)$$

Where:

$p(\mathbf{x}) = \sum_{i=1}^{m}\phi(g_i(x)) + \sum_{i=1}^{l}\psi(h_i(x)$

$= \sum_{i=1}^{m}[\max\{0, g_i(x)\}] + \sum_{i=1}^{l}|h_i(x)|$, is the penalty function.

Pietrgykowski (1969), has shown that function (4.1) is exact in the sense that there is a finite $\mu > 0$ such that any regular local minimizer of (P) is also a local minimizer of the penalized unconstrained problem. In 1970, Luenberger showed that, under convex assumptions, there is a lower bound for μ, equal to the largest Lagrange multiplier in absolute value, associated to the nonlinear problem. In 1978, Charalambous generalized the result of Luenberger for the l_1 penalty function (4.1), assuming the second-order sufficient conditions for (P). The following result shows that, under suitable convexity assumptions, there does exist a finite value of μ that will recover an optimum solution to (P) via the minimization of θ_E. Alternatively, it can be shown that if $\bar{x}$ satisfies the second-order sufficiency conditions for a local minimum of (P) (the Hessian is positive definite). Then, for μ at least as large as the theorem below, $\bar{x}$ will also be a local minimum of θ_E.

Theorem 4

Consider the following primal problem:

Minimize f(x)
subject to $g(x) \leq 0$
$h(x) = 0$. (P)

Let $\bar{x}$ be a KKT point with Lagrangian multipliers $\bar{u}_i$, $i \in I$, and $\bar{v}_i$, $i = 1, \ldots, l$ associated with the inequality and equality constraints, respectively, where $I = \{i \in \{1, \ldots, m\} : g_i(\bar{x}) = 0\}$ is the index set of active constraints.

Furthermore, suppose that f and g_i, $i \in I$ are convex functions and that h_i, $i = 1, \ldots, l$ are affine functions. Then, for $\mu \geq$ maximum $\{\bar{u}_i, i \in I, |\bar{v}_i|, i = 1, \ldots, l\}$, $\bar{x}$ also minimizes the exact l_1 penalized objective function θ_E defined by (4.1).

Proof

Since $\bar{x}$ is a KKT point to (P), it is feasible to (P) and satisfies

$\nabla f(\bar{x}) + \sum_{i\in I}^{m}\bar{u}_i\nabla g_i(\bar{x}) + \sum_{i=1}^{m}\bar{v}_i\nabla h_i(\bar{x}) = 0$, $\bar{u}_i \geq 0$ for $i \in I$ (.4.2) (Moreover $\bar{x}$ solves (P).)

Now, consider the problem of minimizing $\theta_E(x, \mu)$ over $x \in R^n$. This can equivalently be restated as follows, for any $\mu \geq 0$:

$$\text{Minimize } f(x) + \mu\left[\sum_{i=1}^{m} y_i + \sum_{i=1}^{l} z_i\right] \quad (4.3a)$$

subject to $y_i \geq g_i(x)$ and $y_i \geq 0$ for $i = 1, \ldots, m$ (4.3b)

$z_i \geq h_i(x)$ and $z_i \geq -h_i(x)$ for $i = 1, \ldots, l$. (4.3c)

The equivalence follows easily by observing that for any $x \in R^n$, the maximum value of the objective function in (4.3a), subject to (4.3b) and (4.3c), is realized by taking y_i = maximum $\{0, g_i(\bar{x})\}$ for $i = 1, \ldots, m$ and $z_i = |h_i(x)|$ for $i = 1, \ldots, l$. In particular, given $\bar{x}$, define $\bar{y}_i$ = maximum $\{0, g_i(\bar{x})\}$ for $i = 1, \ldots, m$ and $\bar{z}_i = |h_i(\bar{x})| \equiv 0$ for $i = 1, \ldots, l$.

Note that, of the inequalities $y_i \geq g_i(\mathbf{x})$, $i = 1, \ldots, m$, only those corresponding to $i \in I$ are binding, while all the other inequalities in (4.3) are binding at $(\bar{x}, \bar{y}, \bar{z})$. Hence, for $(\bar{x}, \bar{y}, \bar{z})$ to be a KKT point for (4.3), we must find Lagrangian multipliers u_i^+, u_i^-, $i = 1, \ldots, m$, and v_i^+, v_i^-, $i = 1, \ldots, l$, associated with the respective pairs of constraints in (4.3b) and (4.3c) such that

$\nabla f(\bar{x}) + \sum_{i\in I}^{m} u_i^+\nabla g_i(\bar{x}) + \sum_{i=1}^{m}(v_i^+ - v_i^-)\nabla h_i(\bar{x}) = 0,$
$\mu - u_i^+ - u_i^- = 0$ for $i = 1, \ldots, m,$
$\mu - v_i^+ - v_i^- = 0$ for $i = 1, \ldots, l,$
$(u_i^+, u_i^-) \geq 0$ for $i = 1, \ldots, m,$
$(v_i^+, v_i^-) \geq 0$ for $i = 1, \ldots, l,$ $\quad u_i^+ = 0$ for $i \notin I$.

Assumed that $\mu \geq$ maximum $\{\bar{u}_i, i \in I, |\bar{v}_i|, i = 1, \ldots, l\}$, we then have, using (4.2), that $u_i^+ = \bar{u}_i$ for all $i \in I$, $u_i^+ = 0$ for $i \neq I$, $u_i^- = \mu - u_i^+$ for all $i = 1, \ldots, m$, and $v_i^+ = \frac{(\mu + \bar{v}_i)}{2}$ and $v_i^- = \frac{(\mu - \bar{v}_i)}{2}$ for $i = 1, \ldots, l$ satisfy the forgoing KKT conditions. By stated convexity assumptions, it follows that $(\bar{x}, \bar{y}, \bar{z})$ solves (4.3), and, so, $\bar{x}$ minimizes θ_E. This completes the proof. We proof it as follows in detail:

Lemma 5

Suppose (P) is a convex program for which the Karush-Kuhn-Tucker conditions are necessary. Suppose that

$p(x) = \sum_{i=1}^{m} g_i(x)^+ + \sum_{i=1}^{l} |h_i(x)|$.

Then as long as μ is chosen sufficiently large, the sets of optimal solutions of $\theta_E(\mu)$ and (P) coincide. In fact, it suffices to choose $\mu >$ maximum $\{\bar{u}_i, i \in I, |\bar{v}_i|, i = 1, \ldots, l\}$, where $(\bar{u}, \bar{v})$ is a vector of Karush-Kuhn-Tucker multipliers.

Proof

Suppose $\hat{x}$ solves (P). For any $\mathbf{x} \in R^n$ we have:

$\theta_E(\mathbf{x}, \mu) = f(\mathbf{x}) + \mu\left(\sum_{i=1}^{m} g_i(x)^+ + \sum_{i=1}^{l} |h_i(x)|\right)$
$\geq f(\mathbf{x}) + \sum_{i=1}^{m} \bar{u}_i g_i(x)^+ + \sum_{i=1}^{l} |\bar{v}_i h_i(x)|$
$\geq f(\mathbf{x}) + \sum_{i=1}^{m} \bar{u}_i g_i(x) + \sum_{i=1}^{l} \bar{v}_i h_i(x)$

$\geq f(\mathbf{x}) + \sum_{i=1}^{m} \bar{u}_i \left(g_i(\hat{x}) + (\nabla g_i(\hat{x}))^t (x - \hat{x})\right) + \sum_{i=1}^{l} \bar{v}_i (h_i(\hat{x}) + (\nabla h_i(\hat{x}))^t (x - \hat{x}))$
$= f(\mathbf{x}) + \left(\sum_{i=1}^{m} \bar{u}_i \nabla g_i(\hat{x}) + \sum_{i=1}^{l} \bar{v}_i \nabla h_i(\hat{x})\right)^t (x - \hat{x})$
$= f(\mathbf{x}) - \nabla f(x)^t (x - \hat{x}) \geq f(\hat{x})$
$= f(\hat{x}) + \mu\left(\sum_{i=1}^{m} g_i(\hat{x})^+ + \sum_{i=1}^{l} |h_i(\hat{x})|\right) = \theta_E(\hat{x}, \mu)$.

Thus $\theta_E(\hat{x}, \mu) \leq \theta_E(\mathbf{x}, \mu)$ for all $\mathbf{x}$, and therefore $\hat{x}$ solves $\theta_E(\mathbf{x}, \mu)$.

Next suppose that $\bar{x}$ solves $\theta_E(x, \mu)$. Then if $\hat{x}$ solves (P), we have:

$f(\bar{x}) + \mu\left(\sum_{i=1}^{m} g_i(\bar{x})^+ + \sum_{i=1}^{l} |h_i(\bar{x})|\right) \leq f(\hat{x}) + \left(\sum_{i=1}^{m} g_i(\hat{x})^+ + \sum_{i=1}^{l} |h_i(\hat{x})|\right) = f(\hat{x})$

and so

$f(\bar{x}) \leq f(\hat{x}) - \mu\left(\sum_{i=1}^{m} g_i(\bar{x})^+ + \sum_{i=1}^{l} |h_i(\bar{x})|\right)$. (4.3.1)

However, if $\bar{x}$ is not feasible for (P), then

$f(\bar{x}) \geq f(\hat{x}) + \nabla f(\hat{x})^t (\bar{x} - \hat{x})$
$= f(\hat{x}) - \sum_{i=1}^{m} \bar{u}_i \nabla g_i(\bar{x} - \hat{x})) - \sum_{i=1}^{l} \bar{v}_i \nabla g_i(\bar{x} - \hat{x})$
$\geq f(\hat{x}) + \sum_{i=1}^{m} \bar{u}_i (g_i(\hat{x}) - g_i(\bar{x})) + \sum_{i=1}^{l} \bar{v}_i (h_i(\hat{x}) - h_i(\bar{x}))$
$= f(\hat{x}) + \sum_{i=1}^{m} \bar{u}_i g_i(\bar{x}) - \sum_{i=1}^{l} \bar{v}_i h_i(\bar{x})$
$> f(\hat{x}) - \left(\sum_{i=1}^{m} g_i(\hat{x})^+ + \sum_{i=1}^{l} |h_i(\hat{x})|\right)$,

which contradicts (4.3.1). Thus $\bar{x}$ is feasible for (P). That being the case,

$f(\bar{x}) \leq f(\hat{x}) - \mu\left(\sum_{i=1}^{m} g_i(\bar{x})^+ + \sum_{i=1}^{l} |h_i(\bar{x})|\right) = f(\hat{x})$

from (4.3.1.) and so $\bar{x}$ solves (P). Therefore they have the same optimal value.

Example 1

Minimize $x_1^2 + x_2^2$
subject to $x_1 + x_2 - 1 = 0$

$\bar{x} = (\frac{1}{2}, \frac{1}{2})^t$ is the KKT point with the Lagrangian multiplier associated with this point is found as:

$\nabla f(\bar{x}) + \bar{v}\, \nabla h(\bar{x}) = 0$, which follows that $2x_1 + \bar{v} = 0$ and $2x_2 + \bar{v} = 0$.

Equating the two we have $\bar{v} = -2\bar{x} = -2(\frac{1}{2}) = -1$.
The function θ_E defined by (4.1) for $\mu \geq 0$ is:
$\theta_E(x, \mu) = x_1^2 + x_2^2 + \mu|x_1 + x_2 - 1|$.

If $\mu = 0$, $\theta_E(x, \mu)$ is minimized at (0, 0). For $\mu > 0$, minimizing $\theta_E(x, \mu)$ is equivalent to:

Minimizing $x_1^2 + x_2^2 + \mu z$
subject to $-z + x_1 + x_2 - 1 \leq 0$ (4.3.2)
$-z - x_1 - x_2 + 1 \leq 0$

For $(\bar{x}, \bar{z})$ to be a KKT point for (4.3.2) above, we must find Lagrange multipliers v^+ and v^-, associated with the respective constraints such that:

$\begin{pmatrix} 2x_1 + (v^+ - v^-) \\ 2x_2 + (v^+ - v^-) \end{pmatrix} = \begin{pmatrix} 0 \\ 0 \end{pmatrix}$ (4.3.3)
$\mu - v^+ - v^- = 0$
$v^+(-z + x_1 + x_2 - 1) = 0$
$v^-(-z - x_1 - x_2 + 1) = 0$
and, moreover, optimality dictates that $z = |x_1 + x_2 - 1|$.

Now let us consider the cases,

Case 1: if $(x_1 + x_2) < 1$, then
$v^+(-z + x_1 + x_2 - 1) = 0$, from this $v^+ = 0$ since $-z + x_1 + x_2 - 1 < 0$.
And, hence (4.3.3) is:

$\begin{pmatrix} 2x_1 + (-v^-) \\ 2x_2 + (-v^-) \end{pmatrix} = \begin{pmatrix} 0 \\ 0 \end{pmatrix}$

$\mu = v^+ + v^- = v^-$
$2x_1 - v^- = 0$, and
$2x_2 - v^- = 0$
It follows that $x_1 = \frac{v^-}{2} = \frac{\mu}{2} = x_2$.

This is a KKT point, provided that $0 \leq \mu < 1$.

Case 2: if $x_1 + x_2 = 1$, then $z = |x_1 + x_2 - 1| = 0$.

By (4.3.3)
$\begin{pmatrix} 2x_1 + (v^+ - v^-) \\ 2x_2 + (v^+ - v^-) \end{pmatrix} = \begin{pmatrix} 0 \\ 0 \end{pmatrix}$
$\mu - v^+ - v^- = 0$, then

$2x_1 = \frac{(v^- - v^+)}{2} = 2x_2 \quad x_1 = \frac{(v^- - v^+)}{2} = \frac{1}{2} = x_2$.
From this we have;

$v^+ = \mu - v^- = \mu - [v^+ + 1]$ with $v^+ = \frac{\mu - 1}{2}$ and $v^- = \frac{\mu+1}{2}$.
This is a KKT point, provided that $\mu \geq 1$.

Case 3: if $(x_1 + x_2) > 1$, so that (4.3.3) is:

$$\binom{2x_1}{2x_2} + v^+\binom{1}{1} = \binom{0}{0} \quad v^- = 0,$$

which implies that $x_1 = \frac{-v^+}{2} = x_2$, and $v^+ = \mu$. Hence, this means that $x_1 + x_2 = -\mu > 1$, a contradiction to $\mu > 0$. Consequently, as μ increases from 0, the minimum of θ_E occurs at $(\frac{\mu}{2}, \frac{\mu}{2})$ until μ reaches the value 1, after which it remains at $(\frac{1}{2}, \frac{1}{2})$, which is the optimum to the original problem.

Augmented lagrangian penalty function (ALAG)

As we have seen in the above discussion, most "smooth" penalty functions (such as quadratic penalty function) never generate exact solutions to the constrained minimization problem. Therefore, we would need to solve the (penalized) unconstrained problems with very large values of the constant μ in order to obtain solutions that are close to being feasible and optimal. (In theory, we need to let $\mu \rightarrow \infty$ to obtain a solution.) This is unfortunate, since the unconstrained optimization problems one encounters in implementing penalty methods tend to become ill-conditioned when μ increases, and therefore, it will be hard to solve each of the unconstrained problems required by the algorithm. Alternatively, one could employ an exact penalty method, that is, a method that guarantees termination at an optimal solution provided that the value of μ is sufficiently large (but finite). As we have established, linear penalty function is an exact penalty function; unfortunately, it is not differentiable at points at the boundary of the feasible region, and therefore poses difficulties in solving corresponding unconstrained problems.

Motivated by our discussion of exact penalty functions, it is natural to raise the question whether we can design a penalty function that not only recovers an exact optimum for finite penalty parameter values but also enjoys the property of being differentiable. The Augmented Lagrangian Penalty Function (ALAG), also known as the multiplier penalty function, is one such exact penalty function. This approach uses both a Lagrangian multiplier term and a penalty term in the auxiliary function. This approach was independently proposed by Hestenes (1969); Powell (1997). The original proposal of this method may be viewed as a significant milestone in the recent history of the constrained optimization area. As described by Hestenes, augmented Lagrangian methods are not only practically important in their own right, but have also served as the starting point for a chain of research developments centering around the use of penalty functions, Lagrange multiplier iterations, and Newton's method for solving the system of necessary optimality conditions. Again, the motivation here is to avoid the ill-conditioning difficulties encountered by the classical approach as the penalty parameter approaches to infinity.

For simplicity, let us begin by discussing the case with only equality constraints, for which augmented Lagrangians are first introduced, and then readily extend the discussion to include inequality constraints as well.

ALAG penalty function for equality constrained problems

Consider Problem (P) of minimizing f(x) subject to $h_i(x) = 0$ for i = 1, . . . , l. we have seen if we employ the quadratic penalty function problem to minimize f(x) + $\sum_{i=1}^{m} h_i^2(x)$, then we typically need to $\mu \rightarrow \infty$ to obtain a constrained minimum for (P). We might then be curious whether, if we were to shift the origin of the penalty term to $\theta = (\theta_i, i = l, . . . , l)$ and consider the penalized objective function f(x) + $\sum_{i=1}^{l}[h_i(x) - \theta_i]^2$ with respect to the problem in which the constraint right-hand sides are perturbed to θ from 0, it can be shown (Theorem 4.1 below) that if the Lagrange multipliers are fixed at their optimum values $\bar{v}_i$, the minimization of $F_{ALAG}(x, v, \mu)$ gives the solution of the original problem (P) in one step for any value of μ. In such a case there is no need to minimize the function F_{ALAG} for an increasing sequence of values of μ. In expanded form, this latter objective function is

$$f(x) - \sum_{i=1}^{m} 2\mu\theta_i h_i(x) + \mu\sum_{i=1}^{l} h_i^2(x) + \mu\sum_{i=1}^{m}\theta_i^2.$$

Denoting $v_i = -2\mu\theta_i h_i(x)$ for i = 1, . . . , l and dropping the final constant term (independent of x), this can be written as

$$F_{ALAG}(x, v) = f(x) + \sum_{i=1}^{m} v_i h_i(x) + \mu\sum_{i=1}^{l} h_i^2(x), \qquad (4.4)$$

where $v \in R^l$ is some vector of multipliers, that can be either kept constant or updated as we proceed with the penalty algorithm. (Compare this to the usual Lagrangian function $L(x, v) = f(x) + \sum_{i=1}^{m} v_i h_i(x)$.) The usage of this function as a penalty function can be partially motivated by the following observation: suppose that $\bar{x}$ is the optimal solution of (P), and $\bar{v}$ is the vector of corresponding multipliers. Taking the (partial) gradient of the function $F_{ALAG}(\bar{x}, \bar{v})$, we obtain

$$\nabla_x F_{ALAG}(\bar{x}, \bar{v}) = \left[\nabla f(\bar{x}) + \sum_{i=1}^{l} \bar{v}_i \nabla h_i(\bar{x})\right] + 2\mu\sum_{i=1}^{l} h_i(\bar{x})\nabla h_i(\bar{x}) = 0 \qquad (4.5)$$

For all values of μ; whereas this was not necessary the case with the quadratic penalty function, unless $\nabla f(\bar{x})$ was itself zero. Hence, whereas we need to take $\mu \to \infty$ to recover $\bar{x}$ in a limiting sense using the quadratic penalty function, it is possible that we only need to make μ large enough (under suitable regularity conditions as enunciated below) for the critical point $\bar{x}$ of $F_{ALAG}(., \bar{v})$ to turn out to be its (local) minimizer. In this respect, the last term in (4.5) turns out to be a local convexifier of the overall function.

Observe that the function (4.5) is the ordinary Lagrangian function augmented by the quadratic penalty term; hence the name augmented Lagrangian penalty function. Accordingly, (4.5) can be viewed as the usual quadratic penalty function with respect to the following problem that is equivalent to (P):

Minimize $\{f(\mathbf{x}) + \sum_{i=1}^{m} v_i h_i(x) : h_i(x) = 0 \text{ for } i = 1, l\}$. (4.6)

Alternatively, (4.4) can be vied as a Lagrangian function for the following problem which is equivalent to (P):

Minimize $\{f(\mathbf{x}) + \mu \sum_{i=1}^{l} h_i^2(x) : h_i(x) = 0 \text{ for } i = 1, l\}$. (4.7)

inclusion of a "multiplier based term" in the quadratic penalty objective function; it is also sometimes called a multiplier penalty function. These view points lead to a reach theory and algorithmic felicity that is not present in the pure quadratic penalty function.

The following result provides the basis by virtue of which the ALAG penalty function can be classified as an exact penalty function. Namely, if the vector of multipliers $\bar{v}$ is known, one can hope that under some regularity assumptions, the point $\bar{x}$ is the local minimizer of $F_{ALAG}(\mathbf{x}, \bar{v})$ for large (but finite) values of μ.

Theorem 6 (ALAG Theorem)

Consider problem (P) to minimize $f(\mathbf{x})$ subject to $h_i(\mathbf{x}) = 0$ for $i = 1, \ldots, l$, and let the KKT solution $(\bar{x}, \bar{v})$ satisfy the second- order sufficiency conditions for a local minimum (the Hessian is positive definite.) Then, there exists a $\bar{\mu}$ such that for $\mu \geq \bar{\mu}$, $F_{ALAG}(., \bar{v})$ also achieves a strict local minimum at $\bar{x}$. In particular, if f is convex and h_i are affine, then any minimizing solution $\bar{x}$ for (P) also minimizes $F_{ALAG}(., \bar{v})$ for all $\mu \geq 0$.

Proof

Since $(\bar{x}, \bar{v})$ is a KKT solution, we have, from (4.5), that $\nabla_x F_{ALAG}(\bar{x}, \bar{v}) = 0$.

Furthermore, letting $G(\bar{x})$ denote the Hessian of $F_{ALAG}(. , \bar{v})$ at $x = \bar{x}$, we have

$$G(\bar{x}) = \nabla^2 f(\bar{x}) + \sum_{i=1}^{l} \bar{v}_i \nabla^2 h_i(x) + 2\mu \sum_{i=1}^{l} [h_i(\bar{x}) \nabla^2 h_i(\bar{x}) + \nabla h_i(\bar{x}) \nabla h_i(\bar{x})^t]$$
$$= \nabla^2 L(\bar{x}) + 2\mu \sum_{i=1}^{l} \nabla h_i(\bar{x}) \nabla h_i(\bar{x})^t \quad (4.8)$$

where $\nabla^2 L(\bar{x})$ is the Hessian of the Lagrangian function for (P) with a multiplier vector $\bar{v}$ at $x = \bar{x}$. From the second-order sufficiency conditions, we know that $\nabla^2 L(\bar{x})$ is positive definite on the cone

$C = \{d \neq 0 : \nabla h_i(\bar{x})^t d = 0 \text{ for } i = 1, \ldots, l\}$.

Now, on the contrary, if there does not exist a $\bar{\mu}$ such that $G(\bar{x})$ is positive definite for $\mu \geq \bar{\mu}$, then it must be the case that, given any $\mu_k = k$, $k = 1, \ldots, l$, there exists a $\mathbf{d}_k$ with $||\mathbf{d}_k|| = 1$ such that

$$\mathbf{d}_k^t G(\bar{x}) \mathbf{d}_k = \mathbf{d}_k^t \nabla^2 L(\bar{x}) \mathbf{d}_k + 2k \sum_{i=1}^{l} [\nabla h_i(\bar{x})^t \mathbf{d}_k]^2 \leq 0. \quad (4.9)$$

Since, $||\mathbf{d}_k|| = 1$ for all k, there exists a convergent subsequence for $\{\mathbf{d}_k\}$ with limit point $\bar{\mathbf{d}}$, where $||\bar{\mathbf{d}}|| = 1$. Over this subsequence, since the first term in (4.9) approaches $\bar{\mathbf{d}}^t \nabla^2 L(\bar{x}) \bar{\mathbf{d}}$, a constant, we must have $\nabla h_i(\bar{x})^t \bar{\mathbf{d}} = 0$ for all $i = 1, \ldots, l$ for (4.9) to hold for all k. Hence, $\bar{\mathbf{d}} \in C$. Moreover, since $\mathbf{d}_k^t \nabla^2 L(\bar{x}) \mathbf{d}_k \leq 0$ for all k by (4.9), we have $\bar{\mathbf{d}}^t \nabla^2 L(\bar{x}) \bar{\mathbf{d}} \leq 0$. This contradicts the second-order sufficiency conditions. Consequently, $G(\bar{x})$ is positive definite for μ exceeding some value $\bar{\mu}$, and so, $\bar{x}$ is a strict local minimum for $F_{ALAG}(., \bar{v})$.

Finally, suppose that f is convex and h_i are affine, and $\bar{x}$ is optimal to (P). There exists a set of Lagrange multipliers $\bar{v}$ such that $(\bar{x}, \bar{v})$ is a KKT solution. As before, we have $\nabla_x F_{ALAG}(\bar{x}, \bar{v}) = 0$, and since for $F_{ALAG}(. , \bar{v})$ is convex for any $\mu \geq 0$, this completes the proof.

We remark here that without the second-order sufficiency conditions of Theorem 4.3, there might not exist any finite value μ that will recover an optimum $\bar{x}$ for problem (P), and it might be that we need to take $\mu \to \infty$ for this to occur. The following example from (1987) illustrates this point.

Example 2

Consider the following optimization problem:

Minimize $f(x) = x_1^4 + x_1 x_2$
subject to $x_2 = 0$

$\bar{x} = (0, 0)^t$ is the optimal solution. From the KKT conditions, $\nabla f(\bar{x}) + \bar{v} \nabla h_i(\bar{x}) = 0$ and we get $\bar{v} = 0$ as the unique Lagrange multiplier. Note that:

$L(\bar{x}) = f(\bar{x}) + \bar{v}_i h_i(\bar{x}) = f(\bar{x})$. Then,

$\nabla L(\bar{x}) = \begin{pmatrix} 4x_1^3 + x_2 \\ x_1 \end{pmatrix}$ and

$\nabla^2 L(\bar{x}) = \begin{bmatrix} 12x_1^2 & 1 \\ 1 & 1 \end{bmatrix}$

$\nabla^2 L(0,0) = \begin{bmatrix} 0 & 1 \\ 1 & 0 \end{bmatrix} = H$

The eigenvalues of H are found by solving: $|H-\lambda I| = 0$, With $\lambda = 1$ Or $\lambda = -1$. Therefore $\nabla^2 L(0,0)$ is indefinite. This shows the second-order sufficiency condition does not hold at $(\bar{x}, \bar{v})$. Now, consider

$$F_{ALAG}(\bar{x}, \bar{v}, \mu) = F_{ALAG}(\bar{x}, 0, \mu) = f(\bar{x}) + \sum_{i=1}^{m} \bar{v}_i h_i(\bar{x}) + \mu \sum_{i=1}^{l} h_i^2(\bar{x})$$
$$= x_1^4 + x_1 x_2 + 0 + \mu x_2^2.$$

Note that for any $\mu > 0$

$$\nabla F_{ALAG}(x) = \begin{pmatrix} 4x_1^3 + x_2 \\ x_1 + 2\mu x_2 \end{pmatrix},$$

vanishes at $\bar{x} = (0,0)^t$ and $\hat{x} = (\frac{1}{\sqrt{8\mu}}, \frac{-1}{2\mu\sqrt{8\mu}})^t$. Furthermore,

$$\nabla^2 F_{ALAG}(x) = \begin{bmatrix} 12x^2 & 1 \\ 1 & 2\mu \end{bmatrix} \text{ and } \nabla^2 F_{ALAG}(\bar{x}) = \begin{bmatrix} 0 & 1 \\ 1 & 2\mu \end{bmatrix},$$

is indefinite and, hence, $\bar{x}$ is not a local minimizer for any $\mu > 0$. Hence worth it is assumed that second order sufficient conditions hold and μ is sufficiently large.

However,

$$\nabla^2 F_{ALAG}(\hat{x}) = \begin{bmatrix} \frac{3}{2\mu} & 1 \\ 1 & 2\mu \end{bmatrix},$$

The eigenvalues of $\nabla^2 F_{ALAG}(\hat{x})$ are all positive for $\mu > 0$ which shows that $\nabla^2 F_{ALAG}(\hat{x})$ is positive definite, and $\hat{x}$ is in fact the minimizer of F_{ALAG} for all $\mu > 0$. Moreover, as $\mu \to \infty$, $\hat{x}$ approaches the constrained minimum for problem (P).

It is demonstrated in the following examples that if the optimum Lagrange multipliers are known, then the solution of this unconstrained problem corresponds to the solution of the original problem regardless of the value of the penalty parameter.

Example 3

Consider the optimization problem (P) in example 4.1. $\bar{x} = \left(\frac{1}{2}, \frac{1}{2}\right)^t$, with $\bar{v} = -1$ is the unique KKT point and optimum for this problem. Furthermore, $\nabla^2 L(\bar{x}) = \nabla^2 f(\bar{x})$ is positive definite, and thus second-order sufficiency condition holds at $(\bar{x}, \bar{v})$. Moreover from equation (4.4),

$$F_{ALAG}(\bar{x}, \bar{v}) = x_1^2 + x_2^2 - (x_1 + x_2 - 1) + \mu(x_1 + x_2 - 1)^2$$
$$= (x_1 - \tfrac{1}{2})^2 + (x_2 - \tfrac{1}{2})^2 + \mu(x_1 + x_2 - 1)^2 + \tfrac{1}{2},$$

which is clearly uniquely minimized at $\bar{x} = \left(\frac{1}{2}, \frac{1}{2}\right)^t$ for all $\mu \geq 0$. Hence, both assertions of Theorem 4.3 are verified.

Example 4

Consider the following optimization problem:

Minimize $f(x) = \frac{1}{2}x^2 + xy^2$

subject to $x + y^2 = 10$

using KKT conditions, it is easy to compute the optimal solutions as follows (This is computed using Mathematica):

KTSolution[$\frac{1}{2}x^2 + xy^2$,{ $x + y^2$ -10= 0},{x,y}];

***** Lagrangian→$\frac{1}{2}x^2 + xy^2$ + [-10+ $x + y^2$]v_1

***** Valid KT point(s) *****

$f \to 50$

$x \to 10$

$y \to 0$ $v_1 \to -10$

Optimum: x = 10, y = 0 Lagrange multiplier, v = -10

In the augmented Lagrangian approach, the unconstrained function is defined by adding exterior penalty term to the Lagrangian of the original problem. Thus we have the following unconstrained function.

$$F_{ALAG} = \tfrac{1}{2}x^2 + xy^2 + v(x + y^2 - 10) + \mu(x + y^2 - 10)^2$$

The necessary conditions for the minimum of this function give the following equations:

$$\begin{pmatrix} v + x + y^2 - 20\mu + 2x\mu + 2x^2\mu = 0 \\ 2vy + 2yx - 40\mu + 4xyv + 4y^3 v = 0 \end{pmatrix}$$

If v is set to the optimum value of the Lagrange multiplier, we get the following equations:

$$\begin{pmatrix} -10 + x + y^2 - 20\mu + 2x\mu + 2y^2\mu = 0 \\ -20y + 2yx - 40\mu + 4xy\mu + 4y^3\mu = 0 \end{pmatrix}$$

The second equation can be written as follows:

$$y(-20 + 2x - 40\mu + 4x\mu + 4y^2\mu)) = 0.$$

Thus, y = 0 satisfies this equation for any value μ. Substituting y = 0 in the first equation, we get

$$-10 + x - 20\mu + 2x\mu = 0$$

or

$$(-10 + x)(1 + 2\mu) = 0.$$

Thus, x = 10 satisfies this equation. Thus, the Lagrangian penalty function has the property that the optimum solution of the original problem is recovered, if we know the optimum values of the Lagrange multipliers. Therefore, in this sense it is an exact penalty function.

Obviously, when we are solving a problem we don't know the optimum Lagrange multipliers. (If they were known we wouldn't need to spend time in developing new algorithms. We could simply use them with the KKT conditions to get a solution). However, the presence of Lagrange multipliers makes the choice of penalty parameter less critical. In a computational procedure based on the augmented Lagrangian penalty function method, we start with arbitrary values of Lagrange multipliers and develop a procedure that moves the Lagrange multipliers closer to their optimum values. Thus, near the optimum, the function is not as sensitive to the value of μ_i and the procedure converges to the true optimum.

Therefore, to make use of the above result, one attempts to estimate the multipliers by updating the vector v after solving each (or some) unconstrained minimizations of F_{ALAG}. The outline of such an algorithm is given in the following section.

Schema of an algorithm using augmented Lagrangian penalty functions

Method of multipliers

The method of multipliers is an approach for solving nonlinear programming problems by using the augmented Lagrangian penalty function in a manner that combines the algorithmic aspects of both Lagrangian duality methods and penalty function methods. However, this is accomplished while gaining from both these concepts without being impaired by their respective shortcomings. The method adopts a dual ascent step similar to the sub-gradient optimization scheme for optimizing the Lagrangian dual; but, unlike the latter approach, the overall procedure produces both primal and dual solutions. The primal solution is produced via a penalty function minimization; but because of the properties of the ALAG penalty function, this can usually be accomplished without having to make the penalty parameter infinitely large and, hence, having to contend with the accompanying ill-conditioning effects. Moreover, we can employ efficient derivative based methods in minimizing the penalized objective function. The fundamental scheme of this algorithm is as follows.

Schema of the algorithm for equality constraints

Consider the problem of minimizing f(x) subject to the equality constraints $h_i(x) = 0$ for i = 1, . . . , l. (The extension to include inequality constraints is relatively straight forward and is addressed in the following subsection). Below, we outline the procedure first, and then provide some interpretations, motivations, and implementation comments. As is typically the case, the augmented Lagrangian function employed is of the form (4.4), except that each constraint is assigned its own specific penalty parameter μ_i, instead of a common parameter μ. Hence, constraint violations, and consequent penalizations, can be individually monitored. Accordingly, we replace (4.4) by

$$F_{ALAG}(\mathbf{x}, \mathbf{v}) = f(\mathbf{x}) + \sum_{i=1}^{l} v_i h_i(\mathbf{x}) + \sum_{i=1}^{l} \mu_i h_i^2(\mathbf{x}).$$

Although, there are different algorithms to solve this kind of problems the algorithm due to Powell (1997) is given below and ensures global convergence. The outline of such an algorithm is as follows.

Algorithm 1: Algorithm for ALAG with equality constraints

Initialization: Select some initial Lagrangian multipliers v $= \bar{v}$ usually 0 and positive values $\mu_1, \ldots, \mu_l$ for the penalty parameters. Let x_o be a null vector, and denote $VIOL(x_o) = \infty$, where for any $x \in R^n$, $VIOL(x) = \text{maximum}\{|h_i(x)| : i = 1, \ldots, l\}$ is a measure of constraint violations. Put k = 1 and proceed to the "inner loop" of the algorithm.

Inner loop (Penalty function minimization): Solve minimize $F_{ALAG}(\mathbf{x}, \bar{v})$ subject to $\mathbf{x} \in R^n$ and let $\mathbf{x}_k$ denote the optimal solution obtained. If VIOL $(x_k) = 0$, stop with x_k as a KKT point. (Practically, one would terminate if VIOL (x_k) is less than some tolerance $\varepsilon > 0$). Otherwise, if VIOL $(x_k) \le 0.25$VIOL (x_{k-1}), proceed to the outer loop. On the other hand, if VIOL $(x_k) > 0.25$VIOL (x_{k-1}) then, for each constraint i = 1, . . . , l for which $|h_i(x_k)| > 0.25VIOL(x_{k-1})$, replace the corresponding penalty parameter μ_i by $10\mu_i$ and repeat this inner loop step.

Outer loop (Lagrange multiplier update): Replace $\bar{v}$ by $\bar{v}_{new}$,
Where,

$$(\bar{v}_{new})_i = \bar{v}_i + 2\mu_i h_i(\mathbf{x}_k) \text{ for } i = 1, \ldots, l. \tag{4.10}$$

Increment k by 1, and return to the inner loop.

The inner loop of the forgoing method is concerned with the minimization of the augmented Lagrangian penalty function. For this purpose, we can use x_{k-1} (for $k \ge 2$) as a starting solution and employ Newton's method (with line searches) in case the Hessian is available, or else use a quasi-Newton method if only gradients are available, or use some conjugate gradient method for relatively large-scale problems. If VIOL $(x_k) = 0$, then x_k is feasible, and, moreover,

$$\nabla_x F_{ALAG}(\mathbf{x}_k, \bar{v}) = \nabla f(\mathbf{x}_k) + \sum_{i=1}^{l} \bar{v}_i \nabla h_i(\mathbf{x}_k) + 2\sum_{i=1}^{l} \mu_i h_i(\mathbf{x}_k) \nabla h_i(\mathbf{x}_k) = 0 \tag{4.11}$$

implies that $\mathbf{x}_k$ is a KKT point. Whenever the revised iterate $\mathbf{x}_k$ of the inner loop does not improve the measure for constraint violations by selected factor 0.25, the penalty parameter is increased by a factor of 10. Hence, the outer loop will be visited after a finite number of iterations when the tolerance $\varepsilon > 0$ is used in the inner loop, since, as in Theorem 2.2 we have $h_i(\mathbf{x}_k) \to 0$ as $\mu_i \to \infty$ for i = 1, . . . , l.

Observe that the forgoing argument holds regardless of the dual multiplier update scheme used in the outer loop, and that it is essentially related to using the standard quadratic penalty function approach on the equivalent problem (4.6). In fact, if we adopt this view point, then the Lagrange multiplier estimate associated with the constraints in (4.6) is assumed by $2\mu_i h_i(\mathbf{x}_k)$ for i = 1, . . . , l, as (2.8). Since the relationship between the Lagrange multipliers of the original problem (P) and its primal equivalent from (4.6) with $\mathbf{v} = \bar{v}$ is that the Lagrange multiplier vector for (P) equals $\bar{v}$ plus the Lagrange multiplier vector for (4.6), equation (4.10) then gives the corresponding estimate for the Lagrange multiplier associated with the constraints for (P).

This observation can be reinforced more directly by the following interpretation. Note that having minimized $F_{ALAG}(\mathbf{x}, \bar{\mathbf{v}})$, we have (4.11) holding true. However, for $\mathbf{x}_k$ and $\bar{v}$ to be a KKT solution, we want $\nabla_x L(\mathbf{x}_k, \bar{v}) = 0$, where L(x, v) = f(x) + $\sum_{i=1}^{l} v_i h_i(\mathbf{x})$ is the Lagrangian function for (P). Hence, we can choose to revise $\bar{v}$ to $\bar{v}_{new}$ in a manner such that

$$\nabla f(\mathbf{x}_k) + \sum_{i=1}^{l} (\bar{v}_{new})_i \nabla h_i(\mathbf{x}_k) = 0.$$

Super imposing this identity on (4.11), we get

$$\nabla_x F_{ALAG}(\mathbf{x}_k, \bar{v}) = \nabla_x L(\mathbf{x}_k, \bar{v}),$$

which follows that

$$\nabla f(\mathbf{x}_k) + \sum_{i=1}^{l} \bar{v}_i \nabla h_i(\mathbf{x}_k) + 2\sum_{i=1}^{l} \mu_i h_i(\mathbf{x}_k)\nabla h_i(\mathbf{x}_k) = \nabla f(\mathbf{x}_k) + \sum_{i=1}^{l} (\bar{v}_{new})_i \nabla h_i(\mathbf{x}_k)$$

by eliminating like terms, we get

$$\sum_{i=1}^{l} [\bar{v}_i + 2\mu_i h_i(\mathbf{x}_k)]\nabla h_i(\mathbf{x}_k) = \sum_{i=1}^{l} (\bar{v}_{new})_i \nabla h_i(\mathbf{x}_k).$$

From this,

$(\bar{v}_{new})_i = \bar{v}_i + 2\mu_i h_i(\mathbf{x}_k)$, which is the update scheme in (4.10).

Hence, from the view point of problem (4.6), convergence is obtained above in one of the two ways. First, we might finitely determine a KKT point as is frequently the case. Alternatively, viewing the forgoing algorithm as a one of applying the standard quadratic penalty function approach, in sprit, to the equivalent sequence of problems of the type (4.6), each having particular estimates of the Lagrangian multipliers in the objective function, convergence is achieved by letting the penalty parameters approach infinity. In the latter case, the inner loop problems become increasingly ill-conditioned and second-order methods become imperative.

Example 4.5

Consider the optimization problem of Example 4.1. Given any v, the inner loop of the method of multipliers evaluates $\theta(\mathbf{v}) = \min_x\{F_{ALAG}(\mathbf{x}, \mathbf{v})\}$,
Where $F_{ALAG}(\mathbf{x}, \mathbf{v}) = x_1^2 + x_2^2 + v(x_1 + x_2 - 1) + (x_1 + x_2 - 1)^2$.
Solving $\nabla_x F_{ALAG}(\mathbf{x}, \mathbf{v}) = 0$ yields
$x(v) = \frac{2\mu - v}{2(1+2\mu)}$. (The KKT point)
The outer loop then updates the Lagrangian multiplier according to
$(\bar{v}_{new})_i = \bar{v}_i + 2\mu_i h_i(\mathbf{x}_k)$
which gives $v_{new} = v + 2\mu[x_1(v) + x_2(v) - 1] = \frac{v-2\mu}{1+2\mu}$. Note that, as $\mu \to \infty$, $v_{new} \to -1$, the optimal Lagrange multiplier value.
Hence, if we start the algorithm with $\bar{v} = 0$, and $\mu = 1$, the inner loop will determine

$x(0) = \frac{2-0}{2(3)} = (\frac{1}{3}, \frac{1}{3})^t$ with VIOL[x(0)] = $x_1 + x_2 - 1 = \frac{1}{3} + \frac{1}{3} - 1 = \frac{-1}{3}$,

and the outer loop will find $v_{new} = 0 + 2(1)(\frac{-1}{3}) = \frac{-2}{3}$. Next, at the second iteration, the inner loop solution will be obtained as

$x(v) = \frac{2\mu - v}{2(1+2\mu)} = \frac{2(1) - (\frac{-2}{3})}{2(1+2(1))} = \frac{4}{9}$
it follows $x(\frac{-2}{3}) = (\frac{4}{9}, \frac{4}{9})^t$ with VIOL$(x(\frac{-2}{3}))$ = h$[x(\frac{-2}{3})] = \frac{1}{9} > (\frac{1}{4})(\frac{-2}{3})$ with VIOL(x(1)) > VIOL(x(0)).

Hence we will increase μ to 10, and recompute the revised

$\mathbf{x}(\frac{-2}{3}) = \frac{2\mu - v}{2(1+2\mu)} = \frac{2(10) - (\frac{-2}{3})}{2(1+2(10))} = (\frac{31}{63}, \frac{31}{63})^t$ with VIOL$(\mathbf{x}(\frac{-31}{63})) = \frac{-1}{63}$.
The outer loop will then revise the Lagrange multiplier $\bar{v} = \frac{-2}{3}$ to $v_{new} = \frac{-2}{3} + 2(10)(\frac{-1}{63}) = \frac{-62}{63}$.

The iteration will progress in this fashion, using the forgoing formulas, until the constraint violation at the inner loop solution is acceptably small.

ALAG penalty function for problems with mixed constraints

Consider problem (P) to minimize f(**x**) subject to the constraints $g_i(\mathbf{x}) \le 0$ for i = 1, . . . , m and $h_i(\mathbf{x}) = 0$ for i = 1, . . . , l (Bhatti (2000). The extension of the forgoing theory of augmented Lagrangians and the method of multipliers to this case, which also includes inequality constraints, is readily accomplished by equivalently writing the inequalities as the equations $g_i(x) + s_i^2 = 0$ for i = 1, . . . , m. Now suppose that $\bar{\mathbf{x}}$ is a KKT point for problem (P) with optimal Lagrange multipliers $\bar{u}_i$, i = 1, . . . , m, and $\bar{v}_i$, i = 1, . . . , l, associated with the inequality and equality constraints, respectively, and such that the strict complementary slackness condition holds, namely, that $\bar{u}_i g_i(\bar{x}) = 0$ for all i = 1, . . . , m, with $\bar{u}_i > 0$ for each $i \in I(\bar{x}) = \{i : g_i(\bar{x}) = 0\}$. Furthermore, suppose that the second-order sufficiency condition holds at $(\bar{x}, \bar{u}, \bar{v})$, namely, that $\nabla^2 L(\bar{x})$ is positive definite over the cone

$C = \{d \neq 0 : \nabla g_i(\bar{x})^t d = 0 \text{ for all } i \in I(\bar{x}), \nabla h_i(\bar{x})^t d = 0 \text{ for } i = 1, \dots, l\}$.

Then it can be verified that the conditions of Theorem 4.3 are satisfied for problem P' to minimize f(x) subject to $g_i(x) + s_i^2 = 0$ for i = 1, . . . , m, and $h_i(x) = 0$ for i = 1, . . . , l, at the solution $(\bar{x}, \bar{s}, \bar{u}, \bar{v})$, where $s_i^2 = -g_i(x)$ for i = 1, . . . , m. Hence, for μ large enough, the solution $(\bar{x}, \bar{s})$ will turn out to be a strict local minimizer for the following ALAG penalty function at (u, v) = $(\bar{u}, \bar{v})$:

$$f(x) + \sum_{i=1}^{m}(g_i(x) + s_i^2) + \sum_{i=1}^{l} v_i h_i(x) + \mu\left[\sum_{i=1}^{m}(g_i(x) + s_i^2)^2 + \sum_{i=1}^{l} h_i^2(x)\right]. \qquad (4.12)$$

The augmented Lagrangian function defined in (4.12) includes slack variables for inequality constraints. Their presence increases the number of variables in the problem. It is possible to remove these variables by writing the necessary conditions for the minimum with respect to s. Before proceeding it is convenient to combine the two terms involving the slack variables by noting that;

$$\mu\left[g_i(x) + s_i^2 + \frac{u_i}{2\mu}\right]^2 = \mu\left[(g_i(x) + s_i^2)^2 + \frac{u_i^2}{4\mu} + 2(g_i(x) + s_i^2)\left(\frac{u_i}{2\mu}\right)\right].$$

Rearranging the terms gives,

$$\mu[g_i(x) + s_i^2]^2 + u_i(g_i(x) + s_i^2) = \mu[g_i(x) + s_i^2 + \frac{u_i}{2\mu}]^2 - \frac{u_i^2}{4\mu}.$$

For a given penalty parameter μ > 0, let $\theta(u, v)$ represent the minimum of (4.12) over (x, s) for any given set of Lagrange multipliers (u, v). Now let us rewrite (4.12) more conveniently as follows:

$$f(x) + \mu\sum_{i=1}^{m}(g_i(x) + s_i^2 + \frac{u_i}{2\mu})^2 - \sum_{i=1}^{m}\frac{u_i^2}{4\mu} + \sum_{i=1}^{l} v_i h_i(x) + \mu\sum_{i=1}^{l} h_i^2(x)]. \qquad (4.13)$$

Hence, in computing $\theta(u, v)$, we can minimize (4.13) over (x, s) by first minimizing $[g_i(x) + s_i^2 + \frac{u_i}{2\mu}]$ over s_i^2 in terms of x for each i = 1, . . . , m and then minimizing the resulting expression over the $x \in R^n$. The former task is accomplished by writing the necessary conditions for the minimum of θ with respect to the slack variables, we get

$\frac{\partial\theta}{\partial s_i} = 0$ implies that

$$2(g_i(x) + s_i^2 + \frac{u_i}{2\mu})(2s_i) = s_i(g_i(x) + s_i^2 + \frac{u_i}{2\mu}) = 0, \ i = 1, \dots, m.$$

These conditions state that either

$s_i = 0$ Or $g_i(x) + s_i^2 + \frac{u_i}{2\mu} = 0$ which follows

$s_i = 0$ Or $s_i^2 = -(g_i(x) + \frac{u_i}{2\mu}) \geq 0$.

Using this $\theta(u, v)$ can be written as:

$$\theta(u, v) = \text{minimum}_x\{f(x) + \mu\sum_{i=1}^{m}\left(\text{maximum}\left\{g_i(x) + \frac{u_i}{2\mu}, 0\right\}\right)^2 - \sum_{i=1}^{m}\frac{u_i^2}{4\mu} + \sum_{i=1}^{l} v_i h_i(x) + \mu\sum_{i=1}^{l} h_i^2(x)\}$$

$$= \text{minimum}_x\{F_{ALAG}(x, u, v)\}, \text{ say.} \qquad (4.14)$$

Similar to (4.14), the function $F_{ALAG}(x, u, v)$ is sometimes referred to as the ALAG penalty function itself in the presence of both equality and inequality constraints. In particular, in the context of the method of multipliers, the inner loop evaluates $\theta(u, v)$, measures the constraint violations, and revises the penalty parameter(s) in an identical fashion as before.

In order the augmented Lagrangian penalty function to solve constrained optimization problems, we need to determine a procedure that, starting from arbitrary values, leads to near optimum values of Lagrange multipliers. A simple procedure is based on comparing the necessary conditions for the minimum of the Lagrangian function and the augmented Lagrangian penalty function for problem only with equality constraint. In the presence of inequality constraints, the above analysis does not work out as clearly as for the equality case. In practice, the following rule based on similarity with the equality is adopted:

$(\bar{u}_{new})_i = \bar{u}_i + \text{maximum}\{2\mu g_i(x_k), -\bar{u}_i\}$.

If x_k minimizes (4.14), then the sub-gradient component to u_i at (u, v) = $(\bar{u}, \bar{v})$ is found at

$$\nabla_{u_i}\theta(u, v) = 2\mu\sum_{i=1}^{m}\text{maximum}\left\{g_i(x) + \frac{u_i}{2\mu}, 0\right\}\frac{1}{2\mu} - 2\sum_{i=1}^{m}\frac{u_i}{4\mu}$$

and is

$$\text{maximum}\left\{g_i(x) + \frac{u_i}{2\mu}, 0\right\} - \frac{u_i}{2\mu}.$$

Adopting the fixed step length of 2μ along this sub-gradient direction as for the equality constraint case revises u_i to

$(\bar{u}_{new})_i = \bar{u}_i + 2\mu[\text{maximum}\left\{g_i(x) + \frac{\bar{u}_i}{2\mu}, 0\right\} - \frac{\bar{u}_i}{2\mu}]$

$= 0 + \text{maximum}\{2\mu g_i(x_k) + \bar{u}_i, 0\}$

$= \bar{u}_i + \text{maximum}\{2\mu g_i(x_k), -\bar{u}_i\}$ for i = 1, . . . , m. (4.15)

To start the process, arbitrary values, usually zero, are assigned to all multipliers. Also, the multiplier updating is done only after a substantial decrease in constraint violation is achieved. The following algorithm from [6] is used in most literatures.

Algorithm 2: Algorithm for ALAG with mixed constraints

Set iteration counter k = 0. Set multipliers $u_i = 0$, i = 1, …, m and $v_i = 0$, i = 1,…,l. Set multiplier update counter *l* = 0. Choose a penalty parameter μ and a factor $\beta > 1$ to increase the penalty parameter value during iterations. Typically μ = 10 and $\beta = 2$.
Set up the unconstrained minimization problem.

$$\theta(u, v) = \text{minimum}_x \{ f(x) + \mu \sum_{i=1}^{m} \left(\text{maximum} \left\{ g_i(x) + \frac{u_i}{2\mu}, 0 \right\} \right)^2 - \sum_{i=1}^{m} \frac{u_i^2}{4\mu} + \sum_{i=1}^{l} v_i h_i(x) + \mu \sum_{i=1}^{l} h_i^2(x) \}$$

use a suitable unconstrained minimization problem to find x_k the minimum. The derivative of θ with respect to x_j are evaluated according to the following:

$$\frac{\partial \theta}{\partial x_j} = \frac{\partial f}{\partial x_j} + 2\mu \sum_{i=1}^{m} r_i \frac{\partial g_i}{\partial x_j} + 2\mu \sum_{i=1}^{m} h_i \frac{\partial h_i}{\partial x_j} + \sum_{i=1}^{m} v_i \frac{\partial h_i}{\partial x_j} + 2\mu \sum_{i=1}^{m} \frac{u_i}{2\mu}, \quad j = 1, \ldots, n.$$

Check for convergence: A simple convergence criterion is to stop if all constraints are satisfied and the objective function is not changing much between successive iterations. Thus, stop if the following two criteria are satisfied. Otherwise continue to step (iv).

If $\text{Abs}[(\frac{f(x_k) - f(x_{k-1})}{f(x_k)})] < \varepsilon$

$$\text{VIOL}(x_k) < \varepsilon$$

$\text{VIOL}(x_k) = \text{maximum}\{\text{Abs}(h_i(x), i = 1, \ldots, l), g_i(x), i = 1, \ldots, m\}$ is the maximum constraint violation.
Update the multiplier and the penalty parameter:

If $\text{VIOL}(x_k) \le 0.25\text{VIOL}(x_{k-1})$ then update the multipliers
$(u_{l+1})_i = (u_l)_i + \text{maximum}\{2\mu g_i(x_k), -\bar{u}_i\}$ i = 1, …, m
$(v_{l+1})_i = (v_l)_i + 2\mu_i h_i(x_k)$ $i = 1, \ldots, l$
Set *l* = *l* + 1.
Else update the penalty parameter

$$\mu_{k+1} = 10\mu_k.$$

(v) Update the iteration counter k = k +1 and go back to step (ii).

The ALAG has several advantages. As stated earlier, the penalty parameter need not be increased to infinity for convergence. The starting design vector, x_0, need not be feasible. Finally, it is possible to achieve $g_i(x) = 0$ and $h_i(x) = 0$ precisely and the nonzero values of the Lagrange multipliers ($u_i \neq 0$) identify the active constraints automatically. It is to be noted the function F_{ALAG}, assumed by (4.14), is continuous and has continuous first derivatives but has discontinuous second derivatives with respect to x at $g_i(x) = -\frac{u_i}{2\mu}$. Hence, a second-order methods cannot be used to minimize the function F_{ALAG} (Rao, 2009).

SUMMARY AND CONCLUSION

The intent of this section is to point out some of the key points discussed in the previous chapters; and based on that it aims to draw some conclusions.

As discussed in the previous sections all algorithms for constrained optimization are unreliable to a degree. This fact also holds true in the penalty and function methods.

Penalty methods are among the most powerful class of algorithms available for attacking general nonlinear optimization problems. This statement is supported by the fact that these techniques will converge to at least a local minimum in most cases, regardless of the convexity characteristics of the objective function and constraints. They work well even in the presence of cusps and similar anomalies that can stymie other approaches. Penalty methods approximate a constrained problem that assigns high cost to points that are far from the feasible region. As the approximation is made more exact (by letting) the penalty parameter μ tend to infinity) the solution of the unconstrained penalty problem approaches the solution to the original constrained problem from outside of the active constraints. This method is not used in cases where feasibility must be maintained, for example, if the objective function is undefined or ill-conditioned outside the feasible region.

Penalty methods are quite different than other algorithms that they are not iterative in nature. The definition of x_{k+1} in no way depends on that of x_k. From this point of view, if one decides to terminate the sequence at the Nth term corresponding to μ_N, obtaining x_N, the calculation of the previous vectors $x_1, x_2, \ldots, x_{N-1}$ is irrelevant, since x_N could have been calculated directly by solving a single unconstrained problem. Indeed, this is the generally the manner that penalty functions are employed; one selects a large value of μ, solves the unconstrained problem, and takes the resulting solution as the final approximate answer to the original problem. It is sometimes recognized, however, that selecting a single large value of μ can lead to difficulty. First, exactly what is a large value relative to a given problem may not be known in advance and consequently an initial trial may produce a solution point that is not close enough to the feasible region in which case μ must be increased. Second, large values of μ yield, as shown in the above sections, ill-conditioned Hessians which in turn imply slow convergence for many algorithms.

A partial remedy to these difficulties is obtained by noting that the search for x_{k+1} can be initiated from x_k, a starting point that may be fairly close to x_{k+1}. Solution of the k +1th problem will then probably require less time than if the search were initiated from an arbitrary point x_0. For this reason the penalty methods are often regarded as truly iterative algorithms. It has never been determined, however, that solving a sequence of unconstrained problems for increasing value of μ leads to a computational saving over just solving the corresponding to the largest value of μ directly. Indeed, indications are that it does not. The Hessian matrix of $\theta(x, \mu)$ becomes increasingly ill-conditioned as $\mu \to \infty$ and the minimization becomes more difficult. That's why the parameter μ should not be increased too quickly and the previous iterate should be used as a starting point. As $\mu \to \infty$ the Hessian (at the solution) is equal to the sum of L, the Hessian of the Lagrangian associated with the original constrained problem, and a matrix of rank r that tends to infinity (where r is the number of active constraints). This is the fundamental property of these methods.

Though penalty functions are old methods for solving constrained optimization problems, it is, nevertheless, worthy of noticing to recognize the wrong assumption and generalization that everything which is old method is nonsense. We have to be very careful not to trivialize old methods for solving constrained optimization problems and erroneously assume it to be as synonymous to backwardness, as some might misconceive it. In fact, this sequential methods needs to be modified in one way or another so that they would serve for the ever-changing and growing demands of algorithms for certain optimization problems. Though these methods suffer from some computational disadvantages, in the absence of alternative software especially for no-derivative problems they are still recommended. They work well for zero order methods like Powell's method with some modifications and taking different initial points and monotonically increasing parameters.

Finally, In spite of their great initial success, their slow rates of convergence due to ill-conditioning of the associated Hessian led researchers to pursue other approaches. With the advent of interior point methods for linear programming, algorithm designers have taken a fresh look at penalty methods and have been able to achieve much greater efficiency than previously thought possible (Nash and Sofer, 1993).

Exact transformation methods are newer and less well-established as sequential transformation methods and are called the newly established modern penalty methods. Exact transformation methods avoid this long sequence by constructing penalty functions that are exact in the sense that the solution of the penalty problem yields the exact solution to the original problem for a finite value of the penalty parameter. However, it can be shown that such exact functions are not differentiable in most cases. Great consideration should be assumed to the convexity assumption and second-order conditions in using these methods.

ACKNOWLEDGEMENTS

First, the author wishes to acknowledge his family, especially his parents for their unconditional love and faith in him since his birth, without whose support and encouragement, this would not have been a reality.

Also, his warmest and honorable thanks also go to his best friend, Abreha Hailezgi who motivated and told him about his potential, and contributed a lot for the success of this research paper.

Finally, he thanks all his friends who have helped him directly or indirectly in this endeavor, especially those who love him more.

Some notations

The following notations are frequently appearing in this research:

μ = Penalty parameter.
$x = (x_1, x_2, x_3, \ldots, x_n)$ is n-dimensional vector.
$\theta(x, \mu)$ = Unconstrained representation of the primal problem (P).
$\theta(\mu)$ = is the infimum of $\theta(x, \mu)$ with respect to x.
x_μ = A minimum point of $\theta(\mu)$.
X = A nonempty set in R^n.
M(f, S) = Set of minimum points of the constrained optimization problem (P).
M(f, X) = Set of minimum points of the unconstrained optimization problem $\theta(x, \mu)$.
F_{ALAG} = Augmented Lagrangian Penalty Function.
p(x) = Penalty function.
$L_M(\bar{x})$ = L restricted to the subspace M that is tangent to the constraint surface.

REFERENCES

Bazaraa MS, Sherali HD, Shetty CM (2006). Nonlinear Programming: Theory and Algorithms, Second Edition, John Wiley & Sons, New York. pp. 469-500.

Belegundu AD, Chandrupatla TR (1999). Optimization concepts and Applications in Engineering 2nd edition, Pensylvania State University, pp. 278-290.

Bhatti MA (2000). Practical Optimization Methods with Mathematica Applications, Department of Civil and Environmental Engineering University of Iowa, Springer-Verlag New York, Inc. pp. 512-680.

Charalambous CA (1978). Lower Bound for the controling parametres of exact panalty functions, Mathematical Programming, 15:278-290.

Coleman TF, Conn AR (1982). Nonlinear Programming Via an exact penalty function: Asymptotic analysis, Mathematical programming, pp.123-136

Deumlich R (1996). A course in Mathematica, Addis Ababa University, Faculty of science, Department of Mathematics. pp.1-140

Fiacco AV, McCormick GP (1968). Extensions of SUMT for nonlinear programming: Equality constraints and extrapolation. Manage. Sci. 12(11):816-828.

Fletcher R (1987). Practical Methods of Optimization, Second Edition, John Wiley & Sons, New York. pp. 277-318.

Gland ST, Polak E (1979). A multiplier method with Authomatic Limitation of penalty growth. Math. Programming,17:140-155

Hestenes MR (1969). Multiplier and gradient methods. J. Optim. Theory Appl. 4(5):123-136.

Himmelblau DH (1972). Applied Nonlinear Programming, New York, McGraw-Hill, pp. 342-355.

Kiusalaas J (2005). Numerical Methods in Engineering with MATLAB, the Pennsylvania State University, and Cambridge University Press Cambridge, New York, Melbourne, Madrid, Cape Town, Singapore, São Paulo. pp. 391-404.

Luenberger DG (1974). A combined penalty function and Gradient projection method for nonlinear programming. J. Opt. Appl. 14:5.

Luenberger DG (1984). Linear and Nonlinear Programming, 2nd ed., Addison-Wesley Publishing Company, Reading, MA. pp. 401-430.

Nash SG, Sofer A (1993). Linear and Nonlinear Programming, McGraw Hill, New York. pp. 469-765.

Pietrgykowski T (1969). An exact potential method for constrained maxima, SIAM J. Num. Anal. 6:217-238.

Powell MJD (1997). A fast algorithm for nonlinearity constrained optimization calculations, in Lecture Notes in Mathematics, Watson GA et al., Eds., Springer-Verlag, Berlin. pp. 343-357.

Rao SS (2009). Engineering Optimization: Theory and Practice, Fourth Edition, John Wiley & Sons, Inc. pp. 248-318.

Zangwill WI (1967). Nonlinear programming via Penalty Functions. Manage. Sci. 13(5):344-358.

Appendix

General description of the penalty function algorithm

The SUMT iteration involves updating the penalty parameters and initial design vector and calling the unconstrained problem again. In the algorithm Powell's method (which is the zero order method) together with golden-bracket and golden-section method for line minimization is used. The program expects the following files to be available in the path

i. Objective function,
ii. Equality and inequality constraints together,
iii. Unconstrained function,
iv. The flines function (for a line search).

For each an iteration of the penalty method there is an inner iteration of the Powell's method.

The program uses global statements to communicate penalty parameters, initial point, search direction (V), whereas the initial penalty parameters, initial design variable, the number of iterations for penalty method, tolerances for the penalty and Powell's method are given by user automatically.

Several parameters are coded into the program, especially those needed for golden bracket and golden section methods.

Step 0: (Initialization) Choose x_0, number of SUMT iterations (N), penalty parameter (μ), and penalty multiplier (β), tolerance for the penalty method (tol1) and for the Powell's method (tol).
k = 1 (SUMT iteration counter)
Step 1: Start the Powell's method to minimize f(x, μ)
Output x_k.
Step 3: Convergence of exterior penalty method.
Stopping criteria:
$\nabla f = \text{funcnstrained}_k - \text{fobjective}_k,\ \Delta x = x_k - x_{k-1}$.
If $(\nabla f)^2 \leq \varepsilon_1$: stop (they have approximately the same solution)
else if $\Delta x^t \Delta x \leq \varepsilon_1$: stop (design not changing)
else if k = N_ε : stop (max SUMT iteration reached)
continue
$k \leftarrow k + 1$
$x_k \leftarrow x_k^*$
$\mu_{k+1} = \beta \mu_k$
go to step 2

Input for the welded beam example given in example 8 of penalty function method.

```
function f = obweldedbeam(x) % objective function
f=1.10471*x(1).^2*x(2)+0.04811*x(3)*x(4)*(14+x(2));

function [c,ceq] = conweledebeam(x) % constraints

l=(504000./((x(3)).^2*x(4)));
k=64746.022*(1-0.0282346*x(3))*x(3)*x(4).^3;
m =(2.1952./(x(3).^3*x(4)));
t1=(6000./(sqrt(2)*x(1)*x(2)));
t2=6000*(14+0.5*x(2))*sqrt(0.25*(x(2).^2+(x(1)+x(3)).^2));
t3=2*(0.707*x(1)*x(2)*((x(2).^2/12)+0.25*(x(1)+x(3)).^2));
t=t2./t3;
T=sqrt((t1).^2+(t).^2+((x(2)*t1*t)./sqrt(0.25*(x(2).^2+(x(1)+
x(3)).^2))));
c=[T-13600;l-30000;x(1)-x(4);6000-k;m-0.25;-
x(1)+0.125;x(1)-10;-x(2)+0.1;x(2)-10;...
-x(3)+0.1;x(3)-10;-x(4)+0.1;x(4)-10];
ceq =[]; % no equality constraints.

function z = unconweldedbeam(x,miw) %
The corresponding unconstrained problem
l=(504000./((x(3)).^2*x(4)));
k=64746.022*(1-0.0282346*x(3))*x(3)*x(4).^3;
m =(2.1952./(x(3).^3*x(4)));
t1=(6000./(sqrt(2)*x(1)*x(2)));
t2=6000*(14+0.5*x(2))*sqrt(0.25*(x(2).^2+(x(1)+x(3)).^2));
t3=2*(0.707*x(1)*x(2)*((x(2).^2/12)+0.25*(x(1)+x(3)).^2));
t=t2./t3;
T=sqrt((t1).^2+(t).^2+((x(2)*t1*t)./sqrt(0.25*(x(2).^2+(x(1)+
x(3)).^2))));
z=obweldedbeam(x)+miw*(max(0,T-13600)).^2
+miw*(max(0,l-30000)).^2+...
miw*(max(0,x(1)-x(4))).^2          +miw*(max(0,6000-
k)).^2+miw*(max(0,m-0.25)).^2          +miw*(max(0,-
x(1)+0.125)).^2+...
miw*(max(0,x(1)-10)).^2          +miw*(max(0,-
x(2)+0.1)).^2+miw*(max(0,x(2)-10)).^2          +miw*(max(0,-
x(3)+0.1)).^2+...
miw*(max(0,x(3)-10)).^2          +miw*(max(0,-
x(4)+0.1)).^2+miw*(max(0,x(4)-10)).^2;
```

The MATLAB Code for Penalty Function Method:

```
Function penaltyfunction
% Penalty function method for minimizing f(x1,x2, ..., xn).
% Example for Logarithmic function on Example 8.

% input:
% tol and tol1 are error tolerances for Powell's method
and penalty method respectively.
% x = starting point (vector).
% μ = the penalty parameter.
% beta = the penalty multiplier.
% N = number of iterations for the penalty method, we
choose it depending on the problem.
% h = initial step size used in search for golden bracket.
% output:
% xmin = minimum point.
% objmin = miminum value of objective function.
% augmin = minimum of the corresponding unconstrained
problem

% globals (must be declared global in calling program).
```

```
% V = search direction, the same as the unit vectors in the coordinate directions.

% Starting of the program.
clc; % clears the screen.
clear all; % clears all values of variables for memory advantage.
global x μ V
x = [0.4; 6; 0.01; 0.05];
μ = 0.1; beta = 2;
tol = 1.0e-2; tol1 = 1.0e-6; h = 0.1;N = 30;
if size(x,2) > 1; x = x'; end % x must be column vector
n = length(x); % Number of design variables
df = zeros(n,1); % Decreases of f stored here
u = eye (n); % Columns of u store search directions V
disp(sprintf(' μ xmin objmin augmin '))
disp(sprintf(' ------ ------------------ ------------ --------------- '))
for k=1:N % loop for the penalty function method
[c,ceq]= conwelededbeam(x);
obj= obweldedbeam(x);
f= unconweldedbeam(x,μ);
disp(sprintf('%1.5f (%3.12f,%3.12f) %2.10f %2.10f ',μ,x, obj,f))
for j = 1:30 % Allow up to 30 cycles for Powell's method
xold = x;
fold = feval(@unconweldedbeam,xold,μ);
% First n line searches record the decrease of f
for i = 1:n
V = u(1:n,i);
[a,b] = goldbracket(@fline,0.0,h);
[s,fmin] = goldsearch(@fline,a,b);
df(i) = fold - fmin;
fold = fmin;
x = x + s*V;
end
% Last line search in the cycle
V = x - xold;
[a,b] = goldbracket(@fline,0.0,h);
[s,fmin] = goldsearch(@fline,a,b);
x = x + s*V;
if sqrt(dot(x-xold,x-xold)/n) < tol
y = x; % assign the solution to y
end
% Identify biggest decrease of f & update search directions
imax = 1; dfmax = df(1);
for i = 2:n
if df(i) > dfmax
imax= i; dfmax = df(i);
end
end
for i = imax:n-1
u(1:n,i) = u(1:n,i+1);
end
u(1:n,n) = V;
end % end of Powell's method
x=y; % y is the minimum point found using Powell's method in the Kth iteration
μ=beta*μ;
sqrt(dot(f - obj,(f- obj));
if sqrt(dot(f - obj, f - obj)) < tol1
return
end
end % end of SUMT iteration.

% f in the direction of coordinate axes.

function z = flines(s) % f in the search direction V
global x μ V
z = feval(@unconweldedbeam,x+s*V,μ);

% Start of golden bracketing for the minimum.

function [a,b] = goldbracket(func,x1,h)
% Brackets the minimum point of f(x).
% Usage: [a,b] = goldbracket(func,xstart,h)

% input:
% func = handle of function that returns f(x).
% x1 = starting value of x.
% h = initial step size used in search.
% c = a constant factor used to increase the step size h

% output:
% a, b = limits on x at the minimum point.
c = 1.618033989;
f1 = feval(func,x1);
x2 = x1 + h; f2 = feval(func,x2);
% Determine downhill direction and change sign of h if needed.
if f2 > f1
h = -h;
x2 = x1 + h; f2 = feval(func,x2);
% Check if minimum is between x1 - h and x1 + h
if f2 > f1
a = x2; b = x1 - h; return
end
end
% Search loop for the minimum
for i = 1:100
h = c*h;
x3 = x2 + h; f3 = feval(func,x3);
if f3 > f2
a = x1; b = x3; return
end
x1 = x2; x2 = x3; f2 = f3;
end
error('goldbracket did not find a minimum please try another starting point')

% Start of golden search for the minimum.
function [xmin,fmin] = goldsearch(func,a,b,tol2)
% Golden section search for the minimum of f(x).
% The minimum point must be bracketed in a <= x <= b.
% usage: [fmin,xmin] = goldsearch(func,xstart,h).
```

```
% input:
% func = handle of function that returns f(x).
% a, b = limits of the interval containing the minimum.
% tol2 = error tolerance used in golden section.

% output:
% fmin = minimum value of f(x).
% xmin = value of x at the minimum point.
if nargin < 4; tol2 = 1.0e-6; end
nIter = ceil(-2.078087*log(tol2/abs(b-a)));
R = 0.618033989; % R is called golden ratio.
C = 1.0 - R;
% First telescoping
x1 = R*a + C*b;
x2 = C*a + R*b;
f1 = feval(func,x1);
f2 = feval(func,x2);
% Main loop
for i =1:nIter
if f1 > f2
a = x1; x1 = x2; f1 = f2;
x2 = C*a + R*b;
f2 = feval(func,x2);
else
b = x2; x2 = x1; f2 = f1;
x1 = R*a + C*b;
f1 = feval(func,x1);
end
end
if f1 < f2; fmin = f1; xmin = x1;
else
fmin = f2; xmin = x2;
end
```

Scheme for solving ordinary differential equations with derivative discontinuities: A new class of semi- implicit rational, Runge-Kutta

Bolarinwa Bolaji[1]*, Ademiluyi R. A.[1], Oluwagunwa A. P.[1] and Awomuse B. O.[2]

[1]Department of Mathematics and Statistics, Rufus Giwa Polytechnic, Owo, Nigeria.
[2]Department of Mathematical Sciences, Federal University of Technology, Akure, Nigeria.

In this paper, a class of semi- implicit Rational Runge –Kutta scheme is proposed for the integration of differential equations with derivative discontinuities. The method is motivated by varieties of application areas of this class of ordinary differential equations such as electrical transmission network, nuclear reactions, delay problems computer aided designs, economy affected by inflation as well as perturbation problems and dynamic processes in industries and technology fields, and the need to cater for the deficiencies identified in the adoption of the existing methods of solving this class of differential equations. For the development of the scheme, we adopted power series (Taylor and Binomial) expansion, while its analysis and implementation on a micro computer adopts Pade approximation technique and FORTRAN programming respectively. The convergence and stability properties were investigated; it was discovered that the scheme converge and were stable. Numerical result of the adoption of the scheme on some sample problems shows that it is effective and efficient. It compares favourably with modified Euler's scheme.

Key words: Rational Runge - Kutta, derivative discontinuities, semi - implicit, differential equations.

INTRODUCTION

The mathematical models of a large variety of science, engineering and technological problems leads to initial value problems of the form:

$$y' = f(x, y) \qquad y(x_0) = y_0 \quad a \prec x \prec b \qquad (1.1)$$

in which f has some points that is not smooth, or of discontinuities. The derivative in the ordinary differential equation contains some finite jumps other wise referred to as discontinuities in the region of x – y plane defined by: $D = \{(x, y) \text{ such that } a = x = b, -\infty \prec y \prec \infty\}$ at initial point (x_0, y_0). When f(x,y) is infinite or unbounded and the partial derivatives f_x, f_y are large and unbounded, then we say that f(x, y) has low order derivative discontinuities. The state of economy of some third world countries infected by inflation and large foreign debts will lead to equations of this form, when modeled.

At this points where there is derivative discontinuities in the differential equation of the form (1.1), a numerical method adopted for their solution may become either inaccurate, inefficient or both in this region of discontinuities identified. This is due to the fact that these class of differential equations does not satisfy the existence and uniqueness theorem, that is f (x, y) and its partial derivatives f_x, f_y are non-continuous and unbounded in the region of integration; consequently, conventional algorithm that are based on polynomial representation which pre – assumes that the solution to an ordinary differential equation and its derivatives are sufficiently continuous throughout the region of integration will be deficient in solving initial value problem that violates the uniqueness theorem, because they give rise to a solution whose derivatives explodes in the

*Corresponding author. E-mail: bolarinwa.bolaji@yahoo.com.

neighbourhood of this discontinuities (Carver, 1978). The existing methods of solving this class of ODEs evolved from researchers who were motivated to work in this area, after having discovered that the accuracy and efficiency of the methods varies with the location of points of discontinuities, which is state dependent (Paul, 1999). Such methods include: fraction step method proposed by Fatunla and Evans (1975), the switching function technique proposed by Fatunla and Evans (1974), use of discontinuity tracking equation proposed by Paul (1999), use of defect error control method proposed by Paul (1999). The computational algorithm resulting from some of the afore mentioned methods are only valid in the neighbourhood of derivative discontinuities or transient region as long as the mesh points are carefully chosen so as to sandwich the points of discontinuities. There are some other deficiencies of these methods. In this work, we propose a class of semi- implicit one – step scheme which is absolutely stable and capable of handling, effectively, the differential equations of this type (that is, differential equations with derivatives discontinuities). This proposed scheme is built along the line of thought of Hong (1982) by assuming that the approximate numerical solution to equation (1.1) can be represented locally in the interval $(x_n y_n)$ as:

$$y_{n+1} = \frac{y_n + \sum_{i=1}^{R} w_i k_i}{1 + y_n \sum_{i=1}^{S} v_i k_i} \qquad (1.2)$$

$$where\, k_i = hf\left(x_n + c_i h, y_n + \sum_{i=1}^{R} a_{ij} k_j \right) \quad i = 1(1)r \qquad (1.3)$$

$$H_i = hg\left(x_n + d_i h, Z_n + \sum_{i=1}^{R} b_{ij} h_j \right) \quad i = 1(1)s \qquad (1.4)$$

$$g(x_n, y_n) = -z_n^{\ 2} f(x_n, y_n) \qquad (1.5)$$

$$and \quad Z_n = 1/y_n \qquad (1.6)$$

With constraints:

$$c_i = \sum_{i=1}^{R} a_{ij} \qquad i = 1(1) \qquad (1.7)$$

$$d_i = \sum_{I=1}^{R} b_{ij} \qquad i = 1(1) \qquad (1.8)$$

Where h is the step size or grid spacing and h>0 be the denotation for the step size; the consistency of the scheme being ensured by the constraint (1.7) and (1.8). Ademiluyi and Babatola (2000) classified the formula (1.2) to (1.6) into three viz: explicit, semi- implicit and implicit methods. Many researchers have worked on the explicit method, Ademiluyi and Babatola among others have worked on the implicit method, the third method, the semi- implicit method has not been extensively worked upon; hence, we shall be concerned with this semi – implicit method. The formula (1.2) to (1.6) together with the constraints (1.7) and (1.8) are classified to be semi – implicit if the parameters a_{ij} and b_{ij} are chosen to satisfy a_{ij} =0 and b_{ij} =0 for d > i for at least one j > i. We shall however limit ourselves to the case in which R = 1 with its development, following the lines taken by Gill (1951), Butcher (1975) and King (1966) for one – step method, by choosing the parameters so that the resulting algorithm shall have:

i. Adequate order of accuracy,
ii. Minimum error bound,
iii. Adequate interval of absolute stability.

DERIVATION OF THE SCHEME

By setting R = 1 in equation (1.2), the general one stage semi – implicit scheme, is of the form:

$$y_{n+1} = \frac{y_n + w_1 k_1}{1 + y_n v_1 k_1} \qquad (2.1)$$

$$\text{Where } k_1 = hf(x_n + c_1 h, y_n + a_{11} k_1) \qquad i = 1(1)r \qquad (2.2)$$

$$H_1 = hg(x_n + d_1 h, Z_n + b_{11} h_1) \qquad i = 1(1)s \qquad (2.3)$$

$$g(x_n, y_n) = -z_n^{\ 2} f(x_n, y_n). \qquad (2.4)$$

$$\text{And } Z_n = 1/y_n \qquad (2.5)$$

With the constraints

$$c_1 = a_{11}\, and \quad d_1 = b_{11} \qquad (2.6)$$

To determine the unknown parameter a_{11}, b_{11}, c_1 and d_1 we shall adopt the following steps:

(1) Obtain the binomial series expansion of the r.h.s of (2.1) ignoring terms of order higher than one and obtain:

$$y_{n+1} = y_n + w_1 k_1 - y_n^{\ 2} v_1 H_1 \qquad (2.7)$$

(2) Obtain the Taylor series expansion of y_{n+1}, H_1 and k_1 so as to obtain the following results:

$$y_{n+1} = y_n + hf_n + \frac{h^2}{2!} Df_n + \frac{h^3}{3!}\left(D^2 f_n + f_y Df_n\right) + \frac{h^4}{4!}\left(D^3 f_n + f_n D^2 f_n Df_n + 3Df_n Df_y + f_y^2 Df_n\right) + 0\left(h^s\right) \quad (2.8)$$

$$H_1 = hN_1 + h^2 M_1 + h^3 R_1 + 0\left(h^4\right) \quad (2.9)$$

$$K_1 = hA_1 + h^2 B_1 + h^3 D_1 + 0\left(h^4\right) \quad (2.10)$$

Where:

$$Df_n = f_x + f_n f_y$$

$$A_1 = f_n$$

$$B_1 = c_1\left(f_n + f_n f_y\right) = c_1 Df_n$$

$$D_1 = c_1^{\,2}\left(Df_n f_y + \tfrac{1}{2} D^2 f_n\right)$$

$$N_1 = \frac{f_y}{y_n^{\,2}}$$

$$N_1 = \frac{f_y}{y_n^{\,2}}$$

$$M_1 = \frac{-d_1^{\,2}}{y_n^{\,2}}\left(Df_n + 2\frac{f_n^{\,2}}{y_n}\right)$$

$$R_1 = \frac{-d_1^{\,2}}{y_n^{\,2}}\left(C - \frac{Df_n}{y_n} + f_n\right)\left(Df_n + 2\frac{f_n^{\,2}}{y_n^{\,2}}\right) + \tfrac{1}{2} D^2 f_n - 2\frac{f_n}{y_n}\left(\frac{f_n^{\,2}}{y_n} + f_x\right)$$

By inserting (2.9) and (2.10) into (2.8) we have:

$$y_{n+1} = y_n + \left(W_1 A_1 - y_n^{\,2} V_1 N_1\right)\text{h} + h^2 + \left(W_1 A_1 - y_n^{\,2} V_1 R_1\right) h^3 + 0(h^4) \quad (2.11)$$

By comparing the coefficients of equal powers of h in equations (2.8) and (2.11), we obtain:

$$W_1 A_1 - y_n^{\,2} V_1 N_1 = f_n \quad (2.12)$$

$$W_1 B_1 - y_n^{\,2} V_1 M_1 = \frac{Df_n}{2} \quad (2.13)$$

By using the expression for N, M and B in equation (2.12) and (2.13) we obtain the set of linear equations:

$$W_1 + V_1 = 1$$

$$W_1 C_1 + V_1 D_1 = \tfrac{1}{2} \quad (2.14)$$

With $a_{11} = c_1 \; and \, b_{11} = d_1$

This set of linear equations is solved by imposing condition:

$$V_1 = W_1 = \tfrac{1}{2}$$

Then, $c_1 = a_{11} = \tfrac{3}{4}$ $d_1 = b_{11} = \tfrac{1}{4}$

By adopting these values in (2.1) we obtain one stage formula of order 2:

$$y_{n+1} = \frac{y_n + \tfrac{1}{2} K_1}{1 + \tfrac{y_n}{2} H_1}.$$

$$where\; K_1 = hf\left(x_n + \tfrac{3}{4}h, y_n + \tfrac{3}{4}k_1\right)$$

$$H_1 = hg\left(x_n + \tfrac{1}{4}h, Z_n + \tfrac{1}{4}H_1\right) \quad (2.15)$$

By imposing condition $W_1 = \tfrac{1}{5}$ on equation (2.14) and then set:

$V_1 = \tfrac{4}{5}$, *which implies that* $c_1 = d_1 = \tfrac{1}{2}$ *and* $a_{11} = b_{11} = \tfrac{1}{2}$

When these values of the parameters from the set of linear equations (2.14) are adopted in equation (2.1), we obtain one stage formula:

$$y_{n+1} = \frac{y_n + \tfrac{1}{5} K_1}{1 + \tfrac{4}{5} y_n H_1}$$

$$where\; K_1 = hf\left(x_n + \tfrac{1}{2}h, y_n + \tfrac{1}{2}k_1\right)$$

$$H_1 = hg\left(x_n + \tfrac{1}{2}h, Z_n + \tfrac{1}{2}H_1\right) \quad (2.16)$$

These proposed formulae (2.15) and (2.16) are based on a current value y_n of y_{n+1}, its derivative f_n and the step size h. These values are used to compute the next approximation y_{n+1} to y at the point $x = x_{n+1}$.The truncation error T_{n+1} associated with these families of one stage method is of the form:

$$T_{n+1} = y(x_{n+1}) - \frac{y_n + w_1 k_1}{1 + y_n v_1 k_1} + 0\left(h^{p+1}\right)$$

This truncation error is the amount by which the exact solution $y(x_{n+1})$ fails to satisfy the numerical formula (2.1)

PROPERTIES OF THE NEW SCHEME

In the process of the development of the computational

scheme, errors occur, it is therefore important to analyze these errors, convergence and stability properties of the new schemes so that we can examine and know if the method is capable, adequate and efficient towards solving differential equation of our interest, that is, ordinary differential equations with derivative discontinuities. All these are investigated in this section.

Error analysis

Numerical approximation involves iteration process, due to this, there will be propagation of errors from step to step when iterating with the scheme. These propagated errors can grow to the extent of distorting the accuracy of the numerical results. The main feature of an adequate numerical scheme is its ability to control the growth of such error so that the quality of the integration could be guaranteed. Of the two methods of error estimate techniques namely : Richardson extrapolation method and Felhberg error estimation techniques that are relevant to one step schemes, Richardson extrapolation method is adopted in this work because its procedure is less cumbersome, less time and energy consuming relatively, when compared with Felhberg error estimation techniques. By Richardson extrapolation techniques, if we designate the solution by one method, using single step size h by $y(x_{n+1})$, then local error can be estimated from:

$$e_{n+1} = y(x_{n+1}) - y_{n+1} = \Psi(x_n, y(x_n)h)h^{p+1} + 0(h^{p+2}) \quad (3.1)$$

Similarly, by adopting single step size $h/2$, the local error of the method is given by:

$$y(x_{n+1}) - l_{n+1} = \Psi(x_n, y(x_n)h/2)(h/2)^{p+1} + 0(h^{p+2}) \quad (3.2)$$

Where l_{n+1} is the computed solution by the method using step size $h/2$, by subtracting (3.1) from (3.2) and simplifying, we have:

$$\Psi(x_n, y(x_n)h)h^{p+1} = (y_{n+1} - l_{n+1})\left(1 - 1/2^{p+1}\right)^{-1} \quad (3.3)$$

The accuracy of the scheme is estimated from:

$$\mathrm{D} = \left|(y_{n+1} - l_{n+1})\left(1 - 1/2^{p+1}\right)^{-1}\right| \quad (3.4)$$

Thus $\mathrm{D} = |\Psi(x_n, y(x_n)h)|h^{p+1}$ (3.5)

Therefore the, descritization error of the scheme is estimated from:

$$e_{n+1} = [y_{n+1} - l_{n+1}]\left[\frac{2^p}{1-2^p}\right] \quad (3.6)$$

Thus, the approximation from the scheme is accepted as a good approximation to the exact solution if:

$|e_{n+1}| <$ Tolerance

That is, the global error is less than error tolerance; which implies that the scheme is accurate. The truncation error is the error introduced into the scheme as a result of ignoring higher terms of the power series expansion (by either Taylor or Binomial algorithm) .Mathematically, this is defined as the amount by which the actual solution of differential equation (1.1) fails to satisfy the difference equation (2.1), that is:

$$y_{n+1} = (y_{n+1}) - \frac{y(x_n) + w_1 K_1}{1 + y(x_n)v_1 H_1}$$
$$\text{where } K_1 = hf(x_n + c_1 h, y_n + a_{11}k_1)$$
$$H_1 = hg(x_n + d_1 h, Z_n + b_{11}h_1)$$
$$g(x_n, y_n) = -z_n^{\ 2} f(x_n, y_n). \quad (3.7)$$

By adopting Taylor's series expansion for $y(x_{n+1})$, H_1 and K_1 about $(x_n, y(x_n))$ in equation (3.7) term by term and simplifying, the truncation error associated with our one stage method of order 2 is found to be:

$$T_{n+1} = C_0 y_n + C_1 h + C_2 h^2 + C_3 h^3 + 0(h^4) \quad (3.8)$$

Where

$$C_0 = 0$$
$$C_1 = f_n - wf_n - y(x_n)^2 V_1 g_n$$
$$C_2 = Df_n/2 - w_1 c_1 Df_n + y(x_n)^2 V_1 d_1 Dg_n$$
$$C_3 = 1/6 D^2 f_n - w_1 c_1^3 Df_n f_Y + 1/6 Df_n f_y - 1/2 w_1 c_1^3 D^2 f_n + y(x_n)^2 V_1 d_1^2 Dg_n g_z + 1/2 y(x_n)^2 V_1 d_1^2 D^2 g_n$$

By imposing accuracy of order 2 on T_{n+1}, we have C_0 =0, C_1= 0, and $C_2 \neq 0$; so as to have:

$$T_{n+1} = \left(1/6 D^2 f_n - w_1 c_1^3 Df_n f_y + 1/6 Df_n f_y - 1/2 w_1 c_1^3 D^2 f_n + y(x_n)^2 V_1 d_1^2 Dg_n g_z + 1/2 y(x_n)^2 V_1 d_1^2 D^2 g_n\right) h^3$$

The bound of the principal local truncation error T_{n+1} can be found by adopting Lotkin (1951) definition:

$$\left|\frac{d^{i+j}f(x,y)}{dx^i dy^i}\right| < \frac{N^{i+j}}{M^{j-i}} \qquad x\in[a,b] \quad y\in(-\infty,\infty)$$

For bound of f and its partial derivatives. Thus, the bound of T_{n+1} is given by

$$|T_{n+1}| < [N_2|P_1| + M|P_2|]h^3$$

Where

$$P_1 = \tfrac{1}{6} - \tfrac{1}{2}w_1c_1^3 - \tfrac{y_n}{2}V_1d_1^2$$
$$P_2 = \tfrac{1}{6} - \tfrac{1}{2}w_1c_1^3 - y_n^2V_1d_1^2$$

This shows that the bound of the truncation error of one stage method exists. This implies that the error cannot grow as the scheme is used for the integration of ordinary differential equations, thus, showing that the method has some degrees of accuracy.

Stability properties of the scheme

Stability analysis of the scheme is important since it form the basis by which the suitability of the scheme is assessed. Here, Dalquist (1956) and Dalquist (1959) stability scalar test initial value problem:

$$y' = \lambda y, \qquad y(x_0) = y_0. \tag{3.9}$$

This becomes a readily important tool. Consequently, we apply scheme (2.1) to the scalar initial value problem (3.9), under the assumption that Re (λ) <<0: λ being a complex constant with negative real part. We then obtain the recurrent relation:

$$y_{n+1} = \left(\frac{1+w_1\alpha(1-a_{11}\alpha)^{-1}}{1-v_1\alpha(1+b_{11}\alpha)^{-1}}\right)y_n \tag{3.10}$$

For the approximation to the solution and for its convergence, we consider the function:

$$u(\alpha) = \frac{1+w_1\alpha(1-a_{11}\alpha)^{-1}}{1-v_1\alpha(1+b_{11}\alpha)^{-1}} \tag{3.11}$$

This can be shown to satisfy Pade's approximation to e^α and can be expressed in the form:

$$u(\alpha) = \sum_{i=1}^{2} a_i\alpha^i + 0(\alpha^3) \tag{3.12}$$

For example, the associated stability function $u(\alpha)$ is given by:

$$u(\alpha) = \frac{1+\tfrac{1}{2}\alpha}{1-\tfrac{1}{2}\alpha} \tag{3.13}$$

Which is (1,1) Pade's approximation to e^α since:

$$u(\alpha) = 1+\alpha+\tfrac{1}{4}\alpha^2 + \ldots\ldots \tag{3.14}$$

The stability functions (3.13) satisfy the condition for the Pade's approximation with $(-\infty,0)$ as the corresponding interval of absolute stability. This implies that the scheme is A – stable which stimulate the usage of the scheme for integration of ordinary differential equations with derivative discontinuities and stiff ODEs. Also, since any method that is stable is convergent, then the new scheme that is proposed is convergent.

IMPLEMENTATION OF THE SCHEME WITH SAMPLE PROBLEMS

To confirm the applicability of the new scheme and its suitability to integration of ordinary differential equations, we rewrite formula (2.14) in algorithm form and translate it into computer code using FORTRAN programming language and implement with sample problem on a digital computer. These sample problems were solved with the new scheme and the results are shown in Tables 1 to 3. In order to assess the performance of our scheme, the results of our scheme was compared with the result obtained from the other existing method, that is, the modified Euler scheme of the same order, and the results are shown in Table 4.

Problem 1

We consider the initial value problem: $y' = -\tfrac{x}{y};\quad x_0 = -1,\quad y_0 = 1\quad -1 \le x \prec 1$

Whose theoretical solution: $y(x) = \sqrt{2-x^2}$ is a family of a circle centre (0, 0). This differential equation is with derivative discontinuities at $(\sqrt{2},0)$.

This problem was solved numerically using the one- step formula (2.15) and the result is as shown in Table 1.

Problem 2

We consider the initial value problem: $y' = \tfrac{y}{x};$

Table 1. Result of one stage scheme for problem 1.

Mesh size .10000000D+00			
x_n	YEXACT	y_n	ERROR
-0.10000000D+01	0.10000000D+01	0.10000000D+01	0.00000000D+07
-0.90000000D+00	0.10908710D+01	0.10883430D+01	0.41826020D-03
-0.80000000D+00	0.11661900D+01	0.10552338D+01	0.11095620D-02
-0.69999990D+00	0.12288210D+01	0.10782578D+01	0.15056320D-02
-0.59999990D+00	0.12806250D+01	0.12630379D+01	0.17587010D-02
-0.49999990D+00	0.13228760D+01	0.13036342D+01	0.19241740D-02
-0.39999990D+00	0.13564660D+01	0.13361820D+01	0.20283990D-02
-0.29999990D+00	0.13820280D+01	0.13609691D+01	0.21058860D-02
-0.19999990D+00	0.14000000D+01	0.13785968D+01	0.21403148D-02
-0.99999930D-00	0.14142140D+01	0.13889798D+01	0.21694160D-02
0.74505810D-07	0.14142140D+01	0.13925157D+01	0.21698240D-02
0.10000010D+00	0.14106740D+01	0.13891141D+01	0.21559860D-02

Table 2. Result of one stage scheme for problem 2.

Mesh Size .10000000D+00			
x_n	YEXACT	y_n	ERROR
0.10000000D+01	-0.10000000D+01	-0.10000000D+01	0.00000000D+00
0.11000000D+01	-0.11000000D+01	-0.86712549D+00	0.21112590D+00
0.12000000D+01	-0.12000000D+01	-0.72823888D+00	0.45038830D+00
0.13000000D+01	-0.13000000D+01	-0.56249500D+00	0.73749500D+00
0.14000000D+01	-0.14000000D+01	-0.15446630D+01	0.11446630D+01
0.15000000D+01	-0.15000000D+01	-0.15426815D+01	0.39268250D+01
0.16000000D+01	-0.16000000D+01	-0.15611934D+01	0.40119340D+01
0.17000000D+01	-0.17000000D+01	-0.15743918D+01	0.40439118D+01
0.18000000D+01	-0.18000000D+01	-0.15869345D+01	0.40693455D+01
0.19000000D+01	-0.19000000D+01	-0.15986931D+01	0.40869315D+01

Table 3. Result of one stage scheme for problem 3.

Mesh size .10000000D+00			
x_n	YEXACT	y_n	ERROR
0.10000000D+01	0.10000000D+01	0.10000000D+01	0.00000000D+00
0.11000000D+01	0.10953100D+01	0.98976450D+01	0.10538060D+00
0.12000000D+01	0.11823220D+01	0.97857260D+00	0.20348260D+00
0.13000000D+01	0.12623640D+01	0.96628230D+00	0.29605220D+00
0.14000000D+01	0.13364720D+01	0.93785430D+00	0.38354030D+00
0.15000000D+01	0.14054650D+01	0.92159070D+00	0.46749210D+00
0.16000000D+01	0.14700040D+01	0.90406850D+00	0.54826310D+00
0.17000000D+01	0.15306280D+01	0.88420560D+00	0.62640110D+00
0.18000000D+01	0.15877870D+01	0.86439450D+00	0.70249520D+00
0.19000000D+01	0.16418540D+01	0.84176580D+00	0.77726610D+00
0.20000000D+01	0.16931470D+01	0.81797650D+00	0.85069410D+00
0.21000000D+01	0.17419370D+01	0.79086850D+00	0.92365160D+00
0.22000000D+01	0.17884570D+01	0.76358740D+00	0.99637620D+00
0.23000000D+01	0.18329090D+01	0.73286670D+00	0.10681650D+01
0.24000000D+01	0.18754690D+01	0.69835240D+00	0.11414560D+01

Table 4. The result of one stage adopting Richardson method to estimate the local truncation error for problem 2.

Mesh Size .10000000D+00				
x_n	YEXACT	y_n	ERROR	L.T.E
0.10000000D+01	-0.10000000D+01	-0.10000000D+01	0.00000000D+00	0.98656720D-02
0.11000000D+01	-0.11000000D+01	-0.86712549D+00	0.21112590D+00	0.97862520D-02
0.12000000D+01	-0.12000000D+01	-0.72823888D+00	0.45038830D+00	0.93245320D-02
0.13000000D+01	-0.13000000D+01	-0.56249500D+00	0.73749500D+00	0.86425230D-01
0.14000000D+01	-0.14000000D+01	-0.15446630D+01	0.11446630D+01	0.16746320D-02
0.15000000D+01	-0.15000000D+01	-0.15426815D+01	0.39268250D+01	0.14536210D-03
0.16000000D+01	-0.16000000D+01	-0.15611934D+01	0.40119340D+01	0.73214529D-03
0.17000000D+01	-0.17000000D+01	-0.15743918D+01	0.40439118D+01	0.48674920D-03
0.18000000D+01	-0.18000000D+01	-0.15869345D+01	0.40693455D+01	0.36724610D-03
0.19000000D+01	-0.19000000D+01	-0.15986931D+01	0.40869315D+01	0.22657320D-03
0.20000000D+01	-0.20000000D+01	-0.26092830D+01	0.40928300D+01	0.17948610D-03
0.21000000D+01	-0.21000000D+01	-0.26197108D+01	0.40971080D+01	0.11096540D-04
0.22000000D+01	-0.22000000D+01	-0.26285906D+01	0.40859060D+01	0.74869230D-04
0.23000000D+01	-0.23000000D+01	-0.26361110D+01	0.40631110D+01	0.48946520D-04

$y(1) = -1$ whose theoretical solution is y = $-x$. The equation has derivative discontinuity at x = 0. it was solved with the one stage formula (2.15) and the result shown in Table 2.

Problem 3

The third problem considered is: $y' = 1/x$ $x_0 = -1,$ $y_0 = -1$ whose theoretical solution is: $y = \ln x$. The differential equation has discontinuities at x = 0. The numerical solution of this problem is as shown in Table 3. From the results of the solution to the sample problems 1 to 3 as displayed in Tables 1, 2 and 3, it was observed that the discretization error obtained from the solution are sufficiently small, showing that the scheme were accurate, stable and convergent. By considering Table 4 where results obtained from our method was compared with modified Euler's method of the same order; it can be seen that the new method compared well with the said existing method.

Conclusion

Babatola (2000) and Bolarinwa (2005) proposed semi - implicit Rational Runge - Kutta schemes for the numerical integration of ordinary differential equations. The work was motivated by Rational Runge – Kutta scheme proposed by Hong (1982) and a variety of application areas of this class of ODEs and the need to cater for the deficiencies identified in the adoption of the existing methods of solving this class of differential equations. The new scheme was derived using power series expansion technique; it was analyzed, and implemented with sample problems on a micro computer. The results showed that the scheme is absolutely stable, convergent, efficient and effective towards solving ordinary differential equations with derivative discontinuities.

REFRENCES

Ademiluyi RA, Babatola PO (2000). "Implcit Runge – Kutta methods for stiff ODEs". Niger. Math. Soc. (NMS) J. pp. 229-242.

Babatola PO (2000). "Implicit Rational Runge – Kutta scheme for stiff ODEs" M.Tech thesis, Federal University of Technology, Akure, Nigeria, unpublished.

Bolarinwa B (2005). "A class of semi – implicit Rational Runge – Kutta scheme for solving ordinary differential equations with derivative discontinuities"; M. Tech thesis, Federal University of Technology, Akure; Nigeria. Unpublished.

Carver MB (1978). "Efficient integration over discontinuities in ODEs simulation". Math. Comp. Simul. 20:190-196.

Dalquist G (1956). "Convergence and stability in the integration of ODEs" Math. Scand. 4:33-53.

Dalquist G (1959). "Stability and error bounds in the integration of ODEs". Math. Scand. 6:27-43.

Hong YF (1982). "A class of A- stable A – stable explicit scheme, computational and asymptotic method for boundary and interior layer". Proceeding of ball II conference, Trinity College Dublin. pp. 236-241.

Lotkin M (1951). "On the accuracy of Runge – Kutta method". MTAC 5:128-132.

Paul CAH (1999). "The treatment of derivative discontinuities in differential equations." Numerical analysis report No. 337. Manchester centre for computational Mathematics, University of Manchester.

Measuring strength of association in repeated samples

Oyeka I. C. A. and Umeh E. U.*

Department of Statistics, Nnamdi Azikiwe University, Awka, Anambra State, Nigeria.

This paper developed a measure of the strength of the association between populations based on ranks appropriate for the analysis of mixed effects model typed data with one observation per cell. We developed a test statistic for the proposed measure. From the result of the analysis, it was observed that the proposed method is comparable to Kendal's coefficient of concordance which assume the value zero (0) when there is perfect association and the value one (1) when there is no association whatsoever between the variables of interest.

Keywords: Association, ranks, test statistic, observation.

INTRODUCTION

When the assumptions of normality and homogeneity for the use of a parametric two way analysis of variance for data analysis are not satisfied, use of a non-parametric equivalence becomes preferable. One of the methods often used is the Friedman's two-way analysis of variance by ranks (Gibbons, 1971, 1993).

In this paper, we propose to develop a measure of the strength of the association between populations appropriate for the analysis of mixed effects model typed data with one observation per cell and to develop an alternative test statistic for the proposed measure.

THE PROPOSED MEASURE

As in Friedman's test, suppose a random sample of k assessors, judges, observers or teachers are each to observe or assess and rank each of "c" candidates, patients, conditions or situations. As in Friedman's test, this data if treated as a two-way analysis of variance would correspond to a mixed effect model without replication (Oyeka et al., 2010; Hollander and Wolfe, 1999; Siegel, 1956). This means that the data are presented in the form of k × c table with say the column corresponding to one factor with c treatments or respondents which are considered fixed and the row corresponding to a second factor with k blocks, levels or observers which are considered random and there is only "1" observation per cell. The data are therefore arranged in a table with c columns and k-rows just as for the corresponding two way analysis of variance with one observation per cell. As in the analogous analysis of variance, the null hypothesis to be tested is that the "k" judges or observers are in agreement or do not differ in their assessment of c conditions or treatments versus the alternative hypothesis that the assessors do in fact differ. Interest here is also in finding a common measure of association, agreement or concordance between the "k" assessors in their assessment of the c conditions or respondents.

To answer these questions using a non-parametric approach, we first rank the observations in each row (observer) from the smallest to the largest or from the largest to the smallest. That is, within each row (observer) the rank of 1 is assigned to the smallest (largest) value. The rank of 2 is assigned to the next smallest (largest) value and so on until the rank of c is assigned to the smallest (largest) value.

Now, let r_{ij} be the rank assigned by the ith observer or assessor to the jth condition, subject or object for I = 1, 2, ...; j = 1, 2, ...,c. Then the ith row is a permutation of the numbers 1, 2, ..., c in the absence of ties and the jth column represents the ranks assigned to the jth subject by the observers. The ranks in each column are then indicative of the agreement between observers since if the jth object has the same magnitude relative to all other objects in the opinion of each of the k observers; all ranks in the jth column will be the same. Thus, if the

*Corresponding author. E-mail: editus2002@yahoo.com.

null hypothesis is true, we would expect the occurrence of the ranks 1, 2, ..., c to be equally likely in each column (object) across all rows (observers). This implies that we would expect the column sums of ranks to be the same under the null hypothesis. If the observed sums of column ranks are so discrepant that they are not likely to be a result of equal probabilities, then this constitutes an evidence against randomness and hence against the null hypothesis.

If however all the k observers agree perfectly in their ranking of each of the c objects, then the respective column totals $R_{.1}$, $R_{.2}$, ..., $R_{.c}$ will be some permutation of the numbers 1k, 2k, ..., ck. Now since the average column total is $\frac{k(c+1)}{2}$, for perfect agreement between the k observers or their ranking of the c objects, the sum of squares of deviations of column totals from the average column total, we have its maximum value, S^2_{max}which is a constant given as:

$$S^2_{max} = \Sigma_{j=1}^{c}\left(jk - \frac{k(c+1)}{2}\right)^2 = k^2\Sigma_{j=1}^{c}\left(j - \frac{(c+1)}{2}\right)^2$$

That is,

$$S^2_{max} = K^2 c\frac{(c^2-1)}{12} \quad (1)$$

However, in general, the actual sum of squared deviations of observed column totals $R_{.j}$, from the average column total namely S^2_a is:

$$S^2_a = \Sigma_{j=1}^{c}\left(R.j - k\left(\frac{(c+1)}{2}\right)\right)^2$$

That is, $S^2_a = \Sigma_{j=1}^{c} R^2_{.j} - \frac{k^2c(c+1)^2}{4}$ (2)

Note that since S^2_{max} and S^2_a are both the sums of squares, they are both non- negative. However since k and c are both positive integer, $S^2_{max} > 0$ $(c > 1)$ but $S^2_a > 0$ and is equal to 0 if the ranking of the "c" objects by the k observers is completely at random such that $R_{.j}$ = $\frac{k(c+1)}{2}$ for all j = 1, 2, ..., c if the observers are in complete agreement in their ranking of the c objects, then $S^2_a = S^2_{max}$.

Therefore, a good measure D of the strength of association between observers in their ranking of objects is the difference:

$$D = S^2_{max} - S^2_a \quad (3)$$

Note that the smallest value that D can assume is 0 when$S^2_a = S^2_{max} = \frac{k^2c(c^2-1)}{12}$ when there is perfect association or agreement between the judges or assessors in their assessment of the subjects, treatments or conditions. The largest value D can assume is S^2_{max}, when $S^2_a = 0$ meaning there is independence or no association between the judges. The smaller the value of D, the stronger the association; and the larger the value of D, the stronger the disagreement between the judges.

It however seems more illuminating to have an index of association that is normed between 0 and 1with say, 0 indicating perfect association or agreement and 1 indicating independence. To achieve this objective, we divide D by S^2_{max} obtaining:

$$Q = \frac{D}{S^2_{max}} = \frac{S^2_{max} - S^2_a}{S^2_{max}}$$

That is,

$$Q = 1 - W \quad (4)$$

$$\text{Where } W = \frac{S^2_a}{S^2_{max}} \quad (5)$$

Is the so called Kendal's coefficient of concordance (Gibbons, 1971).

SIGNIFICANCE TEST STATISTIC FOR Q

Now the total sum of squared deviations of $r_{ij}^{'s}$ from their mean $\bar{r}$ is $S^2_t = \Sigma_{i=1}^{k}\Sigma_{j=1}^{c}(r_{ij} - \bar{r})^2$

$$= \Sigma_{i=1}^{k}\Sigma_{j=1}^{c} r^2_{ij} - k.c\left(\frac{c-1}{2}\right)^2$$

$$= \frac{kc(c+1)(2c+1)}{6} - \frac{kc(c+1)^2}{4} = \frac{kc(c^2-1)}{12}$$

Note that $S^2_{max} = k.S^2_t$ (6)

Now the total sum of squares S^2_t may be partitioned into its three component parts as:

$$S^2_t = \sum_{i=1}^{k}\sum_{j=1}^{c}(r_{ij} - \bar{r})^2 = \Sigma_{i=1}^{k}\Sigma_{j=1}^{c}\left((r_{ij} - \bar{r}_{i.} - \bar{r}_{.j} + \bar{r}) + (\bar{r}_{i.} - \bar{r}) + (\bar{r}_{.j} - \bar{r})\right)^2$$

$$= c\sum_{i=1}^{k}(\bar{r}_{i.} - \bar{r})^2 + k.\sum_{j=1}^{c}(\bar{r}_{.j} - \bar{r})^2 + \sum_{i=1}^{k}\sum_{j=1}^{c}(r_{ij} - \bar{r}_{i.} - \bar{r}_{.j} + \bar{r})^2$$

Where

$S^2_R = kc\left(\frac{c-1}{2} - \frac{c-1}{2}\right)^2 = 0$ is the sum of squares due to row factor namely observer;

Table 1. Weight gains (in grams) of hogs fed with certain diets. Ranks of weights shown in brackets.

Hogs (blocks)	Diets (treatment)				
	Diet 1	Diet 2	Diet 3	Diet 4	Rank total
1	1 (2)	4 (3)	8 (4)	0 (1)	10
2	2 (2)	3 (3)	13 (4)	1 (1)	10
3	10 (3)	0 (1)	11 (4)	3 (2)	10
4	12 (3)	11 (2)	13 (4)	10 (1)	10
5	1 (2)	3 (3)	10 (4)	0 (1)	10
6	10 (3)	3 (1)	11 (4)	9 (2)	10
7	4 (1)	12 (4)	10 (2)	11 (3)	10
8	10 (4)	4 (2)	5 (3)	3 (1)	10
9	10 (4)	4 (2)	9 (3)	3 (1)	10
10	14 (4)	4 (2)	7 (3)	2 (1)	10
11	3 (2)	2 (1)	4 (3)	13 (4)	10
Total $R_{.j}$	30	24	38	18	110

$$S_C^2 = k\sum_{j=1}^{c}(\bar{r}_{.j} - \bar{r})^2 = k\left(\sum_{j=1}^{c}\frac{R_{.j}^2}{K^2} - c\frac{(c-1)^2}{4}\right) = \sum_{j=1}^{c} R_{.j}^2 - \frac{K^2 c(c-1)^2}{4} \quad (7)$$

is the sum of squares treatments or conditions due to column factor namely subjects, or judges where

$$R_{.j} = \sum_{i=1}^{k} r_{ij}$$

Finally,

And SSE = $S_e^2 = \sum_{i=1}^{k}\sum_{j=1}^{c}\left(r_{ij} - \bar{r}_{i.} - \bar{r}_{.j} + \bar{r}\right)^2$ is the error sum of squares.

Note that,

$$S_e^2 = \frac{S_a^2}{K} \quad (8)$$

And

$$S_e^2 = S_t^2 - S_C^2 = S_t^2 - \frac{S_a^2}{K} \quad (9)$$

It can be shown that these three sums of squares are independently distributed and that S_t^2 has a Chi-square distribution with kc-1 degrees of freedom (Hogg and Craig, 1971); S_R^2 has a Chi-square distribution with k-1 degrees of freedom; S_C^2 has a Chi-square distribution with c-1 degrees of freedom, and S_e^2 has a Chi-square distribution with $(kc-1)-(k-1+c-1)=(k-1)(c-1)$ degrees of freedom.

Hence the statistic F =
$$\frac{\frac{S_C^2}{(c-1)}}{\frac{S_e^2}{(k-1)(c-1)}} = \frac{(k-1)S_C^2}{S_e^2} \quad (10)$$

has an F distribution with c-1 and $(k-1)(c-1)$ degrees of freedom. Using Equations 8 and 9 in Equation 10, we have that:

$$F = \frac{\frac{(k-1)S_a^2}{K}}{S_t^2 - \frac{S_a^2}{K}} = \frac{\frac{(k-1)S_a^2}{S_t^2 .K}}{1-\frac{S_a^2}{S_t^2 .K}}$$

That is,

$$F = \frac{(k-1)W}{1-W}$$

has an F distribution with c-1 and $(k-1)(c-1)$ degrees of freedom which can be used to test the null hypothesis Ho: W = 0 (or Q = 1). That is, the null hypothesis of no association between judges or of independence of judges in their assessment of subjects, treatments or conditions.

ILLUSTRATIVE EXAMPLE

An experiment was conducted to determine the effects of four different types of diets on hogs. The hogs were grouped into eleven blocks in such a way that each block of four had identical environmental conditions. Each block has its four hogs assigned at random to one of the four experimental diets.

Shown in Table 1 are the weights gains (in grams) of each of the 44 hogs. The ranks assigned to the weight gains from the smallest (1) to the largest (4) within each block (hog) are shown in brackets. Interest is in determining whether hogs are different in the weight gains to the various diets and to determine the level of association between diets and weight gain by hogs.

Now from Equation 1, we have:

$$S_{max}^2 = (11)^2(4)\frac{(4^2-1)}{12} = \frac{121 \times 4 \times 15}{12} = 605$$

And from Equation 2, we have that:

$$S_a^2 = (30)^2 + (24)^2 + (38)^2 + (18)^2 - \frac{(11)^2(4)(4+1)^2}{4} = 900+ 576 + 1444 + 324 = 3244 - \frac{121 \times 4 \times 25}{4} = 3244 - 3925 = 219; S_a^2 = 219$$

Hence from Equation 3, we have that:

D = 605 - 219 = 386

The relatively smaller value of D compared with S^2_{max} would seem to suggest the existence of an association.

However, from Equation 4

$Q = 1 - \frac{219}{605} = 1 - 0.362 = 0.638$

Hence from Equation 12; the test statistic for testing Ho: Q = 1.0 is:

$$F = (11 - 1)\frac{(1 - 0.638)}{0.638} = \frac{10 \times 0.362}{0.638} = \frac{3.62}{0.638} = 2.3096$$

which has an F distribution with 3 and 30 degrees of freedom. At α = 0.05, $F_{0.95,3,30}$ = 2.92.

Since the calculated F = 2.310 < 2.92 = F tabulated, we fail to reject the null hypothesis Ho: Q = 1.0(W = 0). That is the null, hypothesis of independence or no association between hogs and types of diets. We may therefore conclude that hogs differ significantly in their response to the four types of diet. Furthermore, since Q is relatively large (Q = 63.8%), we may conclude that the association between hogs and types of diet is small. Note that for the present data, the Kendal's coefficient of concordance from Equation 5, $W = \frac{219}{605} = 0.362 = 1 - 0.638 = 1 - Q$.

Conclusion

This paper developed a measure of the strength of the association between populations based on ranks appropriate for the analysis of mixed effects model typed data with one observation per cell. We also developed a test statistic for the proposed measure.

From the aforementioned result, the proposed method is shown to be comparable to Kendal's Coefficient of Concordance and assume the value zero (0) when there is perfect association and the value one (1) when there is no association whatsoever between the variables of interest. The method is illustrated with some data.

REFERENCES

Gibbons JD (1971). Non- Parametric Statistical Inference. McGraw Hill, New York. pp. 246-250.

Gibbons JD (1993). Non- Parametric Statistical. An Introduction; Newbury Park: Sage Publication. pp. 180-220.

Hogg RV, Craig AT (1971). Introduction to Mathematical Statistics. New York, Macmillan Pub. Coy., Inc. pp. 305-340.

Hollander M, Wolfe DA (1999). Non-Parametric Statistical Methods (2nd Edition). Wiley Inter Science, New York. pp. 79-130.

Oyeka CA, Ebuh GU, Nwankwo CC, Obiora-Ilouno H, Ibeakuzie PO, Utazi C (2010). A Statistical Comparison of Test Scores: A Non-Parametric Approach. J. Math. Sci. 21(1):77-87.

Siegel S (1956). Non-Parametric Statistics for the Behavioural Sciences. McGraw-Hill, Kogakusha, Ltd. Tokyo. pp. 166-172.

Logistic preference function for preference ranking organization method for enrichment evaluation (PROMETHEE) decision analysis

S. K. Amponsah, K. F. Darkwah* and A. Inusah

Department of Mathematics, Kwame Nkrumah University of Science and Technology, Kumasi, Ghana.

Decision problems relate to problems of ranking, choice and detection with regards to whether a decision alternative efficient parameter satisfies some given conditions. The preference ranking organization method for enrichment evaluation (PROMETHEE) methods of decision analysis are recognized as being efficient in solving problems involving ranking. Various preference functions have been established in the literature as being useful in the PROMETHEE methodology. The Gaussian preference function is preferred when the performance data is continuous. This paper presents a new logistic preference function, which can be used for continuous performance data. The proposed logistic preference function was used on telecommunications operators performance data of the National Communication Authority of Ghana. When used in the PROMETHEE methodology, the proposed logistic preference function and the Gaussian preference function produced the same order of ranking. However, the proposed logistic preference function performed more efficiently than the Gaussian preference function.

Key words: Preference ranking organization method for enrichment evaluation (PROMETHEE), multicriteria, preference function, telecommunication.

INTRODUCTION

The most fundamental challenge faced by managers in both public and private sectors is the making of optimal decisions on problems that are multicriteria in nature. In recent times, the giant development in computer technology coupled with advance in theory has made decision analysis an indispensable tool in both government and in business as far as the making of multicriteria decision is concerned (Covaliu, 2001). It is worthwhile to note that the solution of a multicriteria problem does not only depend on the fundamental data employed in the evaluation table, but also on the decision maker (Brans et al., 1986). There exists only a compromise solution, which partly depends on the preferences of each decision maker and as a result additional information representing these preferences is required to provide the decision maker with useful decision aid.

The preference ranking organization method for enrichment evaluation (PROMETHEE) methodology is a family of six outranking methods, which are the PROMETHEE I to VI (Villota, 2009). PROMETHEE I and II were first proposed by Brans (1982). Other multicriteria decision aids (MCDA), such as the PROMETHEE group decision support system (GDSS) for group decision-making (Brans and Mareschal, 2010) and the visual interactive module, geometrical analysis for interactive aid (GAIA), for pictorial representation to complement the algebraic methodology were developed to facilitate the analysis of more complex decision-making problems (Brans and Mareschal, 2010). Two extensions of PROMETHEE have recently been proposed as PROMETHEE TRI for multicriteria decision-making problems involving sorting and the PROMETHEE CLUSTER for problems dealing with nominal

*Corresponding author. E-mail: fordarkk@gmail.com.

classification (Figueira et al., 2004).

RELATED WORKS

PROMETHEE II method was used to solve a facility location problem in which there were eight criteria against four alternative locations solutions (Athawale and Chakraborty, 2010). At the end, the most cost-effective and highest yielding location alternative was identified and selected. Maragoudaki and Tsakiris (2005) identified PROMETHEE methodology as one of the most efficient MCDA outranking techniques that could be used to arrive at the optimal flood mitigation plan for a river basin. Four alternative irrigation projects for the East Macedonia-Thrace district were evaluated using analytic hierarchy process (AHP) and PROMETHEE multicriteria methods (Anagnostopoulos et al., 2005). The project goal was the rational water resources management of Nestos River in relation to the operation of two recently constructed dams. A preventive maintenance decision model based on integrating PROMETHEE method and the Bayesian approach was developed to help decision makers establish replacement intervals (Ferreira et al., 2007). A numerical application example was given to illustrate the proposed decision model and showed the effectiveness of the model in terms of the decision maker's preferences.

Albadvi (2004) formulated national information technology strategies: a preference ranking model using PROMETHEE method. The sole purpose of the research was to define a national strategy model for Information Technology (IT) development in developing countries and to apply the model in a real case of Iran. The model was a multicriteria decision making and in order to solve it and select a set of IT application flagships in different budgeting levels, they used the PROMCALC and GAIA decision support system.

Zhou et al. (2010) developed a fuzzy based pipe condition assessment model using PROMETHEE II. This method was used to calculate pipe breakage risk to reflect the condition assessment in order to enable them rehabilitate the deteriorated pipes in a planned and proactive way. The numerous influential factors they identified as responsible for pipe breakage included ground load, pipe material, soil corrosion, pipe age, construction quality, pipe length, soil condition, breakage history, etc. The authors argued that the proposed model was different from the previous model, being used in that it only required readily usually available data, and that it gave an insight into the uncertainty and preference opinion of the expert as shown in the relation between expert opinion's uncertainty and preference that had a pipe breakage risk signification and in each criterion.

A PROMETHEE based uncertainty analysis of United Kingdom (UK) police force performance rank improvement was designed for a periodic comparison of the units of the police force in the UK with each other in terms of performance by both government and non-government bodies (Barton and Beynon, 2009). The study demonstrated the employment of PROMETHEE in an investigation of the targeted performance rank improvement of individual units of the UK police forces. The graphical representations presented offered an insight into the implications of series of such a PROMETHEE based series of perceived improvement analysis. The goals of their study were two folds: firstly, namely to exposit PROMETHEE based uncertainty analysis in rank improvement and secondly, to show how the subsequent results could form part of the evidence to that aided in their performance strategies.

A new sorting method (flow sort) based on the ranking methodology of PROMETHEE for assigning actions to completely ordered categories, defined either by limiting profiles or by central profiles was established by Nemery and Lamboray (2007). The flow sort assignment rules were based on the relative position of an action with respect to the reference profiles in terms of the incoming, leaving and/or net flows.

Manzano et al. (2011) conducted an economic evaluation of the Spanish port system using the PROMETHEE multicriteria decision method. The work established an ordering relationship among twenty-seven Spanish port authorities at different strategically considered time points.

Aburas et al. (2010) conducted call quality measurement for telecommunication network and proposition of tariff rates research. The idea of their research was basically the measurement of call quality from the end users perspective and could be used by both end user and operator to benchmark the network. The call quality was measured based on certain call parameters as average signal strength, the successful call rate, drop rate, handover success rate, handover failure rate and location area code (LAC). The quality parameters were derived from active calls and the results were analyzed and plotted for detailed analysis and benchmarking as well as used as a base for charging the customer by the operators. The authors suggested charging rates based on the signal quality and the call statistics recorded.

Michailidis and Chatzitheodoridis (2006) proposed a model based on PROMETHEE, a multicriteria decision aid, to be used to evaluate and rank three tourism destinations, located in the Northern and Central Greece. Additionally, innovatory innovative elements were the incorporation of differing levels of socioeconomic data (destination image and destination personality) within the decision frame work and the direct determination of the PROMETHEE II preference thresholds. According to them, the developed methodology provides a user-friendly approach, promotes the synergy between different stakeholders and could pave a way towards consensus. The authors identified the act of describing

Table 1. Relations between alternatives in PROMETHEE partial preorder ranking.

Preference relation	Conditions	Graphical representation
$A_K P A_l$	$\phi^+(A_K) > \phi^+(A_l)$ and $\phi^-(A_K) < \phi^-(A_l)$ $\phi^+(A_K) > \phi^+(A_l)$ and $\phi^-(A_K) = \phi^-(A_l)$ $\phi^+(A_K) = \phi^+(A_l)$ and $\phi^-(A_K) < \phi^-(A_l)$	$A_K \longrightarrow A_l$
$A_K I A_l$	$\phi^+(A_K) = \phi^+(A_l)$ and $\phi^-(A_K) = \phi^-(A_l)$	-
$A_k R A_l$	$\phi^+(A_K) > \phi^+(A_l)$ and $\phi^-(A_K) > \phi^-(A_l)$ $\phi^+(A_l) > \phi^+(A_k)$ and $\phi^-(A_l) > \phi^-(A_k)$	-

the design implementation and use of a decision support system (DSS), which applied new methodological approaches for the evaluation and ranking of several tourism destinations as the main focus of their study.

Due to its reach and capability to share information, the World Wide Web has become an important tool for business (Villota, 2009). According to the author, there were some so-called usability criteria, which should be respected by web designers in order to make websites useful. As a result, using a multicriteria decision making approach, they evaluated the performances, based on seven usability criteria, of five websites from which one could buy books online. Considering usability as a subjective matter, they used two well-known methodologies that deal with this issue: AHP and PROMETHEE. Through PROMETHEE, they related the preference of a decision maker with specially defined criterion functions.

MODEL FORMULATION AND PROMETHEE ALGORITHM

Decision problem statement is stated as follows: given a finite set of alternatives $A = \{A_j\}$, $j = 1, \ldots, m$ against a set of criteria, $C = \{C_j\}$ and weights w_i, $i = 1, \ldots, n$ what alternative A_j is the best alternative?

The PROMETHEE algorithm for ranking the alternatives (Villota, 2009) is given as follows:

Step 1: Input data of performance table and table of weights: The performance data shows in quantitative terms the performance value x_{ij} of each A_j on each criterion, C_i.

Step 2: Calculate deviations of various criteria i:

$$d_i(A_k, A_l) = \begin{cases} x_{ik} - x_{il} & \text{for maximization criteria } i \\ -(x_{ik} - x_{il}) & \text{for minimization criteria } i \end{cases}$$

Step 3a: Select a generalized preference function $P(d_i) = P(d_i(A_k, A_l))$: There are currently eight generalized preference functions from which to choose to reflect the priorities of the decision maker (Podvezko and Podviezko, 2010).

Step 3b: Calculate preference (criterion) value using $P(d_i) = P(d_i(A_k, A_l))$. This measures the intensity of the decision maker's preference for the alternative A_k over A_l on the same criterion C_i.

Step 4: Calculate the aggregate preference index of alternative A_k over A_l for all criteria C_i by using the relation: $\pi(A_k, A_l) = \sum_{i=1}^{n} w_i P_i(A_k, A_l)$, where w_i is the weight of criterion i.

Step 5: Perform partial ranking (PROMETHEE I):

i. Calculate the positive outranking flow of alternative, A_j: over all other alternatives A_k with $A_k \neq A_j$ and using,

$$\phi^+(A_j) = \frac{1}{m-1} \sum_{k=1}^{m} \pi(A_j, A_k) \quad j = 1, 2, 3 \ldots m$$

ii. Calculate the negative outranking flow of all alternatives, A_k over alternatives A_j with $A_k \neq A_j$ and using, $\phi^-(A_j) = \frac{1}{m-1} \sum_{k=1}^{m} \pi(A_k, A_j) \quad j = 1, 2, 3 .. m$

iii. Determine the outranking relation existing between various alternatives by using Table 1 where $A_k P A_l$ signifies the preference of the alternative A_k over A_l, $A_k I A_l$ signifies the indifference between alternatives A_k and A_l and $A_k R A_l$ indicates the incomparability of the two alternatives A_k and A_l over all criteria.

If the resulting incidence table I of the resulting directed graph from column 3 of Table 1, satisfy the condition that:

Table 2. Relations between alternatives in complete ranking.

Preference relation	Cases	Graphical representation
$A_k \, P \, A_l$	$\phi(A_k) > \phi(A_l)$	$A_k \longrightarrow A_l$
$A_k \, I \, A_l$	$\phi(A_k) = \phi(A_l)$	_

Table 3. Performance table of five telecom networks in the Greater Accra region as of June, 2010.

Criteria	Type of criteria	Alternative				
		A_1	A_2	A_3	A_4	A_5
C_1	Min	15.12	12.09	11.67	13.86	15.28
C_2	Max	80	96	41	81	88
C_3	Min	17	3	27	12	10
C_4	Min	3	1	32	8	2

$$\sum_j I_{ij} + \sum_j I'_{ij} = m-1 \quad \text{for all } i = 1,2,3...m$$

with I' being the transpose of I. Then, the alternatives are completely ranked, stop. The alternative represented by the row with the highest sum of entries is the decision. Otherwise the alternatives are partially ranked, go to step 6.

Step 6: Perform complete ranking (PROMETHEE II): Compute the net outranking flow $\phi(A_k)$ for each alternative A_k such that $\phi(A_k) = \phi^+(A_k) - \phi^-(A_k)$:

i. The alternative A_k is preferable to A_l if and only if $\phi(A_k) > \phi(A_l)$

ii. The alternative A_k is indifferent to A_l if and only if $\phi(A_k) = \phi(A_l)$

This is illustrated as shown in Table 2.

PREFERENCE FUNCTION

Podvezko and Podviezko (2010) categorized eight generalized preference functions found in the literature. These include multistage, c-shape and Gaussian preference functions. Villota (2009) suggested that for continuous performance data, the Gaussian preference function is preferred. The Gaussian preference function is given by:

$$P(d_i) = \begin{cases} 0 & d_i \le 0 \\ 1 - e^{\left(-\frac{d_i^2}{2\sigma_i^2}\right)} & d_i > 0 \end{cases}$$

where d_i is deviation of over criterion i over respective pairs of alternatives, A_k, A_l. σ_i^2 is the variance of the data for criterion i.

We introduce a new preference function which we call the logistic preference function. It performs better than the Gaussian preference function. The logistic preference function $P(x)$ is the difference of logistic probabilities for success $p(x)$ and failure $q(x)$.

$$P\ x = p - q = p - (1-p) = 2p - 1$$

$$= 2\left(\frac{1}{1+e^{-x}}\right) - 1 = \frac{2-1-e^{-x}}{1+e^{-x}} = \left(\frac{1-e^{-x}}{1+e^{-x}}\right)$$

$$\text{where} \quad p = \frac{1}{1+e^{-x}}$$

Put $x = \dfrac{d_i^2}{\sigma_i^2}$ to obtain:

$$P\ d_i = \begin{cases} 0 & d_i \le 0 \\ \dfrac{1 - e^{\left(-\frac{d_i^2}{\sigma_i^2}\right)}}{1 + e^{\left(-\frac{d_i^2}{\sigma_i^2}\right)}} & d_i > 0 \end{cases}$$

COMPUTATIONAL EXPERIENCE AND RESULTS

Our preference function was tested on data of performance measure of the National Communications Authority (NCA) of Ghana. Five mobile telecommunications network operators in Greater Accra were selected. Table 3 displays the data and indicates whether a criterion is minimizing or maximizing criterion.

Table 4. The mean and standard deviation of the four criteria.

Criteria	Mean (μ)	Standard deviation (σ)
C_1	13.60	1.67
C_2	77.20	21.23
C_3	13.80	8.93
C_4	10.20	15.22

Table 5. Aggregated preference indices $\pi(A_k, A_l)$.

	A_1	A_2	A_3	A_4	A_5
A_1	0.00	0.00	0.61	0.01	0.00
A_2	0.52	0.00	0.74	0.33	0.33
A_3	0.24	0.01	0.00	0.12	0.25
A_4	0.11	0.00	0.67	0.00	0.09
A_5	0.09	0.00	0.73	0.04	0.00

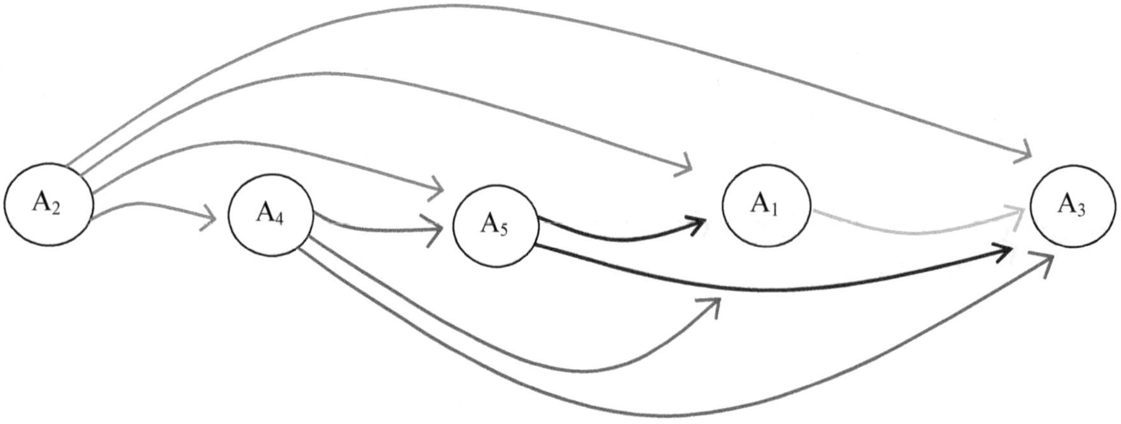

Figure 1. Graph of ordered complete ranking of network operators at partial ranking step of the algorithm when the logistic function is used.

A = {A_j} for j = 1, ...,5 are the set of alternatives and C = {C_j} for i = 1,...,4 are the set of criteria. Table 4 presents the mean (μ_i) and the standard deviation (σ_i) for each of the four criterion C_i.

Going through steps 1 to 4 of the PROMETHEE algorithm, Table 5 shows the aggregate preference indices of pairs of alternatives A_k and A_l. From step 5 of partial ranking, we obtain the directed graph as shown in Figure 1 with the network operators represented as nodes. The resulting incidence matrix of the directed graph satisfies the condition that:

$$\sum_j I_{ij} + \sum_j I'_{ij} = m-1 \quad \text{for all } i, j = 1,2...5 \quad \text{and } m = 5$$

Thus, the alternatives are completely ranked. From Figure 1, the network ranking order is A_2, A_4, A_5, A_1 and A_3 and the ranking is done based on the number of directed arcs that is recorded by each alternative, such that the best alternative (A_2) is the one with the highest number of directed arcs and the alternative A_3 with no directed arc becomes the worst one.

DISCUSSION

The new logistics preference function is the difference between the success and failure probabilities of the logistic function. Applying the proposed preference function in the PROMETHEE algorithm, we had a complete ordered ranking at the partial ranking step 5 of the algorithm.

The same data was used to rank the five network

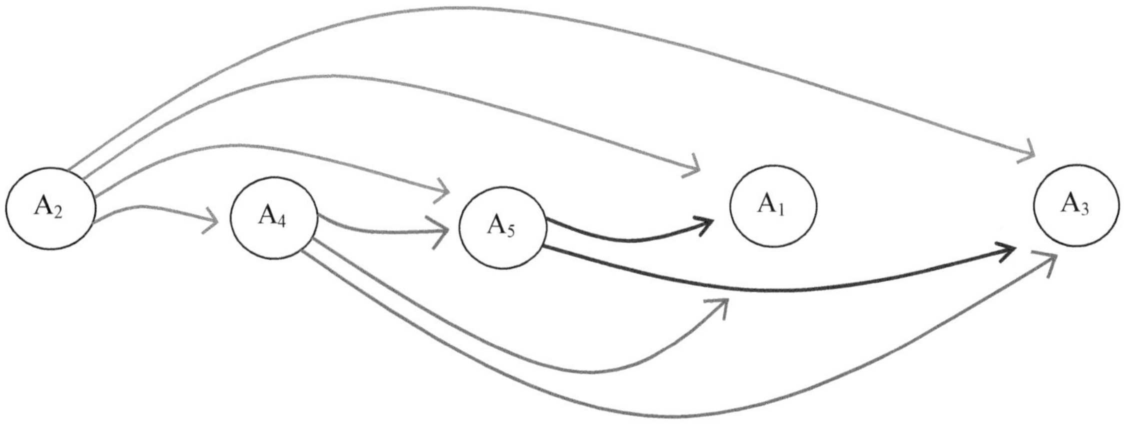

Figure 2. Graph of partial ranking of network operators when Gaussian function is used.

operators using the Gaussian preference function. In this case, step 5 of the algorithm produced partial ranking of the network operators. The directed graph of the partial ranking is as shown in Figure 2, which shows that, the condition,

$$\sum_j I_{ij} + \sum_j I'_{ij} = m-1 \quad \text{for all } i, j = 1,2...5 \quad \text{and } m = 5$$

is not satisfied for nodes A_3 and A_1.

The number of directed arcs terminating on node A_3 of Figure 2 is less than the required number, 4, and node A_1 is missing a directed arc. Complete ranking was achieved at the last step with the ordered ranking A_2, A_4, A_5, A_1 and A_3 being the same as the solution using the logistic preference function.

The PROMETHEE algorithm was also applied to data provided in Villota (2009) as shown in Table A1 of the Appendix. We assigned minimization and maximization characteristics to the criteria of Villota (2009) data as shown in Table A2 of the Appendix. The Gaussian and logistic functions were used for the PROMETHEE calculation and the rankings were the same. Both reached the step of complete ranking and produced the same ranking order of A_5, A_2, A_4, A_1 and A_3.

Conclusion

The new Logistic preference function and the Gaussian preference function yielded the same ordered ranking for the five telecom networks in our case study. The ranking order was A_2, A_4, A_5, A_1 and A_3 under the PROMETHEE methodology. The logistic preference function was more efficient than the Gaussian preference function, in the sense that complete ordered ranking was achieved at step 5 (partial ranking step) for the logistic preference function, while complete ordered ranking was achieved at step 6 (complete ranking step) for the Gaussian preference function. For the decision problem presented in Villota (2009), the Gaussian and logistic functions produced the same ranking order. Both reached the step of complete ranking and produced the same ranking order of A_5, A_2, A_4, A_1 and A_3. The results suggest that for all continuous data for which the Gaussian preference function is applicable, our proposed logistic preference function is equally applicable and can be a perfect and more efficient substitute for the Gaussian preference function.

REFERENCES

Aburas A, Gardiner JG, Al Hokail Z (2010). Call Quality Measurement for Telecommunication Network and Proposition of Tariff Rates, pp. 1–5. http://www.iiis.org/CDs2010/CD2010IMC/CCCT_2010/PapersPdf/TA447AH.pdf (Accessed on 13th June, 2011).

Albadvi A (2004). Formulating National Information Technology Strategy: A Preference Ranking Model Using PROMETHEE Method. Eur. J. Oper. Res., 153: 290–296.

Anagnostopoulos KP, Petalas C, Pisinaras V (2005). Water Resources Planning Using the AHP and PROMETHEE Multicriteria Methods: the Case of NESTOS River –Greece. The 7th Balkans Conference on Operational Research "Bacor 05" Constanta. May 2005, Romania, pp. 1-12. http://fmi.unibuc.ro/balkan-conf/CD/Section4/ANAGNOSTOPOULOS-PETALAS-PISINARAS.pdf. (Accessed on 15th June, 2011)

Athawale VM, Chakraborty S (2010). Facility Location Selection Using PROMETHEE II Method. Proceedings of the 2010 International Conference on Industrial Engineering and Operations Management (Jan. 9-10) Dhaka, Bangladesh, pp. 1-5.

Barton H, Beynon M (2009). A PROMETHEE Based Uncertainty Analysis of UK Police Force Performance Rank Improvement, 14: 1–29. http://www.ipes.info/WPS/WPS%20No%2014.pdf. (Accessed on 15th December, 2010).

Brans JP, Vincke PH, Mareschal B (1986). How to Select And How to Rank Projects: The PROMETHEE Method. Eur. J. Oper. Res., 24: 228–238.

Brans JP, Mareschal B (2010). PROMETHEE methods. https://www.inf.unideb.hu/valseg/dolgozok/anett.racz/docs/.../Promethee.pdf. (Accessed on 25th July, 2010).

Brans JP (1982). The engineering of decision: Elaboration instruments of decision support method PROMETHEE. Laval University, Quebec, Canada. http://www. dss.dpem.tuc.gr/pdf/How% 20to%20Decide

%20with%20PROMETHEE.pdf (Accessed on 10th January, 2011).
Covaliu Z (2001). Decision Analysis: Concepts, Tools and Promise. A Fair Isaac White Paper. 18009992955 from the US, 14154722211. http://www.edmblog.com/weblog/files/decision_analytics_white_paper.pdf. (Accessed on 18th August, 2010).
Ferreira JP, Cavalcante CAV, Almeida AT (2007). A Preventive Maintenance Decision Model Based on a MCDA Approach, pp. 1-6. http://old.ima.org.uk/Conferences/proceedings_mimar2007/proceedings_mimar2007_29.pdf. (Accessed on 11th August, 2010).
Figueira J, de Smet Y, Brans JP (2004). MCDA methods for Sorting and Clustering Problems: PROMETHEE Tri and PROMETHEE Cluster, Free University of Brussels. Department of Mathematics and Management Working Paper. http://www.ulb.ac.be/polytech/smg/indexpublications.htm. (Accessed on 18th July, 2010).
Manzano JIC, Quijada MTA, Nuño MMC (2011). Economic Evaluation of the Spanish Port System Using the PROMETHEE Multicriteria Decision Method. http://www-sre.wu-wien.ac.at/ersa/ersaconfs/ersa04/PDF/647.pdf. (Accessed on 12th May, 2011).
Maragoudaki R, Tsakiris G (2005). Flood Mitigation Planning Using PROMETHEE. Athens. Eur. Water 9/10 E.W. Publ., pp. 51–58. http://www.ewra.net/ew/pdf/EW_2005_9-10_06.pdf. (Accessed on 18th May, 2011)
Michailidis A, Chatzitheodoridis F (2006). Scenarios Analysis of Tourism Destinations. J. Soc. Sci., 2(2): 41-47.
Nemery P, Lamboray C (2007). Flowsort, A Flow-Based Sorting Method with Limiting or Central Profiles, Brussels, Belgium, pp. 1-24. http://code.ulb.ac.be/~pnemeryd/FlowSort_TOP.pdf. (Accessed on 19th July, 2010)
Podvezko V, Podviezko A (2010). Dependence of Multicriteria Evaluation Result on Choice of Preference Functions and their Parameters, Technological and Economic Development of Economy. Baltic J. Sustain., 16(1): 143–158.
Villota ALM (2009). Usability of Websites. Mphil Thesis. University of Birmingham, Birmingham.
Zhou Y, Vairavamoorthy K, Gramshaw F (2010). Development of a Fuzzy Based Pipe Condition Assessment Model Using PROMETHEE, pp. 1-10. http://www.delftcluster.nl/website/files/Development_of_a_Fuzzy_Based_Pipe_Condition_Assessment_Model_Using_PROMETHEE.pdf. (Accessed on 15th January, 2011).

APPENDIX

Table A1. Villota (2009) performance table of five websites (A1 - A5) and seven usability criteria (C1 to C7).

Characteristic	A_1	A_2	A_3	A_4	A_5
C_1	19	23	6	13	39
C_2	27	28	5	16	24
C_3	12	24	29	26	10
C_4	32	10	15	11	32
C_5	29	25	11	13	21
C_6	11	19	13	11	46
C_7	34	11	7	9	39

Table A2. Villota (2009) performance table with added maximization/minimization characteristics.

Characteristic	A_1	A_2	A_3	A_4	A_5
C_1 (max)	19	23	6	13	39
C_2 (max)	27	28	5	16	24
C_3 (max)	12	24	29	26	10
C_4 (min)	32	10	15	11	32
C_5 (min)	29	25	11	13	21
C_6 (max)	11	19	13	11	46
C_7 (max)	34	11	7	9	39

24

On three-dimensional generalized sasakian space – forms

S. Yadav* and D. L. Suthar

Department of Mathematics, Alwar Institute of Engineering and Technology, M.I.A. Alwar-301030, Rajasthan, India.

The object of the present paper is to study locally φ–symmetric three-dimensional generalized Sasakian space forms and such manifolds with Ricci semi symmetric, η-parallel Ricci tensor and cyclic Ricci tensor. Such space forms with non-null concircular vector field are also considered.

Key words: Generalized sasakian space forms, cosymplectic, locally-φ-symmetric, η-parallel ricci tensor, cyclic ricci tensor and non-null concircular vector field.

INTRODUCTION

Generalized Sasakian space forms are considered as special cases of an almost contact metric manifold (Alegre et al., 2004). Three-dimensional LP-Sasakian manifolds and three-dimensional trans-Sasakian manifolds were studied respectively by De and Tripathi (2003), Venkatesha and Bagewadi, 2006). Where as three-dimensional Para-Sasakian manifolds, three-dimensiomal Lorentzian α–Sasakian manifolds and three-dimensional quasi-Sasakian manifolds were studied respectively by Bagewadi and et al. (2007), Yildiz et al. (2009) and De and Sarkar (2009). In this paper we extend same work for three- dimensional generalized Sasakian space forms and obtain some results.

GENERALIZED SASAKIAN SPACE-FORM

A $(2n+1)$-dimensional Riemannian manifold (M,g) is called an almost contact manifold if the following results hold:

(a) $\varphi^2(X) = -X + \eta(X)\xi$, (1)

(b) $\varphi\xi = 0$

(a) $\eta(\xi)=1$, (2)

(b) $g(X,\xi)=\eta(X)$,(c) $\eta(\varphi X)=0$

$g(\varphi X,\varphi Y) = g(X,Y) - \eta(X)\eta(Y)$, (3)

(a) $g(\varphi X,Y) = -g(X,\varphi Y)$ (4)

(b) $g(\varphi X,X)=0$

$(\nabla_X \eta)(Y) = g(\nabla_X \xi, Y)$ (5)

An almost contact metric manifold is called contact metric manifold if

$$d\eta(X,Y) = \Phi(X,Y) = g(X,\varphi Y)$$

Where Φ is called the fundamental two-form of the manifold. If ξ is a killing vector field the manifold is called a k-contact manifold. It is well known that a contact metric manifold is k-contact if and only if $\nabla_X \xi = -\varphi X$, for any vector field X on (M,g). An almost contact metric manifold is Sasakian if and only if $(\nabla_X \varphi)(Y) = g(X,Y)\xi - \eta(Y)X$, for any vector fields X,Y.

Blair (1967) introduced the notion of quasi-Sasakian manifold to unify Sasakian and cosymplectic manifolds.

*Corresponding author. E-mail: prof_sky16@yahoo.com.

Again Olszak (1986) introduced and characterized three-dimensional quasi-Sasakian manifolds. An almost contact metric manifold of dimension three is quasi-Sasakian if and only if

$$\nabla_X \xi = -\beta\varphi X \quad , \tag{6}$$

for all $X \in TM$ and a function β such that $\xi\beta = 0$

As the consequence of (6), we get

$$(\nabla_X \eta)(Y) = g(\nabla_X \xi, Y) = -\beta g(\varphi X, Y) \tag{7}$$

$$(\nabla_X \eta)(\xi) = -\beta g(\varphi X, \xi) = 0 \tag{8}$$

Clearly such a quasi-Sasakian manifold is cosymplectic if and only if $\beta = 0$ .It is known that for a three-dimensional quasi-Sasakian manifold the Riemannian curvature tensor satisfies

$$R(X,Y)\xi = \beta^2\{\eta(Y)X - \eta(X)Y\} + d\beta(Y)\varphi X - d\beta(X)\varphi Y \, , \tag{9}$$

For a $(2n+1)$ -dimensional generalized Sasakian-space-form, we have

$$R(X,Y)Z = f_1\{g(Y,Z)X - g(X,Z)Y\} + f_2\{g(X,\varphi Z)\varphi Y - g(Y,\varphi Z)\varphi X + 2g(X,\varphi Y)\varphi Z\} + f_3\left\{\begin{matrix}\eta(X)\eta(Z)Y - \eta(Y)\eta(Z)X \\ + g(X,Z)\eta(Y)\xi - g(Y,Z)\eta(X)\xi\end{matrix}\right\} \tag{10}$$

$$R(X,Y)\xi = (f_1 - f_2)\{\eta(Y)X - \eta(X)Y\} \, , \tag{11}$$

$$R(\xi, X)Y = (f_1 - f_3)\{g(X,Y)\xi - \eta(Y)X\} \, , \tag{12}$$

$$g(R(\xi, X)Y, \xi) = (f_1 - f_3)g(\varphi X, \varphi Y) \, , \tag{13}$$

$$R(\xi, X)\xi = (f_1 - f_3)\varphi^2 X \tag{14}$$

$$S(X,Y) = (2nf_1 + 3f_2 - f_3)g(X,Y) - (3f_2 + (2n-1)f_3)\eta(X)\eta(Y) \tag{15}$$

$$Q\xi = 2n(f_1 - f_3)\xi \tag{16}$$

$$S(\varphi X, \varphi Y) = S(X,Y) + 2n(f_3 - f_1)\eta(X)\eta(Y) \tag{17}$$

The Conformal curvature tensor vanishes in three-dimensional Riemannian manifold therefore we have

$$R(X,Y)Z = g(Y,Z)QX - g(X,Z)QY + S(Y,Z)X - S(X,Z)Y - \frac{\tau}{2}[g(Y,Z)X - g(X,Z)X] \tag{18}$$

Here S is the ricci tensor and τ is the scalar curvature tensor of the space-forms. It is known that (2006) a $(2n+1)$-dimensional $(n>1)$ generalized Sasakian-space-form is conformally flat if and only if $f_2 = 0$.

BASIC RESULTS

Theorem 1

In a three-dimensional generalizedSasakian space forms $M(f_1, f_2, f_3)^{2n+1}, (n=1)$ we get

$$QX = \left[\frac{\tau}{2} + (1-2n)(f_1 - f_3)\right]X + \left[(4n-1)(f_1 - f_3) - \frac{\tau}{2}\right]\eta(X)\xi \tag{i}$$

$$S(X,Y) = \left[\frac{\tau}{2} + (1-2n)(f_1 - f_3)\right]g(X,Y) + \left[(4n-1)(f_1 - f_3) - \frac{\tau}{2}\right]\eta(X)\eta(Y) \, , \tag{ii}$$

$$R(X,Y)Z = \left[\frac{\tau}{2} + 2(1-4n)(f_1 - f_3)\right]\{g(Y,Z)X - g(X,Z)Y\} + \left[(4n-1)(f_1 - f_3) - \frac{\tau}{2}\right]\left\{\begin{matrix} g(Y,Z)\eta(X)\xi \\ - g(X,Z)\eta(Y)\xi \\ + \eta(Y)\eta(Z)X \\ - \eta(X)\eta(Z)Y \end{matrix}\right\} \tag{iii}$$

Proof 1

Substituting $Z = \xi$ in (18) and using (2-b) (11) and (15) we get

$$(f_1 - f_3)[\eta(Y) - (X)\xi] = \eta(Y)QX - \eta(X)QY + 2n(f_1 - f_3)\eta(Y)X - 2n(f_1 - f_3)\eta(X)Y - \frac{\tau}{2}[\eta(Y)X - \eta(X)Y] \tag{19}$$

Again putting $Y = \xi$ in (19) and using (2-b), we have

$$QX = \left[\frac{\tau}{2} - (1-2n)(f_1 - f_2)\right]X + \left[(4n-1)(f_1 - f_3) - \frac{\tau}{2}\right]\eta(X)\xi \tag{20}$$

And

$$S(X,Y)=\left[\frac{\tau}{2}+(1-2n)(f_1-f_3)\right]g(X,Y)$$
$$+\left[(4n-1)(f_1-f_3)-\frac{\tau}{2}\right]\eta(X)\eta(Y) \quad (21)$$

By virtue of (19) and (20) the equations18) reduces as (iii).

This completes the proof of the theorem1.

Corollary 1

A three-dimensional generalized Sasakian space forms $M(f_1,f_2,f_3)^{2n+1},(n=1)$ with constant function f_1-f_3 is a manifolds of constant curvature if and only if the scalar curvature is $\tau=2(4n-1)(f_1-f_3)$.

Corollary 2

A three-dimensional generalized Sasakian space forms $M(f_1,f_2,f_3)^{2n+1},(n=1)$ with constant curvature is flat if and only if $f_1=f_3$.

RICCI-SEMISYMMETRIC THREE-DIMENSIONAL GENERALIZED SASAKIAN SPACE -FORMS

Theorem 2

A three-dimensional Ricci semi symmetric generalized Sasakian space forms $M(f_1,f_2,f_3)^{2n+1},(n=1)$ with constant function f_1-f_3 is a manifold of constant curvature.

Proof 2

We consider three-dimensional generalized Sasakian space form satisfying the condition

$$R(X,Y)\cdot S=0 \quad (22)$$

From (22), it follows that

$$S(R(X,Y)U,V)+S(U,R(X,Y)V=0 \quad (23)$$

Substituting $X=\xi$ in (23) and using (12) we get

$$4n^2(f_1-f_3)^2[g(Y,U)\eta(V)+g(Y,V)\eta(U)]$$
$$-2n(f_1-f_3)[S(Y,V)\eta(U)+S(U,Y)\eta(V)]=0 \quad (24)$$

Let $\{e_i\}$, $i=1,2,3$ be an orthonormal basis of the tagent space at any point of the manifold then putting $Y=U=e_i$ in (24) and taking summation over i , $1\le i\le 3$, we get

$$g(e_i,e_i)\eta(V)[4n^2(f_1-f_3)^2-2nk(f_1-f_3)]=0, \quad (25)$$

This implies that

$$\tau=2(4n-1)(f_1-f_3), \quad (26)$$

where $k=\left[\frac{\tau}{2}-(1-2n)(f_1-f_3)\right]$

and $g(e_i,e_i)\neq 0$

This completes the proof of the theorem 2.

LOCALLY φ-SYMMETRICTHREE-DIMENSIONAL GENERALIZED SASAKIAN SPACE -FORMS

Definition 1

A generalized Sasakian space-forms is said to be locally φ-symmetric if

$$\varphi^2(\nabla_W R)(X,Y)Z=0,$$

for all vector fields X,Y,Z and W orthogonal to ξ. This notion was introduced by Takahashi (1977) for Sasakian manifolds.

Theorem 3

A three-dimensional cosymplectic (non cosymplectic) generalized Sasakian space forms $M(f_1,f_2,f_3)^{2n+1},(n=1)$ with constant function f_1-f_3 is locally φ –symmetric if and only if the scalar curvature is constant.

Proof 3

Now differentiating (theorem1, iii) covariantly with respect to W we get

$$(\nabla_W R)(X,Y)Z = \frac{d\tau(W)}{2}[g(Y,Z)X - g(X,Z)Y] \tag{27}$$
$$-\frac{d\tau(W)}{2}\begin{bmatrix} g(Y,Z)\eta(X)\xi - g(X,Z)\eta(Y)\xi \\ \eta(Y)\eta(Z)X - \eta(X)\eta(Z)Y \end{bmatrix}$$
$$+\left((4n-1)(f_1-f_3)-\frac{\tau}{2}\right)\begin{bmatrix} g(Y,Z)(\nabla_W\eta)(X)\xi \\ -g(X,Z)(\nabla_W\eta)(Y)\xi \\ +g(Y,Z)\eta(X)\nabla_W\xi \\ -g(X,Z)\eta(Y)\nabla_W\xi \\ +(\nabla_W\eta)(Y)\eta(Z)X \\ +(Y)(\nabla_W\eta)(Z)X \\ -(\nabla_W\eta)(X)\eta(Z)Y \\ -\eta(X)(\nabla_W\eta)(Z)Y \end{bmatrix}$$

Taking X, Y, Z and W orthogonal to ξ and using (6,) and (7), we have from above

$$(\nabla_W R)(X,Y)Z = \frac{d\tau(W)}{2}[g(Y,Z)X - g(X,Z)Y]$$
$$+\left((4n-1)(f_1-f_3)-\frac{\tau}{2}\right)\begin{bmatrix} -\beta g(Y,Z)g(\varphi W,X)\xi \\ +\beta g(X,Z)g(\varphi W,Y)\xi \end{bmatrix}, \tag{28}$$

From (28) it follows that,

$$\varphi^2(\nabla_W R)(X,Y)Z = \frac{d\tau(W)}{2}[g(Y,Z)X - g(X,Z)Y] \tag{29}$$

This completes the proof of the theorem3.

Corollary 3

A three-dimensional Ricci semi symmetric generalized Sasakian space forms $M(f_1, f_2, f_3)^{2n+1}, (n=1)$ is locally φ –symmetric if and only if the scalar curvature is constant.

THREE-DIMENSINAL GENERALIZED SASAKIAN SPACE FORMS WITH η-PARALLEL RICI TENSOR

Definition 2

The Ricci tensor S of generalized Sasakian space-forms is said to be η-parallel if it satisfies

$$(\nabla_W S)(\varphi X, \varphi Y) = 0.$$

for all vector fields $W, X,$ and Y. The notion of Ricci η-parallelity for Sasakian manifolds was introduced by Kon (1976).

Theorem 4

A three-dimensional generalized Sasakian space forms $M(f_1, f_2, f_3)^{2n+1}, (n=1)$ has η–parallel Ricci tensor. Then the scalar curvature is constant.

Proof 4

From (21) we get by virtue of (2.-c) (3), that

$$S(\varphi X, \varphi Y) = \left[\frac{\tau}{2} + (1-2n)(f_1 - f_3)\right]\{g(X,Y) - \eta(X)\eta(Y)\} \tag{30}$$

Differentiating (30) covariantly along W ,we get

$$(\nabla_W S)(\varphi X, \varphi Y) = \frac{d\tau(W)}{2}[g(X,Y) - \eta(X)\eta(Y)]$$
$$-\left[\frac{\tau}{2} + (1-2n)(f_1-f_3)\right]\begin{Bmatrix} \eta(Y)(\nabla_W\eta)X \\ +\eta(X)(\nabla_W\eta)Y \end{Bmatrix} \tag{31}$$

By using (7) in (31) we get

$$d\tau(W)[g(X,Y) - \eta(X)\eta(Y)] + [\tau + 2(1-2n)(f_1-f_3)]\{\beta g(\varphi W, X) + \beta g(\varphi W, Y)\eta(X)\} = 0 \tag{32}$$

Substituting $X = Y = e_i$ in (32) and taking summation over i, $1 \le i \le 3$, we get

$$d\tau(W) = 0, \text{ for all } Z. \tag{33}$$

This completes the proof of the theorem4.

Corollary 4

A three-dimensional generalized Sasakian space forms $M(f_1, f_2, f_3)^{2n+1}, (n=1)$ with η–parallel Ricci tensor is locally φ–symmetric.

THREE-DIMENSINAL GENERALIZED SASAKIAN SPACE FORMS WITH CYCLIC PARALLEL RICI TENSOR

Gray (1978) introduced two classes of Riemannian manifolds determine by the covariant derivative of the Ricci tensor. The first one is class consisting of all Riemannian manifolds whose Ricci tensor is of Codazzi tensor, that is

$$(\nabla_W S)(X,Y) + (\nabla_X S)(W,Y) = 0$$

The second one is the class of consisting of all Riemannian manifold whose Ricci tensor is cyclic parallel, that is

$$(\nabla_W S)(X,Y)+(\nabla_X S)(Y,W)+(\nabla_Y S)(W,X)=0$$

Theorem 5

A three-dimensional non cosymplectic generalized Sasakian space forms $M(f_1,f_2,f_3)^{2n+1},(n=1)$ with cyclic parallel Ricci tensor is a manifold of constant curvature if and only if function f_1-f_3 is constant.

Proof 5

We suppose that a three-dimensional generalized Sasakian space form satisfies the cyclic Ricci tensor. Then we have

$$(\nabla_W S)(X,Y)+(\nabla_X S)(Y,W)+(\nabla_Y S)(W,X)=0 \quad (34)$$

Taking covariant derivative of (21) along W, we obtain

$$(\nabla_W S)(X,Y)=\frac{d\tau(W)}{2}[g(X,Y)-\eta(X)\eta(Y)]$$
$$+\left[(4n-1)(f_1-f_3)-\frac{\tau}{2}\right][\eta(Y)(\nabla_W\eta)(X) \quad (35)$$
$$+\eta(X)(\nabla_W\eta)(Y)$$

By virtue of (7) and (33) Equation (35) take the form

$$(\nabla_W S)(X,Y)=\left[(4n-1)(f_1-f_3)-\frac{\tau}{2}\right] \quad (36)$$
$$[\beta\eta(Y)g(\varphi W,X)-\beta\eta(X)g(\varphi W,Y)]$$

Taking cyclic permutation of (36) and adding them we get by virtue of (34), we get

$$\left[(4n-1)(f_1-f_3)-\frac{\tau}{2}\right][\beta\eta(Y)g(\varphi W,X)$$
$$-\beta\eta(X)g(\varphi W,Y)$$
$$+\beta\eta(W)g(\varphi X,Y)-\beta\eta(Y)g(\varphi X,W)$$
$$+\beta\eta(W)g(\varphi Y,X)-\beta\eta(X)g(\varphi Y,W)]$$
$$(37)$$

Substituting $Y=W=e_i$ in (37) and taking summation over i, $1\le i\le 3$, we get

$$\tau=2(4n-1)(f_1-f_3) \quad , \quad (38)$$

This completes the proof of the theorem.

Corollary 5

The necessary and sufficient condition for three-dimensional generalized Sasakian space forms $M(f_1,f_2,f_3)^{2n+1},(n=1)$ satisfies cyclic condition if the manifold is cosymplectic.

Corollary 6

A three-dimensional non cosymplectic generalized Sasakian space-forms $M(f_1,f_2,f_3)^{2n+1},(n=1)$ with cyclic is Ricci semi symmetric.

THREE-DIMENSINAL GENERALIZED SASAKIAN SPACE FORMS ADMITTING A NON-NULL $(|V|^2\neq 0)$ CONCIRCULAR VECTOR FIELD

Definition 3

A vector field V in generalized Sasakian space-forms $M(f_1,f_2,f_3)^{2n+1},(n=1)$ is said to be concircular vector field if it satisfies an equation of the form

$$\nabla_X V=\lambda X , \quad (39)$$

For all X ,where λ is a scalar function. In particular if $\lambda=0$, then V is parallel.

Theorem 6

If a three-dimensional generalized Sasakian space-forms $M(f_1,f_2,f_3)^{2n+1},(n=1)$ admit a non- null concircular vector field then the manifold is an Einstein manifold.

Proof 6

Differentiating (39) coraiantly we have

$$\nabla_X\nabla_Y V-\nabla_Y\nabla_X V=d\lambda(X)Y-d\lambda(Y)X , \quad (40)$$

By virtue of Ricci identity we get from (40) that

$$R'(X,Y,V,Z)=d\lambda(X)g(Y,Z)-d\lambda(Y)g(X,Z), \quad (41)$$

where $g(R(X,Y,V)Z)=R'(X,Y,V,Z)$

Replacing $Z=\xi$ and using (2.-b), we get

$$R'(X,Y,V,\xi)=\eta(R(X,Y)V)$$
$$=d\lambda(X)\eta(Y)-d\lambda(Y)\eta(X) \quad (42)$$

Taking inner product of (theorem 1.-iii) with ξ and replacing $Z = V$, we obtain

$$\eta(R(X,Y)V) = [(1-4n)(f_1 - f_3)]\begin{Bmatrix} g(Y,V)\eta(X) \\ -g(X,V)\eta(Y) \end{Bmatrix} \quad (43)$$

From (42) and (43), we get

$$d\lambda(X)\eta(Y) - d\lambda(Y)\eta(X) = [(1-4n)(f_1 - f_3)]\{g(Y,V)\eta(X) - g(X,V)\eta(Y)\} \quad (44)$$

Subsisting $X = \varphi X$ and $Y = \xi$ in (44) and using (2. a, c), we get

$$d\lambda(\varphi X) = -[(1-4n)(f_1 - f_3)]g(\varphi X, V) \quad (45)$$

Again putting $X = \varphi X$ in (45) and using (2.), we obtain

$$-d\lambda(X) + \eta(X)d\lambda(\xi) = [(1-4n)(f_1 - f_3)]\{g(X,V) - \eta(X)\eta(V)\}, \quad (46)$$

Multiplying both sides of (46) by $g(X,V)$, we get

$$-d\lambda(X)g(X,V) + \eta(X)d\lambda(\xi)g(X,V) = [(1-4n)(f_1 - f_3)]\{g(X,V) - \eta(X)\eta(V)\}g(X,V), \quad (47)$$

By virtue of (11) and (41), we have

$$d\lambda(X)g(Y,V) = d\lambda(Y)g(X,V), \quad (48)$$

Multiplying both of (48) by $\eta(X) \neq 0$ for all X and putting $Y = \xi$, we obtain that

$$d\lambda(X)\eta(V)\eta(X) = d\lambda(\xi)g(X,V)\eta(X) \quad (49)$$

By virtue of (46) and (49) we get

(i) $d\lambda(X) = [(1-4n)(f_1 - f_3)]g(X,V)$ (50)
for all X or
(ii) $g(X,V) = \eta(X)\eta(V)$ for all X [contradicts our assumption]

From (41) and (50-i), we have

$$R'(X,Y,V,Z) = [(1-4n)(f_1 - f_3)]\{g(X,V)g(Y,Z) - g(Y,V)g(X,Z)\} \quad (51)$$

Substituting $X = Z = e_i$, $i = 1,2,3$ in (51) and taking summation for i, $1 \le i \le 3$, we get

$$S(Y,V) = [2(1-4n)(f_1 - f_3)]g(Y,V), \quad (52)$$

This completes the proof of the theorem 6.

ACKNOWLEDEMENT

The authors are great thankful to the reviewer Associate Professor Kai-Long Hsiao.

REFERENCES

Alegre P, Blair D, Carriago A (2004). On Generalized Sasakian-space-forms. Israel J. Math., 14: 159-183.
Bagewadi CS, Basavarajappa NS, Prakasha DG, Venkatesha (2007). On 3-dimensional Para-Sasakian manifolds. IeJEMTA, 2: 110-119.
Blair DE (1967). Theory of quasi Sasakian structure. J. Differential. Geom., 1: 331-345.
De UC, Sarkar A (2009).On 3-dimensional quasi-Sasakian manifolds. SUT J. Math., 45(1): 59-71.
De UC, Tripathi MM (2003). Ricci tensor in 3-dimensional Trans-Sasakian manifolds. Kyungpook Math. J., 43: 247-254.
Gray A (1978). Two classes of Riemannian manifolds. Geom, Dedicata, 7: 259-280.
Kon M (1976). Invariance sub manifold in Sasakian manifolds. Math. Ann., 219: 227-290.
Olszak Z (1986). Normal almost contact metric manifold of dimension three. Ann. Polon. Math., 47: 41-50.
Takahashi T (1977). Sasakian ϕ–symmetric Spaces. Tohoku Math. J., 29: 91-113.
Venkatesha, Bagewadi CS (2006). On 3-dimensional trans-Sasakian manifolds. Turk. J. Math., 30: 1-11.
Yieldiz A, Mine T, Bilal EA (2009). On 3-dimensional Lorentzian α – Sasakian manifolds. Bull. Math. Anal. Appl., 1(3): 90-98.

An overview of term rewriting systems

Dasharath Singh[1], Ali Maiangwa Shuaibu[2]* and Adeku Musa Ibrahim[1]

[1]Department of Mathematics, Ahmadu Bello University, Zaria-Nigeria.
[2]Department of Mathematics, Statistics and Computer Science, Kaduna Polytechnic, Kaduna, Nigeria.

It is well-known that termination of finite term of rewriting systems is generally undecidable. Notwithstanding, a remarkable result is that, rewriting systems are *Turing complete.* A number of methods have been developed to establish termination for certain term of rewriting systems, particularly occurring in practical situations. In this paper, we present an overview of the existing methods used for termination proofs. We also outline areas of applications of term rewriting systems along with recent developments in regard to automated termination proofs.

Key words: Confluence, rewriting, term, termination, turing complete.

INTRODUCTION

Rewriting is a very powerful method for dealing computationally with equations. However, applying effectively this approach is in general not straightforward. Alternatively, oriented equations, called rewrite rules, are used to replace equals by equals, but only in one direction. A rewrite system is a set of rules used to compute, by repeatedly replacing parts of a given formula with equal ones until the simplest possible form, called normal form, is obtained. For instance, an equation $2+3=5$ can be interpreted as "5 is the result of computing $2+3$", but not vice versa. This directional replacement is expressed by $2+3 \longrightarrow 5$ which reads "$2+3$ reduces to 5".

This computational aspect of equations naturally leads to term rewriting systems (TRSs, for short). Depending on the kinds of objects that are rewritten, there are different kinds of rewrite systems such as string rewrite (Thue or semi-Thue) systems, TRSs and graph rewriting to mention a few (Baader and Nipkow, 1998; Terese, 2003; Dershowitz, 2005).

The formal study of rewriting and its properties began in 1910 with a paper by Axel Thue (Book, 1987). Significantly, most early models of computation were based on notions of rewriting strings or terms. The emergence of Thue systems; Alonzo Church's lambda Calculus; Andrei Markov's normal algorithms, just to mention a few, led to sustained study of rewriting in the context of programming language semantics (Book, 1987). To be more specific, the study of TRSs originated in combinatory logic (CL) and lambda calculus (Curry and Feys, 1958) developed and deeply analyzed half a century ago to investigate the foundation of functions. CL is actually a TRS. One could say that the paradigmatic example of a TRS is the system of CL. As a matter of fact, the roots of the very notion of term rewriting and much of its theory can be found in the system of CL.

In the recent years, a strong impulse for the study of TRSs (including extensions of the usual rewriting format) is given by the design of functional languages such as Miranda (Terese, 2003). Another strong impulse is given by efforts of many researchers to combine logic programming with functional programming (Toyama, 1990; Marché and Zantema, 2007). In this direction, Toyama (1990) proposed and applied Knuth-Bendix completion algorithm for a better performance. The compiling technique proposed in this algorithm is dynamic in the sense that, rewriting rules are repeatedly compiled in the completion process. The execution time of the completion with dynamic compiling is ten or more times faster than the one obtained with a traditional TRS interpreter.

Two of the most central properties of TRSs are

*Corresponding author. E-mail: shuaibuali16@gmail.com.

confluence (the Church-Rosser property) and termination (strong normalization). A confluent and terminating system is called convergent (or complete or canonical) and it defines exactly one normal form for each input term.

Termination proofs play a fundamental role in many applications and the challenges in this area are both practical and theoretical (Marché and Zantema, 2007). From a practical point of view, proving termination is vital issue in software development and formal methods for termination analysis are essential for program verification. From a theoretical point of view, termination is closely connected to mathematical logic and ordinal theory.

The central aspect of attaining the aforesaid goals lies in showing that there is no infinite sequence $u_1, u_2, u_3, \ldots$ such that for all i, u_{i+1} can be obtained from u_i by a replacement using a term rewriting rule. This process is called termination.

Termination, in general, is an undecidable property of TRSs (Terese, 2003). Nevertheless, TRSs possess a very significant property that they are Turing complete; that is, every computable process can be delineated by a rewriting system. Thus, all endeavours made in this regard are intended to discover competing methods that quasi-generally work in cases of practical interest. Most of such methods in vogue are based on well-founded orderings.

Summarily, a TRS is a binary relation over the set of terms of a given signature (or alphabet). The pairs of the relation are used for computing by replacements until an irreducible term is eventually reached. This is how the absence of infinite sequences of replacements grants termination. A TRS is terminating if all rewrite sequences are finite. Rules of a terminating system are called reduction or rewrite rules.

Before we endeavour to present an overview of the researches undertaken in this area, we briefly make clear some elementary illustrations, the notion of a rewrite rule and its action.

Example 1

Consider the following rewrite rules:

R_1: $A(x, S(y)) \longrightarrow S(A(x, y))$,

R_2: $A(x, 0) \longrightarrow x$.

To simplify $A\left(0, S(A(S(0), 0))\right)$, we have

$$A\left(0, S(A(S(0),0))\right) \longrightarrow S\left(A(0, A(S(0),0))\right)$$

$$\longrightarrow S\left(A(0, S(0))\right)$$

$$\longrightarrow S\left(S(A(0,0))\right)$$

$$\longrightarrow S(S(0)).$$

This is terminating. Note that the first rule makes $'S$ move upwards while the second rule makes terms smaller.

Example 2

Using the rewrite rule $f(g(x)) \longrightarrow g(f(x))$, we have

$$f(f\left(g\left(f(g(x))\right)\right)) \longrightarrow f(f\left(g\left(g(f(x))\right)\right))$$

$$\longrightarrow f(g\left(f\left(g(f(x))\right)\right))$$

$$\longrightarrow g(f\left(f\left(g(f(x))\right)\right))$$

$$\longrightarrow g(f\left(g\left(f(f(x))\right)\right))$$

$$\longrightarrow g(g\left(f\left(f(f(x))\right)\right)).$$

The fs moves to the right while the gs moves to the left.

Example 3

$$f(g(x)) \longrightarrow g(g\left(f(f(x))\right))$$

looks terminating with the fs moving to the right and the gs to the left. But it gives rise to an infinite rewrite sequence:

$$f(g(g(x)) \longrightarrow g(g\left(f\left(f(g(x))\right)\right))$$

$$\longrightarrow g(g\left(f\left(g\left(g\left(f(f(x))\right)\right)\right)\right)) \longrightarrow \ldots$$

Remark

We reemphasize that the termination of such derivations is crucial using rewriting in proofs and computations. The difficulty in proving the termination of a system, such as those in the previous examples, stems from the fact that while some rules may decrease the size of a term, other rules may increase its size and duplicate occurrences of subterms. If $x \longrightarrow y$ is a reduction then y is somehow simpler or smaller than x. If it is generative then y is generally more complex or larger than x. Any proof of termination must take into consideration the different possible rewrite sequences generated by the nondeterministic choice of rules.

AN OUTLINE OF TERM REWRITING SYSTEMS

As mentioned earlier, one major property which a TRS needs to satisfy is termination. Generally, termination or halting computing processes explicitly uses dominance orderings in addressing problems relating to termination proofs in theoretical computer science. This aspect of termination started receiving attention in the 1970s. Knuth (1973) applied dominance ordering for demonstrating termination of a sorting algorithm.

Methods of termination

Several methods for proving termination of TRSs have been developed. Most of these methods are based on reduction orderings which are well-founded, compatible with the structure of terms and stable with respect to substitutions. Examples of these methods include, Knuth-Bendix order, polynomial interpretations, multiset order, lexicographic path order, recursive decomposition order, multiset path order, semantic path order, transformation order, forward closures, semantic interpretations, dummy elimination and distribution elimination (Dershowitz, 1987; Hirokawa, 2006; Marché and Zantema, 2007). Proving termination using one of these particular methods, in general, proves more than just the absence of infinite derivation sequences. It turns out that such a proof in many cases implies an upper bound on derivation height, expressed as the function Dh_R on terms (Hofbauer and Lautemann, 1989). Thus, the rate of growth of Dh_R can be used for measuring the strength of termination proof methods.

The use of rewrite systems as termination functions and the formulation of abstract monotonicity conditions are explored in (Bachmair and Dershowitz, 1986). Gorn (1973) uses a stepped lexicographic ordering (under which longer sequences are larger) to prove termination of differentiation. Exponential interpretation method of termination is exploited in (Iturriaga, 1967). The cases where Iturriaga's method works are those which the operators are partially ordered so that the outermost (virtual) operators of the left-hand side of the rules are greater than any other operators.

Singh and Singh (2009) outline an alternative proof of the well-foundedness of the nested multiset ordering. It is shown that the set of nested multisets over a given set forms a cumulative type structure. Also, by exploiting the notion of sets bounded in rank, a necessary and sufficient condition for the well-foundedness of the nested multiset ordering is outlined.

Knuth and Bendix (1970) devised a recursive ordering that combines the notion of precedence with a simple linear weight. The weight is the sum of the weights of all the symbols which are non-negative integers. Furthermore, they point out that their method is applicable to handle duplicating systems (one that has more occurrences of a variable on the right than on the left). Lankford (1979) however suggests a way of extending the method of Knuth and Bendix by using integer polynomial weights (with positive coefficients to guarantee that terms are greater than subterms).

The recursive path ordering (RPO) is shown to be a quasi well-ordering in case of a finite signature and hence well-founded (Toyama, 1990; Dershowitz, 1987). Moreover, it is known to be well-founded for infinite signature and also in the case of the precedence relation, is well-ordering. The RPO has also been adapted to handle associative-commutative operators by flattening and transforming terms (distributing large operators over small ones) before comparing them. The difficulty encountered is that of ensuring monotonicity, since flattening alone may not ensure monotonicity (Bachmair and Dershowitz, 1986; Dershowitz, 1987).

In the work of Bergstra and Klop (1985), an alternative definition of RPO was put forward and proved to be an iterative path order (IPO). The exact relationship between the recursive and iterative approaches to path orders was investigated. It was shown that both approaches coincide in the case of transitive relations (orders). Klop et al. (2006) employed a proof technique due to Buchholz (1995), provides a direct proof of termination for the IPO starting from an arbitrary terminating relation on the signature. Both the proofs essentially rely on a natural number labeled variant ℓex^{ω} of the auxiliary TRS ℓex.

Jouannaud et al. (1982) use the recursive decomposition ordering to prove termination by comparing two terms and the comparison may only stop where two decompositions have incomparable symbols as their first components. The path of subterms ordering is explicitly considered in Dershowitz (1987) to extend the RPO. Also, semantic path ordering (SPO) of Kamin and Lévy (1980) is used to prove termination where terms are compared lexicographically. Furthermore, it was shown that the use of SPO in a termination proof necessarily requires the monotonicity condition to hold.

Another approach, called simple path ordering, defined on multisets for proving termination of differentiation was devised by Plaisted (1983). Here, terms are mapped into multisets of sequences of function symbols: $[\![t]\!] = \{\text{paths in } t\}$, where a path is a sequence of operators, beginning with the outermost one of the whole terms and taking subterms until a constant is reached.

The use of monotonic polynomial interpretations for termination proofs was suggested by Bachmair and Dershowitz (1986) and Dershowitz (1987). Using this method, an integer polynomial of degree n is associated with each n-ary operator f. The choice of coefficients must ensure monotonicity and that the terms are mapped into nonnegative integers only. This is the case if all coefficients are positive. Zantema (1992) provides a classification of termination of TRSs based on types of orderings. The strongest type of termination he considers was polynomial termination. Polynomial terminations are those that can be proved by a polynomial interpretation (PI). Also, Zantema considers the equivalence relation on terms generated by permuting arguments of operation symbols of multiset status. The main difficulty with proving termination using PI technique is that, polynomial terminating TRSs are double-exponentially bounded in the size of the initial term (Hofbauer and Lautemann, 1989).

Toyama (1990) develops a simple method for proving the equivalence of two given TRSs without the explicit use of induction, and demonstrates that the method can be effectively applied to deriving a new TRS from a given one by using equivalence transformation rules. Cropper and Martin (2001) provide a classification of polynomial orderings on monadic terms where they investigate polynomial orderings which are reduction orderings on term algebras determined by the polynomial interpretations of the function symbols. Such orderings offer an apparent flexibility in allowing the choice of polynomials with arbitrarily high degree and large number of coefficients. It also provides the opportunity to use well-understood decision procedures for real arithmetic to verify the polynomial inequalities needed to prove termination.

In automation, we often encounter large search spaces for parameters required by termination criteria and there is a natural trade-off between power and efficiency. In order to optimize the said trade-off, developing efficient search techniques is of cardinal importance. In this regard, increasing emphasis has shifted towards transformation methods like the dependency pair method or semantic labeling. These techniques have significantly increased the possibility of proving termination automatically. Arts and Giesl (2000) while elaborating on termination of TRSs, demonstrate that the application of dependency pairs does exclude dependency inequalities for the right-hand subterms, which also appear on the left. Hirokawa (2006) develops automated termination methods based on the dependency pair technique. These methods are intended to make termination tools more powerful and efficient. Avanzini and Moser (2010) develop techniques to automatically classify the complexity of TRSs and introduce polynomial path orders (POP^*, for short) and its *extensions*. POP^* is a syntactic restriction of the multiset path order on terms, and whenever compatibility of a TRS $\mathcal{R}$ with POP^* can be established, the innermost runtime complexity of $\mathcal{R}$ is polynomially bounded. The runtime complexity of a TRS is a measure of the maximal number of rewrite steps as a function of the size of the initial term, where the initial (or basic) terms are restricted argument normalized terms.

The construction of a PI and the embedding of the rewrite relation into the multiset path order (MPO) or the lexicographic path order (LPO) or the Knuth-Bendix path order (KBO) are among the most prominent methods for proving termination of a (finite) TRS. A termination proof for a TRS using one of these methods is essential for obtaining an upper bound on the derivation length function. This function by mapping a natural number n to the length of a longest derivation, starting with a term of size bounded by n, provides a natural measure for the strength of a termination proof method. Lepper (2001) lists bounds for these methods along with some restrictions pertaining to PI and KBO in a chronological order.

Complexity characterizations for TRSs have been studied by some researchers (Hofbauer, 1992 and Weiermann, 1995). It was shown in Hofbauer (1992) that termination proofs using MPOs imply primitive recursive derivation lengths; and in Weiermann (1995) work that termination proofs using LPOs imply multiply recursive derivation lengths.

In view of the fact that termination of all derivations initiated by a given term is undecidable and termination for all terms is not even partially decidable, all one can hope for, is to develop competing computing termination tools.

The inherent lack of direction in TRSs, computation of a logic program involving TRSs, virtually entails that any non-trivial program would terminate only for certain classes of inputs. Thus, termination analysis in logic programming turns out to be of utmost significance. In recent years, the subject has been widely studied and significant advances have been made. Currently, there exist a number of fully-automated tools to prove termination of a given logic program with respect to a given class of inputs (Hirokawa, 2006). MPO and LPO have been implemented in *REVE* and *RRL* (Dershowitz, 1987). *REVE* and *RRL* are preferred automated termination provers for TRSs in vogue. There are also a number of other tools that has attempt proving termination automatically. These include, *AProVE, Cariboo, CiME, Jambox, Termptation, NTI, Torpa, Matchbox, Mu Term, TPA, T_TT, VMTL* etc. (Marché and Zantema, 2007, for details).

CONCLUSIONS

TRSs are closely related to theorem proving and declarative programs. Termination of a TRS is a desired property proposed to ensure that all computation paths end. The current direction of research is largely towards automation of termination analysis for TRSs. These automated methods are intended to develop competitive termination tools.

The increasing interest in automated termination analysis of TRSs has led to an annual International Competition of Termination Tools initiated in 2004 (Marché and Zantema, 2007). It aims at identifying most talented competitors who could obtain an assigned task by applying appropriate choices of termination proving techniques within a time limit of 60 s.

REFERENCES

Arts T, Giesl J (2000).Termination of term rewriting using dependency pairs. Theor. Comp. Sci. 236:133-178.

Avanzini M, Moser G (2010).Complexity Analysis by Graph Rewriting Revisited. Institute of Computer science, University of Innsbruck, Austria, Technical Report.

Baader F, Nipkow T (1998). Term Rewriting and All That. Cambridge University Press. pp. 61-132.

Bachmair L, Dershowitz N (1986). Communication, transformation and termination. 8th CADE, LNCS 230, J. org. H. Siekmann (ed.), Springer-Verlag. pp. 5-10.

Bergstra J, Klop J (1985). Algebra for communicating process. TCS 37(1):171-199.

Book RV (1987). Thue systems as rewriting systems. J. Symbolic Computat. 3 (1&2):39-68

Buchholz W (1995). Proof-theoretic analysis of termination proofs. APAL 75(1-2):57-65.

Cropper N, Martin U (2001). The classification of Polynomial Orderings on Monadic terms. Applicable Algebra in Engineering communication Comp. 12(3):197-226.

Curry HB, Feys R (1958). Combinatory Logic, Vol.1, North- Holland.

Dershowitz N (1987). Termination of Rewriting. J. Symbolic Comput. 3(1&2):69-115.

Dershowitz N (2005). Open. Closed. Open: Proceedings of Conference on Rewriting Techniques and Applications (RTA). pp. 376 - 393.

Gorn S (1973). On the conclusive validation of symbol manipulation processes (How do you know it has to work?). J. Franklin Institute 296:6.

Hofbauer D, Lautemann C (1989). Termination proofs and the length of derivations: proceedings of the 3rd International Conference on Rewriting Techniques and Applications.LNCS 355. Springer Verlag. pp. 167 - 177.

Hirokawa N (2006). Automated Termination Analysis for Term Rewriting. Dissertation, Faculty of mathematics, computer science and physics, University of Innsbruck.

Hofbauer D (1992). Termination Proofs with Multiset Path Orderings imply Primitive Recursive Derivation Lengths. Theor. Comp. Sci. 105(1):129-140.

Iturriaga R (1967). Contributions to Mechanical Mathematics. Ph.D. Thesis, Department of mathematics, Carnegie - Mellon University, Pittsburgh, Pennsylvania.

Jouannaud JP, Lescanne P, Reinig F (1982).On Multiset Orderings. Information Processing Letters. 15:57 - 63.

Kamin S, Levy JJ (1980). Two Generalizations of the Recursive Path Ordering. Unpublished note, Department of Computer Science, University of Illinois, Urbana, IL.

Klop JW, Van Oostrom V, de Vrijer R (2006). Iterative Lexicographic Path Orders. LNCS 4060, Kafutatsugi et al (eds.), Amsterdam. pp. 541 – 554.

Knuth DE, Bendix PB (1970). Simple Word Problems in Universal Algebras, in Computational Problems in Abstract Algebra, J. Leech (ed.), Pergamon Press.

Knuth DE (1973). The Art of Computer Programming: Fundamental Algorithms, Addison-Wesley 2:2.

Lankford DS (1979). On Proving Term Rewriting Systems are Noetherian. Memo MTP-3, Mathematics Department, Louisiana Tech. University, U.S .A.

Lepper I (2001). Simplification Orders in Term Rewriting: Derivation Lengths, Order Types and Computability, Inaugural-Dissertation universität Münster, Germany.

Marché C, Zantema H (2007). The Termination Competition. Franz Baader (ed.): Proceedings of the 18th International Conference on Rewriting Techniques and Applications, LNCS 4533, Springer Verlag. pp. 303-313.

Plaisted DA (1983). An Associative Path Ordering. Proceedings of NSF Workshop on Rewrite Rule Laboratory, U.S.A. pp. 123-136.

Singh D, Singh JN (2009). An alternative proof of the well-foundedness of the nested multiset ordering. Int. Math. Forum 4(8):359-362.

TERESE (2003). Term Rewriting Systems. Marc Bezem *et al.* (eds.), Vol.55 of Cambridge Tracts in Theoretical Computer Science, Cambridge University Press.

Toyama Y (1990). Term rewriting and the Church-Rosser property. Ph.D Dissertation, Tohoku University.

Weiermann A (1995). Termination proofs for TRS with LPO imply multiply recursive derivation lengths. TCS 139:355-362.

Zantema H (1992). Termination of Term Rewriting by Interpretation. RUU-CS 9214, Department of Computer Science, Utrecht University, Netherlands.

Egoists dilemma with fuzzy data

Sahand Daneshvar[1], Mozhgan Mansouri Kaleibar[2] and Mojtaba Ramezani[3]*

[1]Islamic Azad University, Tabriz Branch, Tabriz, Iran.
[2]Young Researchers Club, Islamic Azad University, Tabriz Branch, Tabriz, Iran.
[3]Islamic Azad University, Bonab Branch, Bonab, Iran.

In this paper, we investigate the problems of consensus–making among individuals or organizations with multiple criteria for evaluating performance when the players are supposed to be egoistic and the score for each criterion for a player is supposed to be fuzzy number. We deal with problems with fuzzy parameters from the viewpoint of experts' imprecise or fuzzy understanding of the nature of parameters in a problem- formulation process. Egoistic means that each player sticks to his/her superiority regarding the criteria. The concept that is developed in optimization leads the problem to a dilemma called 'egoists dilemma'. We examine this dilemma using cooperative fuzzy game theory and propose a solution. The scheme developed in this paper can also be applied to attaining fair cost allocations as well as benefit-cost distributions for fuzzy data.

Keywords: Data envelopment analysis (DEA), fuzzy game, fuzzy linear programming game, game theory.

INTRODUCTION

Consider *n* players each have *m* criteria for evaluating their competency or ability, which is represented by a fuzzy score for each criterion. As with usual classroom examination, the higher score for a criterion is, the better player is judged to perform that criterion. In this paper we formulate a fuzzy cooperative game arising from a linear programming problem with fuzzy parameters (Nishizaki and Sakawa 2000). For example, let the players be three students A, B and C, with three criteria, linear algebra, real analysis and numerical analysis. The scores are their records for the three subjects, are fuzzy parameters. All players are supposed to be selfish in the sense that they insist on their own advantage on the scores. However, they must reach a consensus in order to get the fellowship. Similar situations exist in many societal problems. This paper uses the deterministic situation in order to propose a new scheme for allocating or imputing the given fuzzy benefit under the framework of optimization and fuzzy game. This paper is organized as follows. Firstly, the basic models are described and some properties of problem are proved. Next is a discussion of extensions to the basic model and introduction of coalitions. This is then followed by a numerical presentation of game; Finally, conclusions and some remarks are given.

BASIC MODELS OF THE GAME

We introduce the basic models and structures of the game based on Nakabayashi and Tone (2006) and Jahanshahloo et al. (2006).

Selfish behavior and the egoists dilemma

Let $X = (\tilde{x}_{ij}) = (L_{ij}, x_{ij}, U_{ij})$ be the score fuzzy matrix, consisting of the record $(\tilde{x}_{ij}) = (L_{ij}, x_{ij}, U_{ij})$ of player *j* to the criterion *i* for $i = 1,...,m$ and $j = 1,...,n$. It is assumed that the higher score for a criterion is, the better player is judged to perform as regard to that criterion. Each person *k* has a right to choose a set of nonnegative weights $w^k = (w_1^k,...,w_m^k)$ to the criteria that are most preferable to the player. Using the weight w^k, the relative scores of player *k* to the total score are defined as follows:

*Corresponding author. E-mail: mojtaba.ramezani.53@gmail.com.

$$\frac{\sum_{i=1}^{m} w_i^k \tilde{x}_{ik}}{\sum_{i=1}^{m} w_i^k (\sum_{j=1}^{n} \tilde{x}_{ij})} \quad (1)$$

Thus using the Charnes-cooper transformation scheme by Charnes (1978), and fuzzy game in Nishizaki (2000) this situation can be expressed using a fuzzy linear program as follows:

$$\begin{aligned} \tilde{c}(k) &= Max \sum_{i=1}^{m} w_i^k \tilde{x}_{ik} \\ s.t \quad & \sum_{i=1}^{m} w_i^k = 1 \\ & w_i^k \geq 0 \ (\forall i) \end{aligned} \quad (2)$$

Where $\tilde{x}_{ik}$ is triangular fuzzy number, in this paper, we employ a parametric approach to solving the linear programming problem with fuzzy parameters in order to construct the values of coalitions in Nishizaki (2000).

First we introduce the α-level of the fuzzy number $\tilde{x}_{ik}$ defined as the set $(\tilde{x}_{ik})_\alpha$ in which the degree of their membership functions exceeds the level α:

$$(\tilde{x}_{ik})_\alpha = \{(x_{ik}) \ \mu_{\tilde{x}_{ik}}(x_{ik}) \geq \alpha, \ k = 1,...,n \ , i = 1,...,m\} \quad (3)$$

Now suppose that all players consider that the degree of all the membership functions of the fuzzy number involved in the linear programming problem should be greater than or equal to a certain degree α. Then, for such a degree α, the problem can be interpreted as the following non-fuzzy linear programming problem which depends on a coefficient vector (Sakawa, 1993).

$$\begin{aligned} c(k) &= Max \sum_{i=1}^{m} w_i^k x_{ik} \\ s.t \quad & \sum_{i=1}^{m} w_i^k = 1 \\ & w_i^k \geq 0 \ (\forall i) \end{aligned} \quad (4)$$

Observe that there exists an infinite number of such a problem (4) depending on the coefficient vector $(x_{ik}) \in (\tilde{x}_{ik})_\alpha$ and the value of (x_{ik}) is arbitrary for any $(x_{ik}) \in (\tilde{x}_{ik})_\alpha$ in the sense that the degree of all the membership functions for the fuzzy number in the problem (4) exceeds the level α.

However, if the players think that the problem should be solved by taking an optimistic view, the coefficient vector $(x_{ik}) \in (\tilde{x}_{ik})_\alpha$ in the problem (4) would be chosen so as to maximize the objective functions under the constraints.

From such a point of view, for a certain degree α, it seems to be quite natural to have understood the linear programming problem with fuzzy parameters as the following nonfuzzy α-linear programming problem:

$$\begin{aligned} c(k) &= \underset{w,x}{Max} \sum_{i=1}^{m} w_i^k x_{ik} \\ s.t \quad & \sum_{i=1}^{m} w_i^k = 1 \\ & w_i^k \geq 0 \ (\forall i) \\ & (x_{ik}) \in (\tilde{x}_{ik})_\alpha \end{aligned} \quad (5)$$

It should be noted that the coefficient vector (x_{ik}) is treated as decision variables rather than constants. Therefore, the problem (5) is not a linear programming problem. However, from the properties of the α-level set for the vectors of fuzzy number $\tilde{x}$ it follows that the feasible regions for $\tilde{x}$ can be denoted respectively by the closed interval $[x^L, x^R]$. Thus, we can obtain an optimal solution to the problem (5) by solving the following linear programming problem (Sakawa, 1993):

$$\begin{aligned} & \underset{w,x}{Max} \sum_{i=1}^{m} w_i^k x_{ik}^R \\ s.t \quad & \sum_{i=1}^{m} w_i^k = 1 \\ & w_i^k \geq 0 \ (\forall i) \end{aligned} \quad (6)$$

Conversely the players may think that the problem should be solved by taking a pessimistic view. Then taking opposite extreme points of the closed interval $[x^L, x^R]$, we can formulate the following problem which yields a value of the objective function smaller than that the problem (6):

$$\begin{aligned} & \underset{w,x}{Max} \sum_{i=1}^{m} w_i^k x_{ik}^L \\ s.t \quad & \sum_{i=1}^{m} w_i^k = 1 \\ & w_i^k \geq 0 \ (\forall i) \end{aligned} \quad 7)$$

Let $(w_1^{\alpha kL},...,w_m^{\alpha kL})$ and $(w_1^{\alpha kR},...,w_m^{\alpha kR})$ denote optimal solution to the problem (7) and (6), respectively for given α. Let

$$c_\alpha^L(k) \cup \sum_{i=1}^{m} w_i^L x_i^{\alpha SL} \quad (8)$$

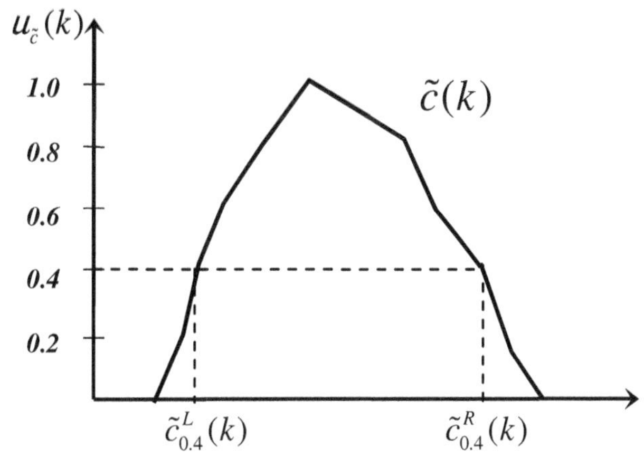

Fig ure 1. The fuzzy value of the player *k*.

$$c^R_\alpha(k) \cup \sum_{i=1}^{m} w_i^R x_i^{\alpha SR} \quad (9)$$

By shifting a parameter $\alpha \in [0,1]$ successively, that is, $\alpha_1 = 0, \alpha_2, ..., \alpha_k = 1$ and connecting points $(c^L_{\alpha_0}(k), \alpha_0), ..., (c^L_{\alpha_k}(k), \alpha_k), (c^R_{\alpha_k}(k), \alpha_k), ..., (c^R_{\alpha_0}(k), \alpha_0)$, we can construct the fuzzy value $\tilde{c}(k)$ of the game expressed by the fuzzy number as depicted in Figure 1 .

By solving the problems (7) and (6) for all k, all the fuzzy numbers $\tilde{c}(k)$ are constructed.

After solving this problems, if the optimal value of this problem is $\tilde{c}(k)$, the problem is to maximize the objective 2 on the simplex $\sum_{i=1}^{m} w_i^k = 1$. Apparently, the optimal solution is given by assigning 1 to $w^k_{i(k)}$ for the criterion *i*(*k*) such that $\tilde{x}_{i(k)} = Max\{\tilde{x}_{ik} | i = 1, ..., m\}$ and assigning 0 to the weight of remaining criteria. We denote this optimal value by $\tilde{c}(k)$.

$$\tilde{c}(k) = \tilde{x}_{ik} \quad k = 1, ..., n \quad (10)$$

The $\tilde{c}(k)$ indicates the highest relative fuzzy score for player *k* which is obtained by the optimal weight selecting behavior. The optimal weight $w^k_{i(k)}$ may differ from one player to another.

Theorem 1

$$\sum_{k=1}^{n} \tilde{c}(k) \geq 1 \quad (11)$$

Proof

Let the optimal weight for player *k* be $w_k^* = (w_{1k}^* ..., w_{mk}^*), w_{i(k)k}^* = 1$ and $w_{ik}^* = 0 \, (\forall i \neq i(k))$ .Then we have

$$\sum_{k=1}^{n} \tilde{c}(k) = \sum_{k=1}^{n}\sum_{i=1}^{m} w_{ik}^* \tilde{x}_{ik} = \sum_{i=1}^{n} \tilde{x}_{i(k)k} \geq \sum_{k=1}^{n} \tilde{x}_{1k} = 1$$

The inequality above follows from $\tilde{x}_{i(k)k} \geq \tilde{x}_{1k}$ and the last equality follows from the row –wise normalization. This theorem assert that , if each player sticks to his egoistic sense of value and insists on getting the portion of the benefit as designated by $\tilde{c}(k)$, the sum of shares usually exceeds 1 and hence $\tilde{c}(k)$ cannot fulfill the role of division of the benefit. If eventually the sum of $\tilde{c}(k)$ turns out to be 1, all players will agree to accept the division $\tilde{c}(k)$, since this is obtained by the players most preferable weight selection. The latter case will occur when all players have the same and common optimal weight selection, we have the following theorem.

Theorem 2

The equality $\sum_{k=1}^{n} \tilde{c}(k) = 1$ holds if and only if our data satisfies the condition $\tilde{x}_{1k} = \tilde{x}_{2k} = ... = \tilde{x}_{mk}$, $\forall k = 1, ..., n$. That is, each player has the same score with respect to the *m* criteria.

Proof

The (if) part can be seen as follows. Since $\tilde{c}(k) = \tilde{x}_{1k}$ for all *k* , we have:

$$\sum_{k=1}^{n}\tilde{c}(k)=\sum_{k=1}^{n}\tilde{x}_{1k}=1$$

The (only if) part can be proved as follows. Suppose $\tilde{x}_{11}>\tilde{x}_{21}$ then there must be column $h\neq 1$ such that $\tilde{x}_{1h}<\tilde{x}_{2h}$, otherwise the second row sum cannot attain 1. Thus we have $\tilde{c}(1)\geq\tilde{x}_{11}$, $\tilde{c}(h)\geq\tilde{x}_{2h}>\tilde{x}_{1h}$ and $\tilde{c}(j)\geq\tilde{x}_{1j}$ $(\forall j\neq 1,h)$. Hence it holds that

$$\sum_{k=1}^{n}\tilde{c}(k)\geq\sum_{j=1,\neq h}^{n}\tilde{x}_{1j}+\tilde{x}_{2h}>\sum_{j=1}^{n}\tilde{x}_{1j}=1$$

This leads to a contradiction. Therefore player1 must have the same score in all criteria. The same relation must hold for the other players.

In the above case, only one criterion is needed for describing the game and the division proportional to this score is a fair division. However, such situation might occur only in rare instances. In the majority of cases, we have

$$\sum_{k=1}^{n}\tilde{c}(k)\geq 1.$$

Coalition with additive property

Let the coalition S be a subset of player set $N=(1,\ldots,n)$. The record for coalition *S* is defined by

$$\tilde{x}_i(S)=\sum_{j\in S}\tilde{x}_{ij}\quad (i=1,\ldots,m \tag{12}$$

These coalitions aim to maximize the outcomes $\tilde{c}(S)$.

$$\tilde{c}(S)=Max\sum_{i=1}^{m}w_i\tilde{x}_i(S)$$
$$s.t\ \sum_{i=1}^{m}w_i=1$$
$$w_i\geq 0\,\forall i \tag{13}$$

Where $\tilde{x}_{ik}$ is triangular fuzzy number, similary we can transform this program to the follow nonfuzzy program:

$$\underset{w,x}{Max}\sum_{i=1}^{m}w_i^k x_i^R(S$$
$$s.t\quad \sum_{i=1}^{m}w_i^k=1$$
$$w_i^k\geq 0\ (\forall i) \tag{14}$$

$$\underset{w,x}{Max}\sum_{i=1}^{m}w_i^k x_i^L(S)$$
$$s.t\quad \sum_{i=1}^{m}w_i^k=1$$
$$w_i^k\geq 0\ (\forall i) \tag{15}$$

Let $(w_1^{\alpha SL},\ldots,w_m^{\alpha SL})$ and $(w_1^{\alpha SL},\ldots,w_m^{\alpha SR})$ denote optimal solution to the problem (14) and (15), respectively for given α. Let

$$c_\alpha^L(S)\bigcup\sum_{i=1}^{m}w_i^L x_i^{\alpha SL}(S) \tag{16}$$

$$c_\alpha^R(S)\bigcup\sum_{i=1}^{m}w_i^R x_i^{\alpha SR}(S) \tag{17}$$

We can construct the fuzzy value $\tilde{c}(S)$ of the game similar to the fuzzy number as depicted in Figure 1. The $\tilde{c}(S)$ with $\tilde{c}(\varphi)=0$, defines a characteristic function of the coalition S. Thus this game is represented by (*N,c*).

Definition 1

A function f is called sub – additive if for any $S\subset N$ and $T\subset N$ with $S\bigcap T=\phi$ the following statement holds:

$f(S\bigcup T)\leq f(S)+f(T)$.

Definition 2

A function f called super – additive if for any $S\subset N$ and $T\subset N$ With $S\bigcap T=\phi$ the following statement holds:

$f(S\bigcup T)\geq f(S)+f(T)$.

Theorem 3

The characteristic function c is sub – additive, for any $S\subset N$ and $T\subset N$ with $S\bigcap T=\phi$ we have

$$\tilde{c}(S\bigcap T)\leq\tilde{c}(S)+\tilde{c}(T) \tag{18}$$

Proof

By renumbering the indexes, we can assume that $S=\{1,\ldots,h\},T=\{h+1,\ldots,k\}$ and $S\bigcup T=\{1,\ldots,k\}$. For these sets, it holds that

$$\tilde{c}(S \cup T) = \underset{i}{Max} \sum_{j=1}^{k} \tilde{x}_{ij} \le \underset{i}{Max} \sum_{j=1}^{h} \tilde{x}_{ij} + \underset{i}{Max} \sum_{j=h+1}^{k} \tilde{x}_{ij}$$
$$= \tilde{c}(S) + \tilde{c}(T) \quad .$$

Theorem 4

$\tilde{c}(N) = 1$.

Proof

$$\tilde{c}(N) = \sum_{i=1}^{m} w_i \sum_{j=1}^{n} \tilde{x}_{ij} = \sum_{i=1}^{m} w_i = 1 \ .$$

DEA minimum game

The opposite side of the game can be constructed by (*N,d*) as follows :

$$\begin{aligned} \tilde{d}(k) = Min \sum_{i=1}^{m} w_i^k \tilde{x}_{ik} \\ s.t \ \sum_{i=1}^{m} w_i^k = 1 \\ w_i^k \ge 0 \quad \forall i \end{aligned} \qquad (19)$$

Similar, program (2) we have:

$$\begin{aligned} \underset{w,x}{Min} \sum_{i=1}^{m} w_i^k x_{ik}^R \\ s.t \quad \sum_{i=1}^{m} w_i^k = 1 \\ w_i^k \ge 0 \ (\forall i) \end{aligned} \qquad (20)$$

$$\begin{aligned} \underset{w,x}{Min} \sum_{i=1}^{m} w_i^k x_{ik}^L \\ s.t \quad \sum_{i=1}^{m} w_i^k = 1 \\ w_i^k \ge 0 \ (\forall i) \end{aligned} \qquad (21)$$

Let $(w_1^{\alpha kL},...,w_m^{\alpha kL})$ and $(w_1^{\alpha kR},...,w_m^{\alpha kR})$ denote optimal solution to the problem (20) and (21), respectively for given α . Let

$$d_\alpha^L(k) \cup \sum_{i=1}^{m} w_i^L x_i^{\alpha kL} \qquad (22)$$

$$d_\alpha^R(k) \cup \sum_{i=1}^{m} w_i^R x_i^{\alpha kR} \qquad (23)$$

The $\tilde{d}(k)$ constructed similar to the fuzzy number as depicted in Figure 1. The optimal value $\tilde{d}(k)$ assures the minimum division that player *k* can expect from the game.

Theorem 5

$$\sum_{k=1}^{n} \tilde{d}(k) \le 1 \qquad (24)$$

Analogously to the max game, for the coalition $S \subset N$, we define

$$\begin{aligned} \tilde{d}(S) = Min \sum_{i=1}^{m} w_i \tilde{x}_i(S) \\ s.t \ \sum_{i=1}^{m} w_i = 1 \\ w_i \ge 0 \quad \forall i \end{aligned} \qquad (25)$$

Then, we have:

$$\begin{aligned} \underset{w,x}{Min} \sum_{i=1}^{m} w_i^k x_i^R(S) \\ s.t \quad \sum_{i=1}^{m} w_i^k = 1 \\ w_i^k \ge 0 \ (\forall i) \end{aligned} \qquad (26)$$

$$\begin{aligned} \underset{w,x}{Min} \sum_{i=1}^{m} w_i^k x_i^L(S) \\ s.t \quad \sum_{i=1}^{m} w_i^k = 1 \\ w_i^k \ge 0 \ (\forall i) \end{aligned} \qquad (27)$$

Let $(w_1^{\alpha SL},...,w_m^{\alpha SL})$ and $(w_1^{\alpha SL},...,w_m^{\alpha SR})$ denote optimal solution to the problem (26) and (27), respectively for given α . Let

$$d_\alpha^L(S) \cup \sum_{i=1}^{m} w_i^L x_i^{\alpha SL}(S) \qquad (28)$$

$$d_\alpha^R(S) \cup \sum_{i=1}^{m} w_i^R x_i^{\alpha SR}(S) \qquad (29)$$

We can construct the fuzzy value $\tilde{d}(S)$ of the game similar to the fuzzy number as depicted in Figure 1.

Theorem 6

The min game *(N,d)* is super – additive we have $d(S \cup T) \geq d(S) + d(T)$ for each *S, T* $\subset N$ with $S \cap T = \phi$

Proof

By renumbering the indexes, we have $S = \{1,...,h\}, T = \{h+1,...,k\}$ and $S \cup T = \{1,...,k\}$. For these sets it holds that

$$\tilde{d}(S \cup T) = Min \sum_{j=1}^{k} \tilde{x}_{ij} \geq Min \sum_{j=1}^{h} \tilde{x}_{ij} + Min \sum_{j=h+1}^{k} \tilde{x}_{ij}$$
$$= \tilde{d}(S) + \tilde{d}(T)$$

Thus these game start from $\tilde{d}(k) > 0, \ k = 1,...,n$ and enlarges the gains by the coalition until the grand coalition *N* with $\tilde{d}(N) = 1$ is reached .

Theorem 7 $\tilde{d}(S) + \tilde{c}(N \setminus S) = 1 \quad \forall S \subsetneq N$

Proof

By renumbering the indexes, we can assume that $S = \{1,...,h\}, N = \{1,...,n\}$ and $N \setminus S = \{h+1,...,n\}$.For this sets, it holds that

$$\tilde{d}(S) + \tilde{c}(N \setminus S) = \underset{i}{Min} \sum_{j=1}^{h} \tilde{x}_{ij} + \underset{i}{Max} \sum_{j=h+1}^{n} \tilde{x}_{ij}$$

$$\tilde{d}(S) + \tilde{c}(N \setminus S) = \underset{i}{Min} \sum_{j=1}^{h} \tilde{x}_{ij} + \underset{i}{Max} \sum_{j=h+1}^{n} \tilde{x}_{ij}$$
$$= \underset{i}{Min} \left(\sum_{j=1}^{n} \tilde{x}_{ij} - \sum_{j=h+1}^{n} \tilde{x}_{ij}\right) + \underset{i}{Max} \sum_{j=h+1}^{n} \tilde{x}_{ij}$$
$$= \underset{i}{Min}\left(1 - \sum_{j=h+1}^{n} \tilde{x}_{ij}\right) + \underset{i}{Max} \sum_{j=h+1}^{n} \tilde{x}_{ij}$$
$$= 1 - \underset{i}{Max} \sum_{j=h+1}^{n} \tilde{x}_{ij} + \underset{i}{Max} \sum_{j=h+1}^{n} \tilde{x}_{ij} = 1$$

EXTENSIONS

Here we extend our fuzzy basic model to a B-C fuzzy game.

A BENEFIT-COST (B-C) GAME

So far we have dealt with a DEA (Cooper et al. 2000) game in which the score matrix *X* represents the superiority (benefits) of players.

However, there are occasions where some criteria exhibit inferiority (costs). Thus, the merit of a player is evaluated by the difference (profit) between benefits and costs.

Suppose that there are *s* criteria for representing benefits and *m* criteria for costs. Let $\tilde{y}_{ij} (i = 1,...,s)$ and $\tilde{x}_{ij} (i = 1,...,m)$ be the benefits and costs of player $j\ (j = 1,...,n)$ respectively. The merit of player *j* with fuzzy data is evaluated by

$$(u_1 \tilde{y}_{1j} + ... + u_s \tilde{y}_{sj}) - (v_1 \tilde{x}_{1j} + ... + v_m \tilde{x}_{mj})$$

where ***u*** $(u_1,...,u_s)$ and ***v*** $(v_1,...,v_m)$ are, respectively, the virtual weights for benefits and costs. Analogous to the expression (1) we define the relative score of player *j* to the total scores as:

$$\frac{\sum_{i=1}^{s} u_i \tilde{y}_{ij} - \sum_{i=1}^{m} v_i \tilde{x}_{ij}}{\sum_{i=1}^{s} u_i \left(\sum_{k=1}^{n} \tilde{y}_{ik}\right) - \sum_{i=1}^{s} v_i \left(\sum_{k=1}^{n} \tilde{x}_{ik}\right)} \qquad (30)$$

Player *j* wishes to maximize his score, subject to the condition that the merit of all players is nonnegative.

$$\sum_{i=1}^{s} u_i \tilde{y}_{ik} - \sum_{i=1}^{m} v_i \tilde{x}_{ik} \geq 0$$

We can express this situation by fuzzy linear program below:

$$\begin{aligned} & Max \sum_{i=1}^{s} u_i \tilde{y}_{ij} - \sum_{i=1}^{m} v_i \tilde{x}_{ij} \\ & s\,t \ \sum_{i=1}^{s} u_i \left(\sum_{k=1}^{n} \tilde{y}_{ik}\right) - \sum_{i=1}^{s} v_i \left(\sum_{k=1}^{n} \tilde{x}_{ik}\right) = 1 \\ & \quad \sum_{i=1}^{s} u_i \tilde{y}_{ik} - \sum_{i=1}^{m} v_i \tilde{x}_{ik} \geq 0 \quad (k = 1,...,n) \\ & \quad u_i \geq 0, v_i \geq 0 \quad \forall i \end{aligned} \qquad (31)$$

Similar to defined basic model of the fuzzy game, we can transform this program to the nonfuzzy program below:

$$\begin{aligned} & Max \sum_{i=1}^{s} u_i y^R_{ij} - \sum_{i=1}^{m} v_i x^R_{ij} \\ & s\,t \ \sum_{i=1}^{s} u_i \left(\sum_{k=1}^{n} y^R_{ik}\right) - \sum_{i=1}^{s} v_i \left(\sum_{k=1}^{n} x^R_{ik}\right) = 1 \\ & \quad \sum_{i=1}^{s} u_i y^R_{ik} - \sum_{i=1}^{m} v_i x^R_{ik} \geq 0 \quad (k = 1,...,n) \\ & \quad u_i \geq 0, v_i \geq 0 \quad \forall i \end{aligned} \qquad (32)$$

$$\begin{aligned}&Max\ \sum_{i=1}^{s}u_i y_{ij}^{L}-\sum_{i=1}^{m}v_i x_{ij}^{L}\\&s\,t\ \sum_{i=1}^{s}u_i(\sum_{k=1}^{n}y_{ik}^{L})-\sum_{i=1}^{s}v_i(\sum_{k=1}^{n}x_{ik}^{L})=1\\&\sum_{i=1}^{s}u_i y_{ik}^{L}-\sum_{i=1}^{m}v_i x_{ik}^{L}\geq 0\quad (k=1,\dots,n)\\&u_i\geq 0, v_i\geq 0\quad \forall i\end{aligned}\tag{33}$$

Following the same scenario as the DEA fuzzy game in the preceding sections, we can develop coalitions of this B-C game, although the row-wise normalization is not available in this game. That is, a characteristic function of the coalition S is defined by the fuzzy linear program below:

$$\begin{aligned}&\underset{u,v}{Max}\ \sum_{i=1}^{s}u_i\sum_{j\in S}\tilde{y}_{ij}-\sum_{i=1}^{m}v_i\sum_{j\in S}\tilde{x}_{ij}\\&s\,t\ \sum_{i=1}^{s}u_i(\sum_{k=1}^{n}\tilde{y}_{ik})-\sum_{i=1}^{s}v_i(\sum_{k=1}^{n}\tilde{x}_{ik})=1\\&\sum_{i=1}^{s}u_i\tilde{y}_{ik}-\sum_{i=1}^{m}v_i\tilde{x}_{ik}\geq 0\quad (k=1,\dots,n)\\&u_i\geq 0, v_i\geq 0\quad \forall i\end{aligned}\tag{34}$$

Then,

$$\begin{aligned}&\underset{u,v}{Max}\ \sum_{i=1}^{s}u_i\sum_{j\in S}y_{ij}^{R}-\sum_{i=1}^{m}v_i\sum_{j\in S}x_{ij}^{R}\\&s\,t\ \sum_{i=1}^{s}u_i(\sum_{k=1}^{n}y_{ik}^{R})-\sum_{i=1}^{s}v_i(\sum_{k=1}^{n}x_{ik}^{R})=1\\&\sum_{i=1}^{s}u_i y_{ik}^{R}-\sum_{i=1}^{m}v_i x_{ik}^{R}\geq 0\quad (k=1,\dots,n)\\&u_i\geq 0, v_i\geq 0\quad \forall i\end{aligned}\tag{35}$$

$$\begin{aligned}&\underset{u,v}{Max}\ \sum_{i=1}^{s}u_i\sum_{j\in S}y_{ij}^{L}-\sum_{i=1}^{m}v_i\sum_{j\in S}x_{ij}^{L}\\&s\,t\ \sum_{i=1}^{s}u_i(\sum_{k=1}^{n}y_{ik}^{L})-\sum_{i=1}^{s}v_i(\sum_{k=1}^{n}x_{ik}^{L})=1\\&\sum_{i=1}^{s}u_i y_{ik}^{L}-\sum_{i=1}^{m}v_i x_{ik}^{L}\geq 0\quad (k=1,\dots,n)\\&u_i\geq 0, v_i\geq 0\quad \forall i\end{aligned}\tag{36}$$

Let $(u_1^{\alpha SL},\dots,u_s^{\alpha SL})$, $(u_1^{\alpha SR},\dots,u_s^{\alpha SR})$, $(v_1^{\alpha SL},\dots,v_m^{\alpha SL})$ and $(v_1^{\alpha SR},\dots,v_m^{\alpha SR})$ denote optimal solution to the problem (35) and (36), respectively for given α. Let

$$c_\alpha^L(S)\bigcup\left(\sum_{i=1}^{s}u_i^L y_i^{\alpha SL}-\sum_{i=1}^{m}v_i^L x_i^{\alpha SL}\right)(S)\tag{37}$$

$$c_\alpha^R(S)\bigcup\left(\sum_{i=1}^{s}u_i^R y_i^{\alpha SR}-\sum_{i=1}^{m}v_i^R x_i^{\alpha SR}\right)(S)\tag{38}$$

We can construct the fuzzy value $\tilde{c}(S)$ of the game similar to the fuzzy number as depicted in Figure 1. In these programs, we keep the condition that the merit of all players is nonnegative. Since the constraints of final program are the same for all coalitions, we have the following theorem.

Theorem 8

The B-C max game satisfies a sub- additive property.

Proof

For any $S\subset N$ and $T\subset N$ with $S\bigcap T=\phi$, we have:

$$\begin{aligned}c(S\cup T)&=\underset{v,u}{Max}\left(\sum_{i=1}^{s}u_i\sum_{j\in S\cup T}\tilde{y}_{ij}-\sum_{i=1}^{m}v_i\sum_{j\in S\cup T}\tilde{x}_{ij}\right)\\&=\underset{v,u}{Max}\left(\sum_{i=1}^{s}u_i(\sum_{j\in S}\tilde{y}_{ij}+\sum_{j\in T}\tilde{y}_{ij})\right)-\left(\sum_{i=1}^{m}v_i(\sum_{j\in S}\tilde{x}_{ij}+\sum_{j\in T}\tilde{x}_{ij})\right)\\&=\underset{v,u}{Max}\left(\left(\sum_{i=1}^{s}u_i\sum_{j\in S}\tilde{y}_{ij}-\sum_{i=1}^{m}v_i\sum_{j\in S}\tilde{x}_{ij}\right)+\left(\sum_{i=1}^{s}u_i\sum_{j\in T}\tilde{y}_{ij}-\sum_{i=1}^{m}v_i\sum_{j\in T}\tilde{x}_{ij}\right)\right)\\&\leq Max\left(\sum_{i=1}^{s}u_i\sum_{j\in S}\tilde{y}_{ij}-\sum_{i=1}^{m}v_i\sum_{j\in S}\tilde{x}_{ij}\right)+Max\left(\sum_{i=1}^{s}u_i\sum_{j\in S}\tilde{y}_{ij}-\sum_{i=1}^{m}v_i\sum_{j\in S}\tilde{x}_{ij}\right)\\&\leq\tilde{c}(S)+\tilde{c}(T)\end{aligned}$$

Theorem 9

The maximal allocated cost game (N,c) and min game (N,d) are dual games, for any

$S\subset N$ we have $\tilde{d}(S)+\tilde{c}(N\setminus S)=1$

Proof

$$\begin{aligned}\tilde{c}(N\setminus S)&=\underset{u,v}{Max}\left(\sum_{i=1}^{s}u_i\sum_{j\in N\setminus S}\tilde{y}_{ij}-\sum_{i=1}^{m}v_i\sum_{j\in N\setminus S}\tilde{x}_{ij}\right)\\&=\underset{u,v}{Max}\left(\sum_{i=1}^{s}u_i(\sum_{j\in N}\tilde{y}_{ij}-\sum_{j\in S}\tilde{y}_{ij})-\sum_{i=1}^{m}v_i(\sum_{j\in N}\tilde{x}_{ij}-\sum_{j\in S}\tilde{x}_{ij})\right)\\&=\underset{u,v}{Max}\left(\sum_{i=1}^{s}u_i\sum_{j\in N}\tilde{y}_{ij}-\sum_{i=1}^{m}v_i\sum_{j\in N}\tilde{x}_{ij}\right)-\left(\sum_{i=1}^{s}u_i\sum_{j\in S}\tilde{y}_{ij}-\sum_{i=1}^{m}v_i\sum_{j\in S}\tilde{x}_{ij}\right)\\&=\underset{u,v}{Max}\left(1-\left(\sum_{i=1}^{s}u_i\sum_{j\in S}\tilde{y}_{ij}-\sum_{i=1}^{m}v_i\sum_{j\in S}\tilde{x}_{ij}\right)\right)\\&=1-\underset{u,v}{Min}\left(\sum_{i=1}^{s}u_i\sum_{j\in S}\tilde{y}_{ij}-\sum_{i=1}^{m}v_i\sum_{j\in S}\tilde{x}_{ij}\right)=1-\tilde{d}(S)\end{aligned}$$

Table 1. Inferiority criteria.

Player j	x_{1j}	x_{2j}	x_{3j}
1	(1.5, 2, 2.5)	(2.7, 3, 3.3)	(7.5, 8, 8.5)
2	(7.5, 8, 8.5)	(3.6, 4, 4.4)	(.5, 1, 1.5)
3	(3.6, 4, 4.4)	(2.7, 3, 3.3)	(5.6, 6, 6.4)
4	(4.2, 5, 5.8)	(1.5, 2, 2.5)	(4.2, 5, 5.8)
5	(5.6, 6, 6.4)	(0.5, 1, 1.5)	(3.6, 4, 4.4)

Table 2. Superiority criteria.

Player j	y_{1j}	y_{2j}	y_{3j}	y_{4j}	y_{5j}
1	(12, 13, 16)	(20, 23, 26)	(32, 36, 41)	(39, 44, 49)	(52, 57, 60)
2	(15, 16, 19)	(25, 26, 28)	(29, 32, 36)	(46, 50, 55)	(51, 57, 59)
3	(12, 14, 17)	(22, 26, 27)	(33, 37,42)	(50, 55, 59)	(60, 66, 70)
4	(11, 13, 16)	(23, 26, 29)	(31, 35, 40)	(39, 42, 47)	(59, 64, 68)
5	(10, 12, 14)	(19, 22, 25)	(27, 30, 35)	(53, 55, 60)	(58, 63, 66)

Table 3. Results.

Player *j*	$\tilde{c}(j)$	$\tilde{d}(j)$
1	0.2118	0.0800
2	0.2353	0.0417
3	0.2236	0.1600
4	0.2114	0.1538
5	0.2236	0.0769

NUMERICAL EXAMPLE

We now apply this approach to below data. There are 5 players in this game. Each player uses 3 inferiority and 5 superiority criteria. Table 1 and Table 2 show all kinds of these inferiority and superiority criteria respectively. The results of using model (13) and (19) shows in Table (3).

As we can see in example, $\sum_{k=1}^{n}\tilde{c}(k)>1$ and $\sum_{k=1}^{n}\tilde{d}(k)<1$. Therefore, in this example the "Egoists dilemma" has occur and the players were not willing to negotiate with each other to attain a reasonable and fair division.

Conclusion

In this paper, we have introduced a societal dilemma called the 'egoists dilemma' and studied its properties by means of data envelopment analysis (DEA) and fuzzy game. The DEA fuzzy game thus defined has two variations, one the original selfish *max* fuzzy game and the *min* fuzzy game. Furthermore, we have studied the common weight issues that connect the fuzzy game solution with arbitrary weight selection behavior of the players for imprecise or fuzzy understanding of parameters in a problem-formulation process and have considered fuzzy linear programming games arising from the linear programming problems. Regarding this subject, we have proposed a method for compute merit of players for said data. In this sense, a numerical example have been calculated with proposed ways, has been considered.

ACKNOWLEDGEMENTS

We are grateful to the anonymous referees and Professors Nakabayashi and Tone for their helpful comments and suggestions. This paper is supported by Islamic Azad University Tabriz Branch and Young Researchers Club.

REFERENCES

Charnes A, Cooper WW, Rhodes E (1978). "Measuring the efficiency of decision making units. Eur. J. Oper. Res., 2: 429-440.

Jahanshahloo GR, Hosseinzadeh FL, Sohraiee S (2006). "Egoists dilemma with interval data. Appl. Math. Comput., 183: 94-10.

Nishizaki I, Sakawa M (2000). "Solution based on fuzzy goals in fuzzy linear programming games. Fuzzy Sets Syst., 115: 105-119.

Nakabayashi K, Tone K (2006). "Egoist's dilemma: A DEA game. Int. Manage. Sci., 36: 135-148.

Sakawa M (1993). "Fuzzy sets and Interactive Multiobjective Optimization. Plenum Press, New York.

Cooper WW, Seiford LM, Tone K (2000). Data envelopment analysis: A comprehensive text with models application references and DEA-solver software, Boston: Klawer Academic Publishers."

Two non-standard finite difference schemes for the Timoshenko beam

Abdul Wasim Shaikh[1]* and Xiao-liang Cheng[2]

[1]Institute of Mathematics and Computer Science, University of Sindh, Jamshoro, Pakistan.
[2]Department of Mathematics, Zhejiang University, Hangzhou, 310028, P.R. China.

In this paper, we derive two non-standard finite difference schemes for the Timoshenko beam problem. The schemes are uniform with respect to the thickness small parameter of the beam, thus, no locking phenomenon occurs. Numerical results are presented.

Key words: Timoshenko beam, non-standard difference scheme, locking phenomenon.

INTRODUCTION

In this paper, we consider the following Timoshenko beam model. According to the Timoshenko beam theory, the in-plane bending of a clamped uniform beam of length *L*, cross section *A*, moment of inertia *I*, Young's modulus *E* and shear modulus *G*, subject to a distributed load $p(\bar{x})$ and a distributed moment $m(\bar{x})$, is governed by the following system of differential equations for $\bar{x} \in (0, L)$:

$$-\frac{dQ}{d\bar{x}} = p, \quad -EI\frac{d^2\theta}{d\bar{x}^2} - Q = 0, \quad -\frac{Q}{\kappa GA} + \frac{dW}{d\bar{x}} - \theta = 0,$$

where $Q(\bar{x})$ is the shear force, $M(\bar{x})$ is the bending moment, $\theta(\bar{x})$ is the cross-sectional rotation, $W(\bar{x})$ is the transverse displacement and κ is the shear correction factor. The boundary conditions are,

$$W\ 0 = W\ L\ = 0;\ \theta\ 0\ = \theta\ L\ = 0$$

We non-dimensionalize the problem by introducing the following change of variables:

$$x = \frac{\bar{x}}{L}, \quad w = \frac{W}{L}, \quad \sigma = \frac{QL^2}{EI}, \quad f = \frac{pL^3}{EI},$$

Then, the original problem is transformed to the following model problem. Find w, θ and σ such that in (0,1),

$$\begin{cases} -\sigma' = f \\ -\theta'' - \sigma = 0 \\ -\varepsilon^2\sigma + w' - \theta = 0 \end{cases} \tag{1}$$

or

$$\begin{cases} -\theta'' + \varepsilon^{-2}(\theta - w') = 0 \\ \varepsilon^{-2}(\theta' - w'') = f \end{cases} \tag{2}$$

together with the boundary conditions:

$$w(0) = w(1) = 0; \quad \theta(0) = \theta(1) = 0 \tag{3}$$

The parameter $\varepsilon^2 = EI/(\kappa GAL^2)$ is a constant proportional to the ratio of the thickness to length of the beam. In most realistic applications $\varepsilon \le 1$.

The numerical approximation of the Timoshenko beam has been frequently used as a starting point for a better understanding of the much more complex Reissner-

*Corresponding author. E-mail: awshaikh786@yahoo.com.

Mindlin plate problem. When solving these problems with the standard Galerkin finite element methods or finite difference methods, some bad behaviors may occur such as the locking phenomenon (Arnold, 1981).

To construct the numerical scheme uniform with respect to the small parameter, Loula et al. (1987a), proposed a Petrov-Galerkin formulation, Arnold (1981), Cheng and Xue (2002), Cheng et al. (1997) and Loula et al. (1987b) used the reduced integration which is equivalent to the mixed formulation. Jou and Yang (2000) discussed the least-squares finite element method and Li (1990) applied the *p* and $h-p$ versions of the finite element method.

In this paper, we derive two non-standard finite difference schemes for the Timoshenko beam. Unlike the standard difference method, we do not use forward, backward or central difference to replace the derivative. We solve the differential equations in each subinterval (one element or two elements), then obtain the equations by some connecting conditions. Numerical experiments are presented for these two schemes.

THE NON-STANDARD DIFFERENCE SCHEME

For simplicity, we consider the uniform partition of (0, 1). Let $h=1/N$ for some positive integer *N*. Denote $x_i = ih,\ i=1,2,\ldots,N$ and $x_{i+\frac{1}{2}} = \frac{1}{2}(x_i + x_{i+1})$

Scheme I

In element $\Delta_i = (x_{i-1}, x_i)$, we let $f \equiv f_{i-\frac{1}{2}} = f(x_{i-\frac{1}{2}})$ be a constant. Then, we solve Equations 1 or 2 in Δ_i.

$$\begin{cases} -\sigma' = f_{i-\frac{1}{2}} \\ -\theta'' - \sigma = 0 \\ -\varepsilon^2\sigma + w' - \theta = 0 \end{cases} \tag{4}$$

We can obtain the solution with four constants,

$$\begin{cases} \sigma(x) = c_1^{(i)} - f_{i-\frac{1}{2}}(x - x_{i-1}) \\ \theta(x) = -\frac{1}{2}c_1^{(i)}(x-x_{i-1})^2 + c_2^{(i)}(x-x_{i-1}) + c_3^{(i)} + \frac{1}{6}f_{i-\frac{1}{2}}(x-x_{i-1})^3 \\ w(x) = -\frac{1}{6}c_1^{(i)}(x-x_{i-1})^3 + \frac{1}{2}c_2^{(i)}(x-x_{i-1})^2 + (c_1^{(i)}\varepsilon^2 + c_3^{(i)})(x-x_{i-1}) \\ \qquad + c_4^{(i)} - \frac{1}{2}\varepsilon^2 f_{i-\frac{1}{2}}(x-x_{i-1})^2 + \frac{1}{24}f_{i-\frac{1}{2}}(x-x_{i-1})^4 \end{cases} \tag{5}$$

Applying the boundary conditions $\theta(x_{i-1}) = \theta_{i-1}$, $\theta(x_i) = \theta_i$; and $w(x_{i-1}) = w_{i-1}$, $w(x_i) = w_i$; we can derive:

$$\begin{cases} c_1^{(i)} = \frac{12}{h(12\varepsilon^2 + h^2)}\left(w_i - w_{i-1} - \frac{1}{2}h(\theta_{i-1} + \theta_i)\right) + \frac{1}{2}hf_{i-\frac{1}{2}} \\ c_2^{(i)} = \frac{6}{12\varepsilon^2 + h^2}\left(w_i - w_{i-1} - \frac{1}{2}h(\theta_{i-1} + \theta_i)\right) + \frac{1}{h}(\theta_{i-1} + \theta_i) + \frac{1}{12}h^2 f_{i-\frac{1}{2}} \\ c_3^{(i)} = \theta_{i-1} \\ c_4^{(i)} = w_{i-1} \end{cases} \tag{6}$$

From the first continuity condition,

$$\lim_{x \to x_i^-} \theta'(x) = \lim_{x \to x_i^+} \theta'(x)$$

we obtain the equation:

$$-hc_1^{(i)} + c_2^{(i)} + \frac{1}{2}h^2 f_{i-\frac{1}{2}} = c_2^{(i+1)} \tag{7}$$

From the second continuity condition,

$$\lim_{x \to x_i^-} w'(x) = \lim_{x \to x_i^+} w'(x)$$

we get:

$$-\frac{1}{2}h^2 c_1^{(i)} + hc_2^{(i)} + \varepsilon^2 c_1^{(i)} + c_3^{(i)} - h\varepsilon^2 f_{i-\frac{1}{2}} + \frac{1}{6}h^3 f_{i-\frac{1}{2}} = c_1^{(i+1)}\varepsilon^2 + c_3^{(i+1)} \tag{8}$$

Thus, we obtain the linear system from Equations 7 and 8 for $i = 1,2,\ldots,N-1$,

$$\begin{cases} \frac{12}{12\varepsilon^2 + h^2}\left(\frac{\theta_{i-1} + 2\theta_i + \theta_{i+1}}{4} - \frac{w_{i+1} - w_{i-1}}{2h}\right) - \frac{\theta_{i-1} - 2\theta_i + \theta_{i+1}}{h^2} = \frac{1}{12}h\left(f_{i+\frac{1}{2}} - f_{i-\frac{1}{2}}\right) \\ \frac{12}{12\varepsilon^2 + h^2}\left(\frac{\theta_{i+1} - \theta_{i-1}}{2h} - \frac{w_{i-1} - 2w_i + w_{i+1}}{h^2}\right) = \frac{1}{2}\left(f_{i+\frac{1}{2}} + f_{i-\frac{1}{2}}\right) \end{cases} \tag{9}$$

and with the boundary conditions:

$$\theta_0 = \theta_N = 0, \qquad w_0 = w_N = 0 \tag{10}$$

The scheme of Equations 8 and 9 is similar to the one derive from the Petrov-Galerkin formulation of Loula et al. (1987a). It is also the scheme which we apply the difference method to the Equation 2 with shear dampening.

Scheme II

Let $\Delta^i = (x_{i-1}, x_{i+1})$, we let $f \equiv \overline{f}_i = \frac{1}{2}\left(f(x_{i-\frac{1}{2}}) + f(x_{i+\frac{1}{2}})\right)$ be a constant. Then, we solve the Equations 1 or 2 in Δ^i,

$$\begin{cases} -\sigma' = \overline{f}_i \\ -\theta'' - \sigma' = 0 \\ -\varepsilon^2\sigma + w' - \theta = 0 \end{cases} \tag{11}$$

Again, we can obtain the solution with four constants,

$$\begin{cases} \sigma(x) = d_1^{(i)} - \overline{f}_i (x - x_{i-1}) \\ \theta(x) = -\frac{1}{2}d_1^{(i)}(x - x_{i-1})^2 + d_2^{(i)}(x - x_{i-1}) + d_3^{(i)} + \frac{1}{6}\overline{f}_i (x - x_{i-1})^3 \\ w(x) = -\frac{1}{6}d_1^{(i)}(x - x_{i-1})^3 + \frac{1}{2}d_2^{(i)}(x - x_{i-1})^2 + (d_1^{(i)}\varepsilon^2 + d_3^{(i)})(x - x_{i-1}) \\ \qquad + d_4^{(i)} - \frac{1}{2}\varepsilon^2 \overline{f}_i (x - x_{i-1})^2 + \frac{1}{24}\overline{f}_i (x - x_{i-1})^4 \end{cases} \tag{12}$$

Applying the boundary conditions $\theta(x_{i-1}) = \theta_{i-1}$, $\theta(x_{i+1}) = \theta_{i+1}$ and $w(x_{i-1}) = w_{i-1}$, $w(x_{i+1}) = w_{i+1}$, we can derive:

$$\begin{cases} d_1^{(i)} = \frac{3}{h(63\varepsilon^2 + 2h^2)}\left(w_{i+1} - w_{i-1} - h(\theta_{i-1} + \theta_{i+1})\right) + h\overline{f}_i \\ d_2^{(i)} = \frac{3}{6\varepsilon^2 + 2h^2}\left(w_{i+1} - w_{i-1} - h(\theta_{i-1} + \theta_{i+1})\right) + \frac{1}{2h}(\theta_{i+1} - \theta_{i-1}) + \frac{1}{3}h^2\overline{f}_i \\ d_3^{(i)} = \theta_{i-1} \\ d_4^{(i)} = w_{i-1} \end{cases} \tag{13}$$

Then, from Equations 12 and 13, we have the relations:

$$\theta_i = \theta(x_i) = -\frac{1}{2}hd_1^{(i)} + hd_2^{(i)} + d_3^{(i)} + \frac{1}{6}h^3\overline{f}_i$$

$$w_i = w(x_i) = -\frac{1}{6}h^3\overline{f}_i + \frac{1}{2}hd_2^{(i)} + h(\varepsilon^2 d_1^{(i)} + d_3^{(i)}) + d_4^{(i)} - \frac{1}{2}\varepsilon^2 h^2 \overline{f}_i + \frac{1}{24}h^4\overline{f}_i$$

Thus, from Equation 13 and continuity conditions, we obtain the system for $i = 1, 2, \ldots, N-1$:

$$\begin{cases} \frac{3}{3\varepsilon^2 + h^2}\left(\frac{\theta_{i-1} + \theta_{i+1}}{2} - \frac{w_{i+1} - w_{i-1}}{2h}\right) - \frac{\theta_{i-1} - 2\theta_i + \theta_{i+1}}{h^2} = 0 \\ \frac{12}{12\varepsilon^2 + h^2}\left(\frac{\theta_{i+1} - \theta_{i-1}}{2h} - \frac{w_{i-1} - 2w_i + w_{i+1}}{h^2}\right) = \overline{f}_i \end{cases} \tag{14}$$

with the boundary conditions:

$$\theta_0 = \theta_N = 0, \qquad w_0 = w_N = 0 \tag{15}$$

We can see that the second equation of Equation 14 is the same as the one in Equation 9, but the first equation of Equation 14 is slightly different with the first equation of Equation 9.

Next we give some error estimates. First, we have the following priori estimates.

Theorem 1

Let θ, w be the solutions of Equations 1 or 2 and 3, then there exists a constant C independent ε such that:

$$\|\theta\|_\infty + \|w\|_\infty \le C\|f\|_\infty \tag{16}$$

where $\|\cdot\|_\infty$ is the uniform norm on the interval (0, 1).

Proof

By the first equation of Equation 1, we have:

$$-\sigma(x) = -F(x) + C_1, \qquad F(x) = \int_0^x f(t)\,dt$$

By the second Equation of Equation 1 and the boundary conditions of Equation 3, we get:

$$\theta(x) = -\frac{1}{2}C_1x^2 + C_1x + G(x)$$

with

$$G(x) = \int_0^x\left(\int_0^s F(t)\,dt\right)ds - \int_0^1\left(\int_0^s F(t)\,dt\right)ds$$

From the third equation of Equation 1, we obtain:

$$w(x) = -\frac{1}{6}C_1x^3 + \frac{1}{4}C_1x^2 + \varepsilon^2 C_1 x - \varepsilon^2\int_0^x F(t)\,dt + \int_0^x G(t)\,dt$$

Applying the conditions $w(0) = w(1) = 0$, we can derive:

$$C_1 = \frac{\varepsilon^2\int_0^1 F(t)\,dt - \int_0^1 G(t)\,dt}{\varepsilon^2 + \frac{1}{12}}$$

Thus for $0 < \varepsilon < 1$, we can verify:

Table 1. The case f = 1; h = 1=10.

		x = 0.1	x = 0.5	x = 0.8
	Scheme I :: $\theta(x)/w(x)$	0.0060/0.0116	0.0000/0.0339	–0.0080/0.0211
$\varepsilon=0.5$	Scheme II:: $\theta(x)/w(x)$	0.0060/0.0116	0.0000/0.0339	–0.0080/0.0211
	Exact solution	0.0060/0.0116	0.0000/0.0339	–0.0080/0.0211
	Scheme I:: $\theta(x)/w(x)$	0.0060/0.0008	0.0000/0.0039	–0.0080/0.0019
$\varepsilon=0.1$	Scheme II:: $\theta(x)/w(x)$	0.0060/0.0008	0.0000/0.0039	–0.0080/0.0019
	Exact solution	0.0060/0.0008	0.0000/0.0039	−0.0080/0.0019
	Scheme I :: $\theta(x)/w(x)$	0.0060/0.0003	0.0000/0.0026	–0.0080/0.0011
$\varepsilon=0.01$	Scheme II:: $\theta(x)/w(x)$	0.0060/0.0003	0.0000/0.0026	–0.0080/0.0011
	Exact solution	0.0060/0.0003	0.0000/0.0026	–0.0080/0.0011

$$\|F\|_\infty \le C\|f\|_\infty, \qquad \|G\|_\infty \le C\|f\|_\infty, \qquad |C_1| \le C\|f\|_\infty$$

The proof is completed.

Denote the piecewise constant function $f_h(x)$ from f(x) by $f_h(x)=f(x_{i-\frac{1}{2}})$, $x_{i-1}<x<x_i$. Consider the equations:

$$\begin{cases} -\tilde{\theta}'' + \varepsilon^{-2}\left(\tilde{\theta}-\tilde{w}'\right)=0 \\ \varepsilon^{-2}\left(\tilde{\theta}'-\tilde{w}'\right)=f_h \end{cases} \qquad (17)$$

Together with the boundary conditions,

$$\tilde{w}(0)=\tilde{w}(1)=0\ , \qquad \tilde{\theta}(0)=\tilde{\theta}(1)=0 \qquad (18)$$

we can see that, $\tilde{\theta}(x_i)=\tilde{\theta}_i$, $\tilde{w}(x_i)=\tilde{w}_i$, $i=0,1,2,\ldots,N$ for the solutions of Equations 9 and 10.

As $\theta(x)-\tilde{\theta}(x)$ and $w(x)-\tilde{w}(x)$ are the solution of Equations 2 and 3 with the replacement f(x) by $f(x)-f_h(x)$, then we apply the Theorem 1 to obtain:

$$\max_i|\theta(x_i)-\theta_i|+\max_i|w(x_i)-w_i|\le C\|f-f_h\|_\infty$$

It is the uniform bounds with respect to the small parameter ε.

For Scheme II, we can not derive the similar bounds of errors but numerical experiments show its uniform bounds with respect to parameter.

NUMERICAL EXPERIMENTS

We first consider the uniform load case *f* = 1; 0 < *x* < 1. The exact solutions are,

$$\theta(x)=\frac{1}{12}x\ \ 1-x\ \ \ 1-2x$$

$$w(x)=\frac{1}{24}x^2\ \ 1-x\ ^2+\frac{1}{2}\varepsilon^2 x\ \ 1-x$$

For both schemes the solution should be exact as shown in Table 1.

We let $f(x)=100(e^x+x)$ as the second example. We do not know the exact solution but we give the approximated solutions for different mesh and ε. We see that no locking phenomenon occurs (Tables 2 and 3).

Conclusion

We consider the numerical approximation of a Timoshenko beam with boundary feedback, and present the non-standard finite difference schemes with a uniform mesh without presenting the problem of the locking phenomenon. These schemes approximate the functions $\theta(x)$ and $w(x)$ under values of *x* and ε. We may easily see the approximate schemes in Table 1.

Table 2. The case $f(x)=100(e^x+x)$, ε = 0.1.

		x = 0.1	x = 0.5	x = 0.8
$h=1/10$	Scheme I: $\theta(x)/w(x)$	1.2214/0.1469	0.1989/0.8400	−1.7749//0.4508
	Scheme II: $\theta(x)/w(x)$	1.2210/0.1471	0.1957/0.8403	−1.7782/0.4508
$h=1/20$	Scheme I: $\theta(x)/w(x)$	1.2210/0.1468	0.1988/0.8398	−1.7745/0.4507
	Scheme II: $\theta(x)/w(x)$	1.2210/0.1469	0.1980/0.8398	−1.7753/0.4507
$h=1/40$	Scheme I: $\theta(x)/w(x)$	1.2210/0.1468	0.1988/0.8397	−1.7744/0.4507
	Scheme II: $\theta(x)/w(x)$	1.2209/0.1468	0.1988/0.8397	−1.7746/0.4507
$h=1/80$	Scheme I: $\theta(x)/w(x)$	1.2209/0.1468	0.1988/0.8397	−1.7739/0.4507
	Scheme II: $\theta(x)/w(x)$	1.2209/0.1468	0.1987/0.8397	−1.7739//0.4507

Table 3. The case $f(x)=100(e^x+x)$, $h=1/10$.

		x = 0.1	*x* = 0.5	*x* = 0.8
$\varepsilon=0.1$	Scheme I:: $\theta(x)/w(x)$	1.2214/0.1469	0.1989/0.8400	−1.7749//0.4508
	Scheme II:: $\theta(x)/w(x)$	1.2210/0.1471	0.1957/0.8403	−1.7782/0.4508
$\varepsilon=0.01$	Scheme I:: $\theta(x)/w(x)$	1.2001/0.0674	0.1397/0.5697	−1.8128/0.2519
	Scheme II:: $\theta(x)/w(x)$	1.2007/0.0674	0.1395/0.5700	−1.8141/0.2520
$\varepsilon=0.001$	Scheme I :: $\theta(x)/w(x)$	1.2001/0.0666	0.1391/0.5670	−1.8131/0.2499
	Scheme II:: $\theta(x)/w(x)$	1.2005/0.0666	0.1389/0.5673	−1.8145/0.2500
$\varepsilon=0.0001$	Scheme I :: $\theta(x)/w(x)$	1.1998/0.0666	0.1391/0.5670	−1.8132/0.2499
	Scheme II:: $\theta(x)/w(x)$	1.2005/0.0666	0.1389/0.5673	−1.8145/0.2500

REFERENCES

Arnold DN (1981). Discretization by finite elements of a model parameter dependent problem. Numer. Math., 37: 405-421.

Cheng XL, Xue W (2002). Linear finite element approximations for the Timoshenko beam and the shallow arch problems. J. Comput. Math., 20: 15-22.

Cheng XL, Han W, Huang HC (1997). Finite element methods for Timoshenko beam, circular arch and Reissner-Mindlin plate problems. J. Comput. Appl. Math., 79: 215-234.

Jou J, Yang SY (2000). Least-squares Finite element approximations to the Timoshenko beam problem. Appl. Math. Comput., 115: 63-75.

Li L (1990). Discretization of the Timoshenko beam problem by the *p* and *h* ¡ *p* versions of the finite element method. Numer. Math., 57: 413-420.

Loula AFD, Hughes TJR, Franca LP (1987a). Petrov-Galerkin formulations of the Timoshenko beam problem. Comput. Meth. Appl. Mech. Eng., 63: 115-132.

Loula AFD, Hughes TJR, Franca LP, Miranda I (1987b). Stability, convergence and accuracy of a new finite element method for the circular arch problem. Comput. Meth. Appl. Mech. Eng., 63: 281-303.

Almost n-multiplicative maps

E. Ansari-Piri* and N. Eghbali

Faculty of Mathematical Science, University of Guilan, Rasht, Iran.

Let A and B be two linear algebras. A linear map $\varphi : A \to B$ is called an n-homomorphism if $\varphi(a_1 \dots a_n) = \varphi(a_1) \dots \varphi(a_n)$ for all $a_1, \dots, a_n \in A$. The continuity of n-homomorphisms between Banach algebras as well as the almost multiplicative linear operators has been recently studied. In this note, we have a verification on the behavior of almost n-multiplicative linear maps with $n > 2$.

Key words: Almost multiplicative maps, n-homomorphism maps, almost n-multiplicative maps, stability.

INTRODUCTION

Let A and B be two linear algebras. A linear mapping $\varphi : A \to B$ is called an n-homomorphism if $\varphi(a_1 \dots a_n) = \varphi(a_1) \dots \varphi(a_n)$ for each $a_1, \dots, a_n$ in A. A 2-homomorphism is then a homomorphism, in the usual sense (Hejazian et al., 2005). In 1985, Jarosz (1985) introduced the concept of ε-multiplicative maps, where he discussed the continuity of ε-multiplicative linear functionals on Banach algebras. Ansari-Piri and Eghbali (2005) proved that every linear almost multiplicative map form a Banach algebra A into a semi-simple Banach algebra B is continuous. In this paper, we introduce a new concept of perturbations, and we call it *almost* n-multiplicative. Also, we examine the relationship between almost multiplicative maps and almost n-multiplicative maps. We will prove that every almost multiplicative linear function is almost n-multiplicative (Corllary 3.5), and by introducing an example, we show that, an almost n-multiplicative map is not necessarily an almost multiplicative one.

The continuity of almost n-multiplicative linear functional on unital Banach algebras as well as the continuity of almost n-multiplicative linear maps from a unital Banach algebra into another semi-simple Banach algebra is also investigated, where by a unital Banach algebra means a Banach algebra with a unit element.

*Corresponding author. E-mail: eansaripiri@gmail.com.

AMS subject classifications: Primary 46H; 46S40; secondary 39B52, 39B82, 26E50, 46S50.

PRELIMINARIES

Here, we provide a collection of definitions and related results which are essential and used in this study's discussion.

Definition 2.1

Let A and B be Banach algebras and, $\varphi : A \to B$ a linear map. We say φ is an almost multiplicative map if there exists an $\varepsilon > 0$ such that for all $x, y \in A$, $\| \varphi(xy) - \varphi(x)\varphi(y) \| \leq \varepsilon \| x \| \| y \|$.

Proposition 2.2

Every almost multiplicative linear functional on a Banach algebra is continuous.

Proof

For proof refer to Jarosz (1985).

Theorem 2.3

Every almost multiplicative linear map from a Banach algebra A to a semi-simple Banach algebra B is continuous.

Proof

For proof refer to Ansari-Piri and Eghbali (2005).

Definition 2.4

Let A and B be two linear algebras and $n>2$ an integer. A linear map $\varphi: A\to B$ is an n-homomorphism if for all $a_1, a_2, ..., a_n \in A$, $\varphi(a_1a_2...a_n) = \varphi(a_1)\varphi(a_2)...\varphi(a_n)$.

THE RELATIONSHIP BETWEEN ALMOST n-MULTIPLICATIVE AND ALMOST MULTIPLICATIVE MAPS

Here, we give a proposition to emphasize the existence of a linear almost n-multiplicative map and then we study the relationship between almost multiplicative and almost n-multiplicative maps.

Definition 3.1

Let A and B be Banach algebras and $n>2$ an integer. A linear map $\varphi: A\to B$ is called an almost n-multiplicative map if there exists $\varepsilon>0$ such that for all $a_1, a_2, ..., a_n \in A,$

$$\| \varphi(a_1a_2..a_n) - \varphi(a_1)\varphi(a_2)...\varphi(a_n) \| \le \varepsilon \| a_1 \|\| a_2 \| ... \| a_n \|.$$

Proposition 3.2

Let A be a Banach algebra, T a linear functional on A, and S a linear map such that $\| S \| \le \varepsilon$. The map $T+S$ is not n-homomorphism where it is almost n-multiplicative.

Proof

It is straightforward.

Theorem 3.3

Let A and B be Banach algebras, $f: A\to B$ a linear map and $n>2$ an integer. If f has one of the following properties, then f is an n-Jordan map.

1) for all $a_1, a_2, ..., a_n \in A,$
$\| \varphi(a_1a_2...a_n) - \varphi(a_1)\varphi(a_2)...\varphi(a_n) \| \le \varepsilon,$

2) for all $a_1, a_2, ..., a_n \in A,$
$\| \varphi(a_1a_2...a_n) - \varphi(a_1)\varphi(a_2)...\varphi(a_n) \| \le \varepsilon \| a_1 \| ... \| a_n \|,$

3) for all $a_1, a_2, ..., a_n \in A,$

$\| \varphi(a_1a_2...a_n) - \varphi(a_1)\varphi(a_2)...\varphi(a_n) \| \le \varepsilon(\| a_1 \| + ... \| a_n \|),$

Proof

The proof of all three parts are similar, so we consider only the second property.

If for all $x_1, x_2, ..., x_n \in A$, $\| \varphi(x_1x_2...x_n) - \varphi(x_1)\varphi(x_2)...\varphi(x_n) \| \le \varepsilon \| x_1 \| ... \| x_n \|,$ so for every $x \in A$

$$| \varphi(x^n) - \varphi(x)^n | \le \varepsilon \| x \|^n.$$

Let $x = 2a$. We have

$$| \varphi(a^n) - \varphi(a)^n | \le \varepsilon 2^{-n} \| a \|^n.$$

Put $\| a \| = 1$. So for all $a \in A$ with $\| a \| = 1$ we have $\varphi(a^n) = \varphi(a)^n$. Therefore for all $a \in A$ if $\| a \| \ne 1$ it is sufficient that we put $\frac{a}{\| a \|}$. So f is an n-Jordan map.

It is easy to check that every bounded linear map between Banach algebras A and B is an almost n- \ multiplicative and there are some elements in $BL(A,B)$ which are not n-homomorphism.

Theorem 3.4

Every almost multiplicative linear map from a Banach algebra A to a semi-simple Banach algebra B is almost n-multiplicative.

Proof

Let $\varphi: A \to B$ be an almost multiplicative linear map. For every $a_1,\ldots,a_n \in A$ we have:

$$\| \varphi(a_1...a_n) - \varphi(a_1)\varphi(a_2...a_n) \| \le \varepsilon \| a_1 \| \| a_2 \| ... \| a_n \| .$$

Continuing this process, we get:

$$\| \varphi(a_1..a_n) - \varphi(a_1)..\varphi(a_n) \| \le \varepsilon(1+\|\varphi\|+\|\varphi\|^2+..+\|\varphi\|^{n-2})\| a_1 \| ...\| a_n \|,$$

and the boundedness of φ (Theorem 2.3) completes the proof.

Corollary 3.5

Every almost multiplicative linear functional on a Banach algebra A is an almost n-multiplicative one.
Here, we give an example to show that an almost n-multiplicative linear map is not necessarily an almost multiplicative one.

Example 3.6

Let $(X; \| . \|)$ be the normed algebra of all polynomials defined on $[0,1]$ and f be a linear unbounded functional on X. Let also $A = \{ \begin{pmatrix} 0 & x \\ 0 & 0 \end{pmatrix} : x \in X \}$ with $\| \begin{pmatrix} 0 & x \\ 0 & 0 \end{pmatrix} \| = \| x \|$ and $B = \{ \begin{pmatrix} 0 & 0 & a \\ b & 0 & c \\ 0 & 0 & 0 \end{pmatrix} : a,b,c \in X \}$ with Euclidean norm be two Banach algebras with the usual matrix operations for addition, scaler multiplication, and product. Define $\varphi: A \to B$ with

$$\varphi\left(\begin{pmatrix} 0 & x \\ 0 & 0 \end{pmatrix}\right) = \begin{pmatrix} 0 & 0 & f(x) \\ f(x) & 0 & f(x) \\ 0 & 0 & 0 \end{pmatrix}.$$

Since $A^2 = B^3 = 0, \varphi$ is a 3-homomorphism and so is a 3-multiplicative linear map. On the other hand:

$$\varphi^2\left(\begin{pmatrix} 0 & x \\ 0 & 0 \end{pmatrix}\right) = \begin{pmatrix} 0 & 0 & 0 \\ 0 & 0 & f^2(x) \\ 0 & 0 & 0 \end{pmatrix},$$

and we have

$$\| \varphi^2\left(\begin{pmatrix} 0 & x \\ 0 & 0 \end{pmatrix}\right) \| = | f(x) |^2 .$$

Hence, there is no $\varepsilon > 0$ such that for all $\begin{pmatrix} 0 & x \\ 0 & 0 \end{pmatrix} \in A,$ one can have $\| \varphi^2\left(\begin{pmatrix} 0 & x \\ 0 & 0 \end{pmatrix}\right) \| \le \varepsilon \| \begin{pmatrix} 0 & x \\ 0 & 0 \end{pmatrix} \|^2,$ and therefore φ is not almost multiplicative.

The next Theorems give some more information on the relationship between almost n-multiplicative linear maps and almost multiplicative.

Theorem 3.7

Let A and B be two unital Banach algebras and $\varphi: A \to B$ a linear almost n-multiplicative map. If $\varphi(1) \in Inv(B)$ then, $\psi(x) = \varphi(1)^{-1}\varphi(x)$ is an almost multiplicative map.

Proof

Suppose $a_1,\ldots,a_n \in A.$ Then,

$$\| \psi(a_1..a_n) - \psi(a_1)..\psi(a_n) \| = \| \varphi(1)^{-1}\varphi(a_1..a_n) - \varphi(1)^{-n}\varphi(a_1)..\varphi(a_n) \|$$

$$\le \| \varphi(1)^{-n} \| \| \varphi(1)^{n-1}\varphi(a_1...a_n) - \varphi(a_1)...\varphi(a_n) \|$$

$$\le \| \varphi(1)^{-n} \| (\varepsilon \| 1 \|^{n-1} \| a_1 \| ... \| a_n \| + \varepsilon \| a_1 \| ... \| a_n \|)$$

$$= \varepsilon \| \varphi(1)^{-n} \| (\| 1 \|^{n-1} + 1) \| a_1 \| ... \| a_n \|$$

and so ψ is almost n-multiplicative.

Now, $\psi(1) = 1$ and for $a,b \in A$ we have:

$$\| \psi(ab) - \psi(a)\psi(b) \| = \| \psi(ab) - \psi(a)\psi(b)\psi(1)..\psi(1) \| \le \delta \| a \| \| b \| \| 1 \|^{n-2},$$

with $\delta = \varepsilon \| \varphi(1)^{-n} \| (\| 1 \|^{n-1} + 1).$

Theorem 3.8

Let A be a unital Banach algebra and φ an almost n-
Let A be a unital Banach algebra and φ an almost n-
multiplicative linear function with $\varphi(1) \neq 0$. Then, φ is an almost multiplicative one.

Proposition 3.9

Let A and B be two Banach algebras without unit and $\varphi: A \to B$ a linear almost multiplicative map. Then, φ has a usual extension $\psi: A_1 \to B_1$ such that ψ is an almost multiplicative map.

Proof

Define $\psi: A_1 \to B_1$ with $\psi(a,\lambda) = (\varphi(a),0) + \lambda(0,1) = (\varphi(a),\lambda)$. We have:

$$\| \psi((a,\lambda)(b,\gamma)) - \psi(a,\lambda)\psi(b,\gamma) \| = \| (\varphi(ab) + \lambda\varphi(b) + \gamma\varphi(a), \lambda\gamma) - (\varphi(a)\varphi(b) + \gamma\varphi(b) + \lambda\varphi(a), \lambda\gamma) \| = \| (\varphi(ab) - \varphi(a)\varphi(b), 0) \| \leq \varepsilon \| a \| \| b \| \leq \varepsilon \| (a,\lambda) \| \| (b,\gamma) \| .$$

So ψ is linear almost multiplicative map.

Proposition 3.9 does not hold for almost n-multiplicative maps, because, if we suppose A and B be two Banach algebras without unit and $\varphi: A \to B$ a linear almost n-multiplicative map. The extension map $\psi: A_1 \to B_1$ is again almost n-multiplicative; then, since $\psi((0,1)) = (0,1) \in Inv(B_1)$, by Theorem 3.6, ψ must be almost multiplicative and then, φ will be almost multiplicative, where the example 3.6 shows that this is not true.

THE CONTINUITY OF ALMOST N-MULTIPLICATIVE MAPS

Here, we prove the continuity of almost n-multiplicative maps.

Proposition 4.1

Let A be a unital Banach algebra. If T is a linear almost n-multiplicative functional on A, then T is continuous.

Proof

If $T(1) = 0$, then

$$| T(x) | = | T(x.1...1) - T(x)T(1)...T(1) | \leq \varepsilon \| x \| \| 1 \|^{n-1};$$

so T is continuous. In the other case by Theorem 3.8 and Proposition 2.2 the proof is complete.

Theorem 4.2

Every linear almost n-multiplicative map from a unital Banach algebra A to a unital semi-simple Banach algebra B is continuous.

Proof

Suppose that $T: A \to B$ is a linear and almost n-multiplicative map. For any multiplicative linear functional F on B, FoT is a linear functional and,

$$| FoT(a_1..a_n) - FoT(a_1)..FoT(a_n) | \leq \| F \| \| T(a_1..a_n) - T(a_1)..T(a_n) \| \leq M\varepsilon \| a_1 \|..\| a_n \|.$$

Therefore FoT is a linear almost n-multiplicative functional. So by Proposition 4.1, it is continuous. Let (a_n) be a sequence with $a = \lim_{n\to\infty} a_n$, and $b = \lim_{n\to\infty} T(a_n)$. We show that $b = T(a)$. For any multiplicative linear functional F we have

$$F(b) = F(\lim_{n\to\infty} T(a_n)) = \lim_{n\to\infty} F(T(a_n)) = FoT(a).$$

So $F(b - T(a)) = 0$. Since B is semi-simple we get $b = T(a)$. Consequently, T is continuous by the closed graph theorem.

REFERENCES

Ansari-Piri E, Eghbali N (2005). A note on multiplicative and almost multiplicative linear maps, Honam Math. J. 27(4):641-647.

Hejazian S, Mirzavaziri M, Moslehian MS (2005). *n*-homomorphisms. Bull. Iran. Math. Soc. 31(1):13-23.

Jarosz K (1985). Perturbation of Banach algebras, Lecture Notes in Mathematics, Springer-verlag.

A study on a novel method of mining fuzzy association using fuzzy correlation analysis

Karthikeyan T.[1]*, Samuel Chellathurai A.[2] and Praburaj B.[1]

[1]Department of Computer Science, PSG College of Arts and Science, Coimbatore, India.
[2]Department of Computer Science, James College of Engineering and Technology, Nagercoil, India.

Two different data variables may behave very similarly. Correlation is the problem of determining how much alike the two variables actually are and association rules are used just to show the relationships between data items. Mining fuzzy association rules is the job of finding the fuzzy item-sets which frequently occur together in large fuzzy data set, where the presence of one fuzzy item-set in a record does not necessarily imply the presence of the other one in the same record. In this paper a new method of discovering fuzzy association rules using fuzzy correlation rules is proposed, because the fuzzy support and confidence measures are insufficient at filtering out uninteresting fuzzy correlation rules. To tackle this weakness, a fuzzy correlation measure for fuzzy numbers, is used to augment the fuzzy support-confidence framework for fuzzy association rules. A practical study over the academic behaviour of a particular school is done and some valuable suggestions are given, based on the results obtained.

Key words: Fuzzy association rules, fuzzy item-sets, fuzzy data sets, fuzzy support-confidence, fuzzy correlation measure.

INTRODUCTION

Frequent patterns are patterns that appear in a data set frequently. Finding such frequent patterns (Agrawal et al., 1993) plays an essential role in mining fuzzy associations, fuzzy correlations, and many other interesting relationships among data. Thus, frequent pattern mining has become an important data mining task and a focussed theme in data mining research. Frequent pattern mining searches for recurring relationships in a given data set. The earliest form of frequent pattern mining for association rules is the market basket analysis (Agrawal and Strikant, 1994).

Frequent item set mining leads to the discovery of associations and correlations among items in large transactional or relational data sets. With massive amounts of data continuously being collected and stored, many industries are becoming interested in mining such patterns from their databases. The discovery of interesting correlation relationships among huge amounts of business transaction records can help in many business decision making processes, such as catalogue design, cross marketing, and customer shopping behaviour analysis (Dunham, 2003). But, since most of the real time databases are fuzzy in nature, it is necessary to explore and discover association rules and correlation rules in a fuzzy environment. To this end many researchers have proposed methods for mining fuzzy association rules, from various fuzzy datasets (Au and Chan, 1998; Dubois et al., 2003). In this paper the fuzzy correlation methods proposed by S.T. Liu and C. Kao is used due its advantages in working with fuzzy numbers in a fuzzy environment.

If a fuzzy item set almost occurs in all records, then it may frequently occur with other fuzzy item-sets also (Chan and Wong, 1997). In order to find out useful relationships between the fuzzy item-sets based on fuzzy statistics, fuzzy correlation rules Chiang and Lin (1999) are generated. By using the fuzzy correlation analysis, the fuzzy correlation rules for fuzzy numbers are generated to see that two fuzzy sets not only frequently occur together in same records, but also are related to

*Corresponding author. E-mail: t.karthikeyan.gasc@gmail.com.

each other.

The rest of the paper is organized as follows: Firstly, the concepts of frequent fuzzy item-sets, closed fuzzy item-sets and fuzzy association rules, the concept of mining fuzzy association rules, the fuzzy correlation techniques, the mining fuzzy association rules and fuzzy correlation rules are explained. Next, a practical study on the academic behaviour of students (higher secondary level) in a particular subject of a school in Nagercoil, Tamilnadu (India) with the help of the aforementioned discussed methods is presented with careful discussions. This is then followed by conclusions and suggestions.

FREQUENT FUZZY ITEM-SETS, CLOSED FUZZY ITEM-SETS AND FUZZY ASSOCIATION RULES

Let $I=\{I_1,I_2,...,I_m\}$ be a set of fuzzy items. Let D, the task-relevant fuzzy data, be a set of database transactions where each transaction T is a set of fuzzy items such that $T \subseteq I$. Let A be a set of fuzzy items. A transaction T is said to contain A if and only if $A \subseteq T$. A fuzzy association rule is an implication of the form $A \Rightarrow B$, where $A \subset I, B \subset I$ and $A \cap B = \phi$. The rule $A \Rightarrow B$ holds in the transaction set D with fuzzy support s, where s is the percentage of transactions in D that contain $A \cup B$ (i.e., both A and B). This is taken to be the probability $P(A \cup B)$. The rule $A \Rightarrow B$ has fuzzy confidence c in the transaction set D, where c is the percentage of transactions in D containing A that also contain B. This is taken to be the conditional probability,

$P(B/A)$. *fuzzysupport* $(A \Rightarrow B) = P(A \cup B)$ *fuzzy confidence* $(A \Rightarrow B) = P(B/A)$ (1)

A set of items is referred to as an item-set. An item-set that contains k items is called a k-item-set. The occurrence frequency of an item-set is the number of transactions that contain the item-set. The fuzzy item-set support defined in Equation (1) is called relative support, whereas the occurrence frequency is called the absolute support. If the relative support of an item-set I, satisfies a pre-specified minimum support threshold, then I is a frequent fuzzy item-set. From (1) we have:

$$\textit{fuzzy confidence } (A \Rightarrow B) = P(B/A) = \frac{\sup port(A \cup B)}{\sup port(A)} = \frac{\sup port\_count(A \cup B)}{\sup port\_count(A)} \quad (2)$$

Equation (2) shows that the fuzzy confidence of rule $A \Rightarrow B$ can be easily derived from the support counts of A and $A \cup B$. Once the support counts of A, B and $A \cup B$ are found, it is straightforward to derive the corresponding association rules $A \Rightarrow B$ and $B \Rightarrow A$, and check whether they are strong. Thus the problem of mining fuzzy association rules can be reduced to that of mining frequent fuzzy item-sets. A fuzzy item-set X is closed in a fuzzy data set S if there exists no proper super-item set Y such that Y has the same support count as X in S. An item-set X is a closed frequent fuzzy item-set in set S if X is both closed and frequent in S.

FUZZY ASSOCIATION RULES

The fuzzy item-sets which frequently occur together in large databases are found using fuzzy association rules (Fu et al., 1998). All the methods used for mining fuzzy association rules are based upon a support-confidence framework where fuzzy support and fuzzy confidence are used to identify the fuzzy association rules. Let $F=\{f_1,f_2,...,f_m\}$ be a set of fuzzy items, $T=\{t_1,t_2,...,t_n\}$ be a set of fuzzy records, and each fuzzy record t_i is represented as a vector with m values, $(f_1(t_i), f_2(t_i),..., f_m(t_i))$, where $f_j(t_i)$ is the degree that f_j appears in record t_i, $f_j(t_i) \in [0,1]$. Then a fuzzy association rule is defined as an implication form such as $F_X \Rightarrow F_Y$, where $F_X \subset F, F_Y \subset F$ are two fuzzy item-sets.

The fuzzy association rule $F_X \Rightarrow F_Y$ holds in T with the fuzzy support (*fsupp*$(\{F_X,F_Y\})$) and the fuzzy confidence (*fconf* $(F_X \Rightarrow F_Y)$). The fuzzy support and fuzzy confidence are given as follows:

$$\textit{fsupp}(\{F_X,F_Y\}) = \frac{\sum_{i=1}^{n} \min(f_j(t_i) / f_j \in \{F_X,F_Y\})}{n} \quad (3)$$

$$\textit{fconf}\ (F_X \Rightarrow F_Y) = \frac{\textit{fsupp}\ (\{F_X,F_Y\})}{\textit{fsupp}\ (\{F_X\})} \quad (4)$$

If the *fsupp*$(\{F_X,F_Y\})$ is greater than or equal to a predefined threshold, minimal fuzzy support (s_f), and the *fconf* $(F_X \Rightarrow F_Y)$ is also greater than or equal to a predefined threshold, minimum fuzzy confidence (c_f), then $F_X \Rightarrow F_Y$ is considered as an interesting fuzzy association rule, and it means that the presence of the fuzzy item-set F_X in a record can imply the presence of the fuzzy item sets F_Y in the same record. If a practical situation is considered where a fuzzy item-set almost occurs in all fuzzy records, then according to the aforementioned framework, many fuzzy association rules can be identified. Interestingly, the presence of this fuzzy item-set does not necessarily imply the presence of other fuzzy item-sets which are also included in these fuzzy association rules. Hence there is an urgent need for analysing the relationships between fuzzy item-sets. Fuzzy correlation analysis is used to determine the linear relationship between any two fuzzy item-sets.

FROM FUZZY ASSOCIATION ANALYSIS TO FUZZY CORRELATION ANALYSIS

As it is seen, the fuzzy support and fuzzy confidence measures are insufficient at filtering out uninteresting association rules. To tackle this weakness, a fuzzy correlation measure Bustince and Burillo (1995), Hong and Hwang (1995) can be used to augment the fuzzy support-confidence framework for fuzzy association rules. This leads to the fuzzy correlation rules of the form $A \Rightarrow B$. Hence the correlation between the fuzzy item-sets A and B becomes necessary. There are many different fuzzy correlation measures from which to choose (Yu, 1993; Kao and Liu, 2002).

In this paper, the method proposed C. Kao and S.T. Liu is followed due to the advantages it has, compared to the earlier proposed fuzzy correlation methods (Chiang and. Lin, 1999). This method works well especially in an environment of fuzzy numbers.

When all the observations are fuzzy, equation for correlation of fuzzy numbers is given by

$$\tilde{\rho}_{X,Y} = \frac{\sum_{i=1}^{n}\left(\tilde{X}_i - \sum_{i=1}^{n}\frac{\tilde{X}_i}{n}\right)\left(\tilde{Y}_i - \sum_{i=1}^{n}\frac{\tilde{Y}_i}{n}\right)}{\sqrt{\sum_{i=1}^{n}\left(\tilde{X}_i - \sum_{i=1}^{n}\frac{\tilde{X}_i}{n}\right)^2 \sum_{i=1}^{n}\left(\tilde{Y}_i - \sum_{i=1}^{n}\frac{\tilde{Y}_i}{n}\right)^2}} \qquad (5)$$

Since it is difficult to derive membership function for $\tilde{\rho}_{X,Y}$ for (5) directly, we rely on Zadeh's extension principle [15] (Zadeh, 1978) which says

$$\mu_{\tilde{\rho}_{X,Y}}(\rho) = \sup_{X,Y}\min\left\{\mu_{\tilde{X}_i}(x_i), \mu_{\tilde{Y}_i}(y_i) \forall i / \rho = \rho_{X,Y}\right\}$$

Equation (5) is used to calculate the correlation coefficient between the fuzzy numbers and the value computed from (5) lies between the interval [-1,1]. According to the aforementioned proposed method we can obtain the strength and type of the linear relationship between two fuzzy item-sets. Hence the fuzzy correlation analysis is of great use in mining only the interesting fuzzy correlation rules.

MINING FUZZY ASSOCIATION AND FUZZY CORRELATION RULES

Mining fuzzy association rules is better done by finding frequent fuzzy item-sets using candidate generation method (Han and Kamber, 2001). Apriori is a seminal algorithm proposed for mining frequent fuzzy item-sets. The algorithm uses prior knowledge of frequent fuzzy item-set properties. Apriori employs an iterative approach known as level-wise search, where k-itemsets are used to explore (k+1) –item sets. First, the set of 1-itemsets is found by scanning the fuzzy database to accumulate the count for each item, and collecting those items that satisfy minimum support. The resulting set is denoted by L1. Next L1 is used to find L2, the set of frequent fuzzy 2-itemset, which is used to find L3, and so on, until no more frequent fuzzy k-item-sets can be found. The finding of each Lk requires one full scan of the database. The algorithm consists of two steps, namely (i) the join step and (ii) the prune step, for candidate generation.

CASE STUDY

A higher secondary school in Trichy keeps the record of the revision exams conducted for the class of 12 students. The school has 650 students in the higher secondary levels, both boys and girls. Repeated exams are conducted prior to the final public exams. The management is interested in performing the market basket analysis with regards to the subjects the students like the most and choose the same in the exams, so that special concentration can be given to those subjects and thereby improving the results of school. A sample of 15 repeated revision exams of the full portions in the subject of Mathematics is taken for the study. The subject has 10 different chapters, connected to each other in one or many means. Association and correlation rules are applied for these different chapters to discover interesting relationships. Table 1 is the fuzzy scores of the overall performance for each individual chapter. In the table f1, f2... f10 are the 10 chapters in Mathematics and t1, t2... t15 are the transactions,(revision exams).

Table 2 represents the fuzzy support of the 10 chapters of the subject Mathematics and Figure 1 gives a clear picture of the same.

Here in the study the fuzzy support is fixed to 0.20; the fuzzy confidence is fixed to 0.85; the minimal fuzzy correlation coefficient is fixed as r_f = 0.20; the level of

Table 1. Fuzzy scores for the performance.

T \ F	f1	f2	f3	f4	f5	f6	f7	f8	f9	f10
t1	0.1	0.2	0.1	0.7	0.6	0.1	0.7	0.7	0.5	0.8
t2	0.1	0.3	0.2	0.8	0.3	0.7	0.9	0.8	0.2	0.7
t3	0.2	0.8	0.7	0.9	0.6	0.1	0.2	0.3	0.8	0.5
t4	0.3	0.2	0.4	0.8	0.8	0.3	0.8	0.9	0.1	0.7
t5	0.4	0.3	0.5	0.7	0.9	0.7	0.9	0.8	0.3	0.8
t6	0.2	0.9	0.3	0.6	0.7	0.2	0.1	0.1	0.9	0.3
t7	0.9	0.1	0.4	0.8	0.2	0.3	0.9	0.9	0.4	0.8
t8	0.3	0.4	0.1	0.7	0.8	0.2	0.1	0.2	0.8	0.4
t9	0.8	0.9	0.2	0.8	0.9	0.2	0.7	0.4	0.1	0.6
t10	0.2	0.9	0.1	0.7	0.1	0.9	0.7	0.9	0.4	0.5
t11	0.1	0.4	0.2	0.9	0.2	0.1	0.9	0.8	0.9	0.8
t12	0.3	0.1	0.3	0.8	0.7	0.2	0.1	0.2	0.8	0.2
t13	0.1	0.9	0.2	0.8	0.4	0.9	0.3	0.1	0.2	0.5
t14	0.1	0.2	0.1	0.9	0.2	0.7	0.9	0.8	0.1	0.7
t15	0.4	0.1	0.2	0.7	0.1	0.3	0.8	0.9	0.7	0.6

Table 2. The fuzzy support of the fuzzy items.

F	Fsupport
f1	0.30
f2	0.45
f3	0.27
f4	0.78
f5	0.50
f6	0.40
f7	0.60
f8	0.59
f9	0.48
f10	0.59

significance for t-distribution is set to 0.01, and the distribution value is 2.65. The calculation of r value in table is done using the fuzzy correlation approach given by Liu and Kao (2002). The calculation of t value in table is done using Arnold (1990) test statistic given by

$$t = \frac{r_{A,B} - r_f}{\sqrt{\frac{1 - r_{A,B}}{n-2}}}$$

C2 consists of 45 fuzzy 2-itemsets, but only those which satisfy the minimum threshold level as earlier discussed is given Table 3. Figure 2 shows the comparison of the items of C2.

From all the fuzzy 2-itemset combinations an element whose Fsupport is greater than or equal to 0.20 and t-value greater then equal to 2.65 is considered as an element of L2. L2={ ({f7,f8},{f7,f10},{f8,f10})}. Now C3 is generated by joining L2 with L2. Table 4 gives a clear picture of the members of C3.

In Table 4 all elements of C3 satisfy the minimum threshold levels. Hence all the elements of C3 are elements of L3. Thus L3 = C3. Now the next C4 cannot be generated by joining L3 with L3, and here the mining procedure stops. By this process some 12 candidate fuzzy correlation rules can be generated out of which only 7 rules are interesting because some do not satisfy the minimum threshold level of confidence 0.85.

$$\{f7\} \rightarrow \{f8\}$$
$$\{f8\} \rightarrow \{f7\}$$
$$\{f7\} \rightarrow \{f10\}$$
$$\{f10\} \rightarrow \{f7\}$$
$$\{f8, f10\} \rightarrow \{f7\}$$
$$\{f7, f10\} \rightarrow \{f8\}$$
$$\{f7, f8\} \rightarrow \{f10\}$$

CONCLUSION

In this paper the method for mining fuzzy correlation rules is based on the fuzzy measures for correlation coefficient of fuzzy numbers. The method of correlation analysis proposed in the fuzzy correlation techniques gives some interesting observations of some 7 fuzzy correlation rules. Here in our study f7, f8 and f10 are the chapters namely Integral-calculus, differential equations and probability distributions. Through this study it is seen that the

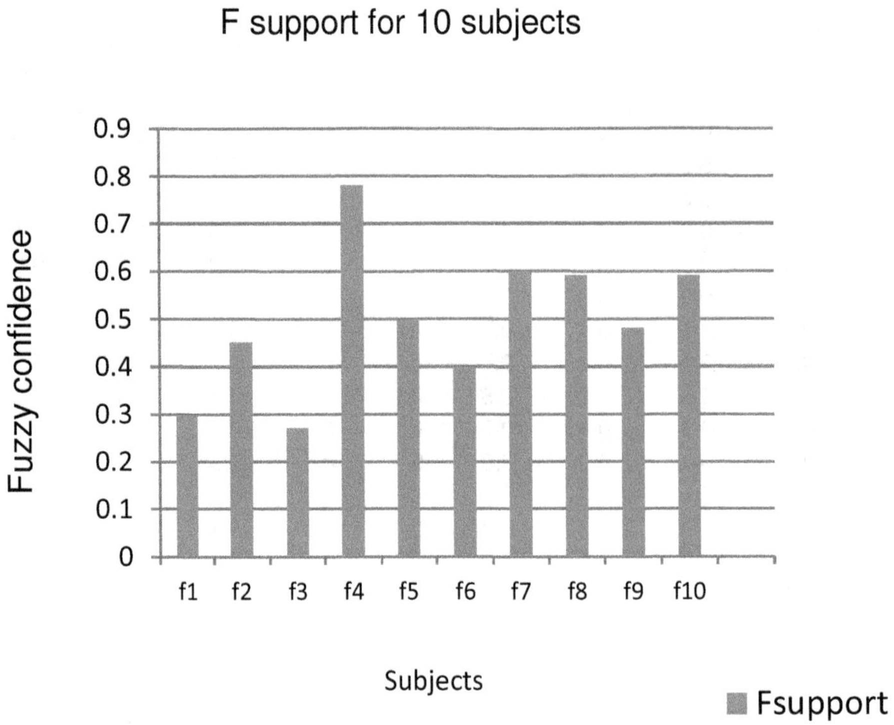

Figure 1. Fuzzy support for the 10 chapters.

Table 3. Candidate Generation of 2-itemsets.

C2	Fsupport	r	t
{f7}{f8}	0.54	0.9156	6.2662
{f7}{f10}	0.51	0.8863	5.7001
{f8}{f10}	0.50	0.7708	3.2303

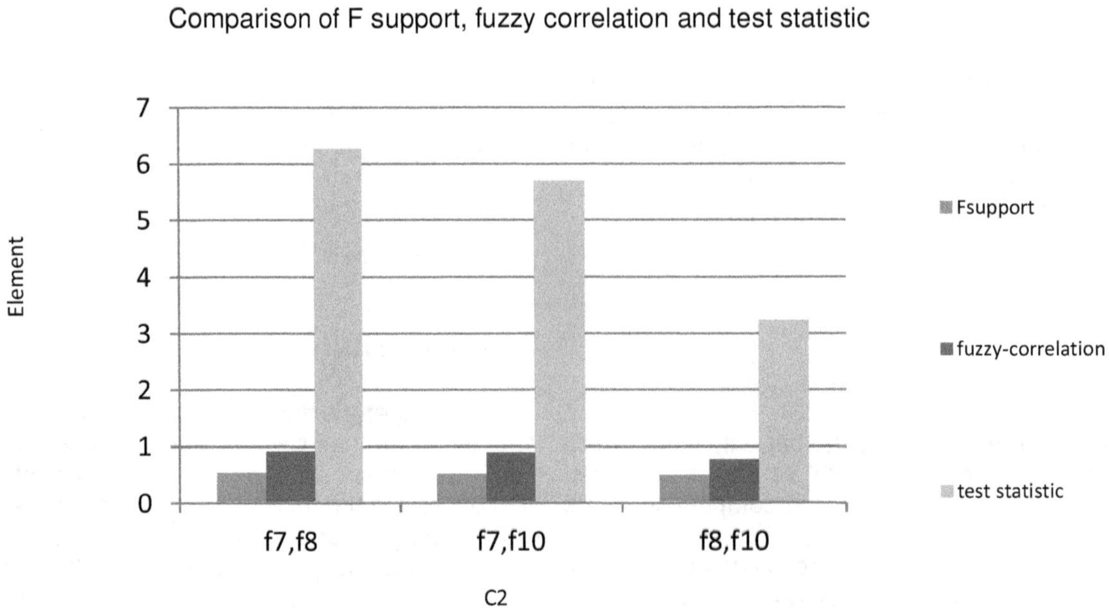

Figure 2. Comparision of F support, r and t of C2.

Table 4. Candidate Generation of 3-itemsets.

C3	Fsupport	r	t
{f7},{f8,f10}	0.48	0.9337	9.2522
{f8},{f7,f10}	0.48	0.8743	5.0076
{f10}{f7,f8}	0.48	0.8523	4.4955

students often prefer questions from these chapters in their examinations.

REFERENCES

Agrawal R, Imielinski T, Swami A (1993). Mining Association Rules between Sets of Items in Large Databases. Proceedings of the ACM SIGMOD International Conference on Management of Data, Washington D.C., May, pp. 207-216.

Agrawal R, Strikant R (1994). Fast algorithms formining association rules, Proceedings of the 20th International Conference on Very Large Databases, Santiago, Chile, Sept., pp. 487-499.

Arnold SF (1990). Mathematical Statistics, Prentice-Hall, New Jersey.

Au W-H, Chan KCC (1998). An effective algorithm for discovering fuzzy rules in relational databases. Proceedings of the IEEE World Congress on Computational Intelligence, pp. 1314–1319.

Bustince H, Burillo P (1995). Correlation of interval-valued intuitionistic fuzzy sets. Fuzzy sets Syst., 74: 237-244.

Chan KCC, Wong AKC (1997). Mining Fuzzy Association Rules. Proceedings of the Sixth International Conference on Information and Knowledge Management, Las Vegas, Nevada, United States, Nov., pp. 209-215.

Chiang DA, Lin NP (1999). Correlation of Fuzzy Sets. Fuzzy Sets Syst., 102: 221-226.

Dubois D, Hullermeier E, Prade H (2003). A Note on Quality Measures for Fuzzy Association Rules. Proceedings of the 10thInternational Fuzzy Systems Association World Congress (IFSA-03), Lecture Notes in Artificial Intelligence 2715, Springer-Verlag, pp. 346-353.

Dunham MH (2003). Data mining, Introductory and Advanced Topics. Pearson Education Inc.

Fu A, Wong M, Sze S, Wong W, Wong W, Yu W (1998). Finding fuzzy sets for the mining of fuzzy association rules for numerical attributes. Proceedings of the First International Symposium on Intelligent Data Engineering and Learning, Hong Kong, October, pp. 263-268.

Han J, Kamber M (2001). Data mining: Concepts and Techniques. Academic Press.

Hong DH, Hwang SY (1995). Correlation of intuitionistic fuzzy sets in probability spaces. Fuzzy Sets Syst., 75: 77-81.

Kao C, Liu ST (2002). Fuzzy measures for correlation coefficient of fuzzy numbers. Fuzzy Sets Syst., 128: 267-275.

Yu C (1993). Correlation of fuzzy numbers. Fuzzy Sets Syst., 55: 303-307.

Zadeh LA (1978). Fuzzy sets as a basis for a theory of possibility. Fuzzy Sets Syst., 1: 3-28.

Permissions

All chapters in this book were first published in AJMCSR, by Academic Journals; hereby published with permission under the Creative Commons Attribution License or equivalent. Every chapter published in this book has been scrutinized by our experts. Their significance has been extensively debated. The topics covered herein carry significant findings which will fuel the growth of the discipline. They may even be implemented as practical applications or may be referred to as a beginning point for another development.

The contributors of this book come from diverse backgrounds, making this book a truly international effort. This book will bring forth new frontiers with its revolutionizing research information and detailed analysis of the nascent developments around the world.

We would like to thank all the contributing authors for lending their expertise to make the book truly unique. They have played a crucial role in the development of this book. Without their invaluable contributions this book wouldn't have been possible. They have made vital efforts to compile up to date information on the varied aspects of this subject to make this book a valuable addition to the collection of many professionals and students.

This book was conceptualized with the vision of imparting up-to-date information and advanced data in this field. To ensure the same, a matchless editorial board was set up. Every individual on the board went through rigorous rounds of assessment to prove their worth. After which they invested a large part of their time researching and compiling the most relevant data for our readers.

The editorial board has been involved in producing this book since its inception. They have spent rigorous hours researching and exploring the diverse topics which have resulted in the successful publishing of this book. They have passed on their knowledge of decades through this book. To expedite this challenging task, the publisher supported the team at every step. A small team of assistant editors was also appointed to further simplify the editing procedure and attain best results for the readers.

Apart from the editorial board, the designing team has also invested a significant amount of their time in understanding the subject and creating the most relevant covers. They scrutinized every image to scout for the most suitable representation of the subject and create an appropriate cover for the book.

The publishing team has been an ardent support to the editorial, designing and production team. Their endless efforts to recruit the best for this project, has resulted in the accomplishment of this book. They are a veteran in the field of academics and their pool of knowledge is as vast as their experience in printing. Their expertise and guidance has proved useful at every step. Their uncompromising quality standards have made this book an exceptional effort. Their encouragement from time to time has been an inspiration for everyone.

The publisher and the editorial board hope that this book will prove to be a valuable piece of knowledge for researchers, students, practitioners and scholars across the globe.

List of Contributors

I. Ahmad
Department of Mathematics, Azad Kashmir University, Muzaffarabad 13100, Pakistan

Stephen Kipkemoi Kibet
Department of Mathematics, Kenyatta University, P. O. Box 43844-00100 Nairobi, Kenya

Kimutai Albert
Kabianga University College, P. O. Box 2030-20200, Kericho, Kenya

Kandie Joseph
Mathematics and Computer Science Department, Chepkoilel University College, P.O. Box 1125-30100, Eldoret

Ali Hussein Al-Marshadi
Department of Statistics, Faculty of Science, King Abdulaziz University, Jeddah, Saudi Arabia

Otto E. Rossler
Institute for Physical and Theoretical Chemistry, University of Tubingen, Auf der Morgenstelle18, 72076 Tubingen, F.R.G., Germany

Navneet Kumar Lamba
Department of Mathematics P.G.T.D. RTM Nagpur University, Nagpur, India

M. S. Warbhe
Department of Mathematics P.G.T.D. RTM Nagpur University, Nagpur, India

N. W. Khobragade
Department of Mathematics P.G.T.D. RTM Nagpur University, Nagpur, India

T. B. Ramkumar
Department of Statistics, St.Thomas' College, Thrissur, Kerala, India. 680001

Mathias A. ONABID
Department of Mathematics and Computer Sciences, Faculty of Sciences, P. O. Box 67 Dschang, University of Dschang, Cameroon

Hamna Parveen
Department of Mathematics P.G.T.D. RTM Nagpur University, Nagpur, India

N. K. Lamba
Department of Mathematics P.G.T.D. RTM Nagpur University, Nagpur, India

N. W. Khobragade
Department of Mathematics P.G.T.D. RTM Nagpur University, Nagpur, India

D. Shukla
Department of Mathematics and Statistics, Dr. H. S. Gour Central University, Sagar, (M.P.), India

D. S. Thakur
School of Excellence, Sagar (M.P.), India

N. S. Thakur
Centre for Mathematical Sciences (CMS), Banasthali University, Rajasthan, India

Xiong Zhang
Department of Mathematics, Shaanxi Institute of Education, Xi'an 710061, China

Stephen Kipkemoi Kibet
Department of Mathematics, Kenyatta University, P. O. Box 43844-00100 Nairobi, Kenya

Ireri N. Kamuti
Department of Mathematics, Kenyatta University, P. O. Box 43844-00100 Nairobi, Kenya

Gregory Kerich
Gregory Kerich, Mount Kenya University, Eldoret Campus P. O. Box 6212-30100, Eldoret Kenya

Albert Kimutai
Kabianga University College, P. O. Box 2030-20200, Kericho, Kenya

Ibrahima Mbaye
Department of Mathematics, University of Thies, Thies, Senegal

OJEDOKUN Olalekan Yinka
Department of Civil Engineering, Faculty of Engineering, the Polytechnic, Ibadan, Oyo State, Nigeria

OLUTOGE Festus Adeyemi
Department of Civil Engineering, Faculty of Engineering, University of Ibadan, Oyo State, Nigeria

Ebiendele Ebosele Peter
Department of Mathematics and Computer Science, Lagos State University, Isolo Campus, Lagos, Nigeria

Kenekayoro Patrick
Department of Mathematics and Computer Science, Niger Delta University, Wilberforce Island, P. M. B. 071, Amassoma, Bayelsa State, Nigeria

Sahand Daneshvar
Islamic Azad University, Tabriz Branch, Tabriz, Iran

Mojtaba Ramezani
Islamic Azad University, Bonab Branch, Bonab, Iran

Mozhgan Mansouri Kaleibar
Islamic Azad University, Tabriz Branch, Tabriz, Iran

Sharmin Rahmatfam
Islamic Azad University, Tehran Central Branch, Tehran, Iran

Sahand Daneshvar
Islamic Azad University, Tabriz Branch, Tabriz, Iran

Mojtaba Ramezani
Islamic Azad University, Bonab Branch, Bonab, Iran

Mozhgan Mansouri Kaleibar
Islamic Azad University, Tabriz Branch, Tabriz, Iran
Young Researchers Club, Islamic Azad University , Tabriz Branch, Tabriz , Iran

G. U. Ebuh
Department of Statistics, Faculty of Physical Sciences, Nnamdi Azikiwe University, Awka, Anambra State, Nigeria

C. Nwoke
Department of Statistics, Faculty of Physical Sciences, Nnamdi Azikiwe University, Awka, Anambra State, Nigeria

A. C. Ebuh
Department of Computer Science, Faculty of Physical Sciences, Nnamdi Azikiwe University, Awka, Anambra State, Nigeria

Abha Teguria
Department of Mathematics, Government M.L.B. PG girl Autonomous College, Bhopal, India

Manindra Kumar Srivastava
Department of Mathematics, School of Management Sciences, Technical Campus, Lucknow, India

Anil Rajput
Department of Mathematics, Sadhu Basbani PG College, Bhopal, India

Trailokyanath Singh
Department of Mathematics, Sir Chandrasekhara Venkata Raman College of Engineering, Bhubaneswar, India

Sudhir Kumar Sahu
Department of Statistics, Sambalpur University, Sambalpur, India

T. L. Grobler
Department of Electrical, Electronic and Computer Engineering, University of Pretoria, South-Africa
Defence, Peace, Safety and Security, Council for Scientific and Industrial Research, South-Africa

A. J. van Zyl
Department of Mathematics and Applied Mathematics, University of Pretoria, South-Africa

J. C. Olivier
School of Engineering, University of Tasmania, Hobart, Australia

W. Kleynhans
Department of Electrical, Electronic and Computer Engineering, University of Pretoria, South-Africa
Meraka Institute, Council for Scientific and Industrial Research, South-Africa

B. P. Salmon
Department of Electrical, Electronic and Computer Engineering, University of Pretoria, South-Africa
Meraka Institute, Council for Scientific and Industrial Research, South-Africa

W. T. Penzhorn
Department of Electrical, Electronic and Computer Engineering, University of Pretoria, South-Africa

Hailay Weldegiorgis Berhe
Department of Mathematics, Haramaya University, Ethiopia

Bolarinwa Bolaji
Department of Mathematics and Statistics, Rufus Giwa Polytechnic, Owo, Nigeria

R. A. Ademiluyi
Department of Mathematics and Statistics, Rufus Giwa Polytechnic, Owo, Nigeria

A. P. Oluwagunwa
Department of Mathematics and Statistics, Rufus Giwa Polytechnic, Owo, Nigeria

B. O. Awomuse
Department of Mathematical Sciences, Federal University of Technology, Akure, Nigeria

I. C. A. Oyeka
Department of Statistics, Nnamdi Azikiwe University, Awka, Anambra State, Nigeria

E. U. Umeh
Department of Statistics, Nnamdi Azikiwe University, Awka, Anambra State, Nigeria

S. K. Amponsah
Department of Mathematics, Kwame Nkrumah University of Science and Technology, Kumasi, Ghana

K. F. Darkwah
Department of Mathematics, Kwame Nkrumah University of Science and Technology, Kumasi, Ghana

A. Inusah
Department of Mathematics, Kwame Nkrumah University of Science and Technology, Kumasi, Ghana

S. Yadav
Department of Mathematics, Alwar Institute of Engineering and Technology, M.I.A. Alwar-301030, Rajasthan, India

D. L. Suthar
Department of Mathematics, Alwar Institute of Engineering and Technology, M.I.A. Alwar-301030, Rajasthan, India

Zhang Xiong
Department of Mathematics, Shaanxi Institute of Education, Shaanxi, xi'an 710061, China

Huang Lihang
College of Mathematics and Computer Science, Fuzhou University, Fuzhou, 350002, China

Dasharath Singh
Department of Mathematics, Ahmadu Bello University, Zaria-Nigeria

Ali Maianguwa Shuaibu
Department of Mathematics, Statistics and Computer Science, Kaduna Polytechnic, Kaduna, Nigeria

Adeku Musa Ibrahim
Department of Mathematics, Ahmadu Bello University, Zaria-Nigeria

Sahand Daneshvar
Islamic Azad University, Tabriz Branch, Tabriz, Iran

Mozhgan Mansouri Kaleibar
Young Researchers Club, Islamic Azad University, Tabriz Branch, Tabriz, Iran

Mojtaba Ramezani
Islamic Azad University, Bonab Branch, Bonab, Iran

Abdul Wasim Shaikh
Institute of Mathematics and Computer Science, University of Sindh, Jamshoro, Pakistan

Xiao-liang Cheng
Department of Mathematics, Zhejiang University, Hangzhou, 310028, P.R. China

E. Ansari-Piri
Faculty of Mathematical Science, University of Guilan, Rasht, Iran

N. Eghbali
Faculty of Mathematical Science, University of Guilan, Rasht, Iran

T. H. Rugumisa
Faculty of Science, Technology and Environmental Studies, Open University of Tanzania, P. O. Box 23409, Dar-es-salaam, Tanzania

W. M. Charles
College of Natural and Applied Sciences, University of Dar-es-salaam, P. O. Box 35062, Dar-es-salaam, Tanzania

J. Y. T. Mugisha
Department of Mathematics, Makerere University, P. O. Box 7062, Kampala, Uganda

T. Karthikeyan
Department of Computer Science, PSG College of Arts and Science, Coimbatore, India

A. Samuel Chellathurai
Department of Computer Science, James College of Engineering and Technology, Nagercoil, India

B. Praburaj
Department of Computer Science, PSG College of Arts and Science, Coimbatore, India

Printed in the USA
CPSIA information can be obtained
at www.ICGtesting.com
JSHW052023301024
72690JS00004B/149